Read This First:
AFRICA

MARY FITZPATRICK

LONELY PLANET PUBLICATIONS
melbourne ◆ oakland ◆ london ◆ paris

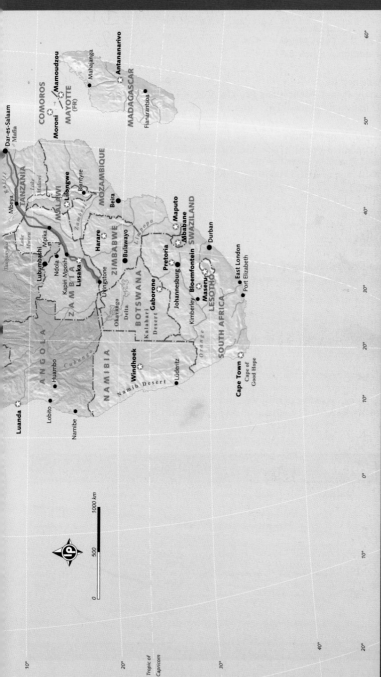

SUGGESTED REGIONAL ITINERARIES
—— Main Car Route
—— Hitch, Train, Bus Travellers Route

DT
2
.H37
2000

Read This First: Africa
1st edition – March 2000

Published by
Lonely Planet Publications Pty Ltd ACN 005 607 983
192 Burwood Rd, Hawthorn, Victoria 3122, Australia

Lonely Planet Offices
Australia PO Box 617, Hawthorn, Victoria 3122
USA 150 Linden Street, Oakland, CA 94607
UK 10a Spring Place, London NW5 3BH
France 1 rue du Dahomey, 75011, Paris

Printed by
The Bookmaker International Ltd
Printed in China

Front cover photograph
Entrance to the Mosque – Mali (David Else, LPI)

ISBN 1 86450 066 2

text, maps © Lonely Planet 2000

LEGEND

BOUNDARIES
International
Regional
Disputed

HYDROGRAPHY
Ocean, Coastline
River, Creek
Intermittent River, Creek
Lake
Salt Lake
Spring, Rapids
Waterfalls
Swamp

TRANSPORT & ROUTES
Ferry Route
Flight Path
One Week Itinerary
Two Week Itinerary
One Month Itinerary
Five Week Itinerary

AREA FEATURES
Park, Reserve
Other Countries

MAP SYMBOLS
CAPITAL — National Capital
Capital — Regional Capital
City — City
Town — Town
Village — Village
Airport
Archaeological Site
Beach
Border Crossing
Camping Ground
Cave
Chalet or Hut
Mine
Mountain or Hill
National Park
Oasis
Pass
Point of Interest
Pyramid
Tomb
Temple

CONTENTS

▶▶

contents

THE AUTHOR

Mary Fitzpatrick

Mary grew up in Washington, DC and has travelled extensively in Africa, Asia and Europe. Her journeys have taken her on foot through remote Malagasy rainforests, on rickety pick-ups to dusty villages in the Sahel, by dhow to palm-fringed East African islands, and on bicycle through Tibet and south-western China. For most of the past six years, she has worked in Africa, first on development projects in Mozambique, and more recently as a freelance writer in Liberia and Sierra Leone. Mary also wrote Lonely Planet's *Tanzania, Zanzibar & Pemba* and has contributed to LP's *West Africa* and *Africa* guidebooks.

From the Author

With thanks to Rick, who has been to so many places on the continent with me, for his enthusiasm during our travels and for his patience and support while I was writing this book.

THIS BOOK

From the Publisher

This book is the second title in Lonely Planet's new series of introductory travel guides. Martine Lleonart oversaw the content and design development of the series based on the original structure and content devised by Pete Cruttenden. Margaret Jung was responsible for developing the design of the series based on an original design concept produced by Penelope Richardson. Margaret laid out this book and Indra Kilfoyle assisted early on in the piece. Penelope designed the cover with assistance from Guillaume Roux and Simon Bracken. Graham Fricke edited this title with assistance from Anne Mulvaney and Russ Kerr. Cartographer Jim Miller produced the colour maps with the assistance of Jackie Rae, Paul Piaia and Paul Clifton. Paul Piaia supplied the climate charts and Tim Uden helped out with Quark. Tass Wilson gave support and advice on design matters.

Isabelle Young and Leonie Mugavin wrote the health content, and LP authors Michelle Coxall, David Else, Frances Linzee Gordon, Paul Greenway, Jon Murray, Miles Roddis and David Willett provided anecdotes from their travels.

Much of the information in this guide (particularly the country profiles) has been drawn and adapted from existing Lonely Planet titles. Thanks to the following authors for their fine work: Geert Cole *(Egypt)*, Geoff Crowther *(Africa, East Africa, Kenya* and *North Africa)*, David Else *(Africa, Africa – the South, The Gambia & Senegal, Malawi, Mozambique & Zambia, Tanzania, Zanzibar & Pemba, Trekking in East Africa* and *West Africa)*, Richard Everist *(South Africa, Lesotho & Swaziland)*, Hugh Finlay *(Africa, East Africa, Kenya* and *North Africa)*, Mary Fitzpatrick *(Africa, Tanzania, Zanzibar & Pemba* and *West Africa)*, Matt Fletcher *(Kenya)*, Frances Linzee Gordon *(Africa* and *Morocco)*, Paul Greenway *(Africa* and *Madagascar & Comoros)*, Andrew Humphreys *(Africa)*, Ann Jousiffe *(Africa, Middle East* and *North Africa)*, Leanne Logan *(Egypt)*, Jon Murray *(Africa, Africa – the South* and *South Africa, Lesotho & Swaziland)*, Alex Newton *(West Africa)*, Miles Roddis *(Africa* and *West Africa)*, Damien Simonis *(Egypt, Morocco* and *North Africa)*, Sarina Singh *(Africa)*, Deanne Swaney *(Africa, Africa – the South, Madagascar & Comoros* and *Zimbabwe, Botswana & Namibia)*, Dorinda Talbot *(Africa* and *Morocco)*, Scott Wayne *(Egypt)*, David Willett *(Africa, North Africa* and *Tunisia)* and Jeff Williams *(Africa, South Africa, Lesotho & Swaziland* and *West Africa)*.

FOREWORD

This book is designed to help you to research and prepare for a trip to Africa. It contains much of the advice that we'd like to include in our regular travel guides, but cannot due to space limitations. It's a compilation of lessons learned by Lonely Planet travel writers and readers on innumerable trips across Africa, and includes detailed advice on planning your route, buying your ticket, choosing and packing your gear, and surviving your first night on the road. Even more importantly, it contains plenty of advice on day-to-day living while you're on the road – things that hold true across the continent – from finding a decent room, eating a good meal, keeping your valuables safe and getting around on some very different forms of transport. In short, this book is the one we wish we'd had before we set out on our first trip to Africa.

It would be irresponsible to suggest that all African countries enjoy political and social stability – some are embroiled in endless rounds of political turmoil – but there's one thing you can be certain of in Africa: there's never a dull moment! You need to keep an eye on the newspapers, your wits together, your eyes and ears open and your mouth in check. Do that, and you're in for the adventure of a lifetime.

Travelling in Africa requires determination, patience and stamina. Always remember to respect other people's customs and sensibilities, and regardless of their politics, religion or whatever else, you will always have a friend. Hospitality is synonymous with Africa. This continent and its people have a great deal to teach and offer to the other people of the world.

This book includes country profiles that provide the basic details and highlights of each country in Africa. These can be used to plan your route, calculate your travel budget and figure out what visas you must get before setting out. These sections will not replace the greater detail you'll need from guidebooks once you're in Africa, but they should serve as a solid start to planning your trip and learning about the cultures you are heading to.

Countries that are not covered in these profiles include Algeria, Angola, Burundi, Congo, Congo (Zaïre), Guinea-Bissau, Liberia, Rwanda, Sierra Leone, Somalia and the Sudan, due to political insecurity or military conflicts in these areas. The islands of Comoros & Mayotte, Mauritius, Réunion and the Seychelles are also excluded as it is assumed that they lie beyond the itineraries of most first-time visitors to the continent. Spanish North Africa receives a brief treatment in the chapter on Morocco. However, each of these countries are covered in Lonely Planet's travel guide series.

We've also included itineraries for each of the countries. The routes we've selected take in the major sights and attractions, plus a few places further off the beaten track, but if you do some further research and come up with your own specific route, you'll encounter the aspects of the region that appeal most to your particular tastes and you'll generally have a more rewarding time.

Also included are loads of web site references and addresses in recognition of the increasing role these resources play in travel planning and information. Inevitably, by the time you read this book, some of these links will have changed or disappeared. A simple keyword search should furnish you with the site's new address.

If you combine the information in this book with some imagination and a healthy sense of adventure, you can't help but fall in love with African travel. Remember, the sooner you get started the sooner you'll be stepping off a plane into your first African adventure.

Warning & Request

Things change – prices go up, schedules change, good places go bad and bad places go bank-rupt – nothing stays the same. So, if you find things better or worse, recently opened or long since closed, please tell us and help make the next edition even more accurate and useful. We genuinely value all the feed-back we receive. Julie Young coordinates a well travelled team that reads and acknowledges every letter, postcard and email and ensures that every morsel of information finds its way to the appropriate authors, editors and cartographers for verification.

Everyone who writes to us will find their name in the next edition of the appropriate guide book. They will also receive the latest issue of Planet Talk, our quarterly printed newslet-ter, or Comet, our monthly email newsletter. Subscriptions to both newsletters are free. The very best contributions will be rewarded with a free guidebook.

Excerpts from your correspondence may appear in new editions of Lonely Planet guide-books, the Lonely Planet web site, Planet Talk or Comet, so please let us know if you don't want your letter published or your name acknowledged.

Send all correspondence to the Lonely Planet office closest to you:

Australia: PO Box 617, Hawthorn, Victoria 3122
USA: 150 Linden St, Oakland, CA 94607
UK: 10A Spring Place, London NW5 3BH
France: 1 rue du Dahomey, 75011 Paris

Or email us at: talk2us@lonelyplanet.com.au

For news, views and updates see our web site: www.lonelyplanet.com

The Lonely Planet Story

The story begins with a classic travel adventure – Tony and Maureen Wheeler's 1972 journey across Europe and Asia to Australia. Useful information about the overland trail did not exist at that time, so Tony and Maureen published the first Lonely Planet guidebook to meet a growing need among the backpacker community.

Written at a kitchen table and hand collated, trimmed and stapled, *Asia on the Cheap* became an instant local bestseller, inspiring thoughts of another book. A further 18 months in South-East Asia resulted in their second guide, *South-East Asia on a shoestring*, which they put together in a backstreet Chinese hotel in Singapore in 1975. The 'yellow bible' as it quickly became known to backpackers around the world, soon became the guide to the region. As we go to print, it has sold almost 750,000 copies, still retaining its familiar yellow cover. A 10th anniversary edition has recently been released and includes a story and photographs by Tony recalling the 1975 trip.

Today Lonely Planet publishes more than 450 titles, including travel guides, city guides, diving guides, city maps, phrasebooks, trekking guides, wildlife guides, travel atlases and travel literature. The company is the largest independent travel publisher in the world; an international company with offices in Melbourne, Oakland, London and Paris.

However, some things haven't changed. Our main aim is still to help make it possible for adventurous travellers to get out there – to explore and better understand the world. At Lonely Planet we believe that travellers can make a positive contribution to the countries they visit – if they respect their host communities and spend their money wisely. Since 1986 a percentage of the income from each book has been donated to aid projects and human rights campaigns across the world.

INTRODUCTION ▶▶

Mention that you're contemplating a trip to Africa, and you're likely to be met with mixed reactions from friends and family. From an enlightened few, it might be amazement or surprise, tinged perhaps with a bit of envy. From most people, however, you'll probably encounter puzzled looks and worried comments. Some would-be travellers to the continent never even make it past the travel section of their local bookshop. A few are put off by visions of wildlife lurking outside their tent (or even more disconcertingly, crawling between their sheets). Others fear mysterious tropical maladies, blistering hot weather, and coups or protracted wars. Still others are simply uncertain about how to take the first step to prepare for their adventure. Whether justified or not, Africa has a reputation as one of the world's most difficult destinations, suitable only for the truly adventurous or for those willing to subject themselves to all sorts of risk.

Happily, however, the realities of travel in Africa are far different. With a bit of advance planning, a willingness to leave your western mindset behind, and an openness to new experiences, you'll find that Africa has almost no closed doors, essentially no boundaries, and an allure which could keep you coming back for a lifetime of visits. It also has attractions enough to appeal to every taste and budget – from colourful, diverse and remarkably accessible cultures, to rich artistic and musical traditions and an untamed vastness and natural splendour. Topping this off are the warmth, generosity and sense of family for which Africans are renowned – which are extended in abundant measure to visitors.

Risky Business

Writing a travel book that tries to bring all the countries of Africa under one roof is a risky undertaking. The continent is so large, and its countries and cultures so diverse, that it is almost impossible to come up with generalisations which apply throughout.

When reading this book, keep in mind that situations in the areas you visit may vary markedly from what is described here. Travellers in South Africa, for example, will likely find that many things – particularly infrastructure – will be very similar to what they are familiar with at home. However, visitors to some of the continent's less developed countries will probably encounter some extreme contrasts.

The best thing is to consider this book as a first step – like coming upon a new house and taking a peek in the window. As the planning for your trip gets under way, and as you determine the regions you will be visiting, other sources of information – particularly country-specific guidebooks – will help you further along. Once in Africa, the door will be wide open and the real fun and fascination of immersing yourself will begin.

The purpose of this book is to allay any initial trepidations you may have about travelling to Africa, to provide you with some practical tools for beginning your trip, and to get you started on your discovery of the continent. The intineraries and highlights suggested in the country profiles offer a great starting point for your trip, with suggestions of what to do if you've only got a week and what to do if you're lucky enough to have two months. By combining its tips and information with imagination and a healthy sense of adventure, you'll not only master the fine art of travel in Africa, but are sure to get hooked on the continent as well. Chances are good that your first trip to Africa won't be your last!

Good planning is the key to fun, informative and smooth travels. By focusing in advance on your expectations, abilities and resources, you will be able to maximise the enjoyment and benefits of your time in Africa. If you are travelling for the first time and don't know what to expect, then this chapter will give you some ideas.

Some general questions to ask during the planning stage include: do you want to travel alone or with others? How much time and money will you have? Would you prefer to see a broad section of the continent or concentrate on getting to know one area in depth? Are there certain activities – for example trekking, or diving and snorkelling – that you enjoy and want to incorporate into your trip? Do you like meeting other travellers or would you rather be out on your own? Are you more interested in exploring Africa's varied landscapes and natural attractions or immersing yourself in its diverse cultures?

Once you've determined the type of trip you're interested in taking, mapped out a rough route and decided when the best time is to go, you can begin more in-depth preparations for your travels. Apart from practical matters such as setting your budget, arranging your visas and buying your ticket (all of which are covered later in this book), these can encompass everything from reading guidebooks and doing background research on your destination to perhaps even learning a bit of the local language.

What Kind of Trip?

At the outset, you'll need to decide whether you want to go on an organised tour, travel independently, or combine both options.

ORGANISED TOURS

Many travellers dismiss organised tours as restrictive or overly programmed. While this can be true, they do have some advantages, the most obvious of which is that all the details are taken care of for you. If run by a well trained guide, organised tours can be highly informative, and can take you to places that would be difficult to reach as an independent traveller, such as longer treks requiring porters and guides, or river trips requiring specialised equipment. They are also a good source of travelling companions and can be ideal for travellers who have a bit of money, but not much time.

Unfortunately, organised tours are often prohibitively expensive. In a few places – for example, some of East Africa's popular national parks – independent travellers may end up paying close to the price of an organised tour anyway. However, in most cases an organised tour will cost several times the amount of independent travel to the same place.

Organised tours also have the drawback of limiting spontaneity and making it harder to come into contact with locals living in the places you are visiting. Not only will you have to put up with the other people in your group for the duration of the trip, but your freedom of movement will be limited and you will spend much of your time surrounded by other visitors, rather than by locals.

If you do opt for an organised tour, try to find a company that suits your style of travel and appeals to your interests. If you enjoy mountain climbing or river rafting, for example, look for tours focused around these activities.

Broadly speaking, organised tours can be divided into three categories: overland tours, all-inclusive tours and adventure tours (a subcategory of all-inclusive tours).

Overland Tours

These tours are organised trips in an overland truck with about 15 to 28 other people, a couple of drivers/leaders, plus tents and other equipment. Food is bought along the way and the group cooks and eats together. Overland tours are very popular, but aren't for everyone. They are designed primarily for those who feel uncomfortable striking out on their own or who prefer guaranteed social interaction to the uncertainties of the road. If you have the slightest inclination towards independence or would feel confined travelling with the same group of people for most of the trip (normally quite a few drop out along the way), think twice before booking something like this.

Most overland truck companies are based in the UK. Trips starting in London enter Africa at Morocco and go from there via the Western Sahara to West Africa. From here, the longer ones may go on to central Africa and — after flying over Congo (Zaïre) — continue into East Africa and then on to Zimbabwe, Botswana and South Africa. An increasing number of overland truck journeys also run shorter routes within Africa. Popular starting points include Nairobi, Johannesburg and Cape Town.

For more information or a list of agents selling overland packages in your home country, contact one of the following African overland tour operators, all of which are based in the UK (Exodus and Encounter also have offices in Australia, New Zealand, the USA and Canada):

Dragoman
(☎ 01728-86 1133; fax 86 1127) Camp Green, Kenton Rd, Debenham, Suffolk IP14 6LA

Encounter Overland
(☎ 020-7370 6845) 267 Old Brompton Rd, London SW5 9JA

Exodus Expeditions
(☎ 020-8673 7966) 9 Weir Rd, London SW12 0LT

Guerba Expeditions
(☎ 01373-82 6689) 101 Eden Vale Rd, Westbury, Wiltshire BA13 3QX

Top Deck
(☎ 020-7330 4555; fax 7373 6201) The Adventure Centre, 131-135 Earl's Court Rd, London SW5 9RH

All-Inclusive Tours

These tours normally include your international flight, as well as transport around the country, accommodation, food, excursions and so on. They are usually about two to three weeks long, and ideal if you want to concentrate on one country or region of Africa but lack the time or inclination to arrange the logistics yourself. For travellers who want something halfway between all-inclusive and completely independent (see Going it Alone later in this chapter), some companies provide self-guided itineraries, including prebooked flights, vehicle hire and accommodation where required, but let you decide on exactly where and when you want to go.

There are literally hundreds of tour companies around the world featuring trips to Africa. Some of the operators listed under Overland Tours (see the previous entry) and Adventure Tours (see the following entry) can provide information. Other good places to check include the travel ads sections of weekend newspapers and travel magazines, the Internet and guidebooks, or speak to other travellers.

Adventure Tours

Planning your trip to Africa around a specific activity is a good way to experience new cultures while doing something you enjoy. The following list of specialist adventure travel agencies can help you get started. Note that with some adventure tours, the international flight may not be included.

Australia

Adventure World
(☎ 02-9956 7766; fax 9956 7707; www.adventureworld.com.au/contact.html) 73 Walker St, North Sydney, NSW 2060
Africa Travel Centre
(☎ 02-9267 3048; fax 9267 3047) Level 11, 456 Kent St, Sydney, NSW 2000
African Wildlife Safaris
(☎ 03-9696 2899; fax 9696 4937) Level 1, 259 Coventry St, South Melbourne, Vic 3205
Peregrine Travel
(☎ 03-9663 8611; fax 9663 8618) Level 2, 258 Lonsdale St, Melbourne, Vic 3000

Canada

Market Square Tours
(☎ 800-661-3830) 54 Donald St, Winnipeg, Manitoba R3C 1L6
Trek Holidays
(☎ 800-661-7265; www.trek.ca) 8412 109th St, Edmonton, Alberta T6G 1E2

New Zealand

Adventure World
(☎ 09-524 5118; www.adventureworld.co.nz) 101 Great South Rd, Remuera, PO Box 74008, Auckland
Africa Travel Shop
(☎ 09-520 2000) 21 Remuera Rd, Newmarket, Auckland
Destinations
(☎ 09-309 0464) 4 Durham St East, PO Box 6232, Auckland

USA

Adventure Center
(☎ 510-654-1879 or 800-227-8747; www.adventurecenter.com/about.htm) 1311 63rd St, Emeryville, CA 91608
Africa Travel Center
(☎ 206-672-3697; fax 672-9678) 23830 Route 99, Edmonds, WA 98026
Safaricentre International Inc
(☎ 310-546-441 or 800-223-6046; www.safaricentre.com) 3201 N Sepulveda Blvd, Manhattan Beach, CA

GOING IT ALONE

If you haven't been to Africa before, the prospect of travelling on the continent by yourself can be daunting. In addition to not having anyone with whom to split transport and accommodation costs, you will need to be self-reliant and fond of your own company. Yet, the luxury of being free to go where you want and when you want can more than outweigh these considerations. More importantly, on your own you will probably find that you are more receptive to new experiences and to the cultures and people surrounding you.

In most areas of Africa, travelling alone poses no particular difficulties. Getting around by public transport is straightforward, and local people are nearly always ready to help (in cities and towns people tend to be more indifferent to foreigners). If you tire of being by yourself, it is usually easy to meet other travellers with whom you can travel either for a while, or for the remainder of your trip. Alternatively, you could combine a short organised tour with a period of solo travel.

If you're tempted by the idea of independent travel, but are unsure as to whether you have the temperament for it, give it a trial run in a brief solo trip at home before heading to Africa. If you find yourself craving companionship after a few days, perhaps it's time to start looking for a travel partner.

TRAVELLING WITH FRIENDS

While travelling with a friend or two may cut you off a bit from local people (you're more likely to talk to each other on the bus, rather than to the locals), it eliminates the potential isolation of solo travel. It also has practical advantages: you can split into teams when looking for rooms, or one person can guard the bags while the other searches; you'll save money on accommodation, taxis and in national parks or wilderness areas where the cost of hiring guides or boats can be shared; and you will have moral support when facing unfamiliar or tricky situations. With a small group, you can also consider options such as hiring a car for a few days in order to reach areas which are more problematic or time-consuming by public transport. It's important, however, to find someone with whom you are compatible, and who shares similar ideas of travel.

While friendship is one thing to consider, it's not the only factor and a good friend (or even a spouse) doesn't necessarily make a good travel companion. It's more critical to determine whether you both enjoy travelling in the same way and have similar priorities for the trip. For example, some people prefer planning their itinerary to the last detail, while others like more spontaneity; some like to travel slowly and stop frequently to savour places, while others would rather keep moving to take in as many new sights as possible.

It usually works best to limit group size to three or four. When travelling with more people, it can be difficult to reconcile all the competing interests and personalities, and organising logistics for a large group can rapidly become the main focus of the trip.

Staying Friends on the Road

Spending 24 hours a day with another person, combined with the normal stresses of travel, can put even the greatest of friendships to the test. In the interest of maintaining good relations with your travel partner, it's often helpful to build some space into your routine so that you can regularly have time alone or pursue your own interests. Some travellers make a habit of separating for a few days and then meeting at a predetermined point further down the road. If you have had an argument or are simply getting on each others' nerves, even an afternoon spent apart can be enough to clear the air. If tensions remain high despite these measures, sit down and discuss your problems, keeping things in perspective. If there is no apparent solution, you always have the option of continuing on alone.

Finding Suitable Travel Partners

There are several ways to find a companion for your trip if you don't happen to know anyone who is interested and able to travel at the same time you are. Good places to start include travel magazines, university and community centre bulletin boards, and Internet travel sites – many of which have advertisements for prospective travel partners. You can also post your own ad through any of these mediums. If you do find a travel partner this way, arrange to meet before setting off and, ideally, do a short trip together closer to home to ensure you are compatible.

Joining an organised tour is another possibility: if you choose your tour carefully, you may find someone to team up with for further travel when it finishes. Alternatively, participating in a short organised tour once at your destination can help you to meet a partner for the remainder of your travels.

Some travellers set off alone and head to a spot with the specific intention of finding a travel partner. Places like Cape Town (South Africa), the Victoria

Great African Travellers

Overland truck caravans across Africa may be a relatively recent development, but travellers have been traversing the continent and exploring its offshore waters since ancient times.

One of the most famous of these travellers was Ibn Battuta, born in 1304 in Tangier, Morocco. When he was just 21, he set out on a pilgrimage to Mecca and didn't return until almost 25 years later. In between, Battuta visited all the countries of the Near East, sailed down the East African coast to Kilwa Kisiwani (off the coast of Tanzania) with stops en route at some of the great ports of the day, and lived for a time in India. After returning to Morocco for a breather, Battuta set off again, first for the Strait of Gibraltar and Muslim Spain, and then across the Sahara to Timbuktu and Gao (Mali). Much of this travel was motivated by his goal of visiting every country in the Islamic world. When he was 50 years old, Ibn Battuta finally settled down in Morocco where he wrote an account of his travels. Even today, this account still offers some of the best available insights into the continent's cultures and peoples during precolonial times.

Falls area in Zimbabwe and Arusha (Tanzania) are full of backpackers seeking other travellers with whom to team up. These and similar places have cafes or hotels frequented by travellers where you can introduce yourself, or which have travellers bulletin boards.

Your Route

One of the most enjoyable parts of planning your trip is setting your route – spreading out the maps, opening the guidebooks and imagining all the possibilities.

An important factor to consider in the initial stages is whether to undertake a point-to-point trip or to fly into and out of one city and use that as a base. Point-to-point trips include overland routes such as the famous 'Cape to Cairo' trail from South Africa up to Egypt (not presently possible due to insecurity in the Sudan), as well as less rigorous journeys that make use of round-the-world fares or open-jaw tickets (allowing you to fly into one city and out of another – see the Tickets & Insurance chapter for details).

Related to this is deciding whether you want to concentrate on one area or cover a broad stretch. Given Africa's size and limited transportation infrastructure, most travellers find it best to pick one or two countries or one region of the continent to explore well, rather than trying to cover too much distance in a single trip.

You will also need to determine your mode of transport. If you're travelling an overland route, you may want to consider taking your own car or motorcycle, although this can involve hassles with paperwork and documentation. Alternatives include organised tours or public transportation, although the latter brings its own brand of frustrations and will require more time. Surface transport can also be combined with air or boat travel.

Wherever and however you decide to travel, it's important to check on the latest travel conditions before leaving home (see the Useful Web Sites section in this chapter for some research pointers). For specific highlights and suggested itineraries within individual countries, see the country profiles later in this book.

OVERLAND ROUTES
Intercontinental & Transcontinental Routes

With the exception of the Israel-Egypt connection, all overland travel to Africa must begin in Europe, and even then there will be a ferry crossing at some point. From Europe, there are traditionally three major routes across the Sahara, although the only feasible one now is that via Morocco and the Western Sahara to Mauritania (see the boxed text 'Crossing the Sahara'). It is possible to do this without your own vehicle, although hitching rides on some sections can be difficult.

Once in Mauritania, you can work your way south-eastward through Senegal, Mali and Niger (or alternatively from Senegal through Guinea, Côte d'Ivoire, Burkina Faso, Ghana, Togo and Benin) to Nigeria and Cameroon and then fly from there to Nairobi (Kenya).

From Nairobi, there are several options for reaching southern Africa. One popular route goes via Mombasa or Arusha and Moshi to Dar es Salaam (Tanzania). From here, drivers follow the Great North Rd, while those without wheels take the TAZARA railway; both lead to Kapiri Mposhi in Zambia, from where Lusaka and Victoria Falls are easily reached. Alternatively you can leave the road/train at Mbeya (in southern Tanzania) and go into northern Malawi.

Another option from Dar es Salaam takes you across Tanzania to Kigoma on Lake Tanganyika, then by ferry to Mpulungu in Zambia, from where you

The Onion Lorry

On a trip through Africa in the mid-1980s, I was heading from Sudan into the Central African Republic (CAR). There were no buses in the border area, in fact there were hardly any roads – just sandy tracks through the bush – so in Nyala, the last town in Sudan, I hitched on a lorry carrying onions to N'Gorou, about 400km away. 'Shouldn't take long', said the driver, and we drove out of town just as the sun was setting. 'How splendid', I thought, 'as we rumbled through the desert with stars overhead, 'travel in Africa is such jolly good fun'.

Next day, it was clear that our progress was very slow as the overloaded Bedford struggled through the sand. It was evening again when we reached the Sudanese border checkpoint, and the immigration police had shut their office. Next day there were more delays, as some other passengers' papers were not in order, so we slept another night at the border – lying on the ground under the lorry.

Day four, and we crossed into the 100km-wide no-man's-land between the border posts. At an innocuous looking river, a few inches of water turned out to be a few inches of mud and we instantly got stuck. We might have been able to push it out, but our driver was a determined man, revving mercilessly until the lorry was neatly buried up to its axles, and completely immovable.

It took two days to unload the cargo, dig out the lorry, push it to dry land, then carry all the sacks across the river. By this time, the onions had started to go mouldy, so we had to spread them in the sun for another day to dry. It then took yet another day to re-fill the sacks and re-load the lorry. By this time, the food we'd brought had long since gone, so we'd started eating the onions.

After re-loading, we drove for another day to the CAR border post, only to discover it was Good Friday – easily overlooked in Muslim northern Sudan. But CAR's French-Catholic colonial heritage means the *fete* was celebrated seriously and everybody (including the border guards) had four days off work. So we simply waited, and once more tucked into the onions. Boiled, fried or raw – that was the only choice.

On the Tuesday after Easter we got through the border, and after another day and night finally rolled into N'Gorou. It had taken almost two weeks to cover the 400km. It was a hard way to learn that travel in Africa always takes longer than expected.

N'Gorou had a notoriously difficult checkpoint, and the policeman on duty looked hot, bored and unfriendly. I was apprehensive, and perspiring profusely. But by now I was sweating pure onion juice. The cop sniffed a few times, then quickly stamped my passport, and couldn't get me out of his office quick enough!

David Else
LP Author, UK

can continue overland to Lusaka, or strike out south-eastward on minor roads to reach northern Malawi at Chitipa. Once in Zambia or Malawi, the rest of southern Africa – including Mozambique and Namibia – is easily accessible.

Other routes south from Nairobi – via Uganda, Rwanda, Burundi and perhaps even Congo (Zaïre) – are currently restricted due to civil strife and political unrest in these countries.

An alternative to entering the continent at West Africa is to fly to Egypt. From here, the traditional route is south into the Sudan via Lake Nasser, or via the Red Sea from Suez to Port Sudan. However, due to the difficulties of travelling in the Sudan, many travellers now fly directly from Cairo to Kenya or Tanzania and proceed south from there.

Overland travel requires careful research into current visa situations, travel advisories and border crossing regulations to ensure your proposed route is feasible. You will also need to continually update your information as you travel, as things in Africa can change rapidly.

Crossing the Sahara

There are three main routes across the Sahara leading to West Africa: the Route de Hoggar (through Algeria and Niger); the Route de Tanezrouft (through Algeria and Mali); and the Western Sahara Route (through Morocco and Mauritania). Since the early 1990s the Tanezrouft and Hoggar routes have been virtually unused by travellers. Initially this was due to an antigovernment Tuareg rebellion in Mali and Niger. More recently, the routes have been restricted because of the situation in Algeria, where foreigners have been targeted by antigovernment terrorists. Thus, all drivers and nearly all independent travellers (hitching or using public transport) now use the Western Sahara Route to reach West Africa. When planning your travels, keep in mind that it's officially prohibited to travel overland northward from Mauritania to Western Sahara.

The Western Sahara Route

The Western Sahara route goes south through Morocco to the town of Agadir on the coast. About 500km south of Agadir you enter the disputed territory of Western Sahara. The main road continues through the Western Sahara, running along the coast to Dakhla, where you can find other vehicles to team up with for the remainder of the journey. If you're hitching, there's a thriving trade in second-hand cars being driven from Europe to sell in West Africa, and these drivers are often happy to give lifts. Hitchers are not allowed in Mauritanian vehicles, and there have been occasional scams where hitchers with local drivers are abandoned in the desert unless they pay a large 'fee'.

South of Dakhla all traffic must join one of the twice-weekly convoys organised by the Moroccan military. The convoy drives for 300km towards Mauritania, but the army vehicles turn back about 8km before the actual border, leaving the tourist vehicles to carefully follow a route through minefields to reach the Mauritanian border post. After border formalities it's another 100km and several checkpoints to the town of Nouâdhibou in Mauritania.

From Nouâdhibou, most vehicles go south down the coast to Nouakchott, through the Parc National de Banc d'Arguin. Some cars, most bikes and hitchers go east on the train to Choûm, and then take the better road via Atar and Akjout to Nouakchott.

Regional Routes

Apart from the long transcontinental routes, there are countless shorter overland journeys which encompass from one to several countries and which will expose you to a diversity of cultures and landscapes. The possibilities for designing your own itinerary are endless. The best way to start is to figure out which countries and sights you are interested in seeing, and then sit down with a guidebook to work out the specifics and see what is feasible. This section outlines a few of the more popular regional itineraries.

East & Southern Africa For travellers with plenty of time who are interested in seeing a broad swath of eastern and southern Africa, one of the most popular routes goes from Kenya or Tanzania to South Africa (or vice versa), as outlined above under Intercontinental & Transcontinental Routes. In addition to stops along the way in Malawi, Zambia, Zimbabwe (if the political situation there stabilises) and Botswana, Mozambique and/or Namibia can be worked in as side trips. International air connections are excellent to both Nairobi and Johannesburg, so entering and exiting is not a problem. Depending on how often you want to stop along the way, you will need at least three months to do justice to this route.

West Africa In West Africa, a tour of the coastal countries (also incorporating a glimpse into Sahelian life in Burkina Faso) could begin and end in Abidjan (Côte d'Ivoire). From Abidjan, head north through Côte d'Ivoire to Burkina Faso, then through Burkina Faso to northern Benin. After making your way south to Cotonou, continue along the coast to Lomé (Togo) and spend some time exploring Togo before continuing into Ghana. After touring Ghana, head back to Abidjan. You could do this itinerary in less than two months if you travel fast, but it would be better to allow about three months.

Another option, which would take in more of the Sahel region (which borders the Sahara desert), could start in Dakar (Senegal) and (after a side trip to The Gambia) continue through Mali and Burkina Faso into Niger. From Niger, head south-east into Nigeria, then south to Lagos. From Lagos go westward along the coast via Benin, Togo, Ghana and Côte d'Ivoire to Abidjan. You could fly out from there, or – to make a full circuit – continue to Guinea and then along rough roads back to Senegal. Allow at least three months for this loop, and ideally closer to four months.

Central Africa To incorporate Central Africa into a larger itinerary, proceed to Nigeria as outlined under West Africa (see the previous entry) and then head to Cameroon and onwards to Gabon and Equatorial Guinea, with a possible detour by plane or boat to São Tomé & Príncipe. From Gabon, which has the best air connections in the region, you can fly over Congo (Zaïre) and continue into southern Africa.

North Africa Given poor security conditions in Algeria and the situation in Libya it is not possible to string together a good overland North Africa itinerary that takes in most of the countries in the region. To get a taste of North Africa, you could start your journey in Morocco and then cross the Sahara into Mauritania and Senegal. From Senegal, follow the West Africa route (see earlier in this section). Alternatively, you could fly to Egypt, spend time there and then fly to another destination within Africa.

Routes in Africa

Following are some suggestions for countries or country groupings that would be feasible to cover within the specified time frames, assuming you travel at a comfortable but steady pace.

Two Weeks to One Month
With a month or less you will be limited to exploring one larger country or smaller sections of several countries. Possibilities include:
- Southern Kenya and northern Tanzania
- Madagascar
- South Africa (possibly also including parts of Lesotho and Swaziland)
- Senegal and The Gambia
- Côte d'Ivoire and Ghana
- Cameroon and Equatorial Guinea
- Egypt
- Morocco
- Tunisia
- Ethiopia
- Niger or Nigeria
- Zimbabwe

Two to Three Months
With up to three months, you will be able to get a good regional overview. Possibilities include:
- Senegal, Mali and Burkina Faso
- Côte d'Ivoire, Burkina Faso and Ghana
- Ghana, Togo, Benin and Burkina Faso
- South Africa, Botswana and Zimbabwe Routes in Africa
- Namibia and South Africa

- Mozambique, Swaziland, South Africa and Lesotho
- Tanzania, Malawi and possibly Zambia
- Tanzania and Kenya
- Mozambique and Malawi
- Cameroon, Equatorial Guinea, São Tomé & Príncipe and perhaps Gabon
- Ethiopia, Eritrea and Djibouti
- Nigeria and Cameroon
- Mali, Burkina Faso and Niger

Three to Six Months
With up to half a year, you will be able to do the full West Africa or East & Southern Africa itineraries outlined under Regional Routes in this chapter. With six months you will also have time to bring Morocco into the itinerary, heading from Morocco south to Mauritania and then into West Africa, as outlined under Intercontinental & Transcontinental Routes.

Alternatively, with six months you could fly into Egypt and then, after travelling there, fly to Kenya and Tanzania and continue south as outlined under Intercontinental & Transcontinental Routes.

Six Months to One Year
With up to one year, and travelling at a steady pace, you will be able to cover a good chunk of the continent, starting in either Morocco or Egypt and working your way southward, or vice versa. With a year, there would be plenty of time to take detours to Madagascar, Mozambique or Namibia in southern Africa, Cape Verde in West Africa, or São Tomé & Príncipe in Central Africa.

Thematic Trips

Planning your travels in Africa around a favourite activity or interest will allow you to get to know landscapes and cultures in one or more regions in some depth while doing something you enjoy. Following are some general suggestions; for more detailed options, consult the activities section of a good guidebook or seek out a specialist guidebook. The Guidebooks section later in this chapter lists some titles.

TREKKING

Africa offers some superb trekking. Among the more popular destinations are Cameroon, Guinea, Lesotho, Malawi, Mali, Morocco, Namibia, South Africa, Tanzania, Uganda and Zimbabwe.

In contrast to mountain or altitude trekking is jungle trekking, which often requires just as much endurance. Many of the best areas to do this in Africa – including the Central African Republic, Congo and Congo (Zaïre) – are presently restricted to travellers due to uncertain political situations. Madagascar, however, offers a few excellent possibilities, along with options for trekking in drier areas. Bioko Island (Equatorial Guinea) also has some good trekking.

If you are planning to trek in Africa, get into shape beforehand, especially for some of the more strenuous mountain climbs. For extended treks, bring any camping equipment you may need from home, as rental equipment is often inferior and expensive. Technical equipment is generally not available, and should also be brought from home. Depending on your route, you may need to hire a guide and porters.

Cameroon – The hills around Bamenda in eastern Cameroon offer many good treks and walks. Northern Cameroon (north of Rumsiki) is another good trekking area. Mt Cameroon (4070m) in the south is easily accessible and popular for climbing.

Equatorial Guinea – While Equatorial Guinea isn't specifically a trekking destination, the mountainous southern part of Bioko Island offers several pleasant walks if you happen to be in the region. The 3106m Pico Malabo also makes an easy but pleasant climb, and there are several decent treks in the area around Luba in the far south.

Ethiopia – Ethiopia, which is sometimes referred to as Africa's largest mountain range, is seldom reached by trekkers although it holds some excellent possibilities. The main goal of those who do come here is a trek to Ras Deshen – Africa's fifth highest summit – through the spectacular Simien mountains.

Guinea – Guinea's Fouta Djalon plateau offers some of the best trekking in West Africa. It's primarily village-based, and on footpaths well used by locals, but the scenery is beautiful and the temperatures a bit cooler than in the lowlands.

Kenya – Mt Kenya is Africa's second highest peak, and one of East Africa's main attractions for trekkers, with a wide range of routes for all tastes and abilities. Other possibilities include the Aberdare Range and Mt Elgon, both of which offer excellent high-altitude wilderness trekking. In contrast, the Cherangani Hills and the Loroghi Hills provide less strenuous and more accessible options.

Lesotho – The entire country of Lesotho exceeds 1000m in altitude, with peaks in the Central Ranges and near the Drakensberg escarpment reaching over 3000m. This all adds up to superb walking and wilderness trekking. Particularly good areas are the Eastern Highlands and the Drakensberg escarpment.

Madagascar – Possibilities range from a challenging rainforest trek across the Masoala Peninsula in the eastern part of the country to village-based walking on the central plateau and trekking through the rugged sandstone massifs of the Parc National de Isalo.

Malawi – The wilderness areas of Mt Mulanje and the Nyika plateau offer high mountains, with deep valleys, sheer escarpments and dramatic peaks, and some of the most enjoyable hill-walking routes in the region.

Mali – The Bandiagara escarpment, which extends some 150km through the Sahel to the east of Mopti, offers stunning landscapes and a fascinating culture. Most visitors explore the region in a series of village-to-village walks, taking it at a slow pace.

Morocco – Morocco is a great destination for mountain lovers, with several year-round trekking possibilities. Jebel Toubkal (4167m) is the highest peak in the High Atlas mountain range and tends to attract most visitors. The Western High Atlas is less developed and offers many challenging walks, while the pink and ochre-coloured mountains of the Anti-Atlas range are excellent for trekking.

Nambia – The best trails include those at Daan Viljoen Game Reserve, the Naukluft, Fish River Canyon, Waterberg Plateau Park and the Ugab River, although at many of these areas treks must be booked and paid for in advance and group size is limited. Bushwalking is permitted in national parks without dangerous animals.

South Africa – South Africa has an excellent system of trails, usually with accommodation. Some good areas include the Wild Coast in Eastern Cape Province, the Drakensberg escarpment which forms the border between KwaZulu-Natal and Lesotho, and the Klein Drakensberg in Mpumalanga.

Tanzania – Mt Kilimanjaro (5896m) tops the list for most trekkers. Mt Meru (4566m), while often overlooked, is pristine and dramatic. The Crater Highlands offer excellent trekking through Maasai lands dominated by the Ol Doinyo Lengai volcano. Many areas of the country are also good for walking, including the Eastern Arc mountains in the north-east and the Kipengere Range in the south-west.

Uganda – Intrepid trekkers (after first checking on the security situation) can head for the wild and vast Ruwenzori Range – the fabled Mountains of the Moon. The lesser known Mt Elgon, until recently a forgotten giant, has good access and good trekking.

Zimbabwe – The main attractions here are trekking and bushwalking. Many of the best areas (including Nyanga, Vumba and Chimanimani national parks) are in the Eastern Highlands. Other good trekking venues include Matobo National Park, Matusadona National Park and the Mavuradonha Wilderness.

DIVING & SNORKELLING

Africa is an excellent destination for diving and snorkelling and has several world-class dive sites. The best regions are in the Red Sea and along the East Africa coast. Specific countries to check out include Eritrea, Kenya, Madagascar, Malawi (lake), Mozambique, São Tomé & Príncipe, Senegal, South Africa, Tanzania and Tunisia.

At most places it is possible to rent equipment, either on-site or through a charter operator in the area, although if you are a serious diver or snorkeller you may want to consider bringing your own masks, regulators and BCDs, snorkels and fins. Some places also offer the opportunity for PADI open-water dive certification, with costs ranging between US$250 and US$350 per course. Two-dive packages for certified divers average about US$50, including equipment.

Egypt – There is some superb scuba diving and snorkelling in the Red Sea. Excellent areas accessible from Egypt include the southern stretch of the Red Sea coast towards the border with the Sudan, and along the southern coast of the Sinai Peninsula. Other possibilities include Dahab and Hurghada. Dive operators abound, and finding rental equipment and dive courses is not a problem.

Eritrea – The waters around the 210 islands of the undeveloped Dahlak Archipelago offer spectacular, unspoiled diving and snorkelling. Rental equipment is available but expensive. Snorkelling is possible from Green Island, off the coast near Massawa.

Kenya – Malindi, Watamu, Shimoni and Wasini Island are the main areas for scuba diving, with Shimoni and Wasini in the far south considered the best. Kenyan diving suffers from a poor reputation for visibility due to plankton in the water, and coral reefs are also often less than spectacular, although there is abundant and interesting marine life. Equipment rental is possible at most places (although snorkelling equipment is often old and substandard), and some operators also offer courses.

Madagascar – Although the coral reefs and marine life are suffering from environmental pressures, Madagascar still has some outstanding diving locations. Among the best sites are the tropical islands and islets around Nosy Be in the north; along the west coast, particularly around Ifaty in the south-west; and the southern end of Masoala Peninsula, in the north-east. Other sites include Île Sainte Marie, Morondava and Mahavelona (Foulpointe). Courses and equipment rental are possible in a few areas.

Malawi – Lake Malawi's population of colourful fish attracts many visitors for snorkelling and scuba diving. The fresh water is warm and generally clear (depending on the season), and weather conditions usually favourable. Several lakeside towns and hotels have scuba gear for hire. Certification courses are also possible.

Mozambique – The Bazaruto Archipelago off the coast between Vilankulo and Inhassoro is one of the best areas. Top-quality boats and all equipment can be hired. Pemba, in the far north, and the waters off Inhaca Island in the far south offshore from Maputo also offer very good diving and snorkelling. While there are many other good spots along Mozambique's long coastline, most are undeveloped.

São Tomé & Príncipe – The main spot for diving is Praia das Conchas on São Tomé; equipment rental is possible. Snorkelling is good at many areas around the island.

Senegal – The main sites are around Dakar, including the rocky reefs and islets around the Pointe des Almadies, and the islands of Gorée and N'Gor. Equipment rental is possible.

Tanzania – The best diving areas include Pemba Island, Unguja (Zanzibar) Island, Mafia Island, some of the smaller islands offshore from Dar es Salaam, and along the south-eastern coast near Mtwara. Rental equipment and certification courses are available in the Zanzibar Archipelago, Mafia and Dar es Salaam. Snorkelling is possible at all these locations, as well as at many other sites along the coast; equipment is generally available.

Tunisia – The best place for diving in Tunisia is near Tabarka on the north coast. Equipment rental and courses for beginners are available.

SURFING

South Africa offers some of the best, least crowded surfing to be found anywhere. Other possible venues on the continent include Côte d'Ivoire and – to a lesser extent – Ghana. Although there are good waves at some of Liberia's beaches, the political situation in the country has restricted access for travellers. In North Africa, Morocco isn't a bad place to take your board.

With the exception of South Africa and Assinie in Côte d'Ivoire, good-quality rental equipment is often not available, so serious surfers should bring their boards from home.

Côte d'Ivoire – Côte d'Ivoire has some of West Africa's better surfing. Popular spots include Grand Lahou, Grand Béréby and Assinie; there are also several spots around Sassandra.

Ghana – The best spots are near the towns of Dixcove and Senya Beraku.

Morocco – While surfing has had little or no attention here, there are some good options. The beaches around Kenitra are safe and enjoyable. Media Beach, just a few kilometres north of Rabat, is said to have a reliable year-round break. Agadir and Essaouira may also be worth trying.

South Africa – Most surfers will have heard of Jeffreys Bay, but there are myriad alternatives, particularly along the east and south coasts. Boards and gear can be bought or rented in most of the big coastal cities. If you plan to surf at Jeffreys Bay, you'll need a decent-sized board as it's a big, very fast wave.

FISHING

For most travellers, deep-sea sports fishing is prohibitively expensive, costing well over US$100 per day per person. For those still interested, facilities are available in some countries, including Cape Verde, Côte d'Ivoire, The Gambia, Guinea, Mauritania and Senegal in West Africa; Kenya, Madagascar, Mozambique, Namibia, South Africa and Tanzania in East and southern Africa; and Gabon in Central Africa. The waters off Liberia and Sierra Leone in West Africa, and off the Congo in Central Africa offer very good fishing, but travel in these countries is presently restricted.

WHITE-WATER RAFTING, KAYAKING & CANOEING

While the white-water rafting industry is not extensively developed in Africa, there are several good opportunities. The best region is southern Africa; many travellers head to Zimbabwe to raft the Zambezi River near Victoria Falls, and there are numerous tour operators here, as well as on the Zambia side, to help you organise a trip. Expect to pay about US$80/100 for a half/full day's rafting on the Zimbabwe side (somewhat less on the Zambia side). Kayaking and canoeing are also possible. There are a few places that rent kayaks, although serious paddlers will probably want to bring their kayak from home. Other areas of the continent offering possibilities include Kenya, Namibia, South Africa and Uganda. West Africa offers canoeing possibilities along the Niger, although there are no outfitters and you will have to organise everything yourself.

Kenya – There are only limited rafting opportunities in Kenya. The main ones are on the Athi/Galana near Sagana and Yatta Gap.

Namibia – White-water rafting is possible on the Kunene River, along the Angolan border, but it's very expensive. More down-to-earth is white-water canoeing through the canyons of the Orange River, along the South African border.

South Africa – The Orange River is the giant among South African rivers, running west across the country for 2340km. Rafting trips are generally on the far north-west section near the Namibian border. The Tugela, another major river, offers more challenging rafting, although it is highly variable depending on rainfall.

Uganda – Rafting is very much in its infancy here. Trips are on the Nile River near Jinja.

Zambia – The main area here is on the Zambezi, near Livingstone and Victoria Falls.

Zimbabwe – The main areas for white-water rafting and kayaking are the Pungwe River near Nyanga National Park and on the Zambezi in the Victoria Falls/Livingstone area.

WILDLIFE VIEWING & BIRDWATCHING

Africa probably offers more and better opportunities than anywhere else in the world for wildlife viewing and birdwatching. There are national parks (such as those in Kenya and Tanzania) with a relatively developed infrastructure, and wilder areas where you will need your own camping equipment and vehicle.

East and southern Africa are the best areas for wildlife viewing, and some spots in West and Central Africa are not bad. The best locations include Botswana, Kenya, Namibia, South Africa, Tanzania and Zambia. For birdwatching, the possibilities are almost endless. Particularly notable are The Gambia, Mauritania, Nigeria and Senegal. Kenya and Tanzania have lakes that attract many species of waterbirds.

Only some of the continent's highlights are listed here. Check in a guidebook for more detailed information about good sites in the country you will be visiting.

Botswana – The Moremi Wildlife Reserve, which incorporates part of the Okavango Delta, and Chobe National Park are both excellent for seeing elephant and other wildlife. Birdwatching is also very good at Moremi. Makgadikgadi & Nxai Pan National Park hosts one of the region's last great wildlife migrations between February and April.

The Gambia – Over 560 bird species have been recorded in The Gambia, and the country's unique shape, with the northern and southern boundaries matching the sinuous path of the Gambia River, makes many good birdwatching sites easily accessible. There is a network of guides, and facilities for birders. The mangrove-lined estuaries of the Gambia River are particularly good locations.

Kenya – One of the best known sites is the Masai Mara National Reserve, which hosts the annual wildebeest migration (July to August) when millions of the animals move north from the Serengeti in search of lush grass. Amboseli National Park doesn't have such a profusion of game, but there are large herds of elephants and the chance of spotting a black rhino. Lake Baringo in the Rift Valley hosts more than 450 of Kenya's 1200 bird species.

Mauritania – Mauritania's Banc d'Arguin is an important crossroads for multitudes of aquatic birds migrating between Europe and northern Asia and most of Africa. Over two million broad-billed sandpipers have been recorded in the winter. Other migrants include black terns, flamingos, white pelicans and spoonbills. August and September, and February and March are the best viewing times.

Namibia – Etosha National Park is the best wildlife viewing venue in Namibia, and one of the best on the continent. It protects 114 mammal species, as well as over 340 bird, 16 reptile and amphibian, one fish and countless insect species. The Namib-Naukluft Park encompasses a variety of habitats. While it does not support the diversity of wildlife found in Etosha, you can see mountain zebra, kudu, leopard and klipspringer, among others; there is also some good birdwatching. The Caprivi national parks and game reserves support a range of wetland wildlife.

Nigeria – Yankari National Park is a stopover for migratory birds, and an ornithologist's dream. Approximately 600 species of bird have been identified here, including savanna, wetland, river and raptor species. Okomo Sanctuary is also good. Gashaka Gumpti National Park near the Cameroon border is Nigeria's largest and most ecologically diverse park, and supports an enormous variety of birdlife.

Senegal – Although Senegal does not have the birding facilities found in The Gambia, it offers a remarkable diversity of species (over 600 have been recorded here). The south-eastern part of the country, where you will see many savanna and woodland species, is particularly good, as are the mangrove swamps of the Casamance River.

South Africa – Kruger is South Africa's most famous national park. It hosts a wide variety of animals and sightings are almost guaranteed. Hluhluwe-Umfolozi is the place to go for rhinos, while the Kalahari Gemsbok National Park supports large populations of birds, reptiles, small mammals and antelope, which in turn support a large population of predators. Among these are Kalahari lion, cheetah, leopard, hyena and jackal.

Tanzania – Tanzania has some of Africa's most famous wildlife viewing areas, including the Ngorongoro Crater and Serengeti National Park, as well as many lesser known protected areas which are just as impressive. These include Katavi, Tarangire, Ruaha and Arusha national parks, as well as Gombe Stream National Park, known for its chimpanzees, and Selous Game Reserve, which hosts one of the largest elephant populations on the continent. Good areas for birdwatching include Rubondo Island National Park and Lake Manyara National Park.

Zambia – The wild and pristine Luangwa Valley is home to a wide diversity of animals. Kafue National Park encompasses many different habitats in which you can find lion, leopard, elephant and buffalo plus many others. Lochinvar National Park with its vast floodplain is excellent for birdwatching.

LEARNING A SKILL

Apart from language courses (see Language later in this chapter), some travellers come to Africa to study drumming and traditional dance. West Africa is one of the best places for this, particularly Senegal and Ghana. Other options include learning how to play local instruments (for example the *kora*, a stringed instrument found in Senegal and other areas of West Africa); arts and crafts; basket weaving; batik-making; cookery; and courses in local storytelling techniques.

Cars of a feather

In Ethiopia we were invited by a farmer to have tea in his village. All the men sat in a circle around us. 'You are researchers?', they hesitated. 'No, no, we are tourists; we are here to see the birds.' 'The birds? Maybe you are scientific or military people or working for the government?' 'No, really, we are here on holiday for the birds.'

The men exchanged glances at one another. 'You have left your families, your homes and your work to travel all the way to Ethiopia to see birds?' 'Yes.' There was a brief discussion between the men: some sat shaking their heads in doubt and suspicion, and a few eyed us up and down as if we we'd arrived from another planet. Then gradually the group began to convulse with laughter. 'But why?', they demanded finally. 'Don't you have birds in your country?'

Ethiopia's birdlife is considered one of the most diverse and abundant in Africa. Over 830 species have been recorded, among them a high number of endemics (birds found only in Ethiopia). Even if you're not naturally a twitcher, the birds are so colourful, so diverse, so beautiful that it's impossible not to get hooked after just a few days in the country. Even the names of the birds are superlative: 'beautiful sunbird', 'superb starling' 'paradise flycatcher' ...

In Addis a few days after our return to the capital, I met a young man who said he had once been to London. He had spent all his time admiring the cars that passed in the street. 'But why?', I asked 'You have cars here in Ethiopia', I said. 'Yes', he replied after pausing to think. 'But not so many; not so colourful, so different and so beautiful ...'

Frances Linzee Gordon
LP Author, UK

OTHER ACTIVITIES

Other activities which you can pursue in Africa include windsurfing, camel trekking, horse riding and pony trekking, rock climbing, mountain biking, soccer and even skiing (both snow and dune skiing).

Windsurfing – Instruction is not commonly offered, but equipment can be hired at most coastal areas with a tourist industry, including in Côte d'Ivoire, Kenya, Ghana, Morocco, Mozambique, South Africa, Tanzania, Togo and many others.

Camel Trekking – Good places to try this include Morocco, Tunisia and Egypt. Possibilities range from one-hour rides to multiday oasis-hopping treks. Prices range from about US$20 to US$30 per person per day.

Horse Riding and Trekking – Try Malawi, South Africa, Zambia and Zimbabwe. Lesotho is the best place in Africa for pony treks, ranging from a few hours to a week or more.

Rock Climbing – Rock climbing is an undeveloped activity in most areas, although it's rapidly growing in popularity. One place to try is the area around Hombori in Mali, where you'll find some spectacular rock formations high above the desert floor that are ideal for serious rock climbing. Mali's Bandiagara escarpment is also good, and is a popular destination for some European climbing groups. In Morocco, the Dadès and Todra gorges provide almost endless climbing possibilities. Areas in the Anti-Atlas and High Atlas offer everything from bouldering to very severe routes. Malawi, Namibia, South Africa and Zimbabwe are among the many other locations you could try.

Mountain Biking – South Africa is one of the few places where there are established paths. Elsewhere on the continent there are endless possibilities, though you'll be on your own.

Soccer – Soccer is Africa's most popular participation and spectator sport, and is played throughout the continent. To join in or just watch, check at universities and municipal stadiums, although in every town there is a patch of ground where informal matches are played most evenings (in coastal areas, the beach is used). Foreigners are usually warmly welcomed and joining in a game

Tips for Travel in Africa

- Travel light. You can buy many things you need on the road, and a heavy pack will only be an encumbrance.
- Don't try to do too much or to cover too large an area. You'll wind up exhausted, and will miss out on getting to know a place in depth. There will always be other opportunities to see the places you miss this time round.
- Don't insulate yourself from Africa and Africans. Travel at least some of the time by public transport, and seek out areas away from major tourist attractions. Even if you spend most of your time in more heavily touristed areas, make it a point to get away from tourist hotels and restaurants to learn more about local life.
- Splurge once in a while, and don't be overly concerned with penny-pinching. If you are feeling run-down, treat yourself to a comfortable hotel or nutritious meal.
- Always treat locals politely, and respect local customs and sensibilities in your behaviour and dress.
- Adjust your clock to 'African time', and remember that things (almost always) do work – just not in the ways you would expect them to.
- Try some unusual foods. Experimenting with different cuisines can be an enjoyable aspect of getting to know a new culture.
- Learn the greetings and at least a few words of the local language(s) of the countries you will be visiting.

is a great way to meet people. If you bring along your own football (deflated for travelling), you'll be a big hit.

Skiing – The higher slopes and peaks of Morocco's High Atlas usually have decent snow cover from February to early April. There are also a few skiing areas around the Middle Atlas, including Mischliffen and Ifrane. Off-piste skiing is gaining in popularity in some sections of the High Atlas, mainly around Toubkal. In South Africa, there is skiing near Rhodes in the Eastern Cape Highlands, with the main centres at Tiffindell and Ben Macdhui. Oxbow in Lesotho used to be popular, but now is fairly dead as a ski resort. Dune skiing is a developing sport in many areas, although it can cause environmental damage, particularly if the dunes are vegetated. Tunisia is one place to try. Sand boarding is another option, and is available commercially at Swakopmund in Namibia.

When to Go

One of the most important factors to consider when planning your trip to Africa is the weather. Other considerations include festivals and special events, seasonal pricing differentials and, in some countries, school holidays.

WEATHER

Africa is so vast – stretching approximately 7000km from north to south, and about as far from east to west – and encompasses such a range of longitudinal and altitudinal zones that at any time of year it is possible to find good weather somewhere on the continent.

Throughout much of Africa the most important climatic factor affecting travel is rainfall, rather than temperature. Rainfall levels can vary dramatically throughout the year. In some areas of West Africa, for example, more than 3000mm of rain can fall during a six or seven month rainy season, with almost none falling during the dry season. While travelling during the rainy season has numerous advantages – including landscapes which are greener, fewer tourists and sometimes lower prices – muddy roads and washed-out bridges mean it is often difficult or impossible to reach many destinations.

Temperatures over much of Africa do not fluctuate dramatically. In fact, across more than half of the continent, the mean annual temperature range is only about 6°C or less. In general, the closer to the equator you are, the less variation you will find. However, there can be significant variations between daytime and night-time temperatures, and marked altitudinal differences. Perhaps even more important than the mercury level is humidity: many people find the dry heat of the Sahel easier to bear than the heavy moist air in regions closer to the equator.

Africa's Four Corners

Africa stretches from Cap Blanc (near the town of Bizerte in Tunisia) in the north to Cape Agulhas, South Africa, in the south. The mainland's westernmost point is Pointe d'Almadies, near Dakar, Senegal. In the east it extends to Ras Hafun (also sometimes spelled Xaafuun), in Somalia. With the exception of Ras Hafun, where access is restricted due to Somalia's poor security situation, all the points can be visited. Don't expect any signs or fanfare, though. While Cap Blanc is near some good beaches, at Pointe d'Almadies and Cape Agulhas there is nothing much other than rocky coastline and unobstructed sea views.

General weather patterns on the continent are summarised in the following sections.

West Africa

Rainfall in most areas of West Africa begins somewhere between March and June, and ends around October or November. In the coastal countries closer to the equator, the rainy season runs from April or May to October, while in the Sahel region, it's from June to September.

Throughout West Africa, temperatures are generally at their highest in the months before the rains begin. At any time of year, coastal areas tend to be cooler than those regions deep in the interior (except for places at altitude, such as Guinea's Fouta Djalon plateau).

In general, November and December are the best months to travel in West Africa as the rains are over and temperatures are relatively pleasant. While travel through to February is possible, the air becomes progressively hazier due to dust-laden harmattan winds (see the boxed text 'Harmattan Winds' in this section). If you are planning to visit national parks and wildlife reserves, note that many are closed during the rainy season because tracks become impassable.

Central Africa

In this region, which includes Cameroon, Chad, the Central African Republic (CAR), Equatorial Guinea, São Tomé & Príncipe and Gabon, rain falls throughout the year, although it is less heavy at certain times. In the Central Africa countries north of the equator (Chad, Cameroon, Equatorial Guinea and much of the CAR), the best time to travel is during the drier months from November to April, although the further north you go, the hotter it will be, especially during March and April. In Gabon and São Tomé & Príncipe, where it rains almost all year round, try to avoid the heavy rainy season from January to May. July and August are the driest months.

Southern Africa

In much of southern Africa, summer (November to April) is hot and wet, while winter (May to October) has limited rainfall and warm to cool or (at altitude) cold temperatures. In some areas there is a spring season from August to October, when rainfall is low but temperatures start to rise. In March and April (southern hemisphere autumn), rainfall and temperature levels begin to drop. This four season pattern is most pronounced in South Africa. Along

Harmattan Winds

'Harmattan' (from a Hausa word meaning 'north wind') refers to the cool, dry winds which originate in the Sahara and blow throughout much of West Africa during the November to March dry season, gaining force from about mid-December onwards. They bring with them dust from the Sahara and cause the air to be hazy. While there is no reason not to travel during this period – in fact, in many countries in the region November to January are considered to be the best travel months – it will not be optimal if you are interested in doing serious photography, or if you will be trekking and want to enjoy good views.

the coast, ocean currents modify the climate: in Mozambique, warm moist air off the Indian Ocean increases both temperature and rainfall levels, while in Namibia and other areas off the western coast, cold air from the Atlantic results in dry areas and the Namibian deserts. If you are planning to travel to the southern part of South Africa's Western Cape Province, note that weather patterns are reversed here, with most rain falling during winter.

In general, the best time to visit southern Africa is between April and August, although March and September are usually fine, and February or October are still OK in some areas. Much of South Africa is pleasant at any time of year. In the southern part of the Western Cape, November to March are the best months.

Madagascar
Ocean currents and topography give Madagascar unique climatic characteristics. The eastern side of the island receives the most precipitation – primarily between January and March – while much of the west remains very dry. Cyclones occur on the east coast, particularly between November and April, and in January and February. They can be very destructive, and make travel in some areas difficult or impossible. The best time to travel is from April to October.

East Africa
In much of East Africa, there are two wet seasons: 'long rains' fall from about March to May and 'short rains' from October/November to December/ January. Temperatures tend to be coolest in June and July, particularly in the highland areas. There is little annual temperature variation along much of the coast, including on offshore islands. Rains can fall on the islands year-round although they are generally limited to short bursts.

The best time to travel is from June to October when the rains have finished and the air is coolest. The second best time is from late December to February or early March, just after the short rains and before the long rains, although temperatures will be higher.

North Africa
Similar to southern Africa, but in reverse, much of North Africa has four seasons. Spring (mid-March to mid-June) is the ideal time to travel. Autumn (mid-September to mid-December) is also OK, but skies can be very hazy. Although summer (mid-June to mid-September) counts as the high season (in part because of European holiday schedules), temperatures can be uncomfortably hot. There are variations within this general pattern. While winter (mid-December to mid-March) on the Mediterranean coast can be wet and dreary, and the mountains can become snowbound, it can be very pleasant in the desert or on the south Moroccan coast.

SPECIAL EVENTS
Watching a festival or special event can be the highlight of a visit to Africa and is one of the best ways to get an introduction to local cultures and

Festivals, Holidays & Special Events

Following is a sampling of some of the continent's major festivals and special events. A country-specific guidebook will have more information about other events unique to the area.

Islamic Holidays

Islamic holidays are observed throughout much of Africa. Their dates are tied to the lunar calendar and are usually about 11 days earlier each year. Some important ones are listed here. Approximate months when these holidays will occur during the period 1999 to 2001 are: Ramadan (December/January); Eid al-Fitr (December/January); Eid al-Adha (March); and Eid al-Moulid (June).

Ramadan – Ramadan is not a holiday, but rather the annual 30 day period of dawn-to-dusk fasting when the Muslim faithful are called upon as a community to renew their relationship with Allah.

Eid al-Fitr – This Feast of the Breaking of the Fast is the second major Islamic holiday, and marks the end of Ramadan. It's a very family-oriented feast and generally lasts four to five days, during which just about everything comes to a halt.

Eid al-Adha (also known as the Great Feast, Eid al-Kebir or Tabaski) – This feast commemorates Abraham's readiness to sacrifice his son in obedience to God's command, only to have God intercede at the last moment and substitute a ram instead. It coincides with the end of the main pilgrimage to Mecca, and is celebrated with the ritual slaying of a sheep and several hours at the mosque, followed by a special meal and visiting with friends. In most countries it is a two day public holiday and the most important and festive day of the year.

Eid al-Moulid (also known as Maulidi or Mouloud, depending where you are) – This is a lesser feast celebrating the birthday of the Prophet Mohammed. It occurs about 10 weeks after Eid al-Adha.

In northern Nigeria, the elaborate Sallah celebrations mark Eid al-Fitr and Eid al-Moulid. The principal event at these is the Durbar, a procession of ornately dressed men mounted on gaily bedecked horses. The major Durbars are in Katsina, Kano and Zaria.

Festivals & Special Events

January
New Year's Day – Celebrated all over Africa.

Paris-Dakar Motor Rally – Africa's biggest auto race, held during the first three weeks of January; the route changes slightly every year, but usually finishes along the beach between St-Louis and Dakar in Senegal.

Mt Cameroon Race – a foot race up and down Mt Cameroon, and one of the continent's toughest athletic events. It is held on the last Sunday in January.

February
Fêtes des Masques (throughout February) – Fascinating festivals with masked dancing, held in the Man region of Côte d'Ivoire.

Argungu Fishing & Cultural Festival – A three day festival held in mid-February on the banks of the River Sokoto in Nigeria; includes displays of fishing, duck hunting and swimming, as well as diving competitions and canoe racing.

Festivals, Holidays & Special Events

FESPACO – International film festival, held in Ouagadougou, Burkina Faso in the last week of February in odd-numbered years; in even-numbered years it is held in October in Carthage, Tunisia.

March

Mardi Gras – Latin-style street festivals and parades held just before Lent (usually between mid-February and early March) in Cape Verde and São Tomé & Príncipe. They are particularly colourful in the towns of Praia and Mindelo (Cape Verde) and São Tomé. Bissau (Guinea-Bissau) also has a famous celebration, but travel to this country is presently restricted.

Easter – Widely celebrated; the date varies from year to year, but is usually in March or April.

April

Fête du Dipri – This is held in Gomon, Côte d'Ivoire and involves masked dancing, healing ceremonies and sacrifices.

Sham an-Nessim – A Coptic Christian holiday celebrated throughout Egypt with family picnics and outings. It falls on the first Monday after Coptic Easter, the date of which varies from year to year.

Santabary – Celebrations of the first rice harvest in Madagascar; held in late April or early May.

May

Deer Hunt (Aboakyer) – Famous festival held in Winneba, Ghana on the first weekend in May; the main event is a competitive antelope hunt between two groups of men.

Moussem of Sidi Mohammed M'a al'Ainin – Part religious festival and part commercial tribal gathering which often attracts Tuareg nomads from the Sahara; usually held in late May or early June.

June

Donia – A traditional music festival held on Nosy Be in Madagascar in early June or late May.

Moussem – Part religious event and part trade fare, with a big camel market; held annually in Goulimine, Morocco.

July

Bakatue Festival – Colourful harvest thanksgiving feast, with music and dancing, held in Elmina, Ghana on the first Tuesday of July.

Zanzibar International Film Festival – A relatively new festival held annually in the Zanzibar Archipelago, generally about the same time as the Zanzibar Music Festival, which features performers from all over Africa.

Mwaka Kogwa – Shirazi new year celebrations, held around late July on Unguja (Zanzibar) Island, and featuring singing and dancing, as well as numerous traditional rituals.

August

Oshun Festival – Famous Yoruba festival in Oshogbo, Nigeria honouring Oshun, the water goddess; it is celebrated on the last Friday in August with music, dancing and ritual sacrifices.

Maherero Day – On this day, Namibia's Red Flag Herero people gather in traditional dress at Okahandjja for a memorial service to the chiefs killed in the Khoi-Khoi and German wars.

Festivals, Holidays & Special Events

It takes place on the weekend nearest 26 August. A similar event is staged at the same location in mid-June by the Green Flag Herero, and in the first half of October at Omaruru by the White Flag Herero.

Umhlanga (Reed) Dance – A week-long ceremony held in Swaziland in August or September in which marriageable young Swazi women journey from all over the kingdom to help repair the queen mother's home at Lobamba. The week culminates with the reed dance on the sixth and seventh day; this is also a showcase of potential wives for the king.

September

Igname Festival – Fire dances are a highlight of this festival in Bassar, Togo, held at the beginning of September.

Biennal – National sport and cultural festival, held in Bamako, Mali in even-numbered years, starting around the second week of September; many regional bands enter the competitions, and it's a good opportunity to hear live music.

La Cure Salée – Annual celebration by the Fula herders in Niger; it is usually held in the first half of September near In-Gall, and is famous all over Africa. The best known part of Cure Salée is the gerewol festival of the Wodaabé people, in which single men participate in a sort of beauty contest to win the attention of eligible women.

October

Carthage International Film Festival – Held in even-numbered years in Tunisia. In odd-numbered years, it is held in Burkina Faso in February.

November

Abissa Festival – Festival of the Prophet Atcho, held at Grand Bassam and Gbregbo, in Côte d'Ivoire in early November.

Nso Cultural Week – Held in mid-November in Kumbo, Cameroon; features wild-horse racing through the streets.

December

Igue/Ewere Festival – A colourful seven day festival with traditional dances, a mock battle and a procession to the palace in which local people reaffirm their loyalty to the Oba (chief). Held in Benin City, Nigeria in early December.

Cattle Crossing – Vibrant annual festival of Fula cattle herders in Diafarabé, Mali in which herders bring their cattle from the Sahara across the Niger River to greener pastures. It takes place around early to mid-December; the exact date is not fixed until November, and depends in large part on water levels. In addition to the main crossing at Diafarabé, there are many smaller crossings at other points along the Niger.

International Music Festival – Held every December in Dakar, Senegal; features both traditional and modern African music.

Christmas – Widely celebrated throughout the continent.

Incwala – The most sacred ceremony of Swaziland's Swazi people, when the king gives permission for his people to eat the first crops of the new year. The celebrations, which last about a week, are held sometime between late December and early January near Lobamba in the Ezulwini Valley.

customs. If you happen to be in an area when one is taking place, it's well worth trying to attend. If you want to plan your trip around particular events, see the boxed text 'Festivals, Holidays & Special Events', which lists some of the more well known events. In addition, there are countless smaller festivals that you will only happen upon by chance, but which can be just as good. Keep in mind that for many of the larger, better known events, businesses may shut down, hotels may be crowded or more expensive, and transport schedules may be disrupted.

TRAVEL PERIODS

When planning your travel to Africa, remember to take into account peak, off-peak and shoulder travel periods. Peak periods are when the majority of travellers want to fly, and usually coincide with school holiday periods in your home country, with certain holidays such as Christmas and New Year, and with favourable times to travel in the destination country. Flights during peak periods are often heavily booked and air fares tend to be more expensive. The peak season in much of East Africa is between June and September. To many areas of West Africa, fares remain fairly even year-round, but planes fill up faster between November and January. In North Africa, the high season for air fares from Europe is from June to September. In southern Africa, hotel costs tend to be highest (and accommodation heavily booked) during the South African school holidays and around Christmas.

BAD TRAVEL TIMES

In southern Africa, the South African school holiday periods (see When to Go in the South Africa country profile) are among the worst times to travel, as hotels and park camp sites in both South Africa and in neighbouring countries can fill completely, and prices skyrocket.

In some West Africa coastal areas (eg in Senegal and The Gambia), resorts are packed with European sunbathers from December to March, and to a lesser extent in November and April. The Casamance region of Senegal and the Dogon area of Mali are also crowded at this time, especially in December and January. That said, there are many areas in these regions which are enough off the beaten track to allow you to travel in relative isolation even at the height of the tourist season.

Throughout the continent in areas of high rainfall, the rainy season is usually not a good time to travel – particularly if you will be relying on public transport – as many roads become impassable and many destinations unreachable.

In Muslim countries, while Ramadan is not necessarily a bad time to travel, restaurants often close during the day and commercial activity grinds to a halt in the afternoon. During Eid al-Fitr, transport is packed as Muslims everywhere journey to be with their families.

Researching Your Trip

Researching your trip beforehand can add tremendously to your enjoyment of your time on the road, and to what you are able to get out of it. In addition to preparing you for what to expect, proper research can give you a good background on culture and customs from which to build while actually at your destination. Research is also important for determining requirements for border crossings, visas and immunisations.

GUIDEBOOKS

Travel guides are invaluable tools, particularly when you're travelling in a country for the first time. They'll help you find places to stay and eat, describe popular attractions, provide vocabulary lists, give insights into the local culture, and include all the transport options between and within countries.

Try to decide on a rough route before buying a guidebook, and allow yourself plenty of time to read it. It's occasionally possible (eg in South Africa, Kenya and Tanzania) to pick up new or second-hand guides (new guidebooks will be more expensive in Africa than at home), or to swap them with fellow travellers on the road. However, it's usually best to bring from home any guidebooks, maps and phrasebooks that you'll need.

Selecting a Guidebook

The travel guide market has mushroomed over the past 20 years and there are thousands of titles on the market. Lonely Planet is a major seller. Other top-selling brands for independent travellers include Rough Guides, Moon, Footprint and Let's Go.

Before buying, ask friends which books they used – a personal recommendation is often the best. Then spend time in a bookshop browsing the guides to a particular destination. Read the author biographies, assess the quality of the maps, look at the edition date, flip through the photographs, and compare some hard information – how each guide describes a particular town or attraction, and the number of places to stay and eat that are covered – and the tone of the writing. If you're basing your trip on an activity such as surfing or diving, read the section that covers it, and see how much prominence is given to it in the index.

Also consider how long you plan to spend in each country, as this will influence the level of detail you will want from your guide. For example, in Lonely Planet's *Africa on a shoestring*, Tunisia merits 20 pages; in the *North Africa* guide the coverage is expanded to 144 pages; while the detailed *Tunisia* guidebook runs to about 300 pages. As the focus is sharpened, a greater level of information is provided; recommendations are more expansive; more maps are included; and cultural, historical and artistic issues are given more prominence.

Complementary Guides

As well as a day-to-day practical guide, consider reading a more general cultural guide. Oona Strathern's *Traveller's Literary Companion to Africa*, Frank Willett's *African Art*, and *Cultural Atlas of Africa* (edited J Murray) are good examples of this genre, with detailed information on the literature, art and other cultural aspects of the countries of Africa.

Specialist Guides

If you plan to pursue a particular activity, such as trekking, surfing or diving, it's worth finding a specialist guide.

Cycle Touring The best cycle touring guide to Africa is *Bicycling in Africa: The Places in Between* by David Mozer, which offers excellent practical and background information on exploring the continent by bike. The International Bicycle Fund (which publishes the *Bicycling in Africa* book) is also a good source of information (ibike@ibike.com). IBF also has a web site www.ibike.org /bikeafrica). *Bicycling* (☎ 800-666-2806; www.bicyclingmagazine.com; 135 N Sixth St, Emmaus, PA 18098, USA) is a monthly magazine covering destinations, training, touring and other topics. Also published by Rodale Press is *Mountain Bike* at www.mountainbike.com.

Diving & Snorkelling Lonely Planet's Pisces diving and snorkelling series covers many premier dive spots, with an Africa-specific book, *The Red Sea*. The series includes detailed information on dive sites, marine life, dive operators, safety and conservation, history, weather, accommodation, transport, dining and money matters. Another book worth looking at on East Africa is *The Dive Sites of Kenya and Tanzania* by Anton Koornhof.

Surfing There's no comprehensive world-wide series of guides. Check your local surf shop or contact *Surfer Magazine* (☎ 714-496-5922; www.surfermag .com), which publishes 'The Surf Report – Journal of World-wide Surfing Destinations'. Copies cost about US$5 per destination; order at PO Box 1028 Dana Point, CA 92629, USA.

Trekking Lonely Planet's *Trekking in East Africa* includes detailed information on trekking in Ethiopia, Kenya, Malawi, Tanzania and Uganda. Information on trekking options is also included in some Lonely Planet regional and country guides, including *Africa – the South*, *West Africa*, *Morocco* and *South Africa, Lesotho & Swaziland*.

Using Your Guidebook

A guidebook is not intended as a 'bible' to be unquestioningly followed every step of the way. Guides are written by people who bring their own experiences and interests to the text, and these may not necessarily coincide with your own. Also, information such as prices and schedules tends to date quite quickly, so expect bus timetables to change or hotels to raise their prices. While a good guide can give you most of the information and advice you'll need, there's no substitute for your own research.

Another point worth considering is that, while it's easy to stay safely within the boundaries laid down by a guidebook, it may tie you to a 'tourist trail' or to heavily touristed areas which increasingly tailor services to western visitors. While this isn't too much of a problem in many areas of Africa, confining your travel to prescribed boundaries can limit your experiences of the real, day-to-day life of the country you are visiting. For more information on this topic, see Getting Off the Beaten Track in the While You're There chapter.

MAPS

If your main method of getting around is public transport, then the regional and city maps in your guidebook should meet your needs. If you plan to hire a car or motorbike, do some independent trekking or an extensive cycle tour, then you will need to purchase more detailed maps either at home or on arrival.

Unfortunately, many areas of Africa, including many cities and towns, are not well mapped. While maps are available for most major urban areas, either from local tourist agencies or in bookshops and news agencies, quality and accuracy often leave a lot to be desired. For towns away from popular tourist areas, maps are usually nonexistent.

For large-scale or regional maps, try the Nelles or Michelin series. Lonely Planet also produces detailed country and regional maps, including travel atlases for Egypt and Kenya, and also the Southern Africa Travel Atlas (comprising Botswana, Lesotho, Malawi, Mozambique, Namibia, South Africa, Swaziland, Zambia and Zimbabwe), which will be published in May 2000.

Contoured maps for cycling or trekking should also be obtained before leaving home, if possible. A good place to look online is Mapquest Mapstore (www.mapquest.com). Other shops with good stocks are listed below. Otherwise, you can try the government Surveys & Mapping Departments once in a particular country in Africa; some produce excellent topographical maps, although they are often a bit dated and sheets covering popular destinations are frequently out of stock.

Australia
　Mapland
　（☎ 03-9670 4383) 372 Little Bourke St, Melbourne, Vic 3000
　Nev Anderson Maps
　（☎ 02-9878 2809) 30 Fawcett St, Ryde, NSW 2112
　The Travel Bookshop
　（☎ 02-9241 3554) 20 Bridge St, Sydney, NSW 2001

Canada
　World of Maps & Travel Books
　（☎ 613-724-6776; maps@magi.com; www.worldofmaps.com) 118 Holland Ave, Ottawa, Ontario K1Y 0X6

New Zealand
　Map World
　（☎ 03-374 5399; maps@mapworld.co.nz) PO Box 13-833, Christchurch
　Whitcoulls
　（☎ 09-356 5400) 210 Queen St, Auckland

UK
　The Map Shop
　（☎ 06-846 3146) AT Atkinson & Partner, 15 High St, Upton-on-Severn, Worcestershire WR8 OHJ
　Stanfords Map Centre
　（☎ 020-7836 1321) 12-14 Long Acre, London WC2E 9LP

USA

The Complete Traveller
(☎ 212-685-9007; completetraveller@worldnet.att.net) 199 Madison Ave, New York, NY 10016

Hagstrom Map and Travel Center
(☎ 212-398-1222; www.hagstromstore.com) 57 West 43rd St, New York, NY 10036

Rand McNally – The Map & Travel Store
(☎ 212-758-7488; www.randmcnallystore.com) 150 East 52nd St, New York, NY 10022;
(☎ 310-556-2202) Century City Shopping Center, 10250 Santa Monica Blvd, Los Angeles, CA 90067;
(☎ 415-777-3131) 595 Market St, San Francisco, CA 94105

US Library of Congress Geography & Map Division
(☎ 202-707-5000; photocopies only – post-1968 maps can be searched for on www.loc.gov) 101 Independence Ave, Washington, DC 20540

TRAVEL AGENCIES
Brochures distributed by travel agents can be a good source of free information. Even if you have no intention of going on an organised tour, you can get a good feel for a country's major sights from the full-colour images in these publications. Travel consultants are often widely travelled and most will be happy to share their experiences with you. Remember, though, that many consultants work on commission, so don't take up too much of their time if you're not planning to book through them.

INTERNATIONAL TOURIST OFFICES
A handful of countries in Africa maintain tourist offices in western countries, which can provide destination information, and sometimes also maps and lists of domestic tour operators. See the Tourist Offices Overseas sections in the country profiles for details, or try the *Tourism Offices Worldwide Directory* (www.towd.com), which has regularly updated links to almost every tourist office web site. For countries without tourist offices, their embassies sometimes have a travel officer, or they may be otherwise able to provide you with basic travel information.

NEWSPAPERS
Many major western newspapers include good-quality weekly or monthly travel sections carrying advertisements for special travel deals and packages. Check out the following papers in your country or access their web sites:

Australia
The *Age* (www.theage.com.au)
The *Australian* (www.news.com.au)
Sydney Morning Herald (www.smh.com.au)

Canada
The *Globe & Mail* (www.theglobeandmail.com)
Vancouver Sun (www.vancouversun.com)

UK
The *Independent* (www.independent.co.uk)
Southern Cross (www.southerncross.co.uk)

Time Out (www.timeout.com/london)
The *Times* (www.the-times.co.uk)
TNT (www.tntmag.co.uk; magazine for young Londoners notable for its travel ads)

USA
Chicago Tribune (www.chicagotribune.com)
LA Times (www.latimes.com)
New York Times (www.nytimes.com)
San Francisco Examiner (www.examiner.com)

BOOKS

Books are an excellent way to research a potential travel destination, and one of the best ways to begin to understand the cultures in the area you will be visiting is to seek out original (or English-translation) works by local authors. These often offer fascinating glimpses into the history, structure and mores of a society.

Travelogues are another good way to learn about the history and society of a country, and to get a feel for life as a traveller in the region. There are innumerable books by western travellers in Africa – both historical accounts and more modern tales. In addition, there is an extensive selection of literature by western authors which has been set in Africa, as well as a wide variety of speciality books covering subjects as diverse as religion, food, trekking, arts, architecture, diving and wildlife.

Finally, academic works on subjects such as sociology, politics, culture or diplomacy – while not always fast reading – will deepen your insights into and intellectual assessment of the issues. For suggested reading on the areas you will be visiting, see the Books & Films sections in the country profiles later in this book.

MAGAZINES

Many travel magazines are directly targeted at a particular market and include a combination of holiday and country profiles; comparative pieces on flights, accommodation and cuisine; articles on specialist activities such as diving, surfing or birdwatching; tips on equipment and clothing; readers' letters; competitions; and reams of travel industry advertisements. Some titles are listed below. Many publications have an e-zine component that you can access on the web. Also look at the magazines produced by travel organisations, such as *STA Escape*, Intrepid Travel's *The Intrepid Traveller* or Trailfinders' *Trailfinder Magazine*.

Adventure Magazine
(☎ 800-846-8575) PO Box 461270, Escondido, CA 92046-1270, USA
(has articles on adventure travel options and loads of practical advice on doing things independently)

Big World Magazine
(☎ 717-569-0217; orders@bigworld.com; www.bigworld.com) PO Box 8743, Lancaster, PA 17604-8743, USA
(a no-frills magazine targeted at the independent budget traveller)

Business Traveller
(☎ 020-7580 9898; www.btonline.com) Russell Square House, 10-12 Russell Square, London WC1B 5ED, England
(tips on managing your finances and how to stay in touch electronically while you're away)

Escape: The Global Guide for the Adventurous Traveler
(☎ 800-738-5571; EscapeMag@aol.com) PO Box 5159, Santa Monica, CA 90409-5159, USA
(a quarterly featuring out-of-the-way destinations, equipment and book reviews and advertising for US-based tour companies)

Geographical Magazine
(☎ 020-7938 4011; geogmag@gn.apc.org) 47c Kensington Court, London W8 5DA, England
(the magazine of the Royal Geographical Society (UK), with a focus on cultural, anthropological and environmental issues)

National Geographic
(☎ 800-647-5463; www.nationalgeographic.com) Box 98198, Washington 20090-8198 USA
(the magazine of the US National Geographic Society with striking photos and good background information. Also try National Geographic Traveler at ☎ 800-437-5521; www.nationalgeographic.com/media/traveler; PO Box 64026, Tampa, FL 33664-4026, USA, which has practical information on getting to the places covered by National Geographic)

Outpost Magazine
(☎ 416-703-5394; outpost@echo-on.net; www.outpostmagazine.com) 490 Adelaide St W, Suite 303 Toronto, Ontario M5V 1T2 Canada
(focuses on active travel and cultural encounters)

Outside
(☎ 800-678-1131; outside.starwave.com) PO Box 54729, Boulder, CO 80322-4729, USA
(focus is on travel by bike, skateboard, kayak and the like. It has a US bias, but includes international destinations)

Travel and Leisure
(☎ 212-382-5600; www.amexpub.com/cgi-bin/WebX.cgi) 1120 Avenue of the Americas, New York, NY 10036, USA
(for the top-end traveller)

Travel Unlimited
(PO Box 1058, Allston, Mass 02134, USA)
(publishes details of cheap air fares, special deals and courier options)

Traveller Magazine
(☎ 020-7589 3315; mship@wexas.com; www.travelmag.co.uk) 45-49 Brompton Rd, Knightsbridge, London SW3 1DE, England
(a quarterly with an emphasis on anthropology, exploration and adventure travel, plus advertising for UK-based tour operators)

Wanderlust
(☎ 01753-620426) PO Box 1832, Windsor, Berkshire SL4 6YP, England
(general travel information on a variety of destinations plus many ads for tours and tour companies)

FILMS

Western films set in African countries and local films made by African industries can sometimes serve as useful supplements to your research.

Unfortunately, western efforts are often lamentably inaccurate and biased, and in many cases are filmed outside the country in which they are fictitiously set. Still, if you can find films shot in the country you will be visiting, they may enhance your appreciation of local landscapes and cityscapes. A good place to start is the Internet Movie Database (www.imdb.com), which allows you to search by location.

African films, by contrast, provide a more accurate picture of the society, culture, scenery and social issues of a country. There may still be an element of fantasy, but even so, they can be useful for conveying information about a society and contemporary issues.

For relevant titles, see the Books & Films sections in the country profiles.

USEFUL WEB SITES

The following web sites are good resources for obtaining information on African countries. There are additional sites mentioned throughout this book with details on visas, accommodation, plane tickets, activities, health, media and other travel needs. For a full list, see the appendix 'Internet Sites' at the back of the book.

Lonely Planet
www.lonelyplanet.com
(destination information, health advice, photographs, bulletin boards and links to all travel-related topics)

Internet Traveller Information Service
www.itisnet.com
(destination information and advice)

Internet Guide to Hostelling
www.hostels.com
(details of hostels across the world, with a good travellers' news section)

World Tourism Organization
www.world-tourism.org/ows-doc/wtich.htm
(the United Nations international organisation dealing with travel and tourism policy and development, with members in numerous countries representing local government, tourism associations, airlines, hotel groups and tour operators)

Hiking & Walking Homepage
www.teleport.com/-walking/hiking.html
(information on international trekking spots, tours and clubs)

World Events Calendar
travel.epicurious.com
(lists of festivals, events and other festivities, which can be searched by theme, country or date)

Travelocity
www.travelocity.com
(general travel information, bookings, equipment and links)

British Foreign & Commonwealth Office
www.fco.gov.uk
(travel advisories written for Brits, but relevant for most travellers)

US State Department Travel Warnings & Consular Information Sheets
travel.state.gov/travel_warnings.html
(mildly paranoid warnings about trouble spots written principally for American citizens)

Rain or Shine
www.rainorshine.com
(five-day weather forecasts for 800 cities around the world)

Africa News On-Line
www.africanews.org
(just what it says it is)

Stanford Library
www-sul.stanford.edu/depts/ssrg/africa
(links to news and other sites)

Orientation Africa
http://af.orientation.com/home.html
(has pages on numerous countries with links to recent news stories, weather reports and news groups)
University of Pennsylvania
www.sas.upenn.edu
(good for background information and for country-specific links)

Language

Although no one is really sure of the exact number, it is estimated that close to 1000 languages are spoken in Africa. Fortunately for travellers, it's not necessary to learn them all. Throughout much of the continent, Arabic or a European language (primarily English, French or Portuguese) functions as the official language. In addition, several African languages have taken on the role of lingua franca as a way of coping with the continent's enormous linguistic diversity. These include Swahili, which is widely spoken throughout East Africa; Hausa, spoken in northern Nigeria and neighbouring areas; Bambara-Maninka, spoken in Mali, Guinea and Côte d'Ivoire; and Wolof, widely spoken throughout Senegal and The Gambia.

Yet, even if the only language you know is English, there's no need to let your enthusiasm for an Africa trip be dampened by visions of studying vocabulary cards and memorising conjugations. In many areas of the continent, particularly in southern and East Africa, you will be able to get by with English alone. In West and Central Africa, where French is the official language in more than half the countries, you'll at least need a French phrasebook, but with this (plus a few phrases of the local African languages), you shouldn't have any trouble. In North Africa, knowing some Arabic would definitely smooth the way, but otherwise you can generally get by with French in many areas. In Mozambique, Cape Verde and São Tomé & Príncipe, you'll need a few phrases of Portuguese.

This said, it is well worth taking the time to learn at least the basics of the official language spoken in the area you want to visit. In addition to making it easier to get around, a rudimentary proficiency will make your travels more fun and – more importantly – will help you gain access to and understanding of the culture. Going a step further and learning even just a few phrases of the local African language will intensify these benefits and enrich your travels even more. In rural areas, a few words of the local African language will often be essential.

LEARNING A LANGUAGE

The vast majority of languages used in sub-Saharan Africa west of the Nile belong to the Bantu subgroup. The most widely spoken is Swahili. Others include Kongo and Zulu. These languages might seem formidable at first. However with many, and Swahili in particular, it is not considered particularly difficult to achieve basic conversational proficiency. Some of the tonal languages, such as Sara (spoken in Chad), Luo (spoken in Kenya) and other members of what is known as the Chari-Nile language family, are more difficult to master. The most difficult of all are the Khoisan, or 'click' languages spoken in a few areas of southern and East Africa.

If you don't have time to learn a language, at least consider trying to master the basic pleasantries, such as 'hello', 'please', 'thank you', 'excuse me' and 'goodbye'. As already noted, these can go a long way in helping you to gain an introduction to African society. Adding a few simple phrases such as 'Where is the ... ?', 'How much does this cost?' and so on, plus learning to count to at least 10, will make day-to-day survival much easier. And, no matter how limited your vocabulary, locals will invariably appreciate your efforts.

To make headway in learning a language, use a textbook with tapes to assist with pronunciation (for study before departure) and a phrasebook (for use on the road; see Phrasebooks following). Good textbook titles include Teach Yourself, Berlitz, Barrons and Routledge. For self-study, set some goals and sit down with the book on a regular basis. Making flashcards of the words and phrases you want to learn, and then drilling yourself, is a very effective method.

If you wish to supplement your study with private tutoring or language classes while at home, contact local universities, many of which offer extension courses and night classes in foreign languages, or which could help you find a private tutor. Community centres are also worth checking out. Other places to look for a tutor include the embassy or consulate of the country you plan to visit, and newspaper advertisements. Searching the Internet under the name of the language you want to learn may also be helpful. Private language schools are another option, although these can be expensive.

If you will be spending an extended time in one area of Africa, consider taking a language course on-site or arranging a local tutor, both of which are often very affordable options. Foreigners frequently go to Africa to study Swahili and Arabic, and study facilities for both languages (in Tanzania and Egypt, respectively) are good.

PHRASEBOOKS

A good phrasebook should be compact and have everything written in both English and the local language. Lonely Planet phrasebooks useful in Africa include those for Amharic, Arabic (both Moroccan and Egyptian versions are available), Swahili, French, Portuguese and Spanish.

Also, don't forget the language sections of your guidebooks. These can be used for learning basic phrases of a language, especially local languages, and often come in handy while you're on the road.

Phrasebooks are difficult to find in most areas of Africa, so acquire one before leaving home.

Work & Travel

If you are interested in working in Africa, it's best to do background research and make some contacts before leaving home. The most likely areas for employment are teaching, the safari industry, journalism and advertising, or international aid work. Countries where a wider choice may be available include Egypt and South

Africa (although in South Africa, due to high levels of unemployment, it is becoming more difficult for foreigners to obtain work or residence permits). A good resource to help you get started is the book, *Work Your Way Around the World* by Susan Griffith, which has an informative chapter on working in Africa.

Keep in mind that work permits can be difficult to arrange in some countries (eg in South Africa, as already mentioned, and in Zimbabwe). Normally, you will need to first line up the job, and then apply for work and residency permits through your employer.

TEACHING

Most teaching positions are either voluntary (arranged through a volunteer agency or mission organisation in your home country) or with the international school system. The more credentials you have (including certification in your home country), the better your chances will be. While teaching positions may be available locally, pay is normally very low.

With the exception of Egypt, where there are many opportunities for teaching English as a second language, English-teaching positions are not common in Africa. Morocco has some opportunities for teaching English, but most schools are fairly small and the chances of just walking into a job are not high. In other countries, check with language schools in the capital cities, although prospects for employment are moderate, at best.

THE SAFARI INDUSTRY

The main countries where positions in the safari industry may be available are Kenya, Tanzania and South Africa. However, operators are a dime a dozen, competition is very stiff and there is a notoriously high turnover. If you are interested in safari work, try to get to know someone already working in the business. If you are contemplating establishing your own operation, you will first need to get a good feel for the country, and find an open market niche in order to survive (plus arrange all the necessary permits and paperwork).

DIVE MASTERS

If you have your dive master certification, you may be able to find work at a dive outfit in Egypt, Kenya or Tanzania, or in other resort diving areas, although the number of available positions is limited. Egypt may be your best bet. However, there and elsewhere, you'll probably need both connections and experience to land a good job. For information on obtaining dive master certification and employment opportunities, check the PADI web site (www.padi.com).

JOURNALISM

Unless you are affiliated with a news agency in your home country, this will all be freelance. For information on how to break into the field, contact news wire services or other media entities in your home country.

In Egypt and perhaps a few other countries, you may be able to find work copy-editing or writing for an English-language publication. Alternatively, publications may be interested in freelance contributions if you have previous experience. In either case, do not expect to earn much money.

TRAVEL WRITING & PHOTOGRAPHY

You may be able to defray a small portion of your travel costs by publishing articles or photos on the places you visit, although expect to put in much more time – at least at the outset – than you will ever be compensated for. If you have ambitions of being a photographer, invest in the appropriate equipment (see the Camera section in the What to Bring chapter) and consider taking a course in photography. The field of travel photography is very competitive. Typically, if you submit 100 shots to a photo library, it might accept fewer than 10. Be sure to use slide film, as transparencies are the industry standard.

The same professional approach should be brought to travel writing. Research the potential markets for your stories and even send away for writers' guidelines before hitting the road. When you're on the road, research your material thoroughly and keep good notes, as it might not be feasible to return to Africa to fill in the gaps.

OTHER PROFESSIONAL WORK

There are often openings in computer science and various business and trade-related areas if you have a university or more advanced degree and some professional experience. Many employers do their recruiting in the west, so start searching in your home country.

For employment with an international aid organisation, most positions are best arranged before leaving home. If you're in Africa, you'll need to establish contacts with expatriates working locally with aid organisations.

VOLUNTEER WORK

There are many opportunities for volunteer work through missions or international organisations. It's best to research the options thoroughly from home before setting off for Africa. In fact, many organisations require applicants to go through their headquarters office (usually in a western country). Some volunteer organisations will give you a small stipend to cover food and lodging expenses; transport from home is generally not included. If you are already in Africa, inquire at local churches or charitable organisations for information about volunteer work.

Following are the contact details of some international aid and placement agencies to help you get started. Consult country-specific guidebooks, the Internet or a local church for additional suggestions.

Australia
Earthwatch Institute
(☎ 03-9682 6828; www.earthwatch.org/australia/html) 126 Bank St, South Melbourne, Vic 3205
Overseas Service Bureau
(☎ 03-9279 1788; www.osb.org.au) PO Box 350, Fitzroy, Vic 3065

New Zealand

Volunteer Service Abroad
(☎ 04-472 5759; www.tcol.co.uk/comorg/vsa.htm) PO Box 12-246, Wellington 1
Switzerland

Voluntary Work Information Service
(☎ 41 22 366 1651; www.workingabroad.com) Case Postale 90, 1268 Begnins, Vaud

UK

Earthwatch Institute
(☎ 01865-311600; www.earthwatch.org/t/Toeuropehome.htm) 57 Woodstock Rd,
Oxford OX2 6JH

International Voluntary Service
(☎ 0131-226 6722) St John's Church Centre, Edinburgh EH2 4BJ

Voluntary Service Overseas (VSO)
(☎ 020-8780 2266; www.oneworld.org/vso) 317 Putney Bridge Rd, London SW15
2PN

USA

Earthwatch Institute
(☎ 800-776-0188; www.earthwatch.org) 680 Mt Auburn St, PO Box 9104,
Watertown, MA 02272

Global Volunteers
(☎ 612-482-0915; www.globalvolunteers.org) 375 E Little Canada Rd, St Paul, MN
55117-1628

Peace Corps of the USA
(☎ 202-606-3970; www.peacecorps.gov) 1990 K St NW, Washington, DC 20526

MONEY MATTERS

Africa can be as expensive or as inexpensive a destination as you wish. All styles of travel – from budget to five star luxury – are possible, although not all types are possible in all places. In many countries, for example, top-end accommodation and upmarket western-style restaurants will only be available in the capital, some resort areas and perhaps one or two major cities. In general, the more comfort and speed you desire, the more costly your trip will be. If you eat at local restaurants, stay in budget or mid-range accommodation and travel by public transport, you will be able to hold your expenses to a very low level.

To maintain a moderate expense level while at the same time enjoying your stay in Africa, determine at the outset what your priorities are: maybe a comfortable hotel at the end of the day with running water and air-con, an organised safari or trek, or simply the occasional splurge at an upmarket restaurant. Then, you can put more emphasis on things that are important for you while striving to save a bit in other areas. For example, taking local transport everywhere may not be so unbearable if you can relax in the evening at a pleasant hotel. Or, the costs of an organised safari during part of your travels could be partially offset by staying in budget lodging during the remainder of the trip.

When setting your budget, always allow enough leeway for unforeseen expenses. Depending on what area you are in, it can be difficult or impossible to have money transferred from abroad, and even where it is possible, it may not be able to be arranged immediately. It's much better to return from a trip with a few unused travellers cheques than to get caught short while on the road.

Also remember that travel costs vary from season to season. If you're travelling during the high season, you can expect to pay up to 50% more than during the low season, especially for accommodation. Airfares will also usually be more expensive.

Pretrip Expenses

Your largest expense will be your plane ticket. Other pretrip expenses will include travel insurance, visas, immunisations and any equipment you may need.

PLANE TICKETS

The following list shows average prices for a return ticket into regional airline hubs for East, West and southern Africa, and into Casablanca (Morocco), though these can vary significantly depending on the season and on the destination city. In West Africa, Abidjan (Côte d'Ivoire) is a major hub, but flights into Dakar (Senegal), Accra (Ghana) or Banjul (The Gambia) are often less expensive. In southern Africa, the best fares are usually to Johannesburg, followed by Harare. In north Africa, the airports to check are Casablanca, and Cairo (Egypt). In East Africa, Nairobi (Kenya) is generally the cheapest. Other popular airports include Dar es Salaam (Tanzania) and (especially if you are transiting from elsewhere in Africa), Addis Ababa (Ethiopia).

Some online sources to check for up-to-date information on air fares include:

Expedia (expedia.msn.com/daily/home/default.hts)
Flight Info.Com (www.flifo.com)
Travelocity (www.travelocity.com)

from Australasia

Sydney - Abidjan	A$2300 to A$2800
Sydney - Casablanca	A$3020 to A$3900
Sydney - Johannesburg	A$1800 to A$2500
Sydney - Nairobi	A$2000 to A$2500

from the UK

London - Abidjan	UK£500 to UK£600
London - Casablanca	UK£200 to UK£300
London - Johannesburg	UK£500 to UK£600
London - Nairobi	UK£400 to UK£600

from North America

New York - Abidjan	US$800 to US$1500
New York - Casablanca	US$900 to US$1100
New York - Johannesburg	US$1000 to US$2000
New York - Nairobi	US$1500 to US$2500

INSURANCE

Good travel/health insurance is a necessity. It's also not an item to cut corners on. Typical rates for a basic travel insurance package, including health, accidental death, baggage and cancellation insurance, are about US$35 for one week, US$115 for one month, US$180 for two months and US$400 for six months. If you are a national of a country with socialised health care, you may be covered while travelling overseas, and may therefore be able to save on some elements of insurance.

See the Tickets & Insurance chapter for more details on buying insurance.

VISAS

Visa costs vary widely among countries in Africa, ranging from about US$10 to US$80, with the average for a one month single-entry visa about US$25. Costs will vary depending on your nationality, and sometimes depending on the place you apply. Gabon has one of the highest visa fees (US$80), while visas for South Africa (if you even need one at all) are free.

IMMUNISATIONS

If you have not previously travelled in Africa, you will likely need to get a full course of immunisations before setting out. This will cost anywhere from US$150 to US$350. Fortunately, many of the immunisations do not need to be repeated or are effective for long periods, so you can view this expense as an investment for future travels. See the Health chapter for details on immunisations.

EQUIPMENT

If you don't already have equipment, it's worth investing in good quality items that will last for other trips as well. Following are typical prices for a few essentials (backpack, torch and pocketknife), plus some big-ticket items you may need if you will be hiking. See the What to Bring chapter for more information.

backpack	US$150 to US$300
camera (automatic)	US$50 to US$300
camera (SLR)	US$250 to US$800
hiking boots	US$70 to US$200
pocketknife	US$15 to US$40
sleeping bag	US$100 to US$250
tent	US$150 to US$250
torch (flashlight)	US$10 to US$30

AVERAGE PRETRIP EXPENSES FOR A TWO MONTH TRIP

The following figures are rough estimates to assist in planning a budget for your trip. Of course, your actual expenses will probably be quite different – you may already have a backpack and don't need to invest in other gear, or you may (or may not) get a good deal on airfare.

gear	US$100 to US$400
immunisations	US$300
insurance	US$180
plane ticket (return)	US$1500
visas	US$75
total	US$2305

Daily On-Road Costs

Your daily travel expenses will depend on a variety of factors, including the style in which you wish to travel (budget vs luxury), whether you incorporate an organised safari, trek or other tour into your trip, how much distance you want to cover within Africa and what method of transport you use, and the cost of living in the areas you visit.

COMFORT LEVELS

It's possible to get by in many countries for US$10 per day or less, although this will mean staying in basic accommodation, eating local food and travelling exclusively by public transport. While this type of travel can be interesting, it can also be exhausting and may detract from your enjoyment of the trip – especially after a few months on the road.

At the other extreme, insulating yourself in five-star hotels, travelling exclusively in rented vehicles or by plane and enjoying expensive western cuisine – while certainly comfortable – will contribute little to your understanding of Africa, its people and cultures.

ORGANISED TOURS

Participating in an organised safari or tour can add significantly to the cost of your trip. Per diem (per day) expenses can easily range from US$80 to US$100 at the lower end to US$300 or more for top-end luxury trips.

If you want to take advantage of some of the benefits of an organised tour without emptying your wallet, a good option may be travelling modestly for most of your trip in order to balance out the costs of a short organised tour for the remainder.

MOVING VS STAYING PUT

Transportation within Africa can eat up a large portion of your travel budget if you fly from one place to another or hire vehicles. However, by utilising buses, taxis and other forms of public transport whenever possible, or by splitting the cost of rental vehicles with others, you can keep expenses in this category to a very reasonable level.

Planning your itinerary to focus on a specific region, rather than trying to fit every corner of the continent into a few months, is another way to minimise transportation costs. Not only will your travels likely be more enjoyable and less expensive, you'll also be able to immerse yourself more deeply in the cultures around you. Any countries you miss this time around will still be there for your next trip.

COST OF LIVING

With a few exceptions, cost of living doesn't tend to vary as much in Africa from country to country as it does in other areas of the world (eg in Asia), although it can vary widely from area to area within a country. Capital cities are often quite pricey, while rural areas are much less expensive. If you are on a tight budget, try to minimise the nights you spend in large cities or resort areas. Also try to stick to local products, including local food and produce, as these will be much less expensive than imported items.

Apart from cost of living, a factor affecting the cost of travel in some areas of Africa is government tourism policy. In Zambia, for example, where the government courts low-impact, high-cost tourism, travel costs can be much

A Matter of Perspective

Just to keep things in perspective, it's worth giving some thought to the value that the money you are spending on your trip would have for a rural African family. According to United Nations statistics, more than half of African countries have an average annual per capita income of US$500 or less. This means that even with a shoestring budget of US$10 per day, you are spending more daily than many rural Africans earn in a week. The money you might drop to stay a few nights in a nice mid-range hotel would cover secondary school tuition costs in many countries for an entire year, while one night in a top-end hotel would probably pay a couple of teachers' salaries for a month. When haggling over the price of fruit with a street-side vendor, consider that the vendor's total profits for the day may well be less than US$1, from which about US$0.10 might need to be deducted for public transport back home in the evening.

higher than in neighbouring Zimbabwe, although actual cost of living figures may be fairly similar.

In North Africa, Libya is probably the most expensive country to visit thanks to its currency exchange regulations (see the Libya country profile). In East Africa, most of the countries are roughly on a par, while in southern Africa, Zambia followed perhaps by Botswana and Namibia (depending on what mode of transport you plan to use in each) are the most expensive. In West Africa, Mauritania can be costly because of the need to hire a vehicle to reach many places. In Central Africa, Gabon is probably the most expensive destination due to high visa costs and the expenses of Libreville. Once outside the capital, however, travelling around Gabon shouldn't cost too much more than anywhere else in the region.

SAVING MONEY ON THE ROAD

While you're travelling, it can be very alarming to see your hard-earned cash trickling away faster than you expected. To prevent serious cash shortfalls, follow some of these thrifty spending policies:

Eat local food – Three or four local meals cost about the same as one western-style meal.

Take public transport – Even though it won't always be very comfortable, you can save significantly by taking buses and share taxis instead of hiring your own cab or renting a car.

Ask for a discount – It's surprising how many hotels will reduce room rates if you ask, especially if you are not travelling during high season.

Learn to bargain effectively – This is a real skill, and a little practice can save you a lot of money.

Get out of the cities – Stay in small towns or rural areas, where prices are almost always cheaper.

Seek out budget lodging – Mid-range and top-end accommodation is often overpriced. However, there are some good budget deals available. Ask other travellers, and look around to get the best deals. Budget lodging doesn't always have to be a flea pit. If camping is possible in the place you are visiting, that will save you even more money.

Travel during low season – If you don't mind the fact that some roads may be closed and others very slow (and that some national parks and other attractions may be closed as well), there are some great lodging and airfare deals available in the low season.

Money Carrying Options

The major hard currencies in Africa are the US dollar, which is widely accepted throughout the continent; the French franc (the most useful currency in West Africa); and the British pound.

If you will be in West Africa, bring at least some of your money in French francs, and in both cash and travellers cheques. In most other areas of the continent, you can get by exclusively with US dollars. Other major currencies will be accepted in larger cities, although often not in rural areas. As a general rule, the less developed the country, the more difficult it will be to exchange currencies other than US dollars.

The main options for carrying money are travellers cheques, credit and/or debit cards and cash. Each has advantages, and most experienced travellers carry a combination of all three (see the following sections).

Always keep your money and other valuables where no one can get them, preferably in a money belt worn under your clothing as unobtrusively as possible, or in some sort of invisible pocket. With a money belt, be sure that the belt clasps are secure and that you can feel it against your skin. You should also bring along a change pouch to carry your daily spending money (separately from your money belt), for convenience and safety, and to be sure you have some money on hand if your money belt is lost or stolen. As an additional fallback in an emergency, keep a US$100 bill and a spare travellers cheque tucked away somewhere safe (eg inside a backpack frame).

TRAVELLERS CHEQUES

Travellers cheques are the most popular and often the most practical way to carry money while travelling. Their biggest advantage is that if they are stolen, they will be replaced by the issuing bank within a few days. Also, in some places you will get better exchange rates for travellers cheques than for cash.

To facilitate replacement if your cheques are lost or stolen, always keep the purchase agreement of the cheques, and keep accurate records of the cheque serial numbers as you spend them, so you can tell the bank which ones are missing. Store the purchase record, spending records and the credit card company's emergency contact number separately from the cheques. It is also a good idea to make a couple of photocopies of the purchase receipt and put one with the photocopy of your passport (see Photocopies in the Passports & Visas chapter) and leave the other with someone at home.

The one caveat to this arrangement is that in some countries, particularly in West Africa, banks and foreign exchange bureaux require you to show the purchase receipt in order to cash a travellers cheque, so you'll need to have this accessible. Be sure to keep a photocopy stored safely somewhere else.

A Numismatist's Delight

Coin collectors will find plenty of variety in Africa – from the Botswanan pula to the Swazi lilangeni – and all sorts of designs and shapes. Some coins are quite attractive, such as the Malagasy one franc piece, which is adorned with a flower. Others are more practical or patriotic – eg the Kenyan one shilling coin, with its depiction of Daniel Arap Moi; or the Tanzanian 10 shilling piece, with Julius Nyerere. Lesotho's 50 lisente piece is a mixture of both, with a Basotho ponyman on one side and King Moshoeshoe II on the other. In rural areas you may find that economies are still primarily barter based and few coins are used.

In some countries you may also encounter the opposite problem: due to high inflation and scarce funds for printing new money, existing denominations are inadequate. Coins will have deflated to the point of being almost useless, while bills will need to be carried around in large wads. When changing money – say, a US$100 travellers cheque – you may receive back a stack of notes several centimetres thick.

In most countries, travellers cheques issued by American Express or Thomas Cook are the most commonly accepted. Barclays cheques are also widely accepted in former British colonies. Ideally, bring along a mixture of several different types, as some banks will only change one brand.

Also try to bring a mixture of both large (US$50 to US$100) and small (US$20) denomination cheques. If you will be in one country for an extended period, cash your large denomination cheques to avoid high per-cheque cashing fees. If you will only be somewhere for a day or two, you can change the smaller denominations to avoid being stuck with too much local currency. It's also handy to have some smaller denomination cheques for those times when you need to pay for something in hard currency but will receive change in local currency. Cheques in amounts greater than US$100 are generally not necessary, and are likely to leave you with too much cash.

CREDIT CARDS

While credit cards are widely used in some countries in Africa (such as South Africa), in most places they are only accepted by some top-end hotels in capital cities and resort areas and by some airline companies. Cash advances against credit cards are possible in many major cities, but the practice is not widespread. They are also often time-consuming and expensive, as exchange rates are generally low and additional fees are often involved. The most realistic way to treat a credit card when travelling in Africa is as a fallback for emergencies or to cover splurges or unexpected expenses (although even here, you should have enough cash reserves in case you are in a place where you cannot use a credit card). The most widely accepted cards are Visa and MasterCard. American Express cards are less useful, although they can be handy for arranging travellers cheque purchases.

In a few countries, such as South Africa and Morocco, you can withdraw cash from automatic teller machines (ATMs) with a credit card and PIN number, although ATMs can be unreliable when it comes to foreign cards. If you don't want to risk having your card swallowed, stick to cash advances. You can search on the Internet for ATMs that accept Visa credit cards (www.visa.com/cgi-bin /vee/pd/atm/main.html) or MasterCard (www.mastercard.com/atm).

If you will be travelling for an extended period and making use of credit cards, don't forget to make arrangements for someone to pay off your account to avoid accumulating interest or exceeding your credit limit.

For any purchases or cash advances that you do make with credit cards, be sure to keep the receipts and check your account statement against these when you return home. Credit card fraud is not widespread in most areas (Nigeria may be an exception) but it does happen. When using your credit card, always try to keep it in sight.

DEBIT CARDS

With a debit card, the money you spend or withdraw is taken directly from your savings or cheque account. If you don't have enough money in your account, you can't make the transaction. Debit cards are of limited or no use in most areas of Africa. If you have a MasterCard or Visa debit card, you can search for ATMs using the web site included in the earlier Credit Cards section.

Another drawback of debit cards is that once the money is taken out of your account, it cannot be replaced. If your card is stolen and transactions or withdrawals are made, you won't see the money again. In contrast, if a credit card is stolen, you can request a 'charge back' and have the money returned to you.

CASH

Obviously, carrying too much cash is not a good idea – if it's stolen or lost, you'll never see it again. However, you will need to have enough cash to cover you in places where travellers cheques are not accepted (which includes many smaller towns and rural areas), for times when you arrive and banks are closed (it's usually possible to change cash on the street, but rarely travellers cheques) and for emergencies. There are also numerous countries that require you to pay for visas with hard currency cash.

Many experienced travellers carry at least a few hundred dollars in cash (US$500 is a good amount). Keep your cash in a very safe place, ideally divided between your money belt and a smaller emergency stash somewhere else.

It's best to bring along a mixture of bills in larger denominations (such as US$50s or US$100s), a good supply of US$20s and some US$5s and US$1s. Keep in mind that in some countries, US$100 notes (and occasionally even US$50s) will not be accepted by banks because of widespread problems with counterfeited notes. Also note that the USA changed the design of the US$100 bill in the mid-1990s and old-style US$100 notes are no longer accepted in some places unless they have a light machine for checking watermarks. It's not a good idea to plan on getting dollars once in Africa, as these are usually expensive and often difficult to buy.

If you will be travelling in West or Central Africa, at least part of your cash supply should be in French francs, in a mixture of denominations. In many places, especially outside of cities, dollars (and pounds) will not be accepted. In a pinch, you can use smaller denomination bills for taxi fares and in hotels and shops.

RUNNING OUT OF MONEY

This is something none of us likes to think about but it is a real possibility, so it helps to be prepared. If you realise you are running out of money, do something before you go flat broke, or you'll have no money to make arrangements for more. If the worse comes to worst, you may be able to borrow money from a fellow traveller (but don't assume this when you start spending your money!).

There are two main ways to have money sent from home: with an international money transfer and through a service like Western Union, which specialises in sending cash to all parts of the world.

Other important aspects of money management relate to changing money, bargaining and tipping.

INTERNATIONAL MONEY TRANSFERS

In theory, it is possible to have money wired from your home country to a local bank in the event that you run out of money. Some travellers also contemplate this option if they plan to be on the road for a long time and don't want to carry too much money from the start of their trip. In practice, however, this method is of dubious utility in much of Africa. Transfers can take weeks to clear, or the bank may deny receiving money that has actually arrived. If you do need to resort to a transfer, arrange for the forwarding bank to send separate confirmation with full details. You can then go into the local bank with the much-needed proof that your money has been sent.

Even when done efficiently, a wire transfer will take at least several days to clear. It will speed up the process if you have details of your home bank account (account number, branch and routing numbers, address and telephone number). Most countries will only give you your money in local currency, normally as cash, while a few may let you have it in US dollars or another hard currency. Be sure to find out the regulations in advance to avoid winding up with a large amount of unconvertible currency that you may not even be allowed to take out of the country.

WESTERN UNION TRANSFERS

Sending cash through a service such as Western Union can be convenient, but it is a hassle and rates are generally significantly higher than those charged by banks for international money transfers. To receive money this way, you'll have to arrange for someone in your home country to take the cash to one of Western Union's offices. For further details, call Western Union in the UK (☎ 0800-833833) or in the USA (☎ 800-325-6000).

Changing Money

Changing money is an inevitable part of travel, and you'll have to do it every few days or weeks on the road. Money can be changed at banks, foreign exchange (forex) bureaus, hotels and (in some countries) on the black market.

Before changing, check a guidebook or ask other travellers or resident foreigners what the best options are. In some countries, banks are the best or only places for foreign exchange, while in others moneychangers are the way to go. Also check a local newspaper for the official exchange rate, and compare the exchange rates and commission fees of several places first, as rates and commissions can vary significantly from place to place. Hotels usually offer poor exchange rates and high commissions. When cashing travellers cheques, be sure to ask whether the commission is per check or per transaction.

It's generally a good idea to save foreign exchange receipts in order to prove you've exchanged your money legally. While it is infrequent that you will be asked to produce the receipts for this purpose, in some countries, you will need to show them upon departure in order to convert any remaining local currency back to hard currency.

Following is some general information about changing money in Africa:

- Rates are often better in major cities, so try to change your money there before heading to rural areas, where you may find it difficult or impossible to change money at all.

- Try not to change at border crossings, where rates are often very low, or change just enough to get to the next major city. In many countries, airports offer poor exchange rates, while in others, rates are similar to or only marginally lower than those in the city centre.

- Each time you change money at a bank or forex bureau, you will be given a slip with the details of the transaction for you to sign. Inspect it carefully. If anything is amiss, you can terminate the transaction immediately. Save the slips for completed transactions for your records.

- Before signing a travellers cheque, verify that the changer will accept it – once signed, the cheque will be difficult to change elsewhere.

- If you will be using a credit card for a cash advance, shop around for the best rates and commission fees. Also, check that the figures are correct on the credit card slip before you sign it.

- Always count the bills carefully after exchanging money, cashing a travellers cheque or getting a cash advance.

- Exercise caution when changing money, especially when using the services of street-side moneychangers, as you will be particularly vulnerable then. If you can, arrange to remove the money you want to exchange beforehand, to avoid having your money belt out in public. At banks and forex bureaux you'll also need to have your passport handy, and in some cases, your travellers cheque purchase receipt. Keep everything together and where you can see it, and check that it's all there before walking away from the bank counter or moneychanger.

- Don't change a large-denomination bill or travellers cheque just before leaving a country, as you'll lose on commissions and exchange rates when you reconvert any unspent money.

- In many countries – due to inflation and/or lack of high denomination notes – you'll receive a small mountain of bills when changing money. It's best to divide this up and store the bills in various places. At banks or forex bureaux always get some small change, as taxi drivers or vendors may not be willing or able to change large bills.

THE BLACK MARKET

In various parts of Africa (as elsewhere in the world), you can sometimes get more local currency for your hard currency by changing on the so-called 'black market'. This is illegal, morally questionable and sometimes dangerous, as it leaves you vulnerable to arrest or bribery attempts from local police and without legal recourse. It's not uncommon for moneychangers on the street to work in cahoots with corrupt police and trap you in a set-up where you may get 'arrested', given a shakedown, and eventually lose all your money. All sorts of other scams exist, ranging from bad exchange rates or folding the notes in half to outright robbery.

Sometimes there isn't any alternative to dealing with unofficial moneychangers. For example, at border crossings there will be moneychangers at the frontier but no banks. In other cases, you may arrive on a day when banks and foreign exchange bureaux are closed. In such cases, if you are in a city, you can usually change money at hotel reception desks, although rates are often low and commissions high. Another option is to try asking discreetly at a shop selling imported items. Saying something like, 'The banks are closed and I have US dollars. Do you know anyone who can help me ...?' is better than 'Do you want to change money?'. As a last resort, moneychangers often hang around markets, banks and post offices, but changing your money here is not advised. Even if the moneychanger is straight up, you don't know who's watching you from the other side of the street. If you do decide to change on the street, ask other travellers or a reliable hotel or shop owner for advice about a trustworthy person to change money with, and keep your wits about you.

Caught Empty Handed

They say you should never do or decide anything that really matters within 24 hours of reeling off a longhaul flight.

But, having decanted into the intense morning sun of Bangui, capital of the Central African Republic after jetting through the night, I couldn't spare myself the luxury of such gradual acclimatisation. Checking into my hotel, I note that the town is about to embark upon three days of national holiday, shops and banks are closing imminently and I haven't a single Central African Franc to my name.

So in the privacy of my room, I hurriedly scribble a quick shopping list, peel off a few high denomination French bank notes, grab my passport, ram everything into my pockets and dash for the door.

Amid the destruction wreaked by the army during its periodic mutinies, the solid concrete mass of the BEAC bank, is, if you except a pockmark or two, reassuringly intact. I mount its crowded steps, squeeze my way in and pick a passage to the foreign exchange counter before which, with barely ten minutes to closing time, an attempt at a queue seethes.

I assess my position. Here I stand, profoundly jetlagged, overheated, pasty mouthed and without a single centime in local currency. And, stuck at the end of the scrum, the only non-national in line, my chances of getting any are receding with each tick of those ten minutes.

A kind Centrafricain interrupted this self-indulgent reverie, beckoning to me and insisting, despite my half hearted protestations, that I should slip in front of him, so gaining several places over the mildly protesting back markers.

The mass surged up to and around the window, behind which sat a particularly surly teller. Snarling at the crowd, he would occasionally and arbitrarily grab a paper from the hand of one of the insurgents as it passed before his booth. But my new found friend graciously protected me with his body, easing me gently forward and remonstrating with his compatriots. Whispering the while into my ear his regrets at their uncouthness, he wished me greater good fortune during the rest of my stay as an honoured guest in his country.

Finally, one of the surges propels me in front of the window, at which I grab to prevent myself being swept back by the ebb. The teller snatches my passport and I know that I've entered the system, that money may well be mine and that I can temporarily relax.

As I turn to thank my protector for his solicitousness towards a visitor, I see him heading low, hunched and at speed for the main exit. I reach instinctively for my back pocket - and find it empty, the button dexterously flicked open.

It remains one of the great regrets of my life that I wasn't present to celebrate with my erstwhile protector when he opened his greedy fist to reveal - nothing more and nothing less than my shopping list.

Miles Roddis
LP Author, Spain

Bargaining

Bargaining over prices is a way of life throughout much of Africa. Outside of fixed-price shops and a few other limited situations, an item's value is generally considered to be whatever the seller can get for it. While bargaining may be a bit intimidating if you are not used to it, it's viewed by locals – vendors and purchasers alike – simply as a business transaction. Done properly, it can be enjoyable for both sides.

Some tips to keep in mind include the following:

- Don't be afraid to bargain – whether out of unfamiliarity with the process or out of guilt about how much money you have compared with locals. Not only might you be considered foolish, you will also be doing other travellers a disservice by creating the impression that all foreigners are willing to pay any price named. There's also a good argument to be made that by paying the asking (inflated) price, you harm the local economy by putting some items out of locals' reach. Particularly at craft shops and other places specifically catering to tourists, bargaining is the norm.

- Try to learn the standard local prices for basic items early in your visit. Although bargaining is common practice in markets, curio shops etc, away from cities and tourist areas sellers will often quote you the same price locals pay. Also keep in mind that prices can vary depending on location and season: fruit and vegetables are generally more expensive in cities, while tinned goods and similar items often cost more in rural areas, as transport costs need be paid. If you are in an area difficult to access (eg due to washed out roads during the rainy season), expect costs to be even higher for any item which needed to be transported.

- When buying crafts or artwork, decide in advance what you want to pay. In addition to your own budgetary limitations, this can be based on what others have told you they have paid, on the price of a similar item in a fixed-price shop or on just being in an area long enough to know what a 'fair' price is considered to be. Your first offer should be about half of what you want to pay. Some vendors may initially ask a price between two and five times higher than they're prepared to accept, and may laugh or feign outrage on hearing your offer. However, they will soon start to come down to a more realistic level, while you'll have to inch up a bit until a mutually agreeable price is reached. If you're not happy with the vendor's 'final offer', there is no need to pay it – just move on.

- Try to keep the exchange friendly and spirited, and never lose your temper. If you feel that you are not getting anywhere with a vendor, just politely take your leave. Sometimes a seller may call you back if they think their stubbornness has been counterproductive; very few will pass up the chance of making a sale, however thin the profit. If a seller won't come down to a price you feel is fair or can afford, it either means they really aren't making a profit, or that if you don't pay the price, they know somebody else will.

Tipping

There are few clear rules for tipping applicable to everyone in Africa. In much of sub-Saharan Africa, tipping is only expected from the wealthy, which means well-to-do locals and nearly all foreign visitors, unless the person obviously looks like a hitchhiker or the setting warrants otherwise. Anyone going to a fancy hotel would be expected to tip, for example, but there would not be the same expectation from a backpacker in a cheap hotel.

At better restaurants throughout the continent all customers, locals and foreigners, are expected to tip around 10%. However, first check the bill closely to see if service is included (it often is). At the other end of the scale are more basic restaurants and eating-houses where no tipping is expected from anyone. There is a grey area between these two classes of restaurants, where tipping is rarely expected from locals but may be expected of wealthy-looking foreigners. Sometimes wealthier Africans will tip at these smaller restaurants, not so much because it's expected but because it's a show of status.

In privately hired taxis, tipping is not the rule among locals; it is almost unheard of for rides in shared cabs.

On treks and safaris, it's usual to tip drivers, guides and porters if service has been good, so be sure to set aside a portion of your budget for this.

In most other situations where a service has been rendered there are no hard and fast rules. If somebody simply points the way to the bus station, tipping would not be appropriate. In contrast, someone helping you for 10 minutes to find a hotel would likely require some sign of gratitude (although many people will help you out of kindness and will not be expecting money). When deciding how much to give, calculate the cost of a bottle of Coke or beer; giving your helper enough 'to have a drink' is usually sufficient. Wherever you are, if you're not prepared to offer a tip, don't ask for significant favours.

In all cases, whenever you are in doubt, try to follow local custom and keep in mind the effect your actions will have when multiplied. This is particularly important when travelling in areas where locals are unaccustomed to foreigners.

NORTH AFRICA

In many areas of North Africa, tipping *(baksheesh)* is a way of life. In Egypt, for example, it is ubiquitous; you will be constantly confronted by demands for baksheesh for anything from having a door opened to being guided against your will. While there is no need to pay baksheesh if you don't think the service warrants it, remember that more things warrant baksheesh here than anywhere in the west. Also keep in mind that baksheesh is an important, and sometimes essential, supplement to income for many people.

In cafes and local restaurants there is usually a saucer for customers to throw their small change into, although this is seldom a significant amount. In tourist restaurants, however, a tip (10% is standard) is expected.

PASSPORTS & VISAS

Passports

Your passport is your most essential travel document. It serves as identification (for banks, foreign exchange bureaux, hotels and many other entities), as well as evidence (via the visa stamps or papers that it contains) of your legal right to be in a country.

Before setting off, make several photocopies of the front page and all pages with pre-arranged visa stamps on them. Carry one set of photocopies separately from your passport and leave a second set with someone at home. (See the Documentation section later in this chapter for more information.) If you will be spending a significant length of time in any one country, you can inquire whether your embassy has arrangements for registration of its nationals in that country. If so, they may also wish to retain a copy of your passport (although most embassies will be unwilling to simply hold copies of your passport or other documents on file for you). Registering will make it easier to replace your passport if it is lost or stolen.

PASSPORT HOLDERS

If you already hold a passport, check its expiry date. If it expires within six months of the date when you plan to enter the final country on your itinerary, get it replaced – many African countries will refuse you entry if you have less than six months left on your passport. Even with a few months leeway, consider getting a new one to give yourself more flexibility on the road. Passports of most western countries are valid for 10 years and are generally much easier to replace in your home country.

In addition to checking the expiry date, be sure there are enough blank pages left for visas and entry and exit stamps – remembering that some African countries use entry and exit stamps that take up at least half a page, and visas normally require a full page. If you're nearing the end, get additional pages inserted, or (if the passport is soon to expire) a new passport. Running out of pages when you are too far from an embassy to have extras added can be a major inconvenience.

APPLYING FOR A PASSPORT

If you need a new passport, apply well in advance, as you will need to submit it with each visa application (which can take anywhere from one day to two weeks to process in each case) and possibly to quote its number to pick up your plane ticket.

Conditions and requirements for passport issue vary from country to country, but most agencies require you to submit the following with the application form:

Proof of citizenship – You need a birth, naturalisation or registration certificate.

Photographs – You will need two recent head-and-shoulder shots taken against a white background, signed and identified.

Proof of identity – Someone must vouch for your identity on the application form and on the photographs. This can be either the holder of a current passport from your country who has known you for two years (but is unrelated to you), or a citizen of good standing such as a Justice of the Peace or notary public. This category can also somewhat arbitrarily include lawyers, employers, doctors and teachers.

Proof of any name change – A marriage or deed poll certificate.

Fee – Fees start at about A$125, C$60, NZ$80, UK£21 or US$65 for a standard adult passport with the minimum number of pages, issued within the usual processing time.

Issuing Period & Rush Jobs
Most agencies will issue a new or replacement passport within 10 days. Express service is usually possible, although it will require an additional fee, which can be paid directly to the national issuing agency or to a commercial expediting agency that will take care of all the details for you. However, even an expedited passport will require at least a couple of days before it is processed and reaches you. Check the phonebook or do a search on the web for a listing of commercial expediters.

Issuing Agencies
The government agencies responsible for issuing passports in Australia, Canada, New Zealand, the UK and the USA are listed below. Some countries also permit you to submit your application to other authorised agencies such as post offices or banks instead.

Australia
Passports Australia, Department of Foreign Affairs & Trade
(☎ 131232; www.dfat.gov.au/passports/passports_faq_contents.html)

Canada
The Passport Office, Department of Foreign Affairs & International Trade
(☎ 800-567-6868; www.dfait-maeci.gc.ca/passport/paspr-2.htm)

New Zealand
The Passport Office, Department of Internal Affairs
(☎ 0800-22 5050; inform.dia.govt.nz/internal_affairs/businesses/doni_pro/fees.html)

UK
UK Passport Agency, The Home Office
(☎ 0870-521 0410; www.open.gov.uk/ukpass/ukpass.htm)

USA
Passport Services, the State Department
(☎ 900-225-5674; travel.state.gov/passport_services.html)

Dual Citizenship
If you have two passports, you'll be able to select the one that will get you the better (and cheaper) visa(s) and will be better received by those countries you plan to enter. However, in most cases you'll only be able to use one passport

for a particular trip, so you will need to decide in advance which is the most advantageous overall. While using two passports on one trip sometimes works, it usually just creates problems, as a passport is supposed to show a logical chain of travel. If, for example, you enter Kenya on a British passport, then try to enter a neighbouring country on an Australian passport, officials are likely to wonder how you managed to get into the region in the first place and, in some cases, may deny you entry. Whatever you decide to do, it's generally best not to advertise the fact to immigration officials that you have dual citizenship.

Hostile Home Countries

With the exception of Israeli passport holders, the identity of your home country generally doesn't affect your reception by officials when you try to enter a country in Africa. Several north African countries, including Tunisia and Libya, refuse entry to Israeli nationals, as well as to anyone with an Israeli stamp in their passport. Apart from this, historical factors and colonial-era connections may affect the tone of the reception. It's more likely, however, that underpaid officials struggling to make ends meet may simply take advantage of the fact that you have a western passport and view you as fair game for bribes. To minimise problems in this area, try to avoid travelling in Africa on a completely empty passport and endeavour to maintain the air of an experienced (but respectful) traveller when passing through customs.

LOST OR STOLEN PASSPORTS

Losing your passport while on the road is a serious inconvenience; replacing it will require time, money and probably lots of patience. To minimise the chances of loss, always keep the passport on your person in an inside pouch or pocket and try to avoid situations requiring you to hand it over for any length of time – whether to a hotel proprietor or anyone else.

If you do lose your passport, contact your embassy immediately. If your home country doesn't have diplomatic representation where you are, contact the embassy in the nearest neighbouring country. Seek advice from embassy staff on whether you should notify the local government of the loss, and how to handle it if you do. It may be that a new passport can be arranged within the time limits of your visa. If, however, the visa was due to expire (and you were due to fly out) shortly after your passport is lost, you will need to arrange a visa extension to cover the period until the new passport is ready and you can leave the country.

If your passport is stolen, inform the local police and get a police report before heading to your embassy. Embassy staff will require some form of identification before issuing a replacement. To be prepared for this, carry a photocopy of your passport with you, as well as a driving licence, student card, an old passport or some other form of photo identification, or a copy of your birth certificate. Although most embassies can generally issue a new passport within a few days, it can be quite expensive.

Visas

Visas are stamps or documents in your passport that permit you to enter a country and stay for a specified period of time. Not everyone needs a visa to enter every country – the rules vary according to your nationality. Some visas are valid for a certain period from when they are issued, while with others you will have to say when you plan to enter, and arrive within a month of that date. Visas are available from the embassies of the country you wish to enter. Depending on the length of your trip, they can be arranged in advance before you leave or with embassies in neighbouring countries during your travels. In addition to single-entry visas, some embassies also issue multiple-entry visas, which can be handy if you are planning to use one country as a base while visiting other attractions in the region.

It's best to research visa requirements when initially planning your itinerary. However, you'll normally need to wait at least until you've booked your ticket before approaching embassies or consulates, as some countries will not issue a visa until you can produce either an itinerary from a travel agent or your plane ticket. Of the countries profiled in this book (see the country profile chapters), only Libya is likely to refuse entry to independent travellers.

VISA REQUIREMENTS

	Australia	Canada	NZ	UK	US
Benin	✓ (30 days)	✓ (30 days)	✓ (30 days)	✓ (30 days)	✓ (30 days)
Botswana	✗ (30 days)	✗ (30 days)	✗ (30 days)	✗ (30 days)	✗ (30 days)
Burkina Faso	✓ (90 days)	✓ (90 days)	✓ (90 days)	✓ (90 days)	✓ (90 days)
Cameroon	✓ (90 days)	✓ (90 days)	✓ (90 days)	✓ (90 days)	✓ (90 days)
Cape Verde	✓ (30 days)	✓ (30 days)	✓ (30 days)	✓ (30 days)	✓ (30 days)
C.A.R.	✓ (30 days)	✓ (30 days)	✓ (30 days)	✓ (30 days)	✓ (45 days)
Chad	✓ (90 days)	✓ (90 days)	✓ (90 days)	✓ (90 days)	✓ (90 days)
Côte d'Ivoire	✓ (90 days)	✓ (90 days)	✓ (90 days)	✗ (90 days)	✗ (90 days)
Djibouti	✓ (30 days)	✓ (30 days)	✓ (30 days)	✓ (30 days)	✓ (30 days)
Equit'l Guinea	✓ (30 days)	✓ (30 days)	✓ (30 days)	✓ (30 days)	✓ (30 days)
Eritrea	✓ (30 days)	✓ (30 days)	✓ (30 days)	✓ (30 days)	✓ (30 days)
Ethiopia	✓ (30 days)	✓ (30 days)	✓ (30 days)	✓ (30 days)	✓ (30 days)
Gabon	✓ (30 days)	✓ (30 days)	✓ (30 days)	✓ (30 days)	✓ (30 days)
The Gambia	✗ (30 days)	✗ (30 days)	✗ (30 days)	✗ (30 days)	✓ (30 days)
Guinea	✓ (30 days)	✓ (30 days)	✓ (30 days)	✓ (30 days)	✓ (30 days)
Ghana	✓ (30 days)	✓ (30 days)	✓ (30 days)	✓ (30 days)	✓ (30 days)
Kenya	✓ (30 days)	✓ (30 days)	✓ (30 days)	✗ (30 days)	✓ (30 days)
Lesotho	✓ (14 days)	✓ (14 days)	✓ (14 days)	✗ (14 days)	✓ (14 days)
Libya	✓ (30 days)	✓ (30 days)	✓ (30 days)	✓ (30 days)	✓ (30 days)
Madagascar	✓ (90 days)	✓ (90 days)	✓ (90 days)	✓ (90 days)	✓ (90 days)
Malawi	✗ (30 days)	✗ (30 days)	✗ (30 days)	✗ (30 days)	✗ (30 days)
Mauritania	✓ (30 days)	✓ (30 days)	✓ (30 days)	✓ (30 days)	✓ (30 days)
Morocco	✗ (90 days)	✗ (90 days)	✗ (90 days)	✗ (90 days)	✗ (90 days)
Mozambique	✓ (30 days)	✓ (30 days)	✓ (30 days)	✓ (30 days)	✓ (30 days)
Namibia	✗ (90 days)	✗ (90 days)	✗ (90 days)	✗ (90 days)	✗ (90 days)
Niger	✓ (30 days)	✓ (30 days)	✓ (30 days)	✓ (30 days)	✓ (30 days)
Nigeria	✓ (30 days)	✓ (30 days)	✓ (30 days)	✓ (30 days)	✓ (30 days)

	Australia	Canada	NZ	UK	US
São Tomé	✓ (15 days)	✓ (15 days)	✓ (15 days)	✓ (15 days)	✓ (15 days)
Senegal	✓ (30 days)	✓ (30 days)	✓ (30 days)	✗ (30 days)	✗ (30 days)
South Africa	✗ (90 days)	✗ (90 days)	✗ (90 days)	✗ (90 days)	✗ (90 days)
Swaziland	✗ (60 days)	✗ (60 days)	✗ (60 days)	✗ (60 days)	✗ (60 days)
Tanzania	✗ (30 days)	✓ (30 days)	✗ (30 days)	✓ (30 days)	✓ (30 days)
Togo	✓ (14 days)	✓ (14 days)	✓ (14 days)	✓ (14 days)	✓ (14 days)
Tunisia	✓ (14 days)	✓ (120 days)	✓ (14 days)	✗ (90 days)	✓ (120 days)
Uganda	✗ (30 days)	✗ (30 days)	✓ (30 days)	✗ (30 days)	✗ (30 days)
Zambia	✗ (30 days)	✗ (30 days)	✗ (30 days)	✓ (30 days)	✓ (30 days)
Zimbabwe	✗ (90 days)	✗ (90 days)	✗ (90 days)	✗ (90 days)	✗ (90 days)

HOME OR AWAY?

For short trips, it's always best to arrange visas at home. For longer trips, this may not be possible, as pre-arranged visas may expire too early, or you may decide to visit a country that wasn't included in your initial itinerary. If a country you wish to visit does not have an embassy in or near your home country, you may have no choice but to wait until you get to the region to apply for a visa. More detailed visa and embassy information is given in the country profiles chapters later in this book.

Getting a Visa on Arrival

Several countries in Africa routinely issue visas on arrival at the airport. A few others that do not have this official policy may occasionally issue one (after some hassling) or send you to the foreign ministry. However, you should never count on this, as there are just as many cases where you will be denied entry. Also, this will not work if you are flying in from outside Africa, as airlines won't let you on the plane without a visa unless a country has an official and published policy (known to the airline) that visas will be issued on arrival.

The situation at land borders is generally more restricted. While there are several countries that will at least issue temporary visas valid until you can get to the capital to arrange an extension, it's best to assume that you will not be able to get a visa at the border.

Where There Is No Embassy

In cases where the country you want to visit has no embassy, it may be possible to arrange a visa through the former colonial government's embassy. For example, French embassies in Africa often issue visas for Côte d'Ivoire and Burkina Faso in places where these countries have no diplomatic representation. While these arrangements have become more restrictive in recent years, it may still be worth asking the local French embassy about visas to former French colonies and with the Portuguese embassy for visas to former Portuguese colonies. British high commissions used to issue visas to most Commonwealth countries (The Gambia, Kenya etc) wherever those countries did not have embassies. Now the situation is more restricted and most high commissions no longer do this.

PLANNING YOUR VISAS

The price of a visa, permitted length of stay and extension requirements vary from country to country. Take note of the following when planning your visas:

- Find out whether the visa is activated on entry or on issue. In some countries visas are activated as soon as the stamp appears in your passport, so if you wait too long between getting the visa and entering, you will have little time left to explore the place.

- The time period can differ depending on whether you arrange the visa at home or on entry. Togo, for example, will issue a 30 to 90 day visa if you apply in your home country, but only a 48 hour temporary visa at the Togo-Ghanaian border near Lomé.

- If you know you will be in a country for a while, try to arrange the maximum length visa (usually 3 months) at the outset. Extensions of shorter-term visas are possible in most places, but can be inconvenient and time consuming.

- Try to determine in advance whether you'll want to enter the country more than once. A circuit-style itinerary in which you plan to arrive and depart from the same airport may require a multiple-entry visa. These are best applied for in your home country.

- Be sure you know the approved entry and exit points for your each of your visas. While many countries in Africa do not require you to specify points of arrival and departure, or whether you plan to arrive by air or overland, some (such as Mauritania) do.

- For details on which countries require visas, see the Visas section of the country profiles chapters. There is a reasonably reliable web site that provides a summary of visa requirements by country of origin (www2.travel.com.au/cgi-bin/clcgi?E=bevisreq). Note that regulations can change, so be sure to verify requirements with the relevant embassy before arriving at the airport or border.

The Application Process

Allow plenty of time for getting your visas. Each one can take anywhere from one day to two weeks to be issued and, regardless of where you apply, it's likely to be a slightly tedious and time-consuming process. Consider these strategies:

- Phone in advance to find out embassy opening hours and requirements for costs, photographs, identification and documents. Also check when the country's public holidays are, as the embassy is likely to be closed on these days.

- Don't wait until the last minute to apply. Some countries take as long as two weeks to issue a visa. Even if the period is shorter, visas are not always processed on the first attempt.

- Arrive early and be prepared to queue.

- Have all your documentation in order and ready to present to the clerk, including your planned entry and departure dates. It pays to have an orderly appearance – embassies are not obliged to grant visas, so first impressions can be important.

- When picking up your visa, be on time and don't leave until checking that the dates, length of stay and other details are correct.

Visa Extensions

Most countries have some sort of process for extending your visa (assuming you do not already have the maximum permissible duration). Sometimes this is straightforward, but more often than not it involves delays of up to a week and hassles with bureaucracy. Also, in many countries visa extensions are only possible in the capital city – of little use if you are in a remote town when your visa is due to expire. In general, if you know you will need to stay a certain length of time in a country, try to arrange the appropriate visa at the outset.

Check a guidebook for information on visa extensions in the country you will be visiting. Normally, the immigration office or – in a few cases – police stations or other authorities are responsible for processing applications.

Photographs

Whether you decide to arrange your visas in advance or on the road, bring plenty of passport-size photographs along. Most countries do not distinguish between black-and-white and colour, but it can help to have a few of each variety with you. Almost all countries require at least two photos to process a visa, and a few require as many as four. Most major cities in Africa have inexpensive instant-photo shops where you can get new photos made in case yours run out.

Other Paperwork

HOSTELLING INTERNATIONAL CARD

Membership in Hostelling International (HI; also still known as YHA in some places) is useful if you plan to combine European travel with your Africa trip. In Africa it is of limited value in most countries, with the exception of South Africa, which has numerous accredited hostels. However, it can be a useful form of secondary identification if you don't have a driving licence or other form of ID that contains your photograph, or to leave with officials rather than leaving your passport or something more valuable.

In other countries which have accredited hostels (eg Egypt and Morocco), you can often stay without a card, although you will be required to pay a bit more. Membership costs around US$25 per year. See the HI web site (www.iyhf.org) for further details.

INTERNATIONAL STUDENT CARDS

The International Student Identity Card (ISIC) is the most widely recognised of the various student cards. It qualifies the holder for discounts on airline tickets, rail passes, accommodation, shopping and entrance to museums and cultural events. The availability and level of discounts vary from country to country. In most African countries, the card is of minimal utility. However, like the Hostelling International Card, it can be a useful form of secondary identification.

The ISIC card is available only to full-time students (there is no age limit) and is issued by accredited travel agencies (such as STA Travel) through the International Student Travel Confederation (ISTC; ☎ 045-3393 9303; web site www.isic.org/index.htm) in Copenhagen, Denmark. You'll need proof of full-time student status from your university.

Travellers who are not full-time students but are under 25 years of age qualify for the International Youth Travel Card, which is also issued by ISTC. Benefits are similar, but it is recognised by fewer countries around the world. A similar card is the GO 25 International Youth Travel Card (known as the GO 25 Card), which has essentially the same benefits as the ISIC card and is issued by representative offices of the Federation of International Youth Travel Organisations (FIYTO; web site www.fiyto.org/index-old.html).

INTERNATIONAL TEACHER CARD

Full-time teachers at recognised educational institutions qualify for the International Teacher Identity Card (ITIC), which is issued by ISTC (www.isic.org /index.htm) and offers similar discounts to student cards.

INTERNATIONAL DRIVING PERMIT

While some African countries recognise national licenses, many require you to have an International Driving Permit (IDP). These are issued only by automobile associations in your home country; occasionally a web site appears claiming to provide IDPs, but these are likely to be counterfeit and more expensive than going through authorised organisations.

To qualify, you normally have to be 18 years of age or older and the holder of a valid driving licence from your home country. You'll need to supply a couple of passport-type photographs and pay a nominal administrative fee. As IDPs are only valid for one year in many western countries, there's no point in getting one too far in advance of your departure (check with your local authority). Make sure your licence states that it is valid for motorcycles if you plan to ride one.

Even if you do get an IDP, bring your home licence along as well. Contact details for major issuing agencies are:

American Automobile Association
(☎ 888-859-5161; www.aaa.com/vacation/idp.html)

Australian Automobile Association
(☎ 02-6247 7311; www.aaa.asn.au)
(for links to the state-based automobile associations that issue IDPs)

British Automobile Association
(☎ 0990-500 600; www.theaa.co.uk/membership/offers/idp.html)

Canadian Automobile Association
(☎ 613-247-0117 ext 2025; www.caa.ca/CAAInternet/travelservices/frames14.htm)

New Zealand Automobile Association
(☎ 0800-500 444; www.aa.org.nz)

BUSINESS CARDS

Having a few business cards along can be useful: Africans like to make friends, and giving someone your card is an indication you want to keep in contact. They can also be helpful in dealing with police and other authorities. You can get cards printed inexpensively in many capital cities.

YELLOW FEVER VACCINATION CERTIFICATE

See the Health chapter for details on this card.

DOCUMENTATION

Before setting out, make two sets of photocopies of all important documents, such as your passport (including any visa stamps), plane tickets, travel insurance, travellers cheque purchase receipt and cheque serial numbers, International Driving Permit, birth and marriage certificates (if you bring them) and credit cards. Keep one copy in your main luggage (assuming the originals are in your money belt) and give the other to a friend or family member at home. If you lose any of the original items, having copies will make them much easier to replace. The copy at home is further insurance, just in case you manage to lose both sets on the road.

A more effective way to store details of vital travel documents such as passport details and travellers cheques numbers is to use Lonely Planet's eKno travel vault. You can access these details by using a password at cybercafes around the world. It's free to join eKno (www.ekno.lonelyplanet.com) and free to use the travel vault.

TICKETS & INSURANCE

Your Ticket
AIR

For most travellers, air tickets are likely to be the largest single expense of a trip to Africa. While shopping around for the best deal will probably never be a very enjoyable task, it will go more smoothly if you first familiarise yourself with airlines and ticketing terms. Most of the information in this chapter applies to the intercontinental airlines and flights that will transport you to and from the continent.

Each country's local carriers have their own set of rules (and some seem to have no rules at all). If you plan on flying within Africa, it's worth trying to learn a bit about domestic and regional air services in the area you will be visiting. General information on these is covered under Getting Around in the While You're There chapter. The best source of country-specific information is someone who has recently lived or spent time in the region you want to visit. Travel agencies specialising in Africa may also be of assistance, although many are not familiar with local carriers. A good guidebook should also have some information about the variety and quality of local airlines.

Travellers who plan to reach Africa overland from Europe and who will not be using airlines at all can skip down to the Travel Insurance section at the end of this chapter.

Airlines

Quality varies widely from one carrier to another. In general, price is a good indicator of the type of service you can expect. However, this may not always hold true, as there are some very good deals available, especially in the European and American carrier markets.

Check with a travel agent if you are interested in learning a bit more about various airlines before booking your ticket. Things to look at include the age and size of the fleet, frequent flier programs, booking and payment options, and cancellation and change policies (although booking and payment options and cancellation policies are likely to vary more depending on the type of ticket you buy than on the airline).

Many airlines flying intercontinental routes have a web site providing information on destinations, schedules and frequent flier programs. A few useful ones include:

Aeroflot (www.aeroflot.com)
Air Afrique (www.travelfile.com/get/aafrica.html)
Air France (www.airfrance.com)
British Airways (www.british-airways.com)
Egypt Air (www.egyptair.com.eg)

Ethiopian Airlines (www.ethiopianairlines.com)
KLM Royal Dutch Airlines (www.klm.com)
Lufthansa Airlines (www.lufthansa.com)
Qantas Airways (www.qantas.com)
Royal Air Maroc (www.royalairmaroc.com)
Sabena (www.sabena.com)
South African Airways (www.saa.co.za)
Swissair (www.swissair.com)
TAP Air Portugal (www.tap.pt)

Partnerships Partnerships are reciprocal arrangements between two or more airlines allowing them each access into designated sectors of the others' markets. As access to sectors is usually jealously guarded and almost always favours the home country airline, these partnership arrangements allow airlines to offer a much broader range of flight options than would otherwise be possible. This applies particularly in the case of special fares such as round-the-world (RTW) tickets that combine flights on several different airlines all belonging to the same partnership. While the concept of partnerships is of little relevance for many flights within Africa, it is important to consider when booking the intercontinental portion of your trip – especially if you will be travelling on more than one airline or visiting Africa as part of a RTW package. If you are gathering information on one carrier, it may also be worth checking out its partner airlines as well.

Frequent Flier Programs Many western airlines and a small but increasing number of African carriers have frequent flier programs that offer rewards (such as free plane tickets or other benefits) based on the number of miles or kilometres you fly with that airline or its partners. Frequent flier points can also be gathered by using associated travel services such as designated car rental companies or hotel chains. If you plan to fly often, it pays to shop around to see which airline will be most useful to you for your travels. Then, try to book most or all of your flights on that airline or its partners in order to earn as many points as possible – although you will need to fly a lot of miles before earning enough points for a free trip to Africa. Many travellers choose a carrier from their home country, as they may then be entitled to use frequent flier points for domestic travel on their return.

Most airlines require that frequent flier points be used within two to five years from the date of your last flight, although many will allow you to redeem them for family members if you are unable to use the points yourself. Other restrictions may include limited 'free' seats available (meaning that you will have to book well in advance for a ticket based on frequent flier miles) and blackout periods where no free seats are available (eg the Christmas holiday season).

Most frequent flier programs are free, though a few levy joining fees and some are also beginning to introduce annual maintenance fees.

After enrolling in a program and receiving your frequent flier member number, keep a record of it with your other travel documents, as you'll need to quote it each time you book a ticket or use an associated service in order to get points credited to your account.

Tickets & Restrictions

There is a wide array of tickets and deals on the market; all are governed by rules and restrictions. Some of the more common restrictions include:

Cancellation or change penalties – Cancelling your ticket or altering your route once it's booked may incur financial penalties (although most travel insurance policies will protect against unavoidable cancellations). In general, the cheaper the ticket, the greater the penalties.

Directional limits – Round-the-world tickets normally allow you to travel only in one direction.

Minimum or maximum limits – You may have to be away a minimum of 14 days or a maximum of 12 months, for example.

Refund policy – Some refunds can only be made through the travel agency that sold the ticket.

Seasonal limits – A ticket may only be available in off-peak or shoulder periods.

Stopover limits – There may be a maximum number of stopovers attached to your ticket.

The basic ticket is a full-price one-way or return ticket between two cities. Airlines typically offer 1st class (coded F), business class (coded J) and economy class (coded Y) tickets. Once the discounting starts, the conditions become more complicated and restrictive as the price drops. The following sections outline some common deals.

Discount Return Tickets If you are planning to visit only one country or region, a simple return ticket may be the best option. The best rates are generally available to major transport hubs such as Nairobi or Johannesburg. Discounted fares can be official (such as APEX fares, which are available from travel agencies or directly from the airline) or unofficial. The lowest prices often impose drawbacks like flying with unpopular airlines, inconvenient schedules or unpleasant routes and connections.

Open-Jaw Tickets These are return tickets that allow you to fly to one destination but return home from another, thus saving backtracking and time. Open-jaw tickets are generally more expensive than standard return fares but enable you to see more of the continent, especially if the distance between the two cities on your ticket is great. For example, if you can arrange a ticket that arrives in Nairobi and departs from Johannesburg, you will be able to explore a wide section of East and southern African without needing to backtrack.

One-Way Tickets One-way tickets are often more expensive than return tickets, but may be useful if you are unsure of your itinerary or return date, or if you want to travel free of deadlines and definite places to be. However, it is generally cheaper to buy a return ticket and just fly one way on it, cancelling the unused portion. One drawback to one-way tickets is that a few embassies in Europe and the USA, and some immigration authorities in Africa require travellers to have an onward airline ticket before they will issue a visa or grant entry. Check the visa and entry requirements before purchasing a one-way ticket.

Round-the-World Tickets If you plan to travel to Africa as part of a larger intercontinental journey, a round-the-world (RTW) ticket is a good deal. This fare gives you a limited period (usually 12 months) to circumnavigate the globe, going in only one direction (no backtracking). While the tickets carry a predetermined number of stopovers, these can often be increased for an extra charge per stop. The biggest constraint is that you're limited to the flight paths of the airline and its partners, but these fares tend to be good enough value (especially when compared with the expense of paying for all of the individual component flights on your route) that having to pay a sector fare to another destination during one of your stopovers is usually worth it. The other great advantage is the air mileage you can accumulate for your frequent flier program, even though RTW fares collect points at the lowest rate.

Group Tickets You may be able to get a discount if you ostensibly travel with a 'group', although these tickets tend to be restrictive and inflexible. The groups can be brought together by a travel agent for the sole purpose of selling a block of cheap fares; there's no need or expectation to stay with your group once you've landed. Once your departure date is booked, it may be impossible to change or you may be restricted to only 60 days away. Check carefully with your travel agent.

APEX Tickets An Advance Purchase Excursion (APEX) ticket is a discounted ticket that must be paid for in advance. It usually costs about 30% to 40% less than the full economy fare, but carries restrictions. Generally, you must purchase the ticket between 14 and 21 days in advance (sometimes more), travel for a minimum period (normally 14 days) and return within a maximum period (ranging from 30 to 180 days). Stopovers are normally not allowed. Changing your return travel date may be permitted, but will incur a penalty. There are also usually stiff cancellation fees.

Student. Teacher & Youth Fares Some airlines offer discounts of up to 25% for holders of student, youth or teacher cards (see Other Paperwork in the Passports & Visas chapter). In addition to the card, some airlines may ask for a letter from your school. These discounts are generally only available on ordinary economy class fares. You probably wouldn't get one, for example, on an APEX or RTW ticket, since these are already discounted.

Courier Flights With these arrangements, an air freight company takes over your entire checked baggage allowance, and you are permitted to bring along only a carry-on bag. In return, you get a steeply discounted ticket. As courier tickets are sold for a fixed date and routing, changes can be difficult or impossible. Tickets are generally not valid for more than a month and refunds are usually not available.

Booking a courier ticket takes some effort. They are limited in availability, and arrangements must be made a month or more in advance. They are also not available to all destinations. Major routes such as London-Nairobi offer the best possibilities.

Courier flights are occasionally advertised in the newspapers, or you could contact air freight companies listed in the phonebook. One possibility (at least for US residents) is to join the International Association of Air Travel Couriers (IAATC). The magazine *Travel Unlimited* (see Magazines in the Planning chapter) is also a good source of information on courier possibilities. Confirm with the courier company that someone will be meeting the plane on arrival in Africa in order to shepherd the freighted goods through customs.

Tickets to Avoid

Back-to-Front Tickets These tickets are return fares purchased in your destination city, rather than in your home city. For example, if you are living in West Africa (where tickets are generally expensive) and want to fly to London for a holiday (where tickets are cheaper), theoretically you could buy a ticket by cheque or credit card in London and get a friend to mail it to you. However, airlines will be able to see in their computers that the ticket was issued in London and may refuse to honour it. Be careful not to fall foul of these back-to-front rules when purchasing plane tickets by post or on the web.

Second-Hand Tickets You'll occasionally see advertisements on youth hostel message boards and sometimes in newspapers for 'second-hand tickets', meaning that somebody purchased a return ticket or one with multiple stop-offs, and now wants to sell the unused portion of the ticket, often at very attractive prices. Unfortunately, these tickets are usually worthless, as the name on the ticket must match the name on the passport of the person checking in. Some people reason that the seller of the ticket can check you in with their passport, and then give you the boarding pass. On international flights, however, immigration officials will check that the boarding pass matches the name in your passport and will stop you from boarding the flight.

If you purchase a ticket and then change your name, make sure you have documentary proof (marriage, divorce or deed poll certificate, or your old passport) to prove that the old you and the new you are the same person.

Buying Your Ticket

Buying a plane ticket can be an intimidating business, so it's worth taking time to research the market. It's also important to start as early as possible, as some cheap tickets must be bought well in advance and popular or high season flights often sell out early.

Have a clear idea of your route and the amount of time you wish to be away, as these factors will affect the type of ticket you purchase and its cost.

Buying from Airlines If you buy your ticket directly from an airline, you probably won't get a discount, as airlines use travel agencies to dispose of tickets they are not confident of selling directly to the public at full price. These tickets are generally sold in discounted blocks to the travel agent and part of the savings are passed on to the traveller. Unless you're trying to organise your ticket at the last minute, you will usually get a better deal by going through a travel agent.

Buying from Travel Agents The lucrative air travel market has attracted a plethora of commercial service providers, ranging from respectable travel agency chains to 'bucket shops' specialising in discounted tickets. Members of the former group will be 'bonded' to a national association, which imposes ethical constraints on its members and generally has refund provisions if the agent goes into liquidation before you've picked up your ticket. Bucket shops, by contrast, are generally unbonded, so the risk of losing your money is higher, although they often offer better deals.

If you buy a ticket from an unbonded agency, it's safer to pay by credit card, as card companies will often cover the loss if the agency goes bankrupt. If you do pay by cash, be sure the ticket is handed over straight away (rather than agreeing to pick it up tomorrow or next week) and call the airline yourself to confirm that the booking was made. Alternatively, arrange to leave a small deposit and pay the balance when you get the ticket. If you are suspicious of an agency and they insist on full cash payment in advance, go somewhere else.

When selecting a travel agency, try to find one that specialises in travel to the region of Africa that you want to visit and check out a few different outfits before deciding. Look for a well travelled agent who is familiar with the routings you intend to fly and has similar inclinations to your own. Finding good deals among the complex network of databases and promotions requires an agent with computer skills and imagination, so be prepared to go elsewhere if you're not satisfied.

Also keep in mind that many travel agencies provide a range of services in addition to booking tickets. They may be able to reserve a particular seat on your flight if you are a smoker/nonsmoker, exceptionally tall, afflicted with chronic travel sickness or travelling with a young child; or to inform the airline if you have a particular dietary requirement and to assist with booking your first night's accommodation. Other services may include currency exchange, travellers cheques, travel insurance, immunisations and visas (although it is generally less expensive to take care of these things yourself), as well as car rental and hotel bookings. If all you are interested in is a ticket at the lowest possible price, go to an agency specialising in discounted tickets. Otherwise, you may need to seek out a full-service agency.

A good place to start your search for a travel agency is in weekend newspapers or travel magazines. Many agents also have ads or web sites. Once you have a list of five or six, start phoning around. Tell them where you want to fly and they will offer you a choice of airline, route and fare. If an agency starts telling you all the cheap flights you've seen advertised are fully booked, 'But we have another one that costs a bit more ...', or that only two seats are left (which they will hold for only two hours), don't fall for it – just ring some of the others.

Some reputable bonded discount travel agencies include:

Australia
Flight Centre
(☎ 131600; www.flightcentre.com)
STA Travel
(☎ 1300 360 960; www.sta-travel.com)

Canada
Travel CUTS
(☎ 800-667-2887; www.travelcuts.com)

New Zealand
STA Travel
(☎ 0800-100 677; www.sta-travel.com)

UK
STA Travel
(☎ 020-7581 4132; www.sta-travel.com)
Trailfinders
(☎ 020-7938 3366; www.trailfinder.com)

USA
Council Travel
(☎ 800-226-8624; www.counciltravel.com)
STA Travel
(☎ 800-781-4040; www.sta-travel.com)

A few other travel agencies with a particular focus on Africa are:

UK
Africa Travel Centre
(☎ 020-7388 4163; email africatravel@easynet.co.uk) 21 Leigh St, London WC1H 9QX
African Travel Specialists
(☎ 020-7630 5434) Glen House, Stag Place, Victoria, London SW1E 5AG
Bridge the World
(☎ 020-7911 0900) 52 Chalk Farm Rd, Camden Town, London NW1 8AN
Campus Travel
(☎ 020-7730 8111) 52 Grosvenor Gardens, London SW1W 0AG; also with offices in large YHA Adventure shops and universities/colleges around the country (for telephone bookings call ☎ 020-7730 2101, 0161-273 1721 or 0131-668 3303)

USA
Falcon Wings Travel
(☎ 800-230-4947 or 310-417-3590) 9841 Airport Blvd, Suite 818, Los Angeles, CA 90045
Flytime Tours & Travel
(☎ 212-760-3737; fax 594-1082) 45 West 34th St, Suite 305, New York, NY 10001
Magical Holidays to Africa
(☎ 800-223-7452) 501 Madison Ave, 14th Floor, New York, NY 10022
Uni Travel
(☎ 314-569-2501) PO Box 12485, St Louis, MO 63132

Buying Online The Internet boom has created a new market for plane tickets and if you spend a lot of time online (the best deals do not last long), it's possible to find some good bargains. However, you may also spend a lot of time tracking down the ticket you want, when you could have found a cheaper option in half the time through a travel agent. At a minimum, the Internet is a good resource for helping you to find out what to expect in the way of budget fares. This can be a good start for negotiating with your travel agent. For some useful web sites, see Pretrip Expenses in the Money Matters chapter.

Getting a Good Deal An airfare is normally determined by the quality of the airline, the popularity of the route, the duration of the journey, the length of any stopovers, the departure and arrival times, and any conditions or restrictions on the ticket. The best way to start your research is by browsing the advertisements in travel magazines and major newspapers and contacting a few of the major airlines and several travel agencies (including some of those listed under Buying from Travel Agents earlier in this chapter). This, together with a look at the web sites listed under Pretrip Expenses in the Money Matters chapter, will give you a good idea of available bargains.

Following are a few tips on getting the cheapest fare available:

- Buy your ticket as early as possible – preferably at least two to three months before you plan to depart – because many of the really good deals will be quickly snapped up. Other tickets may require full payment well in advance of your departure date. Booking early will also allow you plenty of time to arrange visas and immunisations.

- Decide whether you're prepared to accept a roundabout journey to reach your destination. Talented travel agents may get you an inexpensive fare that is made up of several flights (rather than one direct flight), transiting in different countries over a few days. While this can be an exhausting way to travel and you'll spend many hours in transit lounges, it may be the right option if you are looking for every way possible to trim costs. If you plan to travel using a series of flights within Africa, remember to leave enough leeway (which often can mean several days) between connections, as cancellations and delays on local airlines are par for the course.

- Be flexible about your departure date. If you were planning to depart in the peak season, try to delay or bring forward your departure date by a few weeks to take advantage of deals in the shoulder season. Alternatively, if you're planning to be away for several months, consider leaving in the low season, when fares are likely to be cheaper and special deals will be available.

- Be prepared to alter your itinerary to take advantage of particularly good deals. If you're set on visiting a place that cannot be accommodated by the deal, check out the options for arranging a separate sector airfare, or an even cheaper train, boat or bus ride. If you have flexibility with your departure point, consider routing yourself through London, which is normally the best place to buy a ticket to Africa.

- Consider taking a charter flight if you are heading for a destination popular with European package tourists (such as The Gambia and Kenya). Charters are generally cheaper than scheduled flights, and are usually direct routings, although tickets may carry heavy restrictions or be subject to last-minute cancellation. Some charter flights come as part of a package that includes accommodation or other services you may not want. Others, however, have nothing attached and can be good deals.

Once you've decided on a fare type, get a quote from your travel agent and take it to several other agencies to see if they can beat it. The travel industry is not a level playing field – some airlines have preferred agents and send their best deals to them, so different agencies don't necessarily have access to the same flights and deals. Also check out the payment options – some fares only require full payment around six weeks before departure, so many travel agents will request only a small, nonrefundable deposit to ensure that you're a serious buyer.

After purchasing your ticket, keep a note of the number, flight numbers, dates and times and other details, and store the information somewhere separate. Taking a few photocopies (one to carry with you and another to leave at home) will make it easier to replace the ticket should it be lost or stolen.

Your Arrival Time If possible, try to arrange your flights to arrive during daylight hours in order to allow yourself time to clear customs and immigration, change some currency, get into the city centre and find accommodation before nightfall. An additional advantage of arriving during the day is that it's generally easier to adapt to a new time zone – most people find they can manage to stay awake several hours longer than usual, but it can be difficult to fall asleep when your body is convinced it's seven hours until bedtime.

If you can't arrive during daylight hours, ideally have someone you know meet you. Otherwise, resign yourself to spending a bit more that night on accommodation and transport from the airport. (For more on this, see Your First Night in the Touchdown chapter.) Don't count on being able to stay at the airport until morning, as many airports essentially shut down or become too deserted for comfort.

Your First Night's Accommodation

For information on selecting your first night's accommodation see Your First Night in the Touchdown chapter.

Bicycles & Surfboards

If you plan to take a bicycle, surfboard or any other bulky items with you on the plane, you'll need to notify the airline when booking your ticket. Most airlines are surprisingly easy-going about accommodating extra gear, as long as they've been given enough notice. They may charge you a fee – ranging from as little as US$10 to cover packing materials to about US$100 for odd-sized baggage. Remind the airline of your extra requirements when reconfirming your ticket, and get to the airport a little earlier in order to pack your equipment well before the rush; it will be better stored in the luggage compartment if it's not last on the plane.

Bicycles Most airlines don't require you to completely disassemble a bicycle, although you'll have to deflate the tires and will usually need to remove the pedals, front wheel and sometimes the seat, and loosen the nut on the stem in order to turn your handlebars 90°. You may also want to remove any attachments such as lights, pump or bottles. If you value the bicycle, bring some bubblewrap to protect it from dents and scratches. Alternatively, you can pack up your bike in your own box and turn up at the airport with it ready to go (don't forget to deflate the tires). Bicycle shops often have extra cartons, and many will box the bike for you for a small fee (usually about US$10).

Surfboards Airlines are unlikely to have special packaging for surfboards, so look into getting a travel board cover. These have extra padding and generally cost around US$200 to US$300. More expensive models can take up to three boards. It's a good idea to wrap your boards in bubblewrap to prevent damage.

Travel Insurance

Arranging travel insurance to cover theft, loss and medical problems is an indispensable part of pretrip planning, particularly if you will be on the road for a while. While there are some very good medical facilities on the continent,

Tips on Buying Travel Insurance

- Try to buy travel insurance as soon as you've decided on your departure date and itinerary. For example, if you buy it the week before you fly out, you may find that you're not covered for delays to your flight caused by industrial action that may have started or been threatened before you took out the insurance.
- Credit card companies may provide limited insurance if you pay for your airline ticket with their card. For example, you may be able to reclaim the payment if the operator doesn't deliver. Ask your credit card company what it's prepared to cover.
- See whether you can extend your policy if you decide to stay away for a longer period than you anticipated, and whether you can get a cheaper family policy if you're travelling with others.
- Find out what the limits of the policy are. Most policies will have a ceiling on the value of possessions to be insured, especially in the case of high-tech items such as still cameras and video cameras.
- An 'excess' or 'deductible' (an agreed amount of money you must pay for each claim) will be imposed by almost all policies. Be sure to learn how much this amount is, as in some situations it may be cheaper and quicker to pay all expenses out of your own pocket.
- Find out whether your policy obliges you to pay on the spot and redeem the money later, or whether the company will pay the providers directly. If you have to claim later, be sure to keep all documentation, including all receipts and copies of your medical report (in your native language, if possible). If you have a medical problem, some policies will ask you to call back (reverse charges) to a centre in your home country where an immediate assessment of the problem will be made.
- Find out what documentation you will need to provide in the event you are robbed. Most insurance companies require a report from the local police.
- Be forthright with the insurance company about any pre-existing medical condition you may have. If you gloss over a problem in order to try to get a cheaper deal, the company will have grounds not to honour your claims.
- Some policies specifically exclude 'dangerous activities', which can include scuba diving, motorcycling and even trekking. A locally acquired motorcycle licence may not be valid under some policies.

including in South Africa, Kenya (Nairobi) and Côte d'Ivoire (Abidjan), in most places medical resources are inadequate for treating serious illness or accidents. Thus, it is important to have a policy that will at least partially cover medical expenses that may arise from illness or injury, and will cover the costs of an emergency medical evacuation. Travel insurance is also important to protect you against cancellation penalties on advance-purchase flights, theft or loss of your possessions, and the cost of additional plane tickets if you need to arrange an earlier flight due to emergency or illness.

BUYING YOUR INSURANCE

Before arranging a travel insurance policy, check to see whether any personal medical insurance you may already have in your own country (either private or government funded) applies internationally, and specifically in Africa. You also might be automatically covered if you hold a valid International Student Identity Card (ISIC), GO 25 Card or International Teacher Identity Card (ITIC) – ask at the place where you purchased the card (for details on these cards see Other Paperwork in the Passports & Visas chapter). Whatever type of policy you may be covered under, it's important to determine whether it covers emergency medical evacuation (an emergency flight home), as well as treatment in the country you will be visiting. Some policies only cover evacuation to the nearest regional medical facility, rather than back to your home country.

Once you have determined the extent of your existing coverage, you can begin to investigate travel insurance policies. These are offered by travel agencies and student travel organisations, as well as by general insurance companies. Read the fine print carefully to avoid being caught by exclusions; some policies are very cheap, but only offer minimal coverage.

HEALTH

Travel in Africa can expose you to plenty of health hazards, but so long as you are up to date with your immunisations and take some basic preventive measures, you'd have to be pretty unlucky to get anything more serious than a bout of diarrhoea. If you're going to sub-Saharan Africa, malaria is an important risk every traveller needs to be aware of. It's vital to make sure you are informed about this serious disease and to take all possible precautions to prevent it (see the Malaria section later).

Before You Go
INFORMATION SOURCES

Part of your preparation for this trip should be to get up-to-date information and advice on the health risks at your destination and the precautions you can take to stay healthy on the road. You can get this from your family doctor, travel health clinics or national and state health departments. The internet is also a great reference source, both before you go and when you are away.

Specialist travel health clinics are probably the best places to go for immunisations and general travel health advice, although they are often more expensive than going to your health department or family doctor. Some travel health clinics provide specific travel health briefs (usually for a fee), by mail, phone or fax which you can then take to your doctor. Most clinics sell health-related traveller essentials like insect repellent, mosquito nets, and needle and syringe kits.

UK
British Airways Travel Clinics
  (☎ 01276-685040; www.britishairways.com/travelqa/fyi/health/health.html)
  (countrywide network of clinics – plus three in South Africa – and you don't need to be travelling on British Airways to use them)
Hospital for Tropical Diseases Travel Clinic
  (☎ 020-7388 9600; health line ☎ 0839-337733) Mortimer Market Centre, Capper St, London WC1E
Liverpool School of Tropical Medicine Travel Clinic
  (☎ 0151-708 9393; health line ☎ 0906-708 8807) Pembroke Place, Liverpool L3 5QA
Malaria Healthline
  (☎ 0891-600 350)
  (recorded information on malaria risks and avoidance from the Malaria Reference Laboratory at the London School of Hygiene & Tropical Medicine)
MASTA (Medical Advisory Services for Travellers)
  (☎ 0891-224 100) at the London School of Hygiene & Tropical Medicine, Keppel St, London WC1E 7BR
  (no travel clinic but provides information and travel health products)
Nomad Travellers Store & Medical Centre
  (☎ 020-8889 7014; health line ☎ 09068-633414; email nomad.travstore@virgin.net)
  3-4 Wellington Terrace, Turnpike Lane, London N8 0PX

USA & Canada

To find a travel health clinic in your area, you could call your state health department, or try one of the following:

Centers for Disease Control & Prevention (CDC) in Atlanta, Georgia
(☎ 888-232-3228; fax 888-232-3299)
(the central source of travel health information in North America, the CDC has phone travel health information lines and can also advise you on travel medicine providers in your area. The CDC publishes an excellent booklet, Health Information for International Travel – ☎ 202-512-1800 or order it from the Superintendent of Documents, US Government Printing Office, Washington DC)

American Society of Tropical Medicine & Hygiene
(☎ 847-480-9592; fax 847-480-9282; www.astmh.org) 60 Revere Drive, Suite 500, Northbrook, IL 60062
(can also provide you with a comprehensive list of travel health providers in your area)

International Society of Travel Medicine
(☎ 770-736-7060; www.istm.org) PO Box 871089, Stone Mountain, GA 30087
(contact the ISTM for a list of ISTM member clinics)

Health Canada
(fax 613-941-3900; www.hc-sc.gc.ca/hpb/lcdc/osh/)
(the Travel Medicine Program of this government department provides information on disease outbreaks, immunisations and general health advice for travellers, and more detailed information on tropical diseases, as well as information on travel medicine clinics)

The US Department of State Citizen's Emergency Center has travel advisories on a recording. Remember to take a record of the number (☎ 202-647-5225) with you, as they can provide you with access to medical advice and assistance over the phone if you are in an emergency situation overseas.

Australia & New Zealand

The Travellers Medical and Vaccination Centre has a network of clinics in most major cities – use the phone book to find your nearest clinic or check out their web site (www.tmvc.com.au/info.html). They can provide an online personalised travel health report (for a fee) via their web site.

Vaccination Certificates

Apart from some vaccinations being recommended for medical reasons, many countries in Africa require you to be vaccinated against yellow fever (and sometimes cholera, although this is contrary to international law) before you will be allowed into the country. Your doctor or any travel health clinic will be able to advise you on this.

Wherever you're going, it's a good idea to make sure your immunisations are recorded on an official certificate – your doctor or travel health centre will usually issue you with a record. This is useful for your own information and if necessary, you will be able to show it to any doctor treating you.

Internet Resources

Two authoritative web sites are the first point of call for the latest on travel health issues:

WHO
www.who.ch
(the official site of the World Health Organization, this has all the information you'll ever need on the state of the world's health, including disease distribution maps and all the latest health recommendations for international travel. The section that's probably going to be most useful to you is at www.who.int/emc – it has disease outbreak news and health advice for travellers)

CDC
www.cdc.gov
(the official site of the US Centers for Disease Control & Prevention, this has loads of useful information, including disease outbreak news and disease risks according to destination)

Other major sites that are worth checking out include:

African Medical & Research Foundation
www.amref.org
(AMREF is primarily a medical aid organisation based in eastern Africa and maintains an excellent web site, which includes a section on health advice for travellers to Africa. It has a leaflet in print, Health Code for Travellers to Africa, available by contacting the organisation)

MASTA
www.masta.org
(this highly recommended site of the Medical Advisory Services for Travellers – see earlier – is easy to use and provides concise readable information on all the important issues. It also has useful links, including to the Foreign and Commonwealth Office for advice on safe travel)

Medical College of Wisconsin Travelers Clinic
www.intmed.mcw/travel.html
(this site has useful information on all the usual travel health issues, and an impressively comprehensive list of links to a variety of other travel health information sites – browse till you drop)

Shorelands
www.tripprep.com
(this well-organised site is easy to navigate and has lots of good travel health information, as well as a comprehensive directory of travel medicine providers around the world – including South Africa and Tanzania – and handy country profiles that include US State Department travel advisory information)

Travel Health Information Service
www.travelhealth.com
(this chatty site, run by US-based Dr Stephen Blythe, is easy to navigate and has loads of good information and links)

Travellers Medical and Vaccination Centre
www.tmvc.com.au/info.html
(this Australian-based site has lots of useful information, including disease outbreak news and good sections on travelling while pregnant and with children)

Books

For more information on travel health issues you could try include:

Travellers' Health
Dr Richard Dawood, 1995
(comprehensive and authoritative)

Staying Healthy in Asia, Africa & Latin America
  Dirk Schroeder, 1994
  (well organised and easy to use)
Bugs, Bites & Bowels
  Dr Jane Howarth-Wilson
  (full of practical, down to earth advice, this book is aimed at travellers and expatriates)

Where There Is No Doctor
  David Werner, 1994
  (a very detailed guide intended for someone, such as a Peace Corps worker, going to work in an underdeveloped country)

Alternatively, if you're looking for a guide to take on the road, Lonely Planet's *Healthy Travel Africa*, is a handy pocket size and packed with useful information and tips for staying healthy.

Immunisations Details

If you're an adult, you will probably have had the full course of an immunisation before, usually as a child. With most immunisations, it takes two to three weeks to build up maximum protection. There are currently no immunisations available for travellers diarrhoea, dengue fever or malaria.

vaccine	full course	booster	comments
tetanus	three doses given at four-week intervals (usually in childhood); usually given with diphthera	every 10 years	full course usually given in childhood
polio	three doses given at four weekly intervals (usually in childhood)	every 10 years	full course usually given in childhood
hepatitis A vaccine	single dose	booster at six to 12 months	gives good protection for at least 12 months; with booster, protects for more than 10 years
hepatitis A immuno-globulin	single injection; needs to be given close to departure	gives protection only for two to six months, depending on dose	because it's a blood product there's a theoretical risk of HIV and hepatitis B or C
typhoid	single injection, or three or four oral doses	injection every three years; oral every one to five years	the old injectable vaccine was notorious for producing unpleasant side effects, but the new one causes few side effects
meningococcal meningitis	one dose	protection lasts three years	protects against the major epidemic forms of the disease
hepatitis B	two doses one month apart plus a third dose six months later	three to five years	more rapid courses are available if necessary
rabies (pre-exposure)	three doses over one month	two to three years booster at six to 12 months	the old vaccine was extremely unpleasant as it had to be injected into the stomach, but the new vaccine is injected under the skin, and has few side effects
yellow fever	two doses over a month	three years	should be avoided if you have multiple allergies (eg to bee stings or drugs)
BCG (tuberculosis)	single dose	protected for life; no booster required	often given in childhood, so you may already be immune

IMMUNISATIONS

Immunisations help protect you from some of the diseases you may be at risk of getting on your travels. Ideally, you'll need to make your first appointment for advice on immunisations (and other travel-related health risks) about six to eight weeks before you go. This is because you usually need to wait one to two weeks after a booster or the last dose of a course before you're fully protected, and some courses may need to be given over a period of several weeks. For example, a full course of rabies vaccine takes a month. Generally, if you've had a full course of an immunisation before, you will only need a booster injection now.

Don't panic if you have left it to the last minute. Immunisation schedules can be rushed if necessary and most vaccinations you'll need for Africa can be given together two weeks, or even one, before you go. Just bear in mind that you won't be as well protected for the first week or two of your trip as if you'd had them earlier.

You'll need to get individual advice on which immunisations you need to have, as this depends on various factors, including your destination, the length and type of trip, any medical conditions you have, which ones you've had in the past, and any allergies you have.

Whatever your travel plans, you'll need to be up to date with your 'routine' immunisations, including tetanus (often given together with diphtheria), polio and some 'childhood illnesses'. In addition, you'll probably need some of the following travel-related immunisations.

Cholera

Immunisation against this diarrhoeal disease is no longer generally recommended because it only provides short lived and poor protection, and travellers are at very low risk of getting cholera. However, at some borders in Africa, officials may demand to see a certificate of immunisation before allowing you across the border, even though this is contrary to international law. They may even force you to be immunised on the spot, which is probably best avoided. Your best bet is to discuss this issue with your travel health clinic or doctor before you go. You may be able to get a certificate of exemption or some other form of relevant documentation to carry with you just in case.

Hepatitis A

All travellers to Africa should be protected against this common disease which affects the liver. Protection is either with hepatitis A vaccine or immunoglobulin. Although it may be more expensive, the vaccine is recommended as it gives good protection for at least a year (longer if you have a booster). Immunoglobulin needs to be given as close as possible to your departure date. It protects you for a limited time and carries a theoretical possibility of blood-borne diseases like HIV, although this is a minuscule risk in most western countries.

A combined hepatitis A and typhoid vaccine has recently become available, which should be good for cutting down on the number of injections you need to have.

Hepatitis B

Protection against this serious liver infection is recommended for all long-term travellers to Africa, where the disease is common. It is also recommended if you're going to be working as a medic or nurse in Africa or if needle sharing or sexual contact with a local person is a possibility. This immunisation is given routinely to children in some countries, including Australia and the USA, so you may already be protected. If you need both hepatitis A and B immunisations, a combined vaccine is available.

Meningococcal Meningitis

Epidemics of this serious brain infection occur periodically, mainly in the Sahel area in the dry season, although the so-called 'meningitis belt' extends as far south as Zambia and Malawi. Epidemics tend to be widely reported and immunisation is usually recommended if you are travelling in risk areas in the dry season. There have been reports of travellers being required to be immunised at borders into Burkina Faso and possibly other countries in the region – check this out before you go.

Rabies

With rabies, you have the choice of either having the immunisation before you go or just if you are bitten by a potentially rabid animal. If you have the immunisation before you go, you will need to have a course of three injections over a month. This primes your system against rabies, giving you some, but not complete, protection against the disease. If you then get bitten by a suspect animal, you will still need to have two boosters to prevent rabies developing.

Malaria – Did You Know ...

Just bear in mind that the majority of travellers diagnosed with malaria on their return home acquired the infection in sub-Saharan Africa. Some more facts to ponder on:

- Malaria is spread by mosquitoes.
- Malaria is a potentially fatal disease.
- Malaria is becoming more common and more difficult to treat (because of drug resistance).
- Most cases of malaria in travellers occur in people who didn't take antimalarials or who didn't take them as recommended.
- Most malaria deaths in travellers occur because the diagnosis is delayed or missed.
- Malaria is particularly dangerous in children and pregnant women.
- Malaria can be transmitted by transfusion of blood and other blood products, by needle sharing among intravenous drug users and from mother to foetus.

Rabies vaccination is generally recommended if you will be travelling through Africa for more than three months or if you will be handling animals. Children are at particular risk of being bitten, so they may need to be vaccinated even if you're going for a short time; discuss this with your doctor or a travel health clinic.

Tuberculosis

You may already have had this immunisation as a child (although not US travellers). But if you weren't you probably won't need it unless you're going to be living with local people (for example if you're going back to visit relatives) for three months or longer. Although TB is common worldwide, short-term travellers are at very small risk of the disease.

Typhoid

You'll need vaccination against typhoid if you're travelling in Africa for longer than a couple of weeks. Typhoid vaccination is available as an injection or as tablets (oral form), although availability of this may be limited. The oral form can sometimes upset your tummy. If you've had the old injectable typhoid vaccine, you'll know that it can produce some pretty unpleasant reactions (fever, chills, headache) but the new injection causes few effects.

Yellow Fever

Proof of immunisation against yellow fever is a statutory requirement for entry into all African countries if you are coming from a yellow-fever infected country in Africa or South America. As well as this consideration, immunisation is medically recommended if you are planning to visit rural areas of infected countries.

The yellow fever vaccine occasionally causes low-grade fever and a sore arm. It's not recommended if you have severe egg allergy or your immunity is lowered for some reason (for example you are HIV-positive).

MALARIA PREVENTION

If you're going to a malarial area in Africa, especially sub-Saharan Africa, you must take steps to prevent this potentially fatal disease – see the boxed text for some vital facts about this tropical disease.

If you're going to a malarial area:

• Get the latest information on risks and drug resistance from a reliable information source. See Before You Go, Information Sources section earlier in this chapter.

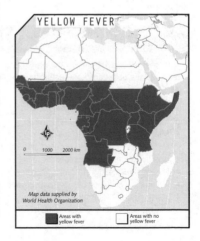

YELLOW FEVER

0   1000   2000 km

Map data supplied by
World Health Organization

Areas with yellow fever   Areas with no yellow fever

- Take suitable malaria preventive drugs or carry malaria treatment with you if appropriate. Discuss this with your doctor or a travel health clinic before you go.
- Take steps to avoid insect bites (see the Insect Bites section in this chapter) this is even more important now that malarial parasites have become resistant to many commonly used antimalarial drugs.
- Make sure you find out a bit about the disease before you go, including what to do if you think you have it. This information is readily available on the internet or from your doctor.

Malaria Preventive Drugs

Recommendations change all the time so you need to get the latest advice from your doctor or travel health clinic before you go. The main options are currently mefloquine or doxycycline (both equally effective for sub-Saharan Africa), or chloroquine (with or without proguanil; chloroquine resistance is widespread in sub-Saharan Africa). For some low-risk malarial areas (for example some parts of North Africa), you may not need to take malaria pills, but instead you may be advised to carry emergency malaria treatment to use if necessary.

Malaria pills need to be started before you leave (a month before in the case of chloroquine; two to three weeks for mefloquine), so that they have a chance to reach maximum protective levels in your body before you arrive at your destination. It also gives any side effects a chance to show themselves so you can change medication before you go if necessary.

Minor side effects are common with all the drugs, but if you get major side effects that make you unsure about continuing the drug, you should seek advice about changing to a medication that suits you better.

As far as possible, it's best to take with you all the malaria pills you think you will need, as some malaria pills may not be available where you're going and you may not be able to get exactly what you want.

Emergency Treatment

If you're going to a high-risk malarial area without access to medical care you'll need to take treatment doses of medication with you to use in an emergency. You should also consider taking a malaria diagnosis kit with you in this situation – they are available from major travel health clinics. Discuss these issues with your doctor before you go, as you need to be clear about when to use emergency treatment and what to do if problems arise. Emergency treatment is a first aid measure only, to tide you over while you seek medical help.

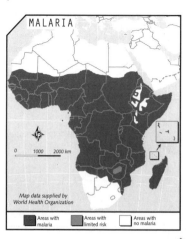

MALARIA

Map data supplied by World Health Organization

| Areas with malaria | Areas with limited risk | Areas with no malaria |

TRAVEL INSURANCE

However lucky (or poor) you're feeling, you don't want to be without this. For more details, see the Tickets & Insurance chapter earlier in the book.

PRETRAVEL CHECKUPS

If you're going to be away for more than about six months or you're going to a remote area, a medical checkup is a good idea to make sure there are no problems waiting to happen. If you've had any niggling problems, now is the time to get them checked out. This goes for your teeth too – make sure you get a dental checkup before you go, to prevent problems arising when you are far from reliable help.

Remember to get any prescription medicines you need from your doctor before you go. If you take any medicines regularly, you'll need to take sufficient

Take Those Tablets

I have an adventurous streak, so I thought travelling across Africa would be fun, but as I was inexperienced, I wisely decided to travel with a London-based overland truck company. I didn't have to worry about transport, accommodation and food in all of those strange-sounding countries – but I also didn't worry about taking antimalarial tablets.

One week before the end of the nine week trip, I started to get a blinding headache, and was unable to move my eyes one degree. Soon, I couldn't keep my eyes open at all, and slept for about 20 hours a day. I was shaking uncontrollably at times, drinking litre after litre of precious drinking water and passing seemingly endless urine the colour of Fanta. I thought I was going to die – and, in a way, I almost wanted to. I gathered enough energy to flick through page after page of the long and disquieting health section in my battered copy of Africa on a shoestring (circa 1986) trying to link my symptoms with some horrible tropical disease.

I initially thought I had hepatitis, which meant going straight home and recuperating for several months. Perhaps I had typhoid, which sounded worse. Maybe, I had contracted both diseases, with a touch of cholera thrown in for good measure. But I was sure that I'd had injections for those diseases.

In a way, I was lucky: I got ill at the end of my trip through Africa, and in Nairobi, which boasts some of the best medical facilities in the continent. The doctor poked and prodded me, went away, eventually came back, and then poked and prodded me again. Twenty minutes after extracting some blood, he calmly told me I had contracted a potentially fatal strain of malaria. The only cure was a course of antimalarial tablets – exactly the sort that I should have taken, but didn't, before getting ill.

I was alone, vulnerable, inexperienced and recovering from a serious illness in a large, strange city. I was hopelessly lethargic, and too tired to stand for more than 10 minutes at a time. I slept for most of three days, and didn't eat anything for five days, but recovered enough to fly back to the UK.

I had tried to avoid being bitten by mosquitoes by wearing long trousers, and using a repellent, but foolishly thought I didn't need to take antimalarial tablets. In Africa, it's difficult to avoid being bitten by mosquitoes, and malaria is rife – every year millions are infected all around the world, and hundreds of thousands of Africans die from the disease. I could have easily been one of the statistics, but thankfully lived to tell the tale.

Paul Greenway
LP Author, Australia

supplies with you, as well as a record of your prescription. If you are going to be travelling to remote areas, you might want to discuss taking emergency treatment for diarrhoea or chest infections with you, which you will need to get on prescription.

If you wear contact lenses, you may want to talk to your optometrist about hygiene and other issues on the road. It's a good idea to take a plentiful supply of any cleaning solutions you use. If you wear glasses, consider taking a replacement pair, and take a copy of your prescription with you. It will be understood in any language in case you need to have a pair made up while you are away.

MEDICAL KIT

Following is a list of items you should consider including in your medical kit – consult you pharmacist for brands available in your country.

Aspirin or paracetamol (acetaminophen in the USA) – for pain or fever.

Antihistamine – useful as a decongestant for colds; for allergies, such as hay fever; to ease the itch from insect bites or stings; and to prevent motion sickness.

Antimalarials. Antibiotics or any regular medication you take.

Antidiarrhoeals and anti-sickness remedies

Rehydration mixture – to prevent dehydration, eg due to severe diarrhoea; particularly . important when travelling with children, but is recommended for everyone.

Insect repellent, sunscreen, lip balm and eye drops.

Calamine lotion, sting relief spray or aloe vera to ease irritation from sunburn and insect bites or stings.

Antifungal cream (or powder) – for fungal skin infections and thrush.

Antiseptic (such as povidone-iodine) – for cuts and grazes.

Bandages, Band-Aids (plasters) and other wound dressings for minor injuries.

Water purification tablets or iodine

Afraid To Take Your Medicine?

Which malaria pills to take and whether to take them at all can be a hot topic of conversation among travellers. Mefloquine is one of the most effective antimalarials available, but it's also one of the most controversial, and there has been much discussion in the media and among travellers about its side effects. These range from common side effects such as sleep disturbance (especially vivid dreams) to uncommon but more serious effects such as panic attacks, hallucinations and fits. Most people who take mefloquine do not, however, have any problems. Perhaps it's simply a case of bad news travelling faster than good.

You can get information on mefloquine and alternative antimalarials from travel health clinics, your doctor or any of the web sites listed under Information Sources at the beginning of this chapter. For a discussion of the issues surrounding mefloquine, try www.travelhealth .com/mefloqui.htm or www.geocities.com/TheTropics/6913/lariam.htm. Or you could visit Lariam Action USA's web site on www.suggskelly.com/lariam.

If you cannot, or would prefer not to, take mefloquine, there are other options, eg chloroquine plus proguanil, or doxycycline, and these may be better than taking nothing at all.

Scissors, tweezers and a thermometer (note that mercury thermometers are prohibited by airlines).

Syringes and needles – in case you need injections in a country with medical hygiene problems. Ask your doctor for a note explaining why you have them.

Cold and flu tablets, throat lozenges and nasal decongestant.

Multivitamins – consider for long trips, when dietary vitamin intake may be inadequate.

FIRST-AID COURSE

Everyone should be familiar with basic first aid techniques, but it is even more important if you are going to places where you cannot rely on rapid response emergency services. If you're going to be spending time in remote areas more than a day or so away from medical help, you should seriously consider doing at least a basic first aid course before you leave. Contact your local first aid organisation for details of courses available. More specialist training in outdoor survival skills is generally offered by organisations concerned with wilderness activities such as mountaineering and trekking.

Travellers with Special Needs

You don't have to be able-bodied or in perfect health to travel, but make sure you know what to expect and be prepared to take extra precautions. A short trip to a tourist centre or a country with well-developed medical services like

Medicines

In many African countries, medicines are much more freely available than they are in the west. Even many prescription medicines are readily available over-the-counter. While this can be very handy if you have run out of something, or become ill on the road, always keep the following points in mind:

Expiry Date – Medicines are frequently sold past their expiry dates; always check these before purchasing.

Storage Conditions & Efficacy – Storage conditions are often not optimal; if the medicine you need is one which requires particular handling (for example, refrigeration), it's generally best to assume that it didn't have this – meaning that the medicine may have lost its efficacy, or may even be detrimental to ingest.

Quality – Quality can be questionable with some medications, and many brands sold in the west may not be available; if you are uncertain about a particular brand or producer of a medication, try to find a knowledgeable pharmacist who can advise you.

Dosages – If you purchase a medicine, be sure you understand the proper dosages and requirements for taking it, as these may not be listed on the packing; try to find a doctor or knowledgeable pharmacist who can advise you.

Outdated Medicines – Remember that drugs no longer recommended in western countries (usually because better alternatives are available) may still be sold in Africa.

It's best to take sufficient supplies of any medication you may need with you. To avoid possible problems at customs, ask your doctor for an official letter stating why you need them.

South Africa may not present you with any major difficulties, but you may want to think more carefully about longer trips, especially to remote areas.

Whatever your plans, you'll need to get advice from your doctor or specialist before you go on problems you may encounter when you're travelling and what to do about them. Take with you a written summary of your medical problems and any treatment you are currently on or have received in the past – you may need to ask your doctor for this before you go.

Check that your travel health insurance covers you for preexisting illnesses. Remember that medical facilities in most countries in Africa are extremely limited, and emergency services are often nonexistent.

Everyday Health

Before you go, find out what precautions you can take to ensure you stay as healthy as possible while you are away. Only a few travel-related illnesses, and none of the more common problems like sunburn, diarrhoea and infected cuts, are preventable by immunisation.

SUN

This is probably the main hazard for most travellers to Africa. Overexposure to the sun can have serious long-term (such as skin cancer) as well as short-term consequences (painful sunburn), so it's worth taking this threat very seriously. Take loose-fitting clothes so that you can cover up against the sun, and wear a hat. Take high protection factor sunscreen with you – and remember to use it on exposed areas. You'll also need to protect your eyes with sunglasses that block out UV rays. The sun is generally at its fiercest between 11 am and 3 pm, so it makes sense to spend this time resting in the shade or indoors. Sun intensity can be particularly fierce at high altitude and near water, so take care in these situations.

HEAT

Remember to give yourself a chance to get used to the heat. You're probably going to feel hot and easily exhausted for about a week. After this, your body will have made adjustments to cope with the heat, and you'll probably find your capacity for activity is about back to normal. Many people find that they sweat heavily in the heat. You'll need to drink plenty of fluids to replace the amount you're sweating out – cool bottled, boiled or purified water is best, but any not-too-sweet soft drinks, fruit juice or green coconut milk are OK. Some more tips are as follows.

- Footwear. Too big is better than too small because your feet can swell up in the heat, and blisters or chafing can easily become infected.

- Help your body out by not doing too much during the heat of the day, and avoid large heavy meals and excess alcohol during the hottest part of the day.

- Avoid prickly heat and fungal infections (both common in hot climates) by washing regularly (but avoid over-using soap, which makes it worse) and drying yourself carefully.

- Learn to recognise the symptoms of heat exhaustion and heat stroke, which are the most serious consequences of heat exposure.

FOOD

It's generally agreed that contaminated food, not water, is the most common source of gut troubles in travellers. The impressive list of diseases you can get in this way includes most forms of diarrhoea, including dysentery, hepatitis A and E, and typhoid (not common in travellers generally but relatively more common if you're travelling in North Africa).

The fact is that you can get sick from food anywhere, but it's more likely when you're travelling. Inadequate or nonexistent sewage systems in many of the less developed nations in Africa, coupled with high levels of disease in the population, makes it much more likely that food, utensils and hands are going to be contaminated with disease-causing microorganisms, mainly from faeces. Travelling usually means you're eating out three meals a day for perhaps weeks on end, relying on other people to prepare your food safely. Most countries in Africa don't have enforceable food safety standards.

If you're on a long trip, or you're budgeting hard, you'll need to take care that your diet is balanced and that you don't lose a huge amount of weight. Consider taking multivitamins with you in case you get run-down.

You can build up immunity to some diarrhoeal diseases, but you can't build up immunity to many of the more serious diseases (like dysentery or food poisoning) or to parasites (like hookworm), so it's worth taking a few precautions to minimise your risks.

- Heating kills germs, so food that's served piping hot is likely to be safer than lukewarm or cold food, especially if it's been sitting around; freezing doesn't kill germs.
- Fruit and vegetables are difficult to clean (and may be contaminated where they are grown), but they should be safe if they're peeled or cooked.
- Well cooked meat and seafood should be OK; raw or lightly cooked meat and seafood can be a source of parasites in many areas.
- Bread and cakes are usually safe, although it's best to avoid cream-filled goodies if you can, as bugs like salmonella love cream.
- Your stomach's natural defences (mainly acid) can cope with small amounts of contaminated foods – if you're not sure about something, don't pig out on it!
- It's best to avoid unpasteurised milk, though powdered or UHT milk should be OK.
- Choose popular, clean-looking eating places as far as possible.

WATER

In countries with good infrastructure and resources, communal water supplies are generally safe from contamination, but you can't rely on this in many countries in Africa. Check your travel guidebook or travel health clinic for information on the reliability of water supplies at your destination. If you're not sure the water is safe, it's best to assume the worst. Never assume that water from rivers, streams or lakes is safe, as even in relatively unpopulated areas it can be contaminated by animals – or trekkers.

For most countries in Africa, this means not drinking tap water and not brushing your teeth in it. Ice is only as safe as the water it's made from, so it's best to avoid this too. Carrying your own cup is a good idea, as the drinking vessels available are frequently sources of infection.

How you deal with the water issue depends on where you are and what sort of travelling you're doing. Drinking bottled water is one obvious option, and it's generally widely available in Africa. But remember that the quality of some local brands is little better than tap water, and plastic bottles can be refilled with any old water and sold to unsuspecting travellers. As a general rule, it's best to stick to major brands of bottled water, preferably with serrated tops; always check the seal carefully.

However, the cost of bottled water can add up over a long trip, especially if you're travelling in hot climates, and there's a very real concern over the environmental – and aesthetic – effect of millions of discarded and unrecycled plastic bottles. If you're trekking or travelling off the beaten track, bottled water is a less practical option anyway.

The simplest and most effective way of making water safe to drink is to boil it, which kills all disease-causing bugs. You just need to bring it to a rolling boil for a minute or two and then let it cool.

If boiling doesn't sound like a practical option, it's easy to disinfect clear water with chemicals. Chlorine and iodine are the chemicals most widely used. Both are available in tablet form, and iodine is also available as a liquid (add five drops of 2% tincture of iodine to every litre of water) or as crystals you can make up into a liquid.

Simple filters or water purifiers are the third choice. While it may seem like a big outlay, it's possibly worth the expense, especially if you are planning a long trip.

PERSONAL HYGIENE

Many diseases you may be at risk for on your travels can be avoided by maintaining good personal hygiene. What this involves is reminding yourself to wash your hands before you eat and always after using the toilet. This is particularly important if you're eating with your hands. Short fingernails are easier to keep clean than long ones. It's a good idea to take your own utensils (plastic cup, bowl, spoon etc) with you so you can use them for street food or eating meals on trains. Try to remember to keep your hands away from your mouth and eyes, especially on public transport, as you can introduce an infection in this way.

INSECT BITES

These are the scourge of travellers to Africa and elsewhere, and you'll probably find they're a popular conversation topic too. Everyone has an opinion on the best way to avoid bites and how to stop the itch if you do get bitten. Although the bites are bad enough in themselves, their main importance is that some serious tropical diseases can be transmitted in this way – see the boxed text for more details.

Most mosquitoes are night-biters, but some (such as the mosquito that transmits dengue) bite mainly during the day. Some tips on how not to get bitten:

- Cover up with long-sleeved tops and long trousers or skirt; light-coloured clothing is thought to be less attractive to mosquitoes than dark colours.
- Use insect repellents on any exposed areas; if you're using sunscreen or other lotions, apply insect repellent last, and reapply after swimming if necessary.
- Sleep in a screened room or, if this is not possible (quite likely), sleep under a treated mosquito net; always cover children's beds or cots with treated mosquito nets; air-conditioned rooms are usually insect-free zones.
- Remember day-biting mosquitoes, and avoid shady conditions in the late afternoon or taking an afternoon siesta without the protection of a mosquito net.
- Spray your room or tent with an insect spray before you retire for the night to get rid of any lurking insects.
- Consider using electric insecticide vaporisers or mosquito coils which you burn – both are widely available in Africa, but you need a power socket for a vaporiser, and both are less effective if you have a fan going.

There are many insect repellent products on the market, but the most effective are those containing the compound DEET (diethyltoluamide) – check the label or ask your pharmacist to tell you which brands contain DEET. These include Autan, Rid, Doom, Jungle Formula, Off and Repel. Remember to try a test dose before you leave to check for allergy or skin irritation.

There have been concerns about the safety of DEET, but it's generally agreed that these are largely unfounded. For children, however, it's best to err on the cautious side – always follow the dosing instructions carefully, and choose a lower strength long-acting cream.

Permethrin is an effective insecticide that can be applied to clothes and mosquito nets. If you're planning on trekking through tick-infested areas (rainforests, scrubland, pastures), consider treating your clothes, particularly trousers and socks, with permethrin before you go.

You may prefer to use one of the new lemon eucalyptus-based natural products, which have been shown to be an effective alternative to DEET, with similar action times (although DEET is probably still your best bet in high-risk areas). Other natural repellents include citronella and pyrethrum, but these tend to be less effective and to have a short action (up to an hour), making them less practical to use.

The quality of screening and nets provided by accommodation in Africa varies from nonexistent to positively airtight, but beware – there always seems to be at least one

Insects & the Diseases They Transmit

Immunisations are currently not available against any of the diseases listed except yellow fever. Don't let yourself get bitten, and you won't get any of these diseases.

mosquitoes – malaria, dengue fever, filariasis, yellow fever
ticks – typhus, relapsing fever and other fevers
lice – typhus
fleas – plague
sandflies – leishmaniasis, sandfly fever
tsetse flies – trypanosomiasis (sleeping sickness)
blackflies – onchocerciasis (river blindness)

mosquito-sized hole in any net or screen. For most of tropical Africa, it's worth taking your own net with you, especially one that has been soaked in permethrin.

SCHISTOSOMIASIS (BILHARZIA)

This parasitic disease is a significant risk to you in most parts of Africa. It's caused by a tiny worm that lives in freshwater snails for part of its life cycle and in humans for the second part. Schistosomiasis can be treated but it's best not to get infected in the first place. For most parts of Africa, this means taking care to avoid swimming, paddling, crossing streams and doing water sports in fresh water (including Lake Malawi and the Nile River). And as the Lake Malawi scare indicates, it's best not to rely on local advice on risk areas, as local hotel operators have their livelihoods to consider, and not necessarily your health. If you do get wet, dry off quickly, as the disease-causing worms can't survive long out of water.

CUTS & SCRATCHES

You need to take more care of these than you would normally. Dust, dirt, lack of washing facilities and hot, humid conditions all make infection of any break in the skin more likely when you're travelling. Take care to prevent injury and insect bites. Keep any skin breaks as clean as possible.

ACCIDENTS & INJURY

Accidents and injury, not tropical diseases, are the leading cause of death in travellers. In addition, accidents are the main reason for needing a blood transfusion or other medical treatment, with all the potential for problems that this entails, including HIV and hepatitis B infection. Make sure you are aware of the risks, and take care to avoid them. Public transport can be risky in most parts of Africa, as a lack of resources and the need to make a living have to take precedence over basic safety considerations. Attacks from wild animals are another great topic for campfire tales among travellers, but you're much more likely to be injured by a marauding bush taxi than a wild animal.

Africa's magnificent coastline is a major drawcard for tourists, but drowning is a common cause of death in travellers, especially children and young adults. Even strong swimmers get taken by unexpectedly strong currents, for example on West Africa's Atlantic coast.

- Avoid alcohol when swimming or driving.
- Beware of strong currents at the seaside – check the local situation and don't swim alone.
- Don't dive into shallow water.
- Use a seat belt if possible.
- If you're riding a motorcycle or moped, wear a helmet and protective clothing.
- Hire cars from reputable firms.
- If you're driving, try not to speed and avoid travelling at night.

SAFE SEX

While it's true that sexually transmitted infections (STIs), including HIV/AIDS and hepatitis B, are a risk anywhere if you're having casual sex, it seems that you're more likely to throw caution to the wind when you are away from home, and are therefore more at risk. Opportunities for casual sex tend to be greater while you're travelling. In addition to the increased opportunties to have sex, the levels of STIs in the countries you are visiting may be much higher than at home.

Avoiding casual sex altogether is the safest option; otherwise, remember to use a condom. Condoms are widely available in most African countries but you may prefer to take a familiar, reliable brand with you. Rubber condoms disintegrate in the heat, so take care to store them deep in your pack and to check them carefully before use.

ALCOHOL & DRUGS

Be a wary of local brews, especially distilled spirits, as they may contain undesirable additives or methanol, a highly toxic form of alcohol which can cause permanent blindness.

If you decide to use drugs, be aware that there's no guarantee of quality, and locally available drugs can be unexpectedly strong or mixed with other harmful substances.

Women's Health

BEFORE YOU GO

Travel can pose problems with certain forms of contraception. The timing of pill-taking can be tricky if you're crossing time zones, and diarrhoea, vomiting and antibiotics used to treat common infections can all reduce its effectiveness – discuss this with your doctor before you go, if necessary. Take a plentiful supply of your medication with you, because it may be difficult to get your brand overseas. In some countries, oral contraceptives may not be readily available at all. International Planned Parenthood Federation (☎ 020-7487 7913; www.ippf.org) Regent's College, Inner Circle, Regent's Park, London NW1 4NS can provide information on the availability of contraception and local attitudes towards birth control and termination of pregnancy in various countries in Africa. If you think you may need to start using contraception while you're travelling, it's a good idea to get this sorted out before you go.

You might want to consider the possibility of stopping your periods temporarily (for example, if you're going to be trekking in a remote area at an inappropriate moment). Another issue you might want to discuss is taking prescription treatment for cystitis or thrush with you, or possibly, emergency contraception.

If you're planning on travelling while you're pregnant, you'll definitely want to discuss this with your doctor as early as possible.

EVERYDAY HEALTH

You may find that your periods stop altogether when you're away – a result of the physical and mental stresses of travelling (but have a pregnancy test done if you think you may be pregnant). You're just as likely to find, however, that travelling brings on the worst period of your life, at the most inconvenient time. If you suffer from PMS, be prepared for it to be worse while you are away and take plentiful supplies of any painkiller or other remedy you find helpful.

Hot weather and limited washing facilities make thrush (yeast infection) more likely when you're travelling. If you know you are prone to thrush, it's worth taking a supply of medication with you.

Unprotected sex with a new partner makes a sexually transmitted infection a possibility. Get any symptoms like an abnormal vaginal discharge or genital sores checked out as soon as possible. Some STIs don't cause any symptoms, even though they can cause long-term fertility and other problems, so if you have unprotected sex, be sure to have a check-up when you return home.

Medical Services

Before you go, you could consider joining an organisation like the International Association for Medical Assistance to Travellers (☎ 519-836 0102; www.sentex.net; 40 Regal Rd, Guelph, Ontario N1K 1B5, Canada). This is a nonprofit organisation (it welcomes donations) which can provide you with a list of reliable doctors in the countries you're planning to visit. A travel health clinic should also be able to advise you on medical care at your destination. If you need a doctor when you are away, your embassy or travel insurance hotline should be able to provide you with names of local doctors. Upmarket hotels can often recommend a doctor, and may even have a doctor attached to the staff.

South Africa has reliable medical care, but elsewhere you will generally find both public and private hospitals and clinics in provincial capitals and large

Traditional Medicine

Most Africans rely at least in part on traditional medicine (which is closely tied together with traditional religion). Even in urban areas where western medicine is usually available, many people prefer traditional methods and will journey long distances to village practitioners for treatment.

Traditional practitioners hold considerable social status in many areas, and jealously guard their turf. In addition to prescribing herbal cures, many practitioners also combine these with potions and rituals aimed at securing help from the ancestors, balancing out negative forces in someone's life, or banishing or communicating with a spirit which has possessed a person.

Many of these things will not be evident unless you are in Africa for a while. However, markets often have a traditional remedies section, which is readily accessible and well worth a look. Here you may see all sorts of powders and plants, as well as fetishes such as birds' skulls and shells. In many parts of Africa, you will also see charms *(grisgris)* – usually worn around the neck or waist. These are believed to ward off evil or bring good luck, but are efficacious only after being blessed by a traditional practitioner.

towns, although rural areas may not be as well served. In many rural areas, the only care available is provided by healthworkers or traditional medical practitioners. In general, public hospitals tend to be under-financed and overstretched, and are probably best avoided unless they are affiliated to a university. Private clinics or hospitals are generally better, although they can be expensive. Mission hospitals or those run by charitable organisations are often of extremely high standard, and may be the only option in more remote areas. In some countries military hospitals are good for emergencies.

Remember that medical care may be very different from what you are used to back home, and this is often exacerbated by language and cultural differences. As a rule, standards of nursing care are very different from those you may be used to – attitudes towards basic hygiene can be alarmingly casual. If you have to stay overnight in hospital, you are often expected to have someone to bring you food and look after you.

Attitudes towards the use of medicines can be very much more cavalier than you may be used to. Western medicines tend to be prescribed very readily, often when there is no need, so be prepared to try a few simple measures first. If you do have to take a medicine while you are away, make sure you know what it is and what it has been prescribed for. Traditional remedies are widely available all over Africa, including herbal remedies, but this doesn't necessarily mean they are harmless.

In many parts of Africa, fees for medical treatment can seem ridiculously cheap. However, you will generally have to pay upfront for all consultations and treatment, and remember that medical evacuation from anywhere costs thousands of dollars. It's vital that you have travel insurance, although you will probably need to come up with the money yourself at the time, and claim it back later. Keep an emergency stash with you just in case, and ask for and keep any receipts.

Medical Problems

We've summarised here some details about the main medical problems (listed in alphabetical order) that may be a risk to you on your travels in Africa. For more in-depth information on any of these problems, try any of the information sources listed at the beginning of this chapter.

ALTITUDE & CLIMATIC EXTREMES
Altitude Sickness

You need to take into account the risk of acute mountain sickness (AMS) if you are planning on trekking in any of Africa's admittedly few high places (by 'high' we mean over about 2500m). Kilimanjaro and Mt Kenya are popular treks that take you to such altitudes. Before you leave, it's a good idea to check that your insurance covers altitude sickness.

You can get advice on preventing AMS from a travel health clinic or expedition organiser, or read up about it in your guidebook or one of the travel health guides listed earlier. Two authoritative web sites with information about AMS and other altitude-related problems are www.princeton.edu/~oa/altitude .html and www.gorge.net/hamg/AMS.html.

Symptoms of mild altitude sickness are common when you first arrive at altitude and include headache, nausea and loss of appetite, difficulty sleeping and lack of energy. They usually respond to rest and simple painkillers.

The best way to prevent AMS is to ascend slowly. Drugs such as acetazolamide (trade name Diamox) are sometimes used to prevent AMS, although this is controversial. The most important point to remember is that taking drugs is no substitute for proper acclimatisation.

The best treatment for AMS is descent, and the golden rule is never to continue to ascend if you have any symptoms of AMS. If mild symptoms persist or get worse, you must descend.

Heat Exhaustion & Heatstroke

Heat can cause a range of conditions from heat cramps and fainting to heat exhaustion and potentially fatal heatstroke. Even if you don't feel too bad, heat and dehydration can affect your physical performance and mental judgement. In a hot climate you can lose an astonishing 2L of sweat in an hour, more if you're doing strenuous physical activity. Sweat contains water and salts, which you need to replace, so drink a lot more than you would in a cool climate, even when you have acclimatised. An adult needs to drink about 3L of fluid a day in a hot climate, or 5L or more if doing a strenuous physical activity such as trekking or cycling. Take a water bottle with you wherever you go, and remember to drink frequently from it.

Both heatstroke and heat exhaustion are caused by prolonged exposure to high temperatures and inadequate fluid intake. In heatstroke, sweating stops and the body temperature rises dangerously, which can be fatal. Symptoms include severe, throbbing headaches, confusion and lack of coordination. This is an emergency situation.

Symptoms of heat exhaustion are headache, dizziness, nausea and feeling weak and exhausted. You may get muscle aches or cramps. If you notice these symptoms in yourself or your travel companions, rest in a cool environment and drink lots of cool fluids.

Needles & Injections

Due to scanty resources and insufficiently rigorous sterilisation procedures, injections in many African countries can carry a risk of HIV/AIDS, malaria or hepatitis B or C transmission. To minimise this risk, avoid injections whenever possible – ask if there is a tablet you can take instead. If you do need an injection, ask to see the syringe unwrapped in front of you. If you will be travelling for extended periods, or in remote areas, also consider carrying sterile needles and syringes with you just in case. You can get packs from most travel health clinics.

Assuming that you are basically healthy, not pregnant and take sensible precautions to avoid accidents, it's unlikely that you would need a blood transfusion while travelling. However, it's worth being aware that most African countries cannot afford to screen blood adequately, so the same diseases can be transmitted in this way. Carry a few sterile needles and syringes in your medical kit (with an official explanatory note). Alternatively, make sure you see the sterile wrapping opened in front of you.

Hypothermia

Although you probably associate Africa more with heat than the opposite extreme, be aware that cold and unpredictable weather are significant hazards in many highland areas, including the Atlas Mountains in North Africa, the Simien Mountains in Ethiopia, the Rwenzoris, highland areas of Malawi and the Drakensbergs in South Africa, as well as obvious risk areas like Kilimanjaro and Mt Kenya. Protect yourself from this hazard by making sure you're always prepared for the worst possible weather, even if you're on a day trip or just planning to cross the mountains on your way somewhere.

INFECTIONS
Cholera

This serious diarrhoeal illness receives much publicity but, as a rule, is unlikely to affect travellers. Cholera is caused by poor sanitation, spread through contaminated food and water, and usually affects the poorest of the poor in developing countries. The best prevention is to take care with food and water. Dehydration is the main risk, and the mainstay of treatment is fluid replacement.

Dengue Fever

This viral disease is transmitted by day-biting mosquitoes. It occurs in Africa, but is not a major problem as it is in other parts of the world such as South-East Asia. Symptoms are fever, headache and severe joint and muscle pains (hence its old name, 'breakbone fever'). Simple dengue can sometimes progress to a more severe form, dengue haemorrhagic fever but this is extremely rare in travellers. There is no specific treatment for dengue. Aspirin should be avoided, as it increases the risk of haemorrhaging. The best prevention is to avoid mosquito bites at all times.

Diarrhoea

This is a great conversation-starter in travellers circles – and sometimes a stopper too. Although the risks vary with your destination, the fact is that diarrhoea affects about 50% of travellers to developing countries. Even if it's relatively mild, you're probably going to feel a tad sorry for yourself for a day or so as it passes through your system, so it's worth building a few rest days into your travel schedule to allow for this. Taking basic precautions with food and drink and paying attention to your personal hygiene are the most important preventive strategies.

If you get it, diarrhoea usually strikes about the third day after you arrive and lasts about three to five days. It's caused by many factors, including jet lag, new food, a new lifestyle and new bugs. It can come back again in the second week, although you do build up immunity to some of the causes. Symptoms are diarrhoea without blood, mild fever, some nausea and stomach cramps.

The most important aspect of treatment is to prevent dehydration by replacing lost fluid – and to rest. You can drink most liquids, except alcohol, very sugary drinks or dairy products. Oral rehydration sachets can be useful

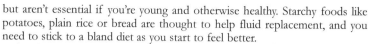

but aren't essential if you're young and otherwise healthy. Starchy foods like potatoes, plain rice or bread are thought to help fluid replacement, and you need to stick to a bland diet as you start to feel better.

Antidiarrhoea tablets are of limited use as they prevent your system from clearing out the toxin and can make certain types of diarrhoea worse, though they can be useful as a temporary stopping measure, for example if you have to go on a long bus journey. They should be avoided in children. Antibiotic treatment for simple travellers' diarrhoea may shorten the illness but side effects are possible, so you might want to discuss this with your doctor before you leave.

Sometimes diarrhoea can be more serious, with blood, a high fever and cramps (bacterial dysentery), or it can be persistent and bloody (amoebic dysentery) or persistent, explosive and gassy *(Giardia)*. All need treatment with specific antibiotics.

If you're going to a remote area far from medical help, you may want to consider taking antibiotics with you for self-treating diarrhoea. However, it's generally better to seek medical advice to diagnose which type of diarrhoea you have and decide which antibiotics you should be taking.

Filariasis

This is a mosquito-transmitted parasitic infection found in many parts of Africa. Possible symptoms include fever, pain and swelling of the lymph glands; inflammation of lymph drainage areas; swelling of a limb or the scrotum; skin rashes; and blindness. Treatment is available to eliminate the parasites from the body, but some of the damage already caused may not be reversible. Medical advice should be obtained promptly if the infection is suspected.

Hepatitis A

Hepatitis A is common and transmitted by contaminated food and drinking water – make sure you are immunised against it. Take care with food, especially shellfish, and water. Symptoms are fever, and sometimes diarrhoea. It can leave you feeling weak for some time after, but has no other long-term effects.

Hepatitis B

This viral infection of the liver is spread through contact with infected blood, blood products or body fluids, for example through sexual contact, unsterilised needles and blood transfusions, or contact with blood via small breaks in the skin. Other risk situations include having a shave, tattoo or body piercing with contaminated equipment. The best prevention is to avoid risk situations. The symptoms of hepatitis B may be more severe than type A and the disease can lead to long term problems such as chronic liver damage, liver cancer or a long term carrier state.

HIV/AIDS

You're at risk wherever you go if you don't take measures to protect yourself. HIV/AIDS is mainly transmitted through heterosexual sex in Africa, and it's a major public health problem in the region, especially sub-Saharan Africa.

Intestinal worms

These parasites are common mainly in rural, tropical areas. The different worms have different ways of infecting people. Some may be ingested on food such as undercooked meat (eg tapeworms) and some enter through your skin (eg hookworms). Taking care with what you eat, especially avoiding undercooked meat, and wearing shoes is the best preventative measure against intestinal worms. Symptoms are often vague and infestations may not show up for some time, and although they are generally not serious, if left untreated some can cause severe health problems later.

Leishmaniasis

This parasitic disease is transmitted by sandflies. Travellers can occasionally get the skin form of the disease, which usually heals up without special treatment. Prevention is through avoiding sandfly bites.

Malaria

Malaria is a parasitic disease carried by infected mosquitoes. It is a major risk to travellers in most parts of sub-Saharan Africa (see map). Prevention is important, and consists of avoiding mosquito bites and taking antimalarial tablets. Symptoms can be nonspecific and include fever, chills and sweating, headache, diarrhoea and abdominal pains or just a vague feeling of ill-health. Without treatment malaria can rapidly become more serious and can be fatal, but if treatment is started promptly, most people recover.

Meningococcal Meningitis

Outbreaks of meningococcal meningitis occur periodically in the Sahel belt of Africa, particularly during the dry season. A fever, severe headache, sensitivity to light and neck stiffness which prevents forward bending of the head are the first symptoms, sometimes also a rash. Although the risk to travellers is small, immunisation is usually recommended if you are going to risk areas.

Rabies

Rabies exists throughout Africa, and pretravel immunisation may be recommended in some circumstances. Practically any warm-blooded animal can be infected, although infected dogs and monkeys are probably the greatest risk to you as a traveller in Africa. Other potentially infected animals include rats, bats, cats, foxes and wolves. Once symptoms have appeared, death is inevitable, but the onset of symptoms can be prevented by a course of injections with the rabies vaccine, which you need whether or not you have been immunised previously.

River Blindness

This parasitic disease occurs in West Africa and some parts of East Africa. It is transmitted by the bite of a small blackfly which lives and breeds around rivers. It causes an itchy rash and severe infections can cause eye damage. It's very unlikely to affect travellers.

Schistosomiasis (Bilharzia)

This disease is caused by tiny worms that live in freshwater snails. It can cause an itchy rash several hours after swimming – swimmer's itch, but it mainly causes long-term problems in your bowel or bladder. You can get it by swimming, bathing or paddling in fresh water. Several cases are reported each year in travellers returning from Africa, even among those who did not consider themselves particularly at risk. Avoid swimming, bathing or paddling in any body of fresh water, including the Nile River and Lake Malawi.

Tetanus

This disease is caused by a germ which lives in soil and in the faeces of horses and other animals. It enters the body via breaks in the skin. The first symptom may be discomfort in swallowing, or stiffening of the jaw and neck; this is followed by painful convulsions of the jaw and whole body. The disease can be fatal. It can be prevented by vaccination.

Tuberculosis

Although tuberculosis (TB) is a major and growing problem in Africa, the risk to short-term travellers is very low unless you will be living in close contact with locals. TB is a bacterial infection usually transmitted from person to person by coughing but which may be transmitted through consumption of unpasteurised milk. Milk that has been boiled is safe to drink, and the souring of milk to make yoghurt or cheese also kills the bacilli. You may need to have a TB test before you travel as this can help diagnose the disease later if you become ill.

Trypanosomiasis

In parts of tropical Africa tsetse flies can carry trypanosomiasis, or sleeping sickness. You're at risk of it if you travel in rural areas, especially near rivers and lakes in West and Central Africa, and on safari in reserves and national parks in East Africa. There's little risk in urban areas. The tsetse fly is about twice the size of a housefly and recognisable by the scissorlike way it folds its wings when at rest. Only a small proportion of tsetse flies carry the disease, but it is a serious disease which can be fatal without treatment. No protection is available except avoiding the tsetse fly bites.

Typhoid

This vaccine-preventable disease is transmitted through contaminated food and water, and is a risk where hygiene standards are low. Symptoms are initially similar to flu, with headache, aches and pains and a fever. Abdominal pain, vomiting and either diarrhoea or constipation can occur. Serious complications such as pneumonia, perforated bowel or meningitis may develop. It can be effectively treated but medical help must be sought.

Typhus

There are several different varieties of typhus, which can be spread by ticks, lice and mites. The different varieties all cause a similar disease but differ in severity. There are no vaccines against any form of typhus, but they respond rapidly to appropriate antibiotic treatment, without any long-term effects.

Yellow Fever

This viral disease is spread by mosquito bites and is mainly a rural disease. It's very unlikely to affect travellers, and the vaccination is considered to be 100% effective.

When You Return

If you were away for a short time only and had no serious health problems, there's probably no need to get a medical check-up when you return, unless you develop symptoms. If you become sick in the weeks following your trip, be sure to tell your doctor that you have been away, which countries you have visited and any antimalarials you may have been taking. Remember that you need to keep taking antimalarials for four weeks after you leave a malarial area.

If you've been on a long trip or are concerned that you may have been exposed to a disease such as bilharzia or an STI that may not show up straightaway, a medical check-up is advisable.

WHAT TO BRING ▶▶

Bring as little as possible with you when travelling in Africa – large or heavy luggage will just be an encumbrance, especially if you'll be relying on public transport. Apart from a few changes of clothes and personal items such as prescription medicines, you'll find you can get most essentials on the road. Clothes can be easily and inexpensively made everywhere in Africa, and re-supplies of basic toiletries can be bought in major cities (unless you are partial to a particular brand, in which case it's better to bring it from home). The exception to this is any specialised equipment you may need, such as a backpack, travel-size mosquito net, sleeping bag, camera, cold-weather gear, or technical equipment for activities such as trekking or rock climbing – all of which should be arranged at home. When purchasing these things, it's generally best to opt for more subdued-looking items that are serviceable without attracting too much attention. Other important criteria are durability and weight; your equipment should be as lightweight as possible. If you will be travelling with others, it's fine to share some items, though it's best not to rely too heavily on your companions for everything.

This chapter contains suggestions for equipment and clothing to consider taking, plus some tips on packing and on recording your trip.

Equipment
BACKPACKS

Your backpack will be central to your comfort and convenience while on the road, so it's worth putting some time and effort into selecting an appropriate design. It's also not something to cut corners on: after a few weeks lifting it on and off buses, and unpacking and re-packing it daily, you won't regret any extra expense. A good-quality backpack will last many years. Important criteria to consider when buying a backpack include design, durability, water repellence and carrying comfort. In general, backpacks are far more practical in Africa than conventional luggage. There are two principle backpack designs – toploaders and travel packs.

Toploaders

Toploaders are essentially a fabric tube. They are generally more durable and watertight than travel packs, since they have fewer seams. They are also better suited to trekking or walking long distances, as they are lighter weight and their design and internal frame structure makes them more comfortable to carry. However, for everyday travel, they are less convenient, as you'll need to unload everything to reach items packed at the bottom. A few manufacturers have tried to address this problem by adding more easily accessible zippered sections and detachable pockets.

Travel Packs

The main advantage of this pack is that it has a zipper running around the edge and top, which allows uncomplicated packing, easy access to your things and makes the pack easier to lock up. Many travel packs also have a zippered flap that is stowed at the base of the pack and can be used to protect the harness when you put your pack on planes, buses, trains or taxis, as well as side handles and a detachable shoulder strap. However, these packs tend to be heavier than proper rucksacks, and not well designed for long-term carrying comfort.

There are a few backpack designs in between travel packs and toploaders that offer easy zippered access, while also being better structured for carrying comfort than the travel pack.

Buying a Pack

The better packs tend to be those made by recognised companies: Macpac, Karrimor, Kelty and others all have ergonomic designs and are made from good-quality fabrics. Prices range from about US$150 to US$300 and more. Following are some points to consider as you investigate the various options.

Capacity It's generally not necessary to buy the largest pack size. If you do need a large pack – eg for a long independent trek on which you will need to carry all your gear and food – it's best to get one with zips or straps that allow

The Trojan Alternative

On my first solo trip to the UK and Europe, I disembarked at Gatwick airport proudly bearing the latest in boy scout-issue backpacks. However, it soon dawned on me that this was not going to be a happy relationship: the external frame rubbed cruelly against my back, the aluminium plumbing gouged into my shoulder blades, and carrying the whole cumbersome edifice engendered excruciating pain – and I'd only got as far as Victoria station. But there, in a small luggage accessory kiosk, I spied my salvation – a set of luggage wheels. To these, after handing over the requisite pounds, I lashed my pack.

There is hardly a moor in that green and fair land that myself and my trusty wheel-borne backpack didn't trundle over, nary a youth hostel up whose stairs we didn't rumble. Admittedly, I received some odd looks (ranging from astonishment to abject scorn) from some members of the backpacking community. A backpack on wheels is, I suppose, a contradiction in terms. Nevertheless, faced with a choice between multiple sessions of physiotherapy and the derision of my fellows (bowed under the weight of their well thumbed Penguin Classic editions of Camus and Nietzsche), I'd make the same choice again.

Years later, while working with the Tibetan community in northern India, I noted with interest a couple who disembarked from a dilapidated bus. This tall, sun-burnished, lean-limbed pair had definite traveller cred: long dreds, stylish grunge gear and a 'don't mess with us: we've crossed the Khyber Pass' attitude. I watched as they strode off up the road towards the Hotel Tibet, heads held high, eyes focused on the mountains, as with studied ease they pulled behind them their matching silver Samsonite suitcases on wheels – and I felt vindicated.

Michelle Coxall
LP Author, Australia

you to change its size, as there will undoubtedly be periods of your trip when you will not need the full capacity. Have a good idea of what you plan to bring with you, then purchase the smallest pack for the job; this will also have the advantage of compelling you to travel light. Many travellers find that a 60L pack allows enough space for equipment, clothes and purchases over a three month trip; if you're carrying a tent, you may want a slightly larger one.

Fabric & Stitching Look for durable material and double stitching at weightbearing places. Also ensure the zippers are strong. If the pack looks flimsy, go to a more expensive model.

Straps & Padding Good packs will be amply padded at the shoulders and hips, as well as lightly padded down the back. The hip pads are the most important, as the bulk of the weight is carried there, not on the shoulders.

Fitting Always try on your pack before purchasing it. Most decent packs have an adjustable internal frame that you can fit to the length of your back. Also keep an eye on the shape of the back. If it's too tall, your centre of gravity will be too high; too wide and it will be difficult to manoeuvre in tight spaces. Some companies also have gender-specific models.

Versatility Look for packs with multiple compartments – a bottom section is ideal for your sleeping bag/sack or dirty laundry and will also protect more fragile items in the main compartment, while front and side pockets are good for regularly needed items such as toiletries, waterproof gear, torch (flashlight), guidebook and map (although outside pockets are more vulnerable to pilfering on public transport). Some packs include a zip-off daypack (see Daypacks below). Loops are useful as tie-down straps for carrying a sleeping bag, sweater or tent outside your pack.

Securing Your Pack

Theft is always a risk, particularly if you have to put your pack up on the roof of public transport, or leave it in a hotel room. Some packs have double zippers on the front and side sections that can be padlocked together. If not, find a strong place in the fabric above the zip where you can make a couple of holes; thread a small padlock through the holes and attach the zip fastener. If you're travelling long distances on trains or ferries, you may want to bring a light chain to attach your pack to the luggage rack or a post so you can sleep with an easy mind.

A good way to protect your pack from petty pilfering (from outside pockets) and to keep dust (and rain) away is to buy a waterproof, elasticised pack cover, which you can just slip over it and fasten down with some rope.

DAYPACKS

Daypacks are useful for carrying everyday items such as a camera, guidebook, map, water bottle, sunscreen etc. Comfort, quality and durability are important. Ensure the shoulder straps and back section are padded and that the fabric is strong and durable. External and internal pockets make smaller items easier to store and find; a side pocket for a water bottle is also useful.

Some backpacks have detachable daypacks, thus saving you the expense of buying a separate unit. However, these are often too small, so make sure it will be big enough to take all your bits and pieces. An overstuffed daypack is cumbersome to carry, as it lacks a solid frame and will end up tiring your shoulders and back. If you plan to reconnect your daypack to your main pack when travelling long distances, use padlocks and remember to remove fragile or valuable items.

MONEY BELT

Your money belt is a vital piece of equipment and the safest way of carrying cash, travellers cheques, credit/debit cards, passport, ticket and other important items. It's crucial to select a money belt that can be worn unobtrusively beneath your clothing – keeping your valuables in a waist pack or otherwise exposed over your clothing is asking for trouble.

The most common types of money belts are worn either around the waist (best option) or hanging from the neck. Neither design is particularly easy to access, so keep enough cash for taxi fares, shopping and other expenses in a separate, more accessible place so you don't need to continually fish out and open the money belt.

Fabric choice is important: plastic sweats and leather is heavy and retains perspiration. Cotton is the best bet, as it's the most comfortable and can be washed, though it's less durable. If you use a cotton money belt, put your ticket, passport and other documents in a plastic bag so they don't deteriorate from your sweat. Don't forget to check the belt's clasp or attachment to be sure it's durable and secure.

MEDICAL KIT

You can buy small medical kits ('conventional' as well as homeopathic) from many travel health clinics, mail order companies and homoeopathic

Travel, African Style

While you're getting all your gear together and mulling over which backpack model you should buy, reflect for a minute on the way a typical rural African travels – even when they are covering just as much, if not more, distance as you will be. It's common in Africa to see people setting off in the back of a crowded pick-up truck with nothing more than a small plastic bag with a bit to eat, a refilled bottle of water and perhaps one other small bag with a change of clothes. On bush taxis or buses you might be overwhelmed with luggage from locals – a basket full of distraught chickens may be on your backpack or a sack of oranges may be taking up leg room. But these will be goods for the market, or similar items; when it comes to personal luggage, locals' bags are invariably extremely modest. After thinking about it for a while, much of what you're contemplating bringing may suddenly seem superfluous.

practitioners, or you can make one up yourself. Use a container that's waterproof, rattle-proof and squash-proof – a transparent plastic box or a zip-up, pocketed plastic case is good.

In addition to any prescription medications you may need (along with copies of the prescriptions), some items to consider including in your medical kit are listed here. Consult your pharmacist for brands available in your country.

For a full Medical Kit list see the Health chapter.

OTHER USEFUL EQUIPMENT

Other items you may want to consider bringing include the following:

Address book – To keep in touch with friends and family, plus those you meet travelling.

Alarm clock – You don't want to miss your flight/bus/train/other appointment. Travel alarm clocks are tough, light and cheap.

Batteries – Bring spares for all your equipment (camera, personal stereo, alarm clock, torch etc) and put new batteries in each before you depart.

Contraception – Condoms can be found in most African countries, but the quality is variable (always check the use-by date). It's easier to bring a supply with you. If you use the pill, then bring enough to cover your whole trip as it is difficult to obtain in many African countries.

Eye wear – Sunglasses are indispensable for both comfort and protection of your eyes. If you wear prescription glasses or contact lenses, take the prescription with you, along with extras such as a case and contact lens solution.

Padlocks & a chain – Apart from securing your backpack, you can use a padlock to fasten the door of your hotel room and give your belongings extra security. Chains are useful for attaching your backpack to the roof rack of a bus.

Pocketknife – A Swiss army knife (or good-quality equivalent) has loads of useful tools, particularly scissors, bottle opener, can opener and straight blade.

Sunscreen – You're likely to spend long hours in the sun and, apart from the long-term risk of melanoma, sunburn is painful. A moisturiser with sunscreen included will save some doubling up.

Tampons or pads – These are available in most African cities, but keep a supply for when you're off the beaten track.

Toilet paper – Never leave home without some! It won't be supplied in some public (and private) toilets in many African countries. Always keep a stash in your daypack.

Torch (flashlight) – Helpful to find stuff late at night in a dorm or in your hotel room, to avoid mishaps in outside toilets in the middle of the night, or if the electricity packs it in.

Toiletries – Basic items are widely available across Africa, but take any specialty products with you.

Towel – For swimming, as well as for showers in budget places (not all will supply one, or at least one you'd want to use). Don't take a beach towel as it'll take ages to dry, weigh a tonne and get very whiffy. A quick-drying travel towel (made from a chamois-like material or one of the new microfibres) is OK, as is the all-purpose sarong.

Travel guides, maps & phrasebooks – See the Planning chapter for details.

Water bottle – You can just refill a standard plastic bottle, but a sturdier model will last longer and be more suitable for purifying water on a regular basis.

Nonessential Equipment

None of the gear listed here is really essential to your travels, but a selection will make life much more pleasant.

Binoculars – Useful on safaris and when birdwatching.

Books – Good for whiling away time on public transport. In many African countries, particularly in French-speaking areas, there is only a limited selection of good books in English.

Camping gear – Only lug this around if you plan to do a lot of camping. While it is possible to rent equipment in trekking and safari centres, it is often of inferior quality and expensive.

Candles – Can lend a nice atmosphere to an otherwise dull room, and are also useful in a long-term blackout.

Earplugs – You'll never regret these if you spend a lot of time in cities, are staying near a mosque or take a 10 hour ride in a bus with a blaring stereo.

Food – It's nice to have a small stash of your favourite food from home, as long as it's a long-lasting product and properly contained.

Inflatable pillow – This will allow you to sleep more comfortably on long trips.

Lighter/matches – For campfires, mosquito coils, candles and cigarettes.

Mosquito net – Malaria is no joke. Most hotels provide mosquito nets, but if you plan to sleep under the stars it's essential to have your own.

Personal stereo/radio – Good for whiling away idle hours and, if you have a record function, you can send audio cassettes home. Short-wave radios can keep you in touch with news from home.

Plug – These are rarely supplied in cheaper accommodation. Double-sided rubber or plastic plugs will fit most bath and basin plug holes.

Sewing kit – Needle, thread, a few buttons and safety pins to mend clothing, mosquito net, tent or sunglasses.

Sleeping bag/sleeping sheet – Only take a sleeping bag if you plan to camp a lot, as this is a bulky item. If you're going to need a bag in only one of the countries on your itinerary, then think about hiring one there. A sleeping sheet is a much better bet. Basically two sheets sewn together, it will give you some protection from insects and dodgy beds, and it's light and easily cleaned. Stick to natural fibres (cotton or silk).

Travel journal & pens – See Recording Your Trip later in this chapter.

Washing line – A piece of string will do the job, but there are relatively cheap lines on the market with suckers, hooks or both on each end, which make them much more versatile.

Washing detergent – For cleaning your clothes in your room. In most African countries laundry services are very cheap, but it can be pretty hard on your clothes.

Specialised Equipment

Diving, snorkelling, surfing and windsurfing equipment can be hired at many areas where these activities are popular, as can some camping and trekking items. However, if you will be pursuing any of them seriously, consider bringing your own equipment from home, unless you are sure of the quality you can obtain in rentals. If you plan to be doing any of these activities in off-the-beaten-track areas, you will need to bring everything with you. For tips on packing your bicycle and surfboard, see Bicycles & Surfboards in the Tickets & Insurance chapter.

Clothing

Lightweight, loose and comfortable clothing is best. Don't pack items you value, because the frequent and rigorous hand-washing and dirt of the road will wear them out quickly. It's easy and relatively inexpensive in most places in Africa to have clothing made. Ask someone living locally to recommend a good tailor.

DAY-TO-DAY

For trousers, skirts, shorts, shirts and underwear, natural fibres (cotton or silk) are best. While synthetics dry faster and wrinkle less, they don't breathe well, will stick to your skin and make you sweat. The chances of contracting a rash or fungal disease are also much higher with synthetic clothes. Avoid nylon, rayon and lycra.

Following are some suggestions. No matter where you're headed, it's a good idea to have one presentable outfit on hand for special occasions or when dealing with officialdom.

For advice on culturally appropriate clothing, see Dressing Appropriately in the Issues & Attitudes chapter.

KEEPING COOL

In most areas of Africa, lightweight, loose-fitting clothes will be the most appropriate. Light colours will keep you cooler than dark ones, but are harder to keep clean. A sarong is a versatile item, as it can function as a skirt, sleeping sheet, beach towel, shadecloth or rope. Jeans, by contrast, are heavy, take up room and take a long time to dry; drawstring or elastic-cotton trousers or long skirts are much lighter and will keep you cooler. Take a couple of short-sleeved shirts if you'd like, but mid-length or long-sleeved shirts are more useful, as they will keep off the sun and be less offensive to local people. Sleeveless tops should be saved

---

African Dress

Africans in general place great importance on dress and spend a large proportion of their non-food budget on clothes. While western informality is making a few inroads with the young in larger cities, it is definitely not the norm.

Over much of the continent, traditional dress for both men and women consists of a long garment. In West Africa, where it is known as the *grand boubou*, it is often embroidered or elaborately sewn, or made from textured cloth. Men generally wear pants and a shirt underneath. Women's garments may be differently stitched and are often worn with a matching headscarf.

For everyday wear, women throughout sub-Saharan Africa wear a loose top and a length of colourful printed cotton cloth around the waist for a skirt. The names for this vary around the continent: *pagne* in West Africa, *kanga* in East Africa, *capulana* in Mozambique, *chitenja* in Malawi – the variations are almost endless. The same cloth used by the women is also frequently used for making men's casual clothes, which often consist of a loose-fitting shirt and trousers made from the same print.

In northern Africa, you will see men – particularly in rural areas – in long, flowing cotton robes (known as *jellaba* in Morocco and *galabiyyas* in Egypt). Similar garments are worn by women, in addition to the *hijab* – the veil and headscarf still widely used in many area.

for the beach. The same applies to shorts. Bring at least one outfit with long sleeves and long trousers (as well as a pair of socks) to put on in the evenings to keep the mosquitoes at bay and decrease your risk of contracting malaria. A wide-brimmed hat is also very useful – a cap won't protect your neck or ears.

KEEPING WARM

If you will be spending much time in areas at altitude, especially during the winter or cool season, or if you will be trekking at altitude, you will need to bring warm clothes; layering is the best principle. For more flexibility, it's better to take several thin layers rather than a few thick layers. A good combination for some of the continent's higher, colder areas starts with thermal underwear, followed by a cotton T-shirt, long-sleeved shirt or sweater, and jacket. The jacket should be reasonably wind-proof and shower-proof. On high mountains, it's recommended to carry a second jacket for when you need an extra layer of warmth. For the legs, light-weight, breeze-proof trousers are ideal in cooler areas; these can be layered over long underwear for colder temperatures. In some areas, waterproof pants will be necessary.

Other things to bring along include gloves, a woollen hat, a brimmed hat, sunscreen, and several pair of socks (with at least one pair made of wool or a fast-drying synthetic).

SPECIALISED CLOTHING

For trekking or other outdoor activities, lightweight, waterproof and breathable fabrics such as Gore-Tex are good. Alternatively, for trekking in Africa's mountains, clothes made from a combination of pile fabric and close-weave nylon such as Pertex are ideal: one layer is fine for the warm, wet conditions on the lower slopes, and two or three layers can cope with the snow and high winds on the summits. Outside South Africa, specialised clothing is not available in most places on the continent, so arrange anything you will need at home.

Clothing Checklist

- light jacket
- long pants/skirts/dress
- long-sleeved shirts
- sarong
- shoes/boots/sandals/thongs (flip flops)
- shorts (can double as swimwear)
- short-sleeved shirt
- socks/underpants/bras
- something presentable
- specialist clothing, such as hat, gloves, shermals, woollen socks
- sweater
- swimwear
- waterproof jacket
- wide-brimmed hat

FOOTWEAR

Footwear can be heavy and bulky to carry around, so try to limit yourself to one main pair, with sandals or something similar for relaxing in the evenings and for showering. For most travel, walking or training shoes are the best, or a sturdy pair of sandals that you can wear with socks. If you'll be doing trekking or serious hiking, consider medium-weight boots.

Packing
BACKPACK

The two most important factors when packing are weight and bulk. Keep things as lightweight as possible, and try to leave some spare room in your pack when you depart, to accommodate things you may pick up during your travels. Following are a few tips for packing your bag.

- Avoid leaving your packing until the night before. A few days before your trip, set everything out that you think you will need, then try to trim this amount down by half. Once you have finalised what you will bring, have a trial run, and try carrying your pack around your apartment or local area to be sure you can maintain the load for an extended period.

- Pack heavy items as close to your spine as possible. This will prevent the pack pulling backwards at your shoulders, maximise the strengths of the design and provide the most comfortable position for long-distance walking.

- Remember that your pack is unlikely to be treated with kid gloves by others, particularly when you're travelling by air. Pack to protect your belongings.

- Make the most of any compartments. Putting your sleeping bag, dirty clothes or other soft items in the bottom compartment will provide a soft, protective layer for more fragile items.

- Use plastic bags to prevent water and dust damage and to compartmentalise your belongings for easier access.

- Keep any items with hard points or angles away from your back. Wrap them in clothes for your comfort and their protection.

- Give some thought to which items you'll need most regularly. Place these near the access points (eg side pockets) of the pack if possible.

DAYPACK

After a few days sightseeing, you'll quickly work out what you want to regularly carry with you in your daypack. Here's a list to start out with:

- book or journal, writing paper and pen
- camera and film
- guidebook
- hat
- lightweight, waterproof jacket
- pocketknife
- sunscreen
- water bottle

ESSENTIALS

The following is a list of essential items that you will need to take with you (although not everyone will need to take everything on this list). It's helpful to make up your own list – and refer to it again just before you leave home.

- cash
- credit card
- driving license
- International Driving Permit

- passport
- photocopies of all important documents
- travellers cheques and purchase receipts
- visas
- yellow fever vaccination certificate

Recording Your Trip
CAMERA

The advantages of having a camera with you on your trip are obvious: even if you're not a serious photographer, you'll be able to record some amazing sights, plus take photos of friends you make on the way. However, there are also some disadvantages. A camera is expensive, and can be a concern on the road if you are constantly worrying about whether it will be stolen, lost or damaged. It can also come between you and the places you've travelled so far to enjoy, if you're constantly wondering if you should be taking a shot of a particular scene or are fumbling to get your camera out of your pack. If you think a conventional camera will only encumber you, alternatives include postcards (available in cities and tourist areas), photo books (sometimes available in tourist areas) and using disposable cameras. You could also arrange for people you meet on the road to send you copies of their pictures (although try not to make this a strictly a one-sided affair).

If you're travelling with a friend, you could consider sharing a camera, especially since you're likely to be taking photos of the same scenes. While you

Tips on Packing Light

Even if you will not be trekking or hiking for extended periods with your pack, it's good to travel as lightly as possible. Other than limiting the overall number of things you bring with you, here are some additional steps you can take to trim ounces and get yourself in a 'travel light' frame of mind:

- If you will not be visiting the entire area or region covered by your guidebook, consider only bringing along the chapters you need.
- Copy out any necessary addresses onto a piece of paper, or use a miniature address book.
- Choose your reading material carefully and try to carry only one book at a time. Longer paperbacks printed on lightweight paper are the best.
- Put your shampoo and other toiletries into small containers. If you will be travelling for an extended period, bring enough for 3-4 weeks at the outset and restock on the road.
- If you will be bringing lots of papers along, copy them in miniature and trim away any excess white space.
- When initially gearing up for your trip, make getting lightweight equipment a priority. ·
- Try to find one or two outfits that are versatile enough for a variety of situations, rather than carrying numerous separate articles of clothing.
- Don't bring any footwear that you don't absolutely need. (But be sure what you do bring is comfortable, good quality and appropriate for the activities you will be pursuing.)
- Avoid jeans, large towels and other heavy, slow-drying items.

may have different ideas on what makes a good photo and who gets to take the shot, a little diplomacy and plenty of film should alleviate most problems.

If you decide to take a camera, and if you plan to use your photos for professional purposes, or want to take high-quality, creative shots, you'll need a single-lens reflex (SLR) camera. If, on the other hand, you just want to take decent shots to show friends and have as memories of your trip, an automatic, point-and-shoot camera is fine.

Weight is another important consideration: SLRs and their lenses are heavy – several times the weight of point-and-shoot cameras – and take up luggage space.

As well as the following information, check out the Photo.net web site (www.photo.net/photo) for information on all aspects of photography.

SLR Cameras

An SLR camera allows you to take creative shots by shooting with the camera on its manual setting (perhaps using the built-in light meter as a guide). Many SLRs also have automatic settings, and also allow you to use different lenses, thus vastly increasing your creative range. It's possible to buy SLRs with lightweight plastic bodies, but these are significantly more fragile than those with metal bodies or frames.

With an SLR, you'll also need the following:

Lenses – Zooms save space and weight. A 24-100mm and an 80-200mm lens should be sufficient for most situations. If you prefer fixed lenses, you'll need three or four to cover the same situations.

Skylight (UV) filters for each of your lenses – These protect your lenses and screen out excess ultraviolet light (which makes pictures look dull).

Camera case – To protect your camera. Many areas of Africa are extremely dusty, especially during the dry season, with a fine dust that permeates everything. Ensure that your equipment is well protected. Even with a case, you may need to further protect it.

Spare camera batteries – These are hard to obtain in some parts of Africa, and impossible in rural areas.

Lint-free lens paper – Difficult to obtain in many parts of Africa.

Silica gel packets – To keep the moisture out of your film and equipment; a necessity in many parts of Africa.

Point-and-Shoot Cameras

Point-and-shoot cameras take the worry out of travel photography. They also make shots of people easier, since they focus almost instantaneously. Point-and-shoot cameras range from cheap disposables to top-of-the-range models with precision lenses and a wide range of features. Since there are so many models on the market, it makes sense to ask at a trustworthy camera shop for a recommendation. A case will protect your camera and some silica gel will keep it moisture-free. You'll also need spare batteries and lint-free paper to clean the lens.

Film

Good-quality film can be hard to find in many areas of Africa, and is often not available outside of larger cities and major tourist areas. In many countries there is a limited selection, and even if you do find what you're looking for, it may have been badly stored or be in poor condition. In general, it's best to bring what you will need from home, especially if you will be using slide film, high-speed film etc. Or you may prefer to purchase some film at the airport before you depart.

Options for film are slide or print film, colour or black and white, and fast or slow. If you have professional aspirations, take slide film. Otherwise, consider print film, as it's easier to view. Some people like the artistic effects they can achieve with black and white film, while others like the realism of colour. You will achieve sharper results with slower films (around 100 ASA) but you may not be able to use these films in dark conditions. To solve this problem, bring several rolls of 400 ASA film or films of several different speeds.

Treatment of film is an important consideration. The sooner you expose your film after purchase the better, because film slowly deteriorates over time. Heat can also damage film – a day in the hot glove box of a car is usually enough. Store your film in as cool a place as possible, out of direct sunlight.

When flying, always carry your film on board with you to protect it from the high-energy X-ray machines used in some airports to inspect baggage. The metal detectors used to check carry-on baggage are usually film-safe. If you're concerned, simply take out your film and ask that it be hand-checked. To make this easier for airport staff, you may want to store your film in a small bag or plastic container.

Photo Etiquette

As with people everywhere, some Africans may enjoy being photographed, while others will not. Particularly in rural areas, you may encounter people who are superstitious about your camera or suspicious of your motives. Many others will see your desire to photograph them from an economic perspective: if you want a picture, you will have to pay. Finally, some people may view it as a matter of pride and may never want to be photographed, money or not. If you can't get a candid shot, always ask permission and don't insist or snap a picture anyway if permission is denied. In a group scene, request permission of the most senior person. The same restraint – if not more – should be exercised with video cameras.

Often people will allow you to photograph them, provided you give them a photo for themselves – this can be a real treasure in rural Africa. If you don't carry a Polaroid camera, take their address and make it clear that you'll send the photo by post once it's processed. Your promise will be taken seriously – never promise to send a copy and then fail to do so. If you think there is a chance you will not be able to come through on your promise, just explain that since so many people ask you for photos, it's impossible to send one to everyone.

A few other tips when photographing in Africa:

- Most African countries are sensitive about official buildings. Wherever you are, avoid taking pictures of airports, bridges, military equipment, police stations, members of the armed forces. In some places you may be arrested or have your film and camera confiscated.

- Places of worship and natural features with traditional religious significance are also sensitive subjects in some areas. If locals don't want you to photograph these, respect their wishes.

- In areas that seldom see tourists, avoid photographing people unless they specifically ask to have their picture taken.

Developing Film

In general, it's best to have film developed as soon as possible after exposing it, to prevent deterioration. However, developing facilities in many areas of Africa are nonexistent or of poor quality, so you may have to wait until you return home.

VIDEO

Video cameras can give a fascinating record of your holiday, but they can be expensive, film is not always available and you'll need a range of plug converters, plus a transformer, to recharge the batteries. In many situations in Africa they can also be obtrusive or attract unwanted attention.

Following are a few tips in case you do decide to use one. As with still cameras, do not film people unless you first have their permission.

- As well as filming the obvious – landscapes, sights and spectacular views – remember to record some of the everyday details of life. Often the most interesting things occur when you're actually intent on filming something else.

- Unlike still photography, video 'flows' – so you can shoot scenes of a winding road from the front window of a vehicle to give an overall impression that isn't possible with ordinary photos.

- Try to film in long takes, and don't move the camera around too much. If your camera has a stabiliser, use it to obtain good footage while travelling on bumpy roads.

- Video cameras have sensitive microphones, and you may be surprised by how much sound is picked up. This can be a pzroblem if there is a lot of ambient noise, such as when filming by the side of a busy road. (On the other hand, it can add interest and colour if there is local music in the background.)

- As already noted, remember to follow the same rules regarding people's sensitivities as for still photography; always ask permission first.

TRAVEL JOURNAL

No matter the length of your journey, there will be experiences, stories, people, sights and events that will be worth recording. A travel journal can serve as a record of your trip, and as a memory of your thoughts, expectations and aspirations at a particular point in time. On a more practical level, a journal is also a good way to keep yourself occupied during long hours on the road or in the evenings. And, if you have particularly good writing skills, a journal can serve as a blueprint for professional travel articles or books. There are plenty of travel journals on the market, including a new one from Lonely Planet that is spiral bound for versatility and includes useful information for international travellers.

CASSETTE RECORDINGS

Cassette recordings can provide you with an audio record of your trip. If you are somewhere with reliable mail, they can also be a good way to send a long letter to friends and family. If you plan to record music or singing, bring your own cassettes from home: in many areas mini-cassettes are difficult to find and larger cassettes are often of poor quality.

Senior Travellers

If you're reasonably fit and have enjoyed travelling in other parts of the world, you will likely enjoy travelling in Africa as well. The following are some considerations to keep in mind.

TRANSPORT

Transport infrastructure in much of Africa is undeveloped and journeys, especially by road, can be long and uncomfortable. If you are the type who values a minimum level of comfort, you may want to consider travelling by hired vehicle or with an organised tour. Bring along a pillow, as cushioning for all those bumpy dirt roads if you have a sensitive back. If you do take public transport, trains (1st class) are often more comfortable than buses, although journeys can be very long.

CLIMATE

Many areas of the continent can be very hot at certain times of year. Humidity is also a problem in coastal regions and in countries near the equator. This, combined with the heat, can be wearing. To avoid problems, try to plan your travels in the cooler dry season of whatever region you wish to visit (see When to Go in the country profile chapters for more details on each country).

ACCESS

Some interesting attractions (eg the Egyptian tombs) are reachable only via many stairs or by passing through narrow, claustrophobic tunnels. Other than top-end hotels, many places do not have lifts and access to upper floors may be via a steep, narrow staircase (some of Zanzibar's most atmospheric hotels are a good example). If this is a problem, try to arrange your accommodation in advance, and request rooms at lower levels.

FOOD

It's possible in almost all major cities to get western food, though it may be quite oily. In rural areas, selection is much more limited and the diet is often not particularly nutritious. If you are particular about what you eat, you may want to consider frequenting tourist or urban areas where there will be more options.

LUGGAGE

Travel as lightly as possible. Although there is always porter service at mid-range and top-end hotels (and at budget establishments as well), a heavy bag will only be a hindrance.

MEDICINES

While at least basic medical care will be available in major cities (and very good care in some places such as Nairobi, Kenya; South Africa; and Abidjan, Côte d'Ivoire), medicines are often not available. Bring adequate supplies of any you may need, especially prescription medications.

SIGHTSEEING

The best time to be out and about is early in the morning, before the day becomes too warm and streets and markets too crowded. Late afternoon is a good alternative, although traffic will be heavy in urban areas.

TOILET FACILITIES

In many places, the only toilets available are squat-style, which can be taxing on the knees. Bringing a folding stool with a 'slipper potty' may be one solution.

SENIOR-FRIENDLY COUNTRIES

Southern Africa is generally good for senior travellers who aren't looking to rough it too much, since facilities such as hotels and restaurants of a good or high standard are generally available. In West Africa, transport and facilities can be a bit rough, although there are some notable exceptions (mostly resort areas). These include coastal areas in The Gambia, Senegal and – to a lesser extent – Côte d'Ivoire. In East Africa, although distances are long and roads often rough, there is a wide offering of organised tours and safaris and a good selection of upper-end (comfortable) lodging, particularly in the popular tourist destinations in Kenya and Tanzania.

Discounts for seniors are rare in most parts of Africa.

Gay & Lesbian Travellers

Despite the fact that an African country (South Africa) was the first country in the world to offer specific constitutional protection for sexual freedom of choice, most areas of the continent are conservative in their attitudes towards gays and lesbians. Even in South Africa, liberalisation of attitudes lags far behind liberalisation of legislation. In many countries, homosexuality is illegal, although statutes are rarely enforced. Even where it is not officially prohibited, homosexual activity is culturally taboo in most areas and is generally conducted clandestinely.

Nevertheless, travel in Africa should pose no particular difficulties for homosexual travellers, as long as you keep things low key and take local sensibilities into account. In a few areas – some of South Africa's urban areas are a good example – it's also not overly difficult to meet other homosexuals, particularly if you do a bit of research before leaving home.

To minimise problems for yourself, keep in mind that throughout the continent, open displays of affection are generally frowned upon, whatever your orientation, and show sensitivity to local feelings. In a few places (eg Morocco), aggression towards gay male travellers is not unheard of, although this is the exception rather than the rule.

RESOURCES

Some organisations that can assist you in identifying places where you are less likely to be hassled and can more easily meet other homosexuals are listed here. The *Spartacus International Gay Guide*, which includes information on some African countries, is also worth checking out.

All Continents Travel
(☎ 800-368-6822 or 310-645-7527; fax 310-645-1071) 5250 West Century Blvd, Suite 626, Los Angeles, CA 90045
(a USA-based tour company offering specialist tours, including some in parts of Africa, for gay men and women)

Gay esCape
(☎ 021-23 9001; fax 23 5907; www.icafe.co.za/gayes) 2nd Floor, 7 Castle St, Cape Town
(this South African-based travel agency has information on gay-oriented accommodation, restaurants, venues and the like throughout South Africa and may also be able to assist with general information for elsewhere in the region)

Travellers with a Disability

Most countries in Africa have few or no facilities for the disabled. While this makes travel in many areas difficult, it doesn't necessarily mean that it is impossible. Counterbalancing the almost complete lack of facilities and infrastructure in many areas is the friendliness and accommodating attitude of many Africans towards the disabled person.

In most places, people will be more than willing to assist you if you explain what you need. Some factors to consider are discussed in the following entries.

TRANSPORT

Public transport tends to be very crowded and drivers often move at dizzying speeds. Bus doors and aisles are usually too narrow to accommodate a wheelchair unless it has been folded up. In general, travelling by hired car is the best road transport option, although this is expensive in most places. For long-distance travel, 1st class on trains might be feasible (apart from the issue of being able to use the bathroom), if you have someone along to assist you. Domestic flights would also be a viable option. Staff are generally very willing to assist disabled travellers to board the plane in advance of other passengers.

GETTING AROUND

For negotiating city footpaths and the like, having a companion along would be a tremendous asset: pavement can be uneven, kerbs high and traffic heavy (making it difficult to cross the street). In some cities (Cotonou, Benin is a notable example), many of the streets are sand. As far as access to buildings and other attractions goes, ramps are nonexistent in most places, though in many cases there will be too many steps, so a wheelchair could be carried up.

ACCESSIBILITY

Most hotels (other than top-end establishments) don't have lifts. In many that do, it's often advisable not to take them as unreliable electricity supplies make getting stuck inside one a real risk. Try booking ground-floor rooms in advance. In most cases, mid-range to top-end options will be your best bet, although exotic lodges or those built to be particularly atmospheric may not be a good choice. For example, some of East Africa's upmarket safari lodges, while built all on one level, are only accessible via rocky or rough paths (designed to preserve the 'natural' ambience). On the other hand, there is usually a large number of staff at these places, many of whom would be willing to assist in carrying a wheelchair.

TOILET FACILITIES

Toilet facilities may present the biggest challenge. There are few bathrooms large enough to manoeuvre a wheelchair in (top-end hotels would be your best bet here) and almost none with grips by the toilet seat. In many places, squat-style (hole-in-the-ground) toilets are the norm. One solution might be to bring along a folding stool with a 'slipper potty'. Bathing may be less of a problem: in many places the shower comes out of a pipe in the wall and there is no cumbersome tub wall to climb over (though top-end hotels will often be an exception to this). Most places will also have a bucket readily available for washing.

ACCESSIBLE COUNTRIES

Some of the easier countries to negotiate as a disabled traveller would likely include The Gambia (distances are short, so vehicle hire would not be prohibitively expensive, and many smarter hotels are on only one or two levels), Ghana (due to its laid-back and friendly pace, and decent infrastructure), South Africa (modern infrastructure and good hotel facilities) and Namibia (road distances are long but infrastructure is modern and efficient). In these and other areas, an organised tour with a company willing to cater to the needs of disabled travellers may be the best option, as all logistics, including transport, would be arranged for you. Whether you opt for an organised tour or independent travel, having a companion along who can help with day-to-day affairs and arrange for assistance if necessary will make your trip much smoother.

USEFUL ORGANISATIONS & RESOURCES

Abilities magazine
(☎ 416-766-9188; fax 762-8716) PO Box 527, Station P, Toronto, Ontario, Canada M5S 2T1 (carries a column called 'Accessible Planet', which offers tips on foreign travel for people with disabilities)

Access (The Foundation for Accessibility by the Disabled)
(☎ 516-887-5798) PO Box 356, Malverne, NY 11565

Mobility International USA
(☎ 541-343-1284) PO Box 10767, Eugene, OR 97440

The Society for the Advancement of Travel for the Handicapped
(SATH; ☎ 718-858-5483) 26 Court St, Brooklyn, NY 11242

Access-Able Travel Source

(☎ 303-232-2979; fax 239-8486; www.access-able.com/about or www.accessable.com/access-able/links.cfm) PO Box 1796 Wheat Ridge, CO 80034

(US-based organisation that provides information for disabled travellers – while there's not too much on Africa, it has helpful general tips and provides online services)

Global Access

www.geocities.com/Paris/1052

(has lots of information for travellers with disabilities, as well as links to related sites)

NICAN

(☎ 02-6285 3713; fax 6285 3714) PO Box 407, Curtin, ACT 2605

(Australians can contact this organisation)

The Royal Association for Disability & Rehabilitation

(RADAR; ☎ 020-7250 3222; fax 7250 0212) 12 City Forum, 250 City Rd, London EC1V 8AF

(this UK company produces three holiday fact packs (UK£2 each) for disabled travellers covering planning, insurance and useful organisations; transport and equipment; and specialised accommodation)

Travelling with Children

Africans in general are very friendly, helpful and protective towards children, and there are no particular reasons for not taking young children on travel with you.

The main considerations would likely include the scarcity of decent medical facilities outside major towns, the length and discomfort involved in many

---

Tips for Travelling with Children

- Consider travelling in an easier region such as southern Africa before heading to a more difficult one such as West Africa. This will give you an idea of how your children hold up to the stresses of travel.
- Bring your children's favourite toys and games to keep them amused on long rides.
- Buses and share taxis can be very overcrowded and often move at excessive speeds. It's best to take trains or private cars instead.
- Children are particularly vulnerable to food-borne illnesses. Be careful about what your children eat and try to avoid street food.
- Bring wide-brimmed hats and plenty of sunscreen. Sunglasses are also a good idea to protect the eyes from glare and dust.
- Make sure your child is fully immunised for the countries you plan to visit.
- Carry a mosquito net with you that your child can sleep under. Some parents prefer a small, lightweight tent (free-standing) with a fine mesh roof (for ventilation) that can be set up over a mattress or on the floor.
- If your children are old enough, consider getting a language cassette. Helping them learn greetings and a few other words of the local language, which they can practice while travelling, can considerably enliven and enrich a journey.
- Children's multivitamins can be a useful supplement to their diet on the road. Seek advice from your paediatrician.

road journeys, the difficulty of finding clean, decent bathrooms outside of mid-range and top-end hotels, and local foods.

In tourist areas in most countries it is not difficult to arrange an extra bed or mattress so children can share a standard adult double. In hotels outside of tourist areas, triple rooms are frequently available for not too much more than a double room.

Powdered milk is available in almost all mid-sized and larger cities, as is bottled water. Nappies (diapers) are available in many capital cities, though generally not in rural areas. Prepared baby food is also available in some capital cities, but not elsewhere. Bring along a supply of handi-wipes from home.

Clothing can be readily stitched up, but good quality shoes in your children's sizes will be difficult to find, so it's best to bring some good ones from home.

While discounts on public transport are not common, assuming the child will occupy a seat, it's often possible to find children's discounts at national parks and even at some hotels (especially those in tourist areas).

If you will be travelling with an infant, strollers (push chairs) are not very practical. Much better is some sort of harness or cloth that allows you to carry the baby on your back (African style) or in front of you.

CHILD-FRIENDLY COUNTRIES & RESOURCES

South Africa, thanks to its good medical facilities and numerous attractions, is one of the easier countries to visit with children. Many resorts, hotels and national park lodges/campsites have facilities for children, and family rooms and chalets are often available for only slightly more than the price of a double. Although there are fewer child-oriented facilities in other southern African countries, opportunities to see elephants and other wildlife, and attractions such as Victoria Falls compensate and make this a good region for travelling with children. The same holds true for many areas of East Africa, although roads are not as good. West Africa has the advantage that distances are often shorter, although many attractions (markets, mosques etc) may not be as appealing to young children as to their parents.

Lonely Planet's *Travel with Children* by Maureen Wheeler contains detailed information about planning successful family holidays.

Most travellers reach Africa by air. Once on the continent, you may have one or more domestic or regional flights, and at the end of your trip you will likely have an international flight to get you home again.

This chapter focuses on preparations before and during your international flight to reach Africa. Much of the information may seem obvious to those who have already travelled frequently by plane. It's included anyway to remind seasoned fliers of a few things and to offer some tips for the uninitiated. For details of what to expect when flying within Africa, see Getting Around in the While You're There chapter.

Before You Fly

The following are things you should take care of before heading to the airport.

SPECIAL NEEDS & REQUESTS

If you have special needs of any sort – whether you've broken a leg, are a vegetarian, travelling in a wheelchair, travelling with a baby or are terrified of flying – let the airline know as soon as possible so that they can make the appropriate arrangements. Remind them when you reconfirm your booking (at least 72 hours before departure) and again when you check in at the airport. It may also be worth checking with several airlines before making your booking to find out which one is best equipped to handle your particular needs. Airports and airlines can be surprisingly helpful, but they do need advance warning.

Most international airports will provide escorts from check-in desk to plane where needed, and there should be ramps, lifts, accessible toilets and reachable phones. Guide dogs for the blind will often have to travel in a specially pressurised baggage compartment with other animals, away from their owner, although smaller guide dogs may be admitted to the cabin. All guide dogs will be subject to the same quarantine laws (six months in isolation etc) as any other animal when entering or returning to countries currently free of rabies such as Britain or Australia. Hearing-impaired travellers can ask for airport and in-flight announcements to be written down for them.

If you are travelling with children, those under two years of age travel for 10% of the standard fare (or free, on some airlines), as long as they don't occupy a seat, although they don't get a baggage allowance. Children aged between two and 12 can usually occupy a seat for half to two-thirds of the full fare, and do get a baggage allowance. For the trip itself, 'skycots', which take a child weighing up to about 10kg, can usually be provided by the airline if requested in advance. Strollers (push chairs) can often be taken as hand luggage.

RECONFIRMING YOUR FLIGHT

Most airlines require that you reconfirm your flight at least 72 hours prior to departure. The ideal time to reconfirm is between three and five days before the flight. If you reconfirm too soon, the airlines may forget about you; if it's too late, they may have already given your seat to another passenger. It never hurts to reconfirm twice – once about a week before the flight and once three days before the flight. Reconfirmation is important for any flight, but it is critical for flights originating in Africa – for regional or domestic flights, as well as for intercontinental flights from Africa to Europe or elsewhere. If you have any dietary restrictions or have ordered a special meal for your intercontinental flight, it's a good idea to remind the airline when you reconfirm.

If the city from which you are departing has more than one airport, verify which one you should use when reconfirming your ticket. If the airport has more than one terminal, ask which one will be handling your flight.

Some airlines issue reconfirmation numbers. Be sure to make a note of this, as it's proof that you reconfirmed your travel and will be useful for getting a refund or a new ticket if you get bumped from the flight anyway. Some airlines allow you to select a seat when reconfirming your flight, which gives you a better chance of getting the seat you want. Always ask if this is possible.

Finally, some airlines or travel agents will tell you that you do not have to reconfirm your flight. Reconfirm anyway! There is nothing worse than getting to an airport and being told that you can't fly because you didn't reconfirm your flight.

CARRY-ON LUGGAGE

Try to put all your breakable and valued belongings in your carry-on bag. Also include a change of clothes to get you by in case your checked luggage doesn't arrive when you do. Remember that there are weight and size limits for carry-on luggage (5kg is enforced by many airlines). There will be a metal frame at many western airports for you to test the dimensions of your bag; nearly all daypacks will meet the criteria. If you exceed the allowable limits, you may be asked to take some things out and put them in your main luggage. If this occurs, it is likely to be just before you board the plane, which will mean inconvenience all around.

Standard items to carry with you when travelling long-distance include the following:

- Passport, tickets, money and all important documents – These should carried with you at all times, preferably in a money belt.
- Fragile or valuable items, such as a camera or binoculars.
- Exposed and unexposed film – Your main luggage may receive a higher dose of X-rays, which could spoil the film.
- A change of clothes that is appropriate for the climate of your destination – If your luggage is put on the wrong plane, you may have to wait several days before it reaches you.
- Simple toiletries – These are useful if your luggage doesn't show up, and for being able to freshen up during the flight.

- A bottle of water – cabin air can get very dry and you can't always rely on cabin crew to keep you properly supplied with drinks, although there are usually taps on board from which you can serve yourself. Moisturiser can also be a good idea to combat the dryness.
- Any medication you take regularly, plus aspirin or paracetamol for headaches.
- Earplugs, if you have difficulty sleeping in a noisy cabin.
- A book, stationery, a personal journal or other items to help pass the time, and your guidebook, so that you can read up more on your destination.

DUTY-FREE ALLOWANCES & RESTRICTED ITEMS

If you're planning to bring stocks of cigarettes, a few bottles of liquor or similar items, you'll need to first check the duty-free allowances of the country you're planning to visit. Quantities in excess of the permitted amount will generally be confiscated on arrival. A few countries (eg Libya) prohibit outright the importation of liquor.

Countries in Africa prohibit the import of firearms, ammunition and narcotics. Some (such as Libya) may also be sensitive to pornography. In the case of narcotics, firearms or ammunition, not only will these items be confiscated, but you run the risk of being arrested.

If you will be bringing medications into the country with you, it's a good idea to carry a note from your doctor explaining why you need them and to bring the original prescription slip.

Some countries require that you declare expensive items such as laptop computers, bicycles, and video equipment on entry. See the Bicycles & Surfboards section in the Tickets & Insurance chapter. You may also be asked to declare how much currency you are carrying (see Arrival in the Touchdown chapter).

Buying Duty-Free

Airport duty-free shops often require you to show your boarding pass when making a purchase. Goods available include liquor, cigars and cigarettes, perfume, beauty products, and sometimes electronic goods, although usually only liquor and cigarettes are good value.

Duty-free shopping is also possible on board, although savings are negligible.

Departure Day

It can be easy to forget things in the rush leading up to departure. If you have little experience with flying and international travel, these sections could be used as a checklist to smooth the departure period.

DRESSING APPROPRIATELY

The best type of outfit for the day you fly is something loose-fitting, comfortable, appropriate for the weather at your destination and relatively presentable. Shorts are not a good option when arriving in Africa, nor are sleeveless tops. If you are flying from a cooler destination, it's better to be a bit chilly before boarding the plane, or to arrange to send winter clothes back with whoever drops you at the airport, than to carry a heavy jacket or pullover around with you during your trip. Having comfortable footwear is also important, since your feet will probably swell during the flight.

BEING ON TIME

This may be obvious, but a surprising number of people arrive late for international flights. In order to get to the airport on time, ie two hours before departure, take things like traffic jams and other eventualities into account when planning. Taking the train is a good option, as it avoids traffic problems. If this isn't possible and you need to go by road, allow plenty of extra time.

Packing your bag the evening before you depart is another good step. Not only will you be more calm and collected on the day of departure and able to arrive earlier at the airport, you'll probably not forget as many things.

NAVIGATING THE AIRPORT

Airports can be crowded and confusing. Many of the larger ones have information desks where you can get an airport map. If think you're going to have problems finding your way, you may want to pick up one of these before heading to the check-in counter. Otherwise, there are usually plenty of people around to ask for directions.

READY MONEY

If you happen to be heading to a destination with an internationally available currency (such as South Africa), it can be a good idea to change some money into the local currency of your destination before leaving home, especially if you will be arriving at a time when banks or exchange bureaux may be closed. This can either be done at a local bank before your departure date or (sometimes) at the airport on the day of your flight. There's no need to change a lot – just enough to get you from the airport to your hotel and to pay for the first night's lodgings and dinner.

As most countries in Africa do not have internationally available currencies, you will likely have to bring your money in the most appropriate hard currency – eg French francs if you will be arriving

Flight Day Checklist

- Turn off the gas and electricity in your home.
- Make sure you've reconfirmed your flight (better late than never).
- Make sure you have your house key for when you return.

Also ensure that you have the following essentials:

- address book
- backpack
- camera
- daypack
- medications you might need
- money belt (with all your credit cards, travellers cheques, cash)
- passport
- plane ticket
- visas you've already received
- wallet/purse

in West or Central Africa, and US dollars elsewhere. In a pinch, you can often pay for taxi rides with these currencies (you will need small denomination notes for this) and then change more after arriving at your hotel.

If you have somehow managed to get local currency for your destination country, despite the fact that it is not internationally available (eg from another traveller), keep in mind that many African countries limit the import (and export) of local currency to a maximum of about US$10.

CHECK-IN

Before checking in, be sure that each piece of your luggage has a tag showing your name, home address and telephone number, airline and flight number. If you have a contact address in your destination country, you may want to add this as well.

As far as possible, prepare your backpack or luggage for the rough treatment it will receive at the hands of baggage handlers, X-rays and conveyor belts. This means tying all pieces of loose webbing and straps, closing all pockets securely, placing liquids (such as shampoo) in plastic bags and making sure your film and camera are in your carry-on bag. Some airlines may be willing to put backpacks and other unwieldy parcels in a large plastic bag on request (and some airlines do this for all backpacks as a matter of course).

At check-in you'll need to show your passport and ticket, so have these out and ready. Unless you've arranged your seat in advance, this is also the time you will make your seat selection for intercontinental flights (see the boxed text for advice). You should also remind the agent of any dietary restrictions or preferences. Once you've taken care of these things, the agent will issue your boarding pass. Be sure to get your passport and remaining tickets back as well.

The Best Seats

Unless you are lucky enough to arrange business or 1st class seats, you're going to have to fight it out in economy class with the rest of the herd. As a rule, economy class seats are designed to be barely distinguishable from medieval torture devices, particularly if you happen to be at all on the tall or large side. Happily, there are a few exceptions to this. When you check in or when you reconfirm your ticket, ask for an exit row seat. These are usually above the wing and have twice the leg room of normal economy class seats. However, these seats are often near the service area where flight attendants prepare meals, so they can be noisy. The other disadvantage is that the armrests on exit row seats often do not lift up, which means that even if no one is sitting next to you, you won't be able to stretch out.

The next-best choices are aisle seats and window seats. Window seats are good if you like to watch the scenery as you travel or if you want to try to sleep. Aisle seats are good if you like to get up and stretch your legs, or if you have a small bladder. Often you will find that the seats you want are taken and you'll be stuck in the middle of a row.

If the plane is empty, look on the bright side – you will have plenty of room. If it's full, try to take a philosophical approach and consider it practice for all the crowded bus and taxi rides you will be taking in Africa.

If you are going to check luggage, see that the appropriate destination tag is affixed to every piece. If you will be changing flights en route, ask whether your baggage will be checked through or if you must collect it and recheck it yourself. Finally, don't forget to get your baggage claim slip. Some African airports are vigilant in checking these before allowing you to leave the airport with your bags.

INSPECTION & IMMIGRATION

Once you have your boarding pass, you can proceed through inspection and immigration. If anyone has accompanied you to the airport, you'll have to say goodbye at this point, as only ticketed passengers are permitted through the gates.

In most airports, inspection for departing passengers is a straightforward procedure. Your carry-on bag will be X-rayed and checked for weapons and other forbidden items (such as spray cans, explosives and flammable substances), and you will have to walk through a metal detector. If you're travelling with a laptop computer, you may have to open it up and turn it on for the inspection officials. If you are nervous about your film, ask that it be hand-checked, although some airports insist on sending it through the machine. Anything that looks like a weapon will be given close scrutiny here and will probably be X-rayed. To avoid problems at this stage, it may be a good idea to stow your pocketknife in your checked baggage.

Immigration formalities are usually very brief when leaving your home country. You'll need to show your boarding pass and passport, and will normally be waved straight through. Sometimes the immigration officer may place a departure stamp in your passport.

Surviving the Flight

Flights to and from Africa are invariably crowded, and – unless you're flying from Europe – often very long. The following sections contain a few suggestions to help pass the time more quickly and comfortably.

ALCOHOL

Alcohol is usually free on airplanes, and you can generally have as much as you want. However, having more than one or two drinks is a bad idea: it will contribute to the dehydration you will already be suffering due to dry cabin air, and is guaranteed to give you a bad headache, or worse, halfway through the flight. (You will be better off drinking loads of water during the flight, to counter the dehydration.) Furthermore, negotiating an unfamiliar city when you arrive is going to be tough enough without doing it hungover.

SLEEP

If you're one of the lucky ones who can sleep on planes, not only will the flight pass relatively quickly, but you'll arrive feeling fairly refreshed. If, however, you are one of those people who could fly for days on end without nodding off, you'll just have to make the best of it. Bring a good book, listen to language tapes, watch the in-flight film, do seat stretches or whatever it takes.

Taking sleeping pills and tranquillisers to get to sleep isn't generally a good idea, as they can leave you feeling groggy and produce an artificial sleep that isn't restful in the first place.

THE BEST MEALS

Despite all the jokes about airplane food, it's generally possible to get decent meals on airplanes if you know what to ask for. Many travellers, whether they're vegetarian or not, request vegetarian meals because these are often better prepared than regular meals. Check with your airline to see what's available. Keep in mind, however, that some airlines don't yet have the hang of vegetarian meals, so there's a chance you'll be served a few limp lettuce leaves, a piece of cheese and a bread roll, while passengers around you tuck into their hot, appetising meals.

If you do want to request a special meal, inform the airline when making your initial reservation. Remind them when reconfirming your ticket and again when checking in.

If the idea of airplane food is unappetising, you can always bring some of your own food on the plane.

TRANSIT BREAKS

If you have a lengthy transit break en route, ask at the airport information counter to see what facilities are available. Many airports (excluding most of those in Africa) have various options for helping you pass the time as agreeably as possible. These often include day rooms where you can lie down and take a nap, or showers where you can freshen up. Alternatively, there may be restaurants and cafes or shopping possibilities. A small number of airports even have fitness rooms, pools or small running tracks where you can stretch your legs a bit.

Fear of Flying

If you've flown before and found the experience unsettling or worse, or have never flown and suspect that you'll suffer from fear of flying, there are some steps you can take to make the flight as painless as possible. First, if you are really terrified of flying, seek out the appropriate counselling before travelling, rather than trying to overcome your fear by yourself.

If you suffer from only mild fear of flying, try to prepare yourself mentally for the flight before boarding. Some people find that aisle seats are more relaxing than window seats, others vice-versa. Whatever the case, make sure to ask for the seat that allows you to feel most comfortable.

Attempting to drown your fears with alcohol is not a good idea, as you will merely be replacing an unpleasant mental condition with an unpleasant physical one. If you feel that you might need something to calm your nerves, speak to your doctor beforehand about getting a mild tranquilliser prescribed.

Finally, some turbulence during the flight is nothing to worry about. Veteran pilots point out that planes can withstand infinitely more stress than most fliers imagine. While it may be disconcerting, you likely have more to fear from the mystery meat in your dinner than from the shaking of the wings.

TOUCHDOWN

While many flights between Europe and Africa are not excessively long, those from North America or Australia may be close to 20 hours. When you arrive, in addition to the unfamiliar surroundings and the heat that will greet you at many airports, you will also need to cope with fatigue and jetlag.

To ensure that everything goes smoothly on arrival, try to familiarise yourself as much as possible in advance with what to expect once you land. The best sources of information are guidebooks and someone who has already been to your destination country. Have a clear idea of airport immigration procedures, as well as a plan for getting yourself into the city and to your first night's accommodation.

Immigration

The first steps on landing will be clearing immigration, collecting your baggage and proceeding through customs.

For immigration, you will need to complete an embarkation/disembarkation card and (sometimes) a customs form. In most cases these will be handed out during your flight. Otherwise, look for them once you disembark – either lying on a table in the immigration hall, or being handed out by an official. Have a pen handy, as there generally won't be any at the airport. The disembarkation card is the one that you'll hand over to the immigration officer upon arrival, together with your passport. The cards of most countries will ask you to state the address where you will be staying. If you don't yet know this, the best thing is to just fill in the name of a mid-range hotel from your guidebook. Many cards also request you to state your occupation. In general, it's best to describe this as innocuously as possible, especially if yours might fall into a 'sensitive' category such as journalist or reporter.

Although you may have to queue in the immigration hall, actual immigration formalities usually take very little time, assuming your passport, visa and international health card are in order.

Possible sources of trouble include not having the necessary visa (although without one, most international airlines will refuse to let you on the plane in the first place), a passport that is due to expire before the visa itself expires or a passport that is in poor condition.

When you are called to the immigration counter, have your embarkation/disembarkation card and your customs form inside your passport, preferably at the first open page or at the page with your visa. After handing over your passport, you may be asked a few simple questions. A few countries may also require that you show an onward ticket.

No matter what country you are visiting, it generally smooths the way if you look halfway presentable when going through immigration and keep your responses to any questions respectful and polite.

Many countries will have a health officer in the immigration hall asking you to show your international health certificate with proof of yellow fever (and possibly also cholera) vaccination, so have this ready together with your passport.

BAGGAGE COLLECTION

Once you've passed through immigration, follow the signs (or the rest of the passengers) to baggage claim. Off-loading is usually not a speedy process, so be prepared for a wait. In many airports you will be besieged by porters eager to assist you. If you do use their services, be prepared with small change for a tip.

As you exit the baggage collection area, you will usually be asked to show your baggage claim tickets (often attached to your flight ticket), so have these handy.

CUSTOMS

The customs form is self-explanatory and it's unlikely you'll have to declare anything unless you are bringing in a video camera, bicycle, laptop computer or other specialised or electronic equipment, which must be declared in some countries. Avoid overestimating the value of your goods on the form, as it is likely to just create difficulties when going through customs inspection. A few countries also require you to declare how much currency you are carrying (see the boxed text).

Customs procedures in many sub-Saharan African countries are relatively informal, although they are often what cause travellers the most hassles. While some countries have the standard system of green (no goods to declare) and red (goods to declare) channels, many process all travellers in the same aisle. If you were given a customs form, you'll need to turn it in here. In some countries – assuming you have nothing to declare – you will just be waved through. In others, you will need to open up your luggage for inspection or explain what is inside. Apart from ensuring that you are not bringing in any prohibited items, the officials want to be sure that what is in your luggage is for personal use (not for sale) and that it will be brought back out with you when you depart. If the customs officer finds any reason for suspicion, they may perform a more detailed search of your bags. It's also not unheard of for enterprising and underpaid customs agents in some countries to use the inspection process as an opportunity to try to elicit some extra cash for themselves, particularly if you are carrying a computer or other flashy, new or expensive equipment, or if they sense you are a novice traveller. No matter how

Currency Declaration Forms

Few African countries still use currency declaration forms, and in most of those that do (eg Ghana), controls are lax. The forms ask you to declare all your money on entry, then on exit, the amount you have remaining will be tallied against your foreign exchange receipts to ensure you did not exchange on the black market. These forms are rarely scrutinised any more, but it's a good idea to hold onto your foreign exchange receipts to avoid any problems. If you think you may be forced to use the black market, hide a small amount of hard currency when entering the country as a safeguard against the unlikely event that your money will be controlled on departure.

onerous a baggage search may be, don't lose your temper; just respectfully but firmly decline to pay any bribes. If they set aside one of your items and insist you pay customs duties (assuming it is part of your personal luggage and not subject to these), it is generally just a bluff to elicit some cash from you – although sometimes, the demands can go as high as 200% or more of the item's declared value. With patience and good humour you should be on your way before too long. If you have been given a customs form, keep whatever copies unitl you depart.

On Your Way

Before leaving the arrivals hall, check that all your valuables are in your money belt and the pockets of your pack are safely closed. Once outside the gates, in many places you'll be greeted by touts offering taxis and accommodation. If you do need a taxi, walk over to where you see the taxi stand and negotiate directly with the driver; with touts, your fare will wind up being more, as they'll want a commission from whichever driver they bring you to.

For accommodation, touts are also best avoided. Know in advance where you want to head and get there on your own. Sometimes, the touts may tell you the place you want to go has gone out of business, which may well be true. However, especially in heavily touristed areas, it's just as likely to be a ploy to get you to go to somewhere else where the tout has a friend or relative, or knows he will get a commission. If you have doubts about whether the place you've selected has closed down, rather than go with a tout, ask the taxi driver to take you to a hotel that you are certain is open, then sort things out from there.

If you need to change money, do it here. Most airports have an exchange booth, ATM or bank in or near the arrivals lobby. Exchange rates at airports are often bad, so change just enough to get you to your hotel and to tide you over until you can get to a bank. Be sure to get some small bills for paying the taxi fare.

LEFT LUGGAGE

Most African airports do not have left luggage facilities. If you really need to, leave it with a trustworthy guesthouse or hotel.

GETTING INTO TOWN

Unless you are being met by someone, you will need to use public transport or taxis. A few airports have special shuttles that go to certain hotels.

Public transport will be much cheaper than a cab, although also slower and very crowded – making it difficult to negotiate with a large backpack. It also normally takes a day or two to become acquainted enough with a city to use its public transport system. If you do decide to take public transport, your guidebook should have a section on getting from the airport to the city centre that spells out your options and what you should expect to pay.

Airport taxi drivers will invariably try to extract as much money from you as possible. If the cab has a meter and the driver is willing to use it, the problem is solved. However, in most places there will be no meters, and you'll have to negotiate. Try to get an idea of reasonable fares in advance from a guidebook, or at least determine how far the airport is from the city or your hotel so you can work out what a reasonable fare would be. In a few airports, official rates will be quoted or posted. While in some cases these really are the correct rate, it's just as likely that they are inflated (or even outdated, as the taxi drivers may claim).

Your First Night

Unless you are travelling during peak season, or arriving in a country during a festival or holiday period, advance reservations are generally not necessary. If you prefer to make a hotel reservation before leaving home, this will make things simpler on arrival – when you may be tired or disoriented – but it will also mean paying a bit more for mid-range or top-end accommodation, as many budget places will not accept or guarantee reservations.

Following are some tips for getting yourself settled as quickly as possible:

- Prior to arriving in Africa, arm yourself with a good guidebook, spend some time studying the map and accommodation possibilities, identify a few options (in case your first choice is full or has closed down) and determine the best way to get there from the airport. Even if you do not know the exact hotel, at least choose the general area of the city where you want to stay. Once you've disembarked and made it

First Night in Africa

Having spent nearly two years in various travels on the Indian sub-continent and in South-East Asia, I figured I had third-world travel down pat.

I flew into Banjul (The Gambia) in the afternoon, checked into a familiarly crummy hotel and wandered into the downtown area in search of entertainment. But where were the crowds? Why were the streets of this capital city unpaved? Why, as darkness, fell, were there no streetlights? The few cafes mentioned in the Lonely Planet guide were all the cafes there were – no wandering around being picky about where I would eat. At least there was no chance of getting lost and spending an exciting hour or two finding my way back to the hotel, as often happened in India.

I was carrying my money belt, which contained everything that I didn't want to leave in the hotel room – tickets, passport, credit card, travellers' cheques. In Asia, this seemed the safest way to go. But when a smiling man lurched out of the darkness, rather gently took hold of the money belt and pulled, I realised that I might have to learn new rules for Africa.

He pulled and I pulled back. 'Give it to me', he said, grinning. He pulled harder and I pulled harder. People were wandering past, not taking much notice. With his free hand he reached for my watch and began to undo it. I didn't want to let go of the money belt to stop him, so he removed the watch, and then strolled away with it. I was dumbfounded.

'Thief!', I tentatively called after him. He turned around, still smiling, and disappeared down an alley.

It took quite a while to stop comparing Africa with Asia, and until I opened up to the surprisingly subtle joys of African travel, the comparison always seemed negative. Poor (and often expensive) accomodation, infrequent transport, few tangible signs of cultural heritage, and above all, no obvious social niche for the independent traveller to inhabit. I never appreciated paying high rates for crummy rooms with no mosquito netting, but I found that waiting a day for a bus to fill up became enjoyable, that you don't need ancient temples to be in a rich culture, and that being treated as an individual meant limitless possibilities for making friends.

Jon Murray
LP Author, Australia

through customs and immigration, head straight for the taxi, bus or whatever transport you have chosen and make your way to the hotel or area you have identified.

- In many sub-Saharan African countries, there is no such thing as a functioning telephone at the airport, so don't plan on calling around once you arrive. If you are stumped for a good place to stay, or if your first few choices are full, ask one of the hotels to suggest another place. If they have a phone, they may also be willing to help you call around. Some upper-end places with luggage services may also be willing to mind your baggage while you go out to search for more options. (A modest tip for the porter will be appreciated.)

- If you are selecting budget or mid-range accommodation, try to choose a place not far from other hotels in case your first choice is full or no longer exists. If you're travelling with someone, one person can then mind the bags in a nearby cafe or hotel lobby while the other goes off on foot in search of a room.

- When you find a likely spot, always ask to see a room – lobbies can be deceptive. Look in the bathroom, see if the water runs, examine the mosquito net for holes, turn on the lights and see that the fan or air-conditioner works. You should also check that the room isn't a firetrap and that emergency exits are available. (For more details on what to look for, see Finding the Right Place in the While You're There chapter.) If a room looks unappealing, you are under no obligation to stay. Either ask for a better room in the same place or head to another hotel.

- Prices in many places will be posted. Whether they are or not, though, it never hurts to ask for a discount. It's often worth spending a bit more on your first night in an unfamiliar city until you can get oriented and settled in – you can always find a cheaper place later.

- The worst plan is to leave things to chance, or to airport touts, who will invariably lead you to dicey or less than optimal lodging (see On Your Way, earlier in this chapter).

Coping With Jetlag

Jetlag may occur when a person travels by air across more than three time zones (each zone usually represents a one hour time difference). It occurs because many of the functions of the human body (temperature, pulse rate and emptying of the bladder and bowels) are regulated by internal 24-hour cycles. After travelling long distances rapidly, our bodies take time to adjust to the 'new time'. Symptoms of jetlag include fatigue, disorientation, insomnia, anxiety, impaired concentration and loss of appetite. These effects will usually be gone within a few days of arrival as your body clock synchronises with the local day and night cycle. Until it does, you may find yourself wide awake in the middle of the night and tired during the day.

Steps to take to minimise the impact of jetlag include:

- Rest as much as possible before your departure.

- Try to select a flight that minimises sleep deprivation. By arriving late in the day, you'll be able to go straight to bed and adjust to local time more rapidly. For very long flights, try to organise a stopover.

- Avoid overeating, especially fatty foods. These will make you feel bloated and slow you down, both of which will add to the feeling of jetlag.

- Avoid alcohol while on the plane and during your first few days in the country. Instead, drink plenty of non-carbonated drinks such as fruit juice or water.

- Avoid smoking.

- Try to go to bed in the evening at the appropriate time at your destination, even if you can't fall asleep right away, and to wake up at a decent hour in the morning (even if it's a struggle the first day or two).

ISSUES & ATTITUDES

Packing your brain is as important as packing your bag. In this chapter we cover issues related to cultural difference, ecotourism, and protecting yourself and your gear from scam artists and thieves. Used wisely, the information in this chapter will come in handier than your Swiss Army pocketknife and will ensure that your trip is a good and a safe one.

Culture Shock

Most first-time travellers, and even many experienced travellers, will suffer some form of culture shock when they set foot in Africa. First encounters with the new and unfamiliar are a kind of traveller's growing pains, but to let culture shock get the better of you would be to miss out on all the wonderful opportunities that African travel offers.

Culture shock describes the confusion and disorientation travellers feel when exposed to new environments. You will find everything in Africa to be vastly different from your known experiences, ranging from the heat, the noise levels, the crowds and the shocking poverty so evident in some areas, to strange languages, food and the curious stares you may get as an outsider. Although these stresses can be quite overwhelming, the best approach is to regard culture shock as an inevitable period of adjustment. Your preconceived values, notions and world-view are all being challenged, but gradually you will adapt as you become more familiar with the world you are travelling in.

The impact of culture shock will vary, depending partly on your previous cross-cultural experiences and your pre-arrival knowledge of the new culture. Culture shock is not the same as homesickness, although homesickness is often one of its symptoms. It's natural to yearn for the familiar when everything seems strange.

Other typical symptoms of culture shock are anxiety, depression, insomnia, feelings of helplessness, an acute sense of isolation and withdrawal, and apathy and lethargy. Take time to ease yourself into the travel experience; catch up on your sleep (on top of everything else, you're probably jet lagged as well) and don't try to cram in too much sightseeing in your first few days.

There are several stages of culture shock, though people experience it differently. The first is the honeymoon stage, characterised by a sense of euphoria and excitement, when everything new seems extraordinary. Inevitably, the novelty wears off – welcome to the disintegration stage. Instead of being thrilled to be thrust into the midst of this new environment, you find yourself disliking and rejecting many aspects of the culture you have come so far to see. To keep yourself out of the 'the pits', it's important to stay motivated by setting yourself realistic goals. Keep an open mind and avoid focusing entirely on the negative.

Soon enough you'll hit the reintegration stage, when you'll be gritting your teeth and getting on with things. You might still feel defensive, vulnerable or hostile, and be tempted to blame every little problem or setback on your host culture, but your survival instinct will have kicked in. By the autonomous stage, you have new goals and objectives based on a more realistic assessment of travel. With more self-confidence, you can relax and be more sensitive to the people around you.

Finally, the interdependence stage arrives, when an emotional bond develops between you and the new culture. This may take some time and effort, but it will happen. To help yourself along, try to do some research before you leave home: read travel and history books, look up the place in an atlas, search the web, and hone up on the art and literature (see Researching Your Trip in the Planning chapter for some specific pointers). Soon enough, time runs out, funds dry up and travel comes to an end – leading to a shock of an altogether different variety on your return home.

Poverty & Begging

According to United Nations statistics, over half of African countries have an average per capita income of US$500 per year or less. Large debt burdens, widespread government corruption, the difficulty of accessing credit for micro-businesses, authoritarian rulers and harsh climatic conditions are just some of the many factors that contribute to the widespread poverty found in many areas of the continent.

Among the manifestations of this are the destitute people you will see on the street, particularly in urban areas – although their numbers are remarkably small considering the overall economic situation on the continent. In most cases, these people are truly needy. Few African countries have the social security systems that exist in many places in the west, and the primary social nets are the community and the extended family. If someone has fallen through the holes because there is no one who is able to take care of them – financially or otherwise – within the community or family, there are few places they can turn. If you choose, carry a bit of small change somewhere easily accessible to help out these people.

Tips on Dealing with Culture Shock

- Read up on your destination before you get there so you have some clear ideas about what to expect.
- Consider travelling with a friend who can lend moral support in unfamiliar circumstances.
- Call home regularly. Familiar voices will help keep you on an even keel.
- Talk to other travellers and expats, to help you put your thoughts and feelings into perspective.
- Try not to compare the country you're in to your home country; accept that it's different and simply observe and analyse the differences.
- If you find yourself getting too stressed or depressed by an unfamiliar culture, find one in which you feel more comfortable. After all, you didn't come to Africa to torture yourself – if you aren't having a good time, find a place where you can.

Another option – particularly if you are concerned that the money you give on the street to charity collectors won't go where it is most needed – is to make a donation to a local mission or charitable organisation. Most African cities have many such organisations. To find out what agencies exist, inquire at a local church or mosque, or ask your church at home for assistance in identifying organisations working in the country or region you will be visiting.

Some charitable organisations that do work in many areas of the continent include:

Don Bosco Programs – These programs, run by the Salesian Fathers, are targeted at providing youth a way to get off the streets, back to school and reintegrated with their communities and families. They usually incorporate vocational or skills training programs, as well as some residential facilities.

Habitat for Humanity – This ecumenical Christian organisation works in numerous countries in Africa and elsewhere to build simple, affordable housing.

Missionaries of Charity – The Sisters of Mother Teresa run homes in many African cities and towns for orphans, children whose families cannot care for them, the elderly, the chronically ill and the dying.

Red Cross – Many countries have local Red Cross chapters that are engaged in a variety of programs aimed at assisting victims of poverty, natural disasters and the like.

Trickle Up Program – The goal of this nonsectarian US-based organisation is to create opportunities for self-employment and economic and social well being among low-income populations. Its particular focus is on promoting small enterprise development.

If you have a bit more time (two to three months is usually the minimum), you may also want to consider contributing your time as a volunteer. For more on this, see Volunteer Work in the Planning chapter.

Other than the sick, elderly and blind, who you may see begging, young children, particularly boys, may attach themselves to you and pester you insistently for money. While some have just come to expect that foreigners will hand them money, pens and the like – in which case the best policy is not to encourage them at all – many have been sent out by their families to help increase an all-too-meagre family income. Others have turned to the streets to escape difficult family situations. A small number are orphans – often AIDS orphans.

In the more genuine cases, particularly with the younger children, you'll find that they want attention even more than money. By making an effort to get to know them, their name and their age, and treating them with interest and respect, you'll find that the pestering for money will stop almost automatically.

Still, exaggerated stories of hardship for the benefit of soft-hearted tourists are not unknown. There are plenty of scams – especially in areas that have many visitors – where you'll be approached by youths with tales of woe about how they would go to school if only they could, and asking you for a donation to their tuition fees or the like. For more on this see the 'Tips to Avoid Being a Scam Victim' boxed text later in this chapter.

A similar issue is local people (not beggars) asking for gifts. This stems from a belief that anyone to whom God has been good should be willing to spread some wealth around. Since foreigners are thought to be rich (which, relatively, they are), generosity is expected. The usual gift asked for is money, but people may ask for your hat, shoes, camera or bicycle, all within a few minutes of meeting you. In this kind of situation you are not really expected to give anything. It's a 'worth a try' situation, and your polite refusal will rarely offend. If a service has been rendered, the gift becomes more like a tip. See Tipping in the Money Matters chapter for guidelines on this.

Avoiding Offence

In general, Africans are very easy-going towards foreigners and any social errors that you might make are unlikely to cause offence (although they may cause confusion or merriment). However, most African cultures tend to be conservative, and public nudity (including scanty dressing), open displays of anger, open displays of affection among people of the same or opposite sex, and vocal criticism of the government or country will be frowned on almost everywhere you go. See the boxed text for some other guidelines that apply across much of Africa.

DRESSING APPROPRIATELY

Clothes such as singlets and shorts or tight trousers are considered offensive, particularly in traditional and Muslim areas. The best clothes to wear are loose-fitting, modest and comfortable items – these will not only avoid offending locals, but will also offer you better protection from the sun. In general, this means trousers, skirts (for women) or at least knee-length shorts, tops with some sort of sleeve, and no tight-fitting garments. Sleeveless or skimpy tops and short shorts are only appropriate on some beaches and at some resorts. Particularly in Muslim areas, women should keep their shoulders and upper arms covered. Africans always dress to a 'T' for special occasions, including church services and any sort of festivities, so having along at least one decent-looking outfit is important.

COUNTRY-SPECIFIC DO'S & DON'TS

In addition to these general guidelines, individual countries have their own local customs. The best way to learn of these is by researching your trip in advance. Good guidebooks should have a section on local society and conduct. Observing locals while you are there is another way to learn the ropes.

Women Travellers

You'll learn pretty quickly in Africa that women keep the continent going. From hoeing the fields, gathering water and cooking the meals to pushing their children to get an education, women play a critical – and in some cases, the only – role. On the other hand, over much of the continent their public place is minimal compared to that of men.

To a large extent, western women are exempt from local norms – and in fact are often treated much like men. Particularly in rural areas, women travellers may also be viewed as a bit of a curiosity: local women rarely travel long distances alone with no apparent destination, and a single foreign female is an unusual sight. There will be little comprehension of the reasons you may not be married, or if you are, why your husband (and children) are not with you. Yet, even for foreign visitors, certain principles still apply. The most important of these is a degree of modesty in behaviour and dress – both to minimise hassles for yourself and to ensure that you are better received during your travels (see Dressing Appropriately in this chapter).

Meeting local women can enrich your trip tremendously, and give you some insight into African notions of women especially. Good places include tourist offices, government departments and similar entities where many of the staff will be formally educated, young to middle-aged women. In rural areas, a good starting point might be women teachers at a local school, or staff at a health centre. Many towns also have women's associations or cooperatives.

Do's & Don'ts

- Dress modestly. In addition to avoiding offence to locals, dressing conservatively will also ensure that you are met with more respect and openness and will help you to gain easier entry into the local culture. See Dressing Appropriately in this chapter for suggestions about dress.
- Always greet people (preferably in the local language) before attempting to transact business or otherwise engage them in conversation.
- Respect local customs and culture in your behaviour and speech.
- Show respect for the elderly, as well as for chiefs and other authority figures.
- Tread lightly and leave as little lasting evidence of your visit as possible. This is particularly important when travelling in remote areas.
- Avoid public displays of affection, among persons of the same or opposite sex.
- Don't lose your temper, and never do anything to insult an official or undermine their authority. Even in trying situations when dealing with officialdom, maintain your patience and a friendly, respectful demeanour.
- Show respect for places of worship. In many areas, mosques in active use are off-limits to non-Muslims. If you do arrange to enter a mosque, dress appropriately, with most or all of your arms and legs covered (whether you are a man or a woman). In some places, women are expected to cover their head and shoulders with a scarf. Also, women may not be allowed to enter some mosques if prayers are in progress or if the imam (Islamic leader) is present.
- Don't criticise the country you are visiting or its government. In some places (such as Libya) it could land you in trouble. Even in countries where locals comment openly about their government or country, the same comments coming from a foreigner may not be well received.
- Don't use the left hand for eating (according to ancient practice in many areas, the left hand is reserved for personal toiletries) or for unnecessary contact with others. Always try to give things with your right hand. When receiving something, the right hand can be used, or both hands, depending on where you are.
- Don't take anyone's photo without first asking for permission. (For more, see the Photo Etiquette boxed text in the What to Bring chapter.)
- When flagging down a taxi, motion by moving your hand up and down (with arm outstretched) at about waist level. The western gesture using the thumb is not used in Africa.
- In rural areas, ask permission to camp and before drawing water from a community well.

SAFETY

Most women travellers find that sub-Saharan Africa poses no particular difficulties, and that sexual harassment is no worse here than in other parts of the world. When it does occur, it's likely to be more of an annoyance (such as a lewd border official or an admirer who won't go away) rather than real harm or rape, which – while not unheard of – are highly unlikely in most areas. In fact, overall, you'll generally find that most places are relatively safe and unthreatening, and that friendliness and generosity are met far more often than hostility. Of course, as in any place in the world there is a certain degree of risk, which can be greatly minimised by following some basic, common-sense precautions.

The following are a few practical safely precautions:

- Muggings can occur, and women (particularly women travelling alone) are seen as easy targets. To minimise the risk of this happening to you, avoid rough or isolated areas and back streets, especially at night. If you have any doubt at all about the safety of an area, take a taxi – it will be money well spent.
- In uneasy situations, putting your nose in a book often works to give your harasser the hint. Having a real or fictitious husband who will be arriving shortly at that particular spot also can do the trick, although some more brazen types will not be deterred by this and may simply want to know how long they have before he arrives. Overall, whatever risks there may be can be significantly reduced if two women travel

---

Greetings & Handshakes

Greetings are of great importance in most areas of Africa and many people spend up to several minutes engaged in them before getting to the substance of their meeting. Common rituals include inquiries as to how the person being greeted is doing, as well as about the welfare of the family, the business and the village. With few exceptions, the response to all such questions is that things are fine, or at least that they are not bad, rather than an outright statement that things are terrible. While foreigners are not expected to go through the whole routine, it is important to use greetings whenever possible. Going a step further and taking the time to learn greetings in the local language is even better – just a few words can make a big difference. Even if you are doing something simple such as changing money or asking directions, it's appropriate to start with a greeting. Don't launch straight into business: you're likely to meet with a negative attitude.

As with greetings, in many areas there is great emphasis on handshakes. There are numerous variations, some of which are quite elaborate. These include linking thumbs or fingers, or shaking with the right hand while touching the right elbow with your left hand. In most situations, however, a western handshake will do fine (although this should be a soft version, not the western knuckle-cracker). In many areas, people who know each other will continue to hold hands throughout their conversation, or at least for a few minutes.

In social settings in most areas, men are expected to shake hands with other men when entering and when leaving a gathering – going around the room and greeting (or taking leave of) everyone. In many Muslim societies, Muslim men may prefer not to shake hands with women, and in traditional areas, whether Muslim or not, local women usually do not shake hands with their male counterparts – although African men often shake the hands of western women.

In French-speaking countries, the thrice-kissed cheek (starting with the left) is the norm for friends and even casual acquaintances of the opposite sex.

together or if a woman travels as part of a mixed-sex couple or group. If you are travelling with a male companion, one of the best ways to avoid unwanted interest is to introduce him as your husband.

- On long journeys it can be more comfortable to sit next to a woman.
- If you are not interested in male attention, don't accept offers of drinks or meals, offers of guide services and the like, and don't go to bars without a male companion.
- In general, women travelling alone should avoid hitching. If you do decide to take a lift, stay away from drunk drivers (a common condition in some areas) and cars full of men (such as military vehicles).
- When in doubt about a situation, ask local women – they will be the best source of advice on what can and cannot be undertaken safely.

North Africa

In contrast to much of sub-Saharan Africa, sexual harassment is a constant problem in North Africa. The harassment may be limited to being stared at in ways that leave little to the imagination, or it may involve being followed and occasionally touched. While this is uncomfortable and annoying, it probably won't go any further. (Tunisia is perhaps the least painful country in this regard.) Actual physical harassment is rare; it may happen in a crowded medina or in a major city, but is extremely unlikely to occur in the countryside.

Even women travelling with a male companion are not immune: it's possible for an Arab man to ask the male member of a western couple if he can take

Feminist Versus Feminine

As a female author, I feel passionately that a woman should never feel afraid to travel alone simply because she is a woman. As a female traveller, I am convinced that women may even have advantages over men when they travel – simply because they are women. Solo women travellers seem to provoke a whole bag of reactions abroad. But not just negative ones. In East Africa recently, the sight of a woman wandering alone seemed to elicit strong reactions of sympathy, sorrow and pity, from women as well as men. This provoked continual invitations, kindnesses and generosity from the local people.

'Aren't you ever afraid as a woman?', is the question I am most often asked when travelling. Anyone who has ever travelled alone knows that learning to judge people and situations fast is essential, as is the calculation of risk. Establishing the status and position of the local women in a society is important too – how they behave and are expected to behave. In Djibouti and Eritrea, for example, drinking alcohol, smoking and wearing excessive make up – as well as inappropriate clothes – were all indications to the male population of 'availability', since this is also the way the local prostitutes behave.

In many countries, women are offered a kind of temporary shelter on their travels; one not necessarily offered to male counterparts. And one that permits a wonderful access to the people and culture. There are darker sides too, undeniably. But even these can be exploited to a woman's advantage. Many the occasion I was denied visas, permission and interviews, with the great, the fat and the powerful until – fluttering an eyelash or two – doors flew right back open again. Essential items along with the mosquito net and torch? One smart skirt and some lippie.

Frances Linzee Gordon
LP Author, UK

liberties with his partner. Despite all this, women can travel, alone or in pairs, throughout most North African countries and still enjoy themselves. There are certain things you can do to minimise the friction. Modest dress is the first and most obvious. Wearing a wedding ring is also a good idea. Women travelling without male companions should not hitchhike. In Libya, where any westerner is a curiosity, you should think twice about travelling without a male companion. (It's often difficult to get a visa as a solo woman anyway.) Finally, avoid eye contact with a man you don't know and ignore any rude remarks.

The best way for female travellers to meet and talk to local women is to go to a *hammam* (bathhouse), although language can be a barrier unless you speak Arabic. Most towns have one, and if there is not one that is exclusively for women, there will be times set aside each day for women.

Holiday Romance

It's hardly news that innumerable long-term relationships have grown from encounters between foreign travellers and Africans. Yet – as when travelling anywhere in the world – until you have a feel for the culture, established yourself a bit and developed a circle of local friends, it's worth exercising a degree of caution. Keep in mind that as a foreigner, you may be viewed by some less savoury types as a means to an end – whether this means a path out of village life, a ticket to Europe, a convenient source of money, or worse. Once you have been in a place for a while, it should be easy to separate the wheat from the chaff. Your own motives are worth a look too – is this new romance simply based on curiosity or adventure? Are you creating some expectations you'd rather not meet? After all, you are likely to be the one moving on.

A dose of caution is also a healthy thing if you are considering a relationship with another traveller you've met on the road. Unless you know the person well, don't let down your guard on your valuables. It's also not worth throwing your own itinerary to the wind to follow after them. If you do this and the romance fizzles – which it is likely to do at some point – you'll likely be left feeling frustrated and resentful that you didn't stick with your own plans.

Ecotourism

While tourism can be the lifeblood of a community, it can also bring with it very negative effects that result in destruction of both natural and social environments. Ecotourism – usually defined as travel that conserves the natural environment and which benefits the well being of local people in a sustainable way – was born as a backlash against destructive travel practices, particularly in more remote regions of the world. Unfortunately, it has rapidly become a meaningless and overused term, with countless companies, particularly in popular trekking and hiking areas, claiming to be 'eco-friendly' although they take no steps to give substance to this assertion.

As a traveller, much of the responsibility rests on you to ensure that whatever activities you engage in protect and support the environment and communities of the areas you visit. In the case of tour operators, this means you'll need to take a bit of extra time to look beyond glossy brochures and vague 'eco-friendly' claims and ask what they are really doing to support the environment (which includes local people, as well as animals and plants). Then, patronise only those companies that make these issues a priority. Also remember that just because an activity is outdoors, it is not necessarily 'eco-friendly'. Depending on how they are carried out, camping, white-water rafting trips, game viewing (especially by car or balloon), or sightseeing excursions to remote or fragile areas can be more environmentally or culturally harmful than a conventional hotel holiday in a specifically developed resort.

Ecologically sound tourism in the broadest sense encompasses people as well as the natural environment, and focuses on your own actions, as well as those of tourism-related entities and of governments – both local and around the world. To familiarise yourself with some of the issues, check the resources listed in the following section before setting off to Africa. The guidelines given in the ecotourism boxed text specify a few concrete steps you can take as an individual to ensure that your impact on the environment and culture are kept to a minimum.

ECOTOURISM RESOURCES

Web Sites

Conservation International's Ecotravel Center
www.ecotour.org/ecotour.htm
(this site has good information on ecotour operators)

The Ecotourism Association of Australia's EcoNETT site
www.wttc.org
(this site contains links to ecotourism sites and ecotourism codes of conduct)

Ecotourism Guidelines

- Don't leave garbage in the places you visit and if you are camping or trekking, ensure that your garbage is going to be disposed of properly or carry it out yourself.
- Take time before your trip to learn about the culture, environment and specific problems of the places you plan to visit.
- Remember that the effect tourists have on the environment is not just financial, and respect the people and cultures of the places you visit. This means encouraging people in their efforts towards sustainable tourism, and not disrupting the fabric of their daily lives. Showing respect for local sensibilities and local etiquette in your behaviour and dress is an important aspect of this.
- Learn about local and international conservation groups working in the area and support their efforts.
- Patronise enterprises that make protection of the environment a priority in action not just in word.
- When possible, patronise locally owned businesses – including locally owned hotels and restaurants – and buy locally produced goods and crafts.
- Never buy products made from endangered species or from local wildlife.
- Stay on designated trails and camping spots.
- Use established toilets or relieve yourself at least 50m from rivers or lakes.
- Try to minimise all aspects of your energy consumption. Switch off lights and air-conditioning when leaving your room.

Organisations

Tourism Concern
(☎ 020-7753 3330; fax 7753 3331) Stapleton House, 277-281 Holloway Rd, London N7 8HN
(this is a membership organisation. If you would like to support its work, it costs UK£18 per year to join)

The Centre for Responsible Tourism
(☎ 415-258-6594; fax 454-2493) Box 827 San Anselmo CA 94979
(this US-based organisation is similar)

Hazards & Safeguards

It's impossible to generalise about personal safety in Africa. While there may be considerable risk in certain areas of some countries, many places are completely safe. In fact, apart from road accidents (which may well be your greatest safety concern in many countries), you will likely be in no greater danger in most areas of the continent than you would be at home. In some places you may even be safer. Even in cities such as Lagos (Nigeria), Abidjan (Côte d'Ivoire), Johannesburg (South Africa) and Nairobi (Kenya), which are notorious for their high crime rates, it is possible to travel safely and enjoyably.

By doing some research before you go to inform yourself well about the countries you intend to visit and taking some basic precautions, you should hopefully have a trouble-free trip. Remember that thousands of travellers enjoy visiting the continent without problem.

THEFT

While theft is no worse in Africa than anywhere else, as a western traveller you will stand out as someone who is wealthy, which increases your vulnerability to crime. In general, the danger of violent robbery is more prevalent in cities and towns than in rural or wilderness areas. While most cities have their dangerous streets and beaches, towns can differ, and there is generally more of a danger in areas frequented by wealthy foreigners than in places off the usual tourist track.

Don't Get Paranoid!

Just to balance the score, this is a lesson for all those who get too carried away with tales of muggings and deception. I was travelling with a group (all first-timers in Tanzania) and we were obviously a bit apprehensive. One day we all set off together to change our travellers cheques. We stood out like sore thumbs walking down a ramshackle road in Arusha with our inconspicuous money belts on. So we were all alarmed when a group of youths suddenly started running after us, shouting and waving their arms. Do you run? Stay calm? We decided on Plan C – stand there like scared rabbits. As one of the boys approached I noticed something shining in his hand ... the room key to one of our hotel rooms! Very grateful and embarrassed, the owner took the key from the boy and we walked on quietly to the bank. At least this taught us early on not to waste our time in a warm and beautiful new country looking over our shoulders every five minutes!

Sarah Tyrrell, Traveller

Some simple precautions to take to minimise whatever risks exist include:

- Keep an eye on your backpack when on long bus trips. If it is placed on the roof or in a luggage compartment, make sure it's placed properly (and secure it with your own lock if possible). During rest stops, watch it to make sure no one tries to walk off with it.
- Thieves will be less interested if you're not carrying a daypack or camera. Consider leaving these in your room if it is safe, or at hotel reception. Even travellers cheques, credit cards and sometimes passports can be left behind at the hotel in a safe box. In many countries you are required to carry your passport at all times – although you're unlikely to be stopped in the street by police and asked for it. Try carrying around a photocopy of your passport instead or some other less valuable ID, in the unlikely event of your being stopped by the police.
- Be discreet. Don't wear any jewellery or watches, no matter how cheap they actually are. Wearing a Walkman is asking for trouble. Use a separate wallet for day-to-day purchases and keep the bulk of your cash out of sight, hidden in a pouch under loose-fitting clothing.
- Avoid back streets and risky areas at night. Take a taxi. A dollar or two for the fare might save you a lot of pain and trouble. In some cases, you may want to consider hiring a local to accompany you when walking around a risky area. It's usually not too difficult to find someone who wouldn't mind earning a few dollars for warding off potential molesters – ask at your hotel.
- Don't jog or walk alone on isolated beaches or stretches of road, even during the day-time.
- Try not to look lost (even if you are), or like a tourist. Walk purposefully and confidently, and don't obviously refer to your guidebook or a map. Tear out the pages you need, or photocopy them, or duck into a shop or cafe to have a look at the map and get your bearings.
- When swimming, diving or snorkelling, either bring your important documents and money with you in a waterproof container or leave them in the safety deposit box of your hotel or guesthouse, if you're sure it's safe.
- Pickpockets sometimes work in teams. If you feel that people are jostling you or crowding you for no reason, stand back and check discreetly to see that your valuables are still on you, without letting on where you carry them. Don't let yourself be distracted by people who bump into you, spill something in front of you or the like.
- Be careful of your valuables while you're taking a shower. If you're not sure that your room is safe, take them into the bathroom with you.
- Remember that it's not just locals who may steal your belongings – there are quite a few travellers around who pay for their trips by ripping off other travellers.

BRIBERY

Bribery is a way of life throughout Africa. In many of the English-speaking countries, particularly in West Africa, a bribe is referred to as a 'dash'. In French-speaking countries it is a *cadeau* (but note that the same word is also used to refer to a tip or gift). Many public officials top up their meagre salaries by extracting extra payments from anyone they can. This can take all sorts of imaginative forms. One of the most common occurs at border posts and customs inspections, where an official – while examining your passport painfully slowly page for page or carrying out an annoyingly full search of your luggage – will ask whether you have anything for him (or her) – implying that if you don't pay up, you could be standing there for hours. Just as bad are the police who demand payments for bogus traffic infractions or for not having your vehicle papers in order. Or, the officials at road checkpoints who explain to you (while keeping the road blocked in front of your vehicle) that they have a brother or other family member in dire need of something, for which your donation would be most appreciated (after which, of course, you will be allowed to proceed smoothly on your way).

There are different ways of dealing with these situations. One method is to feign ignorance and simply bluff your way through. Humour can also be effective – at a

---

Ethiopia – Myth or Reality?

Addis Ababa, Ethiopia's capital city, doesn't seem ordinarily the sort of place where myths are made. But recently, rumours have been rife of locals who lure, siren-like, travellers to their 'doom'.

Various versions seem to be in circulation. Most commonly: a male traveller (alone or with a male companion) is approached by a young, Ethiopian man: 'Hello, my brother(s)', the young man begins, 'Welcome to Ethiopia. I think you like my country ...?' He turns out to be a student. 'You know the Ethiopian coffee?', he continues. 'It is the best in the whole world. I know a lovely place at the university ...' If this invitation fails initially to impress, the student may appeal to his new friends for 'help': perhaps to practice English before an exam, to decipher a letter from a faranji (foreign) friend abroad, to read a difficult medical prescription. Or perhaps to show you a 'special place' – a museum, monument or market ...

'Come in; come in ...' The 'special place' turns out to be a small room in a private house. You are received enthusiastically by the hostess – an ample, middle-aged woman in fine clothes and plenty of make-up. After showing you to a simple table, she offers you – as good Ethiopian hospitality dictates – a beverage. Only, it's alcoholic – and no matter the time of day. Almost simultaneously, some bottles of *tej* (a kind of honey wine), land on the table in front of you.

'And if you don't mind, I think I join you', says the hostess cheerfully. Soon, you will all be chinking cups together and toasting merrily: 'Your lovely country' ... 'May you have much rain, and the harvest be good' ...'To your Prime Minister' ...

Suddenly, an Ethiopian singer appears genie-like from a back room. She treats you to her best, most throaty numbers. 'And if you don't mind, I think ...' she says, helping herself to some tej.

Then, summoned up equally magically, are the Ethiopian dancers. 'And if you don't mind ...', more bottles of tej are brought out. Finally, you are encouraged to 'rest', and in the company of a sympathetic and soothing lady, who appears siren-like from another room.

Suddenly, the afternoon appears to draw to an abrupt halt. The hostess – a little less smiling and jovial – slaps a bill on the table: $50, $100, $200 ..., it depends on her 'hospitality'.

But the least query, the least protest seems to provoke a barrage of hysterics, screams and shouts, as only an Ethiopian hostess knows how. Most travellers pay up, thankful just to escape.

Myth, or reality? I never experienced it myself – possibly because I'm a woman. But one day, at a hotel in the Piazza, I did meet a man who could bear out the story. He was in his mid-seventies, he said, 'seeing a bit of the world and that sort 'a thing ...'

'I had a lovely evening the other night ...', he began wistfully.

Frances Linzee Gordon
LP Author, UK

roadblock where the officer asks what you have for him, simply smiling and asking in a friendly way what he might have for you can defuse the situation. If these tactics don't work, just state clearly that you are not going to give them anything.

Occasionally, the requests for money may become threats, such as not letting you through customs. This is usually just a bluff, although it can last several minutes. No matter how long it goes on, don't lose your cool; just remain respectful and polite. You might ask to see a senior officer, but never return the threats. Give the official you're dealing with plenty of room to back down and save face. In virtually all cases, you'll soon be allowed to continue. Of course, if your passport, vehicle documents, luggage or whatever are not in order, you're more vulnerable. It helps to know the regulations, however, because sometimes officials trump up totally fictitious ones simply to create a bribe situation. Knowing a few words in the local (African) language also can go a long way to smoothing out 'misunderstandings' and ensuring that you are soon on your way.

Another variation you may encounter when dealing with bureaucracy (eg when you apply for a visa extension) is that your paperwork will move at a

Camera? Camera?

I have never been one to believe much in superstition, but perhaps that day in London I should have seen the writing on the wall. I was at the Ethiopian Embassy, trying to get a visa for my forthcoming trip to the Horn. 'One month', the visa official snapped. 'One month?', I protested. 'But I am a journalist ... I have to research a book.' 'A journalist? ... In that case, two weeks', she said taking my passport.

In Eritrea, it took a Herculean effort to set up an interview with a leading archaeologist. His loathing of journalists – particularly female ones – turned out to be almost pathological. Fortunately, we ended up seeing eye to eye – as I did later with the police in Djibouti. We ended up touring together the remarkable archaeological sites of southern Eritrea. Yet all over the Horn, this distrust of the media pervades, transcending race, nationality and sex, in a marvellously indiscriminate way. Not just of journalists, but of any form of reportage. Stories abound in Ethiopia of unsuspecting tourists having cameras or film snatched from them by heavy-handed policemen. And for no apparent reason, other than being in possession of a camera. When entering banks or other official buildings, bags are routinely searched. It is not 'Gun? Gun?' or 'Grenade? Grenade?', that the friskers demand, it is 'Camera? Camera?' No one seems sure why.

Some areas in Ethiopia, including airports, bridges, military camps, and royal palaces, are classed as 'sensitive'. Anyone caught photographing from, at or around these places is likely to unleash a terrible fury – not just from the civil and military police, but from ordinary, Ethiopian civilians too.

And so camera-clutchers travelling in the Horn, are best advised to keep a low profile, particularly if your profession is also media-related. Just before leaving East Africa, I was invited to attend a cocktail party in Addis Ababa. My host introduced me to his other guests, but each time he did, my profession seemed to undergo a slight transformation. From journalist, I became writer, then researcher. Finally, catching a friend by the arm, he said: 'Have you met Frances? She's a poet, you know.'

Frances Linzee Gordon
LP Author, UK

snail's pace (or not at all) unless you find 'something small' to give to the relevant authorities as an incentive to push your paperwork through. Travellers differ in their approaches to this one – some view such payments as just a 'cost of doing business'. However – ethical arguments aside and apart from the fact that this makes it more difficult for others who come after you – if you do

Tips to Avoid Being a Scam Victim

In general:

- Avoid distractions. These can take many forms, ranging from being bumped or jostled to having something spilled or dropped directly in front of you, to being touched, poked or surrounded by a group. In all, the end result is the same: while one person is distracting you, his partners are sizing you up and working the other side to nab your wallet or slash your bag.
- Don't be misled by claims (from street touts or 'guides') that an attraction or market somewhere out yonder is the only one of its kind, or is only available today. Invariably, these will just be attempts to get you into a friend's shop or – worse – to corner you in an isolated alley and relieve you of your wallet.
- Exercise caution when picking up hitchhikers. In a few areas of North Africa (particularly Morocco), professional hitchhikers get in your car and oblige you to accept their thanks for your help with a glass of tea at their house, a carpet-sales session, or worse.
- Beware of con-artists who ask for money to help a sick relative, or to pay for a child's (or their own) school tuition fees or books, or the like. This doesn't mean that everyone who requests these things from you is dishonest (see Poverty & Begging in this chapter). However, in tourist areas and large cities, the chances are good that they are. If you feel the case is genuine, it's better to go (alone) to a local mission or charitable organisation and ask what the best thing would be for you to do, rather than to give money on the street (which will likely never make it into school tuition coffers or wherever it is allegedly going).

A few outright scams are common practice in certain places (keep your eyes and ears open of course, as new scams also spring up):

- Be wary of anyone who asks if you remember them. A popular trick in larger cities and tourist areas is for someone to hang around foreign exchange (forex) bureaux and travel agencies, pretending to be a customs official from the airport. After inquiring whether you have arrived recently, he'll start in by asking if you remember him. Before long, he's demanding a 'tip' if you want to avoid trouble on departure.
- In a variation on this, a man may approach you and say 'Hello, it's me, from the hotel, don't you recognise me?'. Although you don't really remember him, you don't want to seem rude, so you stop for a chat. He may ask if he can walk with you for a while and exchange a few more pleasantries before getting down to the real agenda: how about a visit to his brother's souvenir shop? Do you need a taxi or a tour?
- Yet another variation involves the con-artist pretending to be a hotel employee or 'son of the owner' out to get supplies for the bar or restaurant. He'll explain there's been a mix-up and ask you to lend him some money, which he promises you will later be able to deduct from your hotel bill. He'll know the name of your hotel and perhaps even your name and room number, and will even give you a receipt. Of course, when you get back to the hotel, staff will have never heard of him, and your money will never be seen again.

have a bit of time and are friendly but persistent, you'll find that in most cases, things will ultimately move without the need for any extra payments.

SCAMS

With scams, the general rule is that if someone offers you a deal that seems too good to be true, it almost certainly is. You are most likely to be the victim of a scam when changing money on the street (which is just another name for robbery). See Changing Money in the Money Matters chapter for more suggestions.

While credit card scams are not widespread in Africa, they do exist in some areas. To avoid being a victim, never let your credit card out of your sight and carefully watch what is done with it. If you get home and find charges on your card that don't belong there, call the credit card company.

In general, scams are more likely in tourist areas and large cities. Some common ones and how to avoid them are described in the boxed text.

DRUGS

When buying drugs, you are taking the risk that the dealer may simply rip you off or may be in cahoots with the police. If you're unwise enough to buy from a stranger, don't be surprised if the local authorities soon come around to your hotel room to pay you a visit. In some countries – Morocco is one example – stories abound of travellers being led down alleyways, lured by offers of large quantities of hashish, only to find themselves paying off unpleasant characters not to denounce them to the police (a threat they'd be highly unlikely to carry out). Unless you've been around a long time, the best policy is to ignore these offers completely.

Also, be careful of other travellers or local criminals using you as a mule to smuggle drugs by placing them in your pack. It's a good idea to check your pack carefully before any border crossing or plane flight; never accept gifts from strangers, however charming they may be.

For information on the potential health risks of drug use, see Alcohol & Drugs in the Health chapter.

OTHER HAZARDS

You can avoid almost all of the risks described here through careful research before you travel and by taking the proper precautions.

Unexploded landmines – In Mozambique, Egypt, Eritrea and several other countries, unexploded landmines in some areas are a grim reminder of past wars and ongoing military conflicts. If you are in a country with landmine risk, stick to the beaten path where it is obvious others have walked recently, avoid restricted areas and never trek into an area about which you are unsure.

Road ambushes – In some border areas (eg the Kenya-Tanzania border near Lake Natron/Uganda) or areas of political instability (such as the Chad-Cameroon border), road ambushes and banditry sometimes occur, particularly on desolate stretches of road. Research your trip in advance to learn if such risks exist. Once there, get an update from knowledgeable locals on routes you plan to travel. Try to avoid roads where problems have been reported. If you will be going to trouble spots with your own vehicle, drive in a convoy with others.

Unsafe driving – Road accidents are a serious concern in many countries. Road conditions can be poor, driving substandard and maintenance levels of other vehicles very inadequate. The risk can be just as high where roads are good, as buses and minibuses often move along at dizzying speeds. People, animals and stopped vehicles on the road are additional hazards. To stay safe, avoid road travel at night whenever possible, and at any time of day stay alert for children running onto the road, cyclists, animals and other vehicles. Keep in mind that many Africans don't drive and therefore often don't appreciate concepts such as necessary braking distances. Adjust your own speed accordingly. On routes with a selection of bus companies, ask locals which ones they recommend for safety. Consider taking the train where it is available, as train travel is almost always safer than travelling by road. Alternatively, if you are in a group, consider a rental vehicle with chauffeur, so you can control the speed. Large potholes or similar hazards are often marked with a branch or leaves in the road. If you see something like this, slow down.

Touts, guides & hustlers – In heavily touristed areas (eg Morocco, certain parts of Mali and the old Stone Town on the Zanzibar archipelago), you will be besieged by young men wanting to be your guide, show you to a hotel or in some other way attach themselves to you. While some can very informative and helpful, others can be aggressive and irritating or worse. If you do decide to employ the services of a guide, try to get some sort of recommendation – either from other travellers or through an official tourist bureau, a hotel or the like. Before starting off, be very clear about the price and where you want to go. If you don't want their services, politely but firmly decline all offers of help and just move on. Telling them that you have already employed a guide but now want to be on your own also sometimes works. Exasperated outbursts will never get you anywhere.

Dust – In Mauritania, parts of Niger and other dry areas of the continent, hot, sandy winds can be a problem during the summer and the harmattan season. If you wear contact lenses, bring along a pair of glasses (you should do this anyway). Even those

Your Own Embassy

As a tourist, it's important to realise what your own embassy – the embassy of the country of which you are a citizen – can and cannot do.

Generally speaking, they won't be much help in emergencies if the trouble you're in is remotely your own fault. Remember that you are bound by the laws of the country you are visiting. Embassies will not be sympathetic if you end up in jail after committing a crime locally, even if such actions are legal in your own country.

In genuine emergencies you might be able to get some assistance, but only if other channels have been exhausted. For example, if you need to get home urgently, a free ticket home is exceedingly unlikely – the embassy would expect you to have insurance. If you have all your money and documents stolen, they might assist with getting a new passport, but a loan for onward travel is out of the question.

Embassies used to keep letters for travellers or have a small reading room with home newspapers, but these days the mail holding service has been stopped and even the newspapers tend to be out of date.

On the more positive side, if you are heading into very remote or politically volatile areas, you might consider registering with your embassy so they know where you are, but be sure to tell them when you come back, too.

who don't wear lenses should consider bringing fluid for the eyes. Ensure that cameras and similar equipment are well protected, and bring along some zip-lock plastic bags. In these regions, as well as throughout Africa during the dry season, road dust permeates everything. A lightweight elasticised cover to slip over your backpack, particularly when it is tied to the roof of taxis or buses, will prevent dust from making its way into the cracks.

General problems – Natural disasters, political unrest and the like are generally far less a risk than you might suppose based on reading the news. Doing a bit of research before you travel will alert you in most cases to any potential problem areas. A good guidebook will have a detailed section on the dangers and how to avoid them. Update your information through newspapers, magazines and the Internet just before visiting a country. Once in Africa, some embassies post useful warning notices about local dangers or potential problems. The US embassies are good for providing this information and it's worth scanning their notice boards for 'travellers' advisories' about security, local epidemics and so on. You can also find travel advisories on the Internet (travel.state.gov/travel_warnings.html).

IF YOU DO GET INTO TROUBLE

If something has been stolen or you've been the victim of any other crime, report it to the police. Although this may be time consuming and there will often be little they can do, you will need the report for insurance reimbursement back home, and sometimes also for replacement of travellers cheques.

In the case of lost or stolen passports, you should first go to your country's embassy or consulate (see Lost or Stolen Passports in the Passports & Visas chapter). Your embassy will also be able to advise you about local laws, put you in touch with English-speaking lawyers and contact friends or relatives back home in the event of an emergency. However, don't expect them to lend you money, get you out of jail or pay to fly you home.

If you become ill, your embassy or other foreigners living in the country may be able to recommend the name of a reliable hospital or doctor. Be sure to save all treatment and medication receipts for your insurance.

Accommodation

Finding accommodation in Africa is seldom a problem, although arranging something you like can take a bit of work. This section covers the various types of accommodation available, as well as some tips on locating the right place.

TYPES OF ACCOMMODATION

Accommodation in Africa ranges from the most basic fleapits to luxurious five-star hotels. Prices are equally varied – from US$1 or US$2 for a dormitory bed to US$300 or more per night in an all-inclusive resort.

In the budget range, you can expect the basics: usually just a bed, sometimes with a mosquito net. Few budget rooms come with private bath. Cleanliness standards often leave a lot to be desired, particularly when it comes to shared bathrooms. Some budget places will have good ventilation with a fan or decent-sized windows, while others will have only internal windows opening onto an inner hallway or courtyard. Many budget hotels also double as brothels. Private guesthouses – particularly those run by missions – are an exception to these generalisations (see Guesthouses later in this section). Apart from hotels and guesthouses, other budget options include hostels, village accommodation, and camping. More information on these is given in the following sections.

Mid-range accommodation is generally comfortable and good value, although there are a fair number of overpriced places too. In mid-range establishments you can usually expect a private bathroom (though not always with hot water), a good fan or even air-con, and a reasonable to high standard of cleanliness.

Top-end places tend to be at least as expensive as they would be in the west, and often much more. At this level, you can expect clean rooms with amenities, including private bathrooms with hot showers, functional western-style toilets, air-con and a back-up generator in case there is a power failure. In some of Africa's popular safari areas, top-end lodging comes in the form of luxury tented camps, which offer all the amenities in a more rustic setting.

Hostels & Resthouses

Southern Africa and some parts of North Africa have a decent selection of hostels; in East, West and Central Africa there are very few. The main countries where you will find hostels accredited by Hostelling International (HI) are South Africa, Tunisia, Egypt and Morocco, although there are a few others scattered around the continent. Quality varies widely. Some are clean, well run and well situated, while others are dirty or inconveniently located. Government-run hostels and resthouses tend to fall into the latter category. Prices for a dorm bed range from about US$1 to US$5; some hostels and resthouses also have private rooms, which can cost up to US$15/20 for a single/double.

Guesthouses

In some countries (South Africa for example), the term guesthouse refers to a privately run place, sometimes connected with a private home, which offers rooms – similar to European-style B&Bs. These are generally very comfortable, clean, safe and good value (although not all fall into the budget category). Note that in some countries (Tanzania for example), the word guesthouse refers to a basic budget hotel.

Mission-run guesthouses are scattered throughout sub-Saharan Africa, and are generally simple, but clean, safe and excellent value. They usually cater only to missionaries and aid organisation staff, although some may be willing to accommodate independent travellers if there is extra room.

Hotels

Budget hotels are available almost everywhere except in some resort areas. In smaller towns, they may be the only lodging option. Standards are generally very basic and prices range from about US$3 to about US$15.

You'll find mid-range hotels in almost all capitals and in larger cities or towns. Prices range from about US$20 to US$60.

Almost all African capital cities have at least one top-end luxury hotel. These often belong to one of the major international chains and generally offer the services and facilities (such as a swimming pool, business centre, well appointed rooms) that you would expect from these places anywhere else in the world, although prices are frequently significantly more than those you would pay for a similar establishment at home. Outside of capital cities, top-end hotels may be available in resort areas, and in a few larger cities, particularly in southern and East Africa. In West and Central Africa, there are few top-end options outside the capitals, except in coastal resorts. Expect to pay anywhere from US$70 to US$300 or more for top-end accommodation.

Camping

Camping is possible in most countries and can be a good way to save on accommodation costs, although (with the exception of southern Africa) there are often not good-quality campgrounds in capital cities or major towns. The best camping facilities are found in southern Africa, where many towns also have caravan parks. There are also an increasing number of good, established private sites in East Africa, and almost all national parks in the region have camp sites, although these are often very basic and sometimes very dirty. Some hotels and hostels also permit camping, or provide an area where tents can be pitched. While beach camping is very appealing, it is often not safe. If you are contemplating pitching your tent on the beach or somewhere in the bush, ask around first to find out what the local situation is. If you want to camp anywhere near a village, always ask permission from the chief or village leader.

At established sites, camping generally costs from US$1 to US$5 per person. If showers or other amenities are available, these will usually cost extra.

Village Accommodation

Away from cities and towns, your only lodging option may be with villagers. If you are in a remote area and need to avail yourself of this, you should make your request through the local chief, village leader or most senior person you can find, who in turn will normally arrange something. Africans in general are very welcoming and accommodating, although this generosity should not be taken for granted. If accommodation is offered to you, it is polite to offer some token of your thanks. In some areas, kola nuts or something similar might be appropriate. Otherwise, money is always appreciated: payment should be equivalent to what you would pay for a hostel, simple resthouse or similar hotel room. Do not expect any facilities or much privacy.

Self-Catering

Self-catering apartments are widely available in southern Africa. There are also similar options in East Africa and Morocco, and scattered around other countries on the continent. Facilities vary from comfortable and even luxurious to very basic. Particularly if you are travelling in a group, self-catering options can be a good way to save on lodging and food costs.

Other Types of Accommodation

Apart from the standard accommodation options, individual countries may offer other alternatives. In Tunisia, for example, you can stay in a *ksar* (fortified Berber stronghold). Senegal's Casamance region is known for its local-style lodges *(campements)*, which are ideal for experiencing traditional rural life. In Zimbabwe and elsewhere in southern Africa, accommodation can be arranged at private game ranches; while some of these operate as hunting reserves, the focus at others is on wildlife viewing and photography. In both southern and East Africa you can also find guest farms – converted farmhouses, often in scenic settings or walking areas, which offer comfortable inn-style accommodation. In coastal areas of East and West Africa you'll find simple thatched huts right on the beach, often with only a hammock and a sand floor, and unobstructed sea views.

Other possibilities on the continent are as varied as its many cultures: travellers have arranged overnight lodging in Tuareg nomad tents in Niger; in stilt villages in the rainforests of Madagascar; in mountain refuges in Morocco; on flat-roofed Dogon houses in Mali; in exclusive luxury camps in the Serengeti; and on boats sailing down the Nile.

FINDING THE RIGHT PLACE

Good resources for locating accommodation include your guidebook (assuming you have one that has accurate write-ups which correspond with your own taste), suggestions from other travellers, tourist offices and travel agencies, and local or foreign residents of the area (if they are someone you know or whose recommendations are trustworthy).

In small towns and remote areas, there will probably be only one or two options. Cities and larger towns will offer a wider selection. Factors to consider when deciding on a place include cost, safety, cleanliness and location. Women, particularly those travelling alone, will frequently end up paying a bit more, as the cheapest places often double as brothels or are in unsafe areas.

When choosing a location, consider the distance of the hotel from those attractions or areas you will be visiting, as well as from the bus stand or train station (important if you have an early morning connection, although the hotels closest to the station are often fairly grimy). Also check that the surrounding area is reasonably safe and relatively quiet. Hotels which are only accessed via a dark alley may not be the best bet. Likewise, hotels next to a bus stand or market can be very noisy. If there is a mosque nearby, expect to be woken very early in the morning by prayer calls. If there is a chance your first choice may be full or if you don't have a specific place in mind, select an area with lots of hotels clustered together so that you can walk from place to place to find one.

Inspecting the Room

Once you have found a likely spot, it's always a good idea to ask to see the room; reception areas can be deceptive. If the room is not what you wanted, you are under no obligation to stay – simply ask to see another one, or go to another hotel. If there are shared bathroom facilities, also ask to see these, as many will be in an appalling state even if the rooms are relatively clean.

Some things to check when looking at a room include:

Cleanliness – Look at the overall cleanliness of the room and bathroom. In budget places, check the sheets and bed for cleanliness and insect infestation.

Comfort – Check whether the bed sags or is otherwise uncomfortable. Also determine whether the room is pleasant enough for you to be able to relax in it.

Condition – See if the lights, the fan or air-con, the water taps and the plumbing work. In many dry areas, or during the dry season, water may flow only at certain times of the day. If this is the case, staff are almost always willing to bring a bucket of water for you to wash, but check to be sure. If there are windows in the room, see what they face (an inside hallway offering no ventilation? a noisy bus stop?), whether they open and whether they can be secured shut. Mosquito netting on windows is not common, but it's a great plus.

Safety – Even if the hotel itself is decent, it may not be a good choice if it is in a dicey area or only accessible via isolated streets or alleyways. Alternatively, you may have to calculate a few taxi fares into the room price so that you can get back safely at night. Check the door to see that it can be securely locked, or that it has a place to mount your own padlock. If you are in a multistorey hotel, see if there is an escape route should there be a fire. If the room has windows, see if people can climb into them and whether they are lockable.

Quiet – If sleep is important to you, try to avoid rooms that face a busy street, a market, a bus or taxi stand, a mosque or a noisy courtyard. Also try to avoid hotels or guesthouses with bars, as these tend to be loud. If there is a discotheque, find out what nights it is open. (You definitely won't get any sleep when it is going.) In most hotels, rooms on upper floors near the back of the building will be the quietest.

Negotiating a Rate

Prices are almost always negotiable. Even where there is a posted price list, it never hurts to ask whether a discount is available. It frequently will be, especially if the hotel is not full or if business is slow. In the low season, reductions of up to 50% or more are often possible. If an advertised feature is not working, you could try using this as the basis for a discount. For example, if the hotel has promised running water, but the room you check only has bucket showers, ask for a discount to reflect this.

While most budget places do not attach additional taxes to the tariff (or will already include taxes in the quoted price), many mid-range and top-end hotels do, so be sure to ask what the price is including all taxes.

Also ask whether breakfast is included in the room price. If it is, it's usually on a par with the standard of accommodation, although it is surprising how many upper-end places only serve meagre continental breakfasts. Many budget places serve no breakfast at all.

Checking In

In some countries, you will need to fill out a registration form before checking in. Sometimes you may be asked to leave your passport to ensure that you pay your bill upon check out. However, you will almost always be able to get around this by paying a cash deposit (be sure to get a signed receipt), by paying the bill up front (again, get a receipt), or by leaving some other less valuable form of identification. It sometimes helps to explain to staff that you will need your passport to cash travellers cheques and to carry with you as identification.

At hotels and guesthouses, find out what time you must check out on the day of departure. If you are staying at a private or mission guesthouse or similar type of place, also check to see whether there are any curfews, or what time the gates will be locked.

Security

As in hotels anywhere, avoid leaving valuables – particularly your passport, credit cards and cash – in your room. If you don't want to carry them with you, you can store them in the hotel safe, although these are not always secure. If you have any doubts, one option is to get a signed receipt detailing everything you put in it – although this can serve as some unwanted publicity.

For the room itself, if you have doubts about its security you can sometimes put on your own padlock, although many doors will not have fittings for these. When you go out for the day, be sure that any accessible windows are shut and locked. A small padlock on your bag – while not sufficient to prevent someone who is determined to get into it – will at least deter petty pilfering.

If you are nervous when sleeping, you can always put a lock on the inside of the door or otherwise block the door. Even just placing a chair in front of it will ensure that at least you'll wake up if someone tries to get in.

BATHROOMS & TOILETS
Bathrooms
Most top-end and some mid-range hotels have showers and baths similar to those in hotels back home. Budget places usually just have a simple arrangement – often communal – with a pipe coming out of the wall for a shower, or large buckets from which you scoop water over your body to wash. Very occasionally, you'll find public baths, which generally have a shower, and for which you'll need to pay. Except in South Africa, and in upper-end hotels, hot water is the exception rather than the rule.

In North Africa, you'll frequently find *hammams*, which are Turkish-style bathhouses with sauna and massage. These can be a good alternative to taking a cold shower in a cheap hotel. Sometimes there will be separate hammams for men and women. Elsewhere, there will be one hammam which is open to either sex at different hours or on alternate days. You'll need to bring your own toiletries and towels.

If you're camping or staying in a village, be culturally conscious and don't bathe nude unless you're out of sight of locals. Otherwise, wrap a towel or *pagne* (traditional strip of cloth, like a sarong) around yourself while you wash.

Toilets
In most areas of Africa, particularly in sub-Saharan Africa, public toilets are rare, and in rural areas they're almost nonexistent. Sometimes, the occasional petrol station will have one. Usually the best places to ask are restaurants, hotels or guesthouses; you'll rarely be refused. If you're in a village, ask and someone will usually show you to a private latrine that you can use.

Outside of larger cities, and mid-range and top-end hotels, most toilets are the hole-in-the-ground variety over which you squat. Most have no toilet paper. Instead, you'll often see a bucket of water with a scooper, which is designed for splashing yourself clean. Often these toilets are built over a deep hole in the ground. These are called 'long drops', and the waste matter just fades away naturally, as long as the hole isn't filled with too much other rubbish (such as paper or synthetic materials, including tampons – ideally, these should be burnt separately). Some travellers complain that African toilets are difficult to use, but it just takes a little practice to master a comfortable squatting technique.

In hotels – particularly in the middle to upper range – and in larger cities, you'll also find western-style toilets with a toilet bowl and seat. Standards vary tremendously, from pristine to unusable. Some western toilets are not plumbed in, but just balanced over a long drop. The lack of running water usually makes these cross-cultural mechanisms a disaster.

Even when there is running water, many plumbing systems are not designed to take paper and it's not uncommon to find toilets choked with the stuff. While it's a good idea to carry a roll with you, take care when disposing of it. Often, there will be a bin for used paper next to the toilet. If you're out in the bush or camping, bury the paper or, better still, put it in a strong plastic bag and carry it out with you.

Food

Throughout Africa, the basic meal is a grain-based staple, such as rice, cassava, millet, maize meal or couscous, eaten with some sort of sauce often containing meat, some vegetables or (in coastal areas and by lakes) fish. There are endless variations of sauces, and some are delicious. Along the East African coast, they are often coconut-based. Others (in West Africa for example) are made from groundnuts (peanuts). In southern Africa and in North Africa, sauces are often more like a stew. While some food is quite spicy, in many areas the problem will be that it is too bland. The main complaint that most travellers have about African cuisine – apart from lack of variety – is oil, which is liberally used in preparing many dishes. Generally, you will find the greatest variety of ingredients in coastal areas and in fertile highland regions. Drier areas will have a much more limited selection.

Most cooked food is safe and will not give you trouble, provided you follow basic precautions (see Staying Healthy on the Road in the Health chapter). Be particularly cautious of uncooked or undercooked meat, uncooked and peeled fruits and vegetables, and rice that has been sitting for too long.

If you plan to spend extended periods in remote areas, particularly if you will be trekking or otherwise exerting yourself, it's a good idea to bring along vitamin supplements or dried fruits, nuts or similar items to balance out your diet.

Desserts are not common in most areas of Africa, although sometimes a piece of fruit is eaten after the meal. An exception to this is North Africa, where there is a decent selection of sweets.

LOCAL FOOD

A good way to get acquainted with African cuisine before your trip is to read up on local dishes and ingredients in a guidebook, or in a cookbook specialising on the region you will be visiting. Once in Africa, the best way to sample the food is in the home of a local resident. If you know the hostess, ask if you can accompany her to the market and watch her prepare the meal. Alternatively, ask locals to recommend a place where you can try some good (nonwestern) food, or ask them where they go to eat and what dishes are typical of or unique to the area. To learn more about local dishes, don't be afraid to try food you see being sold on the street, or at least ask vendors what it is that they are selling.

If you are in a village or town during a festival or some other special occasion, you may see some fancy dishes, or others prepared with extras such as meat. For family celebrations, a chicken or other animal is often specially prepared.

Remember that many fruits are seasonal. If you are spending extended time in an area, it can be fun to get to know when mango season is coming or when the best papayas are available.

In North Africa, Morocco is particularly noted for its cuisine, while sub-Saharan Africa, some West African countries and some areas along the East African coast have excellent food.

Types of Eating Places

Apart from being invited to a home, you can also sample local food on the street or in local eateries. Street food rarely involves plates or knives – it's served on a stick, wrapped in paper or in a plastic bag, or pocketed in bread. It is invariably very inexpensive and often excellent. If you are in an area for a while, ask locals where the best cooks are. During the early morning hours in many places the main street food vendors will be ladies with a large pot of piping hot, thin porridge – often made from bean flour and sweetened.

Local eateries are generally very basic places – often just shacks with some benches – serving only one or two menu selections. Ask locals to recommend one. Their biggest attraction is their atmosphere – they are often great places for soaking up a bit of culture and getting to know locals. Another attraction of local eateries in many areas is being able to eat outdoors; the *maquis* (open-air restaurants) in Côte d'Ivoire are a good example of these types of eateries.

A variation on the local eatery is the coffee stall, where clients sit on small benches around a table and drink cups of sweetened Nescafe or something similar, served with bread and butter or some other spread. These are common in West Africa, although you'll find similar places in other regions. You can also get coffee in many areas from the young boys you will see walking around with long-spouted coffee pots fastened onto wire frames with a few smouldering charcoals underneath to keep the coffee hot.

Sit-down restaurants are the next step up from local eateries. You'll usually find at least one in each city and most towns. They are usually more comfortable and generally serve more of a selection, although you miss out on some of the local flavour and the higher prices do not guarantee better food. The less expensive ones tend to be basic chicken and chips outfits. The more expensive a place gets, the more likely it is you will find a range of western and other dishes.

Top-end restaurants are found in all capital cities, in many resort areas and in some larger towns. They will always have a decent selection of western dishes and often some expensive versions of local specialities as well.

Markets & Self-Catering

Africa's colourful and abundant markets is a highlight of a visit to the continent. In larger markets you will find everything from fruits and vegetables to meat, fish, grains and spices for sale. Markets in villages may have a more limited selection – some tomatoes and onions, rice and whatever fruit is in season. Wherever you are, in addition to the daily market, there are likely to be one or two market days each week which attract vendors from the surrounding area and generally offer the best selection of produce (as well as other goods).

In larger towns and cities, you will also be able to purchase food in supermarkets and small convenience shops stocking a range of tinned items and basics. Prices are generally fixed and will almost always be more expensive than at the markets. Supermarkets in larger cities often have a good (though expensive) selection of imported items, including many of the brands you are familiar with from home.

Vegetarian Options

Although vegetarianism as such is often not understood in Africa, it is easy to find food without meat (although self-catering is probably the best option for maintaining balance and variety). Bean dishes are common, as are vegetable sauces, although these almost always have a small bit of meat or animal fat added or are made with a meat stock. In East Africa and parts of southern Africa where there are significant Indian populations the selection is generally better and vegetable curries and similar dishes are fairly easy to find. In North Africa and some other areas, dairy products can be a good fallback; yoghurt is available in many countries.

Fish is easily obtainable in coastal and lakeside areas. Relying on salads and fresh produce is not a good idea, as these are not always available. Salads are also likely to give you stomach troubles, especially if you've just arrived in Africa.

Health Risks

For information on health risks and what you can do to prevent getting sick, see Staying Healthy on the Road in the Health chapter.

WESTERN FOOD

Western food is available at almost all mid-range and top-end hotels and in tourist areas. Apart from this, you will often be able to find local food which comes very close to what you are used to eating at home. Chicken and chips, for example, is available almost everywhere. Senegalese *poulet yassa* (chicken cooked with lemon, onion and garlic) is another meal very similar to western dishes. In West Africa, Lebanese-style *chawarmas* (thin slices of lamb grilled on a spit and served in pita bread with a sauce made from chickpeas) are widely available and can be a pleasant change from rice and sauce. Another change from local fare is Chinese food – there is invariably at least one Chinese restaurant in capital cities.

In areas with large numbers of tourists or expatriates, you may happen across a cafe or restaurant serving European cheeses, home-made wheat breads and jams, and the like. Yoghurt is popular in many areas of Africa and usually inexpensive, though local varieties (which are usually thin enough to drink) may taste different from the packaged brands you may be used to at home.

For breakfast, you can almost always find hard-boiled eggs and some bread. Some coffee stalls also do local versions of scrambled eggs.

Where no western food is available, you can usually vary local fare by seeking out fruit, which is delicious throughout much of the continent.

Drinks

The most common nonalcoholic drinks are soft drinks, tea and coffee. International and local brands of soft drink are sold almost everywhere, including in the most remote villages. You'll also frequently see home-made versions – ginger beer is the most common – although these are often made from unpurified water and best avoided. Outside North Africa (where you can get excellent coffee), coffee is widely available but is usually instant coffee. It is generally served very sweet and often mixed with powdered or canned (condensed) milk. Tea is also available almost everywhere – either made with a teabag or with loose leaves, and is also usually drunk very sweet. In places like Mauritania, northern Mali and Niger, mint tea is the principal drink of the nomads, and it is excellent.

Bottled mineral water is widely available in cities, towns and tourist areas.

Beer – both local and imported brands – is widely available except in Libya and some other parts of North Africa. Local brands are often very good; many travellers prefer them to imported beers. Some better known ones include Star (Ghana and Nigeria), Flag (Côte d'Ivoire) and Castle (southern Africa).

The best wines by far come from South Africa (Western Cape Province), which produces some excellent drops. Other producers include Morocco, which makes some reasonable wines and Zimbabwe, which has some vineyards in the area east and south-east of Harare. Tanzania has a small indigenous wine industry, which is slowly improving though it hasn't yet won any awards for quality. Elsewhere (apart from imported wines, which are available only in top-end restaurants in major cities and tourist areas), the main wine you will find is palm wine, which is especially popular in West Africa. This is made from the sap of the oil palm tree, and comes out of the tree already mildly fermented. Sometimes yeast is added and the brew is allowed to ferment overnight, which makes it much stronger.

Other local brews include millet beer and banana beer. Distilled drinks, such as those made from the fruit of the cashew tree in much of south-eastern Africa, are also fairly common – although also fairly lethal, and in many places illegal as well.

Sightseeing

Outside of North Africa, there are few areas of the continent which are classic 'sightseeing' destinations with magnificent temples, museums or similar sights (although these do exist). Rather, Africa's main attractions are its people, its fascinating cultures, its landscapes and its wildlife. The best way to appreciate these is to take time in a place, get to know locals, visit markets, soak up life on the street, try to attend some festivals or special events, do some trekking or biking, and generally try to leave a more programmed western mentality at home and let the continent's rhythms become your own. Even in North Africa, which abounds in 'sights' – from the Egyptian pyramids and the temples of Luxor to Morocco's imperial cities – the best parts of your visit may well be the times spent away from tourist attractions.

One way to strike a balance is to identify a few sights or regions you'd like to visit, and then plan around that. Don't try to pack in too much. By limiting yourself to one or two attractions a day, and by keeping the overall area you plan to cover on your trip to a manageable size, you will have plenty of time to absorb a bit of the culture. In warmer regions, try to plan your day to have any sight-visiting in the morning when it is cooler, and leave the languid afternoon hours for more leisurely poking around and relaxing.

Guidebooks are one of the best tools for finding out whether there are any sights you'd like to see in a country, and for familiarising yourself in advance

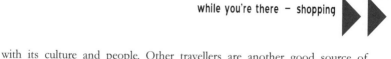

with its culture and people. Other travellers are another good source of information. Guesthouse and hotel proprietors can also be very knowledgeable and helpful.

GETTING OFF THE BEATEN TRACK

While some parts of the continent – for example, East Africa's famous wildlife reserves and some of West Africa's coastal resorts – have become inundated with foreign visitors, there are vast stretches which you can explore in relative isolation (expect facilities outside of the more heavily visited areas to be fairly basic). Even in popular destinations, just taking time to get to know locals and spending a while in one place will give you a different perspective. In some of the continent's tourist hot spots, it is amazing how few visitors actually take time to do this and instead just rush from one 'attraction' to another in an air-con 4WD. Talking to people, getting to know what is important for them, learning how local life is lived – all these can be the most enriching part of a trip, though they require some time and effort.

If you do venture into off-the-beaten track areas where locals may be very unused to tourists it's important to behave in a culturally responsible manner. This means being courteous to local communities, greeting all those whom you encounter with respect and friendliness, and answering questions politely (even if you are asked the same question many times). Always consider how your actions and behaviour would affect the local community if dozens of others visitors came and acted the same way.

Hazards

When travelling in out-of-the-way areas, some prudence is called for. Don't travel in countries experiencing civil or military conflict without first getting a thorough briefing on the situation from your embassy or other knowledgeable sources. Before heading to Africa, research the regions you will be visiting (good sources are guidebooks and the Internet) to find out if there is anything you should be aware of. Update this information once you arrive in the region.

If you are in a country which has landmine problems, stick to well worn paths and don't go trekking off into the bush. If you will be spending extended periods in very remote areas, let someone know where you are going and give some thought to how you would get out in the event of illness or emergency.

Shopping

With its many markets and wide array of textiles and crafts, Africa offers a bounty for shoppers. Before purchasing souvenirs or other items, take time to inform yourself about quality and price. One way to get an idea of quality is to look in an art museum for a standard of comparison. Alternatively, try a good art shop. Compare the quality of their items with that of similar items on the street or in markets, where prices will be more reasonable. To learn what a 'fair' price would be, find out how much other travellers paid or see what the price of the item is in a fixed-price shop (if you can find one). Once you decide to purchase, in most places you'll then need to bargain (see Bargaining in the Money Matters chapter for some tips).

Some other tips for good shopping include the following.

- Do some research before leaving home. If you know in advance that you would like to come back with some African artwork, get a book on African art or on the art of the country you will be visiting, and learn about its symbolism, major craft areas etc. Unlike western art, almost all African art has a use. Knowing the context in which an object is used is important in terms of both appreciation and detecting artificially used or aged pieces.

- Try to save most of your purchases until the end of your trip. This will help you to avoid running short of money. It will also allow you time to get a better idea of what is available, so that you can better distinguish quality from cheap mass-produced items, and determine reasonable prices. Plus, it will save you from having to carry your purchases around with you for the remainder of your travels.

- If you will be purchasing heavier items, consider shipping them home; the process is fairly reliable in most countries. If you plan to purchase expensive items or large quantities, find out before leaving what the duty-free allowances of your home country are and whether there are any exceptions for goods from developing countries. For more on shipping, see Shipping Things Home in the Staying in Touch chapter.

- If you will be flying home, keep airline baggage requirements in mind. If your luggage exceeds the weight limits, you will have to pay an extra fee.

- Most African countries have regulations prohibiting the export of items which are authentic and valuable. Since very little art purchased by nonexperts fits this description, it's more a matter of being hassled by customs than doing something illegal. Nevertheless, in some countries (Mali and Ghana for example), you must get an export permit for genuine antiques (and sometimes also for articles which just look old); these are usually available from the national museum in the capital city. Some countries (Botswana is one example) require export permits for any item made from animal products, such as feathers, ostrich eggshells and game skins.

- If you are buying textiles and plan on having something made up, get a recommendation for a good tailor. Before purchasing cloth, see if the piece is irregular or otherwise flawed, and remember that many of the textiles you may see are imported (from Europe, India or elsewhere). Keep in mind that some cloth (such as Ghanaian adinkra cloth) is not meant to be washed, and some dyes, including indigo, may not be colour-fast. Soaking cloth in vinegar or very salty water may stop the dye running, but this method should only be used on cloth of one colour.

- Many woodcarvings are stained brown or black, usually with shoe polish or hot tar. Some are then passed off as mahogany, ebony or other expensive woods. If you are looking for the real thing, it's worth doing a quick test for genuineness – either wetting your finger and rubbing it on the wood (if it is shoe polish, your finger will be darkened) or, to test for tar, smelling it. If something is being sold as an antique, question whether it really is antique before shelling out a lot of money. Marks made by sandpaper can often 'age' a piece of wood so well that even experts may have difficulty knowing it is genuine.

- Woodcarvings are vulnerable to cracking and insect infestation. New wood must be dried slowly; wrapping your purchases in plastic bags with a small water tray enclosed is one technique. Tiny bore marks with white powder are a sign of powder-post beetles (frequently confused with termites). There are three remedies – zapping the beasts in a microwave oven; putting it in the freezer for a week; or drenching it with lighter fluid. You could also try fumigating items. If customs officials find evidence of insect damage on your wooden objects, they may seize the items and you will have to pay to have them fumigated.

- If you buy cassettes on the street, try to listen to them first or buy only those sealed in cellophane, as these are normally fine. Unscrupulous vendors think nothing of selling blank or very poor-quality tapes.
- Don't buy any items made from protected animals or plants. Never buy items made from ivory, coral, tortoise shell and the like.
- Minerals and gemstones, including malachite, tourmaline, tanzanite and rose quartz, are popular purchases in some areas. Before investing in some of the more expensive

Crafts & Souvenirs

West Africa
- beads and beadwork
- jewellery (mostly gold, but there is some good silverwork in areas near the Sahara; the best is that crafted by the Tuareg and the Moors)
- masks (especially good in Côte d'Ivoire)
- textiles (including kente cloth and adinkra cloth from Ghana; Yoruba textiles from Nigeria; and Korhogo cloth from Côte d'Ivoire)
- traditional musical instruments and drums (Guinea and Senegal are good places to look for the kora – a lute-like stringed instrument; Senegal has a good selection of drums)
- woodcarvings

Southern Africa
- basketry (especially good in Botswana)
- beaded San jewellery (Botswana and Namibia)
- gemstones and minerals
- leatherwork
- mats and woven grassware
- soapstone carvings
- spices (Madagascar)
- textiles
- weavings
- woodcarvings

North Africa
- copper and brassware
- herbs and spices (Morocco)
- leatherwork (Morocco, and to a lesser extent, Tunisia)
- rugs and carpets
- silver jewellery (the tribal jewellery of Morocco is among the most beautiful in Africa)
- textiles

Central Africa
- beads (although the selection is not as good as in West Africa)
- decorated gourds (Cameroon)
- jewellery
- leatherwork (northern Cameroon)
- woodcarvings and masks

East Africa
- baskets
- beaded tribal jewellery (Kenya and Tanzania)
- carved wooden chests (Zanzibar)
- spices (Zanzibar Archipelago)
- decorated gourds
- fabrics and batik
- soapstone carvings
- woodcarvings (Makonde carvings from Tanzania are particularly popular)

stones, be sure you know what you are doing or get recommendations from knowledgeable local residents about an honest dealer. The same precautions apply when buying gold or silver, although in much of sub-Saharan Africa – where the preferred metal in most areas is gold – gold quality tends not to be a serious problem and prices generally don't vary much from country to country. In contrast, quality can be a major problem with silver. Much of the silver you will find in Central and West Africa is not sterling, so it tends to tarnish quickly. The best silver craftsmanship is found in and near the Sahara, where the Tuaregs, the Moors and other nomads prefer silver to gold (which they believe brings bad luck). In most areas of the continent, both silver and gold are sold by the gram, and the artwork is included in the price.

- Try to support local craftsmen. Local artisans cooperatives, where the artist will benefit directly from the sale, are good places to do this. If you can negotiate directly with the artist, not only are you likely to get a better price, but the artist is likely to be able to keep a higher percentage of the profits.

- Look for locally made items, rather than those imported from elsewhere in the region or beyond. The locally made items will generally be less expensive and often of better quality (as opposed to mass-produced 'African' crafts), and you will be supporting local industry.

- If you find the hassling and bustle of markets intimidating, try doing your shopping in the early morning when the stalls are just opening, the vendors are still in low gear, and temperatures are not too hot. If a trader is being too persistent and you don't want what they are selling, just politely decline and move on. Once you move into another trader's pitch they will usually back off. If they keep pulling you and you find it offensive, let them know.

- In a few markets, pickpockets can work the crowds or gangs of youths posing as merchants can surround tourists and snatch bags and cameras. Don't wear jewellery or carry bags in markets, and have your money belt well concealed. See Hazards & Safeguards in the Issues & Attitudes chapter for more information about precautions to take.

- Almost all towns of any size will have daily markets. However, the most colourful markets are those which are held once or twice weekly, and which attract not only local traders but those from a large surrounding area, including neighbouring countries. Try to find out in advance (from a guidebook or by asking locals) when the main market days are in the town where you are heading. (If you are travelling in more remote areas, transport to and from a town is generally much easier immediately before and after market day.) In many places there are also permanent covered markets, as well as tourist-oriented 'craft' markets; sometimes these are in the same place.

Getting Around

Distances in Africa are vast and the means you choose for covering them will be an important element of your trip. In general, comfort and speed correlate directly with price: if you want to get somewhere fast and with a degree of comfort, it will be expensive. In some places, you will not have an option, and there will be only one way of reaching a town or region. Safety is another consideration: trains, for example, are generally safer than buses and taxis. Before heading to a region, research the various transport options. In addition to a guidebook, other travellers are a good source of information.

No matter what form of transport you use, always allow yourself plenty of extra time. Transport seldom runs on schedule, and all sorts of things can come between you and punctual arrival at your destination. Travel during the rainy season — by whatever means — is particularly vulnerable to delays.

AIR

Flying is generally the fastest and the most expensive option, and sometimes the most comfortable. It can spare you hours or days if you're pressed for time, and save you from the exhaustion resulting from travelling hundreds of

---

Numero Uno

'You won't make it', they screamed after me. 'You will die alone in the desert ...' I took my foot off the clutch and the car skidded off. According to my guidebook, it was just 50km to Merzouga and the 'magical desert landscape' of southern Morocco. All I had to do was 'follow the line of telegraph poles'. 'A terrible journey', the boys had threatened. 'Sand storms, hidden holes, treacherous pistes ... '

But the guide fee they were demanding was exorbitant, and it wasn't even open to negotiation. It was a sort of tourism terrorism: threatening, frightening and extorting. 'You think you can cross the great Moroccan hammada in that?' they had shouted next, hooting with laughter at my tiny Fiat Uno. They had picked a bad target; I'd developed an almost fanatical attachment to my little car, as travellers often do to rented vehicles. It had seen me through snow and water, grass, gravel and rock, and now it would see me through the desert sands of Merzouga.

'You're a woman, you'll not last ten minutes in the desert', they had mocked, finally. 'The haze will confuse you; the desert will bewitch you ...' It was the last straw. Off came the handbrake and away we went. And it no longer seemed to matter if we made it or not. A question of honour? Perhaps. After all we were in Morocco. I set my sights on the shimmering telegraph poles ahead, then looked at my watch. Just one hour before dusk. I had driven in the desert once before.

I tried to remember the form: keep a steady course, not too slow, not too fast ... If you hit a sandy patch, drive in curves from side to side ... Never brake, or change gear, or you'll start to sink ... The white, sandy areas were easy to recognise. There was a large one just ahead. I got up a good speed, roared into it weaving like a snake, arrived almost at the end then ground to a halt. The car was up to its gunnels. I began to dig at the sand until my knuckles and fingertips bled. It was packed like concrete under the car and around the axles.

I got up and looked around: not a house, road, person in sight. On the horizon, the sun was beginning to sink from view, and suddenly it felt rather cold. Leaning against the car, I thought for a minute. I hadn't seen another vehicle the entire journey. Would one come tomorrow? Then something caught my eye. Looking up, I saw a small Berber boy with clear eyes, standing before me with his lurcher dog.

In the fast fading light, we began to dig. It was hard work. Two hours later, and now dark, the car was free. In the distance I could see lights: Merzouga was close. I turned back with a smile to the Berber boy. But beyond the footprints and pawprints in the sand, there was nothing of him that remained.

Frances Linzee Gordon
LP Author, UK

Flying in Africa

The capital cities of most African countries are serviced by both international and domestic or regional carriers. Quality varies widely, particularly among regional and domestic carriers, and flights within Africa can range from smooth and pleasant to nightmares of inefficiency and delays. South African Airways, for example, offers topnotch domestic and international service. Ethiopian Airlines also enjoys a very good reputation for both international and domestic service, and is considered to be one of the best airlines in Africa. Other airlines, however, can be fairly precarious operations. Air Ghana and Air Guinée are both notorious for cancellations and delays (although sometimes they offer surprisingly decent service). Many airlines have a bit of both ends of the spectrum: flights which depart on time, run smoothly and are well staffed, as well as those which are delayed for hours or sometimes days for no discernible reason. In general, the less developed the country and the smaller the fleet, the worse the service is likely to be.

Following are some tips about what to expect when flying in Africa.

Tickets – In Africa, it's often better to buy tickets through a travel agency, rather than directly from the airline. Travel agents can explain the various options and the price is usually the same. They may also be able to help you with refunds if something goes wrong. Before purchasing your ticket, find out what the airline's cancellation policy is. While some offer refunds, many will accept no responsibility for delays or cancellations.

Reconfirmation – It's critical to reconfirm any flight originating in Africa – even if the ticket office or travel agency tells you this isn't necessary. If you are flying on an airline with a reputation for cancellations, delays or overbookings, it doesn't hurt to reconfirm several times, including the day before and the day of the flight. When reconfirming, always ask whether the departure time is still as originally scheduled (although in many cases, information about cancellations or major delays won't be available until you are already at the airport).

Check-In – Check-in can be hassle-free, or it can be mass chaos. On smaller airlines with frequent cancellations, flights often get hopelessly backed up. Overbookings are common to start with. Add to this a cancelled or delayed flight, and you will have dozens of people in the check-in hall desperate to get on board the next flight, which invariably will not have enough seats to accommodate demand. No matter what airline you're flying, always arrive promptly for check-in.

Seating – On many national airlines, there is 'free seating' (ie no assigned seats). If you are choosy, try to be among the first to board the plane in order to get the seat you want.

Departure Taxes – Most African countries charge a departure tax, which averages about US$20 for international flights, and between nothing and about US$5 for domestic flights. You will need to pay this after check-in, and before passing through immigration. Find out beforehand (you can check in your guidebook or ask at the local airline office or travel agency when reconfirming your ticket) how much the international departure tax is, and what currencies are permissible. Many countries require this to be paid in US dollars, while others accept local currency. Try to have the exact amount on hand, as getting change can be difficult. Domestic departure tax is always payable in local currency.

Inspection – Many countries have no real system of inspection: you are simply waved through. In others, the process can be onerous. If there is an initial inspection (prior to check-in) it will be to see if you are taking any prohibited or restricted items out of the country. This includes ancient artwork or other items requiring a permit; prohibited items (drugs and the like); and excessively large (vendor-sized) quantities of local items.

Sometimes, underpaid officials use the inspections process as a chance to try to elicit bribes from tourists. After searching your bag, they will ask what you might have 'for them', or alternatively, try to convince you that you've violated some regulation (see Bribery in the Issues & Attitudes chapter for more on this). As long as your luggage is in order, the best thing to do is be compliant with requests to open your baggage, and to maintain a respectful and friendly demeanour. As long as you are not trying to export anything you shouldn't be, there is no need to cough up any cash; just stand your ground politely but firmly. Also remember that in some cases, officials may search your bag simply out of genuine curiosity.

Export Regulations – Many countries have regulations governing export of artwork or other crafts. Be sure to check in advance (your guidebook will be a good source of information) to see whether you will need to arrange any permits before leaving the country.

Exit Permits & Emigration – You will often need to fill out a departures form (available at the airport). Emigration formalities are usually straightforward.

Money – Before heading to the airport, try to exchange or get rid of as much extra currency as possible. While many, but not all, international airports in Africa have foreign exchange counters where you can reconvert local currency, it's best not to count on these being open.

Many countries restrict the amount of local currency you can take out, and some (Guinea for example) are fairly rapacious in confiscating any extra they may find.

Departure Lounges & Airport Facilities – Once you have passed through check-in, inspection and emigration, you will find yourself in the departure lounge. There is usually a TV, a souvenir shop and a duty-free shop.

If you are feeling ill or have special needs, most airports have a more comfortable VIP lounge (often with air-con), which you may be able to use. Despite the lack of special facilities at most airports in Africa, airport staff generally go out of their way to accommodate disabled travellers and others with special needs.

Cancellations & Delays – These happen even under the best of circumstances, but are the norm in many countries in Africa. Small fleet sizes mean that if one airline is down or has been diverted for official use, the whole flight schedule is disrupted. Repairs and maintenance often take longer than they might elsewhere due to scarcity of parts. Weather can also be a factor: violent storms during the rainy season or – in Mauritania and some areas of the Sahel region – severe sand storms during summer and the harmattan season (when dry dusty Sahara winds blow towards the West African coast) can result in cancellations or delays. In countries which rely heavily on the tourism industry to fill planes, there may be frequent cancellations in the low season when flights are emptier. At the other end of the spectrum is the high season when flights may be extremely overbooked, to the point where having a confirmed reservation is no guarantee that you will actually get on the plane. If you are travelling during any of these times, expect more cancellations and delays than normal.

Strategy – Flying in Africa doesn't have to be a traumatic experience. Even if you are unlucky enough to be booked on a flight which is delayed, cancelled or horrendously overbooked, you can minimise the hassles by getting to the airport on time for check-in (this will increase your chances of actually getting your confirmed seat on an overbooked flight). Other steps to take include:

- Bring a good book, a bottle of water and a piece or two of fruit (to while away potentially long hours at the airport).
- Plan at the outset on spending more time in the airport than you want to, and try to get comfortable with the idea.
- Don't schedule other critical plans for the day.
- Avoid having tight connections with other flights.

kilometres along bumpy, dusty roads. It's also sometimes the only feasible way of getting from one country or region to another. This is the case between Morocco and West Africa (where the land route is difficult for those without their own vehicle); between Cameroon or Gabon and São Tomé (boat connections are unreliable); between Egypt and Kenya (civil war in southern Sudan); and between West and East Africa – due to problems with getting into and across Congo (Zaïre). During the rainy season, many areas which are normally accessible by road may be reachable only by air. Since you will miss out on landscapes and cultures when flying, a good option is to combine air travel with surface transport, perhaps by flying one or two of the longest stretches and then using surface transport in between.

While there are some good deals available, flying within Africa is generally not cheap due to the great distances involved. Some sample fares are: Casablanca (Morocco) to Nouakchott (Mauritania) US$420; Cairo (Egypt) to Nairobi (Kenya) US$570; Abidjan (Côte d'Ivoire) to Addis Ababa (Ethiopia) US$780; and Nairobi to Johannesburg (South Africa) US$530. Return fares are usually almost double the one-way fares. Some airlines also offer student or youth fares.

See the boxed text 'Flying in Africa' for more information and tips.

Charter Air Services

Charter air services are a popular transport option throughout Africa for those with a bit of spare cash, and there are privately run charter companies in almost every country. In addition to the fact that charter services are generally reliable, they are also able to reach many areas and towns that are inaccessible to the larger aircraft used by national and regional carriers (which require longer runways). If you are travelling alone or with one other person, charter services may be prohibitively expensive. However, if you have a group of four or five – enough to fill a small plane – costs can be very reasonable. Even if you are a solo traveller, it's worth checking with charter companies about the route you want to fly. If another group has booked an entire plane but will not be filling all the seats, they may be willing to sell (or give) you a place.

BUS, TAXI, MINIBUS & PICK-UP

Bus and taxi are the most common forms of public transport between cities and towns in Africa. They are usually located at bus and bush taxi parks (called *gare routière* in Francophone countries, 'garage', 'lorry park' or 'motor park' in English-speaking countries, and *paragem* in Portuguese-speaking countries) in major towns and cities. In smaller places, you may find them near the market or at the start of the road leading towards the destination. Some bus companies are state-owned and others private; many countries have a mixture of both.

Taxis are always privately owned, although generally not by the driver. Sometimes on buses, and more often on taxis, there will be a small luggage fee. Minibuses are basically just another form of taxi. Pick-ups are used primarily in rural areas where bus, taxi and minibus services are scarce.

Bus

Long-distance buses (also called 'coach', *car* or *grand car*, depending what part of the continent you are in) vary in size from about 35 to 70 seats. In some countries, and on heavily travelled routes, they can be comfortable and efficient, with reliable service and fixed departure times. In other places, especially on lesser travelled routes, vehicles may be in poor condition, tend to break down frequently, stop often to let passengers on and off, and have no discernible schedule: departures are when the bus is full, or when the driver feels like it.

In general, bus travel is usually quicker than going by rail, but more expensive (than 3rd class train travel) and not as safe. On routes serviced by both buses and taxis, bus fares will tend to be cheaper than the taxi fare. In some places you can (or must) book a seat in advance, while in others you just show up. In either case, it's always advisable to arrive at the bus stand about an hour before departure.

When the one-seat-per-person rule is respected, bus travel is usually relatively comfortable (although throughout the continent drivers tend to go disconcertingly fast). However, on many routes, buses are jammed with people, produce and everything else in the aisles, and get only more crowded as the journey progresses.

Taxi

A share taxi or bush taxi (*taxi brousse* and sometimes *grand taxi* or *taxi collectif* in Francophone countries) is essentially a small bus. They are widely used

Tips for Bus Travel

- Fares are almost always fixed. However, on popular routes, or at the end of a day, one bus company may try to undersell its competitors by reducing prices. If you feel you have been quoted too high a fare, just ask the ticket salesman if you can see his receipt book.
- For popular long-distance routes, departure times are often fixed. On less travelled routes, buses leave when full; some can take an entire day (or several days) to fill. Very rough routes or less popular destinations may only be served once or a few times weekly.
- On some international routes, buses do not actually cross the border; you will have to get one bus to the border, walk across, then pick up another bus on the other side.
- In some countries, the same route may be covered by good-quality express services and more basic 'local' or 'ordinary' services. Express will be more expensive, although also more comfortable and faster.
- Bring earplugs along if you want some quiet, as most long-distance buses have either a cassette player or video which will be turned on full volume for most of the trip.
- Many long-distance buses have a compartment underneath the bus for baggage. On the better lines, access is well controlled. On many local buses, baggage will be tied to the roof. In either case, don't leave any valuables in your pack. Putting a small padlock on the fasteners and taping up the whole thing in a waterproof cover is good for deterring petty pilfering and for keeping dust out of your pack. Keep a watch out for your luggage at stops, especially if it is being unloaded and reloaded to access other passengers' bags.
- Food is almost always available at stops along the way (sold by vendors through the windows), so have some small change ready.

throughout Africa (except in southern Africa, where taxi service is generally limited to local transport within towns and cities). Almost without exception, these taxis leave when full, rather than according to a timetable. As soon as one car leaves, the next one starts to fill. Depending on the popularity of the route, the car may take half an hour or several days to fill. Fares are generally slightly higher than bus fares, but are still very reasonable.

Over much of the continent, share taxis are seven-seater Peugeot 504s. In some places (eg Morocco), you'll see old Mercedes or other vehicles. In some countries the seating limits of the car are observed, while in others they are packed to overflowing. If a bush taxi looks like it's going to get uncomfortably full, you can buy two seats for yourself (it's simply double the price). Likewise, if you want to charter the whole car, take the price of one seat and multiply it by the total number of seats available.

Note the distinction between long-distance taxis (taxis brousses), which run between cities and towns, and local taxis, which operate within a city or town.

Minibus

Many routes are served by minibuses, which seat about 12 to 20 passengers and are just a variation on the bush taxi. In some areas (such as parts of southern Africa) they are used instead of taxis, and in other countries in addition to taxis. Names vary throughout the continent. In Kenya, minibuses are called *matatus*, in Mozambique *chapa cem*, in Egypt microbus (or 'meecrobus'), and in parts of southern Africa *taxis*. Fares on minibuses are usually cheaper than in standard bush taxis, as they can take more passengers. However, they are also usually slower, as they stop more and, in countries where there are police roadblocks, there are more passengers to search.

Pick-Up

Pick-ups (*camionette* in Morocco and Tunisia, *bâché* – if it is covered – in some Francophone countries) are sometimes the only form of transport available, especially in rural areas. They officially take about 16 passengers (including two or three in the front cabin), but are invariably stuffed with people and baggage, plus chickens and all sorts of other goods. Some are covered, with wooden seats down the sides, while others are open and all passengers just stand in the back. A ride in a pick-up will invariably be slow and uncomfortable. It's also guaranteed to be unpleasant unless you adopt the African attitude of laughing each time the vehicle descends into yet another pothole or grinds to a stop with yet another mechanical difficulty. To let the driver know when you want to disembark, ask a passenger near the front cabin to bang on the window. Alternatively, on many pick-ups a driver's assistant will ride in the back. Let him know when you want to disembark and he will signal the driver.

TRUCK

In many countries, as you venture further into rural areas the frequency of buses or bush taxis drops dramatically. Sometimes the only option will be to ride on local trucks. In most cases, a fee is payable to the driver, roughly equivalent to the public transport fare; riding up front in the cab will be more expensive than in the back on top of the cargo. Rides in the back can be fairly comfortable if the truck is carrying cotton or rice in sacks, less so if the cargo is logs or oil drums.

HITCHING

As anywhere in the world, hitching in Africa is never entirely safe and is not recommended. Travellers who do decide to hitch are taking a small, but potentially serious risk.

That said, many travellers do hitch their way around Africa, particularly sub-Saharan Africa. To minimise problems, take advice from other hitchers first. Hitching in pairs is obviously safer, and hitching through less salubrious suburbs, especially at night, is asking for trouble. Women should avoid hitching in North Africa unless they have a male companion – and in general on the continent, women should be cautious when hitching alone. In most cases, payment is expected; keep public transport fares in mind when determining the cost.

See also the warning about professional hitchers in the boxed text 'Tips to Avoid Being a Scam Victim' in the Issues & Attitudes chapter.

TRAIN

Train networks are not extensive in Africa, but in some areas they offer a good (and safer) alternative to road travel, both between countries or within a country. Some services are relatively comfortable, with 1st class coaches which may be air-conditioned. Some even have sleeping compartments with two or four bunks. Other trains have 2nd or 3rd class only, and conditions can be very crowded and uncomfortable, with no lights, no toilets and no glass in the windows (no fun on long night journeys). Some trains have a restaurant on board, but you can usually buy food and drink at stations along the way.

First class fares may be as much as double the bus fare; advance booking is almost always required. Second class fares are generally roughly equivalent to bus fares on the same route. Third class will be very inexpensive, and almost never require advance booking.

West African countries with train services include Mauritania, Senegal, Mali, Côte d'Ivoire, Ghana, Burkina Faso, Togo, Benin and Nigeria. In southern Africa, train travel is based largely upon the South African network and its 'extensions' into neighbouring countries, including Namibia, Botswana and Zimbabwe. There is also rail service in Zambia, and between Mozambique and Malawi and Mozambique and South Africa. Madagascar has a small rail network with a few beautiful rides. In East Africa, there are trains in Kenya, Tanzania, Uganda and Ethiopia. In North Africa, there are rail networks in Morocco, Egypt and Libya. In Central Africa, Cameroon and Gabon have rail systems.

Good Train Journeys

The famous South African *Blue Train* running between Pretoria/Johannesburg and Cape Town is one of the world's most luxurious train trips. Other less expensive (and much less luxurious) routes frequently used by travellers include those linking Dar es Salaam (Tanzania) to Kapiri Mposhi (Zambia); Dakar (Senegal) to Bamako (Mali); Ouagadougou (Burkina Faso) to Abidjan (Côte d'Ivoire); Cairo to Aswan (Egypt); Nairobi to Mombasa (Kenya) and Kampala (Uganda); Harare (Zimbabwe) to Gaborone (Botswana) and on to Johannesburg (South Africa); Johannesburg to Maputo (Mozambique); and Fianarantsoa to Manakara (Madagascar).

CAR & MOTORCYCLE

Having access to your own wheels can be a tremendous advantage: you will be able to reach areas that would be difficult to get to by public transport and you will probably travel in greater comfort and speed (as well as more safely). Rentals are fairly straightforward, though expensive. Bringing your own vehicle to Africa requires a certain amount of advance research and paperwork.

Some general information on driving in Africa is outlined below. For information on renting a vehicle, or on bringing your own, see the relevant sections later in this chapter.

- Road conditions vary from excellent (in South Africa for example) to abysmal (throughout vast areas of sub-Saharan Africa). During the rainy season, many roads become impassable or only passable with difficulty, even in a 4WD.
- In addition to poor road conditions, you will frequently encounter people, animals and stopped vehicles on the road. Driving skills in many areas are substandard, and other vehicles are often in very poor condition (no brakes, no windshield etc). Since most Africans in rural areas do not drive, there is little appreciation for concepts such as minimum braking distances and the like. Be especially vigilant for children running onto the road, and for livestock.
- Off-road driving (and driving on gravel or sand roads, or in salt pans) requires skill and practice. Read up on the proper techniques in a good guidebook before setting out.
- Throughout West Africa and in the North African countries covered in this book, driving is on the right-hand side. In most of southern Africa and in East Africa, it is on the left.
- Wherever you are driving, you'll need to ensure that you have a good collection of spares. It's also helpful if you or another passenger are mechanically competent – there are many long, deserted stretches of road. One advantage of renting a car is that these issues will (or should) be taken care of for you.
- Some countries (Mozambique for example) have seat belt laws and look for every opportunity to enforce them against foreign drivers, so buckle up if you want to avoid paying a fine or a bribe.
- Police and military roadblocks are a feature of road travel in many African countries. Sometimes these are harmless and won't delay you at all. In other cases, they are simply ill-disguised attempts to elicit bribes, with onerous searches and long delays. If you get stuck in one of these, maintain your patience and humour and you should soon be on your way (unless, of course, your paperwork is out of order, in which case you will certainly have to pay some sort of 'fee' to clear things up). Before setting off on a journey, make sure the vehicle's insurance and other paperwork is in order, particularly if you will be crossing a border.
- Avoid driving at night whenever possible.

- The vast majority of roads are not more than two lanes (ie just wide enough for two cars to pass each other), which means overtaking is a frequently used manoeuvre – and one of the most frequent causes of accidents. Never overtake unless you can see that the road ahead is completely clear.

Renting a Car or Motorcycle

It's possible to rent a vehicle in most countries in Africa. Many capital cities have representatives of international groups such as Avis or Hertz as well as smaller independent operators. In smaller cities, rentals can often be arranged privately. Places to ask include the reception of your hotel or a travel agency. Motorcycle rental is also generally arranged privately.

Wherever you rent, it is likely to be expensive. In most countries count on at least US$50 per day for 2WD, and up to US$150 per day or more for 4WD. Smaller operators usually charge less than the international chains. Often this is because their vehicles are older and sometimes not well maintained. Sometimes, however, it's simply because their costs are lower and they can do a better deal. In most cases, you will need a credit card to make a large deposit. Be sure you have the proper licence required in the country where you will be driving (either your own or an International Driving Permit).

Rental regulations are often more restrictive than in the west. Unlimited kilometre rates, for example, are rare and often you will not be able to take the car over the border; look into all these things before renting. If you do plan on taking the car over the border, you will need to tell the rental agency in advance so they can arrange the necessary paperwork.

A common option in many countries is to hire a car with driver. In addition to freeing you up for sightseeing, this means that someone else will be able to deal with breakdowns or other problems on the road. In some cases, hiring a chauffeur actually works out to be less expensive as you will pay less for insurance.

If you rent through an established agency, insurance arrangements will generally be specified in the rental contract. In privately arranged deals, however, this aspect is often ignored. To avoid being liable for the bills, be sure to clarify the insurance arrangements in advance; it never hurts to put them in writing. Also with private rentals, be sure that the vehicle or motorcycle you rent is mechanically sound, especially if you will be taking it without a driver.

In general when renting vehicles (especially when contemplating taking a rental without chauffeur), keep in mind that road conditions outside the capitals are often bad, and roads are frequently not tarred. In addition to being aware of the road hazards discussed in the introduction to this section, you'll need to be adept at map reading as there are very few signposts. Should you need to contact your rental company in case of a breakdown, remember that in rural areas phones are very few and far between, and there is no national agency that will rush to your assistance (yet another reason to take along a chauffeur).

Taxi Hire

In many countries, a good alternative to renting a car is to hire a taxi by the day. This will probably cost less (anywhere from about US$20 to US$60 per day in most places), and if the car breaks down it will be the driver's problem. In many countries, you will have the choice of hiring a city taxi (see Local Transport later in this chapter) or a long-distance taxi (bush taxi). Be sure the vehicle is mechanically sound before agreeing to anything. Even if you know nothing about cars, just looking at the bodywork or listening to the engine will give you an idea.

The price you pay will have to be worth the driver taking it out of public service for the day. Unless you have a straightforward journey, it's generally best to work out a fixed daily rate for the car plus extra for the petrol. If you want a deal including petrol, don't be surprised if the driver reduces the speed to a slow trot and complains incessantly at every detour. It can be difficult to find a car with a working petrol gauge, but in most places in sub-Saharan Africa, you can work on the assumption that the tank will be empty when you start. Allow for 10km/L on reasonable roads, and a bit worse on bad roads.

Bringing Your Own Vehicle

Bringing your own car or motorcycle to Africa requires considerable advance research and paperwork. While a *carnet de passage en douane* is not required for

Around Tunisia with a Police Escort

I'd been to Tunisia several times before, but I'd always opted to travel by public transport. This was the first time I'd hired a car, and I was feeling decidedly nervous as I pulled out of the Tunis Airport carpark in a shining new Renault Clio with only 8000 km on the clock. I come from a small country town, and dread city driving – especially in a new car. I was still counting the number of lanes on the airport road when I discovered that I was in the wrong lane. I was trapped in a lane bound for the city centre, and I wanted to turn right onto the main road to Bizerte, 65 km to the north. Changing lanes involved a fair bit of hooting from other motorists, and I wasn't particularly surprised when one of a group of attending policemen waved for me to pull over and wait. I hauled out my passport and driving licence and waited, wondering which element of the driving code I'd violated.

The policeman strolled up, greeted me with a smile and asked where I was going. 'Bizerte,' I said, unsure of his motive. He showed little interest in my documents, but plenty in my destination. 'Can I have a lift,' came the reply. Before I had a chance to reflect on my latest position re hitching, he was seated beside me in the car and we were heading north. He had just knocked off work and was heading home. He was 28, and lived with his wife and two children at his family's home in one of the small villages set amid the rich farming country southeast of Bizerte. He couldn't afford a car on his police wages, and always travelled to and from work this way. So, I was to discover, did a lot of his mates in the police and national guard. He proved to be in no great hurry to get home, and was delighted to act as a guide as we detoured around the countryside searching for good examples of ghorbis, the traditional mud-brick and thatch communal farm dwellings found in the area.

David Willett
LP Author, Australia

some North African countries (including Morocco), it must be prearranged for numerous sub-Saharan countries. Some West and southern African countries, however, issue a free Temporary Import Permit at the border on entry.

The purpose of a carnet is to allow you to take a vehicle into a country without paying the duties which would normally apply. It guarantees that if a vehicle is taken into a country but not exported, the issuing organisation will accept responsibility for payment of import duties. Carnets can only be issued by national motoring organisations. Most require a financial guarantee for the carnet − often well in excess of US$1000. You will also need insurance to get a carnet, and if you decide to sell the vehicle while in Africa, you will need to make arrangements with customs authorities for the carnet to be cancelled.

Since transcontinental overland travel in Africa is restricted (see Overland Routes in the Planning chapter), if you want to drive your vehicle from Europe your only option will be to drive into West Africa via the Western Sahara. If you want to have your own vehicle in other parts of the continent, you will need to ship it to a port such as Mombasa (Kenya) or Cape Town (South Africa). Costs for shipping a vehicle from Europe range from US$500 to US$2000 depending on vehicle size and destination. Apart from cost, your biggest problem is likely to be security − many drivers report theft of items from the inside and outside (such as lights and mirrors) of their car. Vehicles are usually left unlocked for the crossing and when in storage at the destination port, so you should chain or lock all equipment into fixed boxes inside the vehicle. In many countries, getting a vehicle out of port is frequently a nightmare, requiring visits to several different offices where stamps must be obtained and mysterious fees paid at every turn.

Some resources to check for additional information on driving your own vehicle in Africa include: *Africa by Road* by Bob Swain & Paula Snyder; *Africa Overland* by David Brydon; the *Adventure Motorcyclists Handbook* by Chris Scott; and the *Sahara Handbook* by Simon Glen.

Buying a Car or Motorcycle

Some travellers buy a car or motorcycle once in Africa, use it to tour a region, and sell it at the other end of the trip. In addition to arranging purchase, registration, tax and insurance, you may also have to arrange a carnet (see Bringing Your Own Vehicle) and buy additional liability insurance at borders.

BICYCLE

Cycling is an excellent way to travel in Africa. In addition to being inexpensive, healthy and environmentally sound, it will enable you to get closer to the cultures you are visiting. By staying mostly in small towns and villages, you will have more opportunities to interact with local people, eat local foods and experience African life. In general, the more remote the areas you visit, the better your trip will be.

A traditional touring bicycle (fitted with the widest and strongest tyres it will take) is fine for many areas, including most tar roads and some good dirt roads, and may be best if you will be covering long distances. If you plan to do shorter trips off the main roads, or to travel exclusively on secondary roads, a mountain bike may be more suitable. Whichever bike you bring, you will need to be fully self-sufficient with spare parts as, outside South Africa, little is available for western-made bicycles. It's also best to bring your own bike with you from home. While you occasionally will be able to buy a good second-hand bike (try inquiring of expatriate residents), most available locally will be inadequate for long-distance touring.

If you are interested in just doing short day stints, it's better to rent a bike once in Africa. Decent bikes are sometimes available for rent in tourist areas. Otherwise, in villages and towns, local people are often willing to rent their bikes for the day to travellers. Good places to inquire include your hotel, the marketplace or a bicycle repair business (every town has one). Bikes arranged this way will generally be single-speeds and in less than optimal condition, but fine for doing a bit of local sightseeing. Sometimes you may get lucky and find an imported mountain bike, with gearing and in good condition.

Some organisations to contact for additional information on cycling in Africa include:

Cyclists' Touring Club
(☎ 01483-417217; fax 426994; email cycling@ctc.org.uk)
(a British organisation providing members with details on cycling in many parts of the world)

International Bicycle Fund
(☎/fax 206-628-9314; email ibike@ibike.org; www.ibike.org/bikeafrica)
(a US-based, socially conscious organisation which arranges tours and provides information)

Following are some considerations to take into account when contemplating getting around Africa by bicycle:

- Distances are long. In some areas, towns may be widely spaced, with few resources available in between, so you'll need to plan your food, water and lodging needs. If you haven't done much long-distance cycling, consider starting off in an area where distances between major points of interest are manageable.
- Try to plan most of your cycling for early morning or evening hours when temperatures are coolest. The best time of year for cycling is during the dry season when roads are in better shape and temperatures often cooler.
- Carry sufficient reserves of food and water (at least 4L to 5L) with you; in many areas you will not be able to rely on finding purifiable water sources.
- Heavily travelled roads can be dangerous, and trucks lethal. Basic self-preservation skills include staying aware of what is coming up behind you (or on curved roads, in front of you) and being prepared to take evasive action into the brush.
- If you plan to camp near settlements in rural areas, request permission from the village chief. Even if you don't have a tent, he will usually be willing to help find you a place to stay.

- In addition to carrying sufficient spares for your bicycle, you should be versed in bicycle repair. Punctures will be frequent: take at least four spare inner tubes, some tyre repair material and a spare tyre, as well as a large supply of tube patches.
- Consider combining cycling within a region with public transport. In most places, bicycles can be transported on buses (sometimes also on taxis, depending on the size of the vehicle and the rest of the load), as well as on ferries. On trains, you may have to give up the bike to the baggage department; be sure it is well secured. On planes, the normal rules apply (see Bicycles & Surfboards in the Tickets & Insurance chapter), though you may have to do some convincing to get it onto some African airlines.

WALKING

For the majority of Africans, recreational walking is unheard of. However, since walking is the cheapest method of transport, people often resign themselves to foot travel, particularly in rural areas where hitching is difficult. It's not uncommon to meet someone without luggage who's heading off to a market or to visit friends or relatives in a village 30km away.

This said, there are some excellent areas for walking on the continent. These are generally those where villages are closely spaced, and those at altitude (where temperatures are cooler). A good example is Guinea's Fouta Djalon plateau, where you can spend days walking from village to village. Madagascar's central plateau region is another excellent walking area, as are south-western Tanzania near Lake Malawi (Lake Nyasa); the mountains of Morocco; northern and western Cameroon; and parts of South Africa.

If you want to cover large areas of the continent on foot, keep in mind that you will need to carry sufficient food and water to tide you over until the next village. Safety may be a concern in a few areas. Climate is also a consideration.

BOAT & FERRY

Travel by boat or ferry can be a pleasant alternative to the bumps and dust (or mud) of road travel. Some of the more popular ferry trips include those between Tanzania and Zambia along Lake Tanganyika; between Tanzania and Malawi as well as between various points in Malawi on Lake Malawi (Lake Nyasa); between Mwanza and Bukoba (both in Tanzania) on Lake Victoria; and between various points in Ghana on Lake Volta. Many ferries are very crowded, particularly in deck class. For some comfort, it's generally a good idea to book a 1st class cabin, which often is reasonably priced for what you get, and which generally has shower facilities in addition to beds. It's also a good idea to bring along all water and some food; some ships have a basic restaurant, but many do not.

There are countless possibilities for boat trips. Some good ones include those along the Nile (one of the classics); along the River Niger in Mali (another classic) or between Guinea and Mali; along the Gambia and Senegal rivers; along the Ogooué River in Gabon; on the Zambezi in southern Africa; along the Orange River between Namibia and South Africa; and along the

Tsiribihina River in Madagascar. In addition to river trips, locals throughout the continent – especially along the West African coast, and in East Africa between Kenya and Mozambique – frequently use boats to travel between coastal towns. Apart from luxury cruises on some of Egypt's waterways, boat travel is generally very inexpensive, but usually rudimentary, without shade or other amenities. Although you will often be able to buy fruit and other basics at stops along the way, bring whatever food and water you may need. If you will be travelling via nonmotorised boat (eg *dhow* or *pirogue*), count on the journey taking longer than you plan and bring along sufficient reserves.

Both boats and ferries often make frequent stops for loading and unloading cargo and passengers. If you are travelling with several other people, consider renting out an entire boat.

LOCAL TRANSPORT
Bus & Minibus

Almost all capitals and major cities have a network of minibuses connecting the city centre with the suburbs. Some also have a regular city bus (ie large bus) network as well. Vehicles and routes are often not well marked, and it can take a few days until you get oriented enough to be able to get around by public transport. Almost everywhere, vehicles are extremely crowded and prices are very inexpensive. If you're not sure of the price, ask around or watch what locals are paying. In most countries a driver's assistant will collect fares, either during the trip or when you disembark. Sometimes stops are fixed, but in many places you can embark and disembark where you want.

Shared Taxi

Shared taxis are a common form of local transport in many cities. Some run on fixed routes, and are effectively a bus, only quicker and more comfortable. Others go wherever the first passenger wants to go – additional passengers will be picked up only if they are going in the same direction. (For these, shout the name of your destination as the taxi passes; if it is going your way, the driver will stop.) Once you have the hang of the shared taxi system, you'll find it's a quick and inexpensive way to get around cities, and will probably miss it when you're in a country which doesn't have it. Fares generally vary depending on the distance travelled, and are not meter-based in most cases. Check in advance, or watch what other passengers are paying. If you happen to be the first person in the taxi, make it clear that you do not want a private hire (variously known as 'charter', 'town trip' or *deplacement*, depending on where you are).

Private Taxi

In some countries or cities, taxis will have meters. Otherwise, bargaining is required or you will be quoted the legally fixed rate, which in some cases is not negotiable (though in many others it is). Be sure to agree on a fare with the driver before getting in. Try to get an idea of a reasonable fare before negotiating; asking a local with no vested interest is one way. In many places, fares are more expensive at night, although this should be factored into the agreed fare rather than tacked on after the ride. You should not have to pay extra for luggage unless you have a particularly bulky item.

Other Forms of Local Transport

In some areas of Africa, donkey cart or ox cart (*zebu* cart in Madagascar) is used by locals for transport. These are excruciatingly slow and often very uncomfortable, although at least for the first few minutes of the ride they have an exotic appeal.

In a few places in eastern Madagascar you will also see *pousse-pousse* – rickshaws which are used for getting around flat areas of some towns.

Organised Tours

In many countries, especially those which see large numbers of tourists, tour operators can arrange anything from city excursions (not very common) to trips around the country. The disadvantages are cost (organised tours will be much more expensive than using public transport to get around) and that you will miss out on a lot of local colour. The advantages are that getting around will probably be easier and more comfortable, and everything will be arranged for you.

When travelling in Africa, you may hear the term 'bush telegraph' – referring to the fact that no matter how remote or isolated an area may seem, news spreads fast. Not only does news spread fast, but communication lines are far more open than they may appear – though just not using the telecommunications technology you may be familiar with.

When travelling between two towns via bush taxi, it's common to see people along the way stop the cab to give the driver a letter or note to pass on to someone a few villages down the road. If one person in a village is going on a journey, he or she will invariably be asked by others in the village to pass on news and other messages at their destination. Although most rural Africans do not have telephones in their homes, there is usually a telecom facility in most medium-sized to large towns, many of which can even connect internationally.

So, while those at home may think you are journeying to the ends of the earth when you set off for Africa, in reality you are heading for a place where people have their own lives and have been staying in touch and communicating with friends and relatives in distant places – including overseas – for centuries. As a traveller in Africa, it's not particularly difficult to stay in touch with home while you are on the road, and a small amount of effort can go a long way toward easing the concerns of those back home about your welfare. In capital cities and major towns, your main resources will likely be telephone, fax, and – increasingly – the Internet, which is working its way slowly but surely into many African cities. In more remote areas, unless you know someone with a satellite phone, you may have to rely on radioing someone with a telephone who can then pass on your message, or to sending mail back with someone who is heading to a capital city or somewhere else where it can be posted. Whatever method you use, it's important to remember that – unlike at home, where friends or family can usually pick up a phone to call you – in most cases you will need to take the initiative, as they won't be able to track you down while you're on the road.

Following are some general tips on staying in touch for travellers who may be concerned about this part of their journey to Africa. The remainder of the chapter surveys a few of the more common communications options.

- When planning your trip, set aside a portion of your budget for phone calls. International telephone calls from most countries in Africa are much more expensive than they are in the west.
- Contact your telephone company for a list of countries which offer 'direct dial' or call-back service to your home country. You can save money by trying to ring home primarily from places that offer these services, as you will be billed at your home country rates, rather than at expensive African rates.
- Arrange to call home at least sporadically to let others there know you're still alive and well. If you hear that there's been some sort of natural disaster, coup d'etat or

an otherwise unsettling occurrence in the region where you are travelling, let friends and family know you're OK.

- Consider letting friends and family know when you will be in remote areas and out of touch for an extended period. You may also want to call them upon your return to let them know that you made it back in one piece.
- If you are on the road for a long stretch, write up one good detailed letter every month or two and send copies of it to all those at home.

Telephone

Telephone systems in Africa range from excellent satellite networks to ancient lines where all you can hear is static. In most cases, connections are easier from a capital city, although not always. Sometimes it doesn't matter where you call from, and in a few rare cases – eg Zimbabwe – it may even be advantageous to save your calls for rural areas, as rates there are cheaper.

Before phoning internationally, see if the country where you are offers less expensive off-peak rates on evenings or weekends. Also see whether reverse charge (collect) calls are possible, or if it's possible to link up with your home country's direct dial system. Finally, remember that there is likely to be a time difference between where you are and your home country – the person you are calling may not enjoy being awakened at 3.00 am.

WHERE TO CALL FROM

In most countries in Africa (unless you know someone living there who has their own phone), you will need to go either to the telecommunications office (usually at the post office), to a private telecommunications centre or to a hotel to make an international call. Telecom/post offices are usually the least expensive option and hotels the most expensive. While an increasing number of countries have card telephones, these are not widespread; where they do exist, they are often near the telephone office. Lonely Planet's eKno card, specifically aimed at travellers, provides international calls to an increasing number of countries in Africa. In some countries, you can also dial internationally from pay phones, although it's not generally very practical, as you will need a pocketful of coins. A major exception to these generalisations is South Africa, where in many areas you can access Home Country Direct service from pay phones or bill calls on your credit card. Private communication centres generally charge slightly more than the post/telecom and often do not offer discounted weekend or evening rates, even if the national telecom entity does, but are usually more efficient. In some places they also offer fax and even email and Internet facilities.

Various types of calls are possible, including direct (person to person) calls, operator-assisted calls, reverse charge (collect) calls, Home Country Direct calls and credit card calls. No matter which type of calling method you use, it is frequently cheaper if you can arrange to have the person you are dialling ring you back. This will almost always be possible at hotels and frequently also at telecom offices or telecommunications centres (although at the latter you may be required to pay a per-minute fee for receiving a call).

TYPES OF CALLS

Direct (person-to-person) calls – This is the easiest and usually the cheapest way to call. Direct calls can be made in some countries from international pay phones or card phones and from private phones in countries that have International Direct Dialling (IDD) facilities. You first dial the IDD number, then the country code, then the area code and number of the party you want to reach. If you're dialling from a pay phone, be prepared with a pocketful of coins to avoid getting cut off. Card telephones are a better option if they are available. Phone cards are usually sold by the telecom office (usually at or near the post office) or by vendors near the card phone. The cards come in different denominations. Find out before buying one what the minimum charge is for an international call. If you are leaving the country and still have unused value on your card, sometimes you can sell it to enterprising vendors. Otherwise, if you won't be back, you can always give it to some of the young boys who hang out by the phones – they will in turn sell it in increments to people wanting to make shorter, local calls.

Operator-assisted calls – In many African countries you cannot make direct international calls – you'll have to go through an operator. You can place such calls from hotel phones and telecom offices. The normal procedure if you are dialling from a telecom office is that you give the operator the number you need. There will be one or several phone booths (or perhaps just a phone on the counter). Once the operator has gotten through, they will indicate which booth you should go into to pick up your call. In some countries the calls are timed automatically, while in others, or in rural areas, the operator will just look at their watch and tell you the amount you owe afterwards. In some places you'll need to pay for a three minute minimum at the outset; others require you to pay the whole call at the outset and will disconnect the call once you have reached the maximum time for which you've paid.

Reverse-charge (collect) calls – Call an operator and give them the number you'd like to call and your name. If they're able to raise someone at that number who agrees to foot the bill, you'll be connected. This can be expensive, so make sure the other party understands what's involved. Also, if you intend to make a lot of reverse-charge calls to the same party, you may want to arrange a schedule so they know to be there for your call. Many African countries do not offer reverse-charge calling. Where it is possible, you can generally make reverse-charge calls from some pay phones, hotel phones and telephone offices.

Home Country Direct calls – In countries that offer this service, you dial a specific number to bypass local operators entirely and speak directly to an operator in your home country, who can then arrange a credit card or reverse-charge call. Home Country Direct service is available in few African countries. You can find Home Country Direct numbers in most guidebooks or by contacting your telephone company at home. You can place these calls from hotel and pay phones or from communication centres (usually for a small charge). Telephone offices may allow you to make such calls but you should clarify at the outset that the local operator understands what you want and that you will not be charged.

Post

African post offices range from reliable and efficient to lethargic. In general, letters (without enclosures) and most postcards ultimately reach their destinations, although it sometimes takes a long time. Delivery times to Europe, North America or Australia can vary from less than a week to several months.

Post offices in major cities are usually the most reliable and efficient. In some countries there are also specialised international or express post offices, which are your best bet for good, reliable service. As letters sent from rural post offices usually take much longer to reach their intended destinations, you may want to do most of your mailing from the central post offices of larger towns.

RECEIVING MAIL

The best and most common way to receive mail while you're on the road is to have it sent poste restante. If you have an American Express card or American Express travellers cheques, you can also have it sent to American Express offices along your route. In some of the more developed countries, you can try receiving mail through a hotel or guesthouse; check first to be sure the proprietor is willing to hold mail, and arrange to have the mail addressed to a specific person who will ensure that it does not get thrown away. Finally, if you want to have something important sent, or you need something in a hurry, you can have an international courier service like Federal Express or DHL ship it and then pick it up at one of their local offices.

Poste Restante Poste restante is a good way to receive letters while on the road, provided you give those back home a rough idea of your itinerary. You simply ask people to send their letters to the general post office of a city along your route, with your name (surname in block letters and underlined) and the words 'poste restante' written clearly on the envelope. For example, if your name were Jane Blank, a letter addressed to you in Nairobi would look like this:

> <u>BLANK</u>, Jane
> Poste Restante
> General Post Office (GPO)
> Nairobi
> Kenya

In French-speaking countries, substitute 'La Poste Principale (PTT)' for 'General Post Office (GPO)'. In Portuguese-speaking countries, substitute 'Posta Restante' for 'Poste Restante' and 'Os Correios Geral' for 'General Post Office (GPO)'.

Normally, poste restante letters are filed under your surname. However, confusion can arise and letters are sometimes filed under your given name. If a letter you're expecting can't be found by searching under the first letter of your last name, try looking under the first letter of your given name.

In most countries you will need to show your passport when picking up a letter at poste restante. Most post offices also charge a small fee. In some post offices there's a separate room or counter for poste restante; in others, just ask for it at the main desk. As small, rural post offices may be unfamiliar with the concept of poste restante, it's usually better to ask people to send letters to general post offices in larger towns and cities along your route.

Many post offices will only hold mail for a month or so before either discarding it or returning it to the sender, though there are some that will hold it for up to four months. Thus, you'll need to give people a fairly accurate itinerary if you want to receive their letters. If you're not sure of your plans, a good solution is to ask people to send copies of the same letter to two or three different post offices along your route, although the postage for this can add up.

It's possible to receive packages by poste restante, but this is unreliable in most places. In some countries, when you receive a package it will have to be inspected before being turned over to you. You'll usually be notified of a package via a slip of paper in the letter box corresponding to your surname. You'll probably have to fill out some forms when receiving a package this way and you may have to pay some import duties. Of course, any prohibited items will be confiscated and you could land in trouble. As with letters, if you want something important sent or you're in a hurry, you should probably have the item shipped by an international courier service like Federal Express or DHL.

Because some poste restante offices are poorly supervised and other travellers can search through the mail by themselves, it's possible that things will get stolen. As a general rule, never have anything of value sent poste restante.

SENDING MAIL

The procedure for sending letters and postcards in Africa is the same as that for sending mail in your home country. Be sure the address is written clearly; if you want them sent airmail, indicate this clearly somewhere near the address. At the post office you can have the letters weighed and posted with the appropriate amount of stamps. Then, either hand the letter in at the counter or place it in the appropriate bin. Note that in some countries, dishonest postal workers have been known to remove uncancelled stamps from letters and resell them. If you have any doubts, just ask that the stamps be cancelled in front of you. If the post office has a franking machine (which takes the place of stamps and marks the appropriate postage on the letter), you can have the letters franked instead.

While it's cheaper to send letters surface (sea) mail, it's unreliable in many places in Africa and very slow. Important items can be sent by registered mail, which is available at some GPOs for a slightly higher fee than regular airmail. Some countries also offer Express Mail Service (EMS) from larger post offices. Items sent this way usually reach international destinations within a week.

SHIPPING THINGS HOME

In Africa's more developed countries, shipping things home is a relatively painless procedure, but elsewhere, be prepared to spend some time filling out the paperwork and getting things properly packaged.

The three main choices for shipping things home are via air or sea mail from the post office, through shipping agents, and through international couriers such as Federal Express or DHL.

Post Office

For heavy items, air mail can be prohibitively expensive. Surface mail generally takes three to six months and sometimes longer, and is not always reliable.

In most African countries, you will have to package the item yourself before sending it. Packing materials for smaller items are generally available from vendors on the street outside the post office. For larger items, try asking for boxes at a shop selling imported goods. In many countries your package may need to be inspected before shipping, so leave it unsealed until you get to the post office.

Shipping Agent

If you have many things to send home, or even just one very heavy item, it can sometimes be less expensive and often more reliable to have it sent through a shipping agent. Unlike the post office, which charges by weight, shipping agents usually charge by space, with one cubic metre being the minimum. Goods sent by shipping agents take about the same time to reach their destination as goods sent by post office surface mail. In theory, the goods should be shipped to your home address (try to clarify this before shipping).

In practice you may have to go down to the nearest port and pick them up. When the goods arrive at the other end and are inspected by customs, import duties may be levied against you. In some cases, you won't be allowed to pick up the goods until these have been paid; in others you'll be sent a bill. To reduce the risk of incurring import duty on clothing, you should remove all pins and wear the item at least once in Africa before sending it home.

International Courier Services

International courier services such as Federal Express or DHL are available in most capital cities and should be used for any important or valuable items you may want to send home. Although anything larger than a letter will be very expensive, it is the best way to guarantee arrival.

Fax

There are fax machines at most urban post offices in Africa (usually at a separate window or in a building near the post office), as well as at private communications centres and in mid-range and top-end hotels. Some countries charge a flat rate per page, while others charge based on the time it takes for the fax to go through.

It's also possible in most cities and many larger towns to receive faxes at the post office. The system works in a manner similar to poste restante, with incoming faxes (sometimes) registered and then held until you pick them up. More often than not, there is no sort of organised filing system – you will just have to sort through a box. Most post offices charge a fee (usually not more than US$1) for each page received.

Email

Email is the cheapest and most efficient way to keep in touch while you're on the road. Email services are available in an increasing number of major cities and towns in many – though not all – African countries. Some countries, such as South Africa, Tanzania and Egypt, have Internet cafes where you can log onto the Internet or send email, while others have private telecommunication centres with Internet and email facilities. In a few places, where the Internet is just catching on, you will be able to send messages only if you know someone who has a private business with email/Internet facilities.

To receive email while on the road, you can set up an account with a free email service such as Lonely Planet's ekno service, Yahoo or Hotmail. However, with only a few exceptions this will mean an international call to access your Internet service provider (ISP) – see Using Your Existing Account.

Alternatively (or in places where there are no facilities for accessing the Internet), you can have people send email to various Internet centres or email accounts at private communications centres along your route. Once you arrive in a town, seek out email facilities, and then forward the address to those with whom you want to stay in touch.

FREE EMAIL SERVICES

An email account can be easily set up on any Internet-capable computer either back home or while on the road. It doesn't need to be your own – just any one that is hooked up to the Internet. Once you register with one of the services, they will give you an email address and password. Email sent to this address is stored on the service's computer. You can then access this account and read your email from anywhere in the world that has Internet access.

To open an account, simply log onto the online address of ekno (www .ekno.lonelyplanet.com), Yahoo (www.yahoo.com), Hotmail (www.hotmail.com) or another service and follow the instructions on the screen. While in Africa, you can use this account both to send and receive email. If you already have an Internet account with an ISP at home, it's also possible to configure your free email service to access that account, meaning that you can read email sent to your regular email address. Look under the Options menu of your free email service to see how to do this. You can also configure your existing account to forward your email to your free email service account.

USING YOUR EXISTING ACCOUNT

Some of the larger Internet Service Providers, such as CompuServe, AOL and IBM, have dial-ups in cities around the world, including a few in Africa. If you have an account with one of these providers and are in one of these cities it's possible to access your email with a local call. Otherwise, you will need to make a regional or long-distance call. In reality, the international dial-ups are of limited use to travellers in most parts of Africa (unless you are in the city where they are located), as it's often much easier to dial Europe or the USA (where there are also dial-up numbers) than to dial up an ISP within Africa. If you do want to access your own account, it's generally easier to do it through a free email account.

HAVING EMAIL SENT TO YOU WHILE ON THE ROAD

An alternative to setting up a free email account, and an option to use in places where email services are available but no Internet log-ins, is to use the email addresses of Internet cafes or private email centres along your route. To arrange this in advance, you'll need to locate Internet cafes willing to hold email for travellers located in the cities you plan to visit. You can search for these using The Internet Cafe Guide site (www.netcafeguide.com) and can then put together a list of the email addresses of the Internet cafes on your route, along with a rough itinerary of your trip. When you arrive in each city, go to those places and hopefully you'll have a stack of email waiting for you. Be sure that the sender puts your name in the subject box (last name in capital letters) of the message so that the owner of the Internet cafe can file it properly. Just like regular poste restante, you should check under your first name as well in case your message was misfiled. Remember that there is very little privacy with this method.

As there are not yet many Internet cafes in Africa with these services, to receive any email you may need to wait until you arrive in a town to locate a private email centre, then notify those at home of the address, along with the dates that you will be staying there.

Africa Online

While many of your experiences with (tele)communications systems in Africa are likely to leave you wondering how anyone ever gets any business done, there are some happy exceptions. One is the surprisingly fast growth of Internet services. While Internet is not relevant for the vast majority of people on the continent, it has gained a firm – if limited – foothold, particularly in capital cities and within the tourism and hotel industries in some areas.

A few countries – notably South Africa, and to a lesser extent Egypt and perhaps Morocco – are well ahead of the rest, with widespread availability of Internet cafes or other commercial hook-ups in most major cities. In others – such as Tanzania and Senegal – access is possible in capital cities and some major towns, and facilities are rapidly expanding. In many of the approximately 20 countries targeted by the US government's Leland Initiative, which aims at expanding Internet accessibility on the continent, progress is occurring rapidly.

In addition to Tanzania and Senegal, these countries include Guinea, Malawi, Uganda and Zambia. At the other end of the spectrum – Niger is a good example – access exists but is very costly and limited to private subscribers. In a few countries on the continent, including the Central African Republic, Libya and Gabon, no access is possible.

In general, if you want to access the Internet, your best bet is to start your search in the capital city. Check your country guidebook for specific information about Internet facilities in the region you will be visiting and ask around, as the situation changes rapidly in this area. The business centres at top-end hotels are generally good sources of information, as are resident expats and local businesses (especially computer or technology-related businesses).

When you do find access, expect that connection times will be much slower than those you may be used to, lines may frequently fail or that it may take numerous attempts to get a connection. External factors such as heavy rains also often make connections difficult. In most places with Internet facilities, costs are reasonable (averaging between US$2 and US$6 per half hour for Internet access), especially compared to international telephone and fax charges.

Media

It can be easy to lose track of events in the rest of the world while you're travelling. For some people this is a welcome relief, while for others, being cut off from news sources can be unsettling. Yet, although it may be more difficult to keep abreast of local events in your home country, it's often fairly easy in Africa to keep up with global affairs.

RADIO

In most parts of Africa, locals rely much more on the radio for news than on newspapers. In part this is due to low literacy levels, and in part due to the difficulties of circulating papers in rural areas. BBC World Service is probably the most popular news service, along with Voice of America. Both services have feature hours on Africa, and can be valuable sources of information about what is happening in the region you are visiting, as well as for international news. Bringing a portable shortwave radio along with you is a good idea if you like to keep track of events in this way. It's also possible to catch rebroadcasts of some BBC or Voice of America programming on local stations. To find the frequencies of local stations and for scheduling information, check the web sites of the BBC (www.bbc.co.uk/worldservice) and Voice of America (www.voa.gov).

TELEVISION

Many hotels and guesthouses in Africa have a television on which you can watch local programming, some of which may be in English. If they have a satellite dish or cable TV, you'll also be able to watch CNN or BBC world news.

NEWSPAPERS & MAGAZINES

If you are travelling in one of Africa's English-speaking countries, local English-language newspapers can be a source of international news, as well as entertaining and useful means for gaining insights into local life and culture. They are also useful for checking on exchange rates.

In the capital cities of many countries it's also possible to find international newspapers such as the *International Herald Tribune*, as well as international editions of *Time*, *Newsweek* or other magazines. Good places to check for these are top-end hotels, large bookshops and airports. Hotels generally have the most recent editions; copies at airports and bookshops are often dated.

THE INTERNET

If you are in a place with Internet access, this can also be a great source of timely news. Most major newspapers maintain web pages where the day's top stories are posted – see the Internet Addresses appendix for online news service addresses.

COMING HOME

Whether you've been away for a few weeks or a few months, returning home after travelling in Africa will require some readjustment. The longer you have been away, the greater the transition will be. To minimise the 're-entry' shock, try to prepare yourself in advance by knowing what to expect and how to deal with it. By approaching the transition with the right frame of mind, you may even find that your travels act as a springboard to a positive new stage of your life.

Post-Holiday Blues

Post-travel blues affect most travellers to some degree. Some find that life back home seems bleak and boring. Others experience a sense of letdown, or have difficulty focusing on things around them. Many factors contribute to such feelings:

- Not being able to communicate the experiences you've had in a way that makes them exciting to others.
- The difficulty of reconciling the realities of life in Africa with the realities of life in your home country.
- The need to readjust to a daily routine after an extended period of being confronted with the challenges of life on the road and in another culture.

There is no single antidote for overcoming these blues, although many travellers find plunging back into things one of the best remedies. A healthy dose of realism is also a useful tool for fighting the depression caused by these disparities – as you cannot travel all the time, you may as well get on with your regular life.

In some cases, there may also be a physiological component involved, which can manifest itself in depression, fatigue, emotional imbalance or inability to sleep. These symptoms – which can be chemical in nature – are similar to those seen in Seasonal Affective Disorder (SAD), which affects many people each year during autumn and winter. Since they are often rooted in physiological changes brought about by lack of sunlight, a good way to combat both SAD and post-travel blues is to get out in the sunshine and do some exercise. Some people also recommend increasing your daily intake of vitamins B and C, while others prescribe the herbal remedy St John's Wort, which is thought to act as a natural antidepressant.

If the feelings you experience go beyond this, and you find yourself suffering from deep or long lasting depression, seek the assistance of a doctor rather than trying to combat it yourself. Likewise, if you're suffering from any physical symptoms – loose bowels, chronic fatigue, skin inflammations or anything else – seek medical attention as soon as possible, as you may have picked up something while in Africa. If you have spent an extended period in Africa, a physical examination by a tropical medicine specialist is always recommended once you return home, whether or not you are experiencing any symptoms.

Making the Transition

A good way to ease the transition to life back home is to give some thought to it while you're still on the road. You'll have a lot of free time while travelling to think about what you want to do when you get back. You may even want to sit down and make a list of things you want to accomplish. Viewing your time on the road as a period for charging your batteries, getting a new perspective and realigning your priorities will help you in setting up a post-travel framework.

If you've decided to make some changes in your life, the first few months after returning home is a good period in which to implement them. By incorporating some of the things that you have learned during your travels into your daily life, you'll feel that the time spent on the road was not just a holiday or an isolated experience, but contributed something of more lasting value.

Remembering Your Trip

It is surprising how quickly your trip will fade once you return home. The best way to prevent the memories from sliding into oblivion is to try some or all of the following suggestions:

- Make a photo album with prints from your trip. Choose the best ones and put them in chronological order, along with captions or comments. If you've taken slides, sorting them and writing up a few notes and comments will help if you want to give a slide show.
- Keep in touch with people you met along the way. This includes both locals and fellow travellers. If you've promised anyone copies of your pictures, send them as soon as you can. Once a few months go by, you'll never get around to it. You may also want to send thank-you letters to some of the local people who went out of their way to help you.
- Enhance your knowledge of some of the countries you visited. Take a course at your local university or go to the library and take out some books. Even if it's just one small facet of the country or region, such as Moroccan cooking or West African drumming, you'll find that the courses and your reading are much more meaningful once you've encountered the real thing.
- Study the language of a country that particularly interested you. Whether it's just for personal interest or because you'd like to go back some day, learning a language is one of the best ways to deepen your acquaintance with another culture.
- If you kept a journal during your travels, go back and re-read it. Even more than pictures, the words you wrote while on the road can bring your trip alive again months or even years later. If you find that your journal reads like the best travel novel you've ever read, you can always write up some of the better passages and send them off to magazines as potential travel articles.

BENIN

Benin, a small nation on the Gulf of Guinea, doesn't make the headlines much these days. Yet during the 19th century, Dahomey, as the country was known until 1974, was the seat of one of West Africa's most powerful kingdoms, feared far and wide for its slave raids and for its elite female fighting force recruited from the wives of the king. Benin is also the birthplace of voodoo, and was known in Europe and beyond for its occult religious practices. During the 20th century, the country was notorious for its political instability and earned the dubious distinction of having the third highest number of coups in Africa.

Although things are calmer these days, Benin still possesses much of the mystique that captivated earlier imaginations. Its government has stabilised and it's becoming an increasingly popular travel destination, offering voodoo ceremonies, vibrant markets, lagoon stilt villages, and people with a distinct naturalness and vitality. While roads and infrastructure are no better in Benin than in neighbouring countries, its compact size and growing economy make it relatively easy to negotiate.

WHEN TO GO

The best time to visit Benin is between late November and February, when the rains have stopped and temperatures are not yet too high. March and April are also dry, but hotter, and dusty harmattan winds spoil the views. Northern Benin, abutting the Sahel, is less humid than the southern part of the country, but uncomfortably warm during

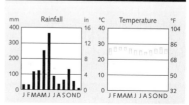

PORTO NOVO

March and April. Its dry season usually lasts into May.

Some secondary roads in the south may become impassable during the heavy rains between April and July. Parc National de la Pendjari is open only from 15 December to 15 May. The best wildlife viewing time is at the end of the dry season, from March to early May.

At a Glance

Full Country Name: Republic of Benin
Area: 112,622 sq km
Population: six million
Capital City: Porto Novo (population 200,000)
People: More than 40 ethnic groups, including Fon (40%), Adja, Yoruba (10%), Bariba (20%) and Somba
Languages: French (official); major indigenous languages include Fon, Adja, Yoruba, Bariba and Dendi
Religions: Most follow traditional religions; about 17% are Christian and about 15% Muslim, while voodoo is practised by about 70% of people
Government: Constitutional republic
Currency: West African CFA franc (CFA)
Time Zone: One hour ahead of GMT/UTC
International Telephone Code: 229
Electricity: 220V 50 Hz; most sockets take plugs with two round pins

HIGHLIGHTS
Culture

Benin's major attraction is its culture. A good place to start is Abomey, the former capital of the Dahomey kingdom and site of the restored Royal Palace and museum. Porto Novo, Benin's present-day capital, is another worthwhile stop, with some colonial-era buildings, an interesting ethnography museum and the Palais du Roi Toffa.

Voodoo

Ouidah is the centre of the voodoo cult in Benin, and has three good museums devoted to voodoo history and culture, as well as the Route des Esclave (Route of the Slaves), which terminates at the port from which slaves were shipped to the Americas.

Modern Attractions

For a glimpse of Benin's more modern attractions, the best place to start is bustling Cotonou, Benin's capital in everything but name. The city has an abundance of good eateries, upbeat nightclubs and the enormous Grand Marché de Dantokpa. From Cotonou, you can easily reach the stilt village of Ganvié, which is accessible only by *pirogue* (dugout canoe).

Outdoor Activities

Nature lovers will enjoy the north of the country. The town of Natitingou makes an excellent base for excursions to Parc National de la Pendjari or for bicycle rides in the surrounding countryside. This area is known for its markets, which attract a colourful mixture of traders. Not far away are the Atakora Mountains, which reach a height of 457m, and the town of Boukoumbé, famous for its market, and for its Whipping Festival, in which, every fourth year, the young men of the area beat each other black and blue.

VISA REQUIREMENTS

Visas are required for all visitors except nationals of Economic Community of West African States (ECOWAS) countries. They are generally issued for either 15 or 30 days, and can be extended in Cotonou. Entry visas, valid for 48 hours and extendible in Cotonou, are

---

Itineraries

One Week

Following a couple of days in Cotonou, you could head to Ganvié, for a look at the bamboo stilt villages, and then Ouidah. After a night or two in Ouidah (with a side trip to the beach at Grand Popo), you could backtrack a bit, then go north to Abomey for the remainder of the week before returning to Cotonou.

Two Weeks

With two weeks, you could follow the one week itinerary, then from Abomey continue north to Natitingou, where you could easily spend three or four days exploring the surrounding countryside before heading further north towards Parc National de la Pendjari for a spot of wildlife viewing. From here, you could continue on to Burkina Faso, or retrace your steps to Cotonou.

One Month

With a month you will have more than enough time to explore the entire country at leisure. Plan on spending at least a week in Natitingou and north-western Benin to allow time for exploring the area on bicycle, and visiting villages and markets, including the one at Boukoumbé. When returning south, you could make stops at Parakou (a bustling town and local administrative centre), Savé and Dassa Zoumé. The latter is a picturesque place with some fascinating rock formations. Savé also has rock formations, many of which are considered sacred.

ENIN HIGHLIGHTS & ITINERARIES

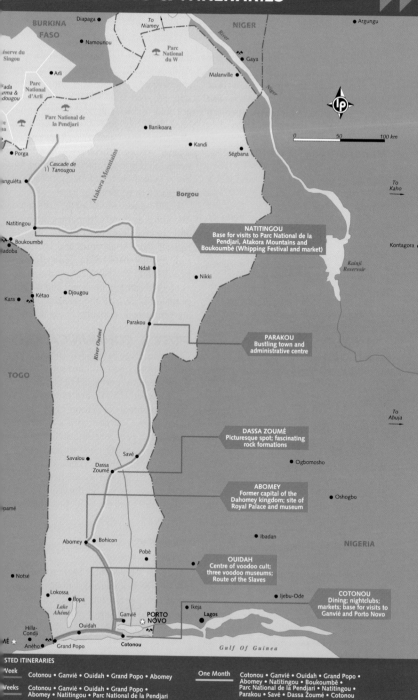

NATITINGOU
Base for visits to Parc National de la
Pendjari, Atakora Mountains and
Boukoumbé (Whipping Festival and market)

PARAKOU
Bustling town and
administrative centre

DASSA ZOUMÉ
Picturesque spot; fascinating
rock formations

ABOMEY
Former capital of the
Dahomey kingdom; site of
Royal Palace and museum

OUIDAH
Centre of voodoo cult;
three voodoo museums;
Route of the Slaves

COTONOU
Dining; nightclubs;
markets; base for visits to
Ganvié and Porto Novo

STED ITINERARIES

Veek   Cotonou • Ganvié • Ouidah • Grand Popo • Abomey

Veeks   Cotonou • Ganvié • Ouidah • Grand Popo •
        Abomey • Natitingou • Parc National de la Pendjari

One Month   Cotonou • Ganvié • Ouidah • Grand Popo •
             Abomey • Natitingou • Boukoumbé •
             Parc National de la Pendjari • Natitingou •
             Parakou • Savé • Dassa Zoumé • Cotonou

issued at the Togo-Benin border on the coastal road. An international health certificate showing proof of yellow fever and cholera vaccinations is also required for entry, although it's often not checked at land crossings.

Benin Embassies

Canada
(☎ 613-233-4429) 58 Glebe Ave, Ottawa, Ontario KIS 2C3

Nigeria
(☎ 234-261 4411) 4 Abudu Smith St, Victoria Island, Lagos

UK
(☎ 0181-954 8800; fax 8954 8844) Dolphin House, 16 The Broadway, Stanmore, Middlesex HA7 4DW

USA
(☎ 202-232-6656; fax 265-1996) 2737 Cathedral Ave NW, Washington, DC 20008

TOURIST OFFICES OVERSEAS

Benin has no overseas tourist offices, but embassies and travel agents will be able to supply you with general information. Also check the web sites listed under Online Services.

HEALTH

Yellow fever can occur in all parts of the country, malaria is present year-round and there are periodic outbreaks of dengue fever. You should take appropriate precautions against these serious diseases. A number of other insect-borne diseases, including filariasis, leishmaniasis, trypanosomiasis (sleeping sickness) and typhus are present in Benin, so take precautions against all insect bites.

Schistosomiasis is widespread, so avoid swimming, paddling or bathing in rivers or streams. There is a risk of meningococcal meningitis, especially during the dry season (November to April/May). Intestinal worms can be ingested in food or enter through the skin, so keep your shoes on whenever possible. Rabies can also occur; avoid bites from any animal, especially dogs, monkeys and bats. Take precautions against sunburn, heat stroke and dehydration if you are travelling during the hot season (March to June), especially in the northern regions.

Food and waterborne diseases, including dysentery, hepatitis, typhoid and cholera all occur in Benin. Stick to treated water at all times and try to eat only freshly cooked, hygienically prepared food.

Medical care in Cotonou is limited, and poor in the rest of the country. If you are seriously ill, consider flying home.

POST & COMMUNICATIONS

Cotonou has a good, reasonably priced postal system, and an efficient poste restante service. Postal services are less reliable outside Cotonou.

International telephone calls can be made from Cotonou with a minimum of hassle. Upcountry, line quality can be poor and you will need to go through an operator. International calls cost between US$4 and US$7 per minute, similar to elsewhere in the region.

Internet access is possible in Cotonou.

MONEY
Costs

It is fairly easy to find basic rooms for about US$5 or less. Mid-range accommodation costs from US$15. Top-end lodging in Cotonou will cost from US$100 per room.

Budget travellers should be able to get by for US$15 or less. Mid-range travel will cost from US$25 to US$50 per day, while top-end travel, including 4WD rental, will cost from US$150 per day.

Changing Money

Changing cash and travellers cheques can be done efficiently in Cotonou, although you may be required to show proof of purchase for your travellers cheques. Upcountry, the best foreign denomination to carry is French francs; changing other currencies may be difficult. Cash withdrawals on Visa card are possible in Cotonou.

ONLINE SERVICES

Lonely Planet has a web site Destination Benin (www.lonelyplanet.com /dest/afr/ben.htm).

For information on getting around in Cotonou, check Cotonou (www .cotonou.com).

The University of Benin has a web site Universite du Benin (www.ub.tg /swintro.htm).

The Norwegian Council for Africa (www.africaindex.africainfo.no/africa index1/countries/benin.html) has a helpful index of links.

BOOKS & FILMS

Photographs & Notebooks by Bruce Chatwin contains an eclectic collection of pictures and observations from his travels in several West African countries, including Benin.

The Viceroy of Ouidah, also by Chatwin, tells the story (partly based on fact) of a Brazilian trader stranded on West Africa's 'Slave Coast' in the 17th century.

For an overview of the region's history, try *West Africa Since 1800* by JB Webster & AA Boahen.

Amazons of Black Sparta: The Women Warriors of Dahomey by Stanley B Alpern

is a detailed study of Dahomey's renowned female army which at its height in the mid 19th century numbered over four thousand.

Benin has a small indigenous film industry. Local productions include *Under the Sign of the Voodoo* (1974) and *Ironou* (1985). The TV movie *Magicians of the Earth: Kings of the Water* (1991) was filmed in Abomey and chronicles events surrounding local voodoo ceremonies.

ENTERING & LEAVING BENIN

There are direct flights to Benin from France, Belgium and many African countries. You can also fly to Lomé in Togo and from there take a taxi to Cotonou (about three hours); it is easy to get a 48 hour entry visa for Benin at the border. Direct taxis run daily between Cotonou and Lomé, although it is cheaper to take a taxi to the border, and another from there to Lomé.

A taxi from Cotonou to Niger takes about 14 hours. The route is via Malanville and Gaya, just over the Niger border.

Taxis between Cotonou and Lagos (Nigeria) take about three hours and run frequently throughout the day.

The route to Burkina Faso is from Natitingou via Tanguiéta to the border, and from there via Tindangou (Burkina Faso) to Fada N'Gourma and Ouagadougou. The trip is normally done in stages; traffic is scarce from Natitingou northward as far as Fada N'Gourma.

With the exception of the road into Burkina Faso, the main roads connecting Benin with most surrounding countries are tarred and in fair condition.

BOTSWANA

Botswana, known as Bechuanaland until 1966, is an African success story, with health, educational and economic standards among the highest on the continent. The majority of the population is concentrated in and near Gaborone in the east of the country. West from here stretches a wilderness of savanna, desert, wetlands and salt pans. To protect these ecosystems, the government courts only high-cost, low-impact tourism, which means that many spectacular wilderness areas are off limits to the budget traveller.

WHEN TO GO
The best time to visit is between June and September, when the days are clear, warm and sunny, and the nights cool to cold. Wildlife viewing is most predictable during the May to August dry season, when the animals tend to congregate near water sources. The best months for viewing animals in Makgadikgadi & Nxai Pan National Park are March and April.

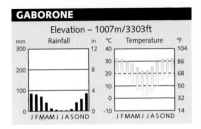

GABORONE
Elevation – 1007m/3303ft

At a Glance

Full Country Name: Republic of Botswana
Area: 582,000 sq km
Population: 1.5 million
Capital City: Gaborone (population 150,000)
People: About 60% are Tswana; other groups include the Herero, Mbukushu, Yei, San, Kalanga and Kgalagadi
Languages: English (official), but Setswana is the most common; other indigenous languages include Kalanga and Yei
Religions: Christian (about 30%); indigenous religions based on ancestor worship are still practised, particularly in more remote areas
Government: Constitutional democracy
Currency: Botswana pula (P)
Time Zone: Two hours ahead of GMT/UTC
International Telephone Code: 267
Electricity: 220V, 50 Hz; most sockets take two-pin round plugs

HIGHLIGHTS
Botswana's appeal lies in its pristine wilderness areas, the friendly, unhurried pace of its rural villages and the stability inherent in its peaceful nature.

Delta & Wildlife
One of the best regions to experience these assets is the Okavango Delta, with its maze of waterways and islands teeming with wildlife.

National Parks & Desert
Other good places include Chobe National Park, Makgadikgadi & Nxai Pan National Park, and the wild expanses of the Kalahari desert.

Hiking & Rock Art
The Tsodilo Hills in the far north-western corner of the country offer

excellent trekking opportunties and harbour a fascinating gallery of ancient San paintings.

VISA REQUIREMENTS

Tourist visas are not required by citizens of the following: Commonwealth countries (except Ghana, India, Mauritius, Nigeria and Sri Lanka), EU countries (except Spain and Portugal), Iceland, Israel, Liechtenstein, Namibia, Norway, Pakistan, San Marino, South Africa, Switzerland, Uruguay, USA and Western Samoa. Others may apply for visas through Botswana diplomatic missions, or a British high commission where there is no Botswana representation. Visas are granted for an initial 30 day period, which may be extended for up to a total of three months.

Botswana Embassies

South Africa
  (☎ 012-342 4760; fax 342 1845) 24 Amos St, Colbyn

UK
  (☎ 020-7499 0031; fax 7495 8595) 6 Stratford Place, London W1N 9AE

USA
  (☎ 202-244-4990; fax 244-4164) 1531 New Hampshire Ave NW, Washington, DC 20008

TOURIST OFFICES OVERSEAS

Botswana has no overseas tourist offices. However the country's embassies and travel agencies should be able to supply you with information. Also check the web sites listed under Online Services.

HEALTH

Malaria is present in Botswana, predominantly in the northern parts of the country, including in the Okavango Delta, between November and June, so take malaria precautions. Dengue fever has not been reported but trypanosomiasis (sleeping sickness) can occur. Filariasis, typhus and leishmaniasis are other insect-borne diseases that occur and although they are generally not a great risk to travellers, you should try to avoid all insect bites.

Pay attention to what you eat and drink as dysentery, typhoid, hepatitis and cholera all occur. Avoid any unwashed fruit and vegetables. Make sure you buy fruit and vegetables with the peel intact, so that you can peel them yourself, and take care with all meat and fish. Tap water is generally OK, but not water from rivers and bores in rural areas.

As schistosomiasis exists, avoid swimming, paddling or bathing in rivers and dams. Other intestinal parasites are common; again take care with what you eat and avoid walking around barefoot. Avoid milk in rural areas due to the risk of tuberculosis. Dogs, bats, monkeys and rats can carry rabies so avoid bites from these and any other animals.

Medical facilities are reasonably good in Gaborone. If you do require serious medical care, you should go to Gaborone, or preferably to Johannesburg or Cape Town.

POST & COMMUNICATIONS

Botswana's postal system is generally reliable, but very slow; allow at least two weeks for delivery to or from an overseas address. Rates for international post are roughly comparable to those in Europe. There is reliable poste restante at the main post office in Gaborone.

The telephone service also is slow but reliable. International phone calls can be made from Gaborone and major towns, and must be placed through an operator; rates are close to US$4 per minute. Reverse charge (collect) calls are not possible. Telephone offices are only open during normal business hours.

There is currently no public Internet access in Botswana.

MONEY

You will need to fill out a currency declaration form upon entry into Botswana, and when departing you must estimate the amount of money you have spent in the country. It is rare that you will be asked to actually show your currency or travellers cheques.

Costs

Botswana is expensive. Supermarket, fast-food and restaurant prices are comparable to those in Europe, North America and Australia. To visit most of the interesting parts of the country, you will need to fly or rent a 4WD – both expensive options by any standards. Flights between Gaborone and Maun (for the Okavango Delta), for example, cost about US$175. Individually organised charters in a five passenger plane cost around US$125 per hour. Rental costs for a 4WD start at about US$50 per day plus kilometre charges.

Budget travellers who forego visits to national parks, self-cater and camp

Itineraries

One Week

With one week, assuming you start in Gaborone and unless you are interested in chartering internal flights, base yourself in the capital and explore the surrounding area. Possible excursions include climbing Mt Kgale, which overlooks Gaborone, taking a game walk through the Mokolodi Nature Reserve 12km south of Gaborone, visiting Mochudi, south-eastern Botswana's most interesting village, and its Phuthadikobo Museum. You could also camp for a couple of nights in the Khutse Game Reserve about 250km north-west of Gaborone.

If you enter Botswana from the north, you could spend a week in the Okavango Delta/Moremi Wildlife Reserve area. Maun is the base for most tours in this area.

Two Weeks

With two weeks, you will have time to visit the attractions listed in the one week itinerary, before continuing on to Francistown and exploring the surrounding area. A good excursion would be to the North-East Tuli Game Reserve, which encompasses Mashatu Game Reserve (Africa's largest private game reserve and an excellent place to view big cats, antelope and large herds of elephant) and the beautifully situated Tuli Game Reserve. Other nearby attractions include the historical village of Serowe (immortalised by writer Bessie Head in *Serowe – Village of the Rain Wind*) and the Khama II Rhino Sanctuary.

One Month

With one month, continue from Francistown north-west towards Nata Sanctuary (good for birdwatching), and then north to Chobe National Park, one of Botswana's main tourist attractions. From Chobe, return to Nata and then head west towards Maun and the Okavango Delta, visiting Makgadikgadi & Nxai Pan National Park en route This section of the trip can easily occupy between one and two weeks. From Maun, drive or fly back to Gaborone or continue overland into Namibia via Ghanzi, Mamuno and Buitepos Namibia).

OTSWANA HIGHLIGHTS & ITINERARIES

OKAVANGO DELTA
Maze of waterways and islands teeming with wildlife

TSODILO HILLS
Great hiking; fascinating ancient San paintings

CHOBE NATIONAL PARK
Myriad birdlife and wildlife; one of Botswana's major tourist attractions

MAKGADIKGADI & NXAI PAN NATIONAL PARK
Beautiful savanna country with plentiful wildlife after the wet season

NORTH-EAST TULI GAME RESERVE
View big cats, antelopes and elephants

GABORONE
Base for visits to Mt Kgale, Mokolodi Nature Reserve, Mochudi and Khutse Game Reserve

KALAHARI DESERT
Solitude and silence. Undulating fossil river valley through vegetated dunes

can probably get by on about US$30 per day. A more realistic budget, including a wildlife tour, will start at around US$75 a day. High-end safaris will cost at least double this figure.

Changing Money

Full banking services are available in all major towns. Many smaller towns often have banking services only once or twice weekly, and often will change only foreign travellers cheques but not cash.

Most major credit cards are accepted at tourist hotels and restaurants in larger cities and towns. Credit card cash advances are available in Gaborone, Lobatse, Maun and Francistown through Barclays Bank or Standard Chartered Bank.

ONLINE SERVICES

Lonely Planet has a web site Destination Botswana (www.lonelyplanet.com/dest/afr/bot.htm).

There is an online version of Botswana Focus magazine (www.africantravel.com/stbrob.html).

Botswana Resource Listings (www.gorp.com/gorp/location/africa/botswana.htm) has numerous links, primarily to safari companies.

National Geographic explores the Okavango Delta in Africa's Savage Oasis (www.nationalgeographic.com/features/96/okavango/index.html).

Additional sites focusing on Botswana's natural wealth include Magnificent Birding in Botswana (www.adventures.co.za/trip_bir.htm) and *Fishing Africa* (www.fishingafrica.co.za/botswana.html).

BOOKS & FILMS

Botswana's most famous modern literary figure is South African-born Bessie Head, whose writings reflect the harshness and beauty of African village life, and the physical attributes of Botswana itself. Her most popular works include *Serowe – Village of the Rain Wind*, which provides an insightful look into village life in Botswana, and *The Collector of Treasures*, an anthology of short stories.

Lost World of the Kalahari by Laurens van der Post, is fascinating reading for anyone interested in the lifestyles of traditional San people.

Cry of the Kalahari by Mark & Delia Owen is a very readable account of an American couple's seven years spent studying brown hyenas in Deception Valley in the Central Kalahari.

History of Botswana by T Tlou & Alec Campbell is a very good history of the country.

The Gods Must Be Crazy (1980), set in the Kalahari, is probably the most well known film to come out of Botswana.

The Greatest Places, a 1998 Imax production focusing on various locations around the world, includes footage from the Okavango Delta.

ENTERING & LEAVING BOTSWANA

There are no intercontinental flights servicing Gaborone. Regional flights are available on Air Botswana, South African Airways, Air Zimbabwe and Air Namibia.

There are overland entry posts at numerous locations between Botswana and Namibia, South Africa and Zimbabwe. The Namibian posts are Mamuno/Buitepos, south-west of Ghanzi in the Kalahari; Ngoma Bridge, between the Caprivi and Chobe National Park; Mohembo/Shakawe in the upper Okavango Panhandle; and

Kasane/Mpalila Island in the far north. There are bus and minibus services between Livingstone (Zambia), Victoria Falls (Zimbabwe) and Windhoek (Namibia) which cross into Botswana at Ngoma Bridge. There is also a bus between Ghanzi and Gobabis (Namibia) via the Buitepos border.

The most frequently used crossings between Botswana and South Africa are at Ramatlhabama/Mmabatho; the Tlokweng Gate, near Gaborone; and Lobatse/Zeerust further south. Other border posts serve backroads across the Limpopo River in the Tuli Block or across the Molopo River in southern Botswana. An easy way to reach Johannesburg is by bus or minibus from Gaborone.

Between Botswana and Zimbabwe the most frequently used crossings are at Ramokgwebana/Plumtree, and the Kasane/Kazungula border west of Victoria Falls. There is a back road crossing at Mpandamatenga/Pandamatengo near Kazuma Forest Reserve in north-eastern Botswana. Border opening hours at most posts change frequently, so be sure to check locally before turning up at the more remote ones. Public transport options include a bus service connecting Gaborone and Francistown with Bulawayo and Harare. The bus and minibus lines between Livingstone (Zambia), Victoria Falls (Zimbabwe) and Windhoek (Namibia) pass through Kasane. Hitching between Bulawayo and Francistown via Plumtree is fairly easy. There are also overnight trains daily between Gaborone and Bulawayo.

From Zambia, the only direct option is the ferry across the Zambezi at Kazungula.

Although few travellers make it to Burkina Faso, those who do invariably rank the country at the top of their lists – proof that here, as in so many places in Africa, people count more than places. Ouagadougou, the country's friendly, bustling capital, is smaller than most Sahelian cities (cities in the region bordering the Sahara desert) and easily negotiated on foot. And, you'll have no trouble meeting the locals – either in the morning at street-side tables where you can get coffee and bread, or in the evening at one of the many bars for which the city is famous.

In the rest of Burkina Faso, village life is fascinating and the landscapes full of contrasts – ranging from waterfalls and greenery in the south to dusty desert panoramas in the north. In the markets, turbaned traders on camels mix with farmers on donkey-drawn carts in a colourful swirl of diverse ethnic groups.

If you have been travelling for a while in West Africa's coastal countries and are looking for a change of pace, Burkina Faso is an ideal place to come.

WHEN TO GO

The best months to visit are between November and mid-February, after the rains end and when temperatures are cooler. If you are planning to take photos, keep in mind that from late November or early December onwards, dusty harmattan winds cause the skies to be hazy. The main rainy season is from June to October, with short rains during March and April, particularly in the south-west.

At a Glance

Full Country Name: Democratic Republic of Burkina Faso

Area: 274,122 sq km

Population: 10.8 million

Capital City: Ouagadougou (population 500,000)

People: About 60 groups, including Mossi (about 48%), Bobo (about 7%), Fulani or Peul (about 10%), Gourma (about 5%), and Lobi-Dagari and Mande (about 14%)

Languages: French (official); major indigenous languages include Moré, Mande, Bobo, Lobi, Dioula, Gourmantché and Peul

Religions: Muslim (nominally about 50%), traditional beliefs (about 30%), Christian (about 15%); adherence to traditional beliefs is probably much stronger than these statistics indicate

Government: Republic

Currency: West African CFA franc (CFA)

Time Zone: GMT/UTC

International Telephone Code: 226

Electricity: 220V; most sockets take plugs with two round pins

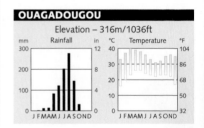

OUAGADOUGOU

Elevation – 316m/1036ft

HIGHLIGHTS
Desert
Burkina Faso's main attractions are its people and its starkly beautiful Sahelian landscape, which is best experienced in the north of the country near Gorom-Gorom. This town also has a fascinating desert market every week, which is well worth a visit.

Greenery
Bobo-Dioulasso, much greener and with all the amenities that Gorom-Gorom lacks, is a complete contrast. Its biennial cultural festival is well worth attending if you are in the area. Nearby Banfora is much smaller, and makes a good base for cycling or hiking in the surrounding countryside.

Rock Formations
About 50km from Banfora are the interesting Peaks of Sindou and villages reminiscent of those in Mali's Dogon region.

Urban
Right in the centre of the country is Ouagadougou, one of the most pleasant of the Sahelian capitals. Film enthusiasts should not miss the Pan-African Film Festival, which is held here every two years. Go if you get the chance!

VISA REQUIREMENTS
Visas are required for all except nationals of Economic Community of West African States (ECOWAS) countries. Burkina Faso's embassies usually issue multiple-entry visas valid for three months on request.

Cholera and yellow fever vaccinations are also required; international health certificates are usually checked on arrival at the airport and at most land borders.

Burkina Faso Embassies
Canada
(☎ 613-238-4796; fax 238-3812) 48 Range Rd, Ottawa, Ontario KIN 8J4

UK
(☎ 020-7738 1800; fax 7738 2820) 5 Cinnamon Row, Plantation Wharf, London SW11 3TW

USA
(☎ 202-332-5577) 2340 Massachusetts Ave NW, Washington, DC 20008

TOURIST OFFICES OVERSEAS
Burkina Faso has no overseas tourist offices. Embassies and travel agents should be able to supply you with general information. Also check the web sites listed under Online Services.

HEALTH
Malaria and dengue fever exist all year round, so you should takes precautions against these serious diseases. Take precautions against sunburn, heat stroke and dehydration if you are travelling in the hot season, March to June. Food and waterborne diseases occur in Burkina Faso, so drink only treated water and try wherever possible to eat only hygienically prepared food.

Medical facilities are basic in Ouagadougou and limited in rural areas. If you require serious medical care, you should leave for home.

POST & COMMUNICATIONS
The postal system is reliable and reasonably priced for letters, though not always fast. There are efficient poste restante services in Ouagadougou and Bobo-Dioulasso.

Telephone service is expensive (about double USA rates), but good. Calls to Europe cost about US$4 per minute (US$5 to the USA and Australia).

Internet access is possible in the capital, and perhaps – by the time this book is published – in Bobo-Dioulasso.

MONEY
Costs

Burkina Faso is relatively inexpensive; it is fairly easy to find basic rooms with fan and shared facilities for under US$10. In Ouagadougou and Bobo-Dioulasso, you can find comfortable accommodation with air-con from about US$20. There's a lodging tax of US$1 per person per night in addition to 18% VAT, except at the cheapest hotels. Both are usually included in the rate you'll be quoted.

For per diem costs, plan on about US$10 to US$15 for budget travel, and from about US$25 for a few mid-range comforts. Car rental and top-end

---

Itineraries

One Week
With one week, you could spend two or three days exploring Ouagadougou, a friendly, relaxed city with an active nightlife, then head south-west towards Bobo-Dioulasso, where you could spend the remainder of your time before continuing south to Côte d'Ivoire (with a stop in Banfora) or returning to Ouagadougou. It's best to take the bus between Ouagadougou and Bobo-Dioulasso; the train is slower and notoriously unpunctual.

Although it's possible to visit the Gorom-Gorom market on a week's visit to the country, you would have to leave from Ouagadougou on Wednesday (the market is on Thursday) and return Thursday evening – an exhausting schedule – because transport on other days is scarce.

Two Weeks
With two weeks, you could easily visit Gorom-Gorom, after which you will have to backtrack to Ouagadougou before heading south-west towards Bobo-Dioulasso and Banfora. Allow about a week for Ouagadougou and Gorom-Gorom, and another week for hiking and relaxing in the south-west.

One Month
With a month you will have time to visit most areas of Burkina Faso. To minimise any backtracking, you could head first to Gorom-Gorom (after getting acclimatised in Ouagadougou). Both Markoye, with its weekly camel market, and Dori, with a small but interesting daily market, make good side trips. From Gorom-Gorom, head via Kaya to Ouahigouya, Burkina Faso's fourth-largest town and a lively place. From Ouahigouya, there are direct buses down to Bobo-Dioulasso, where you can easily spend a week exploring the town and surrounding region. Side trips to Banfora and Sindou can also be worked in. From Bobo-Dioulasso or Banfora, head south-east to Gaoua, where you can see some interesting architecture and learn more about the traditions of the Lobi people who live in the area. From Gaoua, return to Ouagadougou.

If you still have time, you could then head from Ouagadougou south-east to Fada N'Gourma, a laid-back junction town, and from there to Parc National d'Arli, with elephants, warthogs, baboons, monkeys, lions, hippos, leopards, crocodiles and various species of antelopes and birds. The park is part of the same ecosystem as Parc National de la Pendjari in Benin, and is open from mid-December to mid-May. You will need your own vehicle to visit the park. From Arli, you could continue south-west into Togo, or north to Niger via Fada N'Gourma, or return to Ouagadougou.

URKINA FASO HIGHLIGHTS & ITINERARIES

GOROM-GOROM
Starkly beautiful Sahelian landscape; weekly market

OUAGADOUGOU
Interesting Sahelian capital; biennial film festival

BOBO-DIOULASSO
Green landscape; biennial cultural festival

BANFORA
Good base for hiking, cycling

PARC NATIONAL D'ARLI
Diverse wildlife and birdlife

SUGGESTED ITINERARIES

One Week	Ouagadougou • Bobo-Dioulasso • Banfora
Two Weeks	Ouagadougou • Gorom-Gorom • Ouagadougou • Bobo-Dioulasso • Banfora
One Month	Ouagadougou • Gorom-Gorom • Dori • Markoyé • Gorom-Gorom • Kaya • Ouahigouya • Bobo-Dioulasso • Banfora • Sindou • Gaoua • Ouagadougou • Fada N'Gourma • Parc National d'Arli

accommodation (available only in Ouagadougou and Bobo-Dioulasso) will cost from US$100 per day.

Changing Money

Travellers cheques can be easily changed in Ouagadougou and Bobo-Dioulasso, although banks often require you to show proof of purchase. The best denominations are French francs and US dollars. At the time this book was written, some banks were not accepting Thomas Cook, Visa, MasterCard or Citicorp cheques.

Credit cards are only accepted at one or two places in Ouagadougou. Cash advances against a credit card are not possible.

ONLINE SERVICES

Lonely Planet has a web site Destination Burkina Faso (www.lonely planet.com/dest/afr/bur.htm).

Baba's West African Homepage (www.wazobia.com/west/burkina /faso.htm) is a good source of additional links.

The Cityguide (http://cityguide.lycos .com/assist/cityguide/articles/663_t .html) has information on Ouagadougou and Burkina Faso.

To see what is coming up in West Africa's film industry, check FESPACO (www.fespaco.bf/fesengli.htm).

BOOKS & FILMS

The Mossi of Burkina Faso – Chiefs, Politicians and Soldiers by Elliott Skinner makes interesting reading if you can find a copy.

Thomas Sankara Speaks – The Burkina Faso Revolution, 1983-1987 by Thomas Sankara presents the Burkinabè leader's view of events surrounding the 1983 coup d'état.

Burkina Faso – Unsteady Statehood in West Africa by Pierre Engelbert focuses on Burkina Faso's recent history.

The Historical Dictionary of Burkina Faso by Daniel McFarland & Lawrence Rupley contains an extensive bibliography of English and French works on the country.

For an introduction to the literature of the region, the most useful anthology is The Traveller's Literary Companion – Africa edited by Oona Strathern, which contains over 250 prose and poetry extracts from all over the continent.

The Pan-African Film Festival (FESPACO), held in odd-numbered years in Ouagadougou, provides a forum for African film producers. Over the past two decades, several Burkinabè film-makers have won prizes here, including Idrissa Ouedraogo and Gaston Jean-Marie Kaboré.

Ouedraogo's film Tilaï (1990) is set in precolonial times, and chronicles an illicit love affair and its consequences. Yaaba (1989), also by Ouedraogo, is the tale of a young boy's affection for an old woman in his village whom the villagers believe to be a witch.

Kaboré's films include Wend Kuuni (God's Gift) and Zan Boko, about government corruption and censorship.

ENTERING & LEAVING BURKINA FASO

Air France, Sabena, Air Afrique, and several regional airlines have flights to Ouagadougou.

The main route to Côte d'Ivoire is from Ouagadougou via Bobo-Dioulasso and Banfora to Ferkessédougou, Yamoussoukro and Abidjan. Buses connect these cities daily. Alternatively, there is a train three times weekly between Ouagadougou and Abidjan.

To Ghana, there are bus connections several times a week between Ouagadougou and Accra via Hamale (Ghana) and Kumasi. There is also a bus to the Ghanaian border, from where you can find taxis on to Bolgatanga in Ghana. Although there is another route into Ghana from Bobo-Dioulasso via Hamale (Ghana) and Wa, traffic is scarce and you must travel in stages.

To Mali, a weekly direct bus connects Ouagadougou and Bamako. Alternatively, you can travel by bus to Djibasso on the Mali border and change to Malian transport. From Bobo-Dioulasso, there are bus connections with Ségou via Koutiala (both in Mali), and direct to Bamako. Bush taxis also run between Bobo-Dioulasso and Mopti.

To Niger, there are buses a few times a week between Ouagadougou and Niamey. There are also minibuses several times a week to the Niger border, where you can change to local (Niger) transport.

To Togo, there is a sealed road connecting Ouagadougou with Lomé. Direct buses ply the route weekly, but the trip is best done in stages by minibus and taxi.

The road to Benin via Fada N'Gourma is sealed to the border. There are regular connections between Ouagadougou and Fada N'Gourma by bus and bush taxi or minibus. From Fada N'Gourma, minibuses and taxis to the border are infrequent and fill up slowly. Transport is scarce from the border along the dirt road to Tanguiéta (Benin), except on market day.

Cameroon, a fascinating amalgamation of more than 130 ethnic groups, is one of Central Africa's more prosperous nations – although times are harder now than during the economic boom of the early 1980s. It's also an exceptionally diverse country, topographically and otherwise, with something to appeal to everyone. In the north are hobbit-like villages perched on rocky cliffs, and Parc National du Waza, where you can see elephant, giraffe, hippo and many other animals. In the south-west is Mt Cameroon, the region's highest peak, and Foumban, with its Bamoun royal palace. Along the coast near Kribi are some beautiful white-sand beaches.

At a Glance

Full Country Name: Republic of Cameroon
Area: 475,442 sq km
Population: 14.7 million
Capital City: Yaoundé (population 1 million)
People: More than 130 groups, including Bamiléké and Bamoun (together constituting about 19% of the population), Ewondo, Fulani (about 7.5%) and Kirdi (about 11%)
Languages: French and English (official); more than 100 indigenous languages, including Bamiléké, Ewondo, Bamoun and Fulfulde
Religions: Christian (about 33%), Muslim (about 15%); the remainder follow traditional beliefs
Government: Unitary republic
Currency: Central African CFA franc (CFA)
Time Zone: One hour ahead of GMT/UTC
International Telephone Code: 237
Electricity: 110/220V, 50 Hz; most sockets take plugs with two round pins

WHEN TO GO

Cameroon's climate varies widely, with northern areas receiving minimal rainfall, while certain parts of the south, in and around Douala, get over 4000mm.

Overall, the best time to visit is during the cooler, drier months of November to February, although from December to February, dusty harmattan winds cause skies to be hazy. During the rainy season (May to November), many roads in the south-west become muddy and sometimes impassable, except in 4WD.

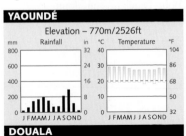

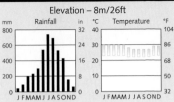

HIGHLIGHTS
Greenery & Culture

Hilly and green Yaoundé is one of Africa's more picturesque capitals and well worth a visit. The Musée d'Art Cameroonais on the outskirts of the city has one of the best collections of Cameroonian art in the world.

Another attractive town with a pleasantly cool climate is Bamenda, set in the highlands to the north-west of Yaoundé. It's a good place to buy handicrafts, and the site of some interesting festivals, as well as one of Central Africa's best hiking areas.

Culture & Architecture

For additional insights into Cameroonian culture, visit the impressive *chefferie* (chief's compound) near Bafoussam at Bandjoun. Bafoussam itself is an interesting place, with many traditional houses in the surrounding countryside, and the German-inspired Palais Royal, with its good museum. Foumban, nearby, is one of Cameroon's major attractions and an important centre of traditional African art. Its main draw is the Palais Royal of the Bamoun tribe.

Outdoors & Wildlife

Those seeking some exercise can head for Mt Cameroon – at 4095m, it's the highest mountain in West and Central Africa. Afterwards, relax on the beautiful beaches near Kribi.

Parc National du Waza offers good wildlife viewing opportunities, although access is presently restricted due to insecurity near the Chad border.

VISA REQUIREMENTS

Visas are required by most visitors. The best place in the region to obtain one is in Malabo (Equatorial Guinea).

You will also need an inter national health certificate with proof of yellow fever vaccination.

Cameroon Embassies

Canada
(☎ 613-236-1522) 170 Clemow Ave, Ottawa, Ontario K1S 2B4

Equatorial Guinea
(☎ 2263) Calle de Rey Boncoro, Malabo

Gabon
(☎ 73 2800) Blvd Léon Mba, Quartier Derrière Prison, Libreville

Nigeria
(☎ 61 2226) Fermi Pearse St, Victoria Island, Lagos. Consulate: Calabar

UK
(☎ 020-7727 0771/4; fax 7792 9353) 84 Holland Park, London W11 3SD

USA
(☎ 202-265-8790/94) 2349 Massachusetts Ave NW, Washington, DC 20008

TOURIST OFFICES OVERSEAS

Cameroon has no overseas tourist offices, but embassies and travel agencies should be able to supply you with information. Also check the web sites listed under Online Services for useful information.

HEALTH

Malaria and dengue fever are present in Cameroon; you will need to take appropriate precautions against these diseases. Drink only treated water and try, wherever possible, to eat only hygienically prepared, fresh food.

As medical facilities are basic in Yaoundé and in rural areas, you should think about going home if you require serious medical care.

POST & COMMUNICATIONS

The post is fairly reliable for letters; rates are similar to those elsewhere in the region. Both Yaoundé and Douala have poste restante services.

International telephone calls can be made with a minimum of hassle at offices of Intelcam (the state telecommunications entity) in Yaoundé, Douala and other major towns. Charges vary depending on distance, but are expensive by any standard. Reverse charge (collect) calls are not possible, but you can make arrangements to receive incoming calls. There are also many privately owned *cabines téléphoniques* in main cities and towns, although their rates can be as much as 50% higher than Intelcam's.

Internet access is possible in Yaoundé.

MONEY
Costs

Cameroon is not as costly as some of its neighbours, but keeping expenses down is still a challenge for the budget traveller. In general, plan on about US$15 to US$25 per day if you stay in simple accommodation and eat local food. To enjoy a few more comforts, budget from US$30 to US$60 per day. Top-end hotels and European cuisine can cost more than US$150 per day.

Itineraries

One Week
Assuming you arrive in Douala, spend a day or so getting acclimatised and visiting the city's sights. Then head to Yaoundé to enjoy the city and art museum. Continue to Bafoussam, where you can see the Royal Palace and nearby chefferie in Bandjoun, then on to Foumban, where you could easily spend a few days visiting the palace and other attractions. Return to Douala. Fitting this all in within a week travelling on public transport will be tight, so ideally allow yourself a few additional days.

Two Weeks
With two weeks, follow the itinerary outlined under One Week, taking a bit more time in each place. From Foumban, backtrack to Bafoussam and continue south to Buea, the starting point for climbing Mt Cameroon. From here, you can make a detour to Kumba in order to visit Barombi Mbo crater lake, five km to the west of the town. Head south-east via Douala to Kribi and spend any time remaining relaxing there on the beaches.

One Month
With one month, do the circle in reverse, going from Douala to Buea and Kumba, then continuing north towards Bafoussam and

Foumban. En route, stop at Bafang to visit the impressive nearby waterfalls. From Foumban, backtrack to Bafoussam. Here you could make a detour north-west to cool and hilly Bamenda for a few days of hiking before continuing on to Yaoundé.

From Yaoundé, go north-east to N'Gaoundal, a pleasant town and site of the Palais du Lamido, a fine example of a traditional chief's compound. Assuming the security situation in the far north of the country near the Chad border is quiet, continue north to Maroua, the starting point for visits to the Parc National du Waza. Maroua is also the centre of Cameroon's leather crafts industry, and its market has a wide selection of leather goods. Nearby is La Dent de Mindif, of interest to serious rock climbers.

From Maroua, you can also visit Mokolo, about 80km to the west. The surrounding area is dotted with the picturesque villages of the Kirdi people, who are distinguished by their round fortress-like houses with tall thatched roofs, which resemble those of the Dogon in Mali. From Maroua, return south by road, or by air from Garoua. Spend any time remaining at the end of your trip relaxing on the beaches near Kribi.

NIGER

Diffa

Lake
Chad

Kousséri

★ N'DJAMENA

PARC NATIONAL DU WAZA
Good wildlife viewing
opportunities

Maiduguri

Bama

Waza

CHAD

Banki

Parc
National
du Waza

Mora

ano

Mokolo

Maroua

Roumsiki

▲ La Dent
de
Mindif

Yagoua

Bongor

NIGERIA

Jos

Léré

Pala

Abuja
Lagos

Yola

Garoua

Lac de
Lagdo

River

Bénoué   River

Moundou

BAMENDA
Handicrafts;
stivals; hiking

Benue

Taraba   River

Faro River

Réserve
du Faro

Parc
National
de la
Bénoué

Parc
National
de Bouba
Ndjida

urdi

MT CAMEROON
ghest mountain in
st and Central Africa

FOUMBAN
Palais Royale (Bamoun
tribe); centre for
traditional African art

N'Gaoundéré

Paoua

Nkambe

Banyo

Retenue de
Mbakaou

Djonong

CENTRAL

Wum

Mt Oko
(3008m) ▲

Kumbo

Tibati

N'Gaoundal

Meiganga

AFRICAN
REPUBLIC

Mbam River

Bamenda

Lac de
Bamending

Garoua-
Boulaï

Baboua

Bouar

Baoro

Ekok

Mamfé

Mbouda

Foumban

BAFOUSSAM
Traditional houses;
museum; chief's
compound at Bandjoun

Sangha   River

Kagéi   River

Dschang

Bafoussam

ondo-Titi

Bafang

Bandjoun

Belabo

Nkongsamba

Kumba

Nachtigal
Falls

Sanaga   River

Bertoua

Batouri

ao   eroon

Mbanga

Obala

Kenzou

Berbérati

Limbe

Buea

Douala

★ YAOUNDÉ

Abong
Mbang

To
Banjui

Ferry

Edéa

Mbalmayo

Réserve du Dja

Yokadouma

TORIAL
NEA

Kribi

Ebolowa

Sangmélima

Mintom

YAOUNDÉ
Picturesque capital;
Cameroonian art
collection

Bayanga

Réserve
de Campo

Ntem   River

Ambam

KRIBI
Beautiful beaches

ANTIC
CEAN

Campo

Yengué

Bata

Ebebiyin

Bitam

GABON

EQUATORIAL
GUINEA

To Oyem &
Libreville

To
Brazzaville

CONGO

0   100   200 km

Changing Money

The best denomination to carry is French francs, followed by US dollars. No banks accept or change Nigerian naira. West African CFA can also be difficult to change, although some shops in Douala and Yaoundé may accept them as payment for a purchase. Travellers cheques can be easily changed in Yaoundé and Douala, but often not in smaller towns. All banks charge commissions for changing travellers cheques. There is no black market.

Credit cards are accepted at some top-end hotels, a few travel agencies and airline offices.

ONLINE SERVICES

Lonely Planet has a web site Destination Cameroon (www.lonelyplanet .com/dest/afr/cam.htm).

The Essence of Cameroon (www .cameroon.net) has hotel booking details and general information on the country.

Welcome to Cameroon (www.rt66 .com/~telp/cam.htm) is an informal look at Cameroon and its people.

Postcards from Cameroon (www .geocities.com/TheTropics/Shores/40 51) has pictures from around the country, and text in English and French.

For other links, see the index of The Norwegian Council for Africa (www .africaindex.africainfo.no/africaindex1 /countries/cameroon.html).

BOOKS & FILMS

One of Cameroon's most famous writers is Mongo Beti, whose novels explore topics ranging from the incompatibility of European and African values as set out during colonial times to post-independence despotism. *Le Pauvre Christ de Bomba*, one of his best known works, tells of the failure of a missionary to convert the people of a small village. His other works include *Remember Ruben* and *Mission to Kala*.

Cameroonian novelist Kenjo Jumbam has written about the country's colonial experience, most notably in *The White Man of God*.

Talking Drums by Shirley Deane focuses on village life near Yaoundé and is a good choice for those seeking to gain insight into Cameroonian culture.

The *Historical Dictionary of Cameroon* (1974) by Victor LeVine & Roger Nye is dated, but useful for reference. Richard A Joseph's *Radical Nationalism in Cameroon* analyses the origins of the Union des populations camerounaises party in the 1950s.

Chocolat (1988), a well known film set in Cameroon, tells of a young French woman who returns to Africa to relive her childhood during the colonial era.

ENTERING & LEAVING CAMEROON

Cameroon is connected with various cities in Africa and Europe by Air Afrique, Air France, Air Gabon, Cameroon Airlines (the national carrier), Sabena and Swissair. Most of these airlines use Douala airport, but some have connections to Yaoundé. Cameroon Airlines flies between Yaoundé/Douala and the capital cities of most of Cameroon's neighbouring countries. Air Affaires Afrique connects Douala with Malabo and Bata (Equatorial Guinea) and with São Tomé & Príncipe.

To Gabon and Equatorial Guinea, the main route is from Yaoundé via

Ebolowa to Ambam. In Ambam, the road splits, with the easterly road going to Bitam, Oyem and Libreville (Gabon) and the westerly road to Ebebiyin and Bata (Equatorial Guinea). On both routes you will need to cross the Ntem River by ferry or *pirogue* (dugout canoe). You can also cross into Equatorial Guinea from Campo on the coast to Lendé or Yenguë and then on to Bongoro and Bata, although this route is very seldom travelled and involves a pirogue crossing at the river and some long walks. If you are heading into Gabon, don't forget to get an entry stamp in Bitam (Gabon) from immigration. There are occasional cargo boats between Douala and Libreville that may take passengers.

To Nigeria, the most popular crossing is in the north-west via Mamfé and Ekok to Mfum (the Nigerian border village) and on to Calabar. The trip is done by bush taxi (and a short stretch on foot), and in stages. There is also a crossing in the far north of Cameroon from Maroua to Maiduguri (Nigeria) via Banki (the border) using bush taxis and minibuses. Another feasible crossing point is from Garoua to Yola (Nigeria). This is mainly of interest to those wanting to visit the Yankari Game Reserve in Nigeria. It is also possible to travel to Nigeria by boat from Idenao, about 50km north-west of Limbe, to Oron (in Nigeria south of Calabar), though this route is currently not advisable for travellers due to the territorial dispute between the two countries over the Bakassi Peninsula.

To São Tomé, there are infrequent cargo ships from Douala.

The border with the Central African Republic (CAR) is closed to foreign travellers. Previously, the most popular routes from Cameroon were via Garoua-Boulaï and Bouar (CAR), and via Bertoua, Batouri and Berbérati (CAR).

To Chad, the usual route is via Kousséri over the Chari River and on to N'Djamena. However, travel is restricted due to insecurity around the Chadian border, so you should get an update on the situation before heading this way.

CAPE VERDE

The Cape Verde islands lie in the Atlantic Ocean, 445km off the coast of West Africa. Geographically they are closer to the Azores and the Canary islands than the African mainland, and they have minimal trade contacts with West Africa, but ethnically there are close connections. Charles Darwin visited here more than a century ago, and it was Cape Verde (and the Galápagos islands) which provided inspiration for his theory of evolution.

For travellers to Africa, Cape Verde's appeal lies in its uniqueness. It's probably the only place on the continent where you will find Mediterranean-style houses with verandas, *praças* (squares) with orchestra stands, and cobbled streets. The country is also notable for its distinctive, fast-paced music which combines Latin and African rhythms, and its relatively well educated populace. While Cape Verde may not be action-packed, its Portuguese ambience, barren and rocky landscape and guaranteed sun may be a welcome change for those who have been travelling around the mainland for a few months.

WHEN TO GO

Cape Verde's is dry, windy and relatively cool. The best time to visit is between August and October, when temperatures are comfortably warm, and winds less strong. From December to February, the air is often hazy due to dusty harmattan winds from the Sahara, and temperatures can be chilly.

At a Glance

Full Country Name: Republic of Cape Verde
Area: 4035 sq km
Population: 407,000
Capital City: Praia (population 65,000)
People: Predominantly mestizo (mixed European and African descent), African (30%) and European (1%)
Languages: Portuguese (official), Krioulo (an Africanised Creole Portuguese) and dialects that vary from island to island
Religions: Roman Catholic (over 90%) and traditional beliefs
Government: Republic
Currency: Cape Verde escudo (CVE)
Time Zone: One hour behind GMT/UTC
International Telephone Code: 238
Electricity: 220V, 50 Hz; most sockets take plugs with two round pins

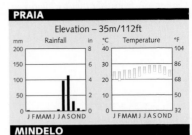

PRAIA — Elevation – 35m/112ft

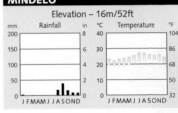

MINDELO — Elevation – 16m/52ft

HIGHLIGHTS
Culture
Cape Verde has a vibrant culture, best experienced during its February Mardi Gras festivals in Praia and Mindelo. Another way to immerse yourself in the local culture is by listening to some lively Cape Verdean music in a Praia nightclub, or enjoying a Portuguese-style meal accompanied by some *vinho verde* (Portuguese wine).

Outdoor Activities
The best outdoor activities are trekking – Santo Antão, Fogo and Brava islands are good for this – and relaxing on the beaches. A good trek is the return trip up Ribeira Grande Mountain, commencing about 10km south of the town of Ribeira Grande on the north-east coast of Santo Antão, which takes a full day.

VISA REQUIREMENTS
Visas are required by everyone. They are usually issued for stays of 30 days, or longer on request. If you are coming from a country which has no Cape Verdean embassy, you may obtain a visa on arrival at the airport. In West Africa, you can get visas at the Cape Verdean embassy in Dakar, Senegal.

You may also be asked to show an international vaccination certificate for proof of cholera and yellow fever vaccination, especially if you are arriving from the African mainland.

Cape Verde Embassies
USA
(☎ 202-965-6820) 3415 Massachusetts Ave NW, Washington, DC 20007

Senegal
(☎ 21 3936) 3 Blvd el Haji Djily Mbaye, Dakar

TOURIST OFFICES OVERSEAS
Cape Verde has no overseas tourist offices. However, tourist information is often available from embassies, and from foreign offices of TACV, the Cape Verdean national airline. Also check the web sites listed under Online Services.

HEALTH
Cape Verde is one of the healthiest of the West African countries, but reasonable health precautions should still be taken. As malaria exists on Santiago, mainly from September to November, you will need to take malaria precautions. Avoid all insect bites, and take care with what you eat and drink as diseases such as dysentery, typhoid and typhus all occur.

Medical facilities in Cape Verde are among the best in West Africa, but if you do require serious medical attention, consider flying home.

POST & COMMUNICATIONS
Cape Verde's postal service is reasonably priced and very reliable, including its poste restante services.

The telecommunications system is also good, and calls can be made easily to the USA, Europe and elsewhere. Rates are comparable to elsewhere in West Africa, and average between US$4 and US$6 per minute to the USA and Europe.

There is currently no public access to the Internet in Cape Verde.

MONEY
Costs
Expect to pay between US$10 and US$25 for budget accommodation, from US$25 for mid-range lodging, and

from US$50 for top-end hotels. Meals cost from US$5 (budget) to US$15 and more (top end). Your main expenses will probably be for trips to other islands, scuba diving and similar excursions.

In general, budget travellers should be able to get by on about US$25 to US$30 per day with careful planning, while mid-range travellers should plan on about US$50 per day.

Changing Money

Travellers cheques in most major currencies can be easily exchanged at banks, although US dollar travellers cheques are the most convenient. Outside of banking hours, some hotels in Praia will change dollars or West African CFA francs into escudos.

Itineraries

One Week

From Sal airport, you could spend a few days on the beach at Santa Maria, or head for Mindelo (on São Vicente Island), one of Cape Verde's most interesting towns. Then take the ferry over to Santo Antão for some trekking before flying to Santiago island and Praia for the remainder of your stay.

Two Weeks

With two weeks or more, you could spend a few extra days hiking on Santo Antão, or you could go to Fogo Island and climb Mt Fogo (2839m, Cape Verde's highest peak and a still-active volcano), followed by a day in sleepy São Filipe town on the southern edge of the island. From Fogo, travel by ferry to tiny but scenic Brava for some more hiking before heading to Praia. With more than two weeks, you could do all of the above at a leisurely pace and also explore some of the less visited islands such as São Nicolau, which is accessible by ferry from Sal or São Vicente.

ONLINE SERVICES

Lonely Planet has a web site Destination Cape Verde (www.lonely planet.com/dest/afr/cap.htm).

Cape Verde Embassy (www.capeverd eusembassy.org) is a good source of official and tourist-related information.

The homepage of the Worldwide Capeverdean Community (www.um assd.edu/SpecialPrograms/caboverde /capeverdean.html) has links to everything even remotely related to Cape Verde.

Photos of Cabo Verde (www.umassd .edu/SpecialPrograms/caboverde/picl ist.html) gives you a glimpse of the islands before you travel.

BOOKS & FILMS

Charles Darwin's *Voyage of the Beagle*, a diary of the trip that led him to develop the theory of natural selection, contains good descriptions of 1830s Cape Verde.

Jen Ludtke's book *Atlantic Peaks: An Ethnographic Guide to the Portuguese-Speaking Islands* is an introduction to the people and culture of Cape Verde.

Cape Verde: Politics, Economics and Society by Colm Foy is another good background work.

The Fortunate Isles by Basil Davidson chronicles Cape Verde's political and social life since independence.

A Birder's Guide to the Cape Verde Islands, edited by Dave Sargeant, is a comprehensive guide to the archipelago's diverse birdlife. Another good choice is *Birds of the Cape Verde Islands* by Cornelius J Hazevoet.

Noxious Beetles of the Cape Verde Islands by Michael Geisthardt & Antonius van Harten is useful for identifying what might be lurking at the bottom of your sleeping bag.

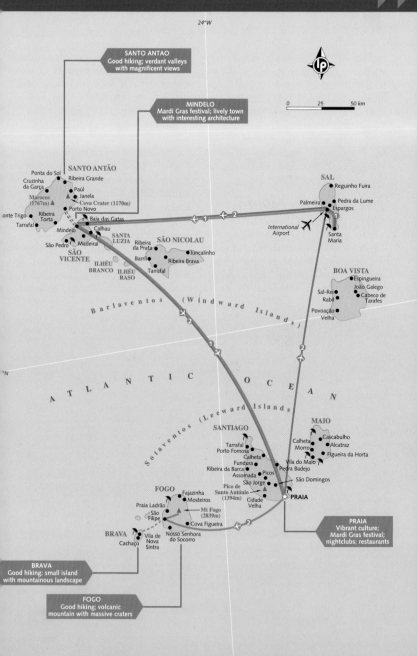

24°W

SANTO ANTAO
Good hiking; verdant valleys
with magnificent views

MINDELO
Mardi Gras festival; lively town
with interesting architecture

0   25   50 km

SAL
Reguinho Fuira

SANTO ANTÃO
Ponta do Sol
Cruzinha da Garça
Ribeira Grande
Paúl
Marocos (1767m)
Janela
Cova Crater (1170m)
Porto Novo
onte Trigo
Ribeira Torta
Tarrafal

Palmeira
Pedra da Lume
Espargos

International Airport

Santa Maria

Baía das Gatas
Calhau
Mindelo
Madeiral
São Pedro
SÃO VICENTE
ILHÉU BRANCO
ILHÉU RASO
SANTA LUZIA
Ribeira da Prata
Barril
Tarrafal
SÃO NICOLAU
Juncalinho
Ribeira Brava

BOA VISTA
Espingueira
Sal-Rei
João Galego
Rabil
Cabeço de Tarafes
Povoação Velha

Barlaventos (Windward Islands)

°N

ATLANTIC OCEAN

Solaventos (Leeward Islands)

MAIO
Calheta
Cascabulho
Morro
Alcatraz
Figueira da Horta

SANTIAGO
Tarrafal
Porto Fomosa
Calheta
Fundura
Ribeira da Barca
Assomada
Picos
São Jorge
Pico de Santo António (1394m)
Vila do Maio
Pedra Badejo
São Domingos
Cidade Velha
★ **PRAIA**

FOGO
Fajazinha
Mosteiros
Praia Ladrão
São Filipe
Mt Fogo (2839m)
Cova Figueira
Nosso Senhora do Socorro

BRAVA
Cachaço
Vila de Nova Sintra

PRAIA
Vibrant culture;
Mardi Gras festival;
nightclubs; restaurants

BRAVA
Good hiking; small island
with mountainous landscape

FOGO
Good hiking; volcanic
mountain with massive craters

The archipelago has a rich literary tradition, although very few works are translated into English. Noted Cape Verdean authors include Jorge Barbosa, Onésima Silveira and Kaoberdiano Dambara.

Most films from the country are also in Portuguese, including *Island of Contempt* (1996) and *Testamento do Senhor Napumoceno* (1997).

ENTERING & LEAVING CAPE VERDE

There are flights connecting Cape Verde with Lisbon daily, and with Amsterdam, Frankfurt and Paris between one and three times weekly. There is also a thrice-weekly direct flight from New York via Johannesburg on South African Airways. All of these flights arrive at Sal Island, from where you can fly on TACV (the national airline) to Praia and Mindelo.

From West Africa, there are flights several times weekly with TACV and Air Senegal between Cape Verde and Dakar (Senegal), and on Gambia Airways between Cape Verde and Banjul (The Gambia). Flights from Dakar are usually heavily booked. Flights from both Dakar and Banjul land at Praia, not Sal.

There is a boat once a month between Dakar and Praia, but the schedule is irregular and the price is almost the same as a return air fare.

CENTRAL AFRICAN REPUBLIC

The Central African Republic (CAR) has suffered decades of plundering and political chaos. As a result, the country today is fragmented, poverty-stricken and, in many areas, lawless. Although the CAR has important mineral deposits and could export significant amounts of produce, little of this potential wealth is realised, and even less makes its way out of the hands of a corrupt government to the people.

The main appeal of the CAR for travellers is its unspoiled, 'off-the-beaten-track' atmosphere. Particularly once outside of Bangui, Central Africans are generally very friendly and generous. The country also has some superb rainforests and fascinating protected ecosystems, although these areas are difficult to reach. The equatorial forests of the south-west are home to some 15,000 Pygmies who still pursue a nomadic hunter-gatherer lifestyle.

Due to high levels of crime and banditry, both in Bangui and up-country, travellers considering visiting the CAR should get a thorough update on the situation first, and should exercise caution while there.

WHEN TO GO

The best time for travel is during the dry months from November to March, although the air can be uncomfortably hot and muggy as the rainy season (May to October) approaches. In Bangui and the south, the rains can start as early as March. During the rainy season, many roads outside the capital become impassable.

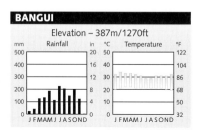

BANGUI

Elevation – 387m/1270ft

HIGHLIGHTS
Cultural & Urban

Bangui is worth a short visit, especially the Musée de Boganda with its interesting collection of musical instruments and displays of the Pygmies and their culture. The butterfly-wing art at the Centre Artisanal is unique.

At a Glance

Full Country Name: Central African Republic
Area: 622,980 sq km
Population: 3.3 million
Capital City: Bangui (population 600,000)
People: More than 80 groups including Baya (35%), Banda (28%), Sara (10%) and Mandja (9%)
Languages: French (official), Sango (national) other indigenous languages
Religions: Roman Catholic (about 25%), Muslim (about 10%) and traditional beliefs
Government: Republic
Currency: Central African CFA franc (CFA)
Time Zone: One hour ahead of GMT/UTC
International Telephone Code: 236
Electricity: 220V 50 Hz; most sockets take two round pins

Outdoors & Wildlife

Outside the capital, the CAR's main attractions are its unspoiled rural areas and friendly people.

The Dzanga-Sangha Reserve in the far south-west protects the country's last remaining virgin rainforests. It also has high densities of lowland gorillas and forest elephants, as well as populations of waterbuck, buffalo, duiker and chimpanzee. The only drawback is that the reserve is difficult to reach without your own 4WD and, once you arrive, there are no facilities for visitors.

Waterfalls

A more accessible destination for outdoor lovers is the 50m-high Chutes de Boali (about 100km north-west of Bangui), where the waterfalls during the rainy season are a dramatic sight.

Itineraries

Be sure to get an update on the political situation in the CAR from your embassy or knowledgeable locals before planning any travel outside Bangui. Only a one week itinerary is given here, due to the poor security situation in many upcountry areas.

One Week
With a week, you could spend a few days in Bangui, followed by an overnight visit to the Chutes de Boali. After returning to the capital, you could then take an excursion to M'Baïki, in the heart of a timber, coffee and tobacco-growing area and a useful base for visiting nearby Pygmy encampments. About 10km north-east of M'Baïki is the village of Sabe, famous for its ebony sculptures.

If the security situation warrants it, and you have the time and equipment (basically your own 4WD), consider extending your itinerary to include the Dzanga-Sangha Reserve.

VISA REQUIREMENTS

All travellers need visas except nationals of France, Germany, Israel and Switzerland. In the USA, visas are usually processed within three days. Elsewhere, allow plenty of time, as embassies must often contact Bangui for permission to issue the visa. Where there is no CAR embassy, visas can generally be obtained from the French embassy.

An international health certificate for proof of yellow fever and cholera vaccination is also required.

CAR Embassies

Cameroon
(☎ 20 2155) Rue 1810, Bastos, Yaoundé

Chad
(☎ 52 3206) Rue 1036, near Rond-Point de la Garde, N'Djamena

USA
(☎ 202-483-7800) 1618 22nd St NW, Washington, DC 20008

TOURIST OFFICES OVERSEAS

The CAR has no overseas tourist offices. See the web sites listed under Online Services for general travel information.

HEALTH

Malaria and yellow fever pose a health risk in CAR, so take appropriate precautions. Other diseases spread by insects, including leishmaniasis, trypanosomiasis (sleeping sickness), filariasis and typhus all occur; avoid all insect bites if possible. During the dry season, from November to April, there is a risk of meningococcal meningitis and schistosomiasis is present in freshwater, so avoid swimming or bathing in rivers and streams. Take care with what you eat;

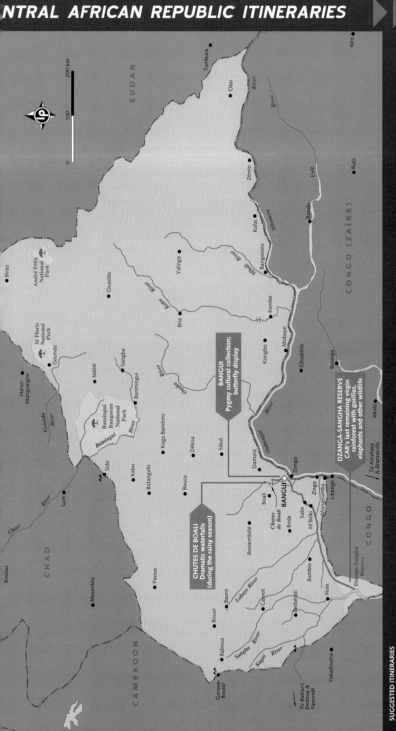

SUGGESTED ITINERARIES

One Week Bangui • Chutes de Boali (waterfalls) • M'Baïki • Sabe • Dzanga-Sangha Reserve

especially avoid undercooked meat and walking barefoot (to prevent intestinal worms). Dysentery, hepatitis, typhoid and cholera are all food or waterborne diseases which can cause serious health problems; drink only treated water and, wherever possible, hygienically prepared, freshly cooked food. Watch out for dogs as they can carry rabies, as can rats, monkeys and bats.

The Night I Slept with the Vicar

There were four of us in the cabin, wedged tight, thigh to thigh. The ample body of Marthe, a jolly market lady who'd commissioned the Benz truck for a little cross-border trade, wobbled with every guffaw ('c'est de la merde, ce camion' – load of shit, this lorry – she hooted at me as the driver winced). Flanking me on the windward side, Jean-Pierre, a gentle Centrafricain pastor, President and Founder (maybe sole?) Member of the Fount of Salvation Evangelical Ministry looked pained as Jacques, the driver, cursed savagely, sotto voce and fluently after each police road block, where generous tribute had to be paid.

We – plus a couple of dozen other passengers, travelling economy in the rear among crates of chickens, sacks of manioc and a solitary pig – were bouncing and swaying over the ruts and potholes of the dirt track linking Bangui, capital of the Central African Republic, and the border with neighbouring Chad.

The driver's fury swelled as each roadblock edged him closer to mental breakdown. More physical were the truck's own breakdowns. Within milliseconds of it spluttering to a stop, he would be out of the cab spitting vile imprecations, heaving up the bonnet (hood), savaging the innards with a giant spanner and removing an entrail or two, after which the vehicle would cough briefly and reluctantly back to life.

Jacques slips a black stocking over his head against the invading dust and I reflect that it's like riding shotgun with an IRA hit team. He seems to be edging ever nearer to meltdown as his left foot performs a lively St Vitus dance. But he's merely pumping the brake pedal every time we need to slow down.

Progressing by fits, starts and frequent total stops, the lorry hacked a terminal tuberculoid cough, shuddered and expired on the outskirts of the small and eminently missable town of Kaga Bandoro.

Leaving the other passengers to bed down around its corpse as though at a wake, Jean-Pierre and I head for the deserted market place, applying the traveller's principle that, if a settlement has a hotel, it will probably be beside the market or bus station – and no bus had ever called by Kaga Bandoro.

Fastidiously rejecting the black hole offered to us, its walls grimy and spattered with the corpses of long-swatted mosquitoes, we set out for the town's only alternative – the aptly named Le Samaritain, each room adorned with an edifying biblical text in large red letters.

Although this should have been right up Jean-Pierre's street, he was clearly not at ease. The cheaper rooms, price US$3, had all been taken and he was distressed by the price of the 'superior' ones, costing a dollar more.

So I say let's share, I'll pay, little knowing that the 'bed' was a small, plain wooden palette. In this constricted space we spent the night, manoeuvring limbs to avoid the mosquito netting and the man-eating insects beyond – and recoiling like opposite poles of a pair of magnets each time our flanks touched.

Sleep was fitful and time plenty for a touch of philosophical reflection: however poor and penniless we folk from the west may think we are, we're still much, much better off than most of those we meet on the road.

Miles Roddis
LP Author, Spain

Medical facilities are basic in Bangui and in rural areas. If you require serious medical care, you should fly home.

POST & COMMUNICATIONS

Poste restante in Bangui is quite efficient, but mail service in general is very slow and it is better to send your letters from outside the country.

Telephone is expensive. Three-minute telephone calls cost US$10 to Europe, and US$20 elsewhere .

There is currently no public access to the Internet in CAR.

MONEY
Costs

Budget travellers can easily get by on about US$15 per day, eating local food and staying in basic accommodation. Mid-range travellers should plan on between US$50 and US$100 per day. Top-end travel will cost from US$150 per day, although facilities outside the capital are extremely limited.

Changing Money

The exchange rate for cash is much lower than for travellers cheques, but commissions on travellers cheques can be very high, so shop around. The only places where you can change money at a bank are Bangui and Berbérati.

ONLINE SERVICES

Lonely Planet has a web site Central African Republic (www.lonelyplanet .com/dest/afr/car.htm).

For some basic facts, see MBendi Central African Republic Profile (http: //mbendi.co.za/cycrcy.htm#top).

Africa News Online – Central African Republic (www.africanews .org/central/centralafricanrepublic) carries a few of the latest news stories.

The Norwegian Council for Africa (www.africaindex.africainfo.no/africai ndex1/countries/car.html) has an index of additional links.

BOOKS & FILMS

Historical Dictionary of the Central African Republic by Pierre Kalck & Thomas O'Toole is a useful reference.

For an overview of major issues in the region, try *Aspects of Central African History* by T Ranger.

African Development Reconsidered by Haskell Ward offers insights into some of the causes of Africa's ongoing problems.

African Tales: Folklore of the Central African Republic, edited by Polly Strong, is hard to find, but interesting.

For an introduction to local literature, a useful anthology is *The Traveller's Literary Companion – Africa* edited by Oona Strathern, which contains over 250 prose and poetry extracts from around the continent.

Few films come out of the CAR.

ENTERING & LEAVING CAR

Air Afrique, Air France, Air Gabon and Cameroon Airlines service Bangui.

All of CAR's land borders are presently closed to foreign travellers. Previously, the most popular routes to Cameroon were via Garoua-Boulaï, and via Berbérati and Batouri.

Between CAR and Chad, the route is from Bangui via Sido to Sarh.

Chad's harsh climate, its poor resource endowment and its history of conflict – including a 25 year war – have given the country the dubious distinction of being one of Africa's poorest. While southern Chad has regained its vitality in recent years, you'll still see many bullet-marked facades and much rubble in N'Djamena, the capital, even today.

Despite this, Chad is an interesting place, and its people exceptionally friendly. Travel in the country's starkly beautiful Tibesti region in the north is not possible at present due to ongoing insecurity, and some areas of the south and south-west are also restricted, including along the border with Cameroon. But a short trip taking in N'Djamena and some nearby attractions is well worth the effort.

WHEN TO GO

The best time to visit is during the dry season between late November and mid-February, when the air is coolest. During the rainy season (June to September), many roads become impassable. While March, April and May are dry, they can be uncomfortably hot.

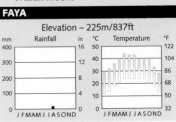

At a Glance

Full Country Name: Republic of Chad
Area: 1,284,000 sq km
Population: 7.3 million
Capital City: N'Djamena (population 700,000)
People: Bagirmi, Sara and Kreish (together constituting 30%), Arabic and Toubou (7.5%)
Languages: French and Turku (often referred to as Chadian Arabic) – official, and Bagirmi and its Sara derivatives
Religions: Christian (33%), Muslim (44%) and traditional beliefs
Government: Republic
Currency: Central African CFA franc (CFA)
Time Zone: One hour ahead of GMT/UTC
International Telephone Code: 235
Electricity: 220V, 50 Hz; most sockets take plugs with two round pins

HIGHLIGHTS
Urban & Archaeological

N'Djamena used to be considered one of the most pleasant cities in the Sahel (the region bordering the Sahara desert). Though it suffered during the war, it's once again lively during the day, with a bustling central market. About 12km out of town in Gaoui is the interesting Sao-Kotoko Museum, which includes finds from 6 BC Sao kingdom whose capital lies under the present-day village.

Ancient Capital

Well to the east (almost 900km from N'Djamena) is Abéché, a cobbled, desert-locked Muslim town which was once the capital of the powerful slave-raiding Ouadaï sultanate and an important staging post on trade routes to Egypt, Sudan and the Indian Ocean.

VISA REQUIREMENTS

Visas are required by all except nationals of France and Germany. They are usually issued for three months, and can be renewed without difficulty. You can obtain a Chadian visa in most countries in West and Central Africa. Notable exceptions are The Gambia, São Tomé & Príncipe, and Rwanda. French embassies no longer issue Chadian visas in countries where Chad has no diplomatic representation.

An international vaccination certificate for yellow fever and cholera is also required. An exit visa *(permit de sortir)* is required for those continuing overland to Niger or the Sudan.

Chadian Embassies

Cameroon
(☎ 21 1624) Rue Mballa Eloumden, Bastos, Yaoundé

USA
(☎ 202-462-4009) 2002 R St NW, Washington, DC 20009

TOURIST OFFICES OVERSEAS

Chad has no overseas tourist offices. Its embassies and travel agencies should be able to provide basic information. Also check the web sites listed under Online Services.

HEALTH

Take appropriate precautions against malaria and yellow fever in Chad. Other diseases spread by insects, including leishmaniasis, trypanosomiasis (sleeping sickness), filariasis and typhus all occur, so avoid all insect bites if possible.

During the dry season, October/November to May, there is a risk of contracting meningococcal meningitis and schistosomiasis is present in freshwater; avoid swimming or bathing in rivers and streams. As intestinal worms are common, take care with what you eat; especially avoid undercooked meat and walking barefoot.

Dysentery, hepatitis, typhoid and cholera are all food or waterborne diseases which occur in Chad; drink only treated water and try wherever possible to eat only hygienically prepared and freshly cooked food. Watch out for dogs, rats, monkeys and bats, which can carry rabies.

Medical facilities are limited in N'Djamena and in rural areas. If you require serious medical care, you should return home.

POST & COMMUNICATIONS

Both the post and telecommunications services are reliable, though inter-national calls are expensive. Expect to pay about US$20 for a three minute call to the USA.

Public access to the Internet is only available in Ndj in Chad.

MONEY
Costs

Although budget travellers can get by on US$10 to $15 per day, lodging standards at this end of the price range are usually abysmal. Mid-range travellers wanting slightly more comfort should plan on spending between US$25 and US$30. Top-end accommodation is available only in N'Djamena.

Changing Money

Cash and travellers cheques can be changed in N'Djamena, though cash is usually quicker. Cash advances on credit cards are not possible.

ONLINE SERVICES

Lonely Planet has a web site Destination Chad (www.lonelyplanet.com /dest/afr/cha.htm).

The World Travel Guide to Chad (www.wtgonline.com/data/tcd/tcd.asp) has factual information on the country.

BOOKS

Chad: A Nation in Search of its Future by Mario Azevedou et al is an examination of past and present political and economic issues in the country.

Limits of Anarchy: Intervention and State Formation in Chad by Sam Nolutshunga is a bit on the dry side, but informative nevertheless.

Country Review Chad, edited by Robert Kelly et al, is good for background information.

Contemporary West African States by Donald O'Brien is a dry but thorough account of conditions and events in Chad and several neighbouring countries.

For an introduction to local literature, a useful anthology is *The Traveller's Literary Companion – Africa* edited by Oona Strathern.

ENTERING & LEAVING CHAD

Chad is serviced by Air Afrique, Air Chad, Air France, Cameroon Airlines, Ethiopian Airlines and Sudan Airways.

To Cameroon, the usual route is across the Chari River to Kousséri and onwards. From Kousséri you can also find bush taxis to Maiduguri in Nigeria. There has been insecurity in the south-west of the country along the border with Cameroon, so get an update on the situation before planning to travel here.

From Chad to the Central African Republic (CAR), the usual route is via Sarh and Sido. Traffic is scarce on this route, and restricted on the CAR side You should make inquiries before undertaking this journey, since this border is closed sometimes.

To Niger, the route is from N'Djamena via Mao and Nokou to Nguigmi, Diffa and Zinder, and takes at least a week. The journey must be done in stages, and you will need to have your own food and water for the leg between Mao and Zinder. However, there is no public transport across the border, and crossing is not possible at present due to banditry and insecurity north-west of N'Djamena.

Itineraries

You should get an update on the security situation from their embassy or knowledgeable locals before following these itineraries.

One Week
With a week, you'll be limited to exploring N'Djamena and the nearby area, including visits to Gaoui and Linia, a village 30km east of the capital with a good Arabic-style market on Sundays.

Two Weeks
With two weeks, you could try your luck hitching a ride out to Abéché – allow about three days each way. Connections with Sarh, Chad's cotton centre and a major town in the southern region, are better and this would be another option.

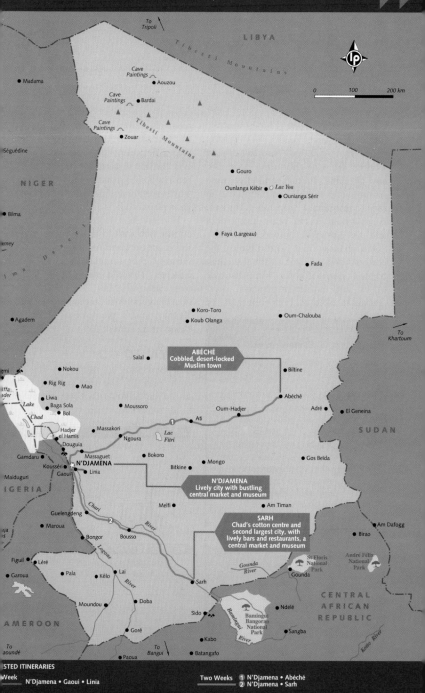

LIBYA

To Tripoli

Tibesti Mountains

Cave Paintings • Aouzou

Cave Paintings ~ • Bardai

Cave Paintings • Zouar

Tibesti Mountains

• Madama

Séguédine

NIGER

• Bilma

Imma Desert

• Agadem

• Gouro

Ounlanga Kébir • ○ Lac Yoa
• Ounianga Sérir

• Faya (Largeau)

• Fada

• Koro-Toro
• Koub Olanga

• Oum-Chalouba

To Khartoum

ABÉCHÉ
Cobbled, desert-locked
Muslim town

Salal •

• Nokou

rmi ·

• Rig Rig   • Mao

affa der

Liwa

Baga Sola

Lake   • Bol

Chad

Gamdaru •

Hadjer el Hamis
Douguia

Massaguet

Koussérri •

Gaoui •   N'DJAMENA ·

Linia

Maiduguri

IGERIA

• Moussoro

Massakori •

Ngoura   *Lac Fitri*

• Bokoro

• Biltine

• Abéché

Adré •   • El Geneina

SUDAN

Oum-Hadjer •

1   • Ati

Bitkine •   • Mongo

• Gos Beïda

N'DJAMENA
Lively city with bustling
central market and museum

Guelengdeng •

• Maroua

Chari

2

River

Bongor •   Bousso •

Logone

Melfi •

• Am Timan

SARH
Chad's cotton centre and
second largest city, with
lively bars and restaurants, a
central market and museum

• Am Dafogg

Figuil •   • Léré

• Garoua

• Pala   • Kélo

Lai •

River

• Doba

Moundou •

Goré •

Guonda   St Floris
National
Park

• Gounda

Gounda River

André Félix
National Park

• Birao

CENTRAL

AMEROON

To aoundé

Kabo •

• Paoua

To Bangui

• Batangafo

Sido •

Sarh •

Bamingui
Bamingui
Bangoran
National
Park

River

• Ndelé

AFRICAN

REPUBLIC

• Sangba

Kotto River

0   100   200 km

CÔTE D'IVOIRE

For many years, Côte d'Ivoire was the jewel of West Africa. Its strong economy attracted thousands of workers from neighbouring countries, and sizeable French and Lebanese communities established themselves in the commercial capital, Abidjan. Although in recent years heavy debt and an autocratic government have cast a shadow over Côte d'Ivoire, the country still gleams, with excellent roads, comfortable long-distance buses and some impressive skyscrapers in Abidjan. Following years of relatively stable government, a coup d'etat in late 1999 thrust the country into a period of political uncertainty. For the most part, the situation has returned to normal, although it's worth getting an update before setting your plans

For travellers, Côte d'Ivoire offers a culture rich with festivals, and some of the most outstanding artwork in West Africa. Other attractions include great beaches, forested mountains in the west around Man, the faded but charming colonial capital of Grand-Bassam and a plethora of colourful open-air restaurants.

WHEN TO GO

The best time to visit is during the early part of the dry season, from about mid-November to February, when temperatures are coolest. The air

At a Glance

Full Country Name: République de Côte d'Ivoire
Area: 322,465 sq km
Population: 14.2 million
Capital City: Yamoussoukro (population 120,000)
People: More than 60 different groups, including Baoulé (12%), Agni (11%), Bété (20%), Malinké (7%), Dan and Senoufo. There are also large numbers of expatriate workers from Burkina Faso, Mali, Guinea, Benin, Togo and Senegal, plus many French and Lebanese nationals
Languages: French (official), Baoulé, Agni, Mandé, Senoufo and Dioula (the universal language of commerce)
Religions: Muslim (25%), Christian (12.5%) and indigenous beliefs
Government: Republic
Currency: West African CFA franc (CFA)
Time Zone: GMT/UTC
International Telephone Code: 225
Electricity: 220V, 50 Hz; most sockets take plugs with two round pins

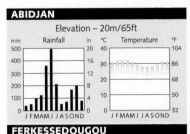

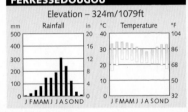

is clearest in November and early December just after the rains end; after this, dusty harmattan winds cause skies to be hazy.

HIGHLIGHTS
Hiking & Festivals

The area around Man is very scenic and offers good hiking. It's also one of the best places to watch the famed masked dancing festivals (Fête des Masques) of the Dan people, which take place in many villages in February. Another festival which is not to be missed is the Fête du Dipri, held in Gomon (100km north-west of Abidjan) in mid-April.

Beaches

Beach lovers should head for Sassandra, which offers beautiful stretches of coastline dotted with small fishing villages. Also along the coast, but east of Abidjan, is the pleasantly dilapidated colonial capital of Grand-Bassam. Further east is Assinié, where you will find more good beaches.

Big Apples

Abidjan itself is worth at least a brief visit, if only because it is such an anomaly in this part of the world. With its gleaming high-rise commercial district, vibrant neighbourhoods and multilane highways, it is undoubtedly the New York of West Africa. Some travellers love it; others cannot wait to leave.

Yamoussoukro has wide, treeless expanses of lawn, long boulevards ending in the bush, and rows of unsightly concrete houses. Yet it has a pleasant central area near the lake, and some good *maquis* (the open-air restaurants for which Côte d'Ivoire is

famed). Most visitors come to see the enormous Basilique de Notre Dame de la Paix, one of the largest churches in the world.

Rainforests & Wildlife

Those interested in seeing what is left of the rainforests which once covered much of West Africa should head to Parc National de Taï in the far southwest of the country (you'll need to arrange a permit first in San Pedro). Parc National de la Comoë in Côte d'Ivoire's north-east corner is the largest game park in West Africa, and also worth a visit. If you are lucky, you may see lion, elephant, baboon, hippo, waterbuck and many other animals. You'll need your own transport to tour the park.

VISA REQUIREMENTS

All travellers need a visa except nationals of the USA, UK, Germany, France, Ireland, Italy, Norway, Sweden, Denmark and Finland.

An international vaccination certificate for yellow fever and cholera is also required.

Côte d'Ivoire Embassies

Burkina Faso
(☎ 31 82 28) cnr Ave Raoul Follereau and Blvd du Faso, Ouagadougou

Canada
(☎ 613-230-0010) 9 Marlborough Ave, Ottawa, Ontario KIN 8EO

Ghana
(☎ 774611) 9 18th Lane, south of Danquah Circle, Accra

UK
(☎ 020-7235 6991) 2 Upper Belgrave St, London SW1X 8BJ

USA
(☎ 202-797-0330) 2424 Massachusetts Ave NW, Washington, DC 20008

TOURIST OFFICES OVERSEAS

Côte d'Ivoire has no overseas tourist offices, but its embassies and travel agents will be able to supply you with ample information on the country.

Itineraries

One Week
If you're visiting Côte d'Ivoire for only a week, plan on a few days in Abidjan including at least a day trip to Grand-Bassam, followed by two or three days at one of the west coast resorts, such as Sassandra. You could then head north to Yamoussoukro (one night), and then take the bus back to Abidjan. Alternatively, you could concentrate only on the coastal area, visiting Grand-Bassam and Assinié to the east for a few days, before heading west for the remainder of the week in Sassandra or at other nearby beaches.

Two Weeks
Follow the one week itinerary, including the coastline both east and west of Abidjan, then from Sassandra continue west to San Pedro and north-west to Man. After spending a few days exploring Man and its scenic surrounds, head east to Yamoussoukro and then back to Abidjan.

One Month
You could follow the two week itinerary, but spend a bit more time in each place, particularly on the western beaches (where you could arrange a detour to Parc National de Taï) and Man. From Man, head north to Korhogo, the home of the Senoufo people who are known for their woodcarvings and textiles. To avoid backtracking, you can go to Korhogo via Odienné, although this route is slow. From Korhogo, head south to Yamoussoukro (with a possible detour first to Parc National de la Comoë), and then to Abidjan. Some travellers prefer to save Grand-Bassam and Assinié until the end of their travels, in order to relax a bit and avoid spending too much time in Abidjan.

Also check the web sites listed under Online Services.

HEALTH

Yellow fever can occur in Côte d'Ivoire and malaria is endemic; you will need to take precautions against these serious diseases. Recently dengue fever epidemics have occurred in Côte d'Ivoire, so cover up, apply repellent and avoid mosquito bites both during the day and at night. Diseases transmitted by ticks, flies and sandflies, such as leishmaniasis, filariasis, trypanosomiasis (sleeping sickness) and typhus all occur; try and avoid all insect bites.

During the dry season (November to June) outbreaks of meningococcal meningitis can occur. Intestinal worms are common – parasites can be ingested in food or through the skin, so take care with what you eat; especially avoid undercooked meat and walking barefoot. As schistosomiasis is found in freshwater, avoid swimming or washing in rivers and streams.

Dysentery, hepatitis, typhoid and cholera are all food or waterborne diseases which occur here. Drink only treated water and try wherever possible to eat only hygienically prepared, freshly cooked food. As in other West African countries, dogs in Côte d'Ivoire as well as bats, monkeys and rodents and other furry animals are potential rabies carriers; avoid bites from all animals.

Reasonable health care is available in Abidjan, but not in the rest of the country. Seriously consider going home if you require medical treatment.

POST & COMMUNICATIONS

The post is reliable for letters, with costs similar to those elsewhere in the

CÔTE D'IVOIRE HIGHLIGHTS & ITINERARIES

PARC NATIONAL DE LA COMOË
Largest wildlife reserve in West Africa

MAN
Scenic area with good hiking and famed dancing festivals

PARC NATIONAL DE TAÏ
Dense rainforest; chimpanzees

ABIDJAN
Gleaming high-rise commercial district with vibrant neighbourhoods

SASSANDRA
Interesting fishing village with superb beaches nearby

GULF OF GUINEA

SUGGESTED ITINERARIES

One Week	Abidjan • Grand-Bassam • Sassandra • Yamoussoukro
	Abidjan • Grand-Bassam • Assinié • Sassandra
Two Weeks	Abidjan • Grand-Bassam • Assinié • Sassandra
	Abidjan • San Pedro • Man • Yamoussoukro
One Month	Abidjan • Grand-Bassam • Assinié • Sassandra • San Pedro • Parc National de Taï • Man • Odienné • Korhogo • Parc Naitonal de la Comoë • Yamoussoukro • Abidjan

region. There is a poste restante service in Abidjan.

International telephone calls can be made easily from Abidjan, and fairly efficiently from other major towns. A three minute call to Australia/USA/UK costs US$10/8/7.

Internet access is possible in Abidjan.

MONEY
Costs

Apart from Abidjan, Côte d'Ivoire is relatively inexpensive, and accommodation and food standards are generally high – even at the low end of the spectrum – in comparison with other countries in the region.

If you eat at local maquis and stay at budget hotels, you should have no trouble keeping your costs to about US$15 per day or less. Mid-range travellers seeking some comforts should plan on about US$30 to US$80 per day. Enjoying western meals and top-end hotels in Abidjan will cost from US$80 to over US$200 per day.

Changing Money

Cash is easily changed at banks in all major towns. Travellers cheques can be changed without much trouble at banks in Abidjan and other large towns, although you will often be required to show proof of purchase. Whether changing cash or travellers cheques, it pays to shop around, as rates and commissions vary. The most convenient denominations are US dollars and French francs.

You can get cash advances against Visa and MasterCard at a couple of banks in Abidjan. Otherwise, credit cards are only useful at a handful of top-end hotels.

ONLINE SERVICES

Lonely Planet has a web site Destination Côte d'Ivoire (www.lonely planet.com/dest/afr/cot.htm).

Côte d'Ivoire (www.execulink.com /~bruinewo/ivory.htm) has news, background information and more.

For a taste of what is to come in your travels, try the Ivoirien Cookbook (www.execulink.com/~bruinewo/reci pies.htm).

BOOKS & FILMS

Côte d'Ivoire's most well known novelist is Bernard Dadié, whose works include *Climbié*, an autobiographical account of a childhood journey to France, *The Black Cloth* and *The City Where No One Dies*.

Aké Loba is best known for *Kocoumbo* (abstracted in *African Writing Today*, 1967), an autobiographical novel of an impecunious, uprooted African in Paris being drawn towards militant communism.

Ahmadou Kourouma's first hit novel was *The Suns of Independence* (1981), the wry, humorous story of a disgruntled village chief, deposed after independence. His second novel, *Monné, Outrages et Défi*, written in 1990 after years of silence (yet to be translated into English), took that year's Grand Prix Littéraire d'Afrique Noire – Francophone Africa's premier literary prize.

Among younger writers, Bandama Maurice won the same honour in 1993 for his novel *Le Fils de la Femme Mâle*. Two novelists and poets who are also widely read throughout Francophone Africa are Véronique Tadjo and Tanella Boni. Tadjo's *Lord of the Dance: An African Retelling* is a good introduction to Senoufo culture, which is known for its elaborate masks and festivals.

Baoulé: African Art, Western Eyes by Susan Mullin Vogel is about the culture of Côte d'Ivoire's Baoulé people.

The Oscar-winning *Black and White in Colour* (1976), the tale of a French expatriate in remote Africa during WWI, and a protest against the madness of war, was filmed in Côte d'Ivoire.

Schweitzer (1990), the story of the Nobel Prize-winning doctor Albert Schweitzer and his life in the African jungle, was partially filmed in Abidjan.

ENTERING & LEAVING CÔTE D'IVOIRE

Abidjan is West Africa's major airline hub. It is serviced by most European airlines, as well as many regional carriers.

Land routes in most directions are unproblematic. Between Côte d'Ivoire and Ghana, the best connections are along the sealed road via Aboisso and Takoradi (crossing at Elubo), which connects Abidjan and Accra. There is a less used crossing to Kumasi in Ghana via Agnibilékrou; you will have to do this trip in stages, and get an exit stamp from the police in Agnibilékrou before crossing into Ghana.

To Burkina Faso, there are daily buses from Abidjan via Ferkessédougou, from where you can get a bush taxi to Bobo-Dioulasso or on to Ouagadougou. There are also direct daily buses between Abidjan and Ouagadougou, and a train which connects the two cities three times weekly.

The route to Mali is via Ferkessédougou to Sikasso using minibus and taxi. There are also some direct minibuses to Bamako, although many drivers who say they are going direct actually only go to the border, where you will have to catch another taxi. Other routes are from Odienné via Bougouni to Bamako (feasible only during the dry season), and from Abidjan by direct bus to Bamako. The latter is at least a 40 hour trip, and best done in stages.

To Guinea, the road is tarred to the border, but rough (and during the rainy season often impassable) on the Guinean side until Nzérékoré. From Nzérékoré, there is a good tarmac road to Conakry.

DJIBOUTI

The area now known as Djibouti was long the grazing land for nomadic tribes such as the Afars from eastern Ethiopia and the Issas from Somalia. It was later controlled by the Arabs for about 700 years, and more recently, by the French. Today, it is a relatively quiet place (except for sporadic outbursts of armed rebel activity), well off the beaten track, but an interesting detour if you are in the region.

In addition to Djibouti City's interesting blend of African, Arabic and French cultures, the country offers some

desolate but beautiful scenery including black lava fields, dormant volcanoes, desert plains, interesting rock formations and pleasant coastline. Lac Abbé in the south-west of the country is a favoured gathering place for flamingos. The Red Sea offers superb coral reefs and very good diving and snorkelling.

All areas of the country are open to travel except the extreme north-west. However, if you plan on venturing outside of the main centres, it's best to get a security update first from your embassy or consulate.

At a Glance

Full Country Name: Republic of Djibouti
Area: 23,000 sq km
Population: 600,000 (Djibouti's population figures are controversial due to the uncertain number of refugees and expatriates, and to sensitivity over the country's ethnic composition)
Capital City: Djibouti City (population 300,000)
People: Afar (just under 50%), Issa, Somalis of the Gadaboursi and Issaq clans, Yemenis and about 8000 French (many of whom are military personnel)
Languages: French and Arabic (official), Afar and Somali
Religions: Muslim (more than 90%). A small percentage is Christian
Government: Republic
Currency: Djibouti franc (DFr)
Time Zone: Three hours ahead of GMT/UTC
International Telephone Code: 253
Electricity: 220V, 50 Hz; most sockets take plugs with two round pins

WHEN TO GO

Djibouti's climate is hot year-round. (It is Africa's warmest city, with a mean annual temperature of 30°C.) The best months to visit are from November through March, when temperatures are a bit cooler (averaging 25°C), and humidity is not too high.

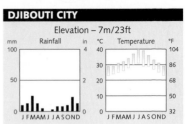

HIGHLIGHTS
Urban Attractions

Djibouti City is a bustling place where the country's different cultures rub elbows. A walk around its centre is a great way to get a feel for the local lifestyle.

Diving & Outdoor Activities

Outside the capital, Djibouti's main attraction is its nature. Diving or snorkelling in the Red Sea, visiting Lac Abbé with its interesting rock formations and flamingos, relaxing on a beach, or enjoying a boat ride across the Gulf of Tadjoura are all enjoyable ways to spend your time.

VISA REQUIREMENTS

Visas are usually valid for one month, and are required by all visitors except French nationals. Where there is no Djibouti embassy, visas can be obtained from the French embassy.

You will also need proof of yellow fever vaccination.

Djibouti Embassies

Ethiopia
(☎ 01-613 200) PO Box 1022, Addis Ababa

France
(☎ 01-454 31 49) 26 rue Emile Menier 751 16, Paris

USA
(☎ 202-331-0270) 1156 15th St NW, Washington, DC 20005

TOURIST OFFICES OVERSEAS

Djibouti has no overseas tourist offices, but its embassies and travel agencies should be able to supply you with information. Also check the web sites listed under Online Services.

HEALTH

Malaria occurs throughout the year and recently there have been outbreaks of dengue fever; take appropriate precautions. Other insect-borne diseases, especially diseases carried by mosquitoes, sandflies, flies and ticks, can occur, so avoid insect bites.

Schistosomiasis may be found in freshwater; avoid swimming or washing in rivers and streams. Dysentery, hepatitis, typhoid and cholera are all food or waterborne diseases which occur here; drink only treated water and try to eat only hygienically prepared, freshly cooked food.

Intestinal worms are common, so take care with what you eat; especially avoid undercooked meat and walking barefoot. Watch out for dogs which can carry rabies, as can rats, monkeys and bats.

In Djibouti City and rural areas, health services are limited. Consider leaving for Nairobi in Kenya or Cairo in Egypt if you need serious medical care.

POST & COMMUNICATIONS

Djibouti's post and telecommunications services are reliable and efficient. Postal rates are roughly equivalent to those in Europe.

International telephone calls are relatively expensive in comparison with rates in Europe and the USA (US$9/12/15 for three minutes to Europe/Australia/USA).

Internet access is not currently available to the public in Djibouti.

MONEY
Costs

Djibouti is expensive; at the lower end of the scale, plan on spending US$25 to US$35 per day for food and lodging. More comfortable hotels and meals in upmarket restaurants will cost between US$40 and US$70 per day, while top-end will cost from US$80.

Changing Money

There is no currency exchange at the airport. Banks in Djibouti City are open Sunday to Thursday from 7.30 am to 1.30 pm. There are also money-changers, mostly on the south-east side of Place Mélénik, which are open throughout the day. The most convenient currencies are French francs and US dollars.

Credit cards are widely accepted at mid-range and top-end hotels and restaurants in Djibouti City. Outside the capital, you will need cash.

ONLINE SERVICES
Lonely Planet has a web site Destination Djibouti (www.lonelyplanet.com/dest/afr/com.htm).

The Djibouti Home Page (www.sesrtcic.org/dir-dji/djihome.htm) has some statistics along with a more interesting photo album.

Djibouti's WWW Sites (www.leb.net/~hajeri/djibouti.html) lists many links.

BOOKS & FILMS
Naval Strategy East of Suez: The Role of Djibouti by Charles Koburger is more readable than its title would suggest. It provides an introduction to Djiboutian military and political history, with some good insights into the country.

Djibouti: Pawn of the Horn of Africa by Robert Tholomier is a helpful analysis of politics during the colonial era and in more recent times.

Country Review, Djibouti, 1998/1999, edited by Robert Kelly et al, is a concise source of political and economic information on Djibouti.

The 1995 film *Total Eclipse* was made in part in Djibouti.

ENTERING & LEAVING DJIBOUTI
Airlines serving Djibouti include Aeroflot, Air France, Ethiopian Airlines, Yemenia and the national carrier, Djibouti Airlines.

There is irregular bus service between Djibouti City and the Ethiopian border, from where you can connect to Dire Dawa in Ethiopia. It's better, however, to take the train to Dire Dawa, where you can stay overnight and continue on the next day to Addis Ababa by bus. Note that all connections with Ethiopia may be disrupted due to the Ethiopian-Eritrean conflict. Be sure to get an update from a reliable source (your embassy or a knowledgeable local) before travelling.

To Eritrea, there are only rough tracks used by nomads. This route is seldom used as there are no formal border posts where you can get your passport stamped.

Due to the security situation in Somalia, overland travel to that region is strictly off limits.

Itineraries

Be sure to get an update on conditions outside of Djibouti City before venturing to the country's more remote areas.

One Week
After three or four days in Djibouti City, including excursions to the nearby beaches, you could spend the rest of the week visiting Lac Abbé, though you will need a 4WD for this. Alternatively, you could take the ferry across the Gulf of Tadjoura to the town of the same name and spend the night there before returning to the capital.

Two Weeks
With two weeks, you can follow the one week itinerary, allowing more time in each place, and for diving and snorkelling in the Red Sea. You can also work in an excursion to Ali Sabieh, one of Djibouti's four district capitals separated from the capital by some beautiful desert plains.

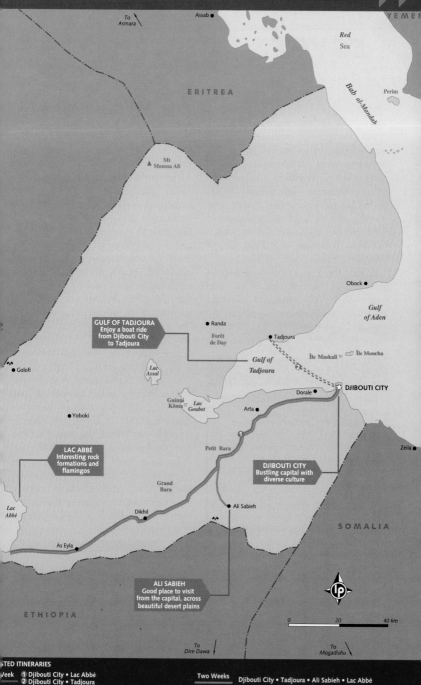

To Asmara

Assab

Red Sea

YEMEI

ERITREA

Bab al-Mandab

Perim

▲ Mt Moussa Ali

Obock ●

Gulf of Aden

GULF OF TADJOURA
Enjoy a boat ride from Djibouti City to Tadjoura

● Randa

Forêt de Day

Tadjoura ●

Île Maskali ◌   ◌ Île Moucha

Gulf of Tadjoura

Lac Assal

Dorale ●

★ **DJIBOUTI CITY**

● Golofi

Guinni Kōma ◌

Lac Goubet

Arta ●

● Yoboki

LAC ABBÉ
Interesting rock formations and flamingos

Petit Bara

DJIBOUTI CITY
Bustling capital with diverse culture

Zeila ●

Grand Bara

Dikhil ●

Ali Sabieh ●

Lac Abbé

SOMALIA

As Eyla ●

ALI SABIEH
Good place to visit from the capital, across beautiful desert plains

ETHIOPIA

0   20   40 km

To Dire Dawa

To Mogadishu

EGYPT

Egypt, birthplace of one of the world's greatest civilisations, still retains much of its ancient glory. This is seen most dramatically in the extraordinary pyramids, temples and other monuments left behind by the Pharaohs in places like Luxor and Aswan, as well as in the remnants of the many other cultures that inhabited the area following the long era of Pharaonic rule.

Today the country is a fusion of ancient and modern, and of east and west. While TV antennae decorate rooftops everywhere – from the crowded apartment blocks of Cairo (Africa's largest city) to the mud-brick homes of farming villages and the goatskin tents of the Bedouins – the *fellahin* (farmers) in the fertile Nile valley still tend their fields using the ancient techniques of their ancestors.

For travellers, Egypt's main attractions – apart from its spectacular architecture and congested capital – are the natural beauty of its countryside and the hospitality of its people. While the noise and chaos of Cairo can come as a bit of a shock, the country has until recently posed no particular difficulties for visitors. Recent episodes of terrorism have modified this picture.

WHEN TO GO

Winter (December through February) is the best time to be in Upper Egypt (the south), including Aswan and Luxor. In the summer months of June to August, this area becomes uncomfortably hot. Spring (March through May) and autumn (October and November) are the most pleasant times to be in Cairo. Summer is the most popular time for destinations along the Mediterranean coast, although they are often crowded then and accommodation is more expensive.

At a Glance

Full Country Name: Arab Republic of Egypt
Area: 1,001,449 sq km
Population: 61.5 million
Capital City: Cairo (the population of Greater Cairo is about 18 million)
People: Hamito-Semitic race, including Berbers (about 90%), Bedouin Arab nomads and Nubians
Languages: Arabic (official); Egyptian colloquial Arabic differs significantly from the Arabic of neighbouring countries
Religions: Muslim (about 90%) and Coptic Christians
Government: Constitutional republic
Currency: Egyptian pound (E£)
Time Zone: Two hours ahead of GMT/UTC (May to September three hours ahead)
International Telephone Code: 20
Electricity: 220V, 50 Hz; sockets take two round pins, although the socket holes are often too narrow to accept European plugs

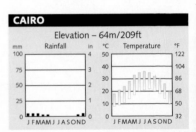

CAIRO

Elevation – 64m/209ft

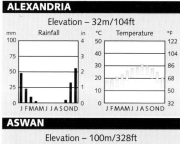

ALEXANDRIA
Elevation – 32m/104ft

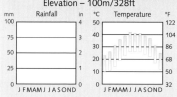

ASWAN
Elevation – 100m/328ft

of the best of Egypt's easily accessible dive locations. The Sinai itself is a region of harsh beauty and well worth visiting. The oases also provide a good escape from Cairo's crowds. Two of the most interesting are lush Siwa, in the northwest, famous for its dates and olives, and Farafra, which is a convenient base for excursions to the White desert.

Other Treasures

Apart from the pyramids, Egypt has many other sights well worth seeing. The medieval labyrinth of 'Islamic Cairo' is a fascinating section where the modern and the centuries-old come together, and the city's Egyptian Museum houses many ancient treasures, including those of Tutankhamun.

HIGHLIGHTS
Pyramids & Monuments

The pyramids are undoubtedly one of Egypt's greatest tourist attractions. Of these, perhaps the most awesome are the Great Pyramids of Giza, about 17km west of Cairo University. The ancient Greeks called these one of the Seven Wonders of the World.

The collection of ancient monuments from Luxor south to Abu Simbel is not to be missed. Luxor's west bank offers everything from the Valley of the Kings (with its tombs, including the Tomb of Tutankhamun) to startling monuments such as the unique Temple of Hatshepsut. The Temples of Karnak on the east bank are also well worth a visit.

Marine Attractions & Oases

Those wanting to escape big cities and tourist throngs could head for the Red Sea, with its coral gardens and fish of every imaginable shape, size and colour. The area around Sharm el-Sheikh and Ras Mohammed in the south of the Sinai peninsula is considered to be one

VISA REQUIREMENTS

All foreigners, except nationals of Malta and Arab countries, must obtain visas from Egyptian consulates overseas or at the airport or port on arrival. Single-entry visas are valid for three months, and entitle the holder to stay in Egypt for one month. Multiple-entry visas are also available. Visas can be obtained in many countries in the region, including Israel, Jordan and Libya.

An international health card with proof of yellow fever and/or cholera immunisation is required if you are arriving from an infected area (such as most of sub-Saharan Africa).

Egyptian Embassies & Consulates

Australia
(☎ 06-273 4437/8) 1 Darwin Ave, Yarralumla, ACT 2600. Consulates: Melbourne and Sydney (Double Bay)

Canada
(☎ 613-234-4931) 454 Laurier Ave East, Ottawa, Ontario K1N 6R3. Consulate: Montreal

EGYPT HIGHLIGHTS & ITINERARIES

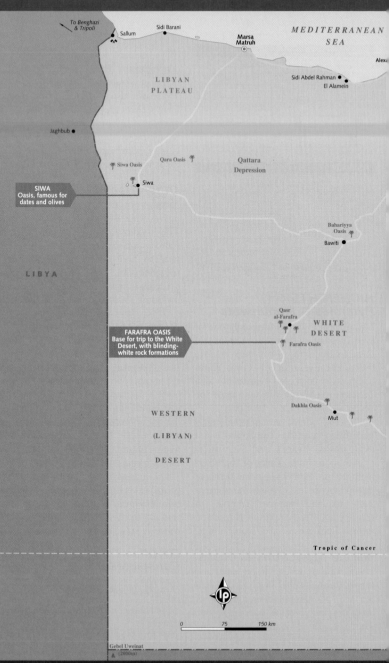

To Benghazi & Tripoli

Sallum

Sidi Barani

MEDITERRANEAN SEA

Marsa Matruh

Alex

LIBYAN PLATEAU

Sidi Abdel Rahman

El Alamein

Jaghbub

Siwa Oasis

Qara Oasis

Qattara Depression

Siwa

SIWA
Oasis, famous for dates and olives

Bahariyya Oasis

Bawiti

LIBYA

Qasr al-Farafra

WHITE DESERT

FARAFRA OASIS
Base for trip to the White Desert, with blinding-white rock formations

Farafra Oasis

WESTERN

(LIBYAN)

DESERT

Dakhla Oasis

Mut

Tropic of Cancer

0   75   150 km

Gebel Uweinat
▲ (2000m)

SUGGESTED ITINERARIES

One Week   Cairo • Giza • Luxor • Thebes • Aswan • Abu Simbel

Two Weeks   Cairo • Luxor • Aswan • Abu Simbel • Temple of Phila Edfu • Hurghada • Mt Sinai

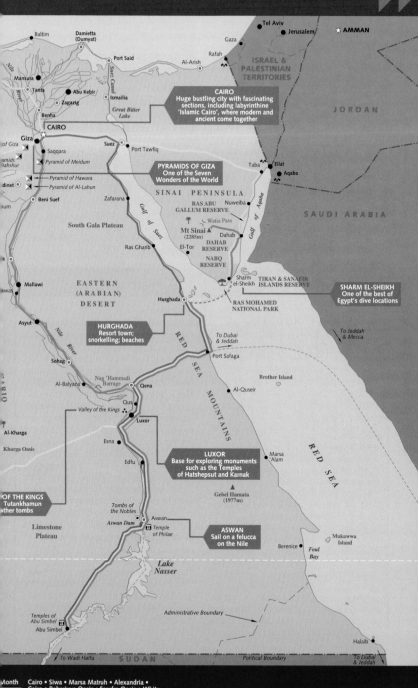

Baltim
Damietta
(Dumyat)
Port Said
Al-Arish
Rafah
Gaza
Tel Aviv
Jerusalem
★ AMMAN

Mansura
Tanta
Abu Kebir
Ismailia
Zagazig
Benha
Great Bitter
Lake
Suez Canal

**ISRAEL &
PALESTINIAN
TERRITORIES**

JORDAN

Nile River

CAIRO

...of Giza
Saqqara
Suez
Port Tawfiq
...ds
ahsur
Pyramid of Meidum
Taba
Eilat
Aqaba

PYRAMIDS OF GIZA
One of the Seven
Wonders of the World

Pyramid of Hawara
...dinet
Pyramid of Al-Lahun
Zafarana
SINAI   PENINSULA

**RAS ABU
GALLUM RESERVE**

Beni Suef
...um

South Gala Plateau

Nuweiba

Watia Pass

Mt Sinai ▲
(2285m)
Dahab

**DAHAB
RESERVE**

El-Tor

**NABQ
RESERVE**

SAUDI ARABIA

Ras Gharib

**EASTERN
(ARABIAN)
DESERT**

Mallawi

...was

Asyut

Nile River

Sharm
el-Sheikh

**TIRAN & SANAFIR
ISLANDS RESERVE**

Hurghada

**RAS MOHAMED
NATIONAL PARK**

To Jeddah
& Mecca

SHARM EL-SHEIKH
One of the best of
Egypt's dive locations

HURGHADA
Resort town;
snorkelling; beaches

Sohag

To Dubai
& Jeddah
Port Safaga

**RED   SEA
MOUNTAINS**

Al-Balyana

Nag 'Hammadi
Barrage
Qena

Brother Island

...RIO

Qus

Valley of the Kings

Luxor

Al-Quseir

Esna

Al-Kharga

Kharga Oasis

Edfu

LUXOR
Base for exploring monuments
such as the Temples
of Hatshepsut and Karnak

Marsa
Alam

**RED
SEA**

Gebel Hamata
(1977m) ▲

...OF THE KINGS
Tutankhamun
...ther tombs

Tombs of
the Nobles

Aswan

**Limestone
Plateau**

Aswan Dam

Temple
of Philae

ASWAN
Sail on a felucca
on the Nile

Mukawwa
Island

Berenice

Foul
Bay

**Lake
Nasser**

Temples of
Abu Simbel

Abu Simbel

Administrative Boundary

SUDAN

To Wadi Halfa

Political Boundary

Halaib

To Dubai
& Jeddah

CAIRO
Huge bustling city with fascinating
sections, including labyrinthine
'Islamic Cairo', where modern and
ancient come together

...onth   Cairo • Siwa • Marsa Matruh • Alexandria •
Cairo • Bahariyya Oasis • Farafra Oasis • White
Desert • Dakhla Oasis • Nile Valley • Qena • Aswan •
Abu Simbel • Hurghada • Sharm el-Skeikh • Sinai

Israel
(☎ 03-546 4151) 54 Basel St, Tel Aviv.
Consulate: Eilat

Jordan
(☎ 6-605202) 4th floor, Karbata Ben el-Dawar St, Amman

Libya
(☎ 61-92488) 5th floor, Omar Khayam Hotel, Benghazi

UK
(☎ 020-7499 2401) 26 South St, Mayfair, London W1Y 6DD

USA
(☎ 202-224-4319/5131) 3521 International Court NW, Washington, DC 20008. Consulates: New York, San Francisco, Houston and Chicago

TOURIST OFFICES OVERSEAS

Egypt has tourist offices in Austria, Canada, France, Germany, Greece, Italy, Japan, Spain, Sweden, Switzerland, the UK and the USA. Following are some addresses:

Canada
(☎ 514-851-4606; fax 861-8071) Egyptian Tourist Authority, 1253 McGill College Ave, Suite 250, Montreal, Quebec H3B 2Y5

UK
(☎ 020-7493 5282; fax 7408 0295) Egyptian Tourist Authority, 3rd floor West, Egyptian House, 170 Piccadilly, London W1V 9DD

Itineraries

One Week
You can see many of Egypt's most famous sights in a week's whirlwind tour. Following a couple of days in Cairo visiting the pyramids and the Egyptian Museum, head to Luxor to explore the ancient necropolis of Thebes and the sites in Luxor itself. Continue to Aswan, where you can spend an afternoon sailing on a *felucca* on the Nile. If you still have energy, you could fit in a trip to Abu Simbel the next day, before taking a train or bus back to Cairo.

Two Weeks
A fortnight will give you sufficient time to explore parts, but not all, of Egypt. If you enjoy ancient monuments, it would be best to stick to the Nile Valley. For more variety, consider a few days in and around Cairo, followed by a couple of days in Luxor and another two days in Aswan, visiting Abu Simbel and the Temple of Philae. Then head back to Aswan, where you could take a felucca trip to Edfu (two nights) to visit the largest and most completely preserved Pharaonic temple in the country. This could be followed by a couple of days snorkelling near Hurghada (Egypt's most popular resort town) on the Red Sea. From Hurghada, take a ferry across the Red Sea to southern Sinai and do some diving or snorkelling before climbing to the peak of Mt Sinai.

One Month
A month will allow you to cover most of Egypt's main sites, although you will have to travel at a steady pace. You could easily fill four days in and around Cairo before heading west to Siwa. After a few days relaxing here, backtrack along the Mediterranean coast, stopping overnight at Marsa Matruh (a large waterfront town built around a charming bay of clear Mediterranean waters and white sandy beaches), then spend a couple of days in Alexandria, once the centre of the Hellenic world.

Head by bus back to Cairo, then on to the Bahariyya Oasis or Farafra Oasis, where you can arrange an overnight trip to the White Desert, an other-worldly region of blinding-white rock formations shaped by wind erosion.

Finish the oasis circuit with two days in the Dakhla Oasis, from where you can take a bus to the Nile Valley and spend a week or so exploring the sights between Qena (a provincial capital about 60km north of Luxor) and Aswan. You will need another day for Abu Simbel. Then head east to Hurghada on the Red Sea Coast, where you could spend a couple of nights before taking the ferry across the Red Sea to Sharm el-Sheikh. You will then have close to a week to explore the delights of Sinai.

USA

Egyptian Tourist Authority
(☎ 212-332-2570; fax 956-6439) 630 5th Ave, Suite 1706, New York, NY 10111; (☎ 213-781-7676; fax 653-8961) 83 Wilshire Blvd, Suite 215, Wilshire San Vincente Plaza, Beverly Hills, CA 90211; (☎ 312-280-4666; fax 4788) 645 North Michigan Ave, Suite 829, Chicago, IL 60611

HEALTH

There is risk of malaria in the Al-Fayoum area only, generally from June until October. Dengue fever outbreaks have been reported; you will need to take precautions against both these mosquito-borne diseases. Schistosomiasis exists in the Nile River delta and in the Nile valley; avoid swimming or bathing in fresh waters in rural areas. Food and waterborne diseases occur here, so pay attention to basic food and water hygiene. Egypt's heat can pose some problems, so take care to avoid sunburn and dehydration.

Health care throughout Egypt is reasonably good. If you do require serious medical attention, Cairo is the best place to go.

POST & COMMUNICATIONS

Most mail gets to its destination, but very slowly; rates are generally cheaper than in the west.

International telephone calls can be made with a minimum of hassle. Rates vary depending on the time of day, with cheaper rates in the evenings. In general, daytime rates are roughly comparable to those in Europe. While hotels often have direct international lines, their rates can be as much as double those at telephone offices. International calls can also be made at card phones, usually located in telephone offices. Collect calls can be made from a few places in Cairo to certain countries, including Canada, the UK and the USA.

Internet access is possible throughout the country, including Cairo, Alexandria, Sharm el-Sheikh, Dahab, Hurghada, Luxor and Aswan, although connections can be very slow. There may also be problems with plugging your laptop into the wall in hotel rooms, as phone sockets vary and in many cases the phone cable is wired into the wall.

MONEY
Costs

Despite high inflation and a steady currency, Egypt is still a relatively cheap place to travel. If you stick to budget hotels and inexpensive food, and limit yourself to one historic site a day, you will have no trouble getting by on US$15 per day or less. More comfortable, but still modest, accommodation and some pricier meals will cost from about US$20 to US$30 per day, while top-end comforts start at about US$100 and more per day.

Changing Money

Most foreign hard currencies, cash or travellers cheques can be readily changed. Money can be officially changed at American Express and Thomas Cook offices, commercial banks, foreign exchange (forex) bureaux and some hotels. The black market for hard currency is negligible.

Major credit cards are accepted in a wide range of shops, and Visa and MasterCard can be used for cash advances from many branches of Banque Misr and the National Bank of Egypt, as well as from Thomas Cook. Outside larger cities and tourist hubs, cash advances are more difficult.

ONLINE SERVICES

Lonely Planet has a web site Destination Egypt (www.lonelyplanet.com /dest/afr/egy.htm).

Egypt – a country study (http://lcweb2 .loc.gov/frd/cs/egtoc.html) has some informative facts and figures.

ArabNet (www.arab.net/egypt/egypt _contents.html) has good information on everything from ancient history to getting around on the Cairo Metro.

Tour Egypt (http://interoz.com /egypt/index.htm) has destination information, travel tips, a monthly newsletter and more.

Look at Cairo city guide (www .openworld.co.uk/cityguides/cairo) before heading to the capital.

The Journeyman Home Page (www .algonet.se/~arvendal/index.htm) has well designed Egyptian travelogues.

For travel tips and water-sports information, look at the Internet Traveller's Guide to the Red Sea (www .red-sea.com).

BOOKS & FILMS

There is an extensive selection of books available on Egypt. Only a small sampling is listed here.

Journey to the Orient by Gerard de Nerval was first published in the 19th century. It is a good book to read for background before you set off to explore Egypt's mysteries.

The Penguin Guide to Ancient Egypt by William J Murnane is one of the best overall books on the life and monuments of ancient Egypt, with numerous illustrations and descriptions of most major monuments in the country.

The Ancient Egyptians – Religious Beliefs & Practices by Rosalie David is a comprehensive history of the evolution of religious beliefs and practices in ancient Egypt.

In an Antique Land by Amitav Ghosh is a superb chronicle of life in a Nile Delta village.

Khul-Khall – Five Egyptian Women Tell their Stories, edited by Nayra Atiya, tells the life stories of five contemporary Egyptian women from a variety of backgrounds.

Egypt's best known writer in the west is Nobel laureate Naguib Mahfouz, who has captured people's imagination with his stories, often of ordinary lives in the poor parts of central Cairo. His works include *The Cairo Trilogy*, *Midaq Alley* and *Miramar*.

Nawal El-Saadawi is another internationally known writer. Her most acclaimed works include *Point Zero* and *Death of an ex-Minister*.

Egypt's first locally produced film was *Laila* (1927) by producer Aziza Amir. One of the nation's best known contemporary film-makers is Youssef

Warning

In September 1997, nine German tourists were shot in Cairo. In November 1997, 67 people (57 of them tourists) were killed by terrorists at Luxor. Fundamentalist Islamic militants have warned that they will continue to target tourists in their campaign against the Mubarak government. In the five years since the campaign began, around 100 tourists have been killed. The Egyptian Ministry of Tourism claims that Egypt is still as safe as any other country, but US and British authorities are advising their nationals to avoid Luxor in particular. The Egyptian government has asked tourists to remember that around one-sixth of Egyptians rely on tourism for their livelihood.

Chahine, whose international break-through came with *Heaven or Hell* starring Omar Sherif. Other works include *The Sparrow* (1973) and the controversial *El-Mohager*.

ENTERING & LEAVING EGYPT

Egypt is serviced by numerous airlines. Cairo is the main international gateway. Lufthansa Airlines and Olympic Airways also have flights to Alexandria, and charter flights are available to Luxor, Aswan, Hurghada and Sharm el-Sheikh.

There are two land crossing points into Israel, one at Taba on the Gulf of Aqaba, and the other at Rafah on the north Sinai coast. Buses connect Cairo and Tel Aviv four times weekly, but it's cheaper to do the trip in stages.

To Libya, there are direct buses connecting both Cairo and Alexandria with Benghazi and Tripoli. Get an update on the security situation in Libya before heading this way.

To Jordan, there are car ferries and a speedboat service between Nuweiba in Sinai and Aqaba, Jordan's only port. The ferry trip takes three hours.

To Saudi Arabia, direct ferries take about three days between Suez and Jeddah. Getting a berth during the haj (pilgrimage to Mecca) is virtually impossible. There are also passenger boats from Port Safaga to Dubai and Jeddah. Service on the steamer between Aswan and Wadi Halfa (Sudan) has been indefinitely cancelled. Overland travel to the Sudan is also not possible due to the security situation in the Sudan.

EQUATORIAL GUINEA

Equatorial Guinea, in the heart of the tropics, is an impoverished and often overlooked but beautiful country. Although not many travellers make it here, those who do are rarely disappointed. Attractive beaches, picturesque landscapes, laid-back people and a slow-paced backwater charm make it an appealing place to explore.

There are few western amenities, and only a handful of other tourists to show you the ropes, so first-timers who venture down here need a healthy sense of adventure. However, if you like exploring places well off the beaten track, you're sure to enjoy yourself.

WHEN TO GO

The best time to travel is during the drier season between November and April, although rain usually falls through December on Bioko Island, and through November on the mainland. During the rainy season, you will find that many roads may be impassable, and this may inhibit your plans.

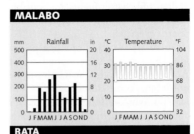

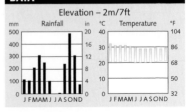

At a Glance

Full Country Name: Republic of Equatorial Guinea
Area: 28,050 sq km
Population: 495,000
Capital City: Malabo (population 15,000)
People: Fang (80% of the mainland population), Kombe, Balengue, Bujeba and Bubi
Languages: Spanish and French (official), Fang and Bubi
Religions: Roman Catholic (80%) and traditional beliefs
Government: Republic
Currency: Central African CFA franc (CFA)
Time Zone: One hour ahead of GMT/UTC
International Telephone Code: 240
Electricity: 220V, 50 Hz; most sockets take plugs with two round pins

HIGHLIGHTS
Dances & Festivals

Witnessing some of the traditional dances and festivals in Equatorial Guinea would be the highlight of any trip to the country. One of the best known of these is the *balélé*, which is commonly performed on national holidays and during the Christmas season, especially on Bioko. Another festival which is common along the coast in Rio Muni is the *ibanga*, for which the dancers are often covered in white powder.

Island Life, Beaches & Hiking

The main attraction on Bioko is Malabo, the capital and the country's most vibrant and tourist-friendly town. It's an attractive place with Spanish architecture, thriving nightclubs and colourful markets. South-west of Malabo along the coastal road are some beautiful beaches, tiny fishing villages and hiking trails, which means that there's plenty to do. Outdoor lovers may want to try climbing Bioko's spectacular Pico Malabo volcano (3106m), although you'll need to get a government permit before starting out.

Mainland Beaches & Villages

Rio Muni on the mainland offers some excellent beaches north and south of Bata, and remote villages which rarely see visitors. One of these villages is Evinayong, about 180km south-east of Bata. The area around this hillside town has several waterfalls and some of the best trekking in Rio Muni.

Rainforests

There are lush rainforests in both Rio Muni and on Bioko. The soil on Bioko, which is itself an extinct volcano, is especially rich. It encourages the rapid growth of trees and vines, to the despair of the cocoa plantation farmers.

VISA REQUIREMENTS

All visitors must have a visa, which is usually valid for 30 days. In Africa, the easiest places to get a visa are Cameroon and Gabon, although it's not very difficult anywhere and same-day service is the norm.

You will also need an international health certificate showing proof of yellow fever and cholera vaccinations.

Equatorial Guinea Embassies

Cameroon
(☎ 20 4149) Rue 1872, Bastos, Yaoundé
Gabon
(☎ 76 3015) Blvd Yves-Digo, before L'Eglise d'Akébé, Akébéville, Libreville
USA
(☎ 202-393-0525, fax 393-0348) Suite 405, 1511 K St NW, Washington, DC 20005

TOURIST OFFICES OVERSEAS

Equatorial Guinea has no overseas tourist offices, though embassies and travel agencies should be able to provide you with basic information. Also check the web sites listed under Online Services.

HEALTH

Both malaria and yellow fever are a risk in Equatorial Guinea; take appropriate precautions against these diseases. Other diseases spread by insects, including leishmaniasis, trypanosomiasis (sleeping sickness), filariasis and typhus all occur; avoid all insect bites if possible.

During the drier season (November to April) there is a risk of meningococcal meningitis, and schistosomiasis is present in freshwater; avoid swimming or bathing in rivers and streams. As intestinal worms are common, take care with what you eat; especially avoid undercooked meat and walking barefoot.

Dysentery, hepatitis, typhoid, lung flukes and cholera are all food or waterborne diseases which occur here; drink only treated water and try wherever possible to eat only hot, fresh food. Watch out for dogs which can carry rabies, as can rats, monkeys and bats.

Medical facilities are basic in Malabo and in rural areas. If you require serious medical care, you should return home.

POST & COMMUNICATIONS

The postal system, with poste restante services in Malabo and Bata, costs somewhat less than in Europe.

International telephone calls can be made easily from Malabo and Bata.

Itineraries

One Week
Assuming you arrive on Bioko, you could spend half a week exploring Malabo and Luba (Bioko's second largest town, set near some superb beaches) before heading to the mainland and visiting the charming, lively town of Bata and nearby villages.

Two Weeks
With two weeks, you could spend close to a week relaxing and hiking on Bioko before heading to the mainland. Using Bata as a base, spend several days exploring the town and surrounding villages and beaches before heading down to Mbini, a pleasant town about 50km south of Bata on the coast.

One Month
With three to four weeks, you will have plenty of time to explore Equatorial Guinea at a leisurely pace. In addition to the two week itinerary, you could venture into the interior, where there is some good hiking around the town of Evinayong. If you plan on exiting the country towards Cameroon, you could then make your way up to Ebebiyin, Rio Muni's second largest town, in the north-east corner of Equatorial Guinea.

Alternatively, from Mbini head south towards Acalayong (the major southern border town), and then over the border into Gabon. Near Acalayong are the rarely visited Islas Elobey, which make a good detour.

Rates are more expensive than in Europe, but cheaper than in many other countries in the region.

There is no public Internet access anywhere in Equatorial Guinea.

MONEY

Costs

Equatorial Guinea is inexpensive, although there is not a very wide choice of upper-end accommodation options. Budget travellers can expect to pay US$5 or less per day for food, and US$10 or less for basic accommodation. Mid-range travel will cost about US$20 to US$40 per day, while top-end standards will cost about US$50 to US$60 per day.

Changing Money

Currency exchange is straightforward, but there is little choice of banks. Only one bank in Malabo and one in Bata have exchange facilities. The best currency to have is French francs, and banks are often reluctant to change other currencies. You will usually be required to show your purchase receipt when changing travellers cheques.

Credit cards are of little use in Equatorial Guinea.

ONLINE SERVICES

Lonely Planet has a web site Destination Equatorial Guinea (www.lonelyplanet.com/dest/afr/eqg.htm).

Bioko (http://bioko.beaver.edu) provides an introduction to the fauna and landscape of the island.

Equatorial Guinea (www.equatorialguinea.org) is an official site with some news and views.

Photos (www.ourdays.com/gallery/africa/eqguinea/EqGuinea.htm) is by Peace Corps volunteer Christine Strater.

MALABO
Vibrant capital; Spanish architecture; nightclubs; colourful markets

BIOKO ISLAND
Festivals; good hiking on Pico Malabo volcano

BATA
Charming, lively town with excellent beaches nearby

EVINAYONG
Pleasant town on top of a small mountain, with cooler climate and nearby waterfalls; good hiking

RIO MUNI

ATLANTIC OCEAN

CAMEROON

GABON

YAOUNDÉ

Douala
MALABO
Pico Malabo (3106m)
Luba
Riaba
Moca
Bioko Island

Edéa

Kribi

Ebolowa

Ambam

Réserve de Campo

Campo
Yengüe
Ntem River
Mary
Ayamiken
Micomeseng
Biyabiyan
Ebebiyin
Bitam
Nsong
Ncue
Nsoc-Nsomo
Mongomo
Niefang
Monte Bata
Bolondo
Ferry
Senye
Río Benito
Nkumekie
Río Uoro
Mbini
Enang
Evinayong
Ebomicu
Oveng
Aconibe
Nsoc
Cabo San Juan
Acalayong
Cogo
Estuaria del Muni
Río Mitémélé
Acurenam
Islas Elobey
Cocobeach
Médouneu
Isla Corisco
Komo River

To Bata (600km)

Pagalu
Palé

LIBREVILLE
Ntoum
Owendo

Ndjolé

To Pagalu

0   25   50 km

Anisoc
Bata

BOOKS

Historical Dictionary of Equatorial Guinea by Max Liniger-Goumaz is useful for reference.

Tropical Gangsters: One Man's Experience with Development and Decadence in Deepest Africa examines the pitfalls of foreign aid in the context of Equatorial Guinea.

Aspects of Central African History by T Ranger is an overview of major issues in the region.

The Art of Equatorial Guinea: The Fang Tribes by Louis Perrois & Marta Sierra Delage provides historical background on the country as well as a comprehensive catalogue of Fang artwork.

For an introduction to local literature, a good anthology is *The Traveller's Literary Companion – Africa* edited by Oona Strathern, which contains prose and poetry extracts from all over Africa, with an introduction to the literature of each country.

ENTERING & LEAVING EQUATORIAL GUINEA

Ecuato Guineana de Aviacion (EGA) and Cameroon Airlines have flights connecting Malabo and Bata with Douala (Cameroon) twice weekly. EGA also connects Malabo and Bata with Libreville (Gabon) weekly. The only direct service to Europe is on Iberia, which flies between Malabo and Madrid.

The usual land route between Cameroon and Equatorial Guinea is from Ebebiyin to Ambam. There is a much more adventurous and seldom travelled route along the coast from Bata across the Ntem River up to Kribi (Cameroon), though this will involve either a very lengthy (40km) walk, or a 10km ride in a *pirogue* (dugout canoe).

To Gabon, the only route is via Mbini and Acalayong. You will need to cross the Estuario del Muni in a pirogue.

Eritrea is Africa's newest country, formed in 1993 when its people voted in a referendum to secede from Ethiopia. This was the final chapter in a war which had lasted for more than 30 years, during which Eritreans fought vigorously to be allowed to fend for themselves. In recent years, this same spirit of self-reliance has been the force behind massive highway construction and rural regeneration programs, including the planting of over one million tree seedlings.

Today, Eritrea is a buoyant, vigorous, though impoverished nation, keen not to become anybody's client. Its cities and towns are graceful and attractive, and its people have a dignity, self-respect and disinterested friendliness that can be a particular tonic if you have just arrived from the hustling and hassles common to many other areas in the region.

Due to ongoing disputes with Ethiopia, hostilities have increased in recent months along the border, and at the time this book went to press, the Ethiopian border was closed to travellers. Be sure to get an update on the situation before planning to head this way. Travel near Eritrea's border with the Sudan is also restricted; there are no diplomatic relations between the two countries.

WHEN TO GO

Eritrea has three climatic zones – the densely populated central highlands, the Red Sea coastal plain to the east,

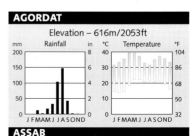

AGORDAT

Elevation – 616m/2053ft

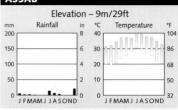

ASSAB

Elevation – 9m/29ft

At a Glance

Full Country Name: State of Eritrea
Area: 124,000 sq km
Population: 3.8 million
Capital City: Asmara (population 460,000)
People: Afar, Bilen, Hadareb, Kunama, Nara, Rashaida, Saho, Tigre and Tigrinya
Languages: Arabic (coastal areas), Tigrinya (highlands) and English –all official; plus Afar, Bilen, To Bedawi, Kunama, Nara, Arabic, Saho, Tigre and Amharic
Religions: Muslims (50%) and Christians (50%)
Government: Transitional government
Currency: Eritrean nakfa (Nfa)
Time Zone: Three hours ahead of GMT/UTC
International Telephone Code: 291
Electricity: 220V, 50 Hz; most sockets take plugs with two round pins

and the western lowlands. In the highlands, the climate is moderate and the main rainy season is from late June to early September, with lighter rains in March and April. On the coast, the most pleasant months are December to February, although light rains often fall during this time. June to August is uncomfortably hot. In the western lowlands, temperatures can reach 40°C during the hottest months of April to June. Overall, probably the best time to visit the country is between October and February.

Itineraries

One Week
You could easily spend at least three to four days relaxing in Asmara and soaking up its graceful ambience. This could be followed by excursions of a day or two to Massawa and Keren, though you'll have to backtrack to Asmara to do both.

Alternatively, head from Asmara to Massawa and build in a trip to the Dahlak Archipelago for some diving and snorkelling, or (if your budget is more limited) to Green Island (half an hour off the coast), which is good for relaxing and snorkelling.

Two Weeks
In two weeks, you could cover all the destinations included in the one week itinerary and extend your time in each area.

More than Two Weeks
With more than two weeks, consider incorporating some of Ethiopia's sights into your itinerary, subject to satisfactory reports about the security situation. From Asmara, head south via Mendefera and Adi Quala to Axum (Ethiopia's holiest city) and even beyond. Before doing this, be sure to get a security update from your embassy or from knowledgeable locals.

HIGHLIGHTS
Urban & Panoramic
Asmara is a pleasant, uncrowded city, with an excellent museum, interesting architecture and a colourful market. The town of Massawa to the north-east is not as interesting, but the 115km road linking it to Asmara is spectacular, winding down from 2300m to sea level and passing briefly through Eritrea's most fertile area.

Diving & Snorkelling
The waters of the Red Sea near Massawa offer some excellent (though expensive) diving and snorkelling.

Markets
Throughout the country are interesting markets. One of the best is the weekly livestock market in Keren, north-west of Asmara. Keren also has a good daily market which is frequented by people of various tribes from the surrounding area, and is renowned for its silversmiths' street.

VISA REQUIREMENTS
All visitors, except nationals of certain eastern and southern African countries, require a visa. The general rule is that you must get your visa from the embassy in your home country, or the one deemed to serve your country, although this is often waived if you can show that you have visited other countries between leaving home and applying. If you are making your visa application en route, you may be asked to produce a letter of recommendation from your embassy or an onward ticket. A one month visa issued by the embassy in Addis Ababa in Ethiopia states that it is valid from the date of issue. However, the Department of

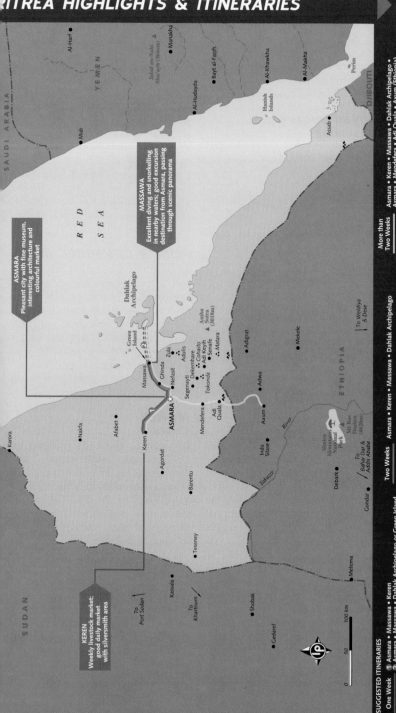

ERITREA HIGHLIGHTS & ITINERARIES

ASMARA
Pleasant city with fine museum, interesting architecture and colourful market

MASSAWA
Excellent diving and snorkelling in nearby waters; good excursion destination from Asmara, passing through scenic panorama

KEREN
Weekly livestock market; good daily market with silversmith area

RED SEA

SAUDI ARABIA

YEMEN

DJIBOUTI

SUDAN

ETHIOPIA

Dahlak Archipelago

Perim

Al-Harf

Jabal an-Nabi Shu'ayb (3666m)

Manakha

Bayt al-Faqih

Al-Khawkha

Al-Makha

Midi

Al-Hudayda

Hanish Islands

Assab

Karora

Nakfa

Atabet

Keren

Agordat

Barentu

Teseney

Kassala

Metema

Shobak

Gedaref

To Port Sudan

To Khartoum

Massawa

Ghinda

Nefasit

Segenayti

Dekemhare

Cohaito

Adi Keyh

Senafe

Tokonda

Matara

Adi Quala

Mendefera

ASMARA

Adwa

Axum

Adigat

Mekele

Inda Silase

Debark

Gondar

Green Island

Zula

Adulis

Amba Soira (3018m)

Takazze River

Simien Mountains National Park

Mt Ras Dashen (4620m)

To Weldiya & Dese

To Bahar Dar & Addis Ababa

0   50   100 km

SUGGESTED ITINERARIES

One Week ① Asmara • Massawa • Keren   ② Asmara • Massawa • Dahlak Archipelago or Green Island

Two Weeks Asmara • Keren • Massawa • Dahlak Archipelago

More than Two Weeks Asmara • Keren • Massawa • Dahlak Archipelago
Asmara • Mendefera • Adi Quala • Axum (Ethiopia)

Immigration in Asmara confirms the more liberal interpretation of 'from the date of arrival in Eritrea'.

Eritrean Embassies & Consulates

Australia
(☎ 02-6282 3489) 26 Guilfoyle St, Yarralumla, ACT 2600

Canada
(☎ 613-234-3989) 75 Albert St, Suite 610, Ottawa, Ontario K1P 5E7

Ethiopia
(☎ 512844) Ras Makonnen Ave, Addis Ababa

UK
(☎ 020-7713 0096) 96 White Lion St, London N1 9PF

USA
(☎ 202-319-1991; fax 319-1304) 1708 New Hampshire Ave NW, Washington, DC 20009

TOURIST OFFICES OVERSEAS

Eritrea has no overseas tourist offices, but travel agents and the information desks at its embassies (usually very helpful) should be able to provide you with information. Also check the web sites listed under Online Services.

HEALTH

Malaria does not occur in Asmara, but does occur in the lowlands, Keren, and on the coastal plain, where dengue fever is also prevalent. Take appropriate precautions and avoid all mosquito bites. Schistosomiasis is present in freshwater; avoid swimming or bathing in river and streams. Contaminated food and water can carry diseases, including, typhoid, hepatitis and cholera. Take extra care with what you eat, and drink only treated water.

Meningococcal meningitis can occur during the dry season (October/November to June). Many diseases which are transmitted by flies, sandflies and ticks occur here, so avoid all insect bites. As rabies can occur, avoid furry animals such as dogs, bats, monkeys and rats.

As medical facilities are poor throughout the country, consider going to Nairobi in Kenya, or Cairo in Egypt if you require serious medical care, or flying home.

POST & COMMUNICATIONS

International mail is slow but reliable and moderately priced.

International telephone calls can be made efficiently in Asmara, less so in the provinces. Rates are somewhat more than those in Europe, with a three minute call costing US$8/9/12 to the USA/Europe/Australia.

Internet access is possible in Asmara.

MONEY
Costs

It is easy to find budget lodging for US$5 or less (single room). More comfortable accommodation is priced from about US$15, while top-end lodging will be about US$50 and up. Good food is available inexpensively throughout the country; meals at restaurants in more expensive hotels will cost from US$10.

Overall, budget travellers should be able to keep their daily costs to about US$15 or less, while mid-range travel will run from US$20 to US$50 per day.

Changing Money

Both cash and travellers cheques can be easily changed in Asmara. The best denomination to have for both is US dollars. Eritrea is refreshingly free of street moneychangers. If you do indulge, be aware that it is a large risk for trivial gain.

Credit cards are only accepted by a few of the top hotels in Asmara, and by Ethiopian Airlines offices.

ONLINE SERVICES

For news and views on Eritrea, there are several web sites (www.dehai.net; www.eritrea.org; http://asmarino.com).

Directory by Nation: Eritrea (www .cs.indiana.edu/hyplan/dmulholl/eritrea /eritrea.html) has a listing of sites on the country.

The Norwegian Council for Africa (www.africaindex.africainfo.no/africai ndex1/countries/eritrea.html) indexes numerous links.

BOOKS & FILMS

Eritrea: Even the Stones are Burning by Roy Pateman is a good survey of Eritrean history and an introduction to the Eritrean independence struggle. The second edition also includes post-independence developments.

The Challenge Road by Amrit Wilson chronicles Eritrean history through the eyes of women.

To Fight and Learn by Les Gottesman examines literacy training during Eritrea's independence struggle, focusing on young Eritreans who worked behind enemy lines to teach nomads to read and write.

Eritrea: Revolution at Dusk by Robert Papstein is an account of the country's history.

A Painful Season and A Stubborn Hope by Abeba Tesfagiorgis chronicles the author's experiences in Eritrea and her odyssey after fleeing Asmara.

The French-made film *Port Djema* (1987) was filmed in Asmara and Massawa.

ENTERING & LEAVING ERITREA

Eritrea is served by Egypt Air, Ethiopian Airlines, Lufthansa and Saudia. Flights between Asmara and Addis Ababa (Ethiopia) are often heavily booked.

To Ethiopia, the main land routes are via Mendefera and Adi Quala to Axum and via Dekemhare and Senafe to Adigrat, although you will need to check on the security situation between the two countries before undertaking any travel; the border was closed when this book went to press. There is also a good road from Assab in southern Eritrea to Addis Ababa, but it is not of much use to independent travellers, as it is so difficult to reach Assab.

The border with the Sudan is officially closed to foreigners.

To Jeddah in Saudi Arabia, there is a weekly boat from Massawa. The journey takes about 32 hours.

ETHIOPIA

While coverage of its persistent famines often dominates the news, Ethiopia has much to offer. It's the only country in Africa that has never been colonised. It's also unusual for its rich Orthodox Christian heritage, which the Ethiopians maintained even when neighbouring peoples embraced Islam in the 7th century. Although facilities in many areas are basic, Ethiopia's spectacular scenery and fascinating culture more than compensate.

Due to ongoing hostilities with Eritrea and Somalia, travel in certain areas of the country is restricted – notably in the north near Axum and the border with Eritrea, and in the east around Dire Dawa and the border

with Somalia. As this book was going to press, the border between Ethiopia and Eritrea was closed. Get an update on the current situation before setting your plans.

WHEN TO GO

Temperatures in most of the country are pleasant year-round, averaging 16°C to 20°C in Addis Ababa and on the central plateau. Travel is good at any time of year, with the exception of the main rainy season between mid-June and mid-September. Light rains also fall during March and April, though all major towns remain accessible.

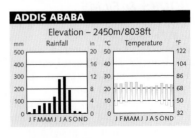

At a Glance

Full Country Name: Federal Democratic Republic of Ethiopia

Area: 1,127,000 sq km

Population: 58 million

Capital City: Addis Ababa (population three million)

People: More than 80 groups including Oromo (40%), Amhara and Tigrayans (together constituting 33%)

Languages: Amharic (official), Tigrinya and Orominya

Religions: Orthodox Christian (40%), Muslim (40%) and traditional religions

Government: Federal republic

Currency: Ethiopian birr (Birr)

Time Zone: Three hours ahead of GMT/ UTC

International Telephone Code: 251

Electricity: 220V, 50 Hz; most sockets take plugs with two round pins

HIGHLIGHTS
Rock Churches & Sacred Monuments

Ethiopia's Orthodox Christian heritage, which was maintained even when all its neighbours embraced Islam in the 7th century, has left it with some unique attractions, the most well known of which are the 11 rock churches of Lalibela. The churches are hewn straight from the bedrock and contain a wealth of treasures including ornamented crosses, illuminated bibles and illustrated manuscripts.

Another place to delve into Ethiopia's rich religious and historical legacy is at Axum. Axum is considered to be the country's holiest city, and it is thought that this is the place where the Ark of the Covenant may reside.

Lakes & Waterfalls

Ethiopia offers some enticing natural attractions. At Bahar Dar – in addition to exploring Lake Tana with its 37 islands and many monasteries – you can visit the impressive Blue Nile Falls (Tis Isat).

Trekking & Wildlife

Simien Mountains National Park in the north of the country is excellent for trekking, with spectacular views and a large variety of wildlife. Bale Mountains National Park in the south-east is also rich in wildlife, including numerous endemic animals and birds.

The scenic Rift Valley Lakes also offers good birdlife and wildlife viewing opportunities. Lake Hora, near Debre Zeit, is another area with plentiful birdlife.

VISA REQUIREMENTS

Everyone except Kenyan nationals needs a visa. You may need to show an onward air ticket or visa for the next country on your itinerary, plus proof that you have sufficient funds. Visas are single entry only and cost about US$65. Extensions are available in Addis Ababa, although they are not always readily granted to travellers.

Proof of yellow fever and cholera vaccinations is also required if you will be arriving from an infected area.

Ethiopian Embassies

Canada
(☎ 613-235-637) 51 Slater St, Suite 210, Ottawa, Ontario K1P 5H3

Eritrea
(☎ 120736) Franklin D Roosevelt St, Asmara

Kenya
(☎ 723027; fax 723401) State House Ave, Nairobi

UK
(☎ 020-7589 7212) 17 Princess Gate, London SW7 1PZ

USA
(☎ 202-234-2281/2; fax 328-7950) 2134 Kalorama Rd NW, Washington, DC 20008

TOURIST OFFICES OVERSEAS

Most Ethiopian embassies have tourist information desks. In some countries, tourist information is handled by the Ethiopian Airlines office. In either case, information is usually limited to mainstream material, but some decent (though dated) glossy brochures on national parks and historical sites may also be available. Also see the web sites listed under Online Services.

HEALTH

Yellow fever can occur in Ethiopia and, except in Addis Ababa, there is a risk of malaria year-round. Take appropriate precautions. There is schistosomiasis in all rivers and lakes, so avoid swimming or bathing in fresh water. Contaminated food and water can carry diseases, including typhoid, hepatitis, cholera and liver flukes; take extra care with what you eat, and drink only treated water.

Meningococcal meningitis can occur during the dry season. Many diseases are transmitted by flies, sandflies and ticks. Stay well away from dogs, bats, monkeys and rats, which carry the risk of rabies infection.

Medical services are poor, so consider leaving for Nairobi, or Cairo if you require serious medical care.

POST & COMMUNICATIONS

The postal service is slow but usually reliable, at least in the capital; try to arrange to send/receive your letters in Addis Ababa. Some post office officials run a flourishing private business selling old stamps to foreigners.

You can make international telephone calls efficiently from Addis Ababa, less so from other major towns. Rates are reasonable in comparison with many other countries in Africa. A three minute call costs about US$6/8/10 to the UK/USA/Australia.

Internet access is not currently available to the public in Ethiopia.

MONEY
Costs

Ethiopia is inexpensive if you stick to public transport, eat local food and stay in budget lodging. Budget travellers can easily get by for US$10 per day. More comforts, including mid-range hotels and some meals in restaurants, will cost from from US$20 to US$40. For about US$70 and more, you can stay in upmarket hotels, fly to many destinations, hire a guide and eat all your meals in restaurants.

Changing Money

Cash in major currencies can be readily exchanged in Addis Ababa. US dollar travellers cheques can also be exchanged in Addis Ababa, although many places are reluctant to accept them. Outside the capital, it can be difficult to exchange anything other than US dollars cash. While there is a black market, it gives you less than a 10% advantage and carries the usual risks.

Credit cards are only used at Ethiopian Airlines and a few upmarket hotels.

ONLINE SERVICES

Lonely Planet has a web site Destination Ethiopia (www.lonely planet.com/dest/afr/eth.htm).

Itineraries

Many of the following suggestions are restricted at present due to the security situation in northern Ethiopia. Internal flight schedules have also been disrupted. Be sure to get an update before settling your plans.

One Week

With a week, spend three to four days getting acclimatised in Addis Ababa, including a day trip to Entoto Natural Park from where you can enjoy good views of the city. With the remainder of the time, you could fly to Axum and then make your way back to the capital by road, with a quick stop at Lalibela. Another option would be a visit to some of the Rift Valley Lakes or an overnight trek in Bale Mountains National Park.

Two Weeks

With two weeks, you will have time to follow Ethiopia's Historic Route (Axum, Gondar, Bahar Dar — with a visit to Blue Nile Falls — and Lalibela), plus take a short trek in Simien Mountains National Park.

One Month

With a month, after taking in the sights included in the two weeks itinerary, you could return to Addis Ababa and then head south to the Rift Valley Lakes and Bale Mountains National Park. The small town of Debre Zeit, south-east of Addis Ababa, makes a good base for visiting some nearby crater lakes, including the attractive Lake Hora with its rich birdlife.

LALIBELA
Ancient rock churches hewn from bedrock

SIMIEN MOUNTAINS NATIONAL PARK
Excellent trekking and wildlife

BAHAR DAR
Explore Lake Tana and visit Blue Nile Falls

ADDIS ABABA
Capital with nearby Entoto Natural Park, from which superb panoramic views can be enjoyed

RIFT VALLEY LAKES
Good birdwatching and wildlife viewing opportunities

BALE MOUNTAINS NATIONAL PARK
Diverse wildlife

0   100   200 km

SUGGESTED ITINERARIES

One Week
1. Addis Ababa • Axum • Lalibela • Addis Ababa
2. Addis Ababa • Rift Valley Lakes • Bale Mountains National Park • Lake Chamo

Two Weeks
Addis Ababa • Bahar Dar • Blue Nile Falls • Gondar • Simien Mountains National Park • Axum • Lalibela • Addis Ababa

One Month
Addis Ababa • Bahar Dar • Blue Nile Falls • Gondar • Simien Mountains National Park • Axum • Lalibela • Addis Ababa • Rift Valley Lakes • Bale Mountains National Park • Lake Chamo • Debre Zeit • Lake Hora • Addis Ababa

A good source of links is Cyber-Ethiopia (www.cyberethiopia.com).

For news try Ethiopian Weekly Press (http://pressdigest.phoenixuniv ersal.com).

For cooking tips, check Ethiopia: Menus and Recipes from Africa (www .sas.upenn.edu/African_Studies/Cook book/Ethiopia.html).

Journey Through Ethiopia (www .casema.net/~spaansen) presents Ethiopia from the traveller's viewpoint.

BOOKS

My Life and Ethiopia's Progress by Haile Selassie is the autobiography of Ethiopia's most famous ruler.

For a general overview of the country's history, try *A History of Ethiopia* by Harold Marcus.

In Ethiopia with a Mule by Dervla Murphy is a classic travel hit.

Woman Between Two Worlds: Portrait of an Ethiopian Rural Leader by Judith Olmstead chronicles the life of a female judge in rural Ethiopia.

ENTERING & LEAVING ETHIOPIA

Airlines serving Ethiopia include Ethiopian Airlines (the reputable national carrier), Air Djibouti, Egypt Air, Kenya Airways, Lufthansa and Saudia.

The border with Eritrea is currently closed. Previously, there were several buses a week between Addis Ababa and Asmara. The journey via Dese, Mekele and Adigrat takes three days. The alternative route, via Bahar Dar, Gondar and Axum, is much more interesting, but also more gruelling. If you will be visiting Eritrea as a side trip from Ethiopia, you could fly one way to Asmara and then return by land, assuming the security situation improves. There is a good tarmac road from Addis Ababa to the Eritrean port of Assab. From Assab, however, it is a tough journey along desert tracks to Massawa (Eritrea) or anywhere else.

To Kenya, there are buses from Addis Ababa to the border at Moyale with an overnight stop in Dila. From the border there are trucks to Nairobi (two to three days). Because of the risk of banditry, the trucks travel in convoys and you may have to wait some time until one assembles. Get an update on the security situation near the border before attempting to cross into Kenya.

To Djibouti, it is possible to travel by road, but wearying. Most travellers prefer to travel by bus from Addis Ababa to Dire Dawa and then by train the following day to Djibouti. Here too, however, you will need to get an update on the security situation before setting off. Alternatively, you can do the whole journey by train in two days, staying overnight in Dire Dawa.

Travel to and from Sudan and Somalia is currently restricted due to the security situation.

GABON

Many travellers avoid visiting Gabon, put off by the expense and the difficulties associated with getting a visa. Nevertheless, it's an interesting place, full of contrasts, and if you are in the region, it is definately a worthwhile stop. The country poses no particular difficulties for the visitor (apart from the expense and visa issues), although many travellers prefer other destinations as more 'typically' African.

Thanks to oil money, Gabon is one of the richest countries in sub-Saharan Africa. This is most obvious in Libreville, the country's modern capital, and a few of the beach resorts. Yet, in some areas of the interior you may feel as if you're in a different world, with dense rainforests, wildlife, and remote villages which rarely see tourists.

WHEN TO GO

The best time to visit Gabon is during the dry season, from May to September. During the rest of the year, there is heavy rainfall and temperatures are uncomfortably hot. Throughout the year, humidity is high.

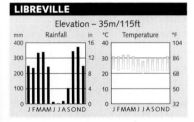

LIBREVILLE
Elevation – 35m/115ft

HIGHLIGHTS
Urban

Even if modern cities were not what you were hoping to see in Africa, glitzy Libreville, with its ocean-view hotels, office buildings and highways, is worth a brief visit. Its Musée des Arts et Traditions is one of the best in Central Africa. Once you get out of the centre, there are lively, vibrant African quarters that will give you more of a flavour of the 'real' Gabon. North of the city are some pleasant beaches and relaxing fishing villages.

River Excursions

Outside the capital, one of Gabon's main attractions is taking a trip by *pirogue* (dugout canoe) down the Ogo-oué River into the lake region, where

At a Glance

Full Country Name: Gabonese Republic
Area: 267,665 sq km
Population: 1.4 million
Capital City: Libreville (population 400,000)
People: Ten major ethnic groups, including Fang (about 33%), Mbédé (about 25%), Eshira (about 20%) and Myéné
Languages: French (official), Fang, Bapunu, Bandjabi, Myéné and Eshira
Religions: Christian (about 50%), Muslim (just under 5%) and traditional beliefs
Government: Republic
Currency: Central African CFA franc (CFA)
Time Zone: One hour ahead of GMT/UTC
International Telephone Code: 241
Electricity: 220V/50 Hz; most sockets take two-pin round plugs

hippos and other wildlife can be seen, especially during the dry season. Lambaréné, built on an island in the river, is the best base. River excursions can be expensive unless you're in a group.

Wildlife

Because Gabon has so few people, wildlife – including gorillas, chimpanzees, leopards, mandrills, monkeys, antelopes and elephants – are still abundant in many areas. The most accessible place to see some of these animals is the Réserve de la Lopé, which borders both the railway and the road, though you will need your own vehicle to explore the park.

If a visit to the reserve is beyond your budget, you can still view crocodiles, hippos and manatees in the river and in Gabon's coastal areas. Offshore, in season, you may even spot a humpback whale if you're lucky.

Another good area for wildlife, as well as for rainforests, is Makokou, 610km east of Libreville.

VISA REQUIREMENTS

All visitors require visas. Except in Equatorial Guinea, allow at least a week for processing, as applications must be referred to Libreville by telex. All visas cost US$80, plus US$10 for the telex. In theory, you also need an invitation from a resident or citizen of Gabon and an onward airline ticket, although these requirements are sometimes waived at embassies in adjoining countries, especially in Equatorial Guinea, where visas are often issued within a few hours.

An international health certificate with proof of yellow fever and cholera vaccinations is also required.

Gabonese Embassies

Cameroon
(☎ 20 2966) Rue 1793, off Rue 1810, Bastos, Yaoundé

Canada
(☎ 613-232-5301) 4 Range Rd, PO Box 368 Ottawa, Ontario K1N 8J5

Equatorial Guinea
(☎ 2420) Calle de Argelia, Malabo

Itineraries

One Week
Following a couple of days in Libreville, including stops at its museum and nearby beaches, head to Lambaréné, where you can easily spend the remainder of the week visiting the town and exploring the nearby lake region by pirogue. Albert Schweitzer built a hospital here shortly after his arrival in 1913. Its well equipped successor, built in 1926, is still a tourist attraction.

Two Weeks
With two weeks, you can do the above, and then, after heading back towards Bifoun (the junction town where the roads to Lambaréné and Franceville split), make your way southeast towards Franceville including stops at the Réserve de la Lopé (if you have your own vehicle), Lastoursville, and other villages along the way. If you have reached Franceville by minibus, take the train or the plane back to minimise backtracking.

One Month
With a month, you will have more than enough time to expand the above itinerary with excursions to Port-Gentil (a bustling town with restaurants, nightclubs and even a casino, and reached only by air or by boat from Libreville or Lambaréné); and Makokou, a town set in an attractive area of rainforests and mountains. From Makokou (after backtracking to the junction town of Booué on the railway line) continue out of the country to Cameroon via the towns of Oyem and Bitam.

ABON HIGHLIGHTS & ITINERARIES

LIBREVILLE
glitzy modern city with
cean-view hotels, office
buildings, highways

MAKOKOU
Town set in
rainforest area

RÉSERVE DE LA LOPÉ
Abundant wildlife

LAMBARÉNÉ
Island town; good
base for canoe trips
down Ogooué River

PORT GENTIL
Bustling town with casino,
restaurants, nightclubs,
accessible by boat from
Libreville or Lambaréné

STED ITINERARIES

Week   Libreville • Lambaréné

Veeks   Libreville • Lambaréné • Bifoun • Réserve de la Lopé •
Lastoursville • Franceville

One Month   Libreville • Lambaréné • Port Gentil •
Bifoun • Réserve de la Lopé • Lastoursville •
Franceville • Bifoun • Makokou

0   50   100 km

(☎ 020-7823 9986) 27 Elvaston Place, London SW7 59L

USA
(☎ 202-797-1000) 2034 20th St NW, Washington, DC 20009

TOURIST OFFICES OVERSEAS

Gabon has no overseas tourist offices, but embassies and travel agencies should be able to provide you with information. Also check the web sites listed under Online Services.

HEALTH

Malaria and dengue fever all both health risks in Gabon, so take appropriate precautions. Dysentery, hepatitis and typhoid are all food or waterborne diseases that occur here; drink only treated water and try wherever possible to eat only hot, freshly cooked food.

Medical facilities are basic in Libreville and in rural areas. If you require serious medical care, you should consider going home.

POST & COMMUNICATIONS

The post is reliable, but expensive. It costs about US$1 to receive a letter at poste restante in Libreville.

International telephone connections are also good, although rates are high – about US$7 per minute to Europe or the USA.

Internet access is not yet available to the public in Gabon.

MONEY
Costs

Gabon – especially Libreville – is expensive. Expect to pay between US$30 and US$40 per day in the capital for budget accommodation and inexpensive meals; outside Libreville, you may be able to reduce this amount by half. Mid-range travel will cost between US$40 and US$70 per day. Those staying in Libreville's notoriously overpriced luxury hotels could easily spend US$200 per day or more. Outside Libreville, there is little available by way of luxury accommodation.

Changing Money

Travellers cheques in US dollars, French francs or CFA francs can be easily changed in Libreville, although commissions can be very high; shop around, and be sure to inquire before cashing your cheques. There are banks in the major towns outside the capital, although many refuse to change money or travellers cheques in denominations other than French francs or CFA francs.

ONLINE SERVICES

Lonely Planet has a web site Destination Gabon (www.lonelyplanet .com/dest/afr/gab.htm).

The government's official web site (www.presidencegabon.com/index-a .html) isn't finished yet, but it has some good social and cultural background information.

The University of Kansas (www.ibrc .bschool.ukans.edu/country/africa /Gabon/gabon.htm) has a short page of links, many of them commercial.

Those wanting to do business in Gabon can check the Florida Data Trade Center site (www.flatrade.org /ccg/gabon.htm).

BOOKS & FILMS

Travels in West Africa by Mary Kingsley is a 19th century classic that details her trip through Gabon in the 1890s, including sailing up the Ogooué River, trekking through the rainforest and gathering specimens for a natural history museum. *One Dry Season* by Caroline Alexander retraces Kingsley's steps nearly a century later.

African Silences by Peter Matthiessen focuses on his journeys through Gabon and other parts of western Africa.

Two films made in part in Gabon are the French *Tomorrow Is Another Day* (1979) and *The Great White of Lambaréné*, about Dr Albert Schweitzer.

ENTERING & LEAVING GABON

Air Gabon (the national airline), Ecuato Guineana de Aviacion, Air São Tomé & Príncipe and Sabena, among others, service Gabon through Libreville. There are good connections with other countries in East and Central Africa, and with various cities in Europe, including Brussels, Paris, Rome, Madrid and Geneva. Air Gabon is considered to be one of the best African airlines serving Central and West Africa.

Overland travel between Libreville and Yaoundé in Cameroon takes about three days using bush taxis and minibuses. The route is via Bitam and Ambam (Cameroon). You will need to cross the Ntem River by ferry or pirogue.

The route connecting Libreville with Bata (Equatorial Guinea) is traversed with pick-up trucks via the border town of Cocobeach, from where there are motorised pirogues across the Estuaire du Muni to Cogo (Equatorial Guinea customs and immigration) and on to Acalayong (again with pick-up).

The major route connecting Libreville and Brazzaville (Congo) is via Lambaréné, N'Dendé and Loubomo, and takes a minimum of six days by road and rail. Travel is restricted now due to the security situation in the Congo.

There are occasional cargo boats between Libreville and Douala (Cameroon) that may take passengers. You will need to bring all your own food and drink.

The Gambia is a small, narrow country, almost completely surrounded by Senegal. Despite its size, it is one of Africa's most low-key and interesting destinations, and a good choice for getting an introduction to the continent. In addition to unspoiled traditional villages and superb beaches, The Gambia has a friendly English-speaking population, a relatively stable political environment and an endless variety of birdlife. Plus, it's easy to traverse the country in a day or two.

WHEN TO GO

The best time to visit is between November and February, when the weather is dry and relatively cool. This is also the local trading season, when the harvest is completed and the markets are at their busiest.

It is also possible to visit The Gambia in the rainy season (June to October). Showers generally last for only a few hours, often falling at night. During this season, the popular tourist areas are less crowded and hotel rates are often cheaper. While roads are muddier, the landscape is lush, birds and flowers are abundant, and the air is clear.

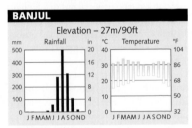

BANJUL

Elevation – 27m/90ft

At a Glance

Full Country Name: Republic of The Gambia

Area: 11,300 sq km

Population: 1.3 million

Capital City: Banjul (population 50,000)

People: Mandinka (Mandingo) (about 40%), Fula (about 20%), Wolof (about 15%), Serer, Jola and Aku

Languages: English (official), Mandinka, Fulani and Wolof (main trading language)

Religions: Muslim (90%), Christian (about 8%) and traditional beliefs (about 1%)

Government: Republic under multiparty democratic rule

Currency: The Gambia dalasi (D)

Time Zone: GMT/UTC

International Telephone Code: 220

Electricity: 220V 50 Hz; most sockets take plugs with two round pins, but some plugs have three square pins

HIGHLIGHTS
Boats, Birds & Beaches

The River Gambia defines the country, and becomes increasingly beautiful as you follow it upstream. The country's other natural highlights include Abuko Nature Reserve, Gambia's flagship protected area, with beautiful forest trails and diverse birdlife; and Ginak Island and Niumi National Park, with beautiful stretches of undeveloped beach, traditional fishing villages and mangrove creeks.

The Gambia is perhaps most famous for the diversity of its birdlife – over 560 species have been recorded within its boundaries. As a result, the country is a mecca for ornithologists, and offers both guides and facilities for birders. A good place for watching birds, as well as monkeys, is Bijilo Forest Park, at the southern end of the Atlantic coast resorts north-west of Serekunda.

Markets

For some glimpses into local culture, try to visit some *lumos* – large weekly markets where Gambians and Senegalese engage in cross-border trade, together with merchants from as far as Guinea, Mali and Mauritania. The lumos at Farafenni and around Basse Santa Su are particularly interesting.

Wrestling

Traditional wrestling matches are another fun sight. They are held in the evening on most weekends in the dry season, particularly in coastal areas – ask locals for directions.

Megaliths

If you like stone monuments, you should visit the enigmatic Wassu Stone Circles, near Kuntaur, on the north side of the River Gambia. Each circle consists of a dozen or two massive, reddish-brown boulders, each of which weighs several tonnes.

VISA REQUIREMENTS

Visas are required by all visitors except nationals of Belgium, Commonwealth countries, Germany, Italy, Luxembourg, the Netherlands, Scandinavia and Spain. They are normally valid for one month, and are available – usually with a minimum of hassle – from Gambian embassies in West Africa and other parts of the world. Citizens of the Republic of Ireland officially need a visa, although immigration officials often seem to

include Ireland as part of the UK and are lax in enforcing this rule. Irish citizens arriving on scheduled flights may be asked to show a visa, but for those arriving on charter flights from the UK, this is generally not required.

Travellers should also have proof of yellow fever and cholera vaccinations.

Gambian Embassies & High Commissions

Canada
(☎ 416-923-2935) 102 Bloor St West, Suite 510, Toronto, Ontario M5S 1N1

Senegal
(☎ 21 4476) 11 Rue de Thiong, one block north of Ave Pompidou, Ponty

UK
(☎ 020-7937 6316) 57 Kensington Court, London W8 5DH

USA
(☎ 202-785-1399) 1155 15th St NW, Washington, DC 20005

TOURIST OFFICES OVERSEAS

The Gambia is represented in the UK by The Gambia National Tourist Office (☎ 020-7376 0093; fax 7938 3644; email info@gambia.itsnet.co.uk), based at the Gambian High Commission, 57 Kensington Court, London W8 5DH. It also has a web site (www.itsnet.co.uk/gambia).

Elsewhere, embassies and travel agencies should be able to provide you with most of what you need. Also check the web sites listed under Online Services.

HEALTH

Malaria is health problem in The Gambia, so take appropriate precautions (see the Health chapter earlier in this book for information on malaria prevention).

Itineraries

One Week
The Gambia's compact size and easy transport system make it ideal for a one or two week visit. If you just have one week, you can spend half of it in Banjul, and the other half visiting one or two of the places listed under the two week itinerary.

Two Weeks
With two weeks, you will have time to visit many of The Gambia's attractions. While Banjul, the small and dusty capital, has little in the way of 'sights', it is a good base for visiting nearby attractions such as the bustling market in Serekunda (The Gambia's largest town), Jufureh (the village where part of Alex Haley's novel *Roots* was set), Abuko Nature Reserve and Bijilo Forest Park – a small wildlife reserve on the coast at Kololi, with pleasant walking trails, lots of monkeys and good birdlife. For birdwatching, fishing or just relaxing, you could also set aside a day for a trip in a *pirogue* (dugout canoe) through the mangroves of Oyster Creek, the main waterway separating Banjul Island and the mainland.

After a few days in and around the capital, head to Farafenni, with its big Sunday market. Wildlife fans can stop en route at Tendaba, a base for visiting Kiang West National Park, one of The Gambia's largest protected areas, with baboon, colobus monkey, bushbuck and many other animals. Another possibility is Baobolong Wetland Reserve, a maze of islands and waterways ideal for observing birdlife and various aquatic mammal species. Allow two to three days to visit both. Further upcountry is peaceful Georgetown, from where you can reach the Wassu Stone Circles or the River Gambia National Park – a scenic area known as the site of a chimpanzee rehabilitation project, although you are unlikely to see any chimps. Also nearby is the lively trading centre of Basse Santa Su, which makes a good excursion for a day or two. From here return to Banjul, or continue into Senegal.

Take care with what you eat and drink, especially outside the main tourist areas, as dysentery, hepatitis, typhoid and cholera all occur here. While most food is generally OK, avoid shellfish, poorly cooked meat and unpurified water.

Medical facilities are limited throughout the country, except in Banjul and at resorts on the Atlantic coast, so seriously consider going home if you suffer a severe illness.

POST & COMMUNICATIONS

The international postal service is reliable and inexpensive. Poste restante at the main post office in Banjul is also reliable.

The telephone system is good and relatively inexpensive. International calls are cheaper after 6 pm and on weekends, and can be placed from offices run by Gamtel (the state telephone company) as well as from private telephone offices (called telecentres). You can buy phonecards at Gamtel offices and use them in public phones, which makes international calls even cheaper. A call to Europe made during the inexpensive weekend hours costs about US$2 per minute. Making reverse charge (collect) calls is possible, although it is easier and cheaper for your caller to get the number of the Gamtel office where you are and then call you back.

Internet access is not currently available to the public in The Gambia.

MONEY
Costs

Accommodation costs start from about US$5 for a bed in a very basic resthouse to about US$10 or US$15 for something a bit more comfortable.

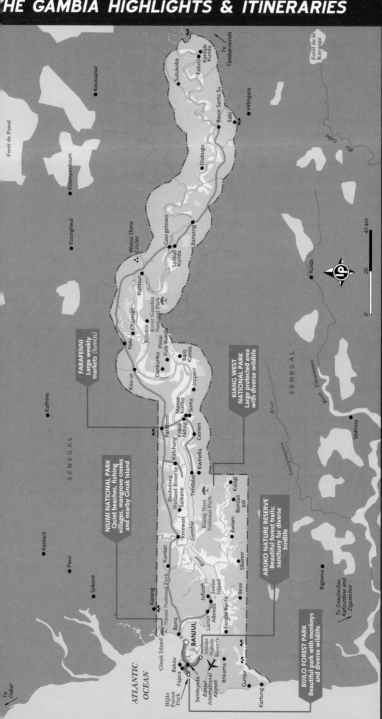

THE GAMBIA HIGHLIGHTS & ITINERARIES

FARAFENNI
Large weekly markets (lumos)

NIUMI NATIONAL PARK
Quiet beaches, fishing villages, mangrove creeks and nearby Ginak Island

KIANG WEST NATIONAL PARK
Large protected area with diverse wildlife

ABUKO NATURE RESERVE
Beautiful forest trails; sanctuary for diverse birdlife

BIJILO FOREST PARK
Beautiful park with monkeys and diverse wildlife

ATLANTIC OCEAN

SENEGAL

SENEGAL

To Dakar

Forêt de Panal

Forêt de la Kayanga

To Tambacounda

To Diouloulou, Karbutline and Ziguinchor

Koussanar

Koungheul

Kaffrine

Passi

Kaolack

Sokone

Karang

Barra

Ginak Island

BANJUL

Abuko Nature Reserve

Banjul International Airport

Serekunda

Bakau

Fajara

Bijilo Forest Park

Brikama

Kartung

Gunjur

Sibanor

Bessi

Faraba Banta

Lamin

Albreda

Jufureh

James Island

Niumi National Park

Kuntair

Kerewan

Salikene

Baobolong Wetland Reserve

Tendaba

Kwinella

Genieri

Soma

Mansa Konko

Pakali Nding

Katchang

Farafenni

Kau-ur

Njau

Dankunku

Pirai

Fula Kunda

Kiang West National Park

Iwiam

Jali

Bondali

Kalagi

Bignona

Sokoto

Kuntaur

River Gambia National Park

Wassu Stone Circles

Sankuli Kunda

Georgetown

Bansang

Diabugu

Sabi

Vélingara

Basse Santa Su

Fatoto

Kantale Kunda

Sutukoba

Baro Kunda

Jappeni

Kolda

Sédhiou

Kolda

Rio Geba

River Casamance

Southorngum

Gambia River

N

0   20   40 km

SUGGESTED ITINERARIES

One Week   Banjul • Serekunda • Abuko Nature Reserve •
Bijilo Forest Park

Two Weeks   Banjul • Serekunda • Jufureh • Abuko Nature Reserve • Bijilo Forest Park •
Banjul • Tendaba • Kiang West National Park • Farafenni • Baobolong Wetland
Reserve • Georgetown • River Gambia National Park • Basse Santa Su

Mid-range hotels cost between US$25 and US$50, while rooms at top-end establishments can be as high as US$100 to US$200. Local food is very inexpensive, while restaurants in Banjul catering for foreigners can easily cost US$15 or more for a meal.

In general, budget travellers should be able to get by on US$10 per day or less. For a bit more comfort, US$15 to US$25 per day is a reasonable budget. With US$30 to US$50 per day, or even more at your disposal, you can stay in decent hotels, eat well and travel quite comfortably. Vacationing in a luxury resort will cost from US$100 to US$200 per day.

Changing Money

In and around Banjul, changing money (cash or travellers cheques) is fairly quick and straightforward. There are numerous banks in the capital, with branches in Serekunda and some of the Atlantic coast resorts, that do foreign exchange. Upcountry, the only place with a bank is Basse Santa Su. Rates and commissions vary, so it pays to shop around. There is a black market, although the minimal difference and the risks of being short-changed or robbed make it hardly worthwhile (unless perhaps the banks are closed).

You can withdraw cash on Visa or MasterCard at all Standard Chartered Bank branches.

ONLINE SERVICES

Lonely Planet has a web site Destination The Gambia (www.lonely planet.com/dest/afr/gam.htm).

There is an official web site Republic of The Gambia (www.gambia .com).

The Gambia Resource Page (http: //persweb.wabash.edu/student/gajig oo/gambia/home.html) is another source of useful information.

The Smiling Face of Africa (www .niica.on.ca/gambia) has pictures, recipes, bulletin boards and more.

Momodou Camara, a Gambian living in Europe, has set up a page on The Gambia (http://home3.inet.tele .dk/mcamara/gam.html).

To get a glimpse of the country before you travel, try the gallery of Norwegian photographer Svend Ole Kvilesjo (www.kvilesjo.no/bilder/gam bia/gambia1.htm).

BOOKS & FILMS

One of The Gambia's best known novelists is William Conton, who was born in Banjul to a Sierra Leonean family. His 1960s classic, *The African*, is a semiautobiographical tale of an African student in Britain who experiences confusion and unhappiness there, and later returns to his homeland and becomes president. The book was an influential bestseller in many parts of Africa.

Lenrie Peters is another Gambian writer with a Sierra Leonean heritage. His best known novel, *The Second Round*, is a semiautobiographical work about an African doctor who lives overseas and has trouble readjusting to local ways when he returns home.

Chaff on the Wind is a more recent work, by Gambian author Ebou Dibba, who is viewed as part of the country's new generation of writers. This book follows the fortunes of two rural boys who come to work in the capital city, both eventually suffering at the hands of fate, despite their attempts to control their own destinies.

Probably the best known work inspired by events in The Gambia is Alex Haley's mix of historical fact and imaginative fiction, *Roots*, describing the black American author's search for his African origins.

In *Our Grandmothers' Drums* by Mark Hudson, the author provides interesting insights into village life based on his stay in central Gambia.

The TV film *Roots*, based on Haley's book, is probably the best known cinematic effort relating to The Gambia.

ENTERING & LEAVING THE GAMBIA

Airlines serving Gambia from Europe include Swissair, Sabena and Austrian Airlines, but most visitors arrive on charter flights as these are cheaper and usually direct. Airlines flying between Gambia and Senegal include Air Dabia and Air Senegal, although few travellers fly because land connections are good.

The Gambia is completely surrounded by Senegal (except for the coast), which you can reach by travelling north towards Dakar, south towards Ziguinchor or east towards Tambacounda. These journeys can be done directly or in stages. The most direct route between Banjul and Dakar is via the Barra ferry, Karang (on the border) and Kaolack (Senegal). The second option between Banjul and Dakar is longer but more interesting: east from Banjul to Soma, across the River Gambia by ferry to Farafenni, and then north on the Trans-Gambia highway to Kaolack and Dakar.

Between Serekunda and Ziguinchor, travel is via minibus and bush taxis. There are also bush taxis from Serekunda and Brikama to Kafountine in Senegal, although these are less frequent and it's usually quicker to get a Ziguinchor taxi to Diouloulou and change there for a local vehicle to Kafountine.

To get to Tambacounda, bush taxis go to the Gambian border post at Sabi and then continue for another few kilometres where you will need to change cars for the Senegalese border post and on to Vélingara (the first town in Senegal).

Some intrepid travellers get rides on ocean-going pirogues from Banjul to Dakar and Ziguinchor, although these boats are notoriously unsafe.

GHANA

For much of its history, Ghana has played a pivotal role in West Africa. From the height of Ashanti power to the more recent era of Kwame Nkrumah's fiery speeches and impassioned pan-Africanism, developments in the country have influenced the course of regional politics and economics. After suffering several decades of decline, Ghana is again on the upswing, with a steadily growing economy and a government cautiously joining the ranks of emerging African democracies.

For travellers, the country is one of the friendliest and easiest to get around in West Africa, making it a good choice for first-time visitors. It offers a variety of attractions, including clamouring, colourful markets, beautiful textiles and crafts, palm-fringed beaches, and towns redolent with ancient culture, such as Kumasi.

WHEN TO GO

The best time to visit Ghana is from December to about February, when the rains have stopped and the air is not yet too hot, although travel at any time of year is possible. The climate along the coast is more humid, with most rain falling between April and June and from September to November. The north is hotter and drier, with rains falling from May to September.

At a Glance

Full Country Name: Republic of Ghana
Area: 238,537 sq km
Population: 17.7 million
Capital City: Accra (population 964,000)
People: Akan (about 44%), Mole-Dagbane (about 16%), Ewe (about 13%), Ga (about 8%) and Guan
Languages: English (official), Akan, Fante-Twi, Nzima, Ga, Ewe, Mole-Dagbane, Grusi and Gurma
Religions: Christian (over 50%), Muslim (about 15%) and traditional religions
Government: Constitutional democracy
Currency: Ghanaian cedi (C)
Time Zone: GMT/UTC
International Telephone Code: 233
Electricity: 220V, 50 Hz. Most sockets take plugs with two round pins, and some take three square pins

---

ACCRA

Elevation – 27m/88ft

Rainfall (mm/in) and Temperature (°C/°F) charts, J F M A M J J A S O N D

TAMALE

Elevation – 194m/635ft

Rainfall (mm/in) and Temperature (°C/°F) charts, J F M A M J J A S O N D

HIGHLIGHTS
Cultural

Ghana's vibrant culture and friendly people are its best assets. Kumasi, the capital of the ancient Ashanti kingdom, is a particularly good place to experience these. Accra, with its bustling Makola market, National Museum and Arts Centre, and many craft shops is another. The relaxing Aburi Botanical Gardens to the north-east offer a pleasant getaway from Accra's hustle and bustle. To the west of the capital, at Kokrobite Beach, is the Academy of African Music & Arts Ltd which attracts well known musicians from all over West Africa.

Fishing Villages & Forts

If you want to relax while also absorbing some history, concentrate your travels along the coast, which is lined with laid-back fishing villages, interspersed with forts from the colonial era. The oldest of these, Fort St Jago and St George's Castle at Elmina, were constructed by the Portuguese in the 15th century. The dungeons, which you can visit, provide a stark reminder of the horrors of the slave trade.

Wildlife

The best place for seeing wildlife is Mole National Park in the north of the country, which is home to antelope, baboon, buffalo, warthog, wild dog, crocodiles and even some elephant. Viewing is best in the dry season between November and May, when the animals tend to congregate around waterholes. The only draw-back here is that you will need your own transport.

Crafts

For those who enjoy places off the beaten track, Bolgatanga, near the border with Burkina Faso, makes a good stop. It's an attractive town and

the craft centre of the north, known particularly for its basketware and leather goods.

VISA REQUIREMENTS

Visas are required for all except nationals of Economic Community of West African States (ECOWAS) countries.

Proof of yellow fever vaccination is checked at the airport and at most land borders.

Ghanaian Embassies

Canada
(☎ 613-236-0871/2/3) 1 Clemow Ave, Ottawa, Ontario KLS 2A

Côte d'Ivoire
(☎ 33 11 24) Immeuble Corniche, Blvd du Général de Gaulle, Le Plateau, Abidjan

Togo
(☎ 21 31 94) behind Gare de Kpalimé, Tokoin, Lomé

UK
(☎ 020-7342 8686) 104 Highgate Hill, London N6 5HE

USA
(☎ 202-686-4520; fax 686-4527) 3512 International Drive NW, Washington, DC 20008

TOURIST OFFICES OVERSEAS

Ghana has no overseas tourist offices, but its embassies generally have a tourism desk which can provide you with background material on the country. Also check the web sites listed under Online Services.

HEALTH

Malaria and dengue fever are both health risks in Ghana; take appropriate precautions against these diseases. Dysentery, hepatitis and typhoid are all food or waterborne diseases which occur here; drink only treated water and eat hot, freshly prepared food wherever possible.

Medical facilities are basic in Accra, and limited in rural areas. If you require serious medical care, you should think about going home.

POST & COMMUNICATIONS

The post is reliable; prices for international mail are far cheaper than in the USA or Europe. Poste restante in Accra and Kumasi is also reliable.

International telephone calls can be made efficiently from the Ghana Telecom offices in Accra and Kumasi.

There are also numerous private telecommunications centres, although they will be more expensive than Ghana Telecom. International calls are less expensive than elsewhere in the region, averaging about US$5/5/6 for three minutes to the USA/Europe/Australia.

Internet access is possible in Accra.

MONEY
Costs

Now that Ghana has a floating exchange rate, prices are generally very reasonable. Although top-end hotels may quote prices in US dollars, most will accept payment in cedis at the current exchange rate.

Itineraries

One Week
With just a week, you will only have time for Accra and one other attraction. Possibilities include a quick visit to Kumasi, a trip along the coast with stops in Kokrobite, Winneba and perhaps Cape Coast, or excursions to Aburi, Akosombo (site of the enormous Lake Volta dam) or Ada (a small town on an attractive beach where the River Volta meets the sea).

Two Weeks
With two weeks, you could spend three to four days in Accra before going westward to Cape Coast, with possible stops en route at Kokrobite and Winneba. From Cape Coast, head on to Elmina and Takoradi, taking in some of the other coastal forts, villages and beaches along the way. From Takoradi, continue via train to Kumasi, where you will probably want to stay at least three nights, before heading back to Accra. From here, you could squeeze in a trip east along the coast to Ada, or up to Akosombo.

One Month
With four weeks to spare, you will have time to visit most of the country. From Kumasi − after

visiting Accra and the coastal towns, including Busua and Dixcove − head north towards to Tamale (one night) and on to Mole National Park (two nights). From here, if you like rough backroads, you could continue north to Wa, and from there to Navrongo and Bolgatanga, though it will be faster to return to Tamale and head up to Bolgatanga from there. If you have plenty of time and don't mind being well off the beaten track, you could work in a side trip for some walks around Nakpanduri, a sleepy village on the Gambaga escarpment with beautiful views, and then head south via very sparsely travelled backroads past Yendi to Kete Krachi on Lake Volta. From here, continue by boat south to Akosombo, and then by road to Accra with a stop at Aburi.

Alternatively, you could leave out the far northern section of this itinerary, and from Mole National Park head back to Tamale and from there to Accra. From Accra, head east to Ada, Akosombo, Ho (a good base for hiking and exploring the surrounding villages) and Hohoe (also a good base for hiking, and a centre of traditional medicine), before making your way back to Accra.

HANA HIGHLIGHTS & ITINERARIES

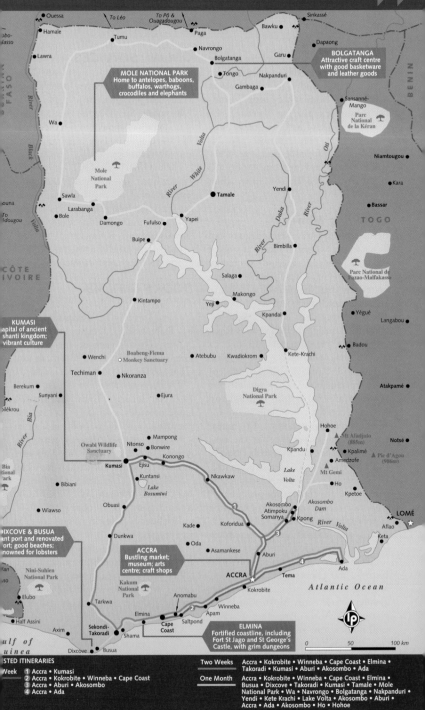

MOLE NATIONAL PARK
Home to antelopes, baboons, buffalos, warthogs, crocodiles and elephants

BOLGATANGA
Attractive craft centre with good basketware and leather goods

KUMASI
Capital of ancient shanti kingdom; vibrant culture

DIXCOVE & BUSUA
ant port and renovated ort; good beaches; nowned for lobsters

ACCRA
Bustling market; museum; arts centre; craft shops

ELMINA
Fortified coastline, including Fort St Jago and St George's Castle, with grim dungeons

0   50   100 km

Towns and places (Burkina Faso side): Ouessa, Hamale, Lawra, Wa, Sawla, Larabanga, Bole, Damongo, Fufulso, Buipe, Kintampo, Wenchi, Techiman, Nkoranza, Ejura, Berekum, Sunyani, Bibiani, Wiawso, Dunkwa, Tarkwa, Sekondi-Takoradi, Shama, Axim, Half Assini, Dixcove, Busua, Elubo, Nini-Suhien National Park, Bia National Park

Tumu, Navrongo, Bolgatanga, Tongo, Gambaga, Nakpanduri, Yendi, Paga

Sinkassé, Bawku, Dapaong, Garu, Sansanné-Mango, Parc National de la Kéran, Niamtougou, Kara, Bassar

Tamale, Yapei, Salaga, Makongo, Yeji, Kpandai, Kete-Krachi, Atebubu, Kwadiokrom

Mole National Park, Boabeng-Fiema Monkey Sanctuary, Digya National Park, Owabi Wildlife Sanctuary

Mampong, Ntonso, Bonwire, Konongo, Kumasi, Ejisu, Kuntansi, Obuasi, Kade, Oda, Asamankese, Aburi, Nkawkaw, Koforidua, Kpong, Somanya, Atimpoku, Akosombo, Akosombo Dam

Bimbilla, Langabou, Badou, Atakpamé, Hohoe, Kpandu, Amedzofe, Kpalimé, Ho, Kpetoe, Notsé, Yégué

TOGO, BENIN, CÔTE D'IVOIRE, BURKINA FASO

Mt Afadjulo (885m), Pic d'Agou (986m), Mt Gemi

Lake Volta, River Volta, River White Volta, River Black Volta, River Oti, River Daka, River Bia

Parc National de Fazao-Malfakasso

LOMÉ, Aflao, Keta, Ada, Tema, ACCRA, Kokrobite, Winneba, Apam, Saltpond, Cape Coast, Elmina, Anomabu, Kakum National Park

Atlantic Ocean

Gulf of Guinea

In general, budget travellers can get by on US$10 per day staying in very basic lodging, and eating local street food. For somewhat more comfortable travel, plan on about US$20 per day. Top-end luxuries (really only possible in and around Accra), including comfortable hotels with air-conditioning and western food, will cost from US$50 to more than US$150 per day.

Changing Money

Both cash and travellers cheques can be easily exchanged in Accra at one of the city's many foreign exchange (forex) bureaux. These usually offer a better rate than the banks for cash and are faster and more efficient, though rates for travellers cheques may be better at banks. There are also forex bureaux in major towns throughout the country, although many outside Accra and Kumasi will not accept travellers cheques. Many forex bureaux give better rates for US$50 and US$100 denomination bills than for smaller denominations. All major currencies are accepted, but the best by far are US dollars, British pounds, French francs or German marks. Don't even give the time of day to the occasional freelance moneychanger who may accost you; the rate won't be superior, and it may be a set-up.

Visa and MasterCard are becoming increasingly widely accepted by major hotels and travel agencies. American Express and Diners Club, by contrast, are next-to-useless. Cash advances against Visa and MasterCard are possible in Accra. American Express card-holders can get cash through the company's Ghanaian affiliate in central Accra.

ONLINE SERVICES

Lonely Planet has a web site Destination Ghana (www.lonelyplanet .com/dest/afr/gha.htm).

Republic of Ghana (www.ghana .com/republic/index.html) has cultural and travel information plus daily news and job vacancies.

Hello Ghana (www.helloghana.com /index.htm) doesn't have the same level of detail, but may be useful if you are making a business trip.

The Ghana Home Page (www .ghanaweb.com) is similar.

For news and views try Ghana Forum (www.ghanaforum.com).

BOOKS & FILMS

The Fall of the Asante Empire: The Hundred-Year War for Africa's Gold Coast by Robert B Edgerton offers an anthropologist's view of the century-long conflict between the British and Ghana's Ashanti people.

The Politics of Reform in Ghana, 1982-1991 by Jeffrey Herbst & Smadar Lavie provides a scholarly look at the country's more recent political history.

Changes: A Love Story by Ama Ata Aidoo is a contemporary novel about a modern Ghanaian woman's life in Accra.

The Beautiful Ones Are Not Yet Born by Ayi Kwei Armah is a sardonic observation of corrupt post-independence politics masquerading as an engaging novel.

This Earth, My Brother is Kofi Awoonor's first and best known novel, telling the story of a young African lawyer who works within the confines of the judicial system inherited from the British.

Ghana has a small, but active film industry producing popular films for the local market. These include *Love*

Brewed in the African Pot (1981) directed by Kwan Ansah and *Nana Akoto* (1985) directed by King Ampaw et al.

ENTERING & LEAVING GHANA

Ghana Airways connects Accra with most regional capitals. Ghana is also well connected with many European capitals, as well as with Johannesburg, South Africa and other cities on the continent. Airlines servicing Accra include Aeroflot, Air Afrique, Alitalia, British Airways, KLM, Lufthansa, South African Airways and Swissair.

To Burkina Faso, the usual land route to Ouagadougou is via Bolgatanga, Navrongo and Pô, crossing at Paga. You will need to do the trip in stages by bus and taxi, and on some sections there is transport only several times a week. Alternatively, there is a weekly direct bus between Accra and Ouagadougou. You can also enter Burkina Faso between Wa and Bobo-Dioulasso via Hamale, although traffic is scarce.

To Côte d'Ivoire, the most convenient route is via Elubo and Aboisso on the coastal road. There are daily direct buses, or you can do the trip in stages by bush taxi. Another crossing is from Kumasi via Agnibilékrou. This route also must be done in stages. On the northernmost route from Bole to Ferkessédougou, there is transport from Bole to the River Volta, which you will need to cross by canoe. From there to Bouna and on to Ferkessédougou, travel is done by taxi and in stages.

To Togo, there are frequent minibuses and taxis along the coastal road between Accra and Aflao/Lomé. There is also a crossing between Kpandu and Kpalimé (Togo) which can either be done by direct share taxi or in stages, which is faster. In the north, you can cross from Tamale via Yendi to Sansanné-Mango or Kara, and from Bawku via Sinkassé to Dapaong, though transport is scarce on these routes.

GUINEA

Guinea (sometimes called Guinea-Conakry to distinguish it from neighbouring Guinea-Bissau) used to suffer under one of the most oppressive regimes in Africa. But during the years since the death of President Sekou Touré in 1984, it has changed radically, and today you can sense its spirit and economic vitality.

One of Guinea's major attractions is the vibrancy of its culture. Across the country, there's a strong tradition of live music, and any evening in Conakry you can find a musical celebration in the streets. Added to this is the spectacular landscape: the Fouta Djalon plateau, in the west of the country, has some of the most striking scenery in West Africa and is an excellent area for trekking.

Despite these attractions, Guinea is not well prepared for tourism. Outside Conakry, most accommodation is basic (although this is beginning to change) and journeys by road can be long and hard. If you insist on creature comforts you may not enjoy Guinea. But if you're prepared to rough it, a visit here can be very rewarding.

WHEN TO GO

The best time to visit Guinea is in November and early December, after the rains end and the air is clearest. The next best time is from December to March, although the air is often hazy, and temperatures can get uncomfortably warm, especially in March. During the rainy season from May to October, secondary roads get very muddy, and many become impassable. Rainfall is heaviest during July and August, especially along the coast.

At a Glance

Full Country Name: Republic of Guinea
Area: 245,855 sq km
Population: 7.2 million
Capital City: Conakry (population approx 1.5 million)
People: Predominantly Malinké (Mandingo), Peul (Fula or Fulani) and Susu (which together constitute about 75% of the population)
Languages: French (official), Malinké, Pular (Fula) and Susu
Religions: Muslim (about 80%), Christian (about 5%) and traditional religions
Government: Republic
Currency: Guinean franc (GF)
Time Zone: GMT/UTC
International Telephone Code: 224
Electricity: 220V, 50 Hz. Most sockets take plugs with two round pins

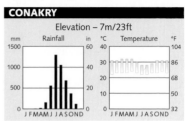

CONAKRY — Elevation – 7m/23ft — Rainfall (mm / in) — Temperature (°C / °F) — J F M A M J J A S O N D

HIGHLIGHTS
Urban & Beaches

Although many travellers prefer to skip Conakry, it is worth at least a brief visit. Offshore are some attractive beaches on the Îles de Los. There are some more beautiful beaches and relaxing fishing villages at Cap Verga, well north of Conakry along the coast, although it's time-consuming to get there without your own transport.

Trekking & Biking

The most scenic region of the country, and one of the best areas in West Africa for trekking, is the Fouta Djalon plateau, where you can wander from village to village while enjoying striking hill panoramas and a pleasantly cooler climate. The forest region around Nzérékoré is also an attractive area, and ideal for biking and relaxing.

Cultural

Delving into Guinean history and culture takes a bit more time, but is well worth the effort. Some places to include on your itinerary are Kankan – once the seat of the ancient Mali empire, base for Guinean hero Samory Touré, and today a relaxed university town; tiny Kouroussa village, north-west of Kankan and birthplace of famous Guinean author Camara Laye; and Kindia, a colourful market town known for its textiles.

VISA REQUIREMENTS

All visitors, except nationals of ECOWAS countries, need a visa. Visas are not available at airports or land borders. Those issued by embassies in Africa are usually valid for a maximum of one month (up to three months for those issued outside Africa). Previously, tourist visas were frequently denied. This is generally not the case now, although a letter of invitation is sometimes requested.

Proof of vaccination against yellow fever and cholera is also required.

Guinean Embassies

Canada
(☎ 613-789-8444) 483 Wilbrod St, Ottawa, Ontario K1N 6N1

Côte d'Ivoire
(☎ 22 25 20) Immeuble Crosson Duplessis, Ave Crosson Duplessis, Le Plateau, Abidjan

Mali
(☎ 22 29 75) South of the centre on Rue 313, Bamako

Senegal
(☎ 824 86 06) Rue 7, Point E, Dakar

UK
(☎ 020-7333 0044) 20 Upper Grosvenor St, London W1X 9PB

USA
(☎ 202-483-9420) 2112 Leroy Place NW, Washington, DC 20008

TOURIST OFFICES OVERSEAS

Guinea has no overseas tourist offices. However, its embassies and travel agencies can provide basic information about the country. Also check the web sites listed under Online Services.

HEALTH

Malaria and dengue fever both pose a health risk in Guinea; take appropriate precautions against these diseases. Dysentery, hepatitis and typhoid are all food or waterborne diseases that occur here; drink only treated water and try wherever possible to eat only hygienically prepared and freshly cooked food.

Medical facilities are basic in Conakry and in rural areas. If you require serious medical care, you should fly home.

POST & COMMUNICATIONS

The post is usually dependable, and prices are standard for the region. However the separate express service is not reliable for sending or receiving mail. There is an unorganised poste restante service in Conakry.

International calls can be made at offices of Sotelgui, the national telecommunications entity, in Conakry and all major upcountry towns. Rates are standard for the region. Upcountry, line quality is often poor. There are also private telecommunications services in Conakry which can be more efficient, but more expensive.

Internet access is possible in Conakry.

MONEY
Costs

In Conakry, budget lodging is limited. Upcountry, most towns have at least one place to stay, often with very basic but cheap facilities, while larger towns generally have a range of hotels. Expect to pay US$10 or less for budget lodging, and from US$15 for a room with amenities. Eating all your meals on the street, you will be able to keep your daily food budget to about US$5 per day. For those willing to spend more, there are some very decent restaurants in most larger

Itineraries

One Week

If you have a week or less in Guinea, a good option would be to spend two days in the capital, then head to Kindia and spend a couple of days exploring the town and nearby attractions, including the Îles de Los. Alternatively, you could fly from Conakry to Labé, the main town in the Fouta Djalon, then travel by road through the Fouta Djalon back to Conakry, with stops en route at Dalaba (a former spa town in an excellent trekking area) and Kindia. If you don't have time to leave Conakry, at least try to take a half-day excursion to the nearby villages of Coyah (the source of Guinea's bottled water) or Dubréka (a quiet town on the mangrove swamps) in order to get a glimpse of upcountry Guinea; it's quite a contrast to the capital.

Two Weeks

With two weeks, head from Kindia east towards the lively junction town of Mamou and then north to the Fouta Djalon, where you could easily spend five to six days or longer walking in the villages, or doing day excursions based in Dalaba.

One Month

With a month or more, you can add north-eastern and south-eastern Guinea to the itinerary:

from the Fouta Djalon region, head east via Dabola (site of the impressive Tinkisso dam) and Kouroussa to Kankan. It's well worth pausing in Kankan for a few days before heading south towards Kissidougou, a friendly market town. From Kissidougou, head south-east via Macenta to Nzérékoré. The region around Nzérékoré can keep you busy for up to a week, including excursions to nearby Lola (known for its traditional medicines) and Mt Nimba. From Nzérékoré you could fly back to Conakry or continue by road into Côte d'Ivoire.

To make this grand loop with the minimum of backtracking, you could start the other way by flying from Conakry to Nzérékoré. From Nzérékoré head towards Kankan via Macenta and Kissidougou. Then, continue from Kankan via Kouroussa towards Dabola and Mamou. Alternatively, from Dabola, you could go south to Faranah (hometown of President Sekou Touré) and then on to Mamou. From Mamou, go north through the Fouta Djalon to Labé. From Labé, you could continue to Mali-ville (a tiny town in a rugged but spectacular trekking area) or Koundara (the base for visits to Parc Transfrontalier Niokolo-Badiar) and on into Senegal or Guinea-Bissau, or else fly or return by road to Conakry.

GUINEA HIGHLIGHTS & ITINERARIES

MAURITANIA

Kaédi

Mbout

Ouro Sogui • Matam

Nguère

Dakar

Nioro

SENEGAL

Bakel

Kidira

Kayes

To Dioubé & Dakar

Tambacounda

Bafoulabé

THE GAMBIA

FOUTA DJALON PLATEAU
Guinea's most scenic region;
good trekking; striking
panoramas; cool climate

SENEGAL

Parc Transfrontalier
Niokolo-Badiar

Sambailo

Koundara

Saréboïdo

Gabú

Kedougou

Kita

MALI

BAMAKO

GUINEA-BISSAU

Massif du
Tamgué

Mali-ville

Kourémalé

KANKAN
University town; former seat of
ancient Malí empire in Niani

Bankan

Koumbia

Gaoual

Source of
the Gambia

Labé

Siguiri

Niger

Niani

To
Bougouni

Boké

Télimélé

Pita

Dinguiraye

Kamsar

Fria

River

Konkouré

Dalaba

Dabola

Mandiana

To Mininian
& Odienné

Kankan

Boffa

Kilomètre 36

Mamou

Parc National
du Haut Niger

Kouroussa

Verga

Kindia

Faranah

Dubréka

CONAKRY

Coyah

Haute Guinée

Îles de Los

Forécariah

KINDIA
Bustling town with busy
market and quality textiles

Kérouané

Pámelap

Kambia

Source of
the Niger

Kissidougou

Guinée Forestière

Sinko
To
Yamoussoukro
& Abidjan

FREETOWN

ÎLES DE LOS
Tranquil beaches popular
for weekend excursions

Guéckédou

Macenta

Beyla

Voinjama

Touba

Kailahun

Bo

SIERRA
LEONE

NZÉRÉKORÉ
Craft centre; good base
for exploring Guinea's
forest region

Zorzor

Lola

Sipilou

Nzo

CAP VERGA
Beautiful beaches;
relaxing fishing villages

Nzérékoré

Bossou

Biankouma

Yekepa

Man

ATLANTIC
OCEAN

Diéké

Danané

Ganta

Sanniquellie

LIBERIA

Nimba
Mountains

CÔTE
D'IVOIRE

To
Monrovia

towns where you can dine in style for US$5 to US$15.

In general, budget travellers should be able to get by without difficulty on US$15 per day or less. Mid-range travel will cost from US$35 to US$60 per day, while top-end food and lodging in Conakry will cost from US$100 per day.

Changing Money

Cash and travellers cheques can be easily exchanged at banks in Conakry. Most banks upcountry exchange only cash. For both cash and travellers cheques, the best denomination is French francs, followed by US dollars. Black market dealers are widely used throughout Guinea (cash only); their rates are usually about 8% better than bank rates.

ONLINE SERVICES

Lonely Planet has a web site Destination Guinea (www.lonelyplanet .com/dest/afr/gui.htm).

International Resources: Guinea (www.mw.klever.net/globe/GUINEA .html) is a bare-bones rundown on facts and figures.

The Norwegian Council for Africa's Index on Africa (www .africaindex.africainfo.no/africaindex1 /countries/guinea.html) is a good source of additional links.

BOOKS & FILMS

Camara Laye is Guinea's most famous author, and one of West Africa's most renowned literary figures. He is known in particular for his autobiographical *L'Enfant Noir* (The African Child) about coming of age among the Malinké. *The Radiance of the King* is another of his works.

Historical Dictionary of Guinea by Thomas O'Toole & Ibrahima Bah-Lalya

is a useful reference book on the country.

A Mission to Civilize: The Republican Idea of Empire in France and West Africa, 1895-1930 by Alice Conklin looks at the arrogance, folly and sometimes good intentions of French empire-builders.

Francophone Sub-Saharan Africa, 1880-1995 by Patrick Manning includes material on developments since 1985, looking at the democratisation movements of the 1980s and 90s and the Francophone movement.

The African Child (1994), filmed in Guinea and directed by Laurent Chevallier, is the film version of Laye's book.

ENTERING & LEAVING GUINEA

International airlines servicing Guinea include Sabena, Air France and Aeroflot. Ghana Airways (via Accra) and Air Afrique (via Dakar) also have flights to and from Europe, and Air Afrique has a direct flight between New York and Dakar with connections to Conakry. Royal Air Maroc flies from Conakry to Casablanca with onward connections to the USA and Europe. There are direct flights from Conakry to many regional capitals, and connections via Abidjan or Accra to southern and eastern Africa.

To Côte d'Ivoire, the most frequently travelled land route is between Lola and Man either via Nzo and Danané or via Sipilou and Biankouma. During the rainy season, the stretches between Lola and the border are usually only passable by 4WD. Alternatively, you can go from Kankan to Odienné via Mandiana. Bush taxis run from Kankan to Mandiana, where you can find transport to Mininian and from there, taxis to Odienné and beyond. There is also a route via Beyla (which has connections north to Kankan and south to Nzérékoré) and Sinko to Odienné. In general, it's better to cover as much distance as possible on the Côte d'Ivoire side, as most secondary roads in Guinea's forest region are in bad shape.

To Mali, there is frequent transport to the border at Kourémalé from both Kankan and Siguiri and a few times weekly from both towns via Kourémalé direct to Bamako. There's also a direct taxi weekly from Conakry to Bamako. Taxis from Siguiri to Bamako sometimes take a less travelled route paralleling the River Niger, via Bankan. You can also go from Kankan via Mandiana to Bougouni, although you'll have to do the trip in stages.

To Senegal, the main route is via Labé and Koundara to Tambacounda and Dakar. During the rainy season the stretch between Labé and Koundara is slow or impassable for 2WD, although trucks ply the route frequently. From Koundara to Dioubé in Senegal, there are several cars a week, and from Dioubé there is daily transport to Tambacounda.

KENYA

Although its reputation has been marred in recent times by political instability and rising crime rates, Kenya has long been one of the most popular tourist destinations in sub-Saharan Africa. Some visitors come for the famous wildlife reserves of Tsavo and Masai Mara, while others are enticed by the Indian Ocean coast – notably the resorts near Mombasa and the exotic Swahili island of Lamu. A wide variety of outdoor activities – including the chance to trek on Mt Kenya (5199m), the continent's second highest peak – will enthuse outdoor activities fans. The chance to experience the colourful and fascinating tribal cultures is an added attraction. To top it all off, good air connections with Europe, Asia and

elsewhere in Africa make getting here a breeze. As long as you keep away from trouble spots and don't flaunt your valuables, a visit to Kenya will most likely be memorable and hassle-free.

WHEN TO GO

The best times to visit Kenya are during the dry seasons – from the end of May to early October when the weather is cooler, and from late November to early March, when it is generally warmer. Between June and September

At a Glance

Full Country Name: Republic of Kenya
Area: 582,645 sq km
Population: 28.2 million
Capital City: Nairobi (population 1.5 million)
People: More than 70 ethnic groups including Kikuyu (about 22%), Luo (about 13%), Meru, Gusii, Maasai, Turkana and Kalenjin
Languages: English and Swahili (official), Kikuyu, Luo, Luhia and Kikamba
Religions: Muslim (about 33%), Christian (about 33%) and traditional religions
Government: Republic
Currency: Kenyan shilling (Ksh)
Time Zone: Three hours ahead of GMT/UTC
International Telephone Code: 254
Electricity: 220V, 50 Hz; most sockets have three square pins, although some older buildings have round-pin sockets

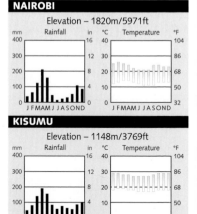

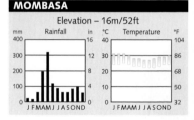

is the best time to see the wildebeest migration in action, while January and February are when you will find the largest concentrations of birdlife on the Rift Valley lakes. This is also a good time to spot animals in the game parks.

HIGHLIGHTS
Wildlife
If you've come to see wildlife, you won't be disappointed. The highlight for many is undoubtedly the annual wildebeest migration (June to September) in the Masai Mara National Reserve when millions of wildebeest move north from the Serengeti in search of lush grass. Apart from the migration, the reserve is a spectacular place abounding in wildlife.

Amboseli National Park, with its dramatic setting against the backdrop of Mt Kilimanjaro (actually in Tanzania), is another good game-viewing area known particularly for its black rhino and large herds of elephants. Lake Baringo in the centre of the country is ideal for bird-watching, containing over 450 of Kenya's 1200 different species.

Kakamega Forest Reserve, a superb patch of tropical virgin rainforest in the heart of an intensively cultivated agricultural area in western Kenya, is home to a large variety of birds and animals including primates such as the red-tailed monkey, black and white colobus monkey and the blue monkey.

Island Life
Away from the wildlife, one of Kenya's top attractions is Lamu Island, which boasts the country's oldest inhabited town, and which is just as exotic as Zanzibar Island to the south.

Urban Experiences
As well as Nairobi, with its bustling markets, there is steamy Mombasa with historic Fort Jesus and an Old Town full of ornate wooden shopfronts and balconies, which is great to explore.

Itineraries

One Week
With a week, spend a few days in Nairobi, including a day white-water rafting on the Athi River. Then either head to the Masai Mara reserve or Amboseli National Park for the remainder of the week.

Two Weeks
The first week could be spent in and around Nairobi and in the Masai Mara National Reserve. For the second week, head towards Mombasa, with possible detours to Amboseli or Tsavo West national parks. You could spend the remainder of the time in and around Mombasa, including diving or snorkelling near Malindi. If you do not stop at the parks, you will also have time to travel along the coast to Lamu Island.

One Month
With a month, you will have time to cover all the ground in the one and two week itineraries, including sufficient time in the national parks and reserves. You could also add a trip to western Kenya to the Kakamega Forest Reserve or Lake Baringo in the Rift Valley – part of a rift system which stretches 6,000 km from the Dead Sea to Mozambique – or alternatively, spend up to a week or more trekking on Mt Kenya. A possible circuit could be from Nairobi to Masai Mara, and then up to Mt Kenya, passing through Naivasha. From here return to Nairobi and then head to Mombasa and the coast. Fly back from Mombasa or return by road. With more than a month, particularly if you have access to a 4WD, you could bring both western and northern Kenya, including the more remote Lake Turkana area, into the itinerary as well.

KENYA HIGHLIGHTS & ITINERARIES

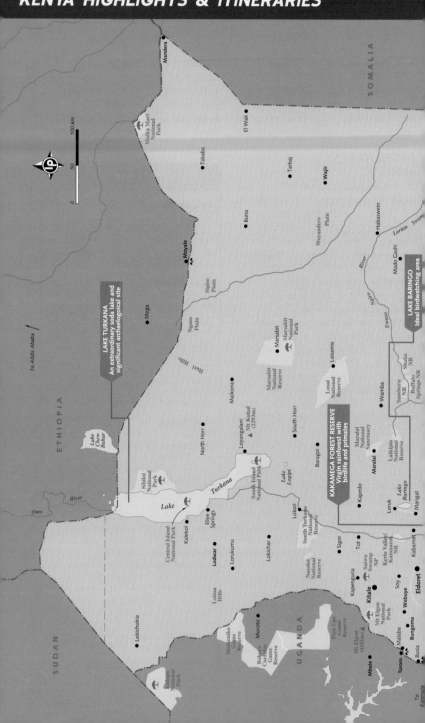

MT KENYA
Beautiful, rugged mountain area; good trekking

LAMU ISLAND
Exotic island; Kenya's oldest inhabited town

MOMBASA
Historic town with Fort Jesus and ornate wooden architecture

MASAI MARA NATIONAL RESERVE
Massive annual wildebeest migration from the Serengeti; abundant wildlife

AMBOSELI NATIONAL PARK
Good game viewing area against backdrop of Mt Kilimanjaro

INDIAN
OCEAN

TANZANIA

SUGGESTED ITINERARIES

One Week ① Nairobi • Athi River • Masai Mara National Reserve
② Nairobi • Athi River • Amboseli National Park

Two Weeks Nairobi • Masai Mara Naitonal Reserve • Amboseli National Park • Tsavo West National Park • Mombasa • Malindi • Lamu Island

One Month Nairobi • Masai Mara National Reserve • Amboseli National Park • Lamu Island • Nairobi • Naivasha • Kakamega Forest Reserve • Lake Baringo • Mt Kenya

Beaches & Trekking

South of Mombasa are some attractive beaches – that at Diani is one of the best. For trekkers, Kenya offers the beautiful and rugged Mt Kenya, as well as the Aberdare Range and Mt Elgon, which straddles the Kenya-Uganda border.

Archaeology

Lake Turkana (the Jade Sea), Kenya's largest lake, is a significant archaeological site. In the 1970s a palaeontologist, Richard Leakey, found a fossilised skull, part of *Homo habilis*, which was 2.5 million years old.

VISA REQUIREMENTS

Visas are required by citizens of most countries, except those from some European countries (including Denmark, Germany, Ireland, Italy, Norway, Spain and Sweden), the UK and citizens of some Commonwealth countries. Citizens of the USA, France, Canada, Australia and New Zealand do need visas.

Visas are available from Kenyan embassies and at Nairobi airport on arrival (although it's better to get one in advance if you can). They are valid for between one and three months, and remain valid if you go to Tanzania or Uganda and return to Kenya.

You also need an international health certificate with proof of yellow fever vaccination.

Kenyan Embassies

Australia
(☎ 02-6247 4788; fax 6257 6613) QBE Building, 33 Ainslie Ave, Canberra, ACT 2601

Canada
(☎ 613-563-1773; fax 233-6599) 415 Laurier Ave, Ottawa, Ontario K1N 6R4

Ethiopia
(☎ 01-610303; fax 611433) Fikre Miriam Rd, PO Box 3301, Addis Ababa

Tanzania
(☎ 051-46362; fax 46519) NIC Investment House, Samora Ave, PO Box 5231, Dar es Salaam

Uganda
(☎ 041-267386; fax 267369) Plot No 2030, Muyenga Kansanga Rd, PO Box 5220, Kampala

UK
(☎ 020-7636 2371; fax 7323 6717) 45 Portland Place, London W1N 4AS

USA
(☎ 202-387-6101; fax 462-3829) 2249 R St NW, Washington, DC 20008

TOURIST OFFICES OVERSEAS

Kenya maintains overseas tourist offices in several countries including:

UK
(☎ 020-7355 3144; fax 7495 8656) 25 Brook's Mews (off Davies St), Mayfair, London W1Y 1LF

USA
(☎ 213-274-6635; fax 859-7010) 9150 Wilshire Blvd, Beverly Hills, CA 90212; (☎ 212-486-1300; fax 688-0911) 424 Madison Ave, New York, NY 10017

HEALTH

Malaria exists in all parts of the country except in Nairobi and in the highlands (above 2500m) of Central, Rift Valley, Eastern, Nyanza and Eastern provinces, where the risk of malaria is very low. Recently epidemics of dengue fever have been reported in Kenya. Take appropriate precautions, including care with what you eat and drink. Avoid shellfish, poorly cooked meat and unpurified water. If you plan to climb Mt Kenya, be prepared for cold conditions and be aware of the symptoms and treatment of altitude sickness.

Medical care is reasonable in Nairobi and in most regional towns. If you do require serious medical care, get to Nairobi at least, but consider going home.

POST & COMMUNICATIONS

Kenya's postal system is reliable, though letters can take up to two weeks to reach Australia or the USA. Prices for international air mail are cheaper than in the USA and Europe. There are poste restante services in Nairobi and in most towns.

The telephone system works reasonably well and international calls can be made from all major towns, although it can sometimes take a number of attempts to get a connection. Rates for international calls are expensive, starting from about US$3 or more per minute. It is possible to make reverse charge (collect) calls, but only to the UK, Europe and the USA.

Internet access is widely available in Nairobi.

MONEY
Costs

Budget travellers in Kenya should plan on about US$15 to US$20 per day if eating local food, using local transport and staying in basic accommodation. Mid-range comforts – including perhaps a low-end organised safari – will cost from US$30 to US$90 per day. Top-end travel, including a luxury safari, can cost from US$100 to more than US$200 per day.

Changing Money

Foreign exchange (forex) bureaux are the best places to change money. Their rates are competitive and they usually don't charge commission. Banks will change money, but their commissions can be steep. All major currencies are accepted, but US dollars are the most convenient. There is no black market, so assume that offers on the street are a set-up. Travellers cheques can be changed without problems in Nairobi. Commissions range from none to about 1%.

Credit cards are accepted by some upper-end hotels and safari companies. Cash advances against Visa card are possible in Nairobi.

ONLINE SERVICES

Lonely Planet has a web site Destination Kenya (www.lonelyplanet .com/dest/afr/ken.htm).

Kenya WWW Newsgroup (www .rcbowen.com/kenya/newsgroup) is a grass-roots discussion forum.

The Nation (www.africaonline.co .ke/nation/index.html) is similar.

Project Elgon (www.abdn.ac.uk /elgon) presents a detailed environmental and social study of Mt Elgon.

Kenya's National Parks & Reserves (www.gorp.com/gorp/location /africa/kenya/parkindx.htm) has up-to-date information.

Both Kenya Travel Guide (www.bwa nazulia.com/kenya/index.html) and About Kenya (www.africaonline.co.ke /AfricaOnline/covertravel.html) have useful safari and travel information.

BOOKS & FILMS

Petals of Blood by Ngugi wa Thiong'o, one of Kenya's most highly regarded authors, is a harrowing criticism of neo-colonialist politics in Kenya. Other worthwhile titles by this author include *A Grain of Wheat* and *Weep Not Child*.

Meja Mwangi is another well known Kenyan author whose books are a good introduction to East African literature. His most famous works include *Going Down River Road*, *Kill Me Quick* and *Carcass for Hounds*.

Elspeth Huxley's *Flame Trees of Thika* tells the story of the white settler experience through the eyes of a young girl. *Out of Africa* by Isak Dinesen (Karen Blixen) covers similar turf from an adult perspective.

Films shot in Kenya include the 1950s Tarzan movies, *King Solomon's Mines* (1950) and, more famously, *Born Free* (1966), based on the Joy Adamson book of the same name. *The Color Purple* (1985), directed by Steven Spielberg and based on the novel by Alice Walker, was filmed in part in Kenya.

Mountains of the Moon (1990) dramatises the historic journey of Burton and Speke in their search for the source of the Nile.

Probably the best known film to be made in Kenya is *Out of Africa*, the 1985 film depiction of the life of Karen Blixen, starring Robert Redford and Meryl Streep.

ENTERING & LEAVING KENYA

Kenya is the main gateway into East Africa and is serviced by airlines from all over the world, including Europe, Asia and the rest of Africa.

To Ethiopia, the main overland crossing point is at Moyale, via Marsabit. The only transport between Marsabit and Moyale are trucks, which usually travel in convoys because of the risk of banditry. The trip takes from two to four days, plus the time you may have to wait until a convoy assembles. Get an update on the security situation near the border before attempting to travel on this route.

Overland travel to both Somalia and the Sudan is restricted due to the security situations in these countries.

The main overland route between Kenya and Tanzania is a tarmac road connecting Nairobi and Arusha via Namanga (the border post). You have a choice of bus, share taxi or (most popular) minibus shuttle. Daily buses connect Mombasa with Tanga and Dar es Salaam, via Horohoro at the border. There is also transport via a 'tourist shuttle' connecting Mombasa with Moshi and Arusha several times weekly.

Other routes into Tanzania are via Taveta to Moshi, through the Masai Mara National Reserve to Bologonya in the northern Serengeti (although there is no public transport on this route), and via Isebania to Musoma. Despite the train lines you may see drawn on maps, there is presently no train service between Kenya and Tanzania. A weekly ferry connects Mombasa with Tanga and Dar es Salaam. There is no ferry service between Kenya and Tanzania on Lake Victoria.

To Uganda, the main route is between Nairobi and Kampala via the border post at Malaba. The roads in both countries are in good condition. There are direct buses or the journey can be done in stages. There is a second route via Kisumu and Busia, which must be travelled in stages (or by direct bus between Kisumu and Kampala). The weekly train from Nairobi to Kampala has ceased to operate, but there is a train service on Saturdays between Malaba on the Ugandan border and Nairobi.

Lesotho, which is completely surrounded by South Africa, is a tiny mountain kingdom with a vibrant culture and spectacular topography. The entire country lies above 1000m, with ranges in the east and centre reaching 3000m in altitude. It's a beautiful and rugged place, ideal for those who enjoy hiking, and who want to meet people living traditional lifestyles.

WHEN TO GO

Lesotho can be visited year-round, but the weather will determine what you can do. In winter be prepared for cold and snow. In summer (October to April), there is rain, mist and sometimes severe thunderstorms. Many roads are blocked by floods during this season. Whatever time of year you go, you need to be well prepared: never go out into the mountains, even for an afternoon, without a sleeping bag, tent and sufficient food for a few days in case you get fogged in. Even in summer, it can be freezing.

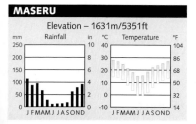

MASERU

Elevation – 1631m/5351ft

HIGHLIGHTS
Hiking & Pony Trekking

The main activities are hiking and pony trekking. Good options include wilderness hiking along the top of the Drakensberg escarpment in eastern Lesotho, and walking up Thabana-Ntlenyana (3482m), southern Africa's highest peak. The rugged and remote Sehlabathebe National Park hosts several rare birds, including the Maloti minnow. It also offers good hiking, climbing and horseback riding.

Villages & Crafts

Lesotho offers the rare opportunity to meet and stay with people living traditional lifestyles. The best way to experience this is on hikes or pony treks. Apart from this, Lesotho's villages make interesting places to visit. Some good destinations include Teyateyaneng (usually known as TY), which is the craft centre of Lesotho; Thaba-Bosiu, Moshoeshoe I's mountain stronghold

At a Glance

Full Country Name: Kingdom of Lesotho
Area: 30,345 sq km
Population: 2.1 million
Capital City: Maseru (population 250,000)
People: Sotho
Languages: Southern Sotho (seSotho) and English
Religions: Christian (about 75%) and traditional beliefs
Government: Constitutional monarchy
Currency: Lesotho maloti (M)
Time Zone: Two hours ahead of GMT/UTC
International Telephone Code: 266 (to call from South Africa, dial 09-266)
Electricity: 220/250V; sockets vary but usually take plugs with three round pins

and the most important historical site in Lesotho; and Leribe (Hlotse), a pleasant market centre.

VISA REQUIREMENTS

Most visitors need a visa, except citizens of Denmark, Finland, Greece, Iceland, Ireland, Israel, Japan, Norway, Sweden and South Africa. Citizens of Commonwealth countries do not need a visa, with the exception of visitors from Australia, Canada, Ghana, India, New Zealand, Nigeria, Pakistan and Namibia.

The nearest Lesotho high commission is in Pretoria, South Africa (address given below). Temporary entry permits are sometimes given at the Maseru Bridge border, which allow you to go to Maseru and apply for a visa there, but don't count on this.

Remember that when you leave South Africa, your South African visa or entry permit will expire. This isn't a problem if you qualify for an entry permit (most people do), or if you have a multiple-entry visa. However, if you only had a single-entry visa you'll need to apply for a new South African visa in Maseru, which can be time-consuming. No vaccination certificates are necessary to enter Lesotho unless you have recently been in a yellow fever area.

Lesotho's Embassies & High Commissions

Canada
(☎ 613-236-9449) 202 Clemow Ave, Ottawa, Ontario H1S 2B4

South Africa
(☎ 012-322 6090) 343 Pretorius St, Momentum Centre, 6th floor, West Tower, Pretoria 001

UK
(☎ 020-7373 8581/2; fax 7235 5686) 7 Chesam Place, Belgravia, London SW1 8AN

USA
(☎ 202-797-5533/4) 2511 Massachusetts Ave NW, Washington, DC 20008

HEALTH

Although malaria is not a great problem in Lesotho, you should cover up and use repellent in order to avoid insect bites. Take care with what you eat and drink to avoid dysentery, cholera and other food and waterborne diseases.

Itineraries

One week
The best option would be to spend the entire week hiking or pony trekking. Alternatively, you could spend a few days visiting Maseru and surrounding urban villages, where you can observe village life and barter for handcrafts.

Thaba-Bosiu, about 16km east of the capital, also makes a good day trip. There's a visitor information centre, and you can arrange a guide to accompany you to the top of the mountain. You could go on excursions to Teyateyaneng to shop for crafts, or to Thaba-Tseka, on the western edge of the Central Ranges, for some modest trekking in the foothills.

Two to Three Weeks
Hiking and pony trekking are the main activities for anyone with some time to spend in Lesotho. Some possibilities are mentioned under Highlights earlier. For the Drakensberg escarpment, you'll need your own 4WD and adequate equipment.

One option here would be to drive to the Sani Top Chalet in the east of the country, from where it's a long day walk to Thabana-Ntlenyana, or a several days walk to Bushman's Nek (in South Africa) and the Sehlabathebe National Park. With two or three weeks, you'll have time for the beautiful walk from the north near new Oxbow Lodge to Sehlabathebe via Mont-aux-Sources (3282m).

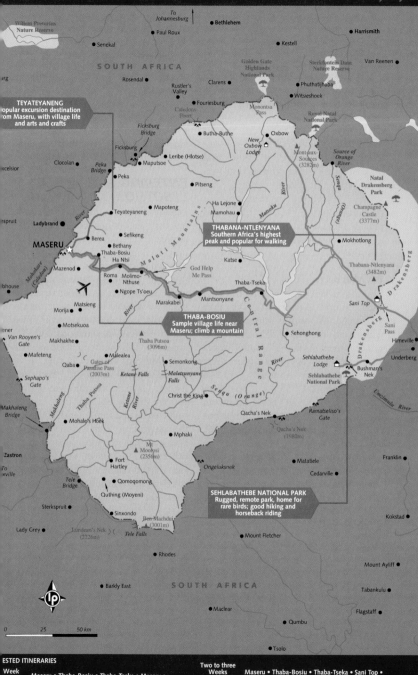

ESOTHO HIGHLIGHTS & ITINERARIES

TEYATEYANENG
opular excursion destination
om Maseru, with village life
and arts and crafts

THABANA-NTLENYANA
Southern Africa's highest
peak and popular for walking

THABA-BOSIU
Sample village life near
Maseru; climb a mountain

SEHLABATHEBE NATIONAL PARK
Rugged, remote park, home for
rare birds; good hiking and
horseback riding

Willem Pretorius
Nature Reserve

To
Johannesburg

Paul Roux   Bethlehem
Senekal   Kestell   Harrismith

SOUTH AFRICA   Sterkfontein Dam
Nature Reserve   Van Reenen

Rosendal   Golden Gate
                  Highlands
                  National Park

Clarens   Phuthatjhaba
Rustler's   Witsieshoek
Valley
Fouriesburg
Clocolan   Caledon
                  Poort   Monontsa
Ficksburg   Pass   Royal Natal
Bridge   National Park
Ficksburg   Butha-Buthe   Oxbow
Maputsoe   Leribe (Hlotse)   New
Peka   Peka   Oxbow
Bridge   Lodge   Mont-aux-
                  Pitseng   Sources   Source of
                                          (3282m)   Orange
Teyateyaneng   Ha Lejone   River   Natal
Mapoteng   Mamohau   Drakensberg
Ladybrand   Sefikeng   Park
Berea   Champagne
MASERU   Bethany   Castle
Thaba-Bosiu   Katse   (3377m)
Ha Ntsi   Mokhotlong
Mazenod   Roma   God Help
                  Molimo-   Me Pass   Thabana-Ntlenyana
                  Nthuse   Thaba-Tseka   (3482m)
Ngope Ts'oeu
Matsieng   Marakabei   Mantsonyane
Morija   Sani Top
Motsekuoa   Sehonghong   Sani
Van Rooyen's   Makhakhe   Pass
Gate   Mafeteng   Thaba Putsoa   Himeville
          Qaba   (3096m)   Underberg
Sephapo's   Malealea   Semonkong   Sehlabathebe
Gate   Gates of   Ketane Falls   Malutsunyane   Lodge
Makhaleng   Paradise Pass   Falls   Bushman's
Bridge   (2003m)   Sehlabathebe   Nek
          Christ the King   Senqu (Orange)   National Park
Zastron   Mohale's Hoek   Qacha's Nek
          Mphaki   Ramatseliso's
          Mt   Gate
Makhaleng   Moorosi   Qacha's Nek
Bridge   (2351m)   (1980m)   Franklin
Tele   Fort   Ongeluksnek   Matatiele
Bridge   Hartley   Cedarville
Sterkspruit   Qomoqomong   Kokstad
          Quthing (Moyeni)
Lady Grey   Sinxondo   Ben Macdhui
          Laisleen's Nek   (3001m)
          (2226m)   Tele Falls   Mount Fletcher

Rhodes

Mount Ayliff

Barkly East   SOUTH AFRICA   Tabankulu

Maclear   Flagstaff

          Qumbu

          Tsolo

0   25   50 km

Medical treatment is limited in Lesotho, but if you suffer a serious illness or injury, consider going to Johannesburg or Cape Town in South Africa for first-class treatment.

POST & COMMUNICATIONS

The postal service is slow and unreliable; it's better to wait until you return to South Africa.

The telephone system works reasonably well in Maseru but is less reliable outside the capital.

There is no access to the Internet in Lesotho.

MONEY

Lesotho is less expensive to travel in than South Africa if you take advantage of opportunities to stay with local people and to camp in remote areas. Otherwise, hotel prices are the same as in South Africa; there are few budget options. Plan on spending about US$5 for a hostel, or from US$30 for a hotel room in Maseru. Transport can add up: a bus ride from Maseru to Thaba-Tseka will cost about US$5.

The maloti is fixed at a value equal to the South African rand, and rands are accepted everywhere; there is no real need to convert your money into maloti. When changing travellers cheques, you can usually get rand notes, which saves you having to convert unused maloti. When receiving change, however, it will invariably be in maloti. The only banks where you can exchange foreign currency, including travellers cheques, are in Maseru.

ENTERING & LEAVING LESOTHO

Lesotho Airways, the national carrier, has daily flights between Moshoeshoe airport (near Maseru) and Johannesburg. In South Africa, it can be booked through South African Airways.

All of Lesotho's land borders are with South Africa. Most travellers enter via Maseru Bridge, which is also the post used by buses from most South African destinations. Minibus taxis run daily between Johannesburg and Maseru. Other border posts include Caledons-Poort, Ficksburg Bridge, Qacha's Nek and Sani Pass. If you are driving via Sani Pass, you can only enter Lesotho with a 4WD, though you can leave via this post in a conventional vehicle. Most of the other entry points in the south and east of the country also involve very rough roads. The easiest entry points are to the north and west.

LIBYA

Despite Libya's reputation as a 'difficult' destination, travel is generally safe for western tourists and most report having a pleasant time – undoubtedly due at least in part to the kindness and hospitality of the people. However, political problems with the outside world can result in sudden changes of policy and regulations governing foreign travellers. Be sure to get up-to-date information about the situation before you travel. See the Online Services section. Once in Libya, be alert, and avoid expressing controversial political opinions or criticising the country's leadership. Also remember that there are stiff penalties for possession or consumption of alcohol.

Travel to Libya is restricted for citizens of some countries, including the USA, which do not maintain diplomatic relations with Libya. It can also be difficult for independent travellers, particularly women travelling alone, to get visas.

WHEN TO GO
The best time to visit Libya is between November and March, when daytime temperatures are moderate. Between April and September, temperatures on the coast average about 30°C, and in the south they sometimes climb as

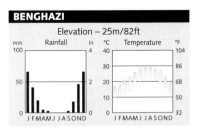

BENGHAZI
Elevation – 25m/82ft

At a Glance

Full Country Name: Socialist People's Libyan Arab Jamahiriya
Area: 1,759,540 sq km
Population: 5.6 million
Capital City: Tripoli (population 1.5 million)
People: Predominantly Arab, with a mixture of other races including Turkish, Berber, Tuareg and sub-Saharan African
Languages: Arabic (official), English, Italian, Hamitic and Tifinagh
Religions: Predominantly Sunni Muslims, mainly conservative but generally not fundamentalist
Government: Jamahiriya (a state of the masses, in theory governed by the people through local councils, though in fact Libya is a military dictatorship)
Currency: Libyan dinar (LD)
Time Zone: One hour ahead of GMT/UTC (two hours ahead from April to September)
International Telephone Code: 218
Electricity: 220V, 50 Hz; various types of plugs are in use – two and three pin, both round and square

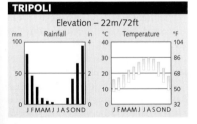

TRIPOLI
Elevation – 22m/72ft

high as 45°C. From May to June and in October, the ghibli, a hot, dry, sand-laden wind, can raise the temperature in a matter of hours to between 40°C and 50°C. These winds last from just a few hours to several days.

Itineraries

One Week
Of all Libyan cities, Tripoli is the most atmospheric and interesting, and is well worth a visit of at least several days. Following this, head out to Leptis Magna. If you still have a day or two left, you could return to Tripoli and then go west to Sabratha, the sister town of Leptis Magna and a finely preserved Roman city.

Two Weeks
With two weeks, if you don't mind a lot of road travel, you could spend several days in Tripoli before heading east to Cyrene, the most splendidly preserved of the five Greek cities of Cyrenaica, and originally modelled on Delphi. Nearby is the ancient port of Apollonia, whose ruins are now partially submerged (and wonderful for diving). After visiting Cyrene, make your way west to Benghazi, Libya's second largest city.

Although there is not much of interest in Benghazi itself, it makes a good base for visiting the Jebel Akhdar, a scenic and refreshing mountain area also known as the Green Mountains. Also in the area is the Greek city of Tocra with its interesting old village square, and Tolmeita, which also has some interesting ruins in a state of partial excavation.

From Benghazi continue westward to Leptis Magna, and then back to Tripoli. Depending on how fast you have travelled, you may have time for a trip to Sabratha and possibly also to Ghadhames. Alternatively, you could make your way down to Ghat and the Acacus Mountain area to view its pre-historic rock art and desert scenery. Note that a permit is needed for travel to the Acacus, and a guide is compulsory.

HIGHLIGHTS
Classical Sites

The Roman cities of Leptis Magna and Sabratha, and the Greek city of Cyrene with the nearby port of Apollonia are fascinating. Leptis Magna is the finest classical site in the country and should not be missed. The Roman remains cover a large area 120km east of Tripoli, next to the modern town of Khoms.

Desert Scenes & Buildings

Ghadhames is a charming oasis settlement about 500km south-west of Tripoli. It's worth visiting for the interesting desert architecture of its old town and the desert scenery.

Rock Art

In the far south in the Acacus Mountain area is some of the finest prehistoric rock art in Africa. It also has some of the most dramatic desert scenery to be found in the Sahara.

VISA REQUIREMENTS

All visitors to Libya require a visa. Nationals of Israel are not admitted, nor are those with Israeli stamps in their passports. Independent tourist visas are not granted to nationals of Australia, New Zealand, UK, USA, Canada or anywhere else without a Libyan People's Bureau. These nationalities need a group tourist visa sponsored by a Libyan tour company. Countries without a Libyan People's Bureau (embassy) often have a Libyan Interests Section working out of another embassy. Visas can be processed through these or another nominated Libyan embassy.

Before applying for a visa you must have your passport details translated into Arabic. Otherwise, the Libyan

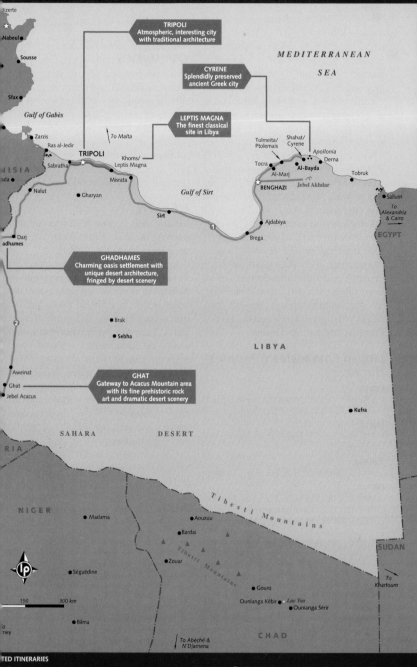

YA HIGHLIGHTS & ITINERARIES

TRIPOLI
Atmospheric, interesting city
with traditional architecture

CYRENE
Splendidly preserved
ancient Greek city

LEPTIS MAGNA
The finest classical
site in Libya

GHADHAMES
Charming oasis settlement with
unique desert architecture,
fringed by desert scenery

GHAT
Gateway to Acacus Mountain area
with its fine prehistoric rock
art and dramatic desert scenery

MEDITERRANEAN

SEA

Bizerte

★ Nabeul

Sousse

Sfax

Gulf of Gabès

Zarzis

Ras al-Jedir

TRIPOLI ★

NISIA

Sabratha

da

Nalut

Gharyan

Gulf of Sirt

Sirt

Misrata

Khoms/
Leptis Magna

Tolmeita/
Ptolemais

Shahat/
Cyrene

Apollonia

Derna

Tocra

Al-Bayda

Al-Marj

BENGHAZI ★

Jebel Akhdar

Tobruk

Sallum

*To
Alexandria
& Cairo*

EGYPT

Darj

adhames

Ajdabiya

Brega

Brak

Sebha

LIBYA

Aweinat

Ghat

Jebel Acacus

Kufra

SAHARA   DESERT

RIA

NIGER

Madama

Aouzou

Bardai

Tibesti Mountains

SUDAN

Séguédine

Zouar

Tibesti Mountains

*To
Khartoum*

150   300 km

Bilma

o

ney

Gouro

Ounianga Kébir   *Lac Yoa*

Ounianga Sérir

CHAD

*To Abéché &
N'Djamena*

embassies will not accept your visa application. You can obtain a stamp in Arabic from most western embassies or passport offices, and the details will then have to be written by hand. Visas are normally valid for one month. Foreigners have to register at a police station within 48 hours of arrival.

The best place to apply for a visa is in Tunis or Malta, but expect to wait a week for processing. It is still difficult, but possible, to persuade the authorities to issue a visa to single unaccompanied women. Married couples should be prepared to supply a copy of their marriage certificate.

Travellers with Australian or New Zealand passports intending to travel from Libya to Tunisia should be aware of the lengthy delays (up to two weeks) in processing visas at the Tunisian embassy in Tripoli.

Libyan Embassies ('People's Bureaux')

Egypt
(☎ 340 1801) 7 Sharia As-Saleh Ayoub, Zamalek, Cairo

Malta
(☎ 356 34947) Dar Tarek, Tower Rd, Sliema

Tunisia
(☎ 780866) 48 rue du 1er Juin, Tunis

UK
(☎ 020-7486 8387) 119 Harley St, London W1 (this is a Libyan Interests Section that works out of the Saudi Arabian embassy)

Warning

There have been several security incidents in the region east of Benghazi. Travellers planning to head to this area, or travel overland towards Egypt, should get a thorough update on the situation before setting off.

TOURIST OFFICES OVERSEAS

Libya has no overseas tourist offices. However, travel agencies should be able to supply you with most of what you need. Also check the web sites listed under Online Services.

There are a small number of private tourism companies in Tripoli which can be very helpful in arranging visas, permits and travel around the country.

HEALTH

Malaria risk is low in Libya; it only occurs in the south-west of the country between February and August. Schistosomiasis is present in freshwater, so avoid swimming or bathing in rivers or streams. Generally water is OK to drink in towns but it's not a bad idea to stick with treated water. Take care with what you eat as well, as dysentery, typhoid and hepatitis can be transmitted via contaminated food and water. Avoid bites from all insects, especially mosquitoes, sandflies and ticks, as these can all carry diseases. Take precautions against the heat to avoid sun stroke and dehydration.

Consider going home if you require serious medical care, as health services in Libya are limited.

POST & COMMUNICATIONS

The postal system is not reliable, and there is a high incidence of undelivered mail. Poste restante services are available in major cities. Prices for international mail are roughly comparable to those in Europe.

The telephone system is fairly reliable, but can be time-consuming as you must wait for an operator to place your call. At the telephone counter, you may be asked for ID, so bring your passport or hotel registration card.

Internet access is not available to the public.

MONEY
Costs

Depending on whether you change your money at the official or unofficial rate, Libya is either very expensive or very cheap. For an average hotel room with a bathroom, you can expect to pay about US$60 at official rates, and about US$10 to US$20 for a meal.

Changing Money

Travellers cheques and credit cards are not accepted in Libya. US dollars cash is the best currency to bring. Major banks and larger hotels provide money-changing services; their rates are similar. A black market exists, but great discretion should be exercised when changing money this way. The current black market rate is six times the bank rate. Better hotels, Libyan Arab Airlines and the ferry companies require foreigners to pay in hard currency at the official exchange rate, or else to produce a bank receipt proving that the money was changed legally.

ONLINE SERVICES

Lonely Planet has a web site Destination Libya (www.lonelyplanet.com /dest/afr/lib.htm).

You can learn more about Gaddafi, plus Libyan news resources at www.geocities.com/Athens/8744 /mylinks1.htm. Another useful site is Libya Mission to the United Nations (www.undp.org/missions/libya).

Tourist information and links to photo galleries are available on the web pages of Mohamed Hassan (http:

//quic.queensu.ca/~hassan/libya/libya .html) and Miftah Shamali (www.i-cias .com/m.s/libya/index.htm).

Finally, check Libya Resources on the Internet (http://members.aol.com /LibyaPage/index.htm).

BOOKS & FILMS

For a list of reprints of old travel and exploration books about Libya, write to Darf Publishers of London (227 West End Lane, London NW6 1QS).

If you are interested in Libyan politics, *Qaddafi & the Libyan Revolution* by David Blundy & Andrew Lycett makes riveting reading.

Desert Encounter by Knud Holmboe, written in 1931, details the author's adventures in Italian Libya.

Lion of the Desert (1980), a film directed by Moustapha Akkad, chronicles the life of a rebel leader who fought against Italian colonisation of Libya between 1911 and WWII.

ENTERING & LEAVING LIBYA

There are currently no international air services to or from Libya due to a UN air embargo.

Libya's land borders with Chad and the Sudan are only open to nationals of those countries.

To Egypt, there are frequent buses from Benghazi to Alexandria and Cairo. The trip can also be done in stages by share taxi and local bus. There are also a few buses from Tripoli direct to Cairo and Alexandria. Get an update on the security situation in north-eastern Libya before travelling.

To Tunisia, there are daily buses as well as share taxis.

There are ferry connections to Malta but the fare is US$200 each way.

MADAGASCAR

Exotic and rugged, Madagascar is the world's fourth largest island and one of Africa's most fascinating destinations. Not only is it unlike anywhere else on the continent – it is also unlike any other region on earth. This is particularly obvious when viewing its plant and animal life, much of which evolved separately from that on the mainland. Culturally also, Madagascar is distinct, with most of its population descended from Malay-Polynesian mariners who first came to its shores about 1500 years ago.

Despite its attractions, Madagascar remains a relatively obscure destination. Tourist facilities in many areas are undeveloped and transport infrastructure is inadequate. Yet the country poses no other difficulties and those that go are rarely disappointed.

WHEN TO GO

Climatic conditions vary across the country, although in general the best time to travel is during the dry winter season (April to October). The east coast and the north, in particular, get a lot of rain from November to March, and are sometimes subject to cyclones, making travel during this time risky.

At a Glance

Full Country Name: Republic of Madagascar
Area: 594,180 sq km
Population: Approximately 14 million
Capital City: Antananarivo (population Greater Antananarivo 1.7 million)
People: Eighteen tribes, whose boundaries are based on old kingdoms rather than ethnic characteristics, including Merina (about 26%), Betsileo (about 12%), Sakalava and Tanala
Languages: Malagasy and French (official). French is often used for business and administrative purposes, but is not widely spoken outside major towns.
Religions: Traditional religions (about 50%), Christian (just over 40%) and Muslim (about 7%)
Government: Republic
Currency: Malagasy franc (FMg)
Time Zone: Three hours ahead of GMT/UTC
International Telephone Code: 261
Electricity: 110V to 220V (assume 220V when in doubt); all outlets take European-style two-pin round plugs

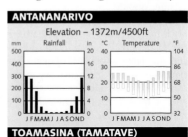

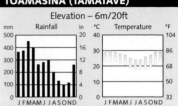

HIGHLIGHTS
Rainforests & Wildlife

Madagascar's unique plant and animal life are one of the island's most fascinating features. Good ways to experience this ecological wealth include taking rainforest treks, and visiting some of the island's national parks, eg Périnet Reserve where you have a chance of spotting lemur monkeys. You can also see the rainforest by taking the train between Fianarantsoa and Manakara, on the coast.

Trekking

Trekking and walking are also good ways to experience Madagascar's fascinating culture. However, you will need to rough it a bit and get out into the villages. If you make it to the south of the country, don't miss the large, colourful carved tombs of the Mahafaly people, west of Ambovombe. Another good place to immerse yourself in Malagasy life is at the huge Zoma market in Antananarivo.

Beaches

For those seeking some luxury, try diving or whale watching (best from July to September) on the beaches of Île St Marie (Nosy Boraha), off Madagascar's eastern coast, or relaxing on the beaches at the resort island of Nosy Be in the north of the country (accessible by plane from Antananarivo). There are gorgeous beaches and excellent diving at Ifaty on the south-west coast.

VISA REQUIREMENTS

All visitors except citizens of several African countries must have a visa. Visas are valid for up to three months from the date of entry. Usually you must have entered and exited Madagascar within six months of the date of issue. Ask your embassy to give you a three month visa, as they are

difficult and expensive to extend. Visas take two to three days to issue at most Malagasy consulates and embassies. You will be required to show a copy of your ticket or itinerary from your travel agent. Proof of yellow fever and cholera vaccinations is also required.

Madagascar Embassies

Australia
(☎ 02-9252 3770; fax 02-9247 8406) 7th floor, 19-31 Pitt St, Sydney, NSW 2000

Canada
(☎ 613-563-2506; fax 231-3261) 282 Somerset St West, Ottawa, Ontario K2P OJ6

Comoros
(☎ 732 290) Opposite Volovolo market, Moroni, Grande Comore (consulate)

South Africa
(☎ 011-442 3322) 13 Sixth St, Hongliton Estate, Johannesburg 2198 (consulate); (☎ 031-239704) 199-201 Percy Osborn Rd, PO Box 1976, Durban 4000

UK
(☎ 020-7746 0133; fax 7746 0134) 16 Lanark Mansions, Pennard Rd, London W12 8DT

USA
(☎ 202-265-5525) 2374 Massachusetts Ave NW, Washington, DC 20008

TOURIST OFFICES OVERSEAS

Madagascar has no overseas tourist bureaux, but Air Madagascar offices act as tourist offices. Both these and Malagasy embassies have basic maps and information, but you'll have to wait until you arrive in Antananarivo for anything specific. There are Air Madagascar offices in Australia, South Africa, the UK and the USA, among other places. Some addresses are:

Australia
(☎ 02-9252 3770; fax 9247 8406) 7th floor, 19-31 Pitt St, Sydney, NSW 2000

Comoros
(☎ 732 290) Opposite Volovolo market, Moroni, Grande Comore (consulate)

South Africa
(☎ 11-784 7724; fax 11-784 7730) Aviation GSA International, 6th floor, Sandton City Office Tower, Sandton City Shopping Centre, Johannesburg

UK
(☎ 01293-526 426; fax 512 229) Aviareps Airline Management, Premiere House, Betts Way, Crawley, West Sussex RH10 2GB

USA
(☎ 800-854-1029; fax 619-481-7474; email cortez-usa@mcimail.com) Cortez Travel, 124 Lomas Santa Fe Drive, Solana Beach, CA 92075

HEALTH

Malaria exists in Madagascar throughout the year, so you will need to take precautions. More information on malaria and other general health matters can be found in the health chapter earlier in this book.

Generally water is OK to drink, but it's not a bad idea to stick with treated water. Take care with what you eat, as dysentery, typhoid and hepatitis are all prevalent.

Health care is poor throughout Madagascar; consider going to Nairobi or Johannesburg if you require serious medical attention.

Itineraries

One Week
With just one week, you could base yourself in Antananarivo and explore the capital and the surrounding area. Interesting nearby sights include Lac Itasy, set in a landscape of volcanic domes, Ambohimanga (the original capital of the Merina royal family) and Parc National d'Andasibe-Mantadia (also known as Périnet), where you may see some lemurs.

Alternatively, after a few days in the capital, you could take a brief trip to Antsirabe, a charming Merina town south of Antananarivo, or head east to the attractive port town of Toamasina, flying one way and taking the train the other.

Two Weeks
With two weeks, after spending some time visiting Antananarivo and other destinations outlined in the one week itinerary, take the train south to Antsirabe to visit nearby villages, lakes and thermal baths. Then continue to Fianarantsoa, a beautiful town regarded as Madagascar's academic and intellectual centre, and the heart of its wine-producing region. Nearby are vineyards and tea plantations, and the interesting Betsileo town of Ambalavao. Once you have explored Fianarantsoa and the surrounding area, head further south to Ihosy – the starting point for a visit to the beautiful Parc National de Isalo with its grassy plains and sandstone ridges. From here, continue to Toliara and Ifaty (about 20km north of Toliara), where there is good diving. From Toliara, you can fly back to Antananarivo.

One Month
With a month, in addition to the two week itinerary, you could add one or more of the following: take the train from Fianarantsoa to Manakara, a pretty town by the sea, and then return to Fianarantsoa with a possible stop at Parc National de Ranomafana enroute; detour from Antsirabe to the town of Miandrivazo, where you can organise a boat trip down the river to the remote town of Belo-Sur-Tsiribihina and explore the surrounding mangrove swamps; the more adventurous could travel overland from Toliara to Taolagnaro (Fort Dauphin), an isolated but very attractive coastal town with a pleasant climate and good beach; another option is to spend a week to 10 days travelling to Île Sainte Marie, via Périnet and Toamasina; or you could finish up with a few days relaxing at Nosy Be.

ADAGASCAR HIGHLIGHTS & ITINERARIES

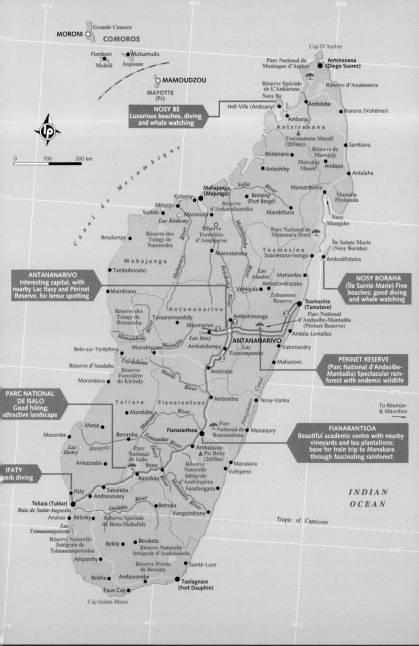

NOSY BE
Luxurious beaches, diving and whale watching

ANTANANARIVO
Interesting capital, with nearby Lac Itasy and Périnet Reserve, for lemur spotting

PARC NATIONAL DE ISALO
Good hiking; attractive landscape

IFATY
perb diving

NOSY BORAHA
(Île Sainte Marie) Fine beaches; good diving and whale watching

PÉRINET RESERVE
(Parc National d'Andasibe-Mantadia) Spectacular rainforest with endemic wildlife

FIANARANTSOA
Beautiful academic centre with nearby vineyards and tea plantations; base for train trip to Manakara through fascinating rainforest

To Réunion & Mauritius

INDIAN OCEAN

Tropic of Capricorn

ESTED ITINERARIES

Week	① Antananarivo • Lac Itasy • Ambohimanga • Périnet Reserve	One Month	Antananarivo • Antsirabe • Fianarantsoa • Manakara • Parc National de Ranomafana • Antsirabe • Miandrivazo • Belo-Sur-Tsiribihina • Toliara • Taolagnaro • Périnet Reserve • Toamasina • Île Sainte Marie • Nosy Be
	② Antananarivo • Antsirabe • Toamasina		
Weeks	Antananarivo • Antsirabe • Fianarantsoa • Ambalavao • Ihosy • Parc National de Isalo • Toliara • Ifaty		

POST & COMMUNICATIONS

The post is reasonably priced and generally reliable for sending letters, but is not recommended for parcels or envelopes containing anything of value. There is a reliable poste restante in Antananarivo. While some smaller towns also have poste restante services, they are usually unreliable and mail is often sent to poste restante in the capital.

International telephone services are good, and calls can be made from private telephones, at hotels, from state Telecom offices next to or in main post offices throughout the country, or from the occasional Agence d'Accueil Telecom (AGATE) office. Rates are high; for a three minute call, expect to pay about US$10/16/20 to France/USA/Australia. Internal calls are much cheaper, but lines are not good and it can be difficult to get through.

Internet access is possible in Antananarivo.

MONEY
Costs

Madagascar is an inexpensive place to travel. Outside the capital, basic but decent budget lodging can be found for well under US$10, and under US$5 if you stay in real dives. Prices in Antananarivo and on Nosy Be may be double these amounts. A meal of Malagasy food will cost less than US$1 at a street stall, and a decent western meal in a good restaurant will cost between US$5 and US$10. While prices for air fares are expensive compared to overland travel, they are still reasonable in comparison with other African countries. Nonresidents must pay for flights in hard currency.

Overall, budget travellers can get by on about US$10 to US$15 per day, while mid-range travel will cost from about US$20 to US$50 per day. Top-end travel (really only possible in Antananarivo and on Nosy Be) will cost from US$100 per day.

Changing Money

The best denominations to carry in cash and travellers cheques are French francs, followed by US dollars, UK pounds and German marks. The country's major banks have branches throughout the country. Most will exchange recognised brands of travellers cheques as well as cash. Most hotels in the capital and major towns also change travellers cheques and cash for their guests, although rates are generally lower than at the banks. Note that most banks and companies such as Air Madagascar will not accept US$100 bills due to problems with forgeries.

Credit cards are of limited use in Madagascar, although they are accepted at some upmarket hotels in major cities and resorts, offices of Air Madagascar, and at larger travel agencies. Cash advances up to the equivalent of 2000 French francs are available with Visa or MasterCard at one or two banks in the capital.

ONLINE SERVICES

Lonely Planet has a web site Destination Madagascar (www.lonelyplanet.com/dest/afr/mad.htm).

Air Madagascar's Explore Madagascar (www.air-mad.com) is a good site with a wide range of subjects and good pictures.

The Madagascar Project (www.pere grinefund.org/Madagscr.html) focuses on conservation and has links to conservation sites worldwide.

The Classification of Natural and Anthropogenic Vegetation in Madagascar (www.mobot.org/MOBOT /Madagasca/vegmad1.html) is strictly for the plant enthusiast.

BOOKS & FILMS

Madagascar, Island of the Ancestors by John Mack provides an excellent overview of Malagasy culture. *The Great Red Island* by Arthur Stratton, and *Madagascar Rediscovered → a History from Early Times to Independence* by Marvyn Brown are good for those seeking more detailed information on the country's history.

Madagascar – A Natural History by Ken Preston-Mafham is one of the best books about Madagascar's natural history, and includes colour photos.

If you are specifically interested in lemurs, try the hefty *Lemurs of Madagascar & the Comoros* by C Harcourt. It helps with identification, and provides a concise history of their discovery and conservation. A more portable choice is the *Field Guide to Mammals of Africa including Madagascar* by T Haltenorth & H Diller.

There is little Malagasy literature available in English. The literary capital of the country is Fianarantsoa. Well known Malagasy writers include Jean Ndema, Rakotonaivo, Rainifihina Jessé and Emilson D Andriamalala.

One of the few contemporary feature-length films produced in Madagascar is the 1988 *Tabataba* by Raymond Rajaonarivelo, a Malagasy director who studied cinema in France. The film, which was shot on the island's south-east coast, is set during the 1947 rebellion against French rule in the small village of Maromena. *When the Stars Meet the Sea* (1996) is another film by Rajaonarivelo.

ENTERING & LEAVING MADAGASCAR

Airlines connecting Antananarivo with Europe include Air France, Air Madagascar and Aeroflot. Air Madagascar also flies to the Comoros, Mauritius, Réunion and the Seychelles. Other regional airlines flying to these islands from Madagascar include Air Mauritius, TAM and Air Austral. Both Interair and Air Madagascar connect Antananarivo with Johannesburg.

Foreigners do not normally travel to Madagascar by boat, but with some determination you can do it. However, the trip will be long, rough and possibly not much cheaper than flying. The two main ports are Mahajanga on the north-west coast (from where ships sail to the Comoros and Mayotte, and possibly on to Zanzibar or Mombasa, Kenya) and Toamasina, from where cargo boats regularly travel to Mauritius and Réunion. From South Africa, you may be able to find a boat to Madagascar from either Durban or Cape Town.

MALAWI

Malawi is one of Africa's most pleasant countries and one of the easiest to negotiate: the scenery is beautiful and varied, Malawians tend to be very friendly towards foreigners, the country's reliable transport and compact size make getting around easy, and there is a broad range of accommodation options and activities.

For most visitors, the country's main attraction is Lake Malawi (also known as Lake Nyasa), stretching some 500km down the eastern border. Malawi's many parks and game reserves are also a big draw, offering endless trekking and outdoor possibilities for nature lovers.

At a Glance

Full Country Name: Republic of Malawi
Area: 118,484 sq km
Population: 11.1 million
Capital City: Lilongwe (population 235,000)
People: Maravi (comprising the Chewa, Nyanja, Tonga and Tumbuka people, together constituting about 60%), Yao, Angoni (Ngoni, about 7%), Chipoka, Lambya and Ngonde
Languages: English (official), Chichewa, Tumbuka and Yao
Religions: Predominantly Christian, with some Muslims in the north (particularly along the lake), and some following both Christian and traditional beliefs
Government: Multiparty democracy
Currency: Malawi kwacha (MK)
Time Zone: Two hours ahead of GMT/UTC
International Telephone Code: 265
Electricity: 220V, 50 Hz; plugs have three square pins

WHEN TO GO

The best time to visit is during the dry season from April/May to October/November. It's coolest in July and increasingly warmer towards September and October. For game viewing, the best time is late in the dry season when vegetation is less dense and animals converge at waterholes, although the heat at this time can be unpleasant. During the rainy season, many roads are impassable except with 4WD.

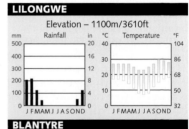

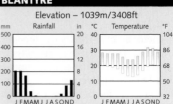

HIGHLIGHTS
Wildlife & Scenery

Malawi's natural attractions are one of its most appealing features. They include the abundant wildlife and beautiful scenery of Liwonde National Park, trekking on Mt Mulanje (3000m), and the wildflowers and scenery of Nyika National Park.

Boating & Diving

Lake Malawi offers innumerable camping and boating options, as well as good diving and snorkelling. Cape Maclear has all of these, including sailing, kayaking and windsurfing, while the scenic Nkhata Bay has slightly cheaper courses in scuba diving.

Isolation

The seldom visited Lower Shire Valley in the far south of the country, with the nearby attractions of Lengwe National Park and Majete Game Reserve, is ideal for those wanting to venture off the beaten path.

VISA REQUIREMENTS

Visas are not required by citizens of Commonwealth countries, Luxembourg, Belgium, Denmark, Finland, Germany, Iceland, Ireland, the Netherlands, Norway, Portugal, South Africa, Sweden and the USA. If you don't need a visa, you will automatically be given a 30 day tourist pass when you enter the country unless you can prove you need a longer stay (eg an air ticket showing a return date), in which case getting two or three months is usually not a problem. If you need a tourist visa for Malawi, allow about three days for processing.

Malawian Embassies & High Commissions

Canada
(☎ 613-236-8932) Malawi High Commission, 7 Clemow Ave, Ottawa, Ontario K1F 2A9

Mozambique
(☎ 491468) Malawi High Commission, 75 Avenida Kenneth Kaunda, Maputo

Tanzania
(☎ 113240) Malawi High Commission, 6th floor, Wing A, NIC Life House Branch, Sokoine Drive, Dar es Salaam

UK
(☎ 020-7491 4172) Malawi High Commission, 33 Grosvenor St, London W1X ODE

USA
(☎ 202-797-1007) Malawi Embassy, 2408 Massachusetts Ave, Washington, DC 20008

Zambia
(☎ 228296) Malawi High Commission, Woodgate House, Cairo Rd, Lusaka

TOURIST OFFICES OVERSEAS

While Malawi has no overseas tourist offices, Malawi embassies and high commissions around the world each have a Tourism Department, which can help with inquiries and send out leaflets. Also check the web sites listed under Online Services.

HEALTH

Malaria exists throughout the year in all areas of Malawi, so you will need to take appropriate precautions. Schistosomiasis exists, so avoid swimming in freshwater lakes and streams, including Lake Malawi. Take care with what you eat and drink, as food and waterborne diseases, including hepatitis, dysentery and typhoid all occur in Malawi.

Medical facilities are reasonable in Lilongwe, but consider leaving Malawi for Cape Town or Johannesburg, in South Africa, if you require serious medical care.

POST & COMMUNICATIONS

Malawi's post office is generally reliable, although international letters can take anywhere from three days to three months to arrive. Rates are inexpensive in comparison with those in most western countries. There are poste restante services in Blantyre and Lilongwe.

International telephone calls can be made with a minimum of hassle from public Telcomms offices or from hotels. Rates average about US$10 for a three minute call. Phone services at hotels are often quicker, but charges can be more than double.

Internet access is possible in Lilongwe.

MONEY
Costs

Accommodation costs in Malawi range from less than US$1 per night for basic resthouses, to US$5 for hostel dorms, US$25 to US$50 for mid-range hotels, and up to US$100 or more for top-end establishments. Transport options are equally varied.

Budget travellers could scrape by on US$5 per day, although even minimum comforts will run closer to US$10. For a bit more luxury, US$20 to US$25 per day is a reasonable budget for living expenses, plus whatever optional extras you may decide on. For luxury travel, including car hire, top-end lodges, and good food and wine, you could easily spend US$200 per day.

Changing Money

You can change both cash and travellers cheques at banks in Lilongwe and most major towns. Banks in smaller

---

Itineraries

One Week
With just a week, assuming you arrive in Lilongwe, spend a day or two there getting acclimatised, then head for the lakeshore – either Senga Bay or the backpackers haven of Cape Maclear, where you could easily spend two to three days relaxing. Then, head back to Lilongwe, or onwards to your next destination.

If you arrive in the north of the country, you could spend a week working your way south, with a stop at Nyika National Park, the historic town of Livingstonia, or Vwaza Marsh Game Reserve, with its hippos, elephants and birdlife.

Two Weeks
With two weeks, assuming you start at Lilongwe, follow the one week itinerary, then continue down the lakeshore to the pleasant town of Mangochi, and on to visit Liwonde National Park and the Upper Shire area. From Liwonde, go to Zomba, famous for its huge market and the nearby Zomba plateau, which offers good walking, excellent views and several good places to stay.

Continue to Blantyre, from where you can head east through the tea plantations to Mt

Mulanje (good for short walks or a longer trek), or south down the escarpment to the Lower Shire area, taking in Lengwe, Majete and possibly the historical town of Chiromo or the Elephant Marsh, one of the best bird-watching areas in Malawi. From there return to Lilongwe via Blantyre.

One Month
One month will give you more than enough time to do the above itineraries at a very leisurely pace, and incorporate some longer treks, or a loop through northern Malawi. One option in the north would be to go from Lilongwe to Kasungu National Park, and then on to Mzuzu, the capital of Malawi's Northern Province.

From Mzuzu you can reach the Vwaza Marsh Game Reserve, the Nyika plateau, with its many opportunities for game viewing, bird-watching and hiking, and Livingstonia town, plus the beaches and quiet villages of the northern lakeshore. Return to Mzuzu and then head to the pleasant town of Nkhata Bay on the lake before following the lakeshore road south towards the towns of Nkhotakota or Salima, from where you can return to Lilongwe.

ALAWI HIGHLIGHTS & ITINERARIES

NYIKA NATIONAL PARK
Beautiful wildflowers and scenery

NKHATA BAY
Lakeside resort town with a 'Caribbean' feel

LAKE MALAWI
Great for boating, diving, snorkelling

CAPE MACLEAR
Backpackers haven; diving and snorkelling

LIWONDE NATIONAL PARK
Beautiful scenery, abundant wildlife

MT MULANJE
Good trekking in this misty 'Island in the Sky'

LOWER SHIRE VALLEY
Isolated area, with nearby attractions of Lengwe National Park and Majete Game Reserve

TANZANIA

ZAMBIA

MOZAMBIQUE

MOZAMBIQUE

ZIMBABWE

Lake Rukwa
To Dodoma
Mbeya
Tunduma
Nakonde
Tukuyu
Kyela
Njombe
Chitipa
Karonga
Kasama
To Dar Es-Salaam
Songea
Chilumba
Chitimba
Livingstonia
Nyika National Park
Shiwa Ngandu
Vwaza Marsh Game Reserve
Rumphi
Mbamba Bay
North Luangwa National Park
Mzuzu
Nkhata Bay
Mpika
Mzimba
Lake Malawi
Likoma & Chizumulo Islands (Malawi)
Cobuè
Lundazi
Nkhotakota Game Reserve
Metangula
South Luangwa National Park
Mfuwe
Kasungu
Nkhotakota
Lichinga
Kasungu National Park
Chipata
Mchinji
Senga Bay
Salima
Cape Maclear
LILONGWE
Chipoka
Monkey Bay
Chanida
Mua
Mandimba
Dedza
To Cuamba & Nampula
Mangochi
Chiponde
Lake Malombe
Liwonde National Park
Balaka
Nayuchi
Liwonde
Lake Chilwa
Zóbuè
Mwanza
Zomba
Lago de Cahora Bassa
Blantyre
Mt Mulanje
Limbe
Tete
Thyolo
Majete Game Reserve
Mulanje
Lengwe National Park
Elephant Marsh
Chiromo
To Mocuba
Mwabvi Game Reserve
Nsanje
To Harare
To Beira & Maputo
Vila de Sena

0   50   100 km

ESTED ITINERARIES

Week
1 Lilongwe • Senga Bay • Cape Maclear
2 Nyika NP • Livingstonia • Vwaza Marsh Game Reserve

Weeks
Lilongwe • Senga Bay • Cape Maclear • Mangochi •
Liwonde NP • Zomba • Blantyre • Mt Mulanje • Chiromo

One Month
Lilongwe • Kasungu NP • Mzuzu • Vwaza Marsh Game
Reserve • Nyika Plateau • Livingstonia • Nkhata Bay •
Nkhotakota • Lilongwe • Senga Bay • Cape Maclear •
Mangochi • Liwonde NP • Zomba • Blantyre •
Mt Mulanje • Chiromo

towns may only be open two or three mornings a week. In rural areas there's a system of 'roving' banks (armoured vans) which only operate for about an hour one or two days weekly. They often do not accept travellers cheques. Foreign exchange (forex) bureaux in cities and larger towns usually offer a slightly better rate than the banks, and often have lower commissions or none at all. There is virtually no black market; offers you may receive on the street are likely to be set-ups.

Cash advances on Visa are available in Blantyre and Lilongwe, although the process can take more than a day. With a Eurocheque card, you can cash personal cheques at the National Bank of Malawi in Lilongwe, Blantyre and a few other major towns. Credit cards can also be used to pay for flight tickets, car hire and many top-end hotels in Lilongwe and Blantyre, but not elsewhere.

ONLINE SERVICES

Lonely Planet has a web site Destination Malawi (www.lonelyplanet .com/dest/afr/mal.htm).

To brush up on your language skills, check the Chichewa language page (www2.humnet.ucla.edu/humnet/aflang //chichewa/chichewa.html).

Llolsten Kaonga's Malawi Home Page (http://spicerack.sr.unh.edu/~llk) has useful information and links.

Thomas Kocher's Evolution of Lake Malawi Cichlid Fishes (http://tilapia .unh.edu/WWWPages/malawi/Malawi .html) and the African Technology Forum's Preserving the Future for Lake Malawi (http://web.mit.edu /africantech/www/articles/Lake_Mal awi.html) are both worth checking for information on Lake Malawi and its inhabitants.

BOOKS

Land of Fire – Oral Literature from Malawi by Scoffeleers & Roscoe is a fascinating collection of traditional stories which have been transcribed into print.

Leading Malawian literary figures include Steve Chimombo, who is best known for his poetic drama, *The Rainmaker*, Jack Mapanje whose first poetry collection *Of Chameleons and Gods* was published in 1981, and Frank Chipasula whose poetic collections include *O Earth Wait for Me* and *Nightsong*. Leading novelists include Legson Kayira, whose semiautobiographical works *I Will Try* and *The Looming Shadow* earned him critical acclaim in the 1970s, and James Ng'ombe, whose novel *Sugarcane with Salt* explores aspects of a changing African society.

For background on Malawi's history, try *A Short History of Malawi* by BR Rafael.

Livingstone by Tim Jeal is a well researched biography of the Scottish explorer David Livingstone, who travelled along the Shire River and into the area now called Malawi in the late 19th century.

A Lady's Letters from Central Africa by Jane Moir was written in the 1890s by 'the first woman traveller in Central Africa', who came to Blantyre and the Shire Highlands as the wife of Frederick Moir, co-founder of the African Lakes Corporation (reprinted in 1991).

Jungle Lovers by Paul Theroux is a light work portraying several aspects of life in Malawi for locals and foreigners.

ENTERING & LEAVING MALAWI

Malawi is well connected by air with cities in Europe and Africa. Airlines servicing the country include Air Malawi, British Airways, Ethiopian Airlines, KLM, Kenya Airways, South African Airways and Air Zimbabwe.

To Mozambique, the overland route is via Blantyre and Mwanza (the Malawian border post) to Zóbuè (the Mozambican border post), Tete and on to Beira and Maputo. The trip is done by local bus in stages. Alternatively, you could take a direct bus between Blantyre and Harare and disembark at Tete.

For northern Mozambique, the route is via Mangochi to the border (by minibus), then from Mandimba (the Mozambican border post) to Cuamba via *chapa* (bush bus) and on to Nampula by train. Traffic is infrequent on this route. You can also reach Cuamba from Malawi by rail.

Another road option between Malawi and northern Mozambique involves travelling by bus, foot and truck from Blantyre via Mulanje (at the border) to Mocuba in Mozambique. By boat, the only connection between the two countries is on the Malawian ferry *Ilala* which stops at Likoma Island in Lake Malawi twice weekly. From here, there is a local boat several times weekly to Cobuè on the Mozambique mainland, from where there are infrequent trucks to Lichinga.

If you're heading for southern Mozambique, there are buses between Mwanza and Zóbuè; other bus routes run via Nsanje and Vila de Sena, just south of the Zambezi River, and via Chiponde and Mandimba.

To Tanzania, the only land crossing is at the Songwe River Bridge at the far north-western tip of Malawi. There are direct buses, or you can do the trip by bus and minibus in stages.

To Zambia, the main border crossing point is about 30km east of Chipata (in Zambia), on the Lusaka to Lilongwe highway. The trip can be done by direct bus, or in stages with local share taxis and minibuses.

To Zimbabwe, there are two international express bus services between Blantyre and Harare, via Tete in Mozambique.

Mali, with its colourful markets, exotic mosque architecture, good trekking and fascinating history, has been a magnet for travellers for years. You can see the legendary Timbuktu, the edge of the Sahara, the great River Niger, nomads on camels crossing the desert, and beautiful mud-brick mosques dating from medieval times.

While the country is one of the region's poorest, and the infrastructure – especially transport – is undeveloped, the culture and vibrant, friendly Malians more than compensate and make Mali one of West Africa's highlights.

WHEN TO GO

The best time to visit Mali is from October to February, after the rains

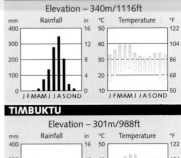

BAMAKO
Elevation – 340m/1116ft

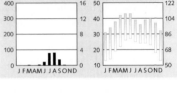

TIMBUKTU
Elevation – 301m/988ft

end but before temperatures become excessively hot. The dusty harmattan wind, which blows from December to February, makes skies hazy, so if you want to take photographs, the best time to visit is November.

HIGHLIGHTS
Cultural

Mali's history and culture are its greatest draws. The best place to experience these is Djenné, possibly the oldest and most impressive of Mali's ancient trading cities. It's a fascinating place – especially its huge mud-brick Grande Mosquée – and a town where little has changed for centuries.

Mali's history comes alive in Timbuktu (Tombouctou), once a great centre of art and learning. Although the town has lost its previous grandeur, its winding streets and alleyways have dusty appeal.

At a Glance

Full Country Name: Republic of Mali
Area: 1,240,140 sq km
Population: 11.5 million
Capital City: Bamako (population 800,000)
People: Bambara, Tuareg, Dogon, Peul, Bozo and Songhaï
Languages: French (official), Bambara, Tuareg, Arabic and Songhaï. The Dogon people have close to 50 dialects.
Religions: Muslim (about 85%), traditional beliefs, plus a small percentage of Christians
Government: Republic
Currency: West African CFA franc (CFA)
Time Zone: GMT/UTC
International Telephone Code: 223
Electricity: 220V, 50 Hz; most sockets take plugs with two round pins, as in Europe

Trekking

Dogon Country – an area to the south-east of Mopti which has long been a major attraction in West Africa – offers some good trekking, along with glimpses into the fascinating culture of the Dogon people, whose multistorey houses and granaries cling precipitously to the sheer rock faces of the Bandiagara Escarpment. Pay particular attention to minimising your impact here.

Urban Attractions

Other highlights include Mopti, a busy river port and the centre of Mali's fledgling tourist industry; and Bamako, the lively capital, which is large enough to have amenities and small enough to cover on foot.

VISA REQUIREMENTS

Visas are required for all except French nationals. They are usually valid for one month and can be extended at main police stations with a minimum of hassle. One-week visas extendible in Bamako are issued at Bamako airport if you fly in from an African country where a visa was unobtainable. However, they are not usually obtainable at land borders.

For both overland and air entries, proof of vaccination against yellow fever and cholera is also required.

Malian Embassies

Côte d'Ivoire
(☎ 32 31 47) Maison du Mali, Rue du Commerce, Le Plateau, Abidjan

Guinea
(☎ 46 14 18) Matam, next to the Office National des Hydrocarbures, Conakry

Senegal
(☎ 823 48 93) 46 Blvd de la République, Dakar

USA
(☎ 202-332-2249 or 939-8950; fax 332-6603) 2310 R St NW, Washington, DC 20008

TOURIST OFFICES OVERSEAS

Mali has no overseas tourist offices, but travel agents will be able to supply you with general information. Check out the web sites listed in Online Services.

HEALTH

Malaria can occur throughout Mali; you should take precautions against this serious disease. For more information on general health issues, see the main health chapter earlier in this book.

Take care with what you eat and drink in Mali, as hepatitis, dysentery, typhoid and cholera all occur here. Drink only treated water and stay away from poorly cooked meat and food which looks reheated. The hot season in Mali is between March and May, and you should take precautions against heatstroke and sunburn at all times.

Medical facilities throughout Mali are generally poor. Consider flying home if you require serious medical treatment.

POST & COMMUNICATIONS

Letters sent from Bamako or Mopti usually reach their destination, though Mali's postal service is not noted for its speed. Poste restante in Bamako is reliable for letters, but not for packages.

International telephone calls can be made at the post office, or at one of the many private telecommunications centres where service is efficient and rates are only slightly more than at the post offices. At all places, however, international calls are expensive. Expect to pay about US$5 per minute to

Europe, and somewhat more to the USA. Reverse-charge (collect) calls cannot be made from anywhere in Mali.

Internet access is possible in Bamako. Sotelma, the state telephone company, is reported to be installing facilities in public telephone offices so that email can be sent and received.

Itineraries

One Week
With one week in Mali, you could spend a day or two in Bamako before heading to Mopti – a good base for visiting the ancient mosque and market at Djenné and for arranging a trip into Dogon Country (though for a trek you will need more than a week).

Two Weeks
Two weeks would make this journey less of a rush, and you could also fit in Timbuktu (although it would probably mean flying there and back).

One Month
With a month, you could really start to do Mali justice, spending a couple of days in Bamako wandering around its lively streets and markets, a day or two at Djenné (ideally tying in with its fascinating Monday market), a couple of days in Timbuktu (plus three or four getting there by boat along the River Niger), and between three and 10 days for some top-quality trekking in Dogon Country.

En route between Bamako and Djenné or Mopti you could stop off at the interesting town of Ségou for a more realistic glimpse of life on the Niger. If you're travelling east from Mopti, you can continue to Gao, an old Sahelian trading city, and on into Niger.

Alternatively, from Ségou you could head south to the towns of Koutiala and Sikasso, where it's easy to find onward transport to Côte d'Ivoire or Burkina Faso. If Senegal is your next destination, you could break the train journey from Bamako at the seldom visited but pleasant towns of Kita and Kayes.

MONEY
Costs
Budget travellers can get by on about US$10 to US$15 per day staying in very basic accommodation and eating local food. Mid-range travellers should budget for a minimum of US$50 per day for food and lodging in the capital, and expect to pay about US$10 or more for meals in western-style restaurants. Outside Bamako, there are few upper-end accommodation options.

Changing Money
Changing cash takes a long time at all banks in Mali, and changing travellers cheques even longer. Bank staff prefer dealing in French francs, and in banks outside Bamako they often refuse to deal in anything else. When changing travellers cheques in Bamako and some other towns you will usually need to show your proof of purchase receipts. If you have French francs in cash, you can also change them at larger hotels, tour companies or traders in main towns, usually with no commission.

Cash advances against a Visa card are available in Bamako, but the process is very time-consuming.

ONLINE SERVICES
Lonely Planet has a web site Destination Mali (www.lonelyplanet.com /dest/afr/mali.htm).

The Washington Embassy (www .maliembassy-usa.org) has only a limited number of facts and figures on Mali but is worth checking for travel and tourism information.

Stephen Buckley's Nomadic by Choice (www.washingtonpost.com /wp-srv/inatl/longterm/nomads /nomad.htm) is a personal account of the Tuaregs' nomadic lifestyle.

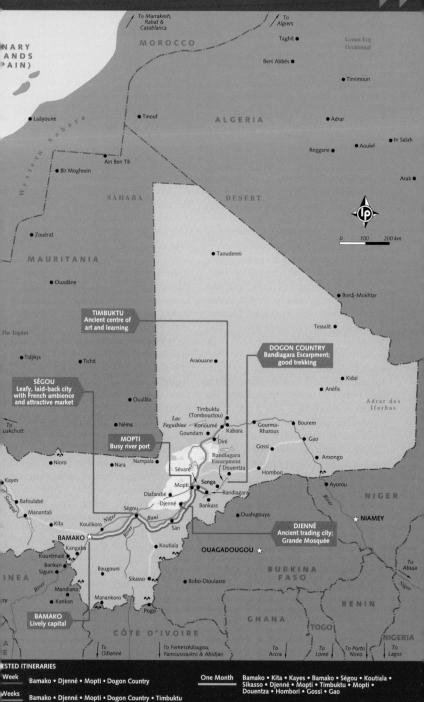

TIMBUKTU
Ancient centre of
art and learning

DOGON COUNTRY
Bandiagara Escarpment;
good trekking

SÉGOU
Leafy, laid-back city
with French ambience
and attractive market

MOPTI
Busy river port

DJENNÉ
Ancient trading city;
Grande Mosquée

BAMAKO
Lively capital

Check Mali Interactive (www.ruf.rice.edu/~anth/arch/maliinteractive/index.html) for the latest from the archaeological digs at Jenné-Jeno (about 3km from Djenné).

BOOKS & FILMS

Ségu by Maryse Condé is an epic novel following the generations of a family living in the trading town of Ségou on the Niger River. It has inspired many Dutch and French travellers to visit Mali.

Lieve Joris captures the essence of the country in *Mali Blues*, published by Lonely Planet's travel literature series, Journeys. The book chronicles Joris' travels to Bamako, Kayes and the Dogon accompanied by famed Malian musician Boubacar 'Kar Kar' Traore.

A popular film to come out of Mali is *Yeelen* (1987), directed by Souleymane Cissé, one of the best known figures in African cinematography. It is set in a Bambara village and portrays events surrounding the initiation rituals of a young man.

Another well known film from Mali is *Guimba the Tyrant* (1985), directed by Cheick Oumar Sissoko, which focuses on life in an African city-state during the precolonial period.

Taafé Fanga (1997), directed by Adama Drabo and in the Bambara language, tells the story of a group of women in a Malian village who find a mask with mystical powers.

ENTERING & LEAVING MALI

Airlines flying between Europe and Mali include Sabena, Air France, Aeroflot, Air Afrique and Ethiopian Airlines. Within Africa, Bamako is connected with Abidjan, Niamey, Dakar, Ouagadougou, Nouakchott and several other West African capitals through Air Afrique.

To Burkina Faso, there are direct buses from Bamako to Bobo-Dioulasso, although many travellers break the trip at Sikasso. You can also get to Bobo-Dioulasso from Ségou on a twice-weekly bus, and there are bush taxis between Mopti and Bobo-Dioulasso.

To Côte d'Ivoire, the main route is via Sikasso and Ferkessédougou. Between Bougouni and Odienné (Côte d'Ivoire) there is little traffic. The bridge at Manankoro, on the Mali side of the border, is usually under water throughout August.

To Guinea, the main route is from Bamako via Siguiri and Kankan to Conakry. There is direct transport several times a week from Bamako to both Siguiri and Kankan. From each of these Guinean towns, you can find bush taxis heading towards Conakry. There is also a direct taxi once-weekly between Bamako and Conakry. Note that taxis from Bamako to Siguiri occasionally take a less travelled route paralleling the River Niger via Bankan. It is also possible to travel from Bougouni to Mandiana (Guinea) and Kankan, although you will need to do the trip in stages. Another option, depending on the season, is the weekly barge which runs when the water level is high enough between Bamako and Siguiri.

See the Mauritania chapter for information about the route from Bamako via Nioro to Nouakchott.

To Niger, the main route is from Gao to Niamey via bus, with an overnight stop at the border.

To Senegal, the overland trip involves innumerable transfers on buses and taxis. Most travellers prefer the twice-weekly Bamako to Dakar express train.

MAURITANIA

Mauritania is the only country in West Africa controlled by people who are traditionally nomads. These Moors are the dominant ethnic group and give Mauritania its special character. In other countries, nomads are often viewed as people out of step with modern times. In Mauritania, however, they are in the majority and their settled descendants call the shots.

Race plays a significant role in everyday life in Mauritania. The Moors look down upon the Blacks, who predominate in the south, and regard them as uncivilised, while the Blacks perceive the Moors as racist and cruel. The delicate balance which exists between the two groups is often disturbed.

Ethics and ethnicities aside, you will enjoy Mauritania if you like venturing through towns half-blanketed in sand, sipping tea with nomads under their colourful tents, crossing plateaux that resemble the moon, and looking at prehistoric rock drawings and ancient Saharan architecture.

WHEN TO GO
The best weather is from December to March, and this is also the best time to visit. Between June and the end of August, it gets extremely hot, with average inland maximum temperatures of 40°C and higher. In Nouakchott and along the coast, trade winds called the alizé blow from the ocean, resulting in average highs which are about 5°C lower than in inland areas. In March and April, hot and sandy winds called the ifiri sometimes blow throughout the country causing sand to permeate everything. If you plan to travel in Mauritania during this time,

At a Glance

Full Country Name: Islamic Republic of Mauritania
Area: 1,030,700 sq km
Population: 2.3 million
Capital City: Nouakchott (population one million)
People: Moors of Arab and Berber descent (just over 40%), Black Africans, comprised of Black Moors or Haratin (descendants of Blacks enslaved by the Moors who have assimilated the Moorish culture) and other Black Africans – mostly Soninké, Fulani or Toucouleur (sedentary Fulani), and Wolof – who live in the south along the Senegal River
Languages: Arabic (official), French, Hassaniya (a Berber-Arabic dialect), Pulaar, Soninké and Wolof
Religions: Sunni Muslim (about 99%) and a very small minority of Christians
Government: Republic
Currency: Mauritanian ouguiya (UM)
Time Zone: GMT/UTC
International Telephone Code: 222
Electricity: 220V, 50 Hz; most sockets take plugs with two round pins

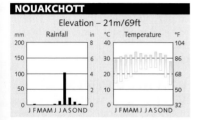

NOUAKCHOTT

Elevation – 21m/69ft

be sure to bring some zip-lock plastic bags and fluid for your eyes.

HIGHLIGHTS
Birdwatching

Mauritania is one of the best birdwatching areas in the world. The 200km-long Arguin Bank (Parc National du Banc d'Arguin), north of Nouakchott, is the mating place for hundreds of thousands of sea birds, which line up side by side on islands of sand as far as the eye can sea. The best viewing times are August and September and (cooler) February and March. You will need your own 4WD vehicle to get here. Another good destination for birdwatching is Cape Tagarit, north of Tidra, though you'll need your own vehicle here as well.

Oases & Canyons

For scenic beauty, head to the Adrar region in the north, encompassing Atâr, Chinguetti and Ouadâne. Here you'll see oases, nomads in their natural habitat, spectacular plateau areas with deep canyons and ancient rock paintings and towns seemingly about to be buried under the encroaching desert. A real treat would be seeing a performance of the *guedra*, a ritual dance of love performed by women for the men.

Rock Paintings & Forts

The Tagânt area east of Nouakchott is another strikingly beautiful region, though more difficult to reach. It offers impressive views from the plateau, prehistoric rock paintings, historical sites including old forts and fortresses, and decaying towns such as Tidjikja and Tichit.

Archaeology

In the far south-eastern corner of the country near the border with Mali is Koumbi Saleh, the legendary capital of Ghana (West Africa's first medieval empire) and Mauritania's most famous archaeological site. Large stone houses and an imposing mosque have been partially excavated here.

VISA REQUIREMENTS

All visitors need a visa except nationals of France, Italy, Arab League countries

---

Itineraries

One Week
With just a week, plan on spending your time in Nouakchott (two days) and the Adrar region. You could take a bush taxi or fly to Atâr and there arrange transport to Chinguetti, the most interesting town in the area. You'll need at least a day and a half in Chinguetti to enjoy a day's camel ride out into the desert.

Two Weeks
With two weeks, from Chinguetti you could try arranging local transport to nearby Ouadâne, another desert village of historical interest. Alternatively you could try the three day overland route from Atâr to Tidjikja along the panoramic Tagânt plateau. Very few travellers take this route and the trip must be conducted by a tour agency because of the danger of getting lost.

One Month
With a month, you will be able to visit the remote Parc National du Banc d'Arguin (you will need to arrange a guide and your own transport for this), as well as explore a bit of southern Mauritania, perhaps including the towns of Kaédi with its colourful market, and Kiffa, capital of the southern Assabe region and an important trading centre. Archaeology buffs could also make a detour to Koumbi Saleh, which is much further away.

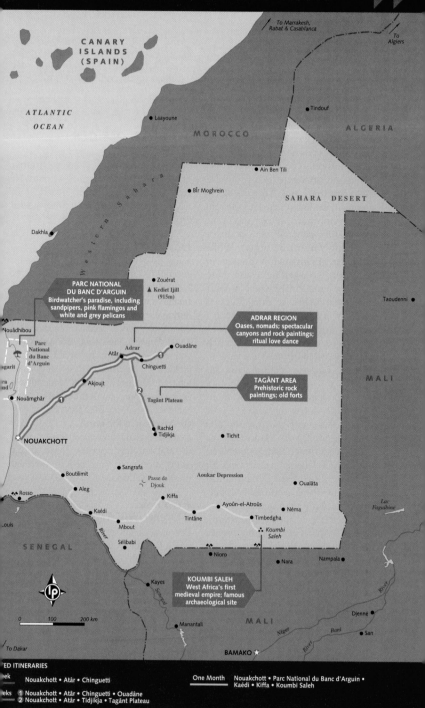

CANARY
ISLANDS
(SPAIN)

ATLANTIC
OCEAN

To Marrakesh,
Rabat & Casablanca

To
Algiers

● Laayoune

MOROCCO

● Tindouf

ALGERIA

● Ain Ben Tili

● Bîr Moghrein

SAHARA   DESERT

● Dakhla

Western Sahara

● Zouérat
▲ Kediet Ijill
(915m)

Taoudenni ●

**PARC NATIONAL
DU BANC D'ARGUIN**
Birdwatcher's paradise, including
sandpipers, pink flamingos and
white and grey pelicans

ADRAR REGION
Oases, nomads; spectacular
canyons and rock paintings;
ritual love dance

● Nouâdhibou

Parc
National
du Banc
d'Arguin

Adrar
Atâr ●   ● Ouadâne

Chinguetti

agarit

ra
and

● Nouâmghâr

Akjoujt

TAGÂNT AREA
Prehistoric rock
paintings; old forts

MALI

Tagânt Plateau

★ **NOUAKCHOTT**

● Rachid
Tidjikja

● Tichit

● Boutilimit

● Sangrafa

Passe de
Djouk

Aoukar Depression

● Oualâta

✈ Rosso

● Aleg

● Kiffa

● Néma

Lac
Faguibine

Kaédi ●

● Ayoûn-el-Atroûs

ouis

● Mbout

Tintâne

● Timbedgha

⚓ Koumbi
Saleh

SENEGAL

● Sélibabi

River

● Nioro

● Nara

Nampala ●

Kayes ●

KOUMBI SALEH
West Africa's first
medieval empire; famous
archaeological site

Senegal River

River

Djenné ●

0   100   200 km

MALI

Niger   River

Bani

San ●

To Dakar

● Manantali

BAMAKO ★

ED ITINERARIES

ek   Nouakchott • Atâr • Chinguetti
1 Nouakchott • Atâr • Chinguetti • Ouadâne
eks 2 Nouakchott • Atâr • Tidjikja • Tagânt Plateau

One Month   Nouakchott • Parc National du Banc d'Arguin •
Kaédi • Kiffa • Koumbi Saleh

and certain African nations. The standard visa is valid for three months and good for a stay of one month from the date of entry, although visas good for stays of up to three months are sometimes available on request. Multiple-entry visas are generally not available. Allow about three days for your application to be processed.

It's usually easier to get your visa before arriving in Africa. Many Mauritanian embassies in Europe will only issue visas to those arriving by air (although they generally do not insist upon seeing your plane ticket). While there is a Mauritanian embassy in Rabat (Morocco), getting a visa there can be problematic. Elsewhere in West Africa getting visas is usually easier, although you may need to present a letter of introduction from your embassy. In Australia, the French consulate in Melbourne issues visas to Mauritania but the requirements are onerous – you must produce A$50, a recent bank statement, itinerary, flight details and a letter from your employer. Make sure they use the title 'Islamic Republic of Mauritania' as some travellers have had problems at borders when 'Islamic' was left out. In other countries without a Mauritanian embassy, the French embassy usually issues visas without requiring a note verbale (a letter of recommendation), but the cost is generally higher (typically about US$40, versus about US$10 at Mauritanian embassies).

Proof of vaccination against yellow fever and cholera is also required.

Mauritanian Embassies

Morocco
(☎ 656678) Souissi II Villa, No 266, OLM, Rabat

Senegal
(no telephone number) Rue 37, Kolobane, Dakar (consulate)

USA
(☎ 202-232-5700; fax 319-2623) 2129 Leroy Place NW, Washington, DC 20008

TOURIST OFFICES OVERSEAS

Mauritania has no overseas tourist offices, but travel agents should be able to supply you with information. Also check the web sites listed under Online Services.

HEALTH

There is a risk of malaria year-round, except in the northern regions of Nouâdhibou and Tiris. In Adrar and Inchiri there is a risk of malaria only during the rainy season (July to October). Take precautions against malaria and avoid all insect bites. Take care with what you eat and drink to avoid diseases including hepatitis, dysentery and typhoid. The hot season in Mauritania is between April to October; take precautions against the heat especially if you are travelling in the north.

As medical care is generally poor throughout the country, think about going home if you require serious medical attention.

POST & COMMUNICATIONS

Post is relatively efficient, and the main post office in Nouakchott is open daily.

The telephone system is connected to satellite, so direct-dial international calls can be made easily from Nouakchott to almost anywhere. Expect to pay from US$5/4 per minute to the USA/Europe.

Internet access is not yet available to the public in Mauritania.

MONEY
Costs

Mauritania is expensive in comparison with other countries in the region. In Nouakchott, plan on at least US$20 to US$30 per day for basic lodging and food. Mid-range accommodation will cost at least US$50, while top-end hotels and meals will cost over US$100 per day.

Changing Money

You can change cash at banks in Nouakchott, Nouâdhibou, Néma and Rosso, but nowhere else. When travelling upcountry, be sure to bring along enough ouguiya; outside Nouakchott, foreign currencies, including the US dollar, will get you nowhere, although the CFA and French franc may be accepted at a pinch. Travellers cheques are only accepted in Nouakchott and Nouâdhibou; the best denomination to have is French francs. Travellers frequently experience difficulty cashing American Express travellers cheques, so consider bringing another type.

Credit cards are accepted at only one or two top-end hotels in the capital.

ONLINE SERVICES

Lonely Planet has a web site Destination Mauritania (www.lonelyplanet .com/dest/afr/maun.htm).

For tourist information, check Miftah Shamali – Mauritania (http://icias .com/m.s/mauritan/index.htm).

For a sobering view of modern Mauritania, see The Coalition Against Slavery in Mauritania and Sudan (http://members.aol.com/casmasalc).

BOOKS

There is very little Mauritanian literature, and most of the works by non-Mauritanians about the country are in French. One of the best of these is *La Mauritanie* by Catherine Belvaude, which offers insights into the country's culture and government.

An English-language work which is set in part in Mauritania is *Impossible Journey: Two Against the Sahara* by Michael Asher. It recounts the first successful west-to-east camel crossing of the Sahara, starting in Mauritania and passing through Mali and Niger before ending at the Nile.

Other selections to look for are *The Songlines* by Bruce Chatwin, which includes brief descriptions of Mauritania's nomadic Namadi people, and his book *Photographs & Notebooks*, which contains an eclectic collection of pictures and observations from his travels in Mauritania, Mali and Benin.

For general history about the region, try *West Africa: An Introduction to its History* by Michael Crowder and *West Africa since 1800* by Webster & Boahen, both part of the Longman West African history series.

A Field Guide to the Birds of West Africa by Serle & Morel would be helpful for those planning a visit to the Arguin Bank.

ENTERING & LEAVING MAURITANIA

Nouakchott is connected with Paris by Air France and Air Afrique, and with Casablanca (Morocco) by Royal Air Maroc and Air Mauritanie. Within West Africa, there are direct flights connecting Nouakchott with Dakar, Bamako, Banjul and Abidjan. During the December to March harmattan season, flights are occasionally cancelled due to sandstorms.

To Senegal, the overland trip between Rosso (on the southern border of Mauritania) and Dakar by bush taxi takes about 12 hours, and entails a ferry or *pirogue* (dugout canoe) crossing over the Senegal River.

To Morocco, the route is via Nouâdhibou and Dakhla. The coastal road between these two towns is mostly tarred, with the exception of one stretch which is sand and marked by stakes. Only about 50km or so is really rough driving. Including waits at the border, the journey can take anywhere from several days to two weeks. Note that this Sahara crossing can only be made going north to south.

To Mali, the main crossings are – east to west – from Néma, Timbedgha (both connecting with Nara in Mali), Ayoûn-el-Atroûs, Tintâne and Kiffa (all connecting with Nioro in Mali). The route via Tintâne is popular as it avoids the worst of the dunes. There are two routes between Nioro and Ayoûn; the westward route is better. The advantage of crossing at Timbedgha is that you can visit the excavations at Koumbi Saleh on the way. Whichever way you go, take everything you'll need, as petrol and supplies are not available en route. Also take a compass. Allow about one and a half days for the trip. The Route de l'Espoir is sealed all the way from Nouakchott to Néma and is in good condition except for the 250km stretch between the Passe de Djouk and Aleg, which is appalling.

MOROCCO

Morocco is separated from Europe by the 15km Strait of Gibraltar. It is at once a crossroads and a frontier state. For many travellers, it is their first taste of Africa. Known to the Arabs as *al-Maghreb al-Aqsa*, the 'furthest land of the setting sun', Morocco has long held a romantic allure for the westerner. Since the 18th century, some of Europe's greatest writers and painters have sought inspiration here. In addition to its rich architectural tradition, medieval cities, Roman ruins, Berber fortresses and Islamic monuments, the country offers beautiful natural attractions, a great diversity of flora and fauna, attractive beaches and, of course, a fascinating culture.

The Western Sahara is still disputed territory between Morocco and Mauritania; it is possible to travel there, but there is little of interest to tourists.

WHEN TO GO

The most pleasant seasons to explore Morocco are spring (April to May) and autumn (September to October). Mid-summer temperatures are comfortable on the coast, but often very hot in the interior. Likewise, winter is often comfortable in Marrakesh and further

At a Glance

Full Country Name: Kingdom of Morocco
Area: 710,000 sq km (including Western Sahara)
Population: 27.7 million
Capital City: Rabat (population 1.3 million, including Salé on the opposite river bank)
People: Arab (about 55%) and Berber (about 44%), though the distinction between these two groups is not always easily made; plus Jewish (about 30,000).
Languages: Arabic (official), French, Spanish, English and Berber dialects. Spoken Moroccan Arabic (darija) is considerably different from the Arabic spoken in the Middle East
Religions: Predominantly Sunni Muslim, plus about 30,000 Jews and a tiny percentage of Christians
Government: Constitutional monarchy, although Morocco is essentially an absolute monarchy
Currency: Moroccan dirham (Dr)
Time Zone: GMT/UTC
International Telephone Code: 212
Electricity: Throughout most of the country, electricity supply is 220V 50 Hz, although in some places you will still find 110V; check before plugging in any appliances. Sockets take plugs with two round pins, as in Europe.

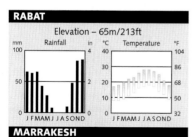

RABAT
Elevation – 65m/213ft

MARRAKESH
Elevation – 460m/1509ft

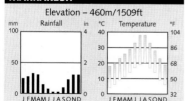

south during the day, but very chilly at night. Along the north coast and in the Rif Mountains, it can get cold, and is frequently wet and cloudy in winter.

HIGHLIGHTS
Trekking

Morocco has so much to offer that it is difficult to highlight just a few attractions. Nevertheless, there are some not to be missed. For outdoor lovers, the top of the list is trekking through remote Berber villages in the High Atlas. The immense ochre-coloured cliffs of the Dadès Gorge are also a fascinating sight. Excellent trekking opportunities are also available in the west from towns south of Agadir.

Architecture & Museums

For those interested in architecture and history, the imperial cities of Fès, Marrakesh and Meknès are among the best preserved medieval cities in the world, and have some excellent museums to visit.

Culture

For an introduction to Moroccan culture, indulge by sampling some of the country's superb cuisine, or search out some performances of traditional music. Moroccan cuisine is justifiably renowned as one of the best in the world. It can be sampled at a number of palace-restaurants, principally in the Imperial cities of Fès and Marrakesh.

Itineraries

One Week

If you have a week or less, but want to fit in a bit of countryside and some Berber towns, as well as seeing something of the major cities, you could travel from Casablanca to Rabat, and then on to Meknès, Fès and the Roman ruins of Volubilis (about 33km west of Meknès).

The town of Sefrou, about 30km south of Fès, makes a good day trip. A bit further south, the French-built alpine town of Ifrane is surrounded by some magnificent cedar forests. Just 17km away is the Berber town of Azrou, a good base from which to explore some of the most attractive country in the Middle Atlas. From Azrou, return via Meknès to Rabat and Casablanca.

Two Weeks

While a tour of Morocco's imperial cities could be accomplished in one week if necessary, you should set aside about two weeks to do them justice. Start with Meknès, then loop around to Marrakesh via Fès, Sefrou, Ifrane and Azrou. From Marrakesh you can then head to Tangier via Rabat and Casablanca by train. If you are in Morocco in spring, you could combine these cities with some travel in the north, which is particularly scenic at this time of year.

One Month

In a month, you will be able to cover a large section of the country. A tour of the imperial cities as outlined in the two week itinerary could be combined with a trek out of Boumalne du Dadès near the stunning Dadès Gorge through the rugged Jebel Sarhro mountain range. From the Dadès Gorge, you could head up into the High Atlas mountains, or from the oasis town of Zagora you could organise a camel trek through the desert.

If you are not particularly interested in the ancient monuments and history of the cities (two or three days in any of them is probably enough), consider combining a coastal trip with forays into the mountains. Starting from Casablanca, wind your way down the Atlantic coast, stopping at the towns of El-Jadida and Oualidia, among others. Taroudannt, inland from Agadir, is a good base for treks into the Western High Atlas, while Tafraoute, to the south, is the place to be based for walks in the Anti-Atlas.

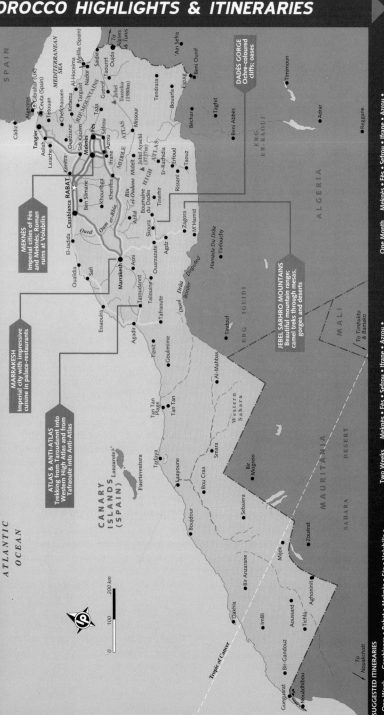

OROCCO HIGHLIGHTS & ITINERARIES

DADÈS GORGE
Ochre-coloured cliffs; oases

MEKNÈS
Imperial cities of Fès and Meknès; Roman ruins at Volubilis

MARRAKESH
Imperial city with impressive cuisine in palace-restaurants

ATLAS & ANTI-ATLAS
Trekking from Taroudannt into Western High Atlas and from Tafraoute into Anti-Atlas

JEBEL SARHRO MOUNTAINS
Beautiful mountain range; camel treks through mesas, gorges and deserts

SUGGESTED ITINERARIES

One Week Casablanca • Rabat • Meknès • Fès • Volubilis •
Sefrou • Ifrane • Azrou

Two Weeks Meknès • Fès • Sefrou • Ifrane • Azrou •
Marrakesh • Casablanca • Rabat • Tangier

One Month Meknès • Fès • Sefrou • Ifrane • Azrou •
Marrakesh • Boumaine du Dadès • Dadès Gorge •
High Atlas Mountains • Zagora • Casablanca •
El-Jadida • Oualidia • Agadir • Taroudannt • Tafraoute

VISA REQUIREMENTS

Most visitors to Morocco do not require visas and are allowed to remain in the country for 90 days on entry. Exceptions to this rule include nationals of Israel, South Africa and Zimbabwe, who can apply for a one month single-entry or three month double-entry visa.

Travellers coming from countries with yellow fever or cholera need proof of vaccination against these illnesses.

Moroccan Embassies

Australia
(☎ 02-9922 4999 or 9957 6717; fax 9923 1053) Suite 2, 11 West St, North Sydney, NSW 2060 (consulate)

Canada
(☎ 416-236-7391) 38 Range Rd, Ottawa, Ontario K1N 8J4

Spain
(☎ 91-563 1090) Calle Serrano 179, Madrid 28002

UK
(☎ 020-7581 5001) 49 Queen's Gate Gardens, London SW7 5NE

USA
(☎ 202-462-7979 through 7982; fax 265-0161) 1601 21st Street NW, Washington, DC 20009

TOURIST OFFICES OVERSEAS

Overseas offices of the Office National Marocain du Tourisme (ONMT) generally stock brochures, some glossy maps and lists of tour operators running trips to Morocco. Some addresses are given below. Also check the web sites listed under Online Services.

Australia
(☎ 02-9922 4999 or 9957 6717; fax 9923 1053) c/o Moroccan Consulate, 11 West St, North Sydney, NSW 2060

Canada
(☎ 514-842-8111; fax 842-5316) 2001 Rue Université, Suite 1460, Montreal, Quebec H3A 2A6

UK
(☎ 020-7437 0073; fax 7734 8172) 205 Regent St, London W1R 7DE

USA
(☎ 212-557-2520; fax 949-8148) Suite 1201, 20 East 46th St, New York, NY 10017

HEALTH

Take appropriate precautions if you travel in the extreme south from May until October, when there is a small risk of malaria. Avoid bites from all insects, especially mosquitoes, sandflies and ticks, as these insects can all carry disease.

Contaminated food and water can present some health problems; stick to treated water and hot, freshly prepared food. Trekkers in the Atlas Mountains need to be prepared for the cold and be aware of the symptoms and treatment of altitude sickness.

More information on general health matters can be found in the main health chapter earlier in this book.

Medical care is reasonable throughout Morocco, and the best medical facilities are in Rabat.

POST & COMMUNICATIONS

The Moroccan postal system is reasonably reliable though not very fast. It can take a week for letters to reach Europe, and two weeks to Australia and North America. Air mail rates are about the same as those in the west. Poste restante counters sometimes hold items for only a couple of weeks before returning them to the sender. There are poste restante services in all major towns.

The telephone system is very good, and most cities and towns have at least one phone office. Rates range from just under US$1 per minute to US$3 or more per minute depending on the country you are calling and the time. Weekend rates are the cheapest. There are also more efficient *téléboutiques* in all major cities and towns. Reverse-charge (collect) calls are possible (except to Australia), but the process can involve long waits in phone offices.

Email and Internet access is widely available in Casablanca and other cities.

MONEY
Costs
Morocco is a relatively inexpensive country, and budget travellers can get by on about US$20 per day. If you'd like more freedom to sample a range of restaurants, take the occasional taxi ride and enjoy a few comforts, plan on spending US$35 to US$45. Top-end travel will cost more than US$100 per day.

Changing Money
Changing cash and travellers cheques is generally a quick process. Rates do not vary much from bank to bank. All major credit cards are widely accepted in main cities and even in many small towns, although their use often incurs a commission of about 5%. Cash advances against Visa and MasterCard are possible at some banks. While Morocco's network of ATMs is increasing and improving all the time, these can be unreliable when it comes to foreign cards.

ONLINE SERVICES
Lonely Planet has a web site Destination Morocco (www.lonelyplanet .com/dest/afr/mor.htm).

MarocNet (www.maroc.net/welcome .html) is a good site with lots of information, including a summary of the country's best museums.

ArabNet (www.arab.net/morocco /morocco_contents.html) provides an overview of Moroccan culture and history.

The One and Only Morocco (www .dsg.ki.se/morocco) has recipes and more.

Ana's Moroccan WWW Sites (www .utoledo.edu/homepages/achraibi /morocco.html) is a compilation of Moroccan web sites.

Morocco Bound (http://tayara.com /club/mrocbd1.htm) lists both print and web resources for independent travellers.

BOOKS & FILMS
Conquest of Morocco by Douglas Porch examines the takeover of Morocco by France and the establishment of the protectorate.

French-speakers can try *Les Almoravides* by Vincent Lagardare, which traces the history of the Berber dynasty from 1062 to 1145.

Patience and Power – Women's Lives in a Moroccan Village by Susan Davies is a fascinating and readable examination of many of the myths surrounding women in Islamic society.

Further insights into the lives of Moroccan women can be found in Elizabeth Warnock Fernea's *A Street in Marrakesh* and Leonora Peet's *Women of Marrakesh*.

The House of Si Abdallah – The Oral History of a Moroccan Family, recorded, translated and edited by Henry Munson Jr, gives a unique insight into the daily lives and thoughts of Moroccans. Munson's *Religion and*

Power in Morocco provides an equally good insight into Islam in Morocco.

The Mellah Society by Shlomo Deshen looks at Jewish community life in Morocco.

Famous Moroccan writers include Driss Chraïbi, Tahar ben Jeloun and the poet Abdu Elaraki. Unfortunately, few of their works have been translated into English. Among the few which have

been are *Year of the Elephant* by Leila Abouzeid, *Si Yussef* by Anouar Majid, and *Silent Day in Tangier* by ben Jeloun.

Most local film-makers concentrate on exploring contemporary issues – in particular, the conflicts that arise between ancient tradition and modern life. *El-Chergui* by Moumem Smihi is a good example of this theme. Other well known Moroccan films include *Le Soiffeur du*

Spanish North Africa

The tiny enclaves of Ceuta and Melilla, along with a handful of islets off the northern Moroccan coast, are all that remain of the Spanish colonies in Africa. Like most harbours along the North African shore, they were founded by Phoenician traders, then colonised successively by a host of foreign powers including the Romans, Byzantines, Arabs, and finally the Spanish in the 15th and 16th centuries. Today, Ceuta and Melilla are administered as city provinces of Spain, but are waiting to be granted autonomous status on an equal footing with the mainland provinces.

The majority of travellers come here for the ferry services to and from Spain, which – in Ceuta – are cheaper than those to and from Tangier. For those with their own transport, there is the added attraction of cheap, tax-free petrol. Beyond this, however, both Ceuta and Melilla are pleasant enough places to spend a couple of days, and offer a good respite if you are feeling travel-fatigued in Africa.

Melilla is probably the more interesting of the two enclaves. Its old town, Melilla la Vieja, is a classic fortress stronghold that until the end of the last century contained virtually the entire town within its walls. It still has a distinctly Castilian flavour, with narrow, twisting streets, squares, gates and drawbridges. Inside its walls is the Museo Municipal, with a good collection of Phoenician and Roman ceramics, coins and historical documents. The new town, considered by some to be Spain's second modernist city (after Barcelona), also merits a stroll.

Ceuta has several interesting attractions including some Baroque churches, a museum with an enormous collection of military paraphernalia, and the Foso de San Felipe – a fortified trench which once formed part of massive ramparts built in the 16th century. It also boasts an extravagant new maritime park on the seafront, and sweeping views over the Mediterranean to Gibraltar from the hill-top convent of Ermita de San Antonio.

Since the enclaves are Spanish territory, anyone requiring a visa to enter Spain (this includes Australians, South Africans and Israelis) will need one to enter Spanish North Africa. There is a Spanish embassy in Rabat (Morocco) at 3-5 Zankat Madnine (☎ 768989) and a consulate at 57 Rue du Chellah (☎ 704147/8; fax 704694), but Spain prefers you to apply for a visa in your country of residence. If they do agree to process your request, it will take at least 24 hours for the visa to be issued.

The currency is the Spanish peseta, and the telephone code is Spain's country code (34) followed by the code of either Ceuta (56) or Melilla (5). If calling from Spain, dial 9, rather than 34.

Ferry and jetfoil services connect Spanish North Africa with mainland Spain. The main sea routes are between Ceuta and Algeciras, Almeria and Melilla, and Málaga and Melilla.

Buses run from Ceuta to the Moroccan border, from where you can catch share taxis to Tetouan. From Melilla, local buses run to the border. After walking across (a few hundred metres), you can find onward transport to Nador and other destinations further inside the country.

Quartier des Pauvres by Mohammed Reggab and *Le Grand Voyage* by Abd er-Rahmane Tazi. Other contemporary film-makers are Souheil ben Barka, Latif Lahlou and Hakim Noury.

Among the most famous foreign films which have been set in Morocco are *Casablanca* (shot completely on location in Hollywood) and *Ali Baba & the Forty Thieves*. Orson Welles shot much of his acclaimed *Othello* in the former Portuguese ports of Essaouira, Safi and El-Jadida. *Lawrence of Arabia* includes scenes filmed on location in the kasbah of Aït Benhaddou.

ENTERING & LEAVING MOROCCO

Morocco is well linked to Europe, Africa and the Middle East by air. Among the airlines serving Morocco are Air Algérie, Air France, Alitalia, British Airways, GB Airways, Iberia, KLM, Lufthansa, Royal Air Maroc (RAM), Royal Jordanian, Sabena, Saudia, Swissair, EgyptAir and Tunis Air. There are international airports at Casablanca, Tangier and Agadir. There are also direct flights from Paris to Fès, Ouarzazate, Oujda and Marrakesh.

Morocco's land borders with Algeria are currently closed.

To Mauritania, the border was open at the time of writing, although you should check the latest political situation before planning to travel this route. See the Mauritania profile for additional information.

Between Morocco and Ceuta in Spanish North Africa, there are plenty of share taxis from Tetouan to the border. Between the border and Plaza de la Constitución in Ceuta there are frequent buses. To Melilla, also in Spanish North Africa, there are frequent buses and share taxis from Nador to the border, and frequent buses from there to the Plaza de España (for more information see the boxed text 'Spanish North Africa' accompanying this profile).

Many visitors travel between Morocco and Europe via bus, train or sea. The main ferry ports on the African side are Tangier, Melilla and Ceuta. These options are covered in more detail in the Overland Routes section in the Planning chapter earlier in this book.

MOZAMBIQUE

For almost 30 years, war and political unrest were the norm in Mozambique. From the early 1960s, the country fought a long battle for independence and was later embroiled in brutal civil fighting that ended in 1992. Now, almost a decade later, Mozambique is regaining its footing and its spirit and vitality are once again obvious.

Many areas of southern and central Mozambique were severely affected by flooding in early 2000. Get an update on the situation before setting your plans.

Among Mozambique's attractions are superb beaches, rich artistic traditions and generous, open people. In much of the country, particularly the

north and north-west, roads are bad and other facilities haphazard. However, for those with an adventurous spirit and plenty of time, travel here is fascinating and well worth the effort required.

WHEN TO GO
The best time to visit is during the cooler, dry season from May to September. During the summer rainy season from October/November to March/April, flooding occurs in some areas and roads often become impassable.

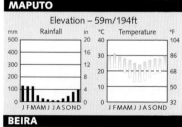

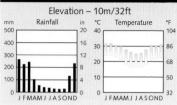

HIGHLIGHTS
Old Buildings
Mozambique Island, one of the earliest settlements in the region, is a crumbling but fascinating place with old churches, mosques and a fort plus a diverse mix of people and cultures.

At a Glance

Full Country Name: Republic of Mozambique
Area: 800,000 sq km
Population: seven million
Capital City: Maputo (population 1.3 million)
People: Sixteen major ethnic groups including Makua/Lomwe (about 52%), Makonde, Sena and Shangaan
Languages: Portuguese (official), Ronga, Shangaan, Makua, Makonde and others
Religions: Christian (about 30%), Muslim (about 20%) and traditional beliefs
Government: Republic
Currency: Mozambique metical (Mt)
Time Zone: Two hours ahead of GMT/UTC
International Telephone Code: 258
Electricity: 220V, 50 Hz; sockets vary, though in most offices they take plugs with three round pins, as in South Africa. You will also frequently find plugs with two round pins, and sometimes three square pins, as in the UK.

The island was declared a UNESCO World Heritage Site in 1991.

Beaches

One of Mozambique's major natural attractions is its coastline. Particularly beautiful spots include the beaches along the southern coast near Inhambane, the islands and surrounding waters of the Bazaruto Archipelago near Vilankulo, and the northern coastline around Pemba.

Visual Arts

The sculpture of the Makonde people from northern Mozambique is recognised as one of Africa's most sophisticated art forms. Mozambique also has numerous renowned painters and sculptors, many of whom have work on exhibit at the National Art Museum in Maputo.

Urban Attractions

For a taste of urban life, the best place by far is Maputo. It has a lively atmosphere, pleasant cafes, interesting architecture and dynamic nightlife, with many pubs, clubs, bars and discos.

VISA REQUIREMENTS

Visas are required by all visitors. They are generally issued for between one and three months. Both single and multiple entry are available.

Proof of yellow fever and cholera vaccinations is also required.

Mozambique Embassies

Malawi
(☎ 784100) Commercial Bank Building, African Unity Ave, Capital City, Lilongwe. Consulate: Limbe

South Africa
(☎ 011-336 1819) 252 Jeppe St, Cape York Bldg, 7th floor, Johannesburg

Tanzania
(☎ 051-33062) 25 Garden Ave, Dar es Salaam

UK
(☎ 020-7383 3800) 21 Fitzroy Square, London W1P 5HJ

USA
(☎ 202-293-7146; fax 835-0245) 1990 M St NW, Suite 570, Washington, DC 20036

Zambia
(☎ 220333) 9592 Kacha Rd, Northmead, Lusaka

Zimbabwe
(☎ 04-253871) 152 Herbert Chitepo Ave, Harare

TOURIST OFFICES OVERSEAS

The Mozambique National Tourist Organisation (ENT) is represented in South Africa by the Mozambique National Tourist Co (☎ 011-339 7275; fax 339 7295) PO Box 31991, Braamfontein, Johannesburg 2017. It can arrange visas, car hire and flights and offer advice on bus travel, camp sites, diving and more. In other countries, such as the UK and USA, Mozambique's embassies can provide general country information on request. Also check the web sites listed under Online Services.

HEALTH

Malaria exists throughout the year in all areas and recently there have been outbreaks of dengue fever, so you will need to take appropriate precautions. See the main health chapter earlier in this book for more information about the prevention of these diseases and other general health matters.

Schistosomiasis exists in freshwater lakes and streams, including Lake Niassa (Lake Malawi), so avoid swimming or bathing in any freshwater. Take care with what you eat and drink, as

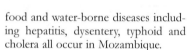
food and water-borne diseases including hepatitis, dysentery, typhoid and cholera all occur in Mozambique.

Medical facilities are limited in Maputo; consider going to South Africa if you require serious medical care.

POST & COMMUNICATIONS

International mail from Maputo is slow but fairly reliable. The best option is the postal system's *ultima hora* express mail service. Letters sent from upcountry may take months to arrive, if at all.

Mozambique's telephone service has been overhauled and efficient public phone offices can be found in most towns. International calls usually connect quickly. Rates are standard for the region, costing about US$13 for three minutes to anywhere in Europe, the USA or Australia.

Internet access is possible in Maputo.

MONEY
Costs

Mozambique is expensive in comparison with other countries in the region, and value for money is poor (particularly with accommodation). Budget travellers can get by on about US$20 per day. Moderate comforts will cost about US$60 to US$80, while luxury lodging and western meals (available only in Maputo) will cost

Itineraries

One Week

With just a week – assuming you arrive in Maputo – spend a few days getting oriented in the capital, including visits to its museums and perhaps a day trip to the small town of Catembe across the bay. Then take an overnight excursion to Inhaca, an island about 40km offshore with some attractive beaches and good snorkelling and diving. Alternatively, go north about 100km to Bilene (Praia do Bilene), also with a good beach. If time remains, continue north from Bilene to Praia do Xai-Xai, a large town with a pleasant beach, before returning to Maputo.

Two Weeks

With two weeks, you will have time to visit all of the above, plus a few other destinations in southern Mozambique. One of the best options would be to head for Inhambane, a sleepy, pleasant town set on a bay. Nearby are the long, beautiful beaches of Tofu and Barra. Well to the north of Inhambane is Vilankulo, the main gateway to the spectacular Bazaruto Archipelago. To have enough time at each of these places, you will need to fly at least one way.

One Month

With a month, you will be able to visit northern Mozambique as well, though you will need to move at a steady pace and perhaps fly at least one way. (You must fly during the rainy season.) After visiting Maputo and environs as outlined in the one week itinerary, fly to Pemba to enjoy its good beaches and then work your way south to Nampula and Mozambique Island. From Nampula, continue southwards, although this journey – which involves some very bad roads between Quelimane and Beira and a ferry crossing over the Zambezi River at Caia – isn't for the faint-hearted. Possible stops along the way include Quelimane (a pleasant coastal town), Beira (Mozambique's second largest city), the Bazaruto Archipeligo and Inhambane.

Another option is a visit to Lago de Cahora Bassa in the north-west. This lake is in a spectacular gorge created in the 1970s by damming the Zambesi River. The goal was to generate hydroelectricity for the region, although it fell far short of its potential. The dam is accessible via Tete by bus from Songo. Tours are available from the power authority offices (HCB) in Tete.

MOZAMBIQUE HIGHLIGHTS & ITINERARIES

PEMBA
Pleasant coastal town set near some beautiful beaches

MOZAMBIQUE ISLAND
Decaying but fascinating architecture; Mozambique's first capital

NAMPULA
Gateway to Mozambique Island; interesting rock formations and topography (to the west)

LAGO DE CAHORA BASSA
Huge dam in spectacular gorge

BAZARUTO ARCHIPELAGO
National park and coral reefs

INHAMBANE
Base for visits to the beautiful beaches of Tofu and Barra

MAPUTO
Vibrant nightlife; base for visits to Catembe, Inhaca Island, Praia do Bilene and Xai-Xai

Tropic of Capricorn

INDIAN OCEAN

0   100   200 km

SUGGESTED ITINERARIES

One Week	**1** Maputo • Inhaca Island
	2 Maputo • Praia do Bilene • Xai-Xai
Weeks	Maputo • Inhaca Island • Bilene • Xai-Xai • Inhambane • Vilankulo • Bazaruto Archipelago
One Month	Maputo • Inhaca Island • Bilene • Xai-Xai • Pemba • Nampula • Mozambique Island • Quelimane • Beira • Bazaruto Archipelago • Inhambane

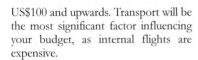

US$100 and upwards. Transport will be the most significant factor influencing your budget, as internal flights are expensive.

Changing Money

Money can be changed at banks (slow) and at some private exchange bureaux in Maputo and larger towns. These are more efficient than the banks and usually give about 5% higher than the bank rate. The most readily accepted currencies are US dollars and South African rand. In the south of the country you can pay for many things directly with rand. Other international currencies will be accepted in Maputo, but with less ease elsewhere. Many supermarkets and shops selling imported goods will also change cash dollars or rands into meticals. Changing on the street is not safe anywhere.

Travellers cheques can be changed at banks (though commissions are high) or private exchange bureaux (more efficient) in Maputo. You are usually required to show your purchase receipt. Credit cards are accepted only at a few top-end establishments in Maputo.

ONLINE SERVICES

Lonely Planet has a web site Destination Mozambique (www.lonelyplanet.com/dest/afr/moz.htm).

Travel & Trade Publishing (www.rapidttp.co.za) has several good sites with frequent and current updates and articles on travel in Mozambique.

Mozambique News Agency (www.poptel.org.uk/mozambique-news) reports on topics of local significance.

Johannesburg's Mail & Guardian frequently has stories on Mozambique on its Open Africa page (www.mg.co.za/mg/oamenu.htm).

WoYaa! (www.woyaa.com/Tree/Regional/Countries/Mozambic) has a collection of links to Mozambican information on the web, much of it in Portuguese. Many of the links are poorly labelled and reappear under different names, so be prepared to be frustrated.

Although the text is in Portuguese, you can get a good idea of what's happening in the contemporary Mozambican arts scene at Exposiçaõ de Pintura – Casa de Moçambique (www.portugalnet.pt/encontro/mocambiq/arte/index.html).

BOOKS & FILMS

Kalashnikovs and Zombie Cucumbers by Nick Middleton is an entertaining book covering the colonial era, South African and superpower involvement in the civil war, and various aspects of the country today.

Other informative and readable choices include *The Harrowing of Mozambique – A Complicated War* by William Finnigan and *Apartheid's Contras* by William Minter.

And Still They Dance by Stephanie Urdang is a study of women's roles in the civil war and struggles for change in Mozambique.

Artistas de Moçambique, a glossy coffee-table book, is a good introduction to the country's principal artists. Other books in the same series include *Mascaras*, on traditional masks, and *Ilha de Moçambique*, on the former island capital.

One of Mozambique's most outstanding literary figures is José Craveirinha, who is known by his poetry about the social reality of the Mozambique people and especially for his work, *Poem of the Future Citizen*.

From the post-independence era, one of the most significant writers is

Mia Couto, whose works include *Voices Made Night* and *The Tale of the Two Who Returned from the Dead*.

A Shattering of Silence is a recent work by Farida Karodia. It describes a young girl's journey through Mozambique following the death of her family.

Full-length feature films from Mozambique are a rarity. Shorter pieces – most of which focus on the war or on the hardships of life – include *Mueda, Memory and Massacre* (1980) and *Borders of Blood* (1987).

ENTERING & LEAVING MOZAMBIQUE

Mozambique's national carrier, Linhas Aéreas de Moçambique (LAM), connects Maputo with Johannesburg (South Africa) and Harare (Zimbabwe). Regional airlines serving Mozambique include SAAirlinks and South African Airways. For long-haul flights, LAM and Air Portugal (TAP) each go to Europe several times weekly, though it's usually cheaper to fly to Johannesburg and get a ticket to Europe there.

Mozambique has land borders with Malawi, South Africa, Swaziland, Tanzania, Zambia and Zimbabwe. The main border crossing with Malawi is at Zóbuè on the Tete Corridor road linking Blantyre (Malawi) and Harare (Zimbabwe). The trip is done in stages, and you'll have to hitch or walk a short distance from the Mozambique border to the Malawi border post. Other border crossing points include Milange, Mandimba and Nsanje. It is also possible to cross between Mozambique and Malawi by boat on Lake Malawi via Likoma Island and Cobuè, although this is a slow and rarely travelled route.

To South Africa, there are minibuses from Maputo to the border, or direct buses all the way to Johannesburg. There is also direct service to/from Durban. Alternatively, there is a South African train connecting Maputo with Johannesburg via Komatipoort, Nelspruit and Pretoria. For those with a lot of time, there are cargo ships between Nacala in northern Mozambique and Durban.

To Swaziland, there are frequent minibuses from Maputo to the border at Namaacha, from where buses go to Mbabane and Manzini.

To Tanzania, the route is via Pemba and Moçimboa da Praia to Palma, Namiranga (the Mozambique border post) and on to the Rovuma River. The trip must be done in stages via pick-up, dugout canoe (across the Rovuma) and on foot, and transport is scarce, particularly north of Moçimboa da Praia and on the Tanzanian side between the river and Kilambo (the Tanzanian border post). During the rainy season the border is effectively closed. Some travellers go between Mozambique and Tanzania by local *dhow* (traditional wooden sailing boat), although these are notoriously unsafe, and can take several days.

To Zambia, there is a crossing between Cassacatiza and Chanida, north-west of Tete, but most travellers prefer to go through Malawi.

To Zimbabwe, there are two main crossing points: one at Nyamapanda on the Tete Corridor, and one at Machipanda on the Beira to Harare road. Both routes are well travelled, so hitching is not too difficult. There are also frequent buses, particularly on the Beira to Harare route.

NAMIBIA

Wedged between the Kalahari and the chilly South Atlantic, Namibia is a country of vast potential and promise. Rich in natural resources and spectacularly beautiful, it has also inherited a solid modern infrastructure and it boasts a diversity of cultures.

For the traveller, Namibia offers fine bushwalking opportunities, rugged seascapes, appealing African and European cities and villages, and nearly unlimited elbowroom – features which until recently have been largely ignored, but are well worth exploring.

At a Glance

Full Country Name: Republic of Namibia
Area: 825,000 sq km
Population: 1.7 million
Capital City: Windhoek (population 190,000)
People: Owambo (about 40%), Kavango (about 7%), Damara (about 6%), Herero (about 6%), Nama (Khoi-Khoi; about 4%), San (about 2%), Himba, Topnaar and Tswana. There are about 85,000 Europeans, mostly of German and Afrikaner heritage.
Languages: English (official), Afrikaans, German and Portuguese. As a first language, most Namibians speak a Bantu language – eg Owambo or Herero – or a Khoisan ('click') language, which may be Nama, Damara or a San dialect.
Religions: Christian (at least 75%) and animist
Government: Republic
Currency: Namibian dollar (N$)
Time Zone: Two hours ahead of GMT/UTC
International Telephone Code: 264
Electricity: 220V, 50 Hz; sockets take either two-pin round plugs, or three-pin round plugs, as in South Africa

WHEN TO GO

Much of Namibia enjoys a minimum of 300 days of sunshine a year. The best time to travel is during the winter dry season from May to October when you can expect clear, warm and sunny days and cold, clear nights, often with temperatures below freezing. The least favourable time to travel is during the main rainy season between January and March, when temperatures in many areas can become uncomfortably hot and roads may be impassable or difficult to negotiate. Note that some resort areas, such as Ai-Ais Hot Springs, close in summer. Others, such as Swakopmund, are booked solid over Christmas and Easter and during school holidays.

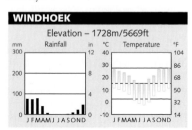

WINDHOEK — Elevation – 1728m/5669ft

HIGHLIGHTS
Wildlife & Birds

Etosha National Park is one of Namibia's most popular attractions. It surrounds a vast salt pan that occasionally holds water and attracts flocks of flamingos, while the surrounding bushveld is dotted with water holes around which congregate an incredible variety of wildlife.

Serenity
Another beautiful area is the Skeleton Coast, characterised by ethereal, fog-bound scenery, and notorious as a graveyard for ships and their stranded crews.

Desert Dunes & Oases
In the centre of the country is the striking Namib desert, with its brilliant waves of red and pink sand dunes. The most popular destination here is the oasis of Sossusvlei, an ephemeral pan surrounded by towering dunes.

Canyon
In the far south is the 161km-long and 550m-deep Fish River Canyon – one of Namibia's (and Africa's) most spectacular natural wonders.

Urban Attractions
If you tire of the open spaces, head for Namibia's 'urban' areas. Windhoek, with its attractive natural setting, Swakopmund, with its colonial architecture, and the small fishing town of Lüderitz are all worth a few days.

VISA REQUIREMENTS
At present, visas are not required by nationals of Australia, New Zealand, France, Germany, Austria, Italy, Spain, Portugal, the UK, Ireland, the Netherlands, Belgium, Luxembourg, Switzerland, Liechtenstein, the CIS, Canada, the USA, Brazil, South Africa, Botswana, Zimbabwe, Zambia, Tanzania, Angola, Mozambique, Kenya, Japan, Singapore or the Scandinavian countries. All EU and Commonwealth countries should soon be excluded from visa requirements.

Tourists are granted an initial 90 days, which may be extended in Windhoek.

Namibian Embassies & High Commissions
South Africa
(☎ 012-344 5922; fax 342 3565) Tulbach Park, Eikendal Flat, Suite 2, 1234 Church St, Colbyn, Pretoria (PO Box 29806, Sunnyside 0132)

UK
(☎ 020-7636 6244; fax 7637 5694) Namibian High Commission, 6 Chandos St, London W1M 0LQ

USA
(☎ 202-986-0540; fax 986-0443) 1605 New Hampshire Ave NW, Washington, DC 20009

Zambia
(☎ 01-252 250; fax 252 497) Namibian High Commission, 6968 Kabanga Rd & Addis Ababa Drive, Rhodes Park, Lusaka

TOURIST OFFICES OVERSEAS
Some of Namibia's overseas tourist offices are listed below. For additional information check the web sites listed under Online Services.

South Africa
(☎ 911-784 8024; fax 784 8340) Namibia Tourism, PO Box 78946, Sandton City, Sandton 2146;
(☎ 021-419 3190; fax 215 840) Ground floor, Main Tower, Standard Bank Centre, Adderley St, PO Box 739, Cape Town 8000

UK
(☎ 020-7636 2924; fax 7636 2969; email namibia@globalnet.co.uk) Namibia Tourism, 6 Chandos St, London W1M 0LQ

USA
(☎ 212-465-0619; fax 868-1654) Kartagener Associates Inc, 12 West 37th St, New York, NY 10018

HEALTH
Malaria occurs in parts of Namibia; take appropriate precautions if your plans include travel in the Caprivi and Kavango regions, the Owambo country and the northern areas of

Kunene Province, especially around Epupa Falls. More information on malaria prevention and other general health matters can be found in the main health chapter earlier in this book.

Take care with what you eat and drink, as food and waterborne diseases occur in Namibia.

Medical care is reasonable through-out Namibia but consider going to South Africa if you require serious medical treatment.

POST & COMMUNICATIONS

While domestic post is slow, overseas air mail is relatively efficient and rates are good value. Poste restante works best in Windhoek; in outlying towns, mail takes longer to arrive.

Namibia has a good, though somewhat expensive telephone service. International calls cost US$3.50 per minute to any foreign country. Cellular phones are gaining in popularity, although they still have not replaced short-wave radio in rural areas.

Internet access is not yet publicly available in Namibia.

MONEY
Costs

Thanks to a favourable exchange rate, Namibia remains a moderately in-expensive country to visit compared

---

Itineraries

One Week
After a couple of days in Windhoek – possibly also including a day hiking in the attractive Daan Viljoen Game Park about 25km west of the city – head to Etosha National Park, where you could easily spend the remainder of the week before returning to Windhoek.

Alternatively, after a day or two in Windhoek, head to Swakopmund and nearby attractions, including the port of Walvis Bay. On the way back stop at the historic town of Karibib. If you have your own vehicle, you may be able to work in a detour to Namib Desert Park (part of Namib-Naukluft Park) and Sossusvlei before returning to Windhoek.

Two Weeks
With two weeks, you will easily have time to visit Windhoek, Swakopmund, and Sossusvlei, as described in the one week itinerary above, with a bit more time at each. From Swakopmund, head north-east to Etosha National Park, and spend the remainder of your time there.

If you have time on your return to Windhoek, you could visit Okahandja, where there are two huge craft markets which

operate daily throughout the year. It also hosts a colourful Maherero Day procession on the weekend nearest 23 August each year.

One Month
With one month, you can add southern Namibia to the itinerary, visiting Lüderitz and hiking at Fish River Canyon, taking in the pleasant hot-springs oasis of Ai-Ais at its southern end. From here, head out of the country to South Africa, or return to Windhoek.

Alternatively, from Swakopmund, if you have your own vehicle you could head north to Skeleton Coast Park. Then, backtrack as far as Torra Bay and continue via Khorixas to Etosha National Park If you happen to be in this area during the wet season – in March or April – Ruacana Falls are worth a visit.

From Etosha, make your way southward via the renowned mining town of Tsumeb and the agricultural and ranching centre of Otjiwarongo – particularly attractive in September and October when the jacaranda and bougainvillea are in bloom. Other options for stops before you return to Windhoek include Omaruru, with its outback feel, and Karibib.

SKELETON COAST
Ethereal fog-bound
scenery and shipwrecks

ETOSHA NATIONAL PARK
Flamingos; incredible
variety of wildlife

WINDHOEK
Capital in attractive
natural setting

MIB-NAUKLUFT PARK
esert dunes, oasis
and wildlife

FISH RIVER CANYON
Spectacular natural
wonder

ANGOLA

ZAMBIA

BOTSWANA

SOUTH AFRICA

ATLANTIC
OCEAN

To Luanda

To Victoria Falls
& Lusaka

To Francistown

To Johannesburg

To Cape Town

Liuwa Plain National Park

Namibe National Park

Bicuan National Park

Mupa National Park

Epupa Falls

Kunene River

Ruacana Falls

Skeleton Coast Park

KAOKOVELD

Etosha National Park

Etosha Pan

Petrified Forest

Huab River

Burnt Mountain

Brandberg (2573m)

Spitzkoppe

al West Coast creation Area

Cape Cross

Daan Viljoen Game Park

Sandwich Harbour

Namib-Naukluft Park

Naukluft (1973m)

Diamond Area 1 (Prohibited Area)

Fish River Canyon National Park

Richtersveld National Park

West Caprivi Game Reserve

Mahango Game Reserve

Popa Falls

Caprivi Strip

Khaudom Game Reserve

Mudumu National Park

Mamili National Park

Chobe River

Linyanti River

Chobe National Park

Ngoma Bridge

Okavango Delta

Gewihaba Caverns

Aha Hills

CENTRAL KALAHARI GAME RESERVE

Ntwetwe Pan

Khutse Game Reserve

GEMSBOK-MABUASEHUBE NATIONAL PARK

Mabuasehube Game Reserve

Kalahari Gemsbok National Park

Gemsbok National Park

Augrabies Falls National Park

Luanda · Lubango · Matala · Capelongo · Menongue · Zambezi · Kalabo · Limulunga · Senanga · Shangombo · Kalongola · Ngonye Falls · Katima Mulilo · Seshoke · Wenela · Kongola · Mohembo · Shakawe · Kasane and Kazungula · Rundu · Divundu · Gumare · Maun · Opuwo · Ondjiva · Namacunde · Santa Clara · Oshikango · Oshakati · Ondangwa · Ruacana · Calai · Sikereti · Tsumkwe · Ghanzi · Orapa · Tsumeb · Grootfontein · Otavi · Khorixas · Outjo · Otjiwarongo · Waterberg Plateau Park · Omaruru · Karibib · Usakos · Okahandja · Swakopmund · Walvis Bay · Rehoboth · Aminuis · Buitepos · Gobabis · Mamuno · Rietfontein · Molepolole · GABORONE · Kanye · Solitaire · Mariental · Sesriem · Sossusvlei · Maltahöhe · Helmeringhausen · Brukkaros (1586m) · Keetmanshoop · Werda · Tshabong · McCarthys Rest · Lüderitz · Aus · Aroab · Rietfontein · Grünau · Nakop · Upington · Karasburg · Ai-Ais · Oranjemund · Vioolsdrift · Noordoewer · Pofadder · Port Nolloth · Springbok · Kimberley · Garies · De Aar · Calvinia

WINDHOEK

Orange River

0   100   200 km

ED ITINERARIES

eek ① Windhoek · Daan Viljoen Game Park · Etosha NP
     ② Windhoek · Swakopmund · Walvis Bay · Sossusvlei

eeks Windhoek · Swakopmund · Walvis Bay · Sossusvlei ·
      Etosha National Park · Okahandja

One Month Windhoek · Swakopmund · Walvis Bay · Sossusvlei ·
           Windhoek · Lüderitz · Fish River Canyon NP ·
           Swakopmund · Skeleton Coast Park · Torra Bay ·
           Khorixas · Etosha NP · Ruacana Falls · Tsumeb ·
           Otjiwarongo · Omaruru · Karibib · Okahandja · Windhoek

with some other destinations in the region. If you are camping or staying in backpackers hostels, cooking your own meals, and hitching or using local minibuses, plan on spending a minimum of US$15 per day. Unfortunately, to get around the country on this sort of budget would be time-consuming and frustrating, since hitching isn't optimal and minibus routes are limited to the main highways.

A plausible mid-range budget, including B&B or inexpensive hotel accommodation and at least one restaurant meal daily, would be around US$30 to US$80 per day plus US$20 to US$50 per person for car hire and petrol expenses.

If you wish to stay at top-end hotels, eat exclusively in restaurants and either take escorted tours or use 4WD, plan on about US$200 to US$300 per person per day.

Changing Money

Major foreign currencies and travellers cheques can be exchanged at any bank. Rates are usually better for travellers cheques, though it pays to shop around for the bank offering the lowest commission. When changing money, you can opt for either South African rand (also legal tender in Namibia at a rate of 1:1) or Namibian dollars. Travellers cheques may also be exchanged for US dollars cash, if the cash is available, but there is a 7% commission. There is no currency black market.

Credit cards are accepted in most shops, restaurants and hotels, and credit card cash advances are available from several banks and ATMs in major towns.

ONLINE SERVICES

Lonely Planet has a web site Destination Namibia (www.lonelyplanet .com/dest/afr/namib.htm).

The Ministry of Tourism's Namibia Page (www.iwwn.com.na/namtour) has commercial links as well as a lot of destination information.

Reader's Digest's The Living Edens (www.pbs.org/edens/etosha) has a feature on Etosha National Park.

Namibia: Some Useful Links (www .members.tripod.com/~nami bia63) is exactly what it says.

For local news, try The Namibian (www.namibian.com.na), the country's independent newspaper.

BOOKS & FILMS

Namibia – The Struggle for Liberation by Alfred T Moleah recounts SWAPO's independence struggle.

For looks at colonisation and independence, see Sam Nujoma's autobiography *To Free Namibia: The Life of the First President of Namibia*, and *The Transition to Independence in Namibia* by L Cliffe et al.

Namib Flora: Swakopmund to the Giant Welwitschia via Goanikontes by Patricia Craven & Christine Marais is excellent for plant identification around northern Namib-Naukluft Park. *The Namib – Natural History of an Ancient Desert* by Mary Seely is a useful handbook by the director of Namibia's Desert Research Unit.

One of contemporary Namibia's most significant writers is Joseph Diescho, known in particular for his largely autobiographical novel *Born of the Sun*. Another significant Namibian voice is David Jasper Utley, whose first publication was a book of short stories entitled *Allsorts*.

Namibia's film industry is in its infancy. The most notable Namibian film to be seen internationally is *Sophia's Homecoming*, which chronicles the life of an Owambo woman forced to work for 12 years in Windhoek in order to support her family.

The 1993 film, *A Far Off Place*, was filmed in Namibia.

ENTERING & LEAVING NAMIBIA

South African Airways operates daily flights between Windhoek, Johannesburg and Cape Town. Air Namibia connects Windhoek with Harare, Lusaka, Maun and Gaborone.

There are three border crossings to Angola – at Ruacana, Oshikango/Santa Clara/Namacunde and Rundu/Calai. You should get an update on the political situation in Angola before deciding to cross.

To Botswana, there are border control posts at Ngoma Bridge, Buitepos/Mamuno, Mohembo/Mahango, and Kasane. The main route between the two countries is via the Trans-Kalahari Highway via Gobabis and the Buitepos/Mamuno border post.

To South Africa, there is a luxury bus service between Windhoek and Cape Town or Johannesburg. There are also bus connections between Swakopmund and Cape Town. The roads between the two countries are good, and are tarred on the two main routes from Cape Town via Noordoewer or from Johannesburg via Nakop. An alternative route is the gravel road into south-eastern Namibia between Rietfontein and Aroab.

The only crossing between Namibia and Zambia is via the Zambezi pontoon ferry at Wenela/Sesheke. If travelling by public transport, plan on doing the trip in stages.

There is no direct border crossing between Namibia and Zimbabwe: to get there you must take the Chobe National Park transit route from Ngoma Bridge through northern Botswana to Kasane/Kazungula, and from there to Victoria Falls. There are several shuttle buses which do this trip.

NIGER

Niger is West Africa's second largest country and one of its most fascinating. Much of the country sits on the edge of the Sahara and the towns in the centre and far north, particularly Agadez, exude a unique desert charm. Separated by hundreds of kilometres of barren, windswept land, these towns are the meeting places for the nation's vibrant mix of people. Their markets, where cattle, camels and other goods have been traded for centuries, are some of the most exciting in Africa. In the far north, the starkly beautiful Aïr Massif rises as if from nowhere.

Niger's wealth lies in uranium exports, and tourism is also important. Yet, tough times in both industries in recent years have forced many people to migrate to the cities, or – in the case of the nomadic Tuareg – to settle. While Niger's shaky economic foundation will be evident to travellers, it is the stoic and resilient nature of its people and the barren beauty of the Niger desert that will create the most lasting impressions.

WHEN TO GO
The best time to visit is between December and February, when temperatures are coolest, although dusty harmattan winds often reduce visibility. The hottest part of the year is March to June. The rainy period (in the south) is from June to August.

At a Glance

Full Country Name: Republic of Niger
Area: 1,267,000 sq km
Population: 9.8 million
Capital City: Niamey (population approx 500,000)
People: Southern Hausa (about 50%), Songhai-Djerma (22%), Tuareg (10%), Peul-Fulani (9%) and Kanouri
Languages: French (official), Hausa, Zarma, Fulani and Tamashek (the language of the Tuaregs)
Religions: Muslim (about 80%), Christian and traditional animist religions
Government: Military government in transition (elections scheduled for early 2000)
Currency: West African CFA franc (CFA)
Time Zone: One hour ahead of GMT/UTC
International Telephone Code: 227
Electricity: 220V, 50 Hz; sockets take plugs with two round pins, as in Europe

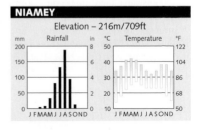

NIAMEY
Elevation – 216m/709ft

HIGHLIGHTS
Mountains & Desert
Among Niger's natural attractions, the remote and exotic Aïr Massif northeast of Agadez would undoubtedly be a high point if the political situation allows a visit. Another would be the Ténéré desert, 500km from Agadez and considered one of the most beautiful parts of the Sahara. However, getting here (if it is possible at all) is

only for the very adventurous. If you don't have a team of camels, you'll need two vehicles – for safety reasons – and several days to make the trip.

Wildlife & Birds

Parc National du W is another good destination for those wanting to immerse themselves in Niger's beauty. While you will not see the profusion of animals that you would in eastern or southern Africa, you will be able to view a large variety of species and many aquatic birds, particularly between February and May. The park is only open from early December to late May.

Urban Attractions, Markets & Festivals

One of the best places to experience the vibrant cultural mix for which Niger is renowned is Agadez, with its maze of narrow alleyways weaving between single storey mud-brick buildings. It's a market town where the nomadic Tuareg come in from outlying areas to barter their goods for those of the Hausa traders from the south.

The surrounding region is known for its festivals, the most important of which is the *gerewol* festival of the Wodaabé people (held in August or September), during which unmarried men adorn and beautify themselves in order to woo women. Other good places for observing Niger's diverse ethnic mix are at the Grand Marché in Niamey, and in Zinder, Niger's second largest city and an old Hausa trading town with a good market.

VISA REQUIREMENTS

Visas are required by all visitors except nationals of Belgium, France, Germany, Italy, Luxembourg, the Netherlands, the

Scandinavian countries, and most West and North African countries. There are few Niger embassies around the world, and French embassies are often not empowered to issue Niger visas, so make sure you plan ahead. Australians and New Zealanders must apply in Paris for a visa. In Africa, visas can be obtained in Algeria, Benin, Côte d'Ivoire, Egypt and Nigeria.

You will also need to show proof of yellow fever and cholera vaccinations.

NIGER EMBASSIES

Benin
(☎ 31 40 30) One block behind the post office, Cotonou

Canada
(☎ 613-232-4291/3; fax 230-9808) 38 Blackburn Ave, Ottawa, Ontario K1N 8A2

France
(☎ 01-45 04 80 60) 154 rue de Long-champ, 75116 Paris

Nigeria
(☎ 261 2300) 15 Adeola Odeku St, Victoria Island, Lagos

USA
(☎ 202-483-4224) 2204 R St NW, Washington, DC 20008

TOURIST OFFICES OVERSEAS

Niger has no overseas tourist offices, but travel agents should be able to supply you with most of what you need. Also check the web sites listed under Online Services.

HEALTH

Yellow fever can occur in all parts of Niger and malaria is present year-round. You should take appropriate pre-cautions against these serious diseases. A number of other insect-borne diseases, including filariasis, leishman-iasis, trypanosomiasis (sleeping sick-ness) and typhus are present in Niger, so you will need to take precautions against all insect bites.

Schistosomiasis is widespread, mainly in the savanna regions; avoid swimming or paddling in rivers or streams. There is a risk of meningococcal meningitis, especially during the dry season from October to May. Intestinal worms are common; take care with what you eat.

Parasites can be ingested in food or enter through the skin, so keep your shoes on whenever possible. Rabies can occur in Niger; avoid bites from any animal, especially dogs, monkeys and bats. Take precautions against sunburn, heat stroke and dehydration if you are travelling during the hot season (March to June), especially in the northern regions.

Food and waterborne diseases including dysentery, hepatitis, typhoid and cholera, occur in Niger; take extra care with what you eat and drink. Stick to treated water at all times and try to eat only freshly cooked, hygienically prepared food.

Medical care is limited in Niamey and poor in the rest of the country. If you are seriously ill, consider going home.

POST & COMMUNICATIONS

Postal services outside Niamey are unreliable, so you should send everything from the capital. Rates for international air mail are about the same as in the west. Poste restante in Niamey is efficient and letters will be held for up to four months or more.

International calls can be made with a minimum of hassle from the post office in Niamey. Rates are about standard for the region, with a three minute telephone call to Europe costing about US$10.

Currently it is almost impossible to send email from Niger by public means (unless you become a monthly subscriber and pay hefty fees), but this may change.

MONEY
Costs

Budget places are relatively expensive in Niger. The cheapest single rooms cost around US$5, and quality is often very poor. Mid-range hotels are more expensive than in neighbouring Nigeria and Benin, although on a par with those

---

Itineraries

Travel in the northern and far eastern sections of Niger is currently restricted for security reasons, so be sure to get an update before planning to travel there.

One Week
It would be easy to spend a week just in Niamey, exploring the town and visiting its good market and museum. Possible excursions include the colourful market towns of Bourbon, Ayorou and Filingué. Alternatively, you could spend two to three days in Niamey and then head south to spend the remainder of the week at Parc National du W, viewing the wild game and birds, though you will need your own vehicle for this.

Two Weeks
With two weeks, you could do all of the above without rushing, and perhaps work in a visit to Zinder. Possible stops enroute include Birni-N'Konni or Maradi, both also with good markets.

One Month
With a month – and if the security situation permits – you will be able to continue on from Zinder to Agadez. Plan on spending at least a few days here as it's a fascinating town. Five weeks would allow you to also take in the beautiful Aïr Massif and Ténéré Desert.

TÉNÉRÉ DESERT
One of the most beautiful parts of the Sahara

ZINDER
Niger's second largest city; old Hausa trading town with a good market and diverse ethnic mix

AÏR MASSIF
Remote, exotic mountain range

AGADEZ
Remote Sahara oasis with vibrant cultural mix and lively festivals; gateway to the Aïr Massif and Ténéré Desert

NIAMEY
Colourful capital with attractive markets (Grand Marché and Petit Marché) and museum

PARC NATIONAL DU W
Park with animals and aquatic birds

Reserve Naturelle Nationale de l'Aïr et du Ténéré

Arbre de Ténéré

0   100   200 km

SUGGESTED ITINERARIES

One Week	**1** Niamey • Bourbon • Ayorou • Filingué **2** Niamey • Parc National du W
Two Weeks	Niamey • Bourbon • Ayorou • Filingué; Parc National du W • Birni-N'Konni • Maradi • Zinder
One Month	Niamey • Bourbon • Ayorou • Filingué; Parc National du W • Birni-N'Konni • Maradi • Zinder • Agadez
Five Weeks	Agadez • Aïr Massif • Agadez • Ténéré Desert

in Mali, with prices ranging from US$10 to US$15 for a double room with fan, and another US$7 to US$10 for air-con. Niamey and a few other towns have comfortable mid-range hotels, where rooms cost from US$25 to US$50 or more. At the country's only international-standard hotel (in Niamey), rooms cost from US$110.

Budget travellers should plan on spending about US$15 to US$20 per day, while mid-range comforts will cost from US$30 to US$80 per day. Top-end accommodation and western-style meals will cost close to US$200 per day.

Changing Money

Both cash and travellers cheques can be changed in Niamey, although it is quicker and easier to change cash; commission on travellers cheques can be high and rates are extremely variable. The best denominations for both cash and travellers cheques are French francs, although US dollars are generally not a problem.

Outside Niamey, finding a bank which will accept travellers cheques can be difficult, and commissions may be ridiculously high. Even changing cash can be difficult, although French francs are acceptable at many places, so bring enough cash (preferably French francs) to cover your trip from the border to Niamey.

ONLINE SERVICES

Lonely Planet has a web site Destination Niger (www.lonelyplanet.com /dest/afr/niger.htm).

Friends of Niger (www.friendsof niger.org) is a good place to start to immerse yourself in the culture.

If you're thinking of travelling in the Ténéré desert, look at Katja

Kreder's site first (www.users.globalnet .co.uk/~ckscott/kat.html).

Focus on Niger (www.txdirect.net /users/jmayer/fon.html) has news, a listing of Internet resources, and more.

BOOKS & FILMS

Impossible Journey: Two Against the Sahara by Michael Asher is a gripping account (documented with some stunning photos) of the first successful west-to-east camel crossing of the Sahara, starting in Mauritania and passing through Mali and Niger before ending at the Nile.

Nomads of Niger by Carol Beckwith & Marion Van Offelen is a beautiful photographic documentary of the authors' travels with Niger's Wodaabé people.

Marriage in Maradi: Gender & Culture in a Hausa Society in Niger, 1900-1989 by Barbara Cooper is dry but has many interesting observations.

For a taste of what life on the road will be like in one of Niger's wildly driven bush taxis, read *Riding the Demon: On the Road in West Africa* by Peter Chilson.

Captive of the Desert (1990) was filmed in Niger and is based on the ordeal of a French woman who was taken hostage by Toubou nomads.

The Sheltering Sky, directed by Bernardo Bertolucci, was filmed in part in Niger.

Films from Niger include *The Exile* (1980) and *Black Dawn* (1983).

ENTERING & LEAVING NIGER

Air Afrique, Ethiopian Airlines, Air Algérie and Air France fly to Niamey. Niamey is also well connected with many West African cities including

Ouagadougou, Bamako, Abidjan, Dakar, Cotonou and N'Djamena.

To Benin, there are buses to Gaya on the border, where you will need to transfer to bush taxis for onward travel to Cotonou or other points.

To Burkina Faso, there are several buses between Niamey and Ouagadougou. The journey can also be done in stages by minibus and bush taxi. The main route is via Foetchango on the border to Kantchari and Fada N'Gourma. There is also a less used crossing to the north via Téra and Dori (Burkina Faso), which involves a ferry over the River Niger.

To Chad, the route is via Zinder, Diffa and Nguigmi to Nokou, Mao and N'Djamena and takes at least a week. The journey must be done in stages, and you will need to have your own food and water for the leg between Zinder and Mao. However, there is no public transport across the border, and crossing is not possible at present due to banditry and insecurity, especially on the Chad side.

The trip to Mali (Niamey to Gao) is also a slow, rough journey, especially from July to September when parts of the route get very muddy. Travel is via direct bus, or in stages by bush taxi and truck.

Between Niger and Nigeria, there are four main bush taxi routes, as well as buses from Niamey to Birni-N'Konni, Maradi and Zinder, all close to the border. The most popular option is from Zinder direct to Kano by taxi. The second route is from Birni-N'Konni to Sokoto, although the road is heavily potholed and the bureaucracy onerous. The other two routes are from Maradi to Katsina and from Niamey to Sokoto via Gaya on the Benin border.

NIGERIA

Nigeria is West Africa's most influential country economically and militarily, and has more than half the region's population and one of its most highly educated workforces. It also suffers from a reputation for attracting only truly masochistic voyagers, and is off most travellers' lists as a place to visit. Apart from corruption, one of the biggest problems throughout the country is lack of fuel, which gives rise to riots, transport difficulties and economic depression. Another problem is the congestion and chaos of Nigeria's urban areas, especially Lagos, which many travellers consider to be the most crime-ridden city in Africa.

Outside the major cities, Nigeria can be fascinating, with a diverse collection of peoples, cultures, histories and religions, as well as attractive landscapes. If you spend most of your time in places such as Kano, Zaria, Jos and Ife, or in the mountains along the Cameroon border (many of these places are prone to sporadic lawlessness and violence) you're sure to enjoy your visit.

WHEN TO GO

The best time to visit is between November and February, after the

At a Glance

Full Country Name: Federal Republic of Nigeria
Area: 924,000 sq km
Population: 118 million
Capital City: Abuja (population 400,000)
People: More than 200 ethnic groups, including Yoruba, Ibo and Hausa-Fulani (together constituting 66%); the Kanuri, Tiv, Edo, Nupe and Ibidio make up about 25%
Languages: English (official) and indigenous languages including Hausa, Yoruba, Ibo, Edo and Efik
Religions: Muslim (about 50%), Christian (about 40%) and traditional religions
Government: Fragile and fledgling multi-party democracy
Currency: Nigerian naira (N)
Time Zone: One hour ahead of GMT/UTC
International Telephone Code: 234
Electricity: 220V, 50 Hz; most sockets take plugs with two round pins, though some take three square pins

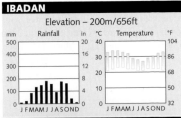

IBADAN

Elevation – 200m/656ft

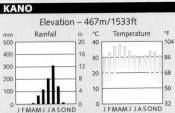

KANO

Elevation – 467m/1533ft

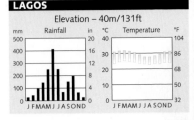

LAGOS

Elevation – 40m/131ft

rains have stopped and before temperatures get too hot.

HIGHLIGHTS
Music Capital
Despite its reputation, Lagos has a lot to offer, particularly for those interested in music. In addition to being one of the region's musical capitals and the home of many African music stars, it has more nightclubs than almost anywhere else on the continent.

Ancient Cities
Mud-walled Kano, the oldest city in West Africa, is the top destination for most visitors to Nigeria. Its main attraction is the Old City with its enormous market, mosque, Emir's palace and ancient dye pits.

South of Kano is cool, green Jos, another highlight with its outstanding museum and large covered market. Oshogbo, in the south-west corner of the country, is another interesting town, housing the Sacred Groves and Shrine of Oshun, the River Goddess. It's also where many of Nigeria's most famous artists have made their homes. Not far away is Ife, the legendary home of the founder of the Yoruba.

Wildlife & Trekking
For a respite from urban crowding, head to Yankari National Park, which is Nigeria's best wildlife reserve – although seeing animals here can be a bit hit-and-miss. The best months to visit are January and February. Eastern Nigeria holds additional attractions for outdoor fans, including Cross River National Park, Obudu Cattle Ranch and Gashaka Gumpti National Park (Nigeria's largest park). There is good trekking along the country's eastern border.

VISA REQUIREMENTS
All visitors require visas except nationals of Economic Community of West African States (ECOWAS) countries. Visas are not available at the border or on arrival at an airport. Most Nigerian embassies issue visas only to residents and nationals of the country in which that embassy is located. Thus, you will need to arrange your visa before leaving for Africa. Visas usually allow a stay of up to one month and remain valid for three months from the date of issue.

Nigerian Embassies
Australia
(☎ 02-6286 1222) 7 Terrigal Crescent, O'Malley, ACT 2606 (consulate)
Canada
(☎ 613-236-0521) 295 Metcalfe St, Ottawa, Ontario K2P IR9
UK
(☎ 020-7353 3776 or 0891-600 199) 76 Fleet St, London EC4Y
USA
(☎ 202-822-1500) 2201 M St NW, Washington, DC 20037. Consulate: New York

TOURIST OFFICES OVERSEAS
Nigeria has no overseas tourist offices, but travel agents should be able to provide you with most of what you need. Also check the web sites listed under Online Services.

HEALTH
Yellow fever can occur in all parts of Nigeria; malaria is present year-round and there are periodic outbreaks of dengue fever in urban areas. You should take appropriate precautions against these serious diseases. A number of other insect-borne diseases,

Itineraries

One Week

Lagos has enough to keep you busy for a week, especially if you are interested in music – an evening at one of the city's great nightclubs is a must.

An alternative for those who want to skip Lagos completely would be to fly in and out of Kano (from Lagos), where you could easily spend at least three days exploring this fascinating city. With the remainder of your time, head to Katsina, an old Hausa city about 175km north-west of Kano, or to other villages closer in, such as Danbatta, which has the largest cattle market in Nigeria.

Two Weeks

With two weeks, you could see both Lagos and Kano, as well as some cities in between, including Kaduna, the northern capital. Alternatively, you could head from Lagos to the far south-eastern section of the country, to spend a week or more trekking and visiting Cross River National Park, Obudu Cattle Ranch and Gashaka Gumpti National Park.

One Month

With a month, you could make a rough circuit, heading from Lagos to Benin City (which has a history dating back to the 10th century) and the nearby Okomu Sanctuary, home to the endangered white-throated monkey and elusive forest elephant, Onitsha, with its famous 'market writers', who produced short and often moralistic paperback novellas, or Abraka, which has white-water rafting and diving, are also worthwhile stops.

Continuing eastward you will come to a more interesting area which encompasses some of the parks included in the two week itinerary, and also offers the country's best trekking. North from Lagos, possible stops include a day or two at Kaduna; Jos, which has a fabulous sprawling ethnographical museum; Yankari National Park; and the town of Zaria, with its interesting old quarter. Finish up with several days in Kano before returning to Lagos.

including filariasis, leishmaniasis, trypanosomiasis (sleeping sickness) and typhus are present in Nigeria, so take precautions against all insect bites.

Schistosomiasis is widespread; avoid swimming or paddling in rivers or streams. There is a risk of meningococcal meningitis, especially during the dry season (November to April). Intestinal worms are common; take care with what you eat.

Parasites can be ingested in food or enter through the skin, so keep your shoes on whenever possible. Rabies can occur in Nigeria; avoid bites from any animal, especially dogs, monkeys and bats. Take precautions against sunburn, heat stroke and dehydration if you are travelling during the hot season (March to May), especially in the northern regions.

Food and waterborne diseases, including dysentery, hepatitis, typhoid and cholera all occur in Nigeria; take extra care with what you eat and drink. Stick to treated water at all times and try to eat only freshly cooked, hygienically prepared food.

Medical care in Lagos is limited, and poor in the rest of the country. If you are seriously ill, consider home.

POST & COMMUNICATIONS

International postal rates are low – about US$0.50 for a letter – but delivery is questionable. Alternatively, try the EMS or DHL services; the documents are insured and are almost guaranteed to arrive at their intended destination. Avoid poste restante in Lagos if possible.

International telephone facilities are generally good and efficient; they are available at the Nigeria Telecom (NITEL) principal office in Lagos and

NIGERIA HIGHLIGHTS & ITINERARIES

YANKARI NATIONAL PARK
Nigeria's best reserve for wildlife and birds

GASHAKA GUMPTI NATIONAL PARK
Nigeria's largest park and highest mountain; diverse ecology

JOS
Pleasantly cool climate; interesting museum complex; good market

SOUTH-EAST
Lush rainforest at Cross River National Park; animals at Obudu Cattle Ranch; good trekking

OSHOGBO
Home for artists, Sacred Groves, Shrine of Oshun and River Goddess

KANO
The oldest city in West Africa, Kano has bustling markets and an impressive mosque

LAGOS
For the adventurous, Nigeria's former capital offers nightclubs and exciting music

SUGGESTED ITINERARIES

One Week
① Lagos
② Lagos • Kano • Katsina • Danbatta

Two Weeks
① Lagos • Ibadan • Ogbomosho • Kaduna • Kano
② Lagos • Cross River National Park • Obudu Cattle Ranch • Gashaka Gumpti National Park

One Month
Lagos • Benin City • Okomu Sanctuary • Onitsha • Abraka • Obudu Cattle Ranch • Gashaka Gumpti NP
Lagos • Ibadan • Ogbomosho • Kaduna • Jos • Yankari National Park • Zaria • Kano

0   100   200 km
0   100

at NITEL offices throughout the country. Rates are reasonable, eg about US$5 for a three minute call to North America.

Internet access is possible in Lagos and Port Harcourt.

MONEY
Costs

Nigeria is relatively inexpensive. Budget travellers staying in basic accommodation and eating local street food can get by on US$10 to US$15 per day. Mid-range travel allowing a few more comforts will cost US$25 to US$50, while top-end travel can easily cost US$150 per day or more.

Rampant inflation in 1999 led the Central Bank to introduce higher-value banknotes (100, 200 and 500 naira). The fall in the value of the naira against the US dollar has been damaging for the locals but a plus for the traveller.

Nigeria is built on the practice of dash (bribe money) so don't even think about avoiding it, and calculate this into your costs. Requests can range from being friendly to downright intimidating, but they are made frequently.

Changing Money

Black market rates are now almost on a par with official rates, and – while the black market is widespread – for the average traveller it is hardly an advantage, especially considering the risks involved (it's illegal).

Cash is more convenient than travellers cheques, as many bureaux de change won't accept cheques, and some banks won't either. If you're very lucky, you might get an exchange rate about 5% to 7% less than that for cash. Although carrying a lot of cash around isn't usually a good idea, you may want to consider having some small bills handy to smooth your way through customs, and to tide you over until the bank changes your travellers cheques (if at all).

Credit cards are virtually useless except at major hotels in Lagos and Abuja. Credit card scams are widespread, so be careful.

ONLINE SERVICES

Lonely Planet has a web site Destination Nigeria (www.lonelyplanet .com/dest/afr/nig.htm).

Motherland Nigeria (www.mother landnigeria.com) has everything that you ever wanted to know about Nigeria and then some.

For a comprehensive listing of texts and sites with brief descriptions of each, see Riikka's Nigeria Links (http://media .urova.fi/~rkorpela/niglink.html).

Washington Post (www.washington post.com/wp-srv/inatl/longterm /nigeria/timeline.htm) has a handy and easy-to-follow timeline of Nigeria's history since the 1960s.

For travel information and tips on what to watch out for in Nigeria try Fielding's Danger Finder (www .fieldingtravel.com/df/dplaces/nigeria /index.htm).

BOOKS & FILMS

Chinua Achebe is probably Nigeria's most famous author. His most famous book is *Things Fall Apart*, which takes place in the mid-1890s and portrays the collision between precolonial Ibo society and western missionaries. *Anthills of the Savannah*, another of his famous works, is an anatomy of political disorder and corruption in a fictional African country resembling Nigeria.

Other excellent Nigerian writers are Wole Soyinka, Ben Okri, Amos Tutuola, Cyprian Ekwensi and Ken Saro-Wiwa. Soyinka, who won the Nobel Prize for literature in 1986, has written three books, including *The Interpreter* and more recently *Ake*, a personal memoir of his childhood, but he is primarily a playwright. *A Dance of the Forests*, *The Man Died* and *Opera Wonyosi* are some of his more well known plays.

The Famished Road by Okri is a winner of the Booker Prize for Fiction, and describes Nigeria as seen through the eyes of a young boy.

Flora Nwapa, an Igbo teacher and administrator, is another well known writer, and the first Nigerian woman to have a novel published. Most of her stories focus on the problems women face in marriage and with children. Her first book, *Efuru* (1966), deals with the role of women in Igbo society. *Idu* (1970) concerns the importance of children in the African family.

Pamela Watson's *Esprit de Battuta: Alone Across Africa on a Bicycle* deals with her experiences as a cycling traveller in Nigeria, Congo (Zaïre) and Rwanda.

Nigeria's film industry does not match its literary scene. Films to come out of the country include *King Roda's Ring* (1962) and *Fight for Freedom* (1979). *Mister Johnson* (1991), a mindless piece about a well educated Nigerian who doesn't fit into colonial-era society, was set and filmed in the country.

ENTERING & LEAVING NIGERIA

Airlines flying into Lagos' international airport include Aeroflot, Air Afrique, Air France, Cameroon Airlines, Ethiopian Airlines, Ghana Airways, KLM, Sabena and Swissair. British Airways and KLM also fly into Kano. Nigerian Airways, the national carrier, flies to many West, Central and East African destinations as well as to Europe. It is also possible to reach Lagos, Port Harcourt and Calabar by boat from London, Liverpool and other European ports.

To Benin, there are frequent bush taxis from Lagos Island to Cotonou. The trip takes between three and six hours, depending on how many times your vehicle is stopped by the police.

To Cameroon, the usual route is from Enugu or Calabar to Mamfé (via Ikom). The trip is made by bush taxi (with a short stretch on foot), and in stages. There is also a crossing in the far north of Cameroon between Maiduguri and Maroua. Travel from Maiduguri to Banki (the Nigerian border) is by bush taxi. On the Cameroon side there are minibuses to Maroua. Still further north is a crossing from Ngala to Kousséri, though this is only useful if you are heading straight for N'Djamena (Chad).

Another feasible crossing point into Cameroon is from Yola to Garoua. It is also possible to travel by boat from Oron (just inside the Nigerian border) to Limbe (just inside the Cameroon border), though this route is currently not advisable due to a territorial dispute between the two countries over the Bakassi Peninsula.

Travellers heading from Maiduguri to N'Djamena in Chad will have to pass through a strip of northern Cameroon and will require a visa. The usual way is by bush taxi and minibus via Ngala on the Nigerian border to Kousséri in Cameroon, and then across the bridge to N'Djamena.

Travel on this route was restricted when this book was being written due to insecurity near the Chad border. Be sure to get an update on the situation before heading this way.

There are four main routes to Niger. The most popular is from Kano to Zinder, which can be done by direct taxi. The second route is from Sokoto to Birni-N'Konni by share taxi, but this road is heavily potholed and there are countless checkpoints along the way. Motorcycle taxis also go from the border village of Illela to Birni-N'Konni. Another route runs from Katsina to Maradi. You will need to travel in stages by bush taxi. The fourth route is from Sokoto to Niamey via Gaya on the Niger-Benin border. This last route is usually the least expensive way to Niamey as you spend less time in expensive Niger.

SÃO TOMÉ & PRÍNCIPE

São Tomé & Príncipe is one of Africa's best-kept secrets. It has remote beaches overlooking turquoise seas, dilapidated but charming Portuguese colonial architecture, a friendly Creole culture, rich birdlife and lush jungle – yet hardly any visitors, despite the country being safer than many other places in the region. Although it lies off normal tourist routes and requires a bit of effort to reach, the detour from Gabon, Equitorial Guinea or Cameroon is well worth it.

WHEN TO GO

The best time to go is between June and September when there is less rainfall and temperatures are coolest. The wettest month is March, when temperatures rise to around 30°C, although there is high humidity and rainfall during most of the year.

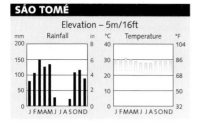

HIGHLIGHTS
Ambience

São Tomé town's delightful ambience, with declining Portuguese colonial buildings and superbly maintained, colourful parks and gardens, makes it a welcome contrast to other capital cities in the region.

Beaches

Good beaches to the north and west of São Tomé town include Praia da Micolo, Praia dos Governadores, Praia dos Tamarindos and Praia das Conchas.

Hiking

In the central part of the island is its highest peak, Pico de São Tomé (2024m), which is surrounded by at least a dozen other volcanic cones all over 1000m high. Also south of São Tomé town is the Boca de Inferno, a dramatic blowhole.

At a Glance

Full Country Name: Democratic Republic of São Tomé & Príncipe
Area: 964 sq km
Population: 150,000
Capital City: São Tomé (population approx 37,000)
People: Filhos da terra (mixed-blood descendants of imported slaves and Europeans who settled the islands in the 16th and 17th centuries); angolares (descendants of Angolan slaves said to have survived a shipwreck in 1540); forros (descendants of freed slaves); serviçais (migrant labourers); and tongas (children of serviçais born on the islands)
Languages: Portuguese (official) and forro (Creole)
Religions: Roman Catholic (about 90%), Evangelical Protestants and Seventh Day Adventists
Government: Republic
Currency: Dobra (Db)
Time Zone: GMT/UTC
International Telephone Code: 23912
Electricity: 220V, 50 Hz; sockets take plugs with two round pins

Birdlife

Tiny Príncipe Island is seldom visited, but is also beautiful, with a rich diversity of birdlife and some attractive stretches of sand.

VISA REQUIREMENTS

All visitors require a visa. The best place to obtain one is in Malabo, Equatorial Guinea, where 15-day visas cost about US$30, although at all embassies they are generally issued promptly and with a minimum of hassle.

Proof of cholera and yellow fever vaccination is also required.

São Tomé & Príncipe Embassies

Equatorial Guinea
(☎ 2997) Avenida de las Naciones Unidas 29, Malabo

Gabon
(☎ 72 0994) Blvd de l'Indépendance

USA
(☎ 212-317-0533) There is no embassy in the USA, but São Tomé & Príncipe has a Permanent Mission to the United Nations at 400 Park Ave, 7th Floor, New York, NY 10022

Itineraries

One Week
In a week, you will have plenty of time to explore São Tomé town and some beaches, as well as to make a trip or two into the interior – possibilities include the pleasant town of Trinidade and the nearby Cascadas da São Nicolau, or the Boca de Inferno.

Two Weeks
With two weeks, you will have time to expand the one week itinerary and see as much of São Tomé as you would like, plus make an excursion to Príncipe (by plane).

TOURIST OFFICES OVERSEAS

São Tomé & Príncipe has no overseas tourist offices, but travel agents and the country's embassies will be able to supply you with information. Also check the web sites listed under Online Services.

HEALTH

Yellow fever can occur and malaria exists year-round, so you will need to take precautions. Avoid all insect bites, and take care with what you eat and drink, as diseases such as dysentery and typhoid occur here. Intestinal worms can be prevented by not walking barefoot and watching what you eat; especially avoid undercooked meat. Rabies can occur here; avoid dogs, monkeys and bats.

Medical services are limited. Consider going home if you require serious medical care.

POST & COMMUNICATIONS

The post is efficient and inexpensive. Poste restante in São Tomé is reliable, although mail takes a long time to arrive.

International telephone calls can be made from São Tomé, but are very expensive, as you must buy a phonecard (US$40).

Internet access is not currently available to the public in this country.

MONEY
Costs

São Tomé & Príncipe is relatively inexpensive, if for no other reason than that there is little to spend your money on. Budget travellers can get by in reasonable comfort for between US$15 and US$20 per day, and mid-range travellers should have no trouble keeping

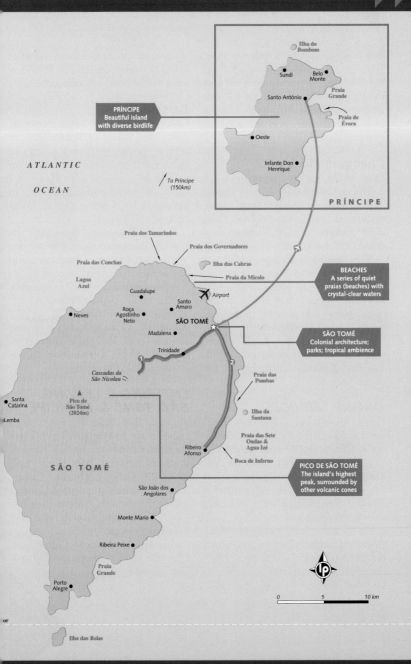

PRÍNCIPE
Beautiful island with diverse birdlife

BEACHES
A series of quiet praias (beaches) with crystal-clear waters

SÃO TOMÉ
Colonial architecture; parks; tropical ambience

PICO DE SÃO TOMÉ
The island's highest peak, surrounded by other volcanic cones

ATLANTIC
OCEAN

To Príncipe
(150km)

PRÍNCIPE

Ilha do Bombom
Sundi
Belo Monte
Santo António
Praia Grande
Praia de Évora
Oeste
Infante Don Henrique

Praia dos Tamarindos
Praia dos Governadores
Ilha das Cabras
Praia das Conchas
Praia da Micolo
Lagoa Azul
Guadalupe
Santo Amaro
Airport
Neves
Roça Agostinho Neto
SÃO TOMÉ
Madalena
Trinidade
Cascadas da São Nicolau
Praia das Pombas
Santa Catarina
Pico de São Tomé (2024m)
Ilha da Santana
Lemba
Praia das Sete Ondas & Agua Izé
SÃO TOMÉ
Ribeiro Afonso
Boca de Inferno
São João dos Angolares
Monte Mario
Ribeira Peixe
Praia Grande
Porto Alegre

or

Ilha das Rolas

0   5   10 km

their expenses to US$60 or less per day. Top-end accommodation options on São Tomé are very limited and will cost roughly US$100 per day. Combined with western-style meals and perhaps a fishing or diving excursion, you may end up spending about US$200 per day.

Changing Money
Most hotels require payment in US dollars or Central African CFA francs. Taxi drivers also prefer these, while restaurants usually want dobra. Thus, don't change too much currency into dobra, and bring plenty of small bills.

Many people exchange money on the black market in the centre of São Tomé, although rates are only marginally better than those at the bank. Money can also be changed at specially licensed shops in the capital. There is only one bank where travellers cheques can be exchanged. The best denomination to have is US dollars.

ONLINE SERVICES
Lonely Planet has a web site Destination São Tomé & Príncipe (www.lonelyplanet.com/dest/afr/sao.htm).

The Democratic Republic of São Tomé & Príncipe (www.geocities.com/RainForest/2619/world/saotome.html) covers environmental concerns, culture and weather.

The Norwegian Council for Africa (www.africaindex.africainfo.no/africaindex1/countries/saotome.html) has a listing of additional links.

Invitation to the African Paradise (www.sao-tome.com/english.html) has some useful travel information.

BOOKS
Country Review – São Tomé & Príncipe, 1998/1999, edited by Robert Kelly et al, is a concise, up-to-date source of political and economic information on the islands.

For an overview of major issues in the region, try *Aspects of Central African History* by T Ranger.

African Development Reconsidered by Haskell Ward offers insights into some of the causes of Africa's ongoing problems.

A good introduction to the literature is the most useful anthology *The Traveller's Literary Companion – Africa* edited by Oona Strathern, which contains over 250 prose and poetry extracts and an introduction to the literature of each country.

ENTERING & LEAVING SÃO TOMÉ & PRÍNCIPE
The only flight from Europe is from Lisbon using Air Portugal (TAP). There are regular flights on Air São Tomé & Príncipe between São Tomé and Libreville (Gabon), Douala (Cameroon) and Malabo (Equatorial Guinea), and on Air Affaires Afrique (based in Douala) between Douala and São Tomé via Príncipe.

You can also sail to São Tomé from Libreville and Douala on the *Solmar II* (Transcolmar).

SENEGAL

Senegal is the buzz place of West Africa – from its hip music and sophistication to its fantastic capital, Dakar. Not surprisingly, it gets more visitors than any other country in the region. Most are package tourists, confined mainly to the string of top-quality hotels on the Atlantic shore. Yet Senegal is also popular with independent travellers, many of whom come to experience the traditional architecture and rural life of the country's Casamance area, or to take advantage of Senegal's bird-watching opportunities, which are among the finest in the world.

WHEN TO GO
The best time to visit Senegal is between November and February when conditions are dry and relatively cool. This is also the local trading season, when the harvest is completed and markets are busier. From March to May, the weather is dry but hotter. The rainy season (June to October) is usually considered to be not as good for travelling, although some visitors prefer this time as tourist areas are less crowded and hotel rates often cheaper. If you do come during the rainy season, keep in mind that secondary roads can be very muddy, or impassable on public transport.

HIGHLIGHTS
Urban Attractions
Cosmopolitan Dakar with its pleasant climate and special mix of Afro-French characteristics is one of Senegal's major drawcards, and most travellers enjoy their time here. A boat trip to the historic Île de Gorée, just three km from Dakar, makes a good excursion.

Beaches, Music & Mangroves
South of the capital are some excellent beaches along the Petite Côte, with traditional fishing villages and plenty of good places to stay. The coastal regions are also ideal for

DAKAR
Elevation – 40m/131ft

At a Glance

Full Country Name: Republic of Senegal
Area: 196,192 sq km
Population: 9.1 million
Capital City: Dakar (population 900,000)
People: Wolof (just over 33%), Sérèr (17%), Fula (12%), Toucouleur, Madinka, Diola and Soninké
Languages: French (official) and Wolof
Religions: Muslim (about 90%), Christian and traditional religions
Government: Multiparty republic
Currency: West African CFA franc (CFA)
Time Zone: GMT/UTC
International Telephone Code: 221
Electricity: 220V, 50 Hz; most sockets take plugs with two round pins

SENEGAL HIGHLIGHTS & ITINERARIES

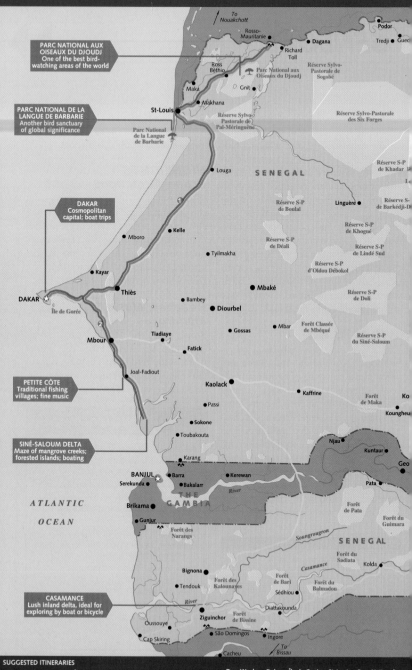

PARC NATIONAL AUX OISEAUX DU DJOUDJ
One of the best bird-watching areas of the world

PARC NATIONAL DE LA LANGUE DE BARBARIE
Another bird sanctuary of global significance

DAKAR
Cosmopolitan capital; boat trips

PETITE CÔTE
Traditional fishing villages; fine music

SINÉ-SALOUM DELTA
Maze of mangrove creeks; forested islands; boating

CASAMANCE
Lush inland delta, ideal for exploring by boat or bicycle

To Nouakchott

Rosso-Mauritanie
Richard Toll
Dagana
Podor
Tredji   Guec

Ross Béthio
Parc National aux Oiseaux du Djoudj
Réserve Sylvo-Pastorale de Sogobé

Maka
Gnit

Makhana
St-Louis
Réserve Sylvo-Pastorale de Pal-Mérinuène
Réserve Sylvo-Pastorale des Six Forges

Parc National de la Langue de Barbarie

Louga
SENEGAL
Réserve S-P de Khadar
Le

Réserve S-P de Boulal
Linguère
Réserve S-P de Barkédji-D

Mboro
Kelle
Tyilmakha
Réserve S-P de Déali
Réserve S-P de Khogué
Réserve S-P de Lindé Sud

Kayar
Mbaké
Réserve S-P d'Oldon Débokol

Thiès
Bambey
Diourbel
Réserve S-P de Doli

DAKAR
Île de Gorée
Gossas
Mbar
Forêt Classée de Mbéqué

Tiadiaye
Fatick
Réserve S-P du Siné-Saloum

Mbour
Joal-Fadiout
Kaolack
Kaffrine
Forêt de Maka
Ko
Koungheu

Passi
Sokone
Toubakouta
Njau
Kuntaur
Geo

Karang
Pata

BANJUL
Barra
Kerewan
Serekunda
Bakalarr
THE GAMBIA   River

Brikama
Forêt de Pata
Forêt du Guimara

ATLANTIC
OCEAN

Gunjur
Forêt des Narangs
Soungrougron
SENEGAL

Forêt du Sadiata
Bignona
Forêt des Kalounayes
Forêt de Bari
Forêt du Balmadou
Kolda

Tendouk
River
Diattakounda
Oussouye
Ziguinchor
Forêt de Bissine
São Domingos
Ingore
Cap Skiring
Cacheu
To Bissau

SUGGESTED ITINERARIES

One Week ① Dakar • Île de Gorée • St-Louis • Parc National aux Oiseaux du Djoudj • Parc National de la Langue de Barbarie
② Dakar • Petite Côte • Siné-Saloum Delta

Two Weeks Dakar • Île de Gorée • St-Louis • Parc National aux Oiseaux du Djoudj • Parc National de la Langue de Barbarie • Petite Côte • Siné-Saloum Delta

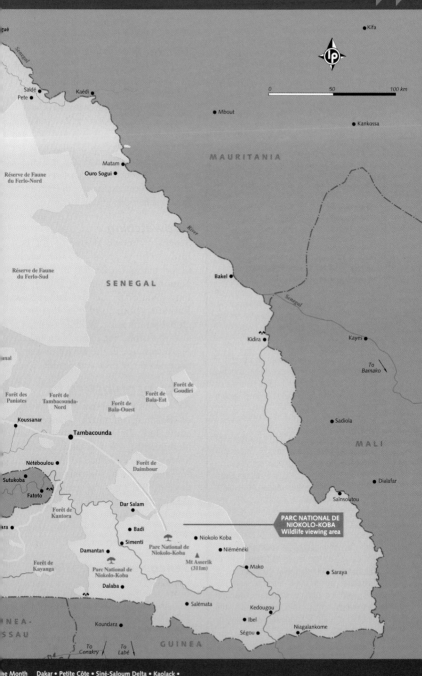

learning more about the country's rich musical traditions and for learning to play traditional instruments or study local dance. Still further south is the Siné-Saloum Delta with its vast maze of mangrove creeks and forested islands, ideal for exploring by boat or on foot.

Itineraries

One Week
Starting in Dakar, you could spend a day or two visiting the capital's frenetic markets and the peaceful Île de Gorée, before heading north to St-Louis, the country's original capital. From here you can visit the spectacular wildlife reserves of Parc National aux Oiseaux du Djoudj and Parc National de la Langue de Barbarie (allow one day each). Alternatively, you could head south to the beaches of the Petite Côte and the Siné-Saloum Delta.

Two Weeks
With two weeks, you could combine the options described in the one week itinerary, visiting St-Louis and the wildlife reserves as well as the Petite Côte and the Siné-Saloum Delta.

One Month
With up to a month, you will have plenty of time to see most of the country. Starting in Dakar, you could do a circular tour, heading south to the Petite Côte, Siné-Saloum Delta and the lively regional capital of Kaolack before going east to Tambacounda, the jumping-off point for visits to Parc National de Niokolo-Koba and the increasingly popular Bassari area (around the town of Kedougou) in the far south-east of the country.

You could then return to Dakar through The Gambia. Alternatively, you could do the eastward leg through Gambia and the westward leg through Senegal's beautiful Casamance region, to Ziguinchor and the beaches at Cap Skiring before returning to Dakar for a flight out.

Village & River Life
Casamance, the region of Senegal south of Gambia, differs geographically and culturally from the rest of the country, and is a magnet for many travellers. It offers rural *campements* where travellers can experience village life while directly benefiting locals; Cap Skiring, with the best beaches in Senegal; Ziguinchor, the laid-back riverside capital of the region; and the River Casamance, an enchanting maze of lagoons and palm groves.

Birdwatching
Senegal is known as one of the best birdwatching areas of the world. Good places for birders include Parc National aux Oiseaux du Djoudj and Parc National de la Langue de Barbarie, both bird sanctuaries of global significance. Wildlife viewing is also possible in Parc National de Niokolo-Koba in the far south-east of Senegal on the Guinean border.

VISA REQUIREMENTS
All visitors need a visa except citizens of Belgium, Denmark, France, Germany, Italy, Ireland, Luxembourg, the Netherlands, the UK and the USA. Visas are usually issued for 30 days and are single-entry. Multiple-entry and three-month visas are generally available upon request. Allow two to three days for processing.

Proof of yellow fever and cholera vaccination is also required.

Senegalese Embassies
Canada
(☎ 613-238-6392; fax 238-2695) 57 Marlborough Ave, Ottawa, Ontario K1N 8E8

The Gambia
(☎ 373752) Kairaba Ave, near the US embassy

Guinea
(☎ 462834) Corniche-Sud, Coléah, Conakry

UK
(☎ 020-7938 4048) 39 Marloes Rd, London W8 6LA

USA
(☎ 202-234-0540) 2112 Wyoming Ave NW, Washington, DC 20008

TOURIST OFFICES OVERSEAS

Senegal has no overseas tourist offices, but its embassies and travel agencies should be able to supply you with information. Also check the web sites listed under Online Services.

HEALTH

Take precautions against yellow fever, malaria (present in Senegal year-round) and dengue fever. A number of other insect-borne diseases, including filariasis, leishmaniasis, trypanosomiasis (sleeping sickness) and typhus are present. You will need to take precautions against all insect bites. Intestinal worms are common; take care with what you eat.

Parasites can be ingested in food or enter through the skin, so keep your shoes on whenever possible. Avoid swimming or bathing in freshwater as schistosomiasis may be present. There is some risk of meningococcal meningitis.

Rabies can occur in Senegal; avoid bites from any animal, especially dogs, monkeys and bats. Food and waterborne disease, including dysentery, hepatitis and typhoid all occur here. Stick to treated water at all times and try to eat only freshly cooked food.

If you are seriously ill, consider going home as medical care is limited in Dakar and poor in the rest of the country.

POST & COMMUNICATIONS

The postal service is good and moderately priced.

International phone connections to and from Senegal are also good. Rates average between US$1.80 and US$2.50 per minute for calls to the USA, Europe and Australia. Cheaper rates are available evenings and on weekends.

Internet access is possible in Dakar. Other large towns, such as Ziguinchor and St-Louis are likely to open Internet offices soon.

MONEY
Costs

Compared with some other parts of Africa, travel in Senegal is not cheap, although it is about on par with travel in much of the surrounding region. Accommodation costs start at about US$5 for a bed in a basic resthouse through to US$10 or US$15 for something a bit more comfortable. Expect to pay from US$25 to US$50 in mid-range hotels, and from US$100 in topnotch establishments. Food is very cheap if you eat from markets and roadside stalls, while western meals at fancy restaurants can easily cost from US$15.

In general, budget travellers could get by on US$10 per day or less. For a bit more comfort, US$15 to US$25 per day is a reasonable budget. With US$30 to US$50 or more per day, you can stay in decent hotels, eat well and travel quite comfortably.

Changing Money

Changing cash of any major currency is no problem in Dakar. Elsewhere, the best currencies to carry are French francs and US dollars. Cashing travellers cheques in any major currency is easy in Dakar, but difficult elsewhere, especially if your cheques are not in French francs. You may be asked to show your purchase receipts.

Credit cards are accepted at major hotels in Dakar and at some of the resorts. You can also get cash advances against a Visa card in Dakar, St-Louis, Ziguinchor and Kaolack.

ONLINE SERVICES

Lonely Planet has a web site Destination Senegal (www.lonelyplanet .com/dest/afr/sen.htm).

Métissicana (www.metissacana.sn), the web site of Dakar's first cybercafe, has a variety of information and tips.

There's the Senegal page of Africa News Online (www.africanews.org /west/senegal).

Dakar is the end-zone for several auto races. For an update, check the Thierry Sabine Organisation site (www .dakar.fr/indexus.html).

BOOKS & FILMS

Ousmane Sembène is probably the most famous Senegalese writer who has been translated into English. His classic *God's Bits of Wood* describes the emergence of a grass-roots political consciousness in pre-independence Africa. His other books include *Black Docker*, based on his experiences in the French port of Marseilles in the 1950s, and *Xala* (The Curse), an attack on the privileged elites of Dakar.

A more recent Senegalese writer is Mariama Bâ, whose brief but incisive novel *So Long a Letter* explores the theme of transition between traditional and modern society. Another female writer is Aminata Sow-Fall. Her 1986 novel *The Beggars Strike* is an ironic story which highlights the differences between rich and poor, and questions the power of the political elite.

Africa Dances by Geoffrey Gorer is a recounting of a white man's journey from Senegal to Benin in 1935, with interesting observations of African customs and lifestyles during colonial times.

Sembène is also a well known film-maker. The ideas expressed in his book *Xala* were portrayed in his film of the same name.

TGV (1998), directed by Moussa Touré, seeks parallels between a bus ride and life.

The French *Hyenas* (1992), a comedy about a once prosperous African village seeking to stop its slide into poverty, was filmed in Senegal.

ENTERING & LEAVING SENEGAL

Airlines connecting Dakar with Europe include Aeroflot, Air Afrique, Air France, Alitalia, Iberia, TAP (Air Portugal), Sabena and Swissair. There are also many charter flights operated by French and Belgian package tour companies. Dakar is also connected by regional airlines with all other capital cities in West Africa.

To The Gambia, there are several places to cross the border. The main route is from Dakar to Banjul via Karang, using taxi, minibus and the ferry at Barra. The route from Ziguinchor to Banjul via Serekunda is also made by bush taxi, as is a third route, from Tambacounda to Basse Santa Su (in The Gambia). As Senegalese vehicles are not allowed to cross the border, you will have to change for all these routes. (Vehicles going through The Gambia on the Trans-Gambia Highway can cross the border, but you can't end your journey in The Gambia.)

To Guinea, there are bush taxis between Dakar and Labé, though most travellers do this journey in stages, breaking at Tambacounda and Koundara (Guinea). During the wet season the stretch on the Guinean side as far as Labé is very slow or impassable.

To Guinea-Bissau (if the political situation in that country settles down), there are bush taxis from Ziguinchor via São Domingos and Ingore to Bissau. There are two ferry crossings on this route. The coastal route via Canchungo is not viable as there is no longer a ferry between Cacheu and São Domingos.

To Mali, the best way to travel is on the Dakar to Bamako express train, as the road is very bad and traffic virtually nonexistent.

To Mauritania, there are regular bush taxis from Dakar to Rosso-Mauritanie (the border), where you will need to take a *pirogue* (dugout canoe) across the river and get onward transport to Nouakchott.

SOUTH AFRICA

Since its first democratic elections in 1994, South Africa has become a popular destination, especially among budget travellers. Political violence is receding into the past and among the vast majority of people there is a desire to get on with building a new nation. It's an exciting time to visit.

Among the country's many attractions are a very good infrastructure, a pleasant climate, and excellent hiking and wildlife-viewing opportunities. While some areas such as Johannesburg are plagued by high crime rates, and the segregation of society is still extreme, South Africa's natural beauty and ease of travel make it a good choice for visitors.

WHEN TO GO

South Africa can be visited at any time of year, although it's best to avoid school holiday periods (two weeks in April, one month around July, one month around September, and about two months from early December to late January, with

At a Glance

Full Country Name: Republic of South Africa
Area: 1,233,000 sq km
Population: 41 million
Capital City: Pretoria (administrative, population 1.1 million), Cape Town (legislative, population 2.2 million) and Bloemfontein (judicial, population 300,000)
People: Black (close to 75%), white (about 15%), coloured (mixed race, about 9%) and Indian (about 2%). About 60% of whites are of Afrikaner descent and about 40% are of British descent.
Languages: The official languages are Afrikaans, English, Zulu, Xhosa, Northern Sotho, Southern Sotho, SeTswana, Venda, Tsonga, SiSwati Ndebele. The most widely spoken are Afrikaans, English, Sotho, Xhosa and Zulu.
Religions: Predominantly Christian, also Hindu, Muslim and traditional religions
Government: Republic
Currency: South African rand (R)
Time Zone: Two hours ahead of GMT/UTC
International Telephone Code: 27
Electricity: 220/250V, 50 Hz; sockets take plugs with three large round pins

CAPE TOWN
Elevation – 17m/56ft
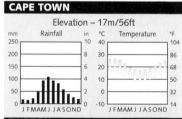

DURBAN
Elevation – 5m/16ft
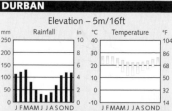

JOHANNESBURG
Elevation – 1665m/5463ft
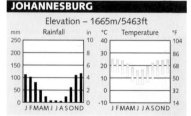

the peak time from mid-December to early January). At these times resorts and national parks are heavily booked and prices often more than double. Also keep in mind that in many places, especially the lowveld, summer (southern hemisphere) can be uncomfortably hot, while in KwaZulu-Natal and Mpumalanga humidity can also be high. Winters are mild almost everywhere except in the highest country, where there are frosts and occasional snow.

HIGHLIGHTS
Hiking
South Africa offers excellent opportunities for hiking, walking and other outdoor activities. Some places to start include the beautiful Drakensberg area in the east of the country, Table Mountain and the Cape of Good Hope Nature Reserve, and Tsitsikamma Coastal National Park and other walking trails in Eastern Cape Province (roughly the area between Plettenberg Bay and Mkambati Nature Reserve).

Wildlife
There are also many superb options for wildlife viewing, most notably Kruger National Park in the north-east and the remote Kalahari Gemsbok National Park in the north-west.

Itineraries

One Week
Assuming you arrive in Johannesburg, spend a day or two seeing the sights there and in nearby Pretoria before heading north-east to Kruger National Park. Use any time remaining for hikes in the Drakensberg.

If you arrive in Cape Town, the entire week can be spent visiting this spectacular city and the surrounding area, including the beautiful Kirstenbosch Botanical Gardens, the Cape Winelands, and perhaps an excursion to the coast at Hermanus to see some whales.

Two Weeks
You could combine both the one week itineraries, spending a week in Cape Town, and a week divided between Kruger National Park and the Drakensberg, with a day or two at the end in Pretoria and Johannesburg.

One Month
Even with a month, you will be hard pressed to see all of South Africa's attractions. After a week or so in the north-east as in the one week itinerary, and at least a week in Cape Town and the surrounding area, continue eastward from Cape Town along the Garden Route – which runs along an attractive, though heavily developed stretch of coast from Still Bay in the west to just beyond Plettenberg Bay in the east.

East of Plettenberg Bay is Tsitsikamma Coastal National Park, which has some beautiful walks. Continue along the coast to Port Elizabeth, which has some interesting historical architecture and a lively nightlife, and then north via Bloemfontein to Johannesburg.

Alternatively, you could continue from Port Elizabeth along the coast to Durban, stopping along the way in Eastern Cape Province to take advantage of some of the excellent walking trails. From Durban, continue north towards the serene wetlands around Greater St Lucia Wetlands, and then head towards Swaziland or on to Johannesburg – although to do this full itinerary, you will need closer to six weeks.

Another alternative, if you have the time and resources, is to fly from Johannesburg or Cape Town into Upington in the north-west, for visits to Namaqualand, near Springbok (especially in spring when you can view a spectacular explosion of wildflowers), and/or Kalahari Gemsbok National Park for wildlife viewing.

SOUTH AFRICA HIGHLIGHTS & ITINERARIES

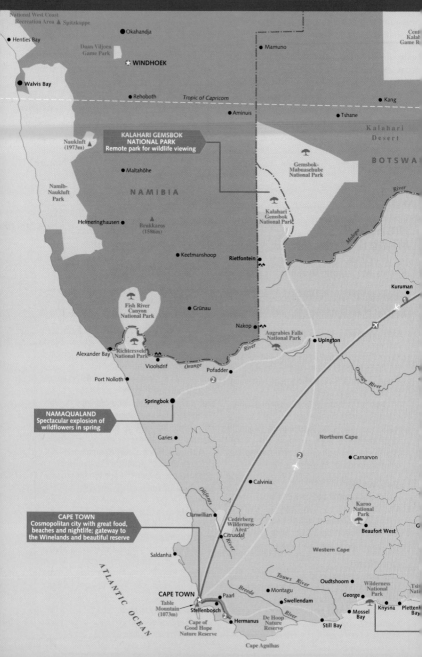

National West Coast
Recreation Area ▲ Spitzkoppe

● Henties Bay

● Okahandja

Daan Viljoen
Game Park

Mamuno ●

☆ WINDHOEK

● Walvis Bay

Cent
Kalah
Game

● Rehoboth   *Tropic of Capricorn*

● Kang

Aminuis ●

Tshane ●

Ka l a h a r i
D e s e r t

Naukluft
(1973m)

**KALAHARI GEMSBOK
NATIONAL PARK**
Remote park for wildlife viewing

Gemsbok-
Mabuasehube
National Park

BOTSWA

● Maltahöhe

N A M I B I A

Namib-
Naukluft
Park

● Helmeringhausen

Brukkaros
(1586m)

Kalahari
Gemsbok
National Park

● Keetmanshoop

Rietfontein ●

Kuruman ●

Fish River
Canyon
National Park

● Grünau

Meloro
River

Nakop ●

Augrabies Falls
National Park

● Upington

Alexander Bay

Richtersveld
National Park

Vioolsdrif ●

Orange   *River*

Orange River

Port Nolloth ●

Pofadder ●

②

NAMAQUALAND
Spectacular explosion of
wildflowers in spring

Springbok ●

● Garies

Northern Cape

Carnarvon ●

②

Karoo
National
Park

Calvinia ●

CAPE TOWN
Cosmopolitan city with great food,
beaches and nightlife; gateway to
the Winelands and beautiful reserve

Clanwillian ●

Cederberg
Wilderness
Area

Beaufort West ●

G

Citrusdal ●

Western Cape

Saldanha ●

Olifants

River

Touws River

Oudtshoorn ●

Wilderness
National
Park

Tsis
Nati

A T L A N T I C   O C E A N

Breede

Montagu ●

George ●

Knysna ●

Plettenb
Bay

CAPE TOWN

Table
Mountain
(1073m)

Paarl ●

Swellendam ●

Mossel
Bay ●

Stellenbosch ●

②

Hermanus ●

De Hoop
Nature
Reserve

Still Bay ●

Cape of
Good Hope
Nature Reserve

River

Cape Agulhas

SUGGESTED ITINERARIES

One Week ① Johannesburg • Pretoria • Kruger National Park •
The Drakensberg
② Cape Town • Kirstenbosch Botanical Gardens •
The Cape Winelands • Hermanus

Two Weeks Cape Town • Kirstenbosch Botanical Gardens •
The Cape Winelands • Hermanus • Cape Town •
Johannesburg • Pretoria • Kruger National Park •
The Drakensberg

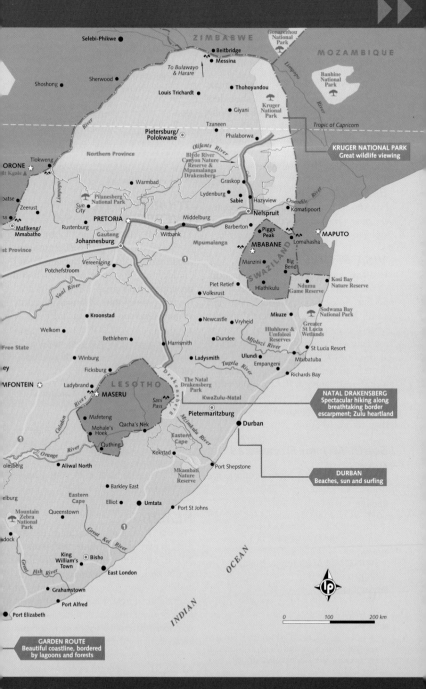

ZIMBABWE

MOZAMBIQUE

Selebi-Phikwe

Beitbridge
Messina

To Bulawayo
& Harare

Sherwood

Gonarezhou
National Park

Banhine
National Park

Limpopo River

Shoshong

Thohoyandou

Louis Trichardt

Giyani

ORONE
Tlokweng

Tzaneen

Pietersburg/
Polokwane

Olifants River

Phalaborwa

Kruger
National
Park

Tropic of Capricorn

t Kgale

oatse

Northern Province

Blyde River
Canyon Nature
Reserve &
Mpumalanga
Drakensberg

Graskop

KRUGER NATIONAL PARK
Great wildlife viewing

Zeerust

Warmbad

Lydenburg

Sabie

Hazyview

Komatipoort

Crocodile River

MAPUTO

na

Mafikeng/
Mmabatho

Pilanesberg
National Park

Sun City

Middelburg

Nelspruit

Barberton

Piggs
Peak

Lomahasha

t Province

Rustenburg

PRETORIA

Witbank

MBABANE

st Province

Gauteng

Mpumalanga

Manzini

Big
Bend

Johannesburg

Potchefstroom

Vereeniging

Piet Retief

Volksrust

Hlathikulu

Ndumu
Game Reserve

Kosi Bay
Nature Reserve

Vaal River

Kroonstad

Newcastle

Vryheid

Mkuze

Sodwana Bay
National Park

Welkom

Free State

Winburg

Bethlehem

Dundee

Hluhluwe &
Umfolozi
Reserves

Mfolozi River

Greater
St Lucia
Wetlands

St Lucia Resort

Harrismith

Ladysmith

Ulundi

Empangeni

Mtubatuba

ey

Ficksburg

LESOTHO

MASERU

Tugela River

Richards Bay

MFONTEIN

Ladybrand

Sani
Pass

Drakensberg

The Natal
Drakensberg
Park

KwaZulu-Natal

NATAL DRAKENSBERG
Spectacular hiking along
breathtaking border
escarpment; Zulu heartland

Caledon River

Mafeteng

Qacha's Nek

Pietermaritzburg

Durban

olesberg

Orange River

Mohale's
Hoek

Quthing

Eastern
Cape

Kokstad

Mkomazi River

DURBAN
Beaches, sun and surfing

Aliwal North

Port Shepstone

Barkley East

Mkambati
Nature
Reserve

elburg

Mountain
Zebra
National Park

Eastern
Cape

Elliot

Umtata

Port St Johns

adock

Queenstown

Great Kei River

King
William's
Town

Bisho

Grey Fish River

East London

Grahamstown

Port Alfred

Port Elizabeth

INDIAN OCEAN

LP

0   100   200 km

GARDEN ROUTE
Beautiful coastline, bordered
by lagoons and forests

e Month   1 Johannesburg • Pretoria • Kruger National Park • The
Drakensberg • Cape Town • Mossel Bay • Plettenberg Bay •
Tsitsikamma Coastal National Park • Port Elizabeth •
Bloemfontein • Johannesburg • Eastern Cape Province •
Durban • Greater St Lucia Wetlands

2 Cape Town • Upington • Springbok • Kalahari
Gemsbok National Park

Urban

Among South Africa's urban areas, Cape Town stands head and shoulders above the rest, and is undoubtedly one of the most attractive cities in the world. The surrounding area – including the Cape Winelands around historic Paarl and Stellenbosch – is also beautiful.

Beaches

For sun and surfing, the best beaches are near Durban. North of Durban is Zululand, home of the Zulu people.

VISA REQUIREMENTS

Visas are not required by most visitors – you will be issued with an entry permit on arrival. Although you are entitled to 90 days, officials usually write the date of your flight home as the date of expiry. Visas are not issued at the border, so if you do need one, get it (free) before departing for Africa. You'll need to request a multiple-entry visa if you plan on going to a neighbouring country (such as Lesotho) and then return to South Africa.

South African Embassies

Australia
(☎ 02-6273 2424; fax 6273 2669) Rhodes Place, Yarralumla, ACT 2600

Canada
(☎ 613-744-0330; fax 744-8287) 15 Sussex Drive, Ottawa, Ontario K1M 1M8. Consulate: Toronto

Malawi
(☎ 09265-73 3722) Impco Building, City Centre, Lilongwe 3

Mozambique
(☎ 01-490059) 745 Avenida Julius Nyerere, Maputo

Namibia
(☎ 061-229765; fax 224140) RSA House, cnr Jan Jonker St and Nelson Mandela Dr, Klein Windhoek, Windhoek, PO Box 23100

UK
(☎ 020-7930 4488; fax 7839 1419) South Africa House, Trafalgar Sq, London WC2N 5DP

USA
(☎ 202-232-4400; fax 265-1607) 3051 Massachusetts Ave NW, Washington, DC 20008. Consulate: Los Angeles

Zimbabwe
(☎ 04-75 3147) Temple Bar House, Baker Ave, Harare

TOURIST OFFICES OVERSEAS

The South African Tourist Corporation (Satour) is the main government tourism organisation (www.africa.com/satour/index.htm). It produces many useful brochures and maps, mostly geared towards short-stay, relatively wealthy visitors. Overseas offices include:

Australia
(☎ 02-9261 3424; fax 9261 3414) Level 6, 285 Clarence St, Sydney NSW 2000

UK
(☎ 020-8944 8080; fax 8944 6705) 5-6 Alt Grove, Wimbledon, London SW19 4DZ

USA
(☎ 212-730-2929, 800-822-5368; fax 212-764-1980) 500 Fifth Ave, 20th floor, New York, NY 10110;
(☎ 310-641-8444, 800-782-9772; fax 310-641-5812) Suite 1524, 9841 Airport Blvd, Los Angeles, CA 90045

HEALTH

Malaria is mainly confined to the eastern part of the country and parts of North-West Province. Schistosomiasis is also present, mainly in South Africa's eastern region. Avoid swimming or bathing in all freshwater. Take care with what you eat and drink. Hikers should take extra care with water supplies and avoid drinking directly from streams.

Medical care is excellent in South Africa. If you require serious medical care, Cape Town and Johannesburg have the best facilities.

POST & COMMUNICATIONS

South Africa's postal service is good and rates are generally cheaper than in Europe and the USA.

International direct dial telephone calls can be made without problem to most parts of the world. Rates are between US$2 and US$4 per minute to the USA/Europe/Australia. Reverse charge (collect) calls are possible, as are 'Dial Direct' numbers which put you through to an operator in your home country (including Australia, New Zealand, the UK and the USA).

Internet and email access is possible in all major cities.

MONEY
Costs

While South Africa is not as inexpensive as many less developed African countries, it is very good value by European, US and Australian standards – due in large part to the collapse in the value of the rand.

Budget travellers who camp or stay in hostels and self-cater can get by on about US$15 to US$20 per day, although travel costs (other than hitching) will increase this amount considerably as public transport can be expensive. Mid-range travel, especially in popular destinations, is not as good value. Plan on about US$40 to US$60 per day. Top-end hotels and sit-down meals will cost from US$100 per day.

Changing Money

Cash and travellers cheques in major currencies can be easily changed at banks in all major cities and towns.

Travellers cheques generally attract a commission of about 1%. There is no black market.

Credit cards, especially Visa and MasterCard, are widely accepted. There are an increasing number of ATMs which give cash advances; many are part of the worldwide Cirrus network.

ONLINE SERVICES

Lonely Planet has a web site Destination South Africa (www.lonely planet.com/dest/afr/saf.htm).

South Africa Online (www.south africa.co.za) has everything from news to travel and sports.

Welcome to South Africa (www .southafrica.net) is the Washington embassy's helpful site.

For South African news try the Independent Online (www.inc.co.za) or the Electronic Mail & Guardian (www.mg.co.za/mg).

To see press statements and policy documents or even write to President Mbeki try the ANC Home Page (www.anc.org.za).

Mike Gregory's Just Backpacking – South Africa includes hostel links and is good for outdoor enthusiasts (www .backpacking.co.za/index.html).

Doorway (www.doorway.co.za) has listings of accommodation and transport companies.

For information on the parks try the South African National Parks Board (http://africa.com/~venture/saparks /npbhome.htm).

BOOKS & FILMS

If you only have time to read one book before travelling to South Africa, it should be *Long Road to Freedom*, Nelson Mandela's auto-biography. Mandela's other works include *The Struggle is My Life* and *Nelson Mandela Speaks*, collections of his writings and speeches.

For a history of the African National Congress (ANC) read *South Africa Belongs to Us* by Francis Meli.

The Mind of South Africa by Allister Sparks is the best introduction to white South African history. Sparks' more recent book, *Tomorrow is Another Country*, is the inside story of the Convention for a Democratic South Africa (CODESA) negotiations.

My Traitor's Heart by Rian Malan is an excellent autobiography of an Afrikaner attempting to come to grips with his heritage and his future.

Nadine Gordimer is South Africa's most lauded fiction writer. She won the Booker Prize in 1974, and the Nobel Prize for Literature in 1991. Her many novels, in which she explores South Africa, its people and their interaction, include *The Lying Days*, *The Conservationist* and *July's People*.

JM Coetzee is another contemporary writer who has received international acclaim. His book *The Life & Times of Michael K* won the 1983 Booker Prize.

Indaba My Children is a book of folk tales, history, legends, customs and beliefs, collected and told by Vusamazulu Credo Mutwa.

Among the many films set in South Africa, one of the best known is the 1951 *Cry the Beloved Country* (with a 1995 remake), based on the famous novel by Alan Paton portraying life under apartheid. *A Good Man in Africa* (1994), based on the William Boyd novel of the same name, is another well known film.

Mandela (1996) is a documentary chronicling the life of Nelson Mandela.

ENTERING & LEAVING SOUTH AFRICA

South Africa is well connected by air with Europe, Asia and other parts of Africa. Most major European airlines fly to Johannesburg, with many flights continuing on to Cape Town. Asian airlines serving Johannesburg include Air India, Cathay Pacific, Malaysia Airlines, Singapore Airlines and Thai Airways. South African Airways has direct flights connecting Johannesburg with New York, Miami and Washington, DC.

To Botswana, the main border posts are at Ramatlhabama, north of Mafikeng, and Tlokweng, north of Zeerust. There are direct buses between Johannesburg and Gaborone and minibus taxis from Mafikeng to Lobatse and Gaborone.

To Mozambique, there are direct buses connecting both Johannesburg and Durban with Maputo. There is also a train three times weekly between Johannesburg and Maputo. Many travellers cross into Mozambique from Swaziland.

To Namibia, there are posts at Rietfontein and Vioolsdrif. Direct buses connect both Cape Town and Johannesburg with Windhoek. There is also indirect service between Pretoria and Windhoek via Upington. Crossing into Namibia from the Kalahari Gemsbok National Park is not allowed.

To Zimbabwe, the only road border post is at Beitbridge (north of Messina) on the Limpopo River. Buses ply the route from Johannesburg to Bulawayo twice-weekly. There are also many buses which connect Johannesburg with Harare. Train service between the two countries was indefinitely cancelled in 1997.

To Swaziland, the best way is via direct bus between Johannesburg and Mbabane. Minibus taxis also do this route.

To Lesotho, there are numerous border posts. Most of those along Lesotho's southern and eastern borders involve very rough roads. The Sani Pass only be negotiated with 4WD coming from South Africa into Lesotho (although a conventional car is OK for the journey from Lesotho into South Africa). Most travellers use the border crossing at Maseru Bridge. The road is well travelled (including by direct minibus taxis from Johannesburg to Maseru) and in good condition.

SWAZILAND

Swaziland, one of the smallest countries in the southern hemisphere, is a pleasant and easy-going place and well worth visiting if you are in the region. Outside of the capital, the country is rural and dotted with small villages. Getting around is easy, and there are attractions enough to keep you busy for a while, including some good national parks.

WHEN TO GO

Swaziland can be visited at any time of year, although some areas – especially the north-east – get hot during summer. Most rain falls between November and March, usually in torrential thunderstorms and mostly in the western mountains. The two most important Swazi cultural ceremonies, the Umhlanga (Reed) Dance and the Incwala ceremony, are held in August or September and late December or

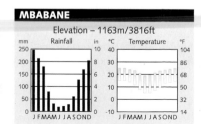

MBABANE

Elevation – 1163m/3816ft

early January, respectively (see Special Events in the Planning chapter).

HIGHLIGHTS
Hiking

Mkhaya Game Reserve (known for its black and white rhino) and Hlane Royal National Park (lions) are both good for hiking. Milwane Wildlife Sanctuary is one of the few places where you can see wildlife on foot, from a bicycle or on horseback. There is also good hiking in Malolotja Nature Reserve in the north-west.

Throughout Swaziland there are generations-old footpaths, which offer the best way to see the country.

Rafting & Royalty

For outdoor fans, there is white-water rafting on the Great Usutu River. The Ezulwini Valley – which begins just outside Mbabane and extends down past Lobamba village, 18km away – is Swaziland's royal heartland. It's here (at Lobamba) that you'll find the palace and parliament.

VISA REQUIREMENTS

Most visitors don't require a visa, with a few major exceptions including

---

At a Glance

Full Country Name: The Kingdom of Swaziland
Area: 17,365 sq km
Population: approximately one million
Capital City: Mbabane (population 50,000)
People: Swazi (about 90%), Zulu, Tsonga-Shangaan and European
Languages: English and siSwati
Religions: Zion Apostolic Church (almost 50%) and traditional religion
Government: Parliamentary monarchy
Currency: Swazi lilangeni (E)
Time Zone: Two hours ahead of GMT/UTC
International Telephone Code: 268
Electricity: 220/230V, 50 Hz; most sockets take plugs with three-point pins

SWAZILAND HIGHLIGHTS & ITINERARIES

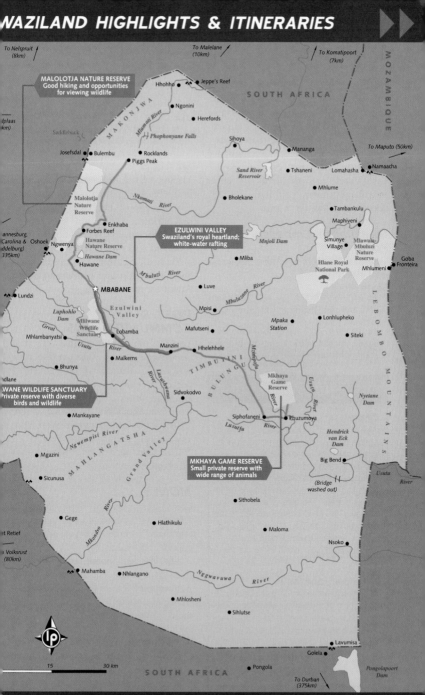

To Nelspruit (8km)
To Malelane (10km)
To Komatipoort (7km)

MOZAMBIQUE

MALOLOTJA NATURE RESERVE
Good hiking and opportunities for viewing wildlife

SOUTH AFRICA

Hhohho
Jeppe's Reef
Ngonini
Herefords
MAKONJWA
Mlumati River
Phophonyane Falls
Sihoya
Mananga
To Maputo (50km)
Josefsdal • Bulembu
Rocklands
Piggs Peak
Sand River Reservoir
Tshaneni
Lomahasha
Namaacha
Mhlume
Bholekane
Tambankulu
Maphiveni
Malolotja Nature Reserve
Nkomati River
Simunye Village
Mlawula-Mbuluzi Nature Reserve
Goba Fronteira
Enkhaba
Forbes Reef
EZULWINI VALLEY
Swaziland's royal heartland; white-water rafting
Mnjoli Dam
Hlane Royal National Park
Mhlumeni
Hawane Nature Reserve
Hawane Dam
Hawane
Mbuluzi River
Mliba
Oshoek
Ngwenya
★ MBABANE
Luve
Mbulucane River
Lundzi
Ezulwini Valley
Luphohlo Dam
Mpisi
Mpaka Station
Lonhlupheko
Siteki
Milwane Wildlife Sanctuary
Lobamba
Mafutseni
Mhlambanyatsi
Great Usutu River
Manzini
Hhelehhele
Bhunya
Malkerns
Mbuluzi
LEBOMBO MOUNTAINS
MLILWANE WILDLIFE SANCTUARY
Private reserve with diverse birds and wildlife
TIMBUTINI BULUNGU
Mkhaya Game Reserve
Usutu River
Nyetane Dam
Mankayane
Sidvokodvo
Lusushwana River
Siphofaneni
Phuzumoya
Hendrick van Eck Dam
Mgazini
MAHLANGATSHA
Ngwempisi River
Grand Valley
Lusutfu River
MKHAYA GAME RESERVE
Small private reserve with wide range of animals
Big Bend
(Bridge washed out)
Usutu River
Sicunusa
Gege
Hlathikulu
Sithobela
Maloma
Mkondvo River
Nsoko
Mahamba
Nhlangano
Nggwavuma River
Mhlosheni
Sihlutse
Lavumisa
Golela
SOUTH AFRICA
Pongola
To Durban (375km)
Pongolapoort Dam

15   30 km

Austrian, French, Swiss and German citizens. However, citizens of these and other EU countries can get free visas at the border or the airport. Anyone staying for more than 60 days must apply for a temporary residence permit in Mbabane. No vaccination certificates are required to enter Swaziland, unless you have recently been in a yellow fever area

Swaziland's Embassies

Canada
(☎ 613-567-1480) 130 Albert St, Ottawa, Ontario K1P 5G4

South Africa
(☎ 012-342 5782/4; fax 342 5682) Suite 105, Infotech Building, 1090 Arcadia St, Arcadia, Pretoria 0083;
(☎ 011-29 9776/7; fax 29 9763) Swaziland Trade Attache, 165 Jeppe St, PO Box 8030, Johannesburg 2000

Itineraries

One Week
With a week, you'll have plenty of time to explore the Ezulwini Valley, including visits to Lobamba, Mlilwane Wildlife Sanctuary, and a day rafting on the Great Usutu River. There are numerous campgrounds, caravan parks and hotels in the area that you could use as a base. The area is also ideal for shopping for handcrafts. With any extra time, you could head for Mbabane for a day to look around. The market at Manzini is recommended; you should try to get there at dawn.

More than One Week
With more than one week, you'll be able to cover most of the country, including a visit to Mkhaya Game Reserve, some hiking in Malolotja Nature Reserve, and a visit to Piggs Peak – a small town in Swaziland's scenic north-western corner with some good handcrafts.

UK
(☎ 020-7630 6611) 20 Buckingham Gate, London SW1E 6LB

USA
(☎ 202-362-6683/4) 3400 International Dr NW, Suite 3M, Washington, DC 20008

HEALTH
Malaria is a risk in Swaziland, especially in the Big Bend, Mhulme, Simunye and Tsanei regions; take the appropriate precautions. Food and waterborne diseases occur, so pay attention to basic food and water hygiene.

Medical treatment is limited in Swaziland. Consider heading to South Africa for treatment of serious illness.

POST & COMMUNICATIONS
You can make international calls (but not reverse charge calls) at the post office in Mbabane between 8 am and 4 pm on weekdays and until noon on Saturday. International calls to and from Swaziland are expensive. There are no area codes within Swaziland. The country code is 268.

Internet access is possible at Mbabane.

MONEY
Costs are similar to those in South Africa, with food a little cheaper. Swaziland's game reserves are particularly good value.

The lilangeni (plural, emalangeni) is fixed at a value equal to the South African rand. Rands are accepted everywhere and there is no need to change them, although many places will not accept South African coins. Several banks change travellers cheques. There are also a number of automatic teller machines (ATMs) which accept some (but not all) credit cards.

ENTERING & LEAVING SWAZILAND

Royal Swazi Airlines flies between Matsapha international airport north of Manzini to Johannesburg (South Africa), Maputo (Mozambique), Harare (Zimbabwe), Lusaka (Zambia), Dar es Salaam (Tanzania) and Nairobi (Kenya). Lesotho Airways links Swaziland with Maseru (Lesotho).

Swaziland's border posts are all with South Africa, with the exception of the Lomahasha/Namaacha border post in the extreme north-east, which is the entry point to Mozambique. Crossing points into South Africa include Lavumisa in the south, Lundzi in the west and Jeppe's Reef in the north. There is bus service linking Mbabane with Maputo and Johannesburg. Buses also link Johannesburg with Manzini and Hlathikulu. You can also travel between Johannesburg and Mbabane via minibus taxi, changing at the border.

TANZANIA

Tanzania is East Africa's largest country, and one of its most diverse, being home to more than 100 different ethnic groups, as well as some of the largest wildlife herds on the continent. It also has some of Africa's most spectacular topography, including the Great Rift Valley, Mt Kilimanjaro (the continent's highest peak at 5895m) and the vast Serengeti plains. Offshore are idyllic islands with beautiful palm-fringed beaches and Zanzibar, East Africa's most exotic Swahili city-state. Topping it off are the Tanzanians themselves, who are known throughout the region for their warmth and openness.

For travellers – apart from long distances and an inadequate transport infrastructure – Tanzania is one of the easier places on the continent to negotiate, and is rapidly becoming East Africa's top travel destination.

WHEN TO GO

The best time to visit Tanzania is between late June and October when the rains have finished and the air is coolest. However, this is also when hotels and park lodges are full and air

At a Glance

Full Country Name: United Republic of Tanzania

Area: 943,000 sq km (including the Zanzibar Archipelago)

Population: 31 million

Capital City: Dar es Salaam (population 2.5 million)

People: About 120 tribal groups, including Sukuma (about 13%), Nyamwezi, Makonde, Haya and Chagga

Languages: Swahili and English (official), Sukuma, Makonde, Haya, Ha, Gogo and Yao

Religions: Christian (45%), Muslim (40%) and traditional religions

Government: Multiparty republic

Currency: Tanzanian shilling (Tsh)

Time Zone: Three hours ahead of GMT/UTC

International Telephone Code: 255

Electricity: 220V, 50 AC; sockets vary but usually take plugs with three square pins (as in the UK) or two round pins (as in Europe)

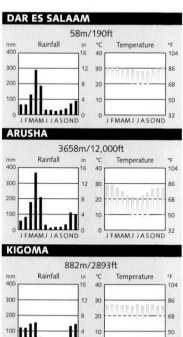

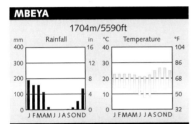

MBEYA

1704m/5590ft

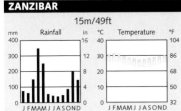

ZANZIBAR

15m/49ft

fares most expensive. The second best time is from late December to February or early March, just after the short rains and before the long rains, though temperatures are higher.

HIGHLIGHTS
Trekking

Highlights for outdoor enthusiasts include trekking on Mt Kilimanjaro, Mt Meru, or in the beautiful Crater Highlands, hiking around Tukuyu near Lake Nyasa (Lake Malawi) or in the beautiful Usambara and Pare mountain ranges. For something off the beaten track, try exploring the relatively unknown Udzungwa Mountains National Park, which is accessible only on foot.

Beaches & Diving

For more relaxing pastimes head to the beaches. Among the best are those in the Zanzibar Archipelago, which also boasts the old Stone Town on Unguja Island, and offers some superb diving and snorkelling.

Itineraries

One Week
Assuming that you will be arriving in Dar es Salaam, spend a day or two in the capital getting oriented, followed by a night at Mikumi National Park and the remainder of the week on Unguja, dividing your time between Zanzibar Town and one of the beaches.

Two Weeks
With two weeks, you could expand this base, staying longer on Unguja and adding a few days hiking in the Usambaras or visiting the Selous Game Reserve or Ruaha National Park. Travellers seeking a more rugged adventure can replace this with a few days in Udzungwa Mountains National Park.

Alternatively, you could head from Dar es Salaam towards Moshi and Arusha, spending a day or two walking in the villages around Marangu at the base of Mt Kilimanjaro and several days visiting one of the northern parks or the Ngorongoro Crater before heading to Unguja.

One Month
With a month or more, you will have time to bring some of Tanzania's more distant attractions into the itinerary. One option would be a leisurely trip through the Southern Highlands, which stretch south and west from Morogoro. Possible stops along the way include Iringa (one of the major towns in the region), Ruaha National Park, the Uluguru Mountains, Mbeya (the major town in southwestern Tanzania) and Tukuyu.

From Mbeya you could continue on to Malawi or Zambia. Alternatively, you could head north-west towards Katavi National Park and then (from the nearby town of Mpanda) take the Central Line train back to Dar es Salaam, finishing the trip with some time on the Zanzibar Archipelago – although to do this you will need closer to five weeks.

If you do have more than a month, you might consider a visit to Lake Tanganyika or Lake Victoria, each of which is scenic and provides opportunities for relaxation.

TANZANIA HIGHLIGHTS & ITINERARIES

INDIAN OCEAN

Mafia Island

Kilindoni

Kibiti

Mohoro

Nangurukuru

Kilwa Kivinje

Kilwa Masoko

Mchinga

Lindi

Mingoyo

Mtwara

Mikindani

Quionga

Palma

Mocímboa da Praia

Pemba

To Nampula

Mueda

SOUTH-EASTERN TANZANIA
Remote area with beautiful beaches and the rugged Selous Game Reserve

Masasi

Newala

Nachingwea

Masuguru

Montepuez

Ruvuma River

Liwale

Selous Game Reserve

Mangula

Rufiji River

Mkumi National Park

Mkumi

Ifakara

Lupiro

Mahenge

Malinyi

Ilonga

Iringa

Makumbako

Taveta

Msembe

Ruaha National Park

Great Ruaha River

Kungwa Game Reserve

Rungwa

Kipembawe

Chunya

Tunduru

Songea

Njombe

Mbamba Bay

Liuli

Lichinga

Metangula

To Maputo

MOZAMBIQUE

UDZUNGWA MOUNTAINS NATIONAL PARK
Adventurous hiking, accessible only on foot

Udzungwa Mountains National Park

Livingstone Mountains

Lake

Matema

Itungi

Songwe River Bridge

Karonga

Nyika NP

Livingstonia

Nkhata Bay

Mzuzu

M A L A W I

To Lilongwe

To Blantyre

To Lilongwe

Lake Malawi

Mbeya

Tukuyu

SOUTHERN HIGHLANDS
Pleasant climate, striking scenery and colourful markets

Shiwa Ngandu

Mpika

North Luangwa NP

South Luangwa NP

Mtuwe

Luangwa River

To Lusaka

Kanona

To Kapiri Mposhi

Z A M B I A

Tunduma

Kasama

Mbala

WESTERN TANZANIA
Historical towns, relaxing Lake Tanganyika and three national parks

Sumbawanga

Namanyere

Uwanda Game Reserve

Lake Rukwa

Kipembawe

Nkamba

Rukwa River

Katavi National Park

Moba

Kapona

Chiengi

Mweru Wantipa NP

Lusenga Plain National Park

Lake Mweru

Mansa

C O N G O (Z A I R E)

Lake Tanganyika

Mpulungu

0   100   200 km

Wildlife

Wildlife fans have an array of choices. Tanzania's spectacular national parks include the vast Serengeti and tiny but beautiful Arusha in the north, relaxing Rubondo Island in Lake Victoria, remote Mahale Mountains in the far south-west, and the rugged Ruaha National Park near Iringa. In the south-east is the magnificent Selous, Africa's largest game reserve.

Scenery & Markets

To get to know Tanzania's colourful cultures away from major tourist areas, one of the best regions is the Southern Highlands with its abundant markets and diverse ethnic mix. Tanzania's remote south-eastern corner is ideal for the more adventurous, with a spectacular shoreline, a wealth of history and striking savanna panoramas.

VISA REQUIREMENTS

Visas are required by most visitors to Tanzania except nationals of some Commonwealth countries; Canadian and British citizens do require visas. Visas are usually issued for a maximum of three months, although length of stay is determined at the border, and one month is the norm.

It's best to obtain a visa before arrival, or they are usually issued at Dar es Salaam, Kilimanjaro and Zanzibar airports, and at the Kenyan border post of Namanga.

Proof of yellow fever vaccination is also required.

Tanzanian Embassies

Canada
(☎ 613-232-1500; fax 232-5184) 50 Range Rd, Ottawa, Ontario K1N 8J4

Kenya
(☎ 02-331056; fax 218269) Continental House, cnr Uhuru Hwy and Harambee Ave, Nairobi

Mozambique
(☎ 258-1-490110) Ujamaa House, PO Box 4515, Maputo

South Africa
(☎ 012-323 9041, 342 4393; fax 323 9042) PO Box 56572, Arcadia 0007, Pretoria

Uganda
(☎ 256-41-256292, 256272; fax 242890) 6 Kagera Rd, PO Box 5750, Kampala

UK
(☎ 020-7499 8951; fax 7491 9321) 43 Hertford St, London W1Y 8DB

USA
(☎ 202-939-6125; fax 797-7408) 2139 R St NW, Washington, DC 20008

Zambia
(☎ 260-1-253320, 227698) Ujamaa House, 5200 United Nations Ave, Lusaka

TOURIST OFFICES OVERSEAS

In the UK, the Tanzania Tourist Board is represented by the Tanzania Trade Centre (☎ 020-7407 0566; fax 7403 2003; email director@tanzatrade.co .uk), 80 Borough High St, London SE1 1LL. In other countries, it is represented by Tanzanian embassies and high commissions. Also check the web sites listed under Online Services.

HEALTH

As in other East African countries, malaria occurs throughout the country. For more information on precautions against this serious disease and other general health matters, see the main health chapter earlier in this book.

Food and water-borne diseases occur here, so pay particular attention to basic food and water hygiene.

Trekkers to Mt Kilimanjaro, Mt Meru and other high-altitude areas should be prepared for cold conditions and be aware of the symptoms and treatment of altitude sickness.

Medical facilities are generally limited. If you require medical care, try and get to Dar Es Salaam, or better still, Nairobi in Kenya.

POST & COMMUNICATIONS

The post is reliable and relatively efficient. Rates for international air mail are comparable to those in Europe and the USA. There is poste restante service in Dar es Salaam and most major towns.

International telephone calls can be made without difficulty from Tanzania Telecom offices in all larger towns, although outside major centres the exchange is often unreliable. Rates are expensive, starting at about US$4 per minute. There are also private tele-communications centres in the capital and most larger towns which are more expensive, but generally more efficient. When dialling from hotels, expect to pay at least double the Tanzania Telecom rates.

Internet access is possible in Dar es Salaam and major towns.

MONEY
Costs

Staying only in budget accom-modation, eating local food and travelling via public transport, you should have no trouble keeping costs to about US$15 to US$20 per day or less (not including safaris or other organised activities). In contrast, organised tours and tourist-class hotels can be very pricey – costs can easily exceed US$200 per person per day on an organised safari. Travellers

seeking a degree of comfort and western-style meals in pleasant surroundings should plan on spending between US$20 and US$60 per day for lodging, and between US$10 and US$15 for a full-course meal.

Changing Money

Cash and travellers cheques can be easily changed at banks or foreign exchange (forex) shops in all major towns and cities; rates and commissions vary, so it pays to shop around. Exchange rates for travellers cheques are generally slightly lower than for cash. Most smaller towns do not have forex shops; your only option is the bank, which will often change cash only. US dollars are the most convenient foreign currency, although other major currencies are accepted in larger towns. There is essentially no black market for foreign currency.

Credit cards are accepted by many top-end hotels, some tour operators and increasingly by mid-range establishments. However, most places charge a commission of 5% to 15%. Cash advances against Visa or MasterCard are possible in Dar es Salaam, Arusha and Zanzibar Town.

ONLINE SERVICES

Lonely Planet has a web site Des-tination Tanzania (www.lonelyplanet .com/dest/afr/tan.htm).

The tourist bureau has a web site, Tan-zania (www.tanzania-web.com/home2 .htm).

For information on Tanzanian wildlife, check Serengeti National Park (www.gorp.com/gorp/location/africa /tanzania/ser_intr.htm) and Tarangire National Park (www.gorp.com/gorp /location/africa/tanzania/tar_intr.htm).

To brush up on your Swahili, use the Swahili Online Dictionary (www.yale.edu/swahili).

The Zanzibar Travel Network's Zanzibar (www.zanzibar.net) is good for those heading to the archipelago.

Moja (www.moja.com) has East African news.

BOOKS & FILMS

Tanzania's most significant 20th century author is Shabaan Robert. Among his best known works is the autobiographical *Maisha yangu* (in Swahili).

Peter Palangyo is a well known contemporary Tanzanian author of English-language works. His novel *Dying in the Sun* tells the story of a young Tanzanian who, after questioning his existence, comes to terms with his family and his heritage in rural Tanzania.

William Kamera has authored several collections of poetry, as well as *Tales of the Wairaqw of Tanzania*, containing stories of the Iraqw people.

North of South: An African Journey by Shiva Naipaul chronicles the author's trip through Tanzania and several other African countries in the 1970s.

The very readable *Memoirs of an Arabian Princess* by Emily Said-Ruete is the autobiography of a Zanzibari princess who eloped with a German to Europe. In recalling her early life, Said-Ruete paints an intriguing historical portrait of Unguja in the days of the sultans.

Through a Window by Jane Goodall is a vivid portrayal of the author's research and life with the chimpanzees of Gombe Stream National Park, while *African Voices, African Lives* by Patricia Caplan focuses on village life on Mafia Island.

Tanzania's tiny indigenous film industry received a boost in 1998 with the opening of the first annual Zanzibar International Film Festival, which premiered *Maangamizi*, shot in Tanzania and co-directed by Tanzanian Martin M'Hando. Another M'Hando film is *Women of Hope* (1986).

Numerous documentaries of Tanzania's wildlife have been shot on location, including *Africa: The Serengeti* (1994), filmed in both Tanzania and Kenya, and focusing on the annual wildebeest migration.

ENTERING & LEAVING TANZANIA

Regional and international carriers servicing Tanzania include Air India, Air Tanzania, Air Zimbabwe, British Airways, EgyptAir, Ethiopian Airlines, Gulf Air, Kenya Airways, KLM and Swissair. Most of these, as well as Air France, Lufthansa and others, also fly to Nairobi, from where there are daily connections to Dar es Salaam.

The main overland route between Tanzania and Kenya is the tarmac road connecting Arusha and Nairobi via Namanga (the border post). You have a choice of bus, share taxi or (most popular) minibus shuttle. Daily buses connect both Dar es Salaam and Tanga with Mombasa via Horohoro (north of Tanga). There is also transport connecting Moshi and Arusha with Mombasa several times a week. Other routes into Kenya are via Taveta, east of Moshi, via Bologonya in the northern Serengeti (although there is no public transport on this route), and via Isebania, north-east of Musoma. Despite the railway lines you may see drawn on maps, there is presently no train service between

Tanzania and Kenya. A weekly ferry connects Dar es Salaam, Unguja and Tanga with Mombasa.

To Malawi, the only crossing is at the Songwe River bridge, south-east of Mbeya. Direct buses run between Mbeya and Mzuzu (Malawi) and Lilongwe. This trip can also be done in stages via minibus and on foot. There are also occasional direct minibuses between Mbeya and the border, where you can get Malawian transport, and there is a direct bus service connecting Dar es Salaam and Lilongwe. Remember that there is no Tanzanian embassy in Malawi, and visas are not issued at the border. As an alternative to road travel, you can take the ferry between Mbamba Bay and Nkhata Bay (Malawi).

To Mozambique, the main crossing is at Kilambo, south of Mtwara. The trip must be done in stages via pick-up, dugout canoe (across the Rovuma) and on foot. Allow plenty of time; during the rainy season the border is effectively closed. There is another border post further west, just south of Masuguru, but this puts you 150km away from Mueda, the nearest town in Mozambique. Some travellers go between Mozambique and Tanzania by local *dhow* (an East African boat), although these are notoriously unsafe and can take several days.

To Rwanda, the main crossing is at Rusumu Falls, south-west of Bukoba. The trip must be done in stages, changing vehicles at the border. Be sure to get an update on the political situation in Rwanda before heading this way.

To Uganda, the most commonly used post is at Mutukula, north-west of Bukoba. There is also a crossing at Nkurunga, to the west of Mutukula, but the road is bad and little transport passes this way. Direct buses link Dar es Salaam and Kampala (Uganda) via Nairobi. There is also a direct bus several times weekly between Bukoba and Kampala.

To Zambia, the main crossing is at Tunduma, south-west of Mbeya. A direct bus connects Dar es Salaam and Lusaka twice-weekly. There are also buses between Mbeya and Lusaka, and minibuses between Mbeya and Tunduma, where you can change to Zambian transport. Tanzania is also linked with Zambia via the TAZARA rail line which runs several times weekly between Dar es Salaam and Kapiri Mposhi. Kigoma is also connected with Mpulungu (Zambia) via a weekly ferry on Lake Tanganyika.

The border between Tanzania and Burundi is officially closed, and there is no regular passenger service between Tanzania and Congo (Zaïre).

TOGO

For many years, Togo was one of West Africa's hot spots for travellers. Deserted beaches, trekking and butterfly spotting in the highlands, a fascinating cultural mix and generally enthusiastic and friendly people all made the country an overlander's goal. Then, political turbulence in the early 1990s, together with improving situations in neighbouring Ghana and Benin, reduced the stream of travellers to a trickle.

Fortunately, the tide seems to be turning, with the establishment of a fragile political stability and a surge in economic growth. Despite an entrenched and oppressive government autocracy, Togo is a lively place, especially once you get outside Lomé.

Although the country still doesn't see as many travellers as it did before, its compact size and friendly people make it popular among those who do come.

WHEN TO GO
The best time to visit is in the dry season between December and February, before temperatures become too warm. During the main rainy season from April to July, secondary roads can become very muddy.

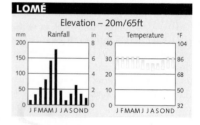

At a Glance

Full Country Name: Republic of Togo
Area: 56,600 sq km
Population: 4.6 million
Capital City: Lomé (population 600,000)
People: About 30 tribal groups, the largest of which are the Ewé in the south and the Kabyé in the north.
Languages: French (official), Ewé, Kabyé and Mina (widely used in commerce)
Religions: Animism (more 50%), Christian (about 25%) and Muslim
Government: Republic
Currency: West African CFA franc (CFA)
Time Zone: GMT/UTC
International Telephone Code: 228
Electricity: 220V, 50 Hz; sockets take plugs with two round pins as in e as Europe pins, as in Europe

HIGHLIGHTS
Culture
Togo's main attractions are its interesting culture and scenic landscapes, which offer good possibilities for outdoor enthusiasts. To immerse yourself in the culture, one of the best places to start is around Lac Togo, where there are many colourful market towns. This area is also the centre of Togo's voodoo cult; the famous Friday market at Vogan, on the north-eastern lakeshore, has a fascinating voodoo section. Another good place is Atakpamé, once a favoured hill station of German colonial administrators. It is from here that Togo's famous stilt dancers originate.

Trekking

Trekkers should head for Kpalimé, where there are many possibilities for good walks in the surrounding hills, as well as trips into the forest at Klouto, 10km north-east of Kpalimé, to see the masses of colourful butterflies. Another relaxing and scenic destination is Kara, in the north of the country. Still further north is the Vallée de Tamberma, with its unique collection of fortified villages founded in the 17th century by people fleeing the slaving forays of the kings of Abomey. As the valley remained isolated until recent times, the local culture is relatively intact. The best way to visit these villages is by bicycle or on foot.

Beaches

For beaches, try Aného (the former colonial capital) east of Lomé. There is a pleasant lagoon dividing the town.

VISA REQUIREMENTS

Visas are required for all except nationals of Economic Community of West African States (ECOWAS) countries. They are rarely issued at the airport. However, 48-hour temporary visas are generally available on land entry through Aflao on the Ghanaian-Togo border near Lomé.

Visas can be issued for up to three months. It is best to request the maximum time you may need, as extensions in Lomé take at least three days to process.

Proof of yellow fever vaccination is obligatory for entry at the airport, but is not generally required at land crossings.

Togolese Embassies

Canada
  (☎ 613-238-5914/5917; fax 235-6425) 12 Chemin Range, Ottawa, Ontario K1N HJ3

Ghana
  (☎ 777950) Togo House, Cantonments Rd, 1km north of Danquah Circle, Accra

USA
  (☎ 202-234-4212) 2208 Massachusetts Ave NW, Washington, DC 20008

TOURIST OFFICES OVERSEAS

Togo has no overseas tourist offices but embassies and travel agencies should be able to supply you with most of what you need. Also check the web sites listed under Online Services.

HEALTH

Malaria exists year-round in Togo, so you should take precautions against this serious disease.

Dysentery, hepatitis and typhoid are all food or water-borne diseases which occur in Togo; stick to treated water and hot, freshly cooked food wherever possible. See the main health chapter earlier in this book for more information on general health matters.

As health care throughout most of Togo is basic, consider flying home if you require serious medical attention.

POST & COMMUNICATIONS

The post is generally reliable for letters, but not parcels. Rates for international mail are about the same or somewhat more than in the west. Poste restante in Lomé will hold mail for one month.

International telephone calls can be made easily in Lomé at the telecommunications building behind the main post office. Direct dial using a card phone is also possible. Making calls from outside the capital is more difficult, but not impossible. International calls cost between US$3 and US$5 per minute.

Internet access is possible in Lomé.

MONEY

Costs

Accommodation in Togo is among the least expensive in West Africa – finding a room for under US$5 is not difficult. For between US$10 and US$15, you'll get a spacious hotel room with bathroom and fan. Top-end hotels with swimming pools and other amenities can be found in Lomé, on Lac Togo (Agebodrafo) and in Kara, and will cost from US$50. Local food is also inexpensive, and budget travellers will be able to keep their daily food budgets to US$5 or less. For dining in western-style restaurants, plan on about US$10 or more per meal.

Overall, expect to spend about US$10 per day for budget travel, US$20 to US$35 for mid-range travel, and from US$60 for top-end accommodation and meals in Lomé.

Changing Money

Cash and travellers cheques can be easily exchanged at banks in Lomé and major towns. French franc or US dollar denominations are best. Proof of purchase is generally required for travellers cheques.

It may be possible to withdraw cash against a Visa card in Lomé, but it is best not to count on this.

ONLINE SERVICES

Lonely Planet has a web site Destination Togo (www.lonelyplanet.com /dest/afr/tog.htm).

Republic of Togo (www.republicof togo.com) is the official web site, with news and more.

Griot in Kansas (http://hometown .aol.com/Dzrekpo/griotinks2.html) is by a Peace Corps volunteer who worked in Togo.

BOOKS & FILMS

The *Historical Dictionary of Togo* by Samuel Decalo is a hefty but interesting compendium of the country's history, culture, politics and development.

If you can get your hands on a copy, Allan Wolsey Cardinal's *Tales Told in Togoland* contains a cornucopia of African myths and legends. Would-be literary anthropologists will want to

---

Itineraries

One Week
After a day or two in Lomé, head for Lac Togo, where you can spend the remainder of the week visiting nearby villages such as Togoville and Vogan, and the beach at Aného.

Two Weeks
With two weeks, in addition to the above, you can head to Atakpamé for a day or two, with a possible excursion to see the Cascades d'Akloa near the town of Badou (west of Atakpamé). Finish up with a few days hiking around Kpalimé.

One Month
A month will be more than enough time to explore Togo. After visiting Lomé and Lac Togo, head to Kpalimé and then on to Atakpamé. From here, continue north to Kara, with stops in Sokodé (Togo's second largest city) and the nearby Parc National de Fazao-Malfakassa in the beautiful Malfakassa mountains.

Using Kara as a base, you can spend a day or two cycling around the Vallée de Tamberma in the far north. Sansanné-Mango and Dapaong are worth brief stops, as is Parc National de la Kéran, although you are unlikely to see many animals. To finish, you could either head out of Togo into Burkina Faso, Benin or Ghana, or return to Lomé.

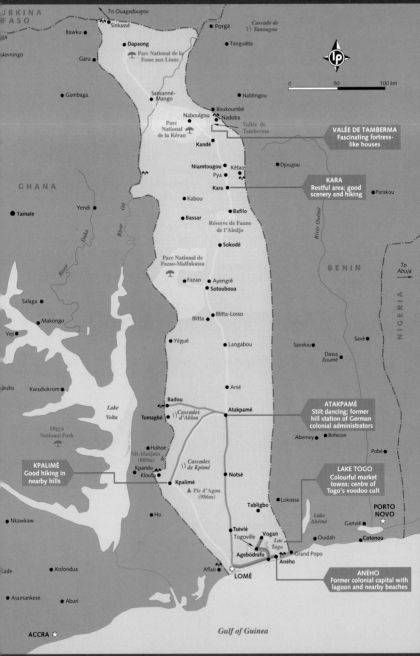

OGO HIGHLIGHTS & ITINERARIES

VALÉE DE TAMBERMA
Fascinating fortress-like houses

KARA
Restful area; good scenery and hiking

ATAKPAMÉ
Stilt dancing; former hill station of German colonial administrators

LAKE TOGO
Colourful market towns; centre of Togo's voodoo cult

KPALIMÉ
Good hiking in nearby hills

ANÉHO
Former colonial capital with lagoon and nearby beaches

BURKINA FASO

GHANA

BENIN

NIGERIA

To Ouagadougou
Sinkassé
Bawku
Porga
Cascade de Tanougou
Dapaong
Tanguiéta
Garu
Parc National de la Fosse aux Lions
Navrongo
Gambaga
Sansanné-Mango
Natitingou
Boukoumbé
Nadoba
Naboulgou
Vallée de Tamberma
Parc National de la Kéran
Kandé
Niamtougou
Kétao
Djougou
Pya
Kara
Parakou
Kabou
Bafilo
Tamale
Yendi
Bassar
Réserve de Faune de l'Aledjo
Sokodé
Parc National de Fazao-Malfakassa
Fazao
Ayengré
Sotouboua
Salaga
Makongo
Blitta
Blitta-Losso
Yeji
Yégué
Langabou
Savalou
Savé
Dassa Zoumé
Kwadiokrom
Badou
Anié
Lake Volta
Cascades d'Akloa
Tomagbé
Atakpamé
Digya National Park
Abomey
Bohicon
Pobè
Hohoe
Mt Afadjato (885m)
Kpandu
Cascades de Kpimé
Kloufo
Notsé
Lokossa
Nkawkaw
Kpalimé
Pic d'Agou (986m)
Tabligbo
Lake Ahémé
PORTO NOVO
Ho
Ganvié
Tsévié
Vogan
Togoville
Lac Togo
Ouidah
Koforidua
Agbodráfo
Grand Popo
Cotonou
Aflao
LOMÉ
Aného
Asamankese
Aburi

ACCRA

Gulf of Guinea

River Oti
River Daka
River Mono
River Oualé

To Abuja

0   50   100 km

pick up *Ewé Comic Heroes: Trickster Tales in Togo* by Zinta Konrad, which includes the Ewé and English versions of 30 traditional stories.

George Packer's experiences as a Peace Corps volunteer in Togo in the early 1980s are chronicled in *The Village of Waiting*.

An African in Greenland is the most famous book by Togo's most famous author, Tété-Michel Kpomassie, giving the author's outlook on Arctic life.

The Birds of Togo: An Annotated Check-List by Robert A Cheke & J Frank Walsh will be of interest to birdwatchers.

Togo's film industry is insignificant. Two films to come out of the country are *Bawina* (1985) and *Kovami* (1972).

ENTERING & LEAVING TOGO

Airlines servicing Lomé include Air France, Corsair, KLM, Aeroflot, Ghana Airways and Air Afrique.

To Benin, minibuses ply the coastal road between Lomé and Cotonou throughout the day. The trip can also be made in stages via share taxi. Other crossings are near Kétao, north-east of Kara, and at Nadoba in Vallée de Tamberma, but transport on these routes is infrequent.

To Burkina Faso, there are direct minibuses between Lomé and Ouagadougou, but it is more comfortable and slightly cheaper to do the trip in stages.

The most popular route to Ghana is via Aflao on the coastal road. There are direct minibuses between Lomé and Accra, or the trip can be done in stages by share taxi. There are also several vehicles a day from Kpalimé to the border, from where you can catch onward transport to Kpandu and Accra. Other crossings are via Badou to Hohoe and Yendi, from Kara or Sansanné-Mango to Tamale via Yendi, and from Dapaong via Sinkanse to Bawku. These routes are sparsely travelled.

TUNISIA

Tunisia, the smallest of the three Maghreb states, has a rich cultural and social heritage stemming from the many empires that have come and gone in this area – from the Phoenicians to the Romans, Byzantines, Arabs, Ottoman Turks and the French. While little remains of ancient Carthage, there are some magnificent Roman ruins, plus impressive Islamic architecture.

Apart from its archaeological treasures, Tunisia's major drawcard is its beaches, which entice millions of sun-starved northern Europeans to its shores every year. Another attraction for travellers is the opportunity to explore the world's greatest desert, the Sahara, which covers the southern tip of the country.

WHEN TO GO

The best time to visit is between mid-March and mid-May when the days are pleasantly warm and the countryside at its prettiest after the winter rains. During July and August – the main tourist season for Europeans – hotel prices go up, rooms can be hard to find, and it's often too hot for serious activity during much of the day.

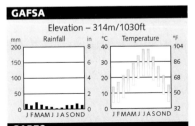

GAFSA

Elevation – 314m/1030ft

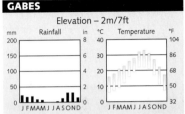

GABES

Elevation – 2m/7ft

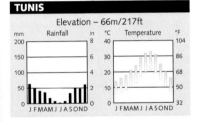

TUNIS

Elevation – 66m/217ft

At a Glance

Full Country Name: Republic of Tunisia

Area: 164,150 sq km

Population: 9.4 million

Capital City: Tunis (population 1.5 million)

People: Arab-Berber (about 98%), Europeans and Jews

Languages: Arabic, French, plus a few English speakers outside the main tourist centres

Religions: Predominantly Muslim, plus small Jewish and Roman Catholic communities

Government: Republic

Currency: Tunisian dinar (TD)

Time Zone: One hour ahead of GMT/UTC

International Telephone Code: 216

Electricity: 220V, 50 Hz, although the occasional hotel in Tunis and some of the smaller towns in the south are still on 110V – check before plugging in any appliance; sockets take plugs with two round pins

Winter is wet and dreary in the north, but it is the best time to see the migratory birds at Lake Ichkeul. It's also the perfect time to visit the Saharan south.

HIGHLIGHTS
Beaches

Beaches are the major attraction most tourists come to Tunisia. The best ones are in the north around

Itineraries

One Week

Assuming you arrive in Tunis, spend a few days in and near the capital, including two days at Carthage. Then catch a bus to Dougga, site of the best preserved Roman ruins in the country. After exploring the site, continue to the ancient fortress town of Le Kef before heading on to the regional centre of Jendouba, from where you can visit the ruins at Bulla Regia.

Continue to the attractive hill station of 'Ain Draham, and then travel slowly up to the small resort town of Tabarka on the coast. Spend a day relaxing on the beach here before returning to Tunis.

Two Weeks

With two weeks you will have time to see some of central Tunisia as well. Following about three days in Tunis and Carthage, catch the train north to the port town of Bizerte, with its interesting architecture.

From here, travel west along the north coast to Tabarka and then on to 'Ain Draham and Bulla Regia. Continue via Jendouba to Le Kef. After exploring Le Kef, head to Dougga, then travel south-east to Kairouan (one of Islam's holiest cities), stopping at Makthar to visit the ruins of ancient Mactaris on the way.

Continue eastward to Sousse, with its huge *medina* (Arab section of town) and interesting museum. From Sousse, head north along the coast to the town of Nabeul, a good base for side trips to Kelibia (known for its ancient fort) and El-Haouaria, a quiet town with some beaches and Roman caves.

One Month

In addition to the two week itinerary outlined above, you will have plenty of time to work in visits to some other attractions. When you reach Kairouan, head south-west to Sbeitla, the site

of the ancient town of Sufetula, famous for its remarkably well preserved Roman temples.

Then, continue on to Gafsa, an uninspiring place but the starting point for rides on the Lezard Rouge train through the spectacular Seldja Gorge. Continue south-west to the interesting town of Tozeur, one of the most popular travellers' destinations in Tunisia thanks to its extremly attractive setting, labyrinthine old quarter and excellent museum.

After visiting Tozeur, you can make side trips to the nearby mountain oases of Chebika, Midès and Tamerza before heading across the Chott el-Jerid salt lake towards Douz, a small town on the edge of the Sahara from where you can organise a few days of camel trekking.

If you are craving some company after the sparseness of the desert, continue to Matmata, a small village which seems to attract more tourist buses than anywhere else in Tunisia. From Matmata, head to the small village of Metameur, where you can stay overnight in a 13th century ksar (plural ksour, a fortified Berber stronghold used for storing grain).

Continue south to Tataouine, from where you can visit several other ksour in the surrounding area, including the impressive Ksar Ouled Soltane. Then head north to the town of Houmt Souq on the island of Jerba, one of Tunisia's most popular tourist destinations, with a superb climate and an interesting history.

After a couple of days on Jerba, continue up the coast to Sfax, Tunisia's second largest city with an unspoiled old medina which was used in the film The English Patient. From Sfax, make your way to the coastal town of Mahdia, and then on to Sousse via the ancient coliseum of El-Jem, one of the most impressive Roman monuments in Africa. Wind up your journey by returning to Tunis.

NISIA HIGHLIGHTS & ITINERARIES

MEDITERRANEAN SEA

BIZERTE & CAP FARINA
Attractive beaches

TUNIS
Laid-back capital, base for exploring Carthage, site of Roman ruins and museum

DOUGGA
an ruins - Capitol ougga and theatre

TOZEUR
Oasis town with labyrinthine old quarter and fine museum

HOUMT SOUQ
Popular tourist destination with superb climate and interesting history

DOUZ
Camel trekking in the Sahara desert

Cap Serrat
Cap Blanc
Bizerte
Sidi Ali el-Mekki
Cap Farina
Lake Ichkeul
Utica
Gulf of Tunis
Cap Bon
El-Haouaria
Kerkouane
Tabarka
Mateur
Carthage
Kelibia
Skikda
Annaba
Mountains
TUNIS
Hammam Lif
Tebersouk
Ain Draham
Beja
Oued Medjerda
Bulla Regia
Nabeul
Jendouba
Mountains
Hammamet
Ghardimao
Thuburbo Majus
Hammamet
Guelma
Kroumirie
Tebersouk
El-Fahs
Zaghouan
Gulf of Hammamet
antine
Souq Ahras
Dougga
Siliana
Le Kef
Jugurtha's Table
Sousse
Monastir
Ain-Beida
Kalaat Khasba
Makthar
Mactaris
Kairouan
Haidra
Raqqada
Tébessa
Jebel Chambi (1544m)
Sufetula
Mahdia
El-Jem
ALGERIA
Kasserine
Sbeitla
Sfax
Kerkennah Islands
Seldja Gorge
Meknassy
Midès
Tamerza
Gafsa
Jebel Biada (1163m)
MEDITERRANEAN SEA
Chebika
Metlaoui
Chott el-Gharsa
Chott el-Fejej
Gulf of Gabès
Houmt Souq
Nefta
Tozeur
Gabès
Jerba
Kebili
Matmata
Ajim
Jorf
Gightis
Zarzis
Chott el-Jerid
Douz
Ras Ajdir
Zaafrane
Metameur
Medenine
Ben Guerdane
ed
Ghomrassen
Jebel Dahar
Tataouine
Zuara
Ksar Ghilane
Nouvelle Chenini
To Tripoli
Grand Erg Oriental
Remada
ALGERIA
Nalut
LIBYA
Rebaa
Borj el-Khadra
0   50   100 km
Ghadhames

Tabarka and Bizerte and at Sidi Ali el-Mekki.

Archaeology
The country's other big attraction is its history, and archaeology enthusiasts will not want to miss exploring the ruins of Roman Carthage, El-Jem, Dougga and Bulla Regia. The old Berber granaries at Tataouine are also well worth a visit.

Oasis Town
For a taste of life in modern Tunisia, take a stroll through the delightful old quarter of the oasis town of Tozeur. Against a backdrop of desert dunes, this laid-back town has colourful shops with extensive displays of rugs.

Camel Trekking
Camel trekking in the Sahara desert around Douz is an experience not to be missed. Go for three or four days to get a real taste of desert adventure.

VISA REQUIREMENTS
Nationals of most western European countries can stay for up to three months in Tunisia without a visa. Americans, Canadians, Germans and Japanese can stay for up to four months. Australians and New Zealanders travelling independently can get a two week visa at the airport on arrival at a nominal cost, although some travellers have reported being given a month. South Africans can stay one month.

Travellers wanting to stay beyond these limits should get a three month visa before they arrive; these are available wherever Tunisia has diplomatic representation. Israeli nationals are not allowed into the country.

Tunisian Embassies
Australia
(☎ 02-9363 5588) GPO Box 801, Double Bay, NSW 2028 (honorary consulate)

Canada
(☎ 613-237-0330/2) 515 O'Connor St, Ottawa, Ontario K1S 3P8

UK
(☎ 020-7584 8117) 29 Prince's Gate, London SW7 1QG

USA
(☎ 202-862-1850) 1515 Massachusetts Ave NW, Washington, DC 20005

TOURIST OFFICES OVERSEAS
The government-run Office National du Tourisme Tunisien (ONTT) handles tourist information. It has a network of offices throughout Tunisia as well as overseas (some addresses are listed below). Some addresses are listed below. In places without ONTT offices, Tunisian embassies will be able to provide information. Also check out the web sites listed under Online Services.

Canada
(☎ 514-397-1182) 1253 McGill College, Montreal, Quebec H3A 3B6

UK
(☎ 020-7224 5561; fax 7224 4053) 77A Wigmore St, London W1H GLJ

HEALTH
Food and waterborne diseases occur in Tunisia, so pay particular attention to basic food and water hygiene. The extreme heat can pose some health problems; take care to avoid sunburn and dehydration. Watch out for snakes, especially in the south, and avoid bites from any animal, in order to prevent rabies.

Medical facilities are poor throughout most of Tunisia. Consider going home if you require extensive medical care.

POST & COMMUNICATIONS

The Tunisian postal service is slow, but inexpensive and reliable. Poste restante services are available at any post office in the country, and are also reliable.

The Tunisian telephone system is modern and efficient. Public telephones known as Taxiphones are everywhere, and usually work. Making international calls is straightforward and rates average between US$1 and US$2 per minute. Almost all public phones are equipped for international direct dialling.

There are no public places yet where you can send or receive email.

MONEY
Costs

Tunisia is a cheap country to travel in. It's usually possible to find a clean room for about US$5 per person, main meals in local restaurants seldom cost more than US$3, and transport is inexpensive. If you are fighting to keep costs down, you can get by on between US$15 and US$20 per day. You will have more fun with a budget of about US$25 to US$30 per day, and can be quite lavish for US$50.

Changing Money

All major currencies are readily exchangeable, but Australian and NZ dollars and South African rand are not accepted. Exchange rates are regulated, so the rate is the same everywhere. Banks charge a standard commission per travellers cheque. Post offices will change cash only. There is no black market.

Credit cards (particularly MasterCard and Visa) are widely accepted in major towns and tourist areas. They can also be used to draw Tunisian dinars from the ATMs of affiliated Tunisian banks.

ONLINE SERVICES

Lonely Planet has a web site Destination Tunisia (www.lonelyplanet.com/dest/afr/tun.htm).

Focus on Tunisia (www.focusmm.com/tunisia/tn_anamn.htm) has everything from an introduction to Tunisian music to a primer on the national cuisine.

At Tunisia Online (www.tunisiaonline.com) you can read the local papers in French and Arabic, plus link up with Radio Tunis.

Travel & Tourism Guide to Tunisia (www.tourismtunisia.com) is the web site of the ONTT.

For some good photographs of the country check Postcard from Tunisia (www.harlon.demon.co.uk/tpcard/index.html).

BOOKS & FILMS

Salammbô by Gustave Flaubert is a historical epic set at the time of the mercenaries' rebellion against Carthage in the 3rd century BC.

A rather more recent work is *The Pillars of Hercules* by Paul Theroux, which contains a chapter on Tunisia.

For insights into the Arab psyche, read *The Arabs* by Peter Mansfield, which includes a section on Tunisia.

Few Tunisian writers have been translated into English. One who has and whose work is available internationally is Mustapha Tlili, whose novel *Lion Mountain* tells the story of the disasters wrought upon a remote village by progress and tourism.

Sleepless Nights by Ali Duaji is a collection of short stories and sketches about life in and around Tunis during the first half of the 20th century.

Tunisia has a busy film industry, but few locally produced films make it beyond the Arab world. The best known director is Ali Laâbidi, who is known particularly for his films *Halfouine*, *The Silence of the Palace* and *Redeyef 54*. Tunis hosts the biennial Carthage International Film Festival in October of even-numbered years.

Besides its own film industry, Tunisia has long been a popular spot for international film-makers. Films made or set in the country include *The English Patient*, Monty Python's *The Life of Brian* and *Star Wars*.

ENTERING & LEAVING TUNISIA

Most tourists arrive by air. The main airports for international flights are Tunis-Carthage, Monastir and Jerba. A few flights also go into Tozeur and Tabarka. Tunis Air, the national airline, flies to a range of destinations in Europe, the Middle East and North Africa, but there are no direct flights between Tunisia and North America, Asia or Oceania. Other airlines serving Tunisia are Air France, British Airways, Lufthansa and Royal Air Maroc.

Overland travel between Tunisia and Algeria is currently restricted due to the security situation in Algeria. The road between Tunis and Tripoli (Libya) via Ras Ajdir is well travelled, although obtaining a tourist visa to Libya can be almost impossible for independent travellers. The best approach is to go through one of the tour companies specialising in trips to Libya.

Crossing into Tunisia by ferry from France or Italy is a popular option. There are year-round ferry connections between Tunis and Trapani (Sicily) and Genoa, and summer connections between Tunis and Naples, as well as year-round services between Marseilles (France) and Tunis.

UGANDA

During the dark days of Idi Amin and the various civil wars that followed his rule, Uganda was restricted for travel. But the long years of terror ended in the late 1980s, and the country reopened to visitors. While the level of comfort may not be as high as elsewhere in the region, Uganda offers beautiful scenery and friendly people, and is well worth visiting.

In the light of insecurity resulting from the activities of antigovernment rebel forces in the north, west and south-west of the country you should be sure to get an update on the situation before planning travel in these areas.

WHEN TO GO

The best time to visit Uganda is from the end of May to early October, when the weather is dry and cool, and from late November to February, when it is

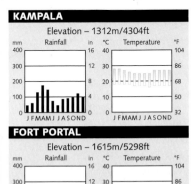

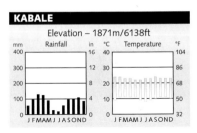

still dry, although warmer. If you are planning to visit the Rwenzori Mountains, note that they are wet, even in the dry season.

HIGHLIGHTS
Scenery & Trekking

Uganda's striking scenery is one of its major attractions. Good places to

At a Glance

Full Country Name: Republic of Uganda
Area: 236,580 sq km
Population: 22.5 million
Capital City: Kampala (population 774,000)
People: Baganda (about 20%), Lango, Acholi, Teso, Karamojong, Maasai and Pygmies (in the forests of the west)
Languages: English (official), Luganda and Swahili
Religions: Christian (about 66%), traditional religions and Muslim
Government: Republic
Currency: Ugandan shilling (USh)
Time Zone: Three hours ahead of GMT/UTC
International Telephone Code: 256
Electricity: 220V, 50 Hz; most sockets take plugs with three square pins, as in the UK, although some older buildings may have round-pin sockets

appreciate this are at Murchison Falls on the Victoria Nile River, on the mellow Ssese islands in Lake Victoria, and while trekking in the rugged Rwenzori mountains in the west of the country.

Another good trekking area is Mt Elgon (4321m), the second largest crater in the world.

Itineraries

Be sure to get an update on the security situation in Uganda before setting off. Many of Uganda's attractions are in the south-west, where travel is presently restricted. You should make careful inquiries about security in this area before embarking on the One Month itinerary.

One Week
After spending a day or two in Kampala, take a ferry to the Ssese islands, where you can spend a few more days relaxing and enjoying the unhurried pace. Head back to the mainland for a visit to the bustling market town of Jinja with its many old Asian-style buildings. Return to Kampala or continue out of the country into Kenya.

Two Weeks
With two weeks, you can spend close to a week trekking on Mt Elgon. From here, make your way back to Kampala via Jinja, and then relax for a few days on the Ssese islands. If you have time, head north to Murchison Falls National Park to see the magnificent falls on the Victoria Nile River and perhaps some of the fishing villages on Lake Albert.

One Month
Following the Murchison Falls option in the two weeks itinerary, and assuming you receive reassuring reports on security in the south-west, you could continue south to Kibale National Park (or Rwenzori Mountains National Park), and then to Bwindi National Park. Either return to Kampala or – if security improves and you are adventurous – continue south into Rwanda.

Rainforest Gorillas

Visiting the mountain gorillas deep in the rainforest of Bwindi National Park can be an unforgettable experience, although this area is presently restricted following the murder of eight foreign tourists by an insurgent group in March 1999. Another big attraction is the chimpanzees at Kibale National Park near Fort Portal.

VISA REQUIREMENTS

Visas are not needed by citizens of most countries including European Union members, several other European and Scandinavian countries, Israel, Japan, the USA, plus Australia, New Zealand, Canada and most other Commonwealth countries. If your own country is not on this list, one to three-month tourist visas are easily available from Ugandan embassies.

A yellow fever vaccination certificate is required to enter Uganda. Officials at the airport in Kampala are especially vigilant in checking these, so make sure yours is in order.

Ugandan Embassies

Canada
(☎ 613-233-7797; fax 232-6689) 231 Cobourg St, Ottawa, Ontario K1N 8J2

Kenya
(☎ 02-330801; fax 330970) Uganda House, Baring Arcade, 4th floor, Kenyatta Ave, Nairobi

Tanzania
(☎ 051-117646) Extelecoms Building, 7th floor, Samora Ave, Dar es Salaam

UK
(☎ 020-7839 5783; fax 7839 8925) Uganda House, 58/59 Trafalgar Square, London WC2N 5DX

USA
(☎ 202-726-0416; fax 726-1727) 5909 16th St NW, Washington, DC 20011-2896

GANDA HIGHLIGHTS & ITINERARIES

MURCHISON FALLS NATIONAL PARK
Spectacular waterfalls in the Victoria Nile River; boating and hiking

RUWENZORI MOUNTAINS
Challenging, misty trekking conditions on the 'Mountains of the Moon'

KIBALE NATIONAL PARK
Opportunity to view chimpanzees in lush surroundings

MOUNT ELGON NATIONAL PARK
Trekking in huge extinct volcano amongst cliffs, caves, gorges and waterfalls

SSESE ISLANDS
Dozens of tranquil, unspoilt islands; interesting wildlife, beautiful views and scope for fishing

BWINDI NATIONAL PARK
Gorilla viewing at close range in the hidden surroundings of a natural rainforest

ESTED ITINERARIES

Week	Kampala • Ssese Islands • Jinja
Weeks	Kampala • Mt Elgon • Jinja • Kampala • Ssese Islands • Kampala • Murchison Falls National Park

One Month   Kampala • Murchison Falls National Park • Kibale National Park • Ruwenzori Mountains National Park • Bwindi National Park • Kampala

TOURIST OFFICES OVERSEAS

While Uganda does not maintain a separate tourist office, there are tourist information desks attached to some of its embassies. The Uganda Tourist Board in Kampala also has an email address (utb@starcom.com.ug). Check the web sites listed under Online Services.

HEALTH

As in other East African countries, yellow fever can occur in Uganda and malaria occurs throughout the country. Take precautions against these serious diseases. Schistosomiasis is widespread in freshwater rivers, lakes and dams. Avoid bites from all insects, especially mosquitoes, sandflies, flies and ticks, as they can all carry diseases, including trypanosomiasis (sleeping sickness), which occurs mainly in the north-west.

Food and waterborne diseases, including dysentery, hepatitis, typhoid and cholera occur here, so pay particular attention to basic food and water hygiene. Trekkers too should be prepared for cold conditions and be aware of the symptoms and treatment of altitude sickness. To reduce the chance of intestinal worms, watch what you eat, avoid all undercooked meat, and wear shoes whenever possible. Watch out for dog, rats, monkeys and other furry animals, as rabies is present in Uganda.

Medical facilities are generally limited. If you do require serious medical care, go to Kampala or, even better, Nairobi in Kenya.

POST & COMMUNICATIONS

The post is relatively reliable and inexpensive. Poste restante in Kampala is efficient.

International telephone connections are fairly good, though expensive – averaging more than US$6 per minute at public phone boxes. You may be able to get cheaper rates (between US$2 and US$3 per minute) through some private operators in Kampala.

Internet access may now be possible in Kampala.

MONEY
Costs

Although Uganda is one of the more expensive countries in the region, it is still possible to keep your costs to a reasonable level. Budget travellers should expect to pay between US$15 and US$20 per day for basic accommodation and local food. Mid-range comforts will cost from US$25 to US$60, while top-end luxury will cost from US$100 per day. A trip to see the gorillas, and other similar excursions will cost from US$150 per day.

Changing Money

Money can be changed in foreign exchange (forex) bureaux, which offer a better rate than the banks, although many banks also have forex desks. Most towns have a bank and forex bureau. There is no black market. Some banks also issue 'Smart Money' debit cards which are accepted in major tourist hotels, and can be handy if you want to avoid carrying around a large wad of local currency.

ONLINE SERVICES

Lonely Planet has a web site Destination Uganda (www.lonelyplanet.com/dest/afr/uga.htm).

Uganda Tourist Board has a site (www.tomco.net/~jssemwog/utb/utb.htm).

Uganda Pages (www.ugandapages .com) has links to the few sites based in Uganda, including some tour companies.

Project Elgon (www.abdn.ac.uk /elgon) presents a highly detailed environmental and social study of Mt Elgon.

For news, try The Monitor (www .africanews.com/monitor) and for news on wildlife, check African Primates at Home (www.indiana.edu /~primate/primates.html) and Rhino Fund Uganda (www.ugandapages.com /rhino_fund/index.html).

BOOKS

Uganda Since Independence by Phares Mutibwa and *Uganda: Landmarks in Rebuilding a Nation* (various authors) are both useful but fairly dry accounts of the country's recent history.

Uganda – From the Pages of Drum is an interesting compilation of articles which appeared in the now defunct *Drum* magazine. These chronicle the rise of Idi Amin and the atrocities he committed, and President Museveni's bush war and rise to power.

Ian Clarke's *The Man With the Key Has Gone!* is an account of the time spent in the Luwero Triangle district (north of Kampala) by a British doctor and his family.

Fong and the Indians by Paul Theroux is set in a fictional country that bears a remarkable likeness to Uganda.

ENTERING & LEAVING UGANDA

Few travellers enter Uganda by air, preferring to fly into Nairobi where discounted air fares are more readily available. Airlines serving the region include British Airways, KLM, Lufthansa and Swissair. Ethiopian Airlines offers good-value international service in East Africa. Also look out for flights on Alliance Air. For regional flights to Uganda, check Kenya Airways, Uganda Airlines and Air Tanzania.

To Kenya, the main border post is at Malaba, which is linked to Kampala and Nairobi by tar roads. Direct buses run the route. You can also do the trip in stages by bus and minibus. There is a less frequently used border crossing at Busia. There is also a direct train between Kampala and Nairobi weekly.

To Tanzania, there is sporadic transport between Kampala and Bukoba (this trip is usually done in stages). Most travellers take one of the direct buses that connect Kampala with Dar es Salaam via Nairobi. There is no longer a ferry connecting Uganda and Tanzania on Lake Victoria.

To Rwanda, the two main routes are Kabale to Kigali via Gatuna, and Kisoro to Ruhengeri (done in stages). Get an update on the security situation.

Overland routes between Uganda and Congo (Zaïre) and the Sudan are currently restricted due to the security situations in these countries.

ZAMBIA

Zambia can be a challenge for the independent traveller. Distances between major towns are long, getting around by public transport takes persistence (particularly once you get off the main routes) and budget accommodation is limited, especially outside the few tourist centres that do exist. But for many, the challenge of Zambia – as well as its genuinely wild national parks and outstanding scenery – is the main reason for visiting. In the south of the country are the Victoria Falls and the Zambezi River – two of the continent's major highlights.

WHEN TO GO

For wildlife viewing, the best time is August to October, though it can get quite warm during the day. For cooler weather and greener landscapes, visit

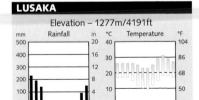

during the cool, dry months from May to August. During the November to April rainy season many rural roads become impassable and many of the national parks are closed, although November and December are the best months for birdwatching.

HIGHLIGHTS
Wilderness & Wildlife

Most travellers come to Zambia to enjoy its superb wilderness areas. One of the best of these is South Luangwa National Park in the east of the country, where you can see lion, buffalo, zebra, elephant and leopard, among others. Walking safaris and night drives are the best way to visit.

The Kafue National Park in the west is another impressive wilderness area. It contains a wide variety of animals and more than 400 species of birds.

Canoeing & Waterfalls

For the chance to watch elephants on the banks and eagles soaring overhead, try canoeing down the Zambezi River.

Away from the animals, Zambia's premier attraction is Victoria Falls, which provides an entirely different experience than its Zimbabwean

At a Glance

Full Country Name: Republic of Zambia
Area: 752,615 sq km
Population: 9.5 million
Capital City: Lusaka (population 1.5 million)
People: About 35 different groups including Bemba, Tonga, Nyanja and Lozi
Languages: English (official), Bemba, Nyanja, Tonga and Lozi
Religions: Christian (more than 50%), Muslim (less than 33%) and traditional beliefs
Government: Republic
Currency: Zambian kwacha (ZK)
Time Zone: Two hours ahead of GMT/UTC
International Telephone Code: 260
Electricity: 220V, 50 Hz; most sockets take plugs with three square pins

counterpart. While the panoramas may not be as spectacular, you can get closer to the water and the atmosphere is more pristine.

Culture

For immersion into Zambian culture, head for Barotseland, centred on the town of Mongu and the traditional kingdom of the Lozi people. It's a fascinating and culturally intact area. A highlight would be the chance to observe the Kuomboka ceremony, held near Mongu in years with good rain fall.

In this ceremony, the Lozi king is transported on the royal barge – a huge wooden canoe painted with black and white stripes – for a journey which takes six hours, while subjects pound away on large war drums. During the journey the king changes from traditional dress into the uniform of a British admiral – a uniform which was presented to King Lewanika by the British king (Edward VII) in 1902.

VISA REQUIREMENTS

All visitors need a visa except citizens of any Commonwealth country or Ireland. The only exception is British citizens who must now have a visa unless they are going to Zambia as part of a fully organised tour. Visas are obtainable from Zambian embassies, or at the Kariba and Victoria Falls border posts (although sometimes only seven-day transit visas are issued here, which must be later extended in Lusaka if you plan to stay longer). The maximum period of validity for a visa is three months.

Zambian Embassies

Botswana
(☎ 351951) Zambia House, The Mall, PO Box 362, Gaborone

Malawi
(☎ 782100/635) Convention Drive, Capital City, Lilongwe

Mozambique
(☎ 492452) 1266 Avenida Kenneth Kaunda, Maputo

Namibia
(☎ 237610; fax 228162) 22 Sam Nujoma Drive, cnr Republic Rd, PO Box 22882, Windhoek

Tanzania
(☎ 118481) 5/9 Sokoine Drive at Ohio St, Dar es Salaam

UK
(☎ 020-7589 6655) 2 Palace Gate, London W8 5NG

USA
(☎ 202-265-9717; fax 332-0826) 2419 Massachusetts Ave NW, Washington, DC 20008

Zimbabwe
(☎ 790851) 6th floor, Zambia House, Union Ave, PO Box 4698, Harare

TOURIST OFFICES OVERSEAS

Zambia has no overseas tourist offices, but embassies and travel agencies will be able to supply you with most information. Also check the web sites listed under Online Services.

HEALTH

Malaria occurs in all parts of Zambia year-round, so take appropriate precautions. Take care with what you eat and drink, as food and waterborne diseases all occur in Zambia.

Medical care is poor; consider leaving for South Africa if you require serious medical treatment.

POST & COMMUNICATIONS

International air mail is surprisingly quick from Lusaka (three to four days to Europe), though a bit more expensive than elsewhere in the region. From elsewhere in Zambia, mail is less reliable and much slower. There is a reliable poste restante service in Lusaka.

International telephone calls can be made from Lusaka and most major towns without hassle, although rates are very expensive – about US$25 for three minutes to Australia or Europe.

Internet access is possible in Lusaka.

MONEY
Costs

For travellers on a tight budget, good inexpensive accommodation is rare. Combined with entrance fees for national parks and the cost of boat or vehicle transfers to places which cannot be reached by public transport, this means that Zambia can be an expensive place to visit.

In general, budget travellers should plan on spending about US$20 to US$25 per day. For mid-range accommodation and perhaps a safari, plan on US$30 to at least US$60. Comfortable travel is available for US$100 per day, though luxury hotels and chartered planes will add significantly to this figure.

Changing Money

Cash and travellers cheques can be changed at banks or foreign exchange

---

Itineraries

One Week
With a week, it would work well to enter Zambia from Zimbabwe at Victoria Falls. From here, head to Lake Kariba for a day or two, and then (via Lusaka) to Lower Zambezi National Park for some canoeing (although it will be tight to fit all three places in within a week).

Two Weeks
With two weeks, you will have time to do justice to the attractions in the one week itinerary. From Lower Zambezi National Park, continue north-eastward to South Luangwa National Park for the remainder of your stay. Continue into Malawi (via Chipata) or return to Lusaka.

One Month
If you enter the country at Livingstone, spend a day or so at the falls before heading to Sesheke, the former capital of Barotseland, and then up to Mongu with possible stops en route at the impressive Ngonye Falls and the dusty but pleasant town of Senanga. Exploring Mongu and the surrounding area can easily occupy close to a week, if not more. Sights to see include the palaces of the Lozi paramount chief at Limulunga and

Lealui, and the small Liuwa Plain National Park to the north.

From Mongu, head to Kafue National Park (depending on your budget and mode of transport you may have to retrace your steps from Mongu back to Livingstone and then to Kafue via Lusaka). After visiting Kafue, head south again via Lusaka to Lake Kariba. After a few days here, continue east to Lower Zambezi National Park for canoeing and game viewing. Continue on to South Luangwa National Park and then exit Zambia into Malawi via Chipata.

Alternatively, from South Luangwa National Park backtrack to Lusaka and then head north via Kapiri Mposhi to Kasanka National Park. Continue north-eastward and exit the country via Nakonde into Tanzania, or head to Mpulungu and take the ferry up Lake Tanganyika to Kigoma (Tanzania).

With any additional time you could add on visits en route to Lake Bangweulu, a fascinating and seldom visited wildlife area north of Kasanka National Park, or (for the well heeled) North Luangwa National Park. Access to both of these places is restricted to fly-in visitors or drivers.

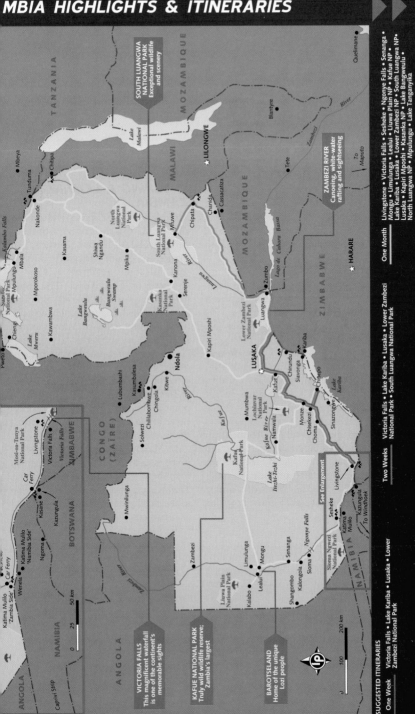

MBIA HIGHLIGHTS & ITINERARIES

SOUTH LUANGWA NATIONAL PARK
Exceptional wildlife and scenery

ZAMBEZI RIVER
Canoeing, white-water rafting and sightseeing

VICTORIA FALLS
This magnificent waterfall is one of the continent's memorable sights

KAFUE NATIONAL PARK
Truly wild wildlife reserve; Zambia's largest

BAROTSELAND
Home of the unique Lozi people

SUGGESTED ITINERARIES

One Week Victoria Falls • Lake Kariba • Lusaka • Lower Zambezi National Park

Two Weeks Victoria Falls • Lake Kariba • Lusaka • Lower Zambezi National Park • South Luangwa National Park

One Month Livingstone • Victoria Falls • Sesheke • Ngonye Falls • Senanga • Mongu • Limulunga • Lealui • Liuwa Plain NP • Kafue NP • Lake Kariba • Lusaka • Lower Zambezi NP • South Luangwa NP • Lusaka • Kapiri Mposhi • Kasanka NP • Lake Bangweulu • North Luangwa NP • Mpulungu • Lake Tanganyika

(forex) bureaux in Lusaka and most large towns. Rates at forex bureaux are generally about 5% better than at banks. There is no real black market. While you may get a few kwacha more on the street, the chances of being robbed or scammed make it not worth the risk.

Credit cards are accepted by some top-end hotels and tour operators in Lusaka, but are not much use outside the capital. It is possible to get a cash advance against a Visa card in Lusaka, although the process can take all day.

ONLINE SERVICES

Lonely Planet has a web site Destination Zambia (www.lonelyplanet .com/dest/afr/zam.htm).

There is an official Zambia site (www.gozambia.com).

Welcome to Zambia (www.africa-in sites.com/zambia/travel/default.htm) has information travel in Zambia, including places to visit, ways to get around, contacts and links.

In addition to some background information, Travel & Tourism in Zambia (www.zamnet.zm/zamnet/zntb .html) has many links to accommodation and safari providers.

For news, try the Times of Zambia (www.zamnet.zm/zamnet/times /times2.html).

BOOKS

Kakuli by Norman Carr is a memoir of a lifetime spent working with animals and people in the South Luangwa National Park.

Delia and Mark Owens have made a name for themselves by relentlessly fighting poachers. Their *Survivors' Song* details their efforts in North Luangwa National Park.

If you're thinking of driving in Zambia or spending some time in the national parks, Chris McIntyre's *Zambia* is a good resource.

North of South: An African Journey by Shiva Naipaul chronicles the author's trip through Zambia, Tanzania and Kenya in the late 1970s.

ENTERING & LEAVING ZAMBIA

Airlines serving Zambia include Air Zimbabwe, British Airways, Ethiopian Airways, KLM, Kenya Airways, Air France and South African Airways, as well as some regional airways in southern or East Africa. The international airport is in Lusaka, although some regional flights use Livingstone (near Victoria Falls) or Mfuwe (South Luangwa National Park).

Zambia shares borders with eight other countries so there are many crossing points.

To Botswana, the only crossing point is the ferry across the Zambezi River at Kazungula, about 60km west of Victoria Falls.

To Malawi, the main border crossing point is east of Chipata, on the main road between Lusaka and Lilongwe. The other possible route, via Chitipa in the north, is rarely used as the road is in bad condition.

To Mozambique, the main route is via Chanida and Cassacatiza, though most travellers prefer to go through Malawi.

To Namibia, the only border crossing point is at the Zambian village of Katima Mulilo, on the west bank of the Zambezi River, near Sesheke. There is a direct bus between Livingstone and Windhoek, and buses between Livingstone and Sesheke via

Kazungula. You will need to cross the Zambezi via ferry.

The main Zambia-Tanzania border crossing point is between Nakonde and Tunduma, used by the Great North Road and the TAZARA railway line. Most travellers take the train, as bus rides can be long and slow, and often involve changing at the border. The train runs several times weekly between Kapiri Mposhi (with connections to Lusaka) and Dar es Salaam (Tanzania). It is also possible to travel by ferry on Lake Tanganyika from Mpulungu to Kigoma (Tanzania).

The main Zambia-Congo (Zaïre) crossing point is between the towns of Chililabombwe and Kasumbalesa on the main road between Ndola and Lubumbashi, though travel is restricted now due to the security situation in Congo (Zaïre).

To Zimbabwe, the main crossing points are at Chirundu, on the main road between Lusaka and Harare (daily buses); at Kariba, about 50km upstream from Chirundu; and at Victoria Falls, which is the crossing used by most travellers, and which offers great views of the falls from the Zambezi Bridge. It is also possible to travel between Livingstone and Victoria Falls by freight train.

ZIMBABWE

Zimbabwe, with its beautiful scenery, friendly people, vibrant musical and artistic traditions and fine national parks, has long been a favourite destination of visitors to southern Africa. Thanks to decent infrastructure, most areas are relatively accessible. Good-value accommodation is an additional plus. Unfortunately, due to recent political violence, enjoyment of these attractions has been put on hold. While principal tourist areas have been largely unaffected, numerous game reserves and lodges around the country have closed and road travel – particularly in rural areas – has been curtailed. If the situation stabilises, Zimbabwe may again become a popular destination. In the meantime, get a thorough update before setting any plans to travel here.

WHEN TO GO

The most comfortable time to visit is during the dry winter months from May to October. Winter is also the best time for wildlife viewing.

National parks and tourist sites can get crowded during the South African school holidays (mid-April to mid-May and mid-July to mid-September) and the Namibian school holidays in December to early January.

HARARE

Elevation – 1473m/4831ft

[Rainfall and temperature chart for Harare, showing months J F M A M J J A S O N D. Rainfall in mm (0–300) and inches (0–12); Temperature in °C (-10–40) and °F (14–104).]

HIGHLIGHTS
Scenery, Wildlife & Hiking

For most visitors, Victoria Falls are the main draw. Other natural attractions include the Eastern Highlands (roughly between Nyanga and Chimanimani), with their lush vegetation and dramatic landscapes, wildlife viewing at Hwange National Park, and bushwalking in rugged Chimanimani National Park.

Ruins & Rock Art

The mysterious ruins of Great Zimbabwe in the country's heartland are

---

At a Glance

Full Country Name: Republic of Zimbabwe

Area: 390,310 sq km

Population: 11.9 million

Capital City: Harare (population 1.5 million)

People: Shona groups including the Ndau, Rozwi, Korekore and Karanga (totalling about 75%), Ndebele (about 18%), Batonka (2%), Shangaan (1%), plus European, Asian and Coloured (totalling 2%)

Languages: English (official), Shona and Ndebele

Religions: Christian (almost 50%) and traditional beliefs

Government: Republic

Currency: Zimbabwe dollar (Z$)

Time Zone: Two hours ahead of GMT/UTC

International Telephone Code: 263

Electricity: 220V, 50 Hz; Zimbabwe has both three-pin rectangular and three-pin round plug sockets

perhaps the most impressive historical site in sub-Saharan Africa, while the Matobo Hills in the heart of Matabele country have one of the greatest concentrations of rock art in the world as well as some rare wildlife species.

VISA REQUIREMENTS

Visas are not required by nationals of Commonwealth countries, members of the European Union, Japan, Norway, Switzerland or the USA. South African citizens can pick up entry cards at the port of entry. Unless you arrive by car, immigration officials at land borders may want to see an onward ticket, although a ticket out of a neighbouring country or even Kenya will usually suffice. The normal length of stay is 90 days, which can be extended to a maximum of six months.

An international health certificate with proof of yellow fever vaccination is required if you're entering from a country where the disease is endemic.

Zimbabwe Embassies

Australia
(☎ 02-6286 2270; fax 290 1680) 11 Culgoa Circuit, O'Malley, ACT 2606

Botswana
(☎ 314495; fax 305863) 1st floor, IGI Building, PO Box 1232, Gaborone

Canada
(☎ 613-237-4388; fax 563-8269) 332 Somerset St West, Ottawa, Ontario K2P 0J9

Kenya
(☎ 02-721071) 6th floor, Minet ICDC Building, Mamlaka Rd, PO Box 30806, Nairobi

Mozambique
(☎ 1-499404; fax 492239) Avenida Kenneth Kaunda 816/820, Caixa Postal 743, Maputo. Consulate: Beira

Namibia
(☎ 061-227738; fax 226859) Gamsberg Building, PO Box 23056, Windhoek

South Africa
(☎ 012-342 5125) 798 Mertons, Arcadia, Pretoria. Consulates: Johannesburg and Cape Town

UK
(☎ 020-7836 7755; fax 7379 1167) Zimbabwe House, 429 The Strand, London WC2R 0SA

USA
(☎ 202-332-7100; fax 438-9326) 1608 New Hampshire Ave NW, Washington, DC 20009

Zambia
(☎ 01-229382; fax 227474) 4th floor, Ulendo House, Cairo Rd, PO Box 33491, Lusaka

TOURIST OFFICES OVERSEAS

Some of Zimbabwe's overseas tourist offices are listed below. Also check the web sites listed under Online Services.

Australia
(☎ 02-9959 4922) Zimbabwe Travel Bureau, Level 7, 75 Miller St, North Sydney, NSW 2060

South Africa
(☎ 011-331 6970) Zimbabwe Tourist Board, Tower Mall, Upper Shopping Level, Carlton Centre, Commissioner St, PO Box 9398, Johannesburg 2001;
(☎ 011-788 1748) Zimbabwe Tourist Board, 2 President Place, Jan Smuts Ave, Rosebank, Johannesburg 2196

UK
(☎ 020-7836 7755; fax 7379 1167) Zimbabwe Tourist Board, Zimbabwe House, 429 The Strand, London WC2R 0SA

USA
(☎ 212-332-1090; fax 332-1093) Zimbabwe Tourism Office, Rockefeller Center, Suite 1905, 1270 Avenue of the Americas, New York, NY 10020

HEALTH

In Harare and Bulawayo the risk of malaria is low, but in most other parts of the country malaria occurs from November until June. In the Zambezi Valley malaria occurs year-round. As dengue fever has been reported in Zimbabwe, you will need to take precautions against both these mosquito-borne diseases. Pay attention to what you eat and drink, as dysentery, typhoid and hepatitis all occur in Zimbabwe. Tap water is generally OK in towns in Zimbabwe, but not water from rivers and bores in rural areas.

Itineraries

Before undertaking these itineraries, get an update on the political situation.

One Week

With a week, you could combine a few days in and around Harare with an excursion to the Eastern Highlands. Attractions here include Nyanga National Park, where you can climb Mt Nyangani (2592m) or do some trekking; Chimanimani National Park, also excellent for hiking; and the scenic Vumba Botanical Reserve.

Alternatively, if you enter the country at Victoria Falls, combine a visit there with a few days canoeing on the Zambezi followed by a short visit to Hwange National Park. Continue south to Bulawayo.

Two Weeks

With two weeks, you could start at Victoria Falls for some canoeing on the Zambezi. Continue south-east to Bulawayo with a stop en route at Hwange National Park. Spend the rest of the time exploring Bulawayo and the surrounding area, including a visit to Matobo National Park if time permits.

One Month

With a month, follow the two week itinerary, then from Bulawayo make your way over to Masvingo and visit the Great Zimbabwe ruins. Continue north-east towards Chimanimani and the Eastern Highlands for several days, or even a week, of trekking. From Mutare (the main town in the Highlands), head to Harare to finish off your trip. If you enter the country at Harare, this itinerary can be done in reverse.

Medical facilities are reasonably good in Zimbabwe. If you do require serious medical care, you should get yourself at least to Harare, or better still to either Johannesburg or Cape Town in South Africa.

POST & COMMUNICATIONS

International postal services are fairly reliable and relatively inexpensive. Poste restante services are available in all major cities and towns but Harare is probably the best and most efficient.

International telephone calls can be made with a minimum of hassle, with coins or phonecards from public phones, or more expensively from private phones. Rates are cheaper when dialling from rural areas rather than from urban centres. In general, calls to Australia, Europe and the USA cost about US$9 for the first three minutes, and US$2 for each subsequent minute.

Internet access is possible in Harare and Victoria Falls.

MONEY
Costs

Hotels, national parks and tour operators employ a two tier (or three tier) pricing system, in which foreigners pay considerably more for goods and services than Zimbabwe residents. However, Zimbabwe is still an inexpensive country for foreigners not frequenting international-class hotels or taking upmarket package safaris.

Budget travellers staying in inexpensive lodging and eating at small local establishments or self-catering can get by on about US$15 per day or less. Mid-range travel will average from US$20 to US$50 per day, while top-end comforts will cost from US$80 to US$150 and up.

ZIMBABWE HIGHLIGHTS & ITINERARIES

NYANGA NATIONAL PARK
A fine example of the lush, beautiful Eastern Highlands

VICTORIA FALLS
Canoeing; spectacular views

HWANGE NATIONAL PARK
Superb wildlife viewing and opportunity for walking trips

MATOBO NATIONAL PARK
Haunting rock formations, ancient San paintings and rare wildlife

GREAT ZIMBABWE
Mysterious ruins; impressive historical site

CHIMANIMANI NATIONAL PARK
Rugged mountain wilderness with excellent bushwalking opportunities

100   200 km

Ndola • | CONGO (ZAIRE) | • Kanona | South Luangwa National Park
Chanida
Kapiri Mposhi • | Cassacatiza
To Tete & Zóbuè

ZAMBIA
MOZAMBIQUE

Kafue National Park

Lake Itezhi-Tezhi

Kafue River

LUSAKA ☆
Lower Zambezi National Park
Kafue River
Lochinvar National Park
Zambezi River
• Zumbo
Lake Cabora Bassa

Zambezi/ Victoria Falls National Park

Mana Pools National Park
• Chirundu
Muzerabani •
Mavuradonha Wilderness

• Kariba
Chisekezi •
Centenary • • Mount Darwin
Nyamapanda
Kotwa

Livingstone
Batoka Gorge

Matusadona National Park
Mvurwi • | Myarwi Range
Hippo Pools
Shamva • • Mutoko

Lake Kariba
Sengwa •
• Siabuwa
Chinhoyi Caves National Park
• Chinhoyi
Lake Chivero
Mt Nyangani (2592m)

azungula (15km) iasane, Caprivi Strip & Vindhoek

Binga •
Chizarira National Park
Lake Chivero Recreational Park
Chitungwiza
HARARE ☆
Nyanga NP
• Nyanga

amatenga

Mlibizi •
• Gokwe
Chegutu •
Kadoma •
Marondera •
Juliasdale
Mtarazi Falls NP

Victoria Falls
• Deka Drum
• Hwange
Sinamatella Camp
Dete •
Main Camp
Gwaai River
Shangani River
Ngezi Recreational Park
• Chivhu
Rusape •
Mutare
Vumba Botanical Reserve
To Chimoio & Beira

Kazuma Pan National Park

Robins Camp

Hwange National Park

akgadikgadi & Nxai Pan National Park

2
Main Camp
• Lupane
Kwe Kwe •
• Mvuma
Wengezi Junction
Chimani-Mani NP

Gwaai River
Shangani •
Somabhula •
• Gweru
• Shurugwi
Lake Mutirikwe
Birchenough Bridge •
• Chimanimani

Rundе River
Masvingo •
Mutirikwe (Kyle) Rec Park
Chipinge •
Mt Selinda

Bulawayo •
Zvishavane •
• Great Zimbabwe National Monument
Chirinda Forest Botanical Reserve

Khami •
Matobo National Park
Mushandike Sanctuary

wetwe Pan

Sua Pan

Plumtree •
• Gwanda
Chiredzi •

Ramokgwebana •
Triangle •

apa •
• Lethlakane
Francistown •
• Rutenga
Gonarezhou National Park

BOTSWANA
Shashe River
• Thuli
Bubi River
MOZAMBIQUE

• Serule
Beitbridge
Selebi-Phikwe
• Baines Drift
Limpopo River
• Messina

ral hari ne rve

Zanzibar
Thohoyandou •
Kruger National Park
Tropic of Capricorn

• Shoshong
• Groblersbrug
SOUTH AFRICA
• Giyani

Limpopo River
Pietersburg/ Polokwane ○
To Johannesburg
• Tzaneen

To Gaborone

Changing Money

Cash and travellers cheques can be easily changed at banks in Harare and all major towns. The best denominations are US dollars and British pounds, although all major international currencies are accepted. Note that no one currently accepts US$100 notes due to rampant counterfeiting. There is no black market. While informal currency exchange exists, it is illegal as well as risky, as it is almost certainly a set-up.

Credit cards are accepted at many establishments catering to tourists and businesspeople. Cash advances against a credit card are possible in Harare and major towns, although you may have to wait a while for authorisation. You can draw cash with a Visa card at some ATMs, but it is best not to rely on this as your main source of money.

ONLINE SERVICES

Lonely Planet has a web site Destination Zimbabwe (www.lonelyplanet .com/dest/afr/zim.htm).

For local news, check the *Zimbabwe Independent*'s site (www.samara.co.zw /zimin).

The Norwegian Council for Africa has a helpful index of links at (www .africaindex.africainfo.no/africaindex1 /countries/zimbabwe.html).

BOOKS & FILMS

Mugabe by Colin Simpson & David Smith is a biography of Robert Mugabe tracing his rise to the office of executive president of Zimbabwe.

The Struggle for Zimbabwe – The Chimurenga War by David Martin & Phyllis Johnson is a popular history of the Second Chimurenga which describes in detail the Zimbabwean perspective of the tragic war that led to the country's independence.

Tsitsi Dangarembga's *Nervous Conditions* is the tale of a young black woman attending a mission school in 1960s Rhodesia.

One of Zimbabwe's first internationally recognised black writers is Charles Mungoshi, whose works include the acclaimed *Coming of the Dry Season*.

Songs to an African Sunset: A Story of Zimbabwe by Sekai Nzenza Shand tells of her childhood in Zimbabwe and her return to the country after spending many years living in the west. The book is part of Lonely Planet's Journeys travel literature series.

Doris Lessing sensitively portrays the country and its people in *The Grass is Singing*, *African Laughter* and other works.

One of the most successful films to come out of Zimbabwe is *Flame*, by British director Ingrid Sinclair. *Jit*, directed by Michael Raeburn, is a romantic comedy about a young man's travels in search of fame, fortune and the woman of his dreams.

Everyone's Child directed by author Tsitsi Dangarembga, Zimbabwe's first female director, is the story of two children who are catapulted into the world of adult responsibility when their family is struck by AIDS.

Neria tells the story of a successful Zimbabwean family who worked their way into the good life in Harare before enduring tragedy.

ENTERING & LEAVING ZIMBABWE

There are frequent air connections between Harare, Johannesburg and other South African cities on Air Zimbabwe, Zimbabwe Express

Airlines, South African Airways and Air Namibia. The cheapest flights between Europe and Harare are with Balkan Airways, which flies via Sofia, but there are also competitively priced flights from London. Qantas flies from Sydney and Perth, Australia, to Harare once a week. North American visitors will probably have to connect through Johannesburg.

To Botswana, the main border crossings are Victoria Falls/Kazungula and Plumtree/Francistown. Buses run between Harare and Gaborone via Bulawayo and Francistown, and from Victoria Falls to Kasane. There is also a daily train from Bulawayo to Gaborone.

To Mozambique, there are direct buses from Harare via Mutare and Chimoio to Beira, and minibuses between Nyamapanda, Tete and Zóbuè.

There is no direct route between Namibia and Zimbabwe. The most straightforward way is between Victoria Falls and the Caprivi Strip via Botswana. Direct buses connect Victoria Falls and Livingstone with Windhoek.

The only border crossing to South Africa is at Beitbridge by road. The train service has been indefinitely cancelled.

Most travellers cross into Zambia at Victoria Falls/Livingstone. There are also crossings at Kariba and Chirundu. Direct buses from Harare to Lusaka take about nine hours.

INTERNET ADDRESSES

AIR FARES
Expedia: www.expedia.msn.com/daily/home/default.hts
Flight Info.Com: www.flifo.com
Travelocity: www.travelocity.com

AIRLINES
Air New Zealand: www.airnz.com
Alitalia: www.alitalia.com/english/index.html
American Airlines: www.americanair.com
Ansett Australia: www.ansett.com.au
British Airways: www.british-airways.com
Canadian Airlines: www.cdnair.ca
Cathay Pacific: www.cathaypacific.com/index.html
Continental Airlines: www.flycontinental.com
International Association of Air Travel Couriers (IAATC):
  www.courier.org/index.html
Lauda Air: www.laudaair.com
Lufthansa: www.lufthansa.com
Qantas: www.qantas.com
Singapore Airlines: www.newasia-singapore.com; www.singaporeair.com
United Airlines: www.ual.com
Virgin: www.fly.virgin.com

CAR & MOTORCYCLE
American Automobile Association: www.aaa.com/vacation/idp.html
Australian Automobile Association: www.aaa.asn.au
British Automobile Association: www.theaa.co.uk/membership/offers/idp.html
Canadian Automobile Association:
  www.caa.ca/CAAInternet/travelservices/frames14.htm
New Zealand Automobile Association: www.aa.org.nz

EMAIL ACCOUNTS
eKno: www.ekno.lonelyplanet.com
Internet Cafe Guide: www.netcafeguide.com
Opening Accounts: www.yahoo.com; www.hotmail.com

FILM & RADIO

BBC World Service: www.bbc.co.uk/worldservice

Internet Movie Database: www.imdb.com

Radio America: www.voa.gov

Radio Australia: www.abc.net.au/ra

HEALTH

African Medical & Research Foundation: www.amref.org

Altitude Sickness: www.princeton.edu/~oa/altitude.html;
www.gorge.net/hamg/AMS.html

American Society of Tropical Medicine & Hygiene: www.astmh.org

British Airways Travel Clinics:
www.britishairways.com/travelqa/fyi/health/health.html

CDC (US Centers for Disease Control & Prevention):
www.cdc.gov/travel/travel.html

Emergency & Wilderness Medicine: www.gorge.net/hamg/AMS.html

Health Canada: www.hc-sc.gc.ca/hpb/lcdc/osh

International Association for Medical Assistance to Travellers (Canada):
www.sentex.net

The International Planned Parenthood Federation: www.ippf.org

International Society of Travel Medicine: www.istm.org

Lariam Action USA: www.suggskelly.com/lariam

Marie Stopes: www.mariestopes.org/uk

MASTA (Medical Advisory Services for Travellers): www.masta.org

Medical College of Wisconsin Travelers Clinic: www.intmed.mcw/travel.html

Mefloquine: www.travelhealth.com/mefloqui.htm;
www.geocities.com/TheTropics/6913/lariam.htm

Princeton University Outdoors Action Program:
www.princeton.edu/~oa/altitude.html

Shorelands: www.tripprep.com

Travel Health Information Service: www.travelhealth.com

Travellers Medical and Vaccination Centre: www.tmvc.com.au/info.html

WHO (World Health Organization): www.who.ch

MAGAZINES & NEWSPAPERS

Bicycling: www.bicyclingmagazine.com

Big World Magazine: www.bigworld.com

Chicago Tribune: www.chicagotribune.com

LA Times: www.latimes.com

Mountain Bike: www.mountainbike.com

National Geographic: www.nationalgeographic.com

New York Times: www.nytimes.com
Outside: http://outside.starwave.com
San Francisco Examiner: www.examiner.com
Southern Cross (UK): www.southerncross.co.uk
Surfer Magazine: www.surfermag.com
Sydney Morning Herald: www.smh.com.au
The Age (Melbourne): www.theage.com.au
The Australian: www.news.com.au
The Globe & Mail (Toronto): www.theglobeandmail.com
The Independent (UK): www.independent.co.uk
The Times: www.the-times.co.uk
Time Out: www.timeout.com/london
TNT: www.tntmag.co.uk
Traveller Magazine: www.travelmag.co.uk
Vancouver Sun: www.vancouversun.com

MAPS
Hagstrom Map and Travel Center: www.hagstromstore.com
Mapquest Mapstore: www.mapquest.com
Rand McNally — The Map & Travel Store: www.randmcnallystore.com
World of Maps & Travel Books: www.worldofmaps.com

MONEY MATTERS
Credit Cards: www.mastercard.com/atm;
  www.visa.com/cgi-bin/vee/pd/atm/main.html
Oanda Online Currency Converter: www.oanda.com/site/cc_index.html

PASSPORTS & VISAS
Passports Australia, Department of Foreign Affairs & Trade:
  www.dfat.gov.au/passports/passports_faq_contents.html
Passport Office, Department of Foreign Affairs & International Trade (Canada):
  www.dfait-maeci.gc.ca/passport/paspr-2.htm
Passport Office, Department of Internal Affairs (New Zealand):
  www.passports.govt.nz/pports_home.html
Passport Services, the State Department (USA):
  travel.state.gov/passport_services.html
UK Passport Agency, the Home Office: www.open.gov.uk/ukpass/ukpass.htm

TRAVEL ADVISORIES
British Foreign & Commonwealth Office: www.fco.gov.uk
Conservation International's Ecotravel Center: www.ecotour.org/ecotour.htm
Council Travel: www.counciltravel.com
Ecotour: www.ecotour.org/ecotour.htm

Encounter: www.encounter.co.uk
Exodus: www.exodustravels.co.uk
Global Exchange: www.globalexchange.org
Intrepid Travel: www.intrepidtravel.com.au
Journeys International: www.journeys-intl.com
Monkey Business: www.monkeyshrine.com
Serious Sports: www.serioussports.com/core.html
STA Travel: www.sta-travel.com
The Ecotourism Association of Australia: www.wttc.org
Tourism Offices Worldwide Directory: www.towd.com
Trailfinders: www.trailfinder.com
Travel CUTS: www.travelcuts.com

TRAVEL EQUIPMENT

Karrimor: www.karrimor.co.uk
Macpac: www.macpac.co.nz
Photo.net: www.photo.net/photo
REI: www.REI.com

TRAVELLERS WITH DISABILITIES

Mobility International USA: www.miusa.org
Society for the Advancement of Travel for the Handicapped (SATH): http://sath.org/index.html
Royal Association for Disability & Rehabilitation (RADAR): www.radar.org.uk
The Access-Able Travel Source: www.access-able.com/about

VOLUNTEER ORGANISATIONS

Australian Volunteers International: www.ozvol.org.au
Earthwatch Institute: www.earthwatch.org/australia/html; www.earthwatch.org/t/Toeuropehome.htm
Global Volunteers: www.globalvolunteers.org
International Voluntary Service: www.ivsgbn.demon.co.uk
Oxfam International: www.oxfaminternational.org
Peace Corps of the USA: www.peacecorps.gov
Voluntary Service Overseas (VSO): www.oneworld.org/vso
Volunteer Service Abroad: www.tcol.co.uk/comorg/vsa.htm

OTHER USEFUL SITES

Federation of International Youth Travel Organisations: www.fiyto.org/index-old.html
Gay esCape: www.icafe.co.za/gayes
Hostelling International: www.iyhf.org
International Student Travel Confederation: www.isic.org/index.htm

International Bicycle Fund: www.ibike.org/bikeafrica
Internet Guide to Hostelling: www.hostels.com
Internet Traveller Information Service: www.itisnet.com
Lonely Planet: www.lonelyplanet.com
Rain or Shine: www.rainorshine.com
US State Department Travel Warnings & Consular Information Sheets:
  http://travel.state.gov/travel_warnings.html
World Events Calendar: www.travel.epicurious.com
World Tourism Organization: www.world-tourism.org/ows-doc/wtich.htm

The following is a list of words that are used in this book and that you are likely to come across in Africa. A country or region in brackets indicates that the word is principally used there. Included are glossaries of food terms and air travel terms.

ANC – African National Congress

animism – the base of virtually all traditional religions in Africa; the belief that there is a spirit in all natural things and the worship of those spirits which are thought to continue after death and have the power to bestow protection

asantehene – Ashanti king (Ghana)

askari – guard (East Africa)

auberge – traditionally a simple guesthouse; used (occasionally) in West Africa to mean any small hotel

bab – Islamic gate (North Africa)

bâché – covered pick-up vehicle used as a basic bush taxi (West Africa)

banda – thatched hut with wooden or earthen walls (East Africa)

benzin aadi – normal petrol (Egypt)

BIAO – Banque International pour l'Afrique Occidentale

bijou – service taxi (Egypt)

boda-boda – bicycle taxi (Kenya)

boîte – nightclub

Boîte Postale (BP) – post office box

braai – a barbecue which normally includes lots of meat grilled on a braai stand or pit (South Africa)

buvette – refreshment stall (West Africa)

cadeau – bribe; also a tip or gift

camion – truck (Mozambique)

camionette – pick-up vehicle (West Africa)

campement – hostel or local style lodge (West Africa)

caravanserai – courtyard inn

careta – donkey-drawn cart (Egypt)

carnet – (carnet de passage en douane) permit to take a vehicle into a country

carnival – (in Portuguese-speaking countries, carnaval) Latin-style street festival or parade held in Cape Verde for Mardi Gras

chambre d'hôte – guesthouse

chapa – (full name chapa cem) bush bus (Mozambique)

chop bar – streetside restaurant selling inexpensive local food (West Africa)

colectivo – share-taxi (São Tomé & Príncipe and Mozambique)

commissariat – police station

couchette – two-person train compartment

dalla dalla – pick-up or minibus (Tanzania, especially Dar es Salaam)

dash – bribe

déplacement – private hire of taxi (West Africa)

dhow – traditional wooden sailing boat (East Africa)

douche – public shower

duka – shop (East Africa)

ECOMOG – ECOWAS Monitoring Group

ECOWAS – Economic Community of West African States

felucca – Nile River sailing boat

forex – foreign exchange bureau

gare lagunaire – ferry terminal

gare routière – bus or train station

gargotte – cheap restaurant (West Africa)

ghibli – sandstorms, particularly in the desert regions of Libya

ghorbi – traditional mud-brick and thatch communal farm dwelling (Tunisia)

gîte – hiker's accommodation, similar to auberge, campement (Morocco)

grand taxi – long distance share or bush taxi (Morocco)

hammam – Turkish-style bathhouse (Morocco)

hantour – horse-drawn carriage (Egypt)

harmattan – dry dusty Sahara wind which blows towards the West African coast particularly from November to March

hôtel de ville – town hall

IMF – International Monetary Fund

ISIC – International Student Identity Card

juju – an object used as a charm or fetish

kasbah – fort or citadel often outside the administrative centre; also spelt qasba (North Africa)

kente cloth – probably the most expensive material in West Africa, made with finely woven cotton and sometimes silk by Ghana's Ashanti people

kola nuts – bitter nuts sold on the streets, known for their mildly hallucinogenic and caffeine-like effects (West Africa)

konjo – millet beer (Mali)

kopje – prominent isolated hill or mountain

kora – lute-like stringed instrument

koubba – Islamic sanctuary (North Africa)

kraal – livestock enclosure or hut village (southern Africa)

ksar – (plural ksour) fortified stronghold

louage – share taxi (Tunisia)

lycée – high school

maghreb – west (literally 'where the sun sets'); used to describe the area covered by Morocco, Algeria, Tunisia and sometimes Libya

mairie – town hall (West Africa)

maquis – small open-air restaurant with low wooden tables, sandy floors and good music (Côte d'Ivoire)

marabout – a religious saint (animist) or holy man (Muslim)

marché – market (West Africa)

marginal – waterfront or coastal road (Mozambique)

matatu – minibus (Kenya)

matola – vehicle (usually a pick-up van) acting as an unofficial public transport service (Malawi)

medersa – college for teaching theology, law, Arabic literature and grammar (Morocco)

medina – old town; usually Arab (North Africa)

mellah – Jewish quarter of a medina (Morocco)

MET – Ministry of Environment & Tourism (Namibia)

mihrab – prayer niche

mobylette – moped (Burkina Faso)

mokoro – dugout canoe (Botswana)

muezzin – mosque official who does the call to prayer from the minaret

mumtaz – super petrol (Egypt)

NGO – nongovernmental organisation

OAU – Organisation of African Unity

occasions – trucks (Central African Republic)

pagnes – traditional strips of cloth (Togo)

PAIGC – African Party for the Independence of Guinea-Bissau and Cape Verde

paillotte – thatched sun shelter (usually on a beach or around an open-air bar-restaurant (West Africa)

palmeraie – oasis-like area around a town where date palms, vegetables and fruit are grown (North Africa)

paragem – bus or taxi station

pensão – cheap hotel (Mozambique, Cape Verde, São Tomé)

pinasse – motorised boat (Mali)

pirogue – dugout canoe

plat du jour – dish of the day (West Africa)

pont – bridge (West Africa)

poulet yassa – chicken cooked with lemon, onion and garlic

pousada – better-grade cheap hotel (Mozambique)

pousse pousse – rickshaw (Madagascar)

praça – square

praia – beach

prefecture – administrative headquarters

PTT – post office

qasba – *see* kasbah

Ramadan – ninth month of the Islamic year; a period of fasting

rice bar – streetside restaurant selling inexpensive local food (West Africa)

RMS – Ruwenzori Mountaineering Services

rondavel – circular building often thatched (southern Africa)

Sahel – dry savannah region bordering Sahara desert to the south

Sahelian – *see* Sahel

shari'a – Islamic law

sharia – street (Arabic)

shifta – bandit (Kenya and Somalia)

souk – outdoor market; also spelt souq (North Africa)

sûreté – police station

SWAPO – South-West African People's Organisation

syndicat d'initiative – government-run tourist office

taxi-brousse – bush taxi

taxi collectif – *see* taxi-brousse

toiles – rough, painted textiles

tro-tro – small wooden bus (Ghana)

UNITA – National Union for the Total Independence of Angola

vila – town (Malawi)

ville nouvelle – 'new city' towns built by the French alongside existing towns and cities of the Maghreb

voodoo – the worship of spirits with supernatural powers widely practised in Benin, Togo and Pemba island (Tanzania)

ZANU – Zimbabwe African National Union

ZAPU – Zimbabwe African Peoples' Union

zawiyya – shrine (Morocco)

FOOD GLOSSARY

brochettes – kebabs

capitaine – fish
chai – tea (East Africa)
chapati – Indian-style bread (Kenya and Somalia)
chawarma – a popular snack of grilled meat in bread served with salad and sesame sauce originally from Lebanon; also spelt shawarma
couscous – semolina

foutou – boiled and pounded yams or plantains eaten as a staple food with sauce (West Africa)
fuul – fava beans with a variety of ingredients added to spice them up, eg oil, lemon, meat, egg (Egypt)

groundnuts – peanuts (West Africa)

harissa – spicy chilli sauce
hummus – chickpea paste mixed with sesame puree (tahina), lemon and garlic

karkaday – hibiscus tea
kedjenou – chicken and vegetable stew served with rice or foutou (West Africa)
kushari – popular and cheap dish; oil-based mixture of noodles, rice, black lentils, fried onions, chickpeas and spicy tomato sauce (Egypt)

mafé – groundnut-based stew (West Africa)
mandazi – semi-sweet African doughnut (East Africa)

manioc – cassava

nsima – maize porridge; the regional staple (Malawi)

palava sauce – a sauce made from pounded leaves, palm oil and seasonings
poisson – fish
poulet brais – fish or chicken cooked over the embers of a low fire
poulet yassa or **poisson yassa** – marinated and grilled chicken or fish

riz sauce – very common basic meal (rice with meat sauce)

sahleb – sweet milky drink made from rice flour, grapes, coconut and nuts (North Africa)
suya – spiced brochette (Nigeria)

ta'amiyya – Egyptian version of felafel (chickpea burgers)
tajine – stew usually with meat as the main ingredient (Morocco)
tej – a kind of honey wine (Ethiopia)
tiéboudienne – rice baked in a thick sauce of fish and vegetables with pimiento and tomato sauce
tô – millet or sorghum-based pâté (Burkina Faso)

ugali – staple East African food made by mixing maize and/or cassava flour with water; it's always eaten with a sauce

yaourt – yoghurt (Burkina Faso)

AIR TRAVEL TERMS

baggage allowance – Written on your ticket and usually includes one 20kg item to go in the hold, plus one item of hand luggage.

bucket shops – Unbonded travel agencies specialising in discounted plane tickets.

cancellation penalties – If you have to cancel or change a discounted ticket, there are often heavy penalties involved; insurance can sometimes be taken out against this. Some airlines impose penalties on regular tickets as well, particularly against 'no-show' passengers.

check-in – If you fail to check in on time (usually one to two hours before departure time on international flights) and the flight is overbooked, the airline can cancel your booking.

confirmation – Having a ticket written out with the flight and date you want doesn't mean you have a seat until the agent has checked with the airline that your status is 'OK' or confirmed.

full fares – Airlines traditionally offer 1st class (coded F), business class (coded J) and economy class (coded Y) tickets. With so many promotional and discounted fares available, few passengers pay full economy fare.

ITX – An ITX, or 'independent inclusive tour excursion', is often available on tickets to popular holiday destinations. Officially it's a package deal combined with hotel accommodation, but many agents will sell these for the flight only and give you phoney hotel vouchers in the unlikely event that you're challenged at the airport.

lost tickets – If you lose your plane ticket an airline will usually treat it like a travellers cheque and, after inquiries, issue you with another one. Legally, however, an airline is entitled to treat it like cash and if you lose it then it's gone forever.

MCO – An MCO, or 'miscellaneous charge order', is a voucher that looks like a plane ticket but carries no destination or date. It can be exchanged through any International Association of Travel Agents (IATA) airline for a ticket on a specific flight. It's a useful alternative to an onward ticket in those countries that demand one, and is more flexible than an ordinary ticket if you're unsure of your route.

no-shows – These are passengers who fail to show up for their flight. Full-fare passengers who fail to turn up are sometimes entitled to travel on a later flight. The rest are penalised.

on request – An unconfirmed booking for a flight.

onward tickets – An entry requirement for many countries is that you have a ticket out of the country. If you're unsure of your next move, the easiest solution is to buy the cheapest onward ticket to a neighbouring country or a ticket from a reliable airline which can later be refunded if you don't use it.

open-jaw tickets – Return tickets where you fly into one place but out of another.

overbooking – Since every flight has some passengers who fail to show up, airlines often book more passengers than they have seats. Occasionally somebody gets 'bumped' onto the next available flight and this is most likely to be passengers who check in late.

point-to-point tickets – Discount tickets that can be bought on some routes in return for passengers waiving their rights to a stopover.

promotional fares – Officially discounted fares available from travel agencies or direct from the airline.

reconfirmation – If you don't reconfirm your flight at least 72 hours prior to departure, the airline may delete your name from the passenger list.

restrictions – Discounted tickets often have various restrictions on them – such as needing to be paid for in advance, incurring a penalty to be altered, or restrictions on the minimum and maximum period you must be away.

round-the-world tickets – RTW tickets give you a limited period (usually a year) in which to circumnavigate the globe. You can go anywhere the carrying airlines go, as long as you don't backtrack. The number of stopovers or total number of separate flights is decided before you set off and they usually cost a bit more than a basic return flight.

stand-by – A discounted ticket where you only fly if there is a seat free at the last moment, and usually available only on domestic routes.

transferred tickets – Plane tickets cannot be transferred from one person to another. Travellers sometimes try to sell the return half of their ticket, but officials can ask you to prove that you are the person named on the ticket. This is less likely to happen on domestic flights, but on an international flight tickets will always be compared with passports.

travel periods – Ticket prices vary depending on the time of year – low (off-peak) season, high (peak) season or shoulder season. Usually the fare depends on your outward flight – if you depart in the high season and return in the low season, you pay the high-season fare.

INDEX

Italics indicates maps

Italics indicates maps

LONELY PLANET

ON THE ROAD

Lonely Planet **travel guides** explore cities, regions and countries in depth, with restaurants, accommodations and more for every budget. With reliable, easy-to-use maps, practical advice, great cultural background and sights both on and off the beaten track. There are over 200 titles in this classic series covering nearly every country in the world.

 Lonely Planet Upgrades extend the usefulness of existing travel guides by detailing any changes that may affect travel in each region since the book has been published. Upgrades can be downloaded for free on www.lonelyplanet.com/upgrades

For travellers with more time than money, **Shoestring guides** offer dependable, first-hand information with 100s of detailed maps, plus insider tips for stretching money as far as possible. Covering entire continents in most cases, the six-volume shoestring guides have been known as 'backpackers' bibles' for over 25 years.

For the discerning short-term visitor, **Condensed** guides highlight the best a destination has to offer in a full-colour pocket-sized format designed for quick access. From top sights and walking tours to opinionated reviews of where to eat, stay, shop and have fun.

Lonely Planet **CitySync** lets travellers use their Palm™ or Visor™ handheld computers to quickly search and sort hundreds of reviews of hotels, restaurants, major sights, and shopping and entertainment options, all pinpointed on scrollable street maps. CitySync can be downloaded from www.citysync.com

ESSENTIALS

Read This First books help travellers new to a destination hit the road with confidence. These invaluable pre-departure guides give step-by-step advice on preparing for a trip, from budgeting and arranging a visa to planning an itinerary, staying safe and still getting off the beaten track.

Healthy Travel pocket guides offer practical advice for staying well on the road, with user-friendly design and helpful diagrams and tables.

Pocket-sized, with colour tabs for quick reference, extensive vocabulary lists easy-to-follow pronunciation keys and two-way dictionaries, Lonely Planet **Phrasebooks** cover the essential words and phrases travellers may need.

Lonely Planet's eKno is a communication card developed especially for travellers, with low phone rates, free email and a toll-free voicemail service so that you can keep in touch while on the road. Check it out on www.ekno.lonelyplanet.com

LONELY PLANET

OUTDOOR GUIDES

For those who believe the best way to see the world is on foot, Lonely Planet's **walking guides** detail everything from family strolls to difficult treks, with expert advice on when to go and how to do it, reliable maps and essential travel information.

Cycling guides map out a destination's best bike tours, long and short, in day-by-day detail. With all the information a cyclist needs, including advice on bike maintenance, places to eat and stay, and innovative maps with detailed cues to the rides and elevation charts.

The **Watching Wildlife** series is perfect for travellers who want authoritative information but don't want to tote a field guide. Packed with advice on where, when and how to view a region's wildlife, each title features photos of over 300 species and engaging insights on their lives and environments.

With underwater colour photos throughout, **Pisces Books** explore the world's best diving and snorkelling areas. Each book contains listings of diving services and dive resorts and detailed information on depth, visibility, levels of difficulty and marine life you're likely to see.

MAPS & ATLASES

Lonely Planet's **City Maps** feature downtown and metropolitan maps as well as transit routes, walking tours and a complete index of streets and sights. Plastic-coated for extra durability.

Road Atlases are an essential navigation tool for serious travellers. Cross-referenced with Lonely Planet guidebooks, they also feature distance and climate charts and a complete site index.

LONELY PLANET

FOOD & RESTAURANT GUIDES

Lonely Planet's **Out to Eat** guides recommend the brightest and best places to eat and drink in top international cities. Arranged by neighbourhood and packed with dependable maps, scene-setting photos and quirky features, Out to Eat serves up the lot.

For people who live to eat, drink and travel, **World Food** guides explore the culinary culture of each country. Entertaining and adventurous, each guide is packed with detail on staples & specialities, regional cuisine and local markets, as well as sumptuous recipes, comprehensive culinary dictionaries and lavish photos good enough to eat.

OFF THE ROAD

Journeys is a travel literature series that captures the spirit of a place, illuminates a culture, recounts an adventure or introduces a fascinating way of life. These books are tales to read while on the road or at home in your favourite armchair.

Lonely Planet's new range of lavishly illustrated **Pictorial** books is just the ticket for both travellers and dreamers. Quirky tales and vivid photographs bring the adventure of travel to life, before the journey begins or long after it is over.

Entertaining and adventurous, Lonely Planet **Videos** encourage the same independent approach to travel as the guidebooks. Currently airing throughout the world, this award-winning series features all original footage and music.

TRAVELLERS NETWORK

Lonely Planet online. Lonely Planet's award-winning web site has insider information on hundreds of destinations from Amsterdam to Zimbabwe, complete with interactive maps and colour photographs. The site also offers the latest travel news, recent reports from travellers on the road, guidebook upgrades and a lively traveller's bulletin board www.lonelyplanet.com or AOL keyword: lp

Lonely Planet produces two free newsletters. **Planet Talk** is the quarterly print version, **Comet** comes via email once a month. Each is loaded with travel news, advice, dispatches from authors and letters from readers. Contact your nearest Lonely Planet office to subscribe.

LONELY PLANET

Guides to the Region

L onely Planet is known worldwide for publishing practical, reliable and no-nonsense travel information in our guides and on our web site. The Lonely Planet list covers just about every accessible part of the world. Currently there are fifteen series: travel guides, Shoestrings, Condensed, Phrasebooks, Read This First, Healthy Travel, Walking guides, Cycling guides, Pisces Diving & Snorkeling guides, City Maps, Travel Atlases, Out to Eat, World Food, Journeys travel literature and Pictorials.

AFRICA Africa on a shoestring • Africa – the South • Arabic (Egyptian) phrasebook • Arabic (Moroccan) phrasebook • Cairo • Cape Town • Cape Town city map • Central Africa • East Africa • Egypt • Egypt travel atlas • Ethiopian (Amharic) phrasebook • The Gambia & Senegal • Healthy Travel Africa • Kenya • Kenya travel atlas • Malawi, Mozambique & Zambia • Morocco • North Africa • Read This First Africa • South Africa, Lesotho & Swaziland • South Africa, Lesotho & Swaziland travel atlas • Swahili phrasebook • Tanzania, Zanzibar & Pemba • Trekking in East Africa • Tunisia • West Africa • Zimbabwe, Botswana & Namibia • Zimbabwe, Botswana & Nambia Travel Atlas • World Food Morocco

Travel Literature: The Rainbird: A Central African Journey • Songs to an African Sunset: A Zimbabwean Story • Mali Blues: Traveling to an African Beat

MIDDLE EAST & CENTRAL ASIA Bahrain, Kuwait & Qatar • Central Asia • Central Asia phrasebook • Dubai • Hebrew phrasebook • Iran • Israel & the Palestinian Territories • Israel & the Palestinian Territories travel atlas • Istanbul • Istanbul to Cairo on a shoestring • Jerusalem • Jerusalem City Map • Jordan • Jordan, Syria & Lebanon travel atlas • Lebanon • Middle East • Oman & the United Arab Emirates • Syria • Turkey • Turkey travel atlas • Turkish phrasebook • Yemen

Travel Literature: The Gates of Damascus • Kingdom of the Film Stars: Journey into Jordan • Black on Black: Iran Revisited

Mail Order

L onely Planet products are distributed worldwide. They are also available by mail order from Lonely Planet, so if you have difficulty finding a title please write to us. North and South American residents should write to 150 Linden St, Oakland CA 94607, USA; European and African residents should write to 10a Spring Place, London, NW5 3BH; and residents of other countries to PO Box 617, Hawthorn, Victoria 3122, Australia.